LEGIONS OF
ROME

LEGIONS OF
ROME

THE DEFINITIVE HISTORY OF
EVERY IMPERIAL ROMAN LEGION

STEPHEN DANDO-COLLINS

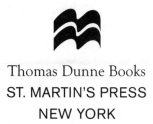

Thomas Dunne Books
ST. MARTIN'S PRESS
NEW YORK

www.thomasdunnebooks.com
www.stmartins.com

ISBN 978-1-250-00471-0

First U.S. Edition
10 9 8 7 6 5 4 3 2

Designed by Hugh Adams
Picture research by Elaine Willis
Illustration by William Donohoe

Printed and bound in China

Picture acknowledgements are reproduced on p. 608

For Louise, who soldiers at my side,
and Richard, who always fights the good fight.

CONTENTS

II. THE LEGIONS

III. THE BATTLES

INTRODUCTION

The Roman legion of the imperial era was a triumph of organization. Its basic structure was so effective that it continues to be used to this day, by armies whose squads, platoons, companies and battalions reflect the contubernium, century, cohort and legion of old. The imperial legion created by Augustus was like a giant Lego set, with each component, from heavy infantry to cavalry, artillery to supporting auxiliary light infantry, fitting neatly together to form a solid, self-contained military machine.

The fearsome effectiveness of the organizational structure, training, and tactics of the legions were so universally acknowledged that several of Rome's greatest foes used them against her. Men who had formerly served in Rome's army and went on to raise rebellions against her not only organized their own forces along Roman lines, their intimate knowledge of how the legions operated allowed them to employ tactics which exploited their few weaknesses. As a result, Arminius destroyed Varus and his three legions in Germany's Teutoburg Forest, Tacfarinas was able to terrorize North Africa for years, and Civilis took the Rhine and seven legions from Rome and threatened to remove all of Gaul from Roman control.

The legions' make-up, originally homogeneous as a result of mass enlistments in specific provincial areas, became increasingly ethnically diverse, with men from opposite ends of the Roman world bringing greatly varying customs, dialects, and religious observances to their legions without any detrimental effect to the serviceability of the overall unit. This can be put down, in part, to the fact that, like a modern military unit, legions had for centuries possessed a strong corporate identity, with the battle honours of previous enlistments being cited by commanders to rouse their troops to greater battlefield deeds.

It is remarkable that even though all the imperial legions sprang from common roots and used common training and equipment, their performance varied. Some were consistently reliable while others were fated to disappoint. Others that had once failed later grabbed glory with spectacular victories. Others still did not live up to earlier reputations. The legions destroyed with Varus in the Teutoburg Forest, for example, had been, up to that time, considered by Velleius, an officer who served with them on the Rhine, among Rome's best and bravest. Yet clever tactics by their attackers and poor leadership by their commander led to their destruction.

The question of leadership emerges time and again in the history of the legions. The 12th Fulminata Legion, for example, poorly led in Rome's initial confounded attempt to put down the first-century Jewish Revolt, disgraced itself by losing its eagle standard to the rebels. A century later, this same legion regained its reputation by standing firm in a thunderstorm to save its leader Marcus Aurelius from surrounding German hordes. Vastly outnumbered but under firm leadership, the 14th Gemina Martia Victrix Legion similarly gained fame, by defeating Boudicca's rebels in Britain.

The first century and the early part of the second century represented the golden age of the legions, when massive armies of up to 100,000 legionaries and a similar number of auxiliaries swept all before them, and a legionary could expect to retire rich with the spoil of conquest. From the death of the emperor Trajan in AD 117, the situation changed. Stretched thin along porous borders, Roman forces were forced permanently on to the defensive. Internal divisions would soon regularly rend the empire. Central control was frequently lost, reasserted, and lost again.

In the process, the quality of the men and their units declined, as their leaders increasingly adopted foreign mercenaries and foreign methods, created ever more new units, and changed the legions' organizational structure. And with change came regular defeat, stimulating even more debilitating change. Only the occasional emergence of a great commander stemmed the tide of decline and even offered hope of a return to the glory days, but always just for the duration of his lifetime.

The long existence of the Roman Empire had everything to do with the legions. While the legions were strong, Rome was strong. Conversely, the disintegration of the Late Empire had everything to do with the disintegration of the legions as effective fighting forces. At the end of the fourth century, the Notitia Dignitatum listed several hundred legions and auxiliary units of the day, yet these units were small, with many no more than border police and some perhaps existing only on paper. Even the most elite units then in existence paled in comparison to the Augustan legions. Vegetius' plea to his emperor Valentinian, just prior to the creation of the Notitia Dignitatum, for a return to the legion structure, weapons and training of old, fell on deaf ears.

When, in AD 398, Rome's last great general, Stilicho, son of a Vandal cavalry commander, put together a task force in northern Italy to wrest Africa back from rebel governor Gildo, the state of the legions then mirrored the state of the empire. Stilicho's force was organized from Mediolanum (Milan), which had superseded Rome as imperial capital in the West, and it sailed from Pisa in Tuscany, not from one of the old imperial naval bases of Misenum or Ravenna. This army consisted of legions including the Jovian, Herculian, and 3rd Augusta, plus several auxiliary units – although the distinction between legionary and auxiliary had blurred since Commodus' AD 212 decree had made Roman citizenship universal.

Yet, this task force's seven units totalled no more than 5,000 men, most of them Gallic veterans. Rome's once proud legions had shrunk to complements of some 1,000 men each, less than a fifth the size of the Augustan legions. Training, equipment, and tactics had also changed drastically since the days of Augustus. Legionaries were now using light equipment and light arms. Not long before this, entire units had thrown away their armour and helmets, claiming they were too heavy, to fight unprotected, with predictably fatal results.

Stilicho's task force won back Africa without having to lift a sword – the very sight of their disciplined ranks caused the rebel governor's troops to run. But it would be a different story just three years later, when Alaric's Visigoths invaded Italy. Stilicho's legions, withdrawn from Britain and the Rhine to save Italy, would, under his inspiring leadership, fight bloody battles and conduct gritty sieges, driving the Visigoths out of Italy. Yet once Stilicho died, soon after, those same legions were devoured by Alaric, who, in AD 410, achieved his ambition of sacking Rome.

This, then, is the comprehensive story of Rome's imperial legions. From the army moulded by Augustus through the heady early phase of the empire's expansion, with its conquests, revolts, and self-destructive civil conflicts, to the long, grinding decline as the quest to maintain the gains of old sometimes stemmed the barbarian tide but inevitably gave way to it.

Despite their inglorious end, the legions remain to this day, thousands of years after their creation, the most pre-eminent example of how detailed organization, tight discipline, and inspiring leadership can take a group of individuals and turn them into a winning team.

STEPHEN DANDO-COLLINS
March 2010

· I ·

THE MEN

'Every country produces both brave men and cowards, but it is equally certain that some nations are naturally more warlike than others.'

Vegetius, *De Re Militari*, FOURTH CENTURY

Down through the centuries, millions of men served with the army of imperial Rome; half a million during the reign of Augustus alone. The history of the legions is the collective story of those individuals, not just of Rome's famous generals. Men such as Titus Flavius Virilis, still serving as a centurion at the age of 70. And Titus Calidius, a cavalry decurion who missed military life so much after retiring he re-enlisted, at the reduced rank of optio. And Novantius, the British auxiliary from today's city of Leicester, who was granted his discharge thirteen years early for valiant service in the second century conquest of Dacia. Any analysis of the legions must begin with the men, their organization, their equipment, and their service conditions.

I. WHERE IT ALL BEGAN

The origins of the legions of Pompey, Caesar, Augustus, Vespasian, Trajan and Marcus Aurelius go back to the Roman Republic of the fifth century BC. Originally, there were just four Roman legions – *Legio*s I to IIII (the legion number 4 was written as IIII, not IV). Each of the two consuls, 'who were charged both singly and jointly to take care to preserve the Republic from danger', commanded two of these legions. [Vege., III]

All legionaries were then property-owning citizens of Rome, conscripted in the spring of each year into the armies of the two consuls. Legio, the origin of the word 'legion', meant 'levy', or draft. Service ordinarily ended with the Festival of the October Horse on 19 October, which signalled the termination of the campaigning season.

Men of 'military age' – 16 to 46 – were selected by ballot for each legion, with the 1st Legion considered to be the most prestigious. Rome's field army was bolstered by legions from allied Italian tribes. Legionaries of the early Republic were appointed to one of four divisions within their legion, based on age and property qualifications. The youngest men were assigned to the *velites*, the next oldest to the *hastati*, men in the prime of life to the *principes* and the oldest to the *triarii*, with the role and equipment of each group differing. By Julius Caesar's day, the conscripted infantry soldier of the Republic was required to serve in the legions for up to sixteen years, and could be recalled in emergencies for a further four years.

Originally, republican legions had a strength of 4,200 men, which in times of special danger could be brought up to 5,000. [Poly., VI, 21] By 218 BC and the war between Rome and Carthage, the consuls' legions consisted of 5,200 infantry and 300 cavalry, which approached the form they would take in imperial times. From

104 BC, the Roman army of the Republic underwent a major overhaul by the consuls Publius Rutilius Rufus and Gaius Marius. Rutilius introduced arms drill and reformed the process of appointment for senior officers. Marius simplified the requirements for enrolment, so that it was not only property owners who were required to serve. Failure to report for military service would result in the conscript being declared a deserter, a crime subject to the death penalty.

A legionary would be paid for the days he served – for many years, this amounted to ten asses a day. He was also entitled to the proceeds from any arms, equipment or clothing he stripped from the enemy dead, and was entitled to a share of the booty acquired by his legion. If a legion stormed a town, its legionaries received the proceeds from its contents – human and otherwise – which were sold to traders who trailed the legions. If a town surrendered, however, the Roman army's commander could elect to spare it. Consequently, legionaries had no interest in encouraging besieged cities to surrender.

Republican consul Gaius Marius remodelled the legions in the first century BC. After he took much of the baggage off the baggage train and put it on the backs of his legionaries, they became known as 'Marius' mules'.

Marius focused on making the legions independent mobile units of heavy infantry. Supporting roles were left to allied forces. To increase mobility, Marius took most of the legionaries' personal equipment off the huge baggage trains which until then had trailed the legions, and put it on the backs of the soldiers, greatly reducing the size of the baggage train. With the items hanging from their baggage poles weighing up to 100 pounds (45 kilos), legionaries of the era were nicknamed 'Marius' mules'. Until that time, the maniple of 160–200 men had been the principal tactical unit of the legion, but under Marius' influence the 600-man cohort became the new tactical unit of the Roman army, so that the legion of the first century BC comprised ten cohorts, with a total of 6,000 men.

Half a century later, Julius Caesar fashioned his legions around his own personality and dynamic style. Of the twenty-eight legions of Augustus' new standing army in 30 BC, some had been founded by Caesar, others moulded by him. The civil war, between the rebel Caesar and the forces of the republican Senate led by their commander Pompey the Great, created an insatiable demand for military manpower. At

Republican legionaries. From the altar of Domitius Ahenobarbus.

the Battle of Pharsalus in 48 BC, Caesar led elements of nine legions; Pompey, twelve. For the 42 BC Battle of Philippi, two years after Caesar's murder, when Mark Antony, Marcus Lepidus and Octavian took on the so-called Liberators, Brutus and Cassius, more than forty legions were involved.

II. SOLDIERING FOR AUGUSTUS

The emperor Augustus, as Octavian became known from 27 BC, totally reformed the Roman army after he finally defeated Antony and Cleopatra in 30 BC.

In the professional army of Augustus, the legionary was a full-time soldier, sometimes a volunteer but more often a conscript, who signed on, initially for sixteen and later twenty years. Towards the end of his forty-three-year reign, Augustus was to boast: 'The number

A cameo showing Augustus early in his reign.

of Roman citizens who bound themselves to me by military oath was about 500,000. Of these I settled in colonies or sent back into their own towns more than 300,000, and to all I assigned lands or gave money as a reward for military service.' [*Res Gest.*, 1, 3] That retirement payment was standardized by Augustus at 12,000 sesterces for legionaries, 20,000 for men of the Praetorian Guard. After the completion of his enlistment, an imperial legionary could be recalled in an emergency to the Evocati, a militia of retired legionaries.

On Antony's death, Augustus controlled approximately sixty legions. Many of these were promptly disbanded. 'Others,' said Cassius Dio, 'were merged with various legions by Augustus', and as a result 'such legions have come to bear the name Gemina', meaning 'twin'. [Dio, LV, 23] By this process, Augustus created a standing army of 150,000 legionaries in twenty-eight legions, supported by 180,000 auxiliary infantry and cavalry, stationed throughout the empire. He also created a navy with two main battle fleets equipped with marines, and several smaller fleets. In addition, Augustus employed specialist troops at Rome – the elite Praetorian Guard, the

A copy of the *Res Gastae*, Augustus' personal testament to his achievements, inscribed on brass tablets at the Temple of Rome and Augustus in modern Ankara, Turkey.

City Guard, the Vigiles or Night Watch, and the imperial bodyguard, the German Guard.

In AD 6, Augustus set up a military treasury in Rome, initially using his own funds, which were given in his name and that of Tiberius, his ultimate successor. To administer the military treasury he appointed three former praetors, allocating two secretaries to each. The ongoing shortfall in the military treasury's funds was covered by a death duty of 5 per cent on all inheritances, except where the recipient was immediate family or demonstrably poor.

III. ENLISTING AND RETIRING

Some volunteers served in Rome's imperial legions – 'the needy and the homeless, who adopt by their own choice a soldier's life', according to Tacitus. [Tac., *A*, IV, 4] But most legionaries were conscripted. The selection criteria established by Augustus required men in their physical prime. A recruit's civilian skills would be put to use by the legion, so that blacksmiths became armourers, and tailors and cobblers made and repaired legionaries' uniforms and footwear. Unskilled recruits found themselves assigned to duties such as the surveyor's party or the artillery. When it was time for battle, however, all took their places in the ranks.

A slave attempting to join the legions could expect to be executed if discovered, as happened in a case raised with the emperor Trajan by Pliny the Younger when he was governor of Bithynia-Pontus. Conversely, during the early part of Augustus' reign it was not uncommon for free men to pose as slaves to avoid being drafted into the legions or the Praetorian Guard when the *conquisitors*, or recruitment officers, periodically did the rounds of the recruitment grounds. This became such a problem that Augustus' stepson Tiberius was given the task of conducting an inquiry into slave barracks throughout Italy, whose owners were accepting bribes from free men to harbour them in the barracks when the conquisitors sought to fill their quotas. [Suet., III, 8]

Once Tiberius became emperor the task of filling empty places in the legions became even more difficult. Velleius Paterculus, who served under Tiberius, made a sycophantic yet revealing statement about legion recruitment in around AD 30: 'As for the recruiting of the army, a thing ordinarily looked upon with great and constant dread, with what calm on the part of the people does he [Tiberius] provide for it, without any of the usual panic attending conscription!' [Velle., II, CXXX] Tiberius, who followed Augustus' policy of recruiting no legionaries in Italy south of the River Po, broadly extended the draft throughout the provinces.

Legionaries were not permitted to marry. Recruits who were married at the time of enrolment had their marriages annulled and had to wait until their enlistment expired to take a wife officially, although in practice there were many camp followers and many de facto relationships. The emperor Septimius Severus repealed the marriage regulation, so that from AD 197 serving legionaries could marry.

For many decades, each imperial legion had its own dedicated recruitment ground. The 3rd Gallica Legion, for example, was for many years recruited in Syria, despite its name, while both 7th legions were recruited in eastern Spain. By the second half of the first century, for the sake of expediency, recruiting grounds began to shift; the 20th Legion, for instance, which had up to that time been recruited in northern Italy, received an increasing number of its men from the East.

When a legion was initially raised, its enlistment took place en masse, which meant that a legion's men who survived battle wounds and sickness were later discharged together. As a result, as Scottish historian Dr Ross Cowan has observed, Rome 'had to replenish much of a legion's strength at a single stroke'. [Cow., *RL* 58 – 69] When a legion's discharge and re-enlistment fell due, all its recruits were enrolled at the same time. Although the official minimum age was 17, the average age of recruits tended to be around 20.

Some old hands stayed on with the legions after their discharge was due, and were often promoted to optio or centurion. There are numerous gravestone examples of soldiers who served well past their original twenty-year enlistment. Based on such gravestone evidence, many historians believe that all legionaries' enlistments were universally extended from twenty to twenty-five years in the second half of the first century, although there is no firm evidence of this.

Legions rarely received replacements to fill declining ranks as the enlistments of their men neared the end of their twenty years. Tacitus records replacements being brought into legions on only two occasions, in AD 54 and AD 61, in both cases in exceptional circumstances. Accordingly, legions frequently operated well under optimum strength. [Ibid.]

By AD 218, mass discharges would be almost a thing of the past. The heavy losses suffered by the legions during the wars of Marcus Aurelius, Septimius Severus and Caracalla meant that the legions needed to be regularly brought up to strength again or they would have ceased to be effective fighting units. The short-lived emperor Macrinus (AD 217–218) deliberately staggered legion recruitment, for 'he hoped that these new recruits, entering the army a few at a time, would refrain from rebellion'. [Dio, LXXIX, 30]

In 216 BC, two previous oaths of allegiance were combined into one, the *ius iurandum*, administered to legion recruits by their tribunes. From the reign of Augustus, initially on 1 January, later on 3 January, the men of every legion annually renewed the oath of allegiance at mass assemblies: 'The soldiers swear that they will obey the emperor willingly and implicitly in all his commands, that they will never desert, and will always be ready to sacrifice their lives for the Roman Empire.' [Vege., II]

On joining his legion, the legionary was exempt from taxes and was no longer subject to civil law. Once in the military, his life was governed by military law, which in many ways was more severe than the civil code.

IV. SPECIAL DUTIES

Legions' headquarters staff included an adjutant, clerks and orderlies who were members of the legion. The latter, called *benificiari*, were excused normal legion duties and were frequently older men who had served their full enlistment but who had stayed on in the army.

Legionaries served as clerks, armourers, tailors and so on, as well as in the ranks. It has long been known that the legions were supported by medical orderlies; in this scene from Trajan's Column, the medics tending both legionaries and auxiliaries during a battle in Dacia, are themselves auxiliaries.

V. DISCIPLINE AND PUNISHMENT

'I want obedience and self-restraint from my soldiers just as much as courage in the face of the enemy.'
JULIUS CAESAR, *The Gallic War*, VII, 52

Tight discipline, unquestioning obedience and rigid training made the Roman legionary a formidable soldier. Roman military training aimed not only to teach men how to use their weapons, it quite deliberately set out to make legionaries physically and mentally tough fighting machines who would obey commands without hesitation.

As one of the indications of his rank, every centurion carried a vine stick, the forerunner of the swagger stick of some modern armies. Centurions were at liberty to use their sticks to thrash any legionary mercilessly for minor infringements. A centurion named Lucilius, who was killed in the AD 14 Pannonian mutiny, had a habit of brutally breaking a vine stick across the back of a legionary, then calling 'Bring another!', a phrase that became his nickname. [Tac., *A*, 1, 23]

For more serious infringements, legionaries found guilty by a court martial conducted by the legion's tribunes could be sentenced to death. Polybius described the crimes for which the death penalty was prescribed in 150 BC – stealing goods in camp, giving false evidence, homosexual offences committed by those in full man-hood, and for lesser crimes where the offender had previously been punished for the same offence three times. The death penalty was later additionally prescribed for falling asleep while on sentry duty. Execution also awaited men who made a false report to their commanding officer about their courage in the field in order to gain a distinction, men who deserted their post in a covering force, and those who through fear threw away weapons on the battlefield. [Poly., VI, 37]

If whole units were involved in desertion or cowardice, they could be sentenced to decimation: literally, reduction by one tenth. Guilty legionaries had to draw lots. One in ten would die, with the other nine having to perform the execution. Decima-tion sentences were carried out with clubs or swords or by flogging, depending on the whim of the commanding officer. Survivors of a decimated unit could be put on barley rations and made to sleep outside the legion camp's walls, where there was no protection against attack. Although both Julius Caesar and Mark Antony decimated their legions, this form of punishment was rarely applied during the imperial era.

First-century general Corbulo had one soldier brought out of the trench he was digging and executed on the spot for failing to wear a sword on duty. After this, Corbulo's centurions reminded their men that they must be armed at all times, so one cheeky legionary went naked while digging, except for a dagger on his belt. Not famed for his sense of humour, Corbulo had this man, too, pulled out and put to death. [Tac., XI, 18]

VI. LEGIONARY PAY

Julius Caesar doubled the legionary's basic pay from 450 to 900 sesterces a year, which was what an Augustan recruit could expect. This was increased to 1,200 by Domitian in AD 89. [Dio, LXVII, 3] Before this, Roman soldiers were paid 300 sesterces three times a year, instalments which Domitian raised to 400 sesterces each. [Ibid.]

The legionary's annual salary was infinitesimal compared to the 100,000 ses-terces a year earned by a *primus pilus,* the most senior centurion of a legion, and the 400,000 a year salary of the legate commanding the legion. Deductions were made from the legionary's salary to cover certain expenses, including contributions to a funeral fund for each man. Conversely, he also received small allowances for items such as boot nails and salt.

Another source of legionary income was the donative, the bonus habitually paid to the legions by each new emperor when he took the throne – 300 sesterces per man was common. The legionaries normally received another, smaller, bonus on each subsequent anniversary of the emperor's accession to the throne. In addition, emperors frequently left several thousand sesterces per man to

their legionaries in their wills. Profits from war booty could also be substantial. After Titus completed the Siege of Jerusalem in AD 70, so much looted Jewish gold was traded in Syria that the price of gold in that province halved overnight.

A legionary could lodge his savings in a bank maintained at his permanent winter base; his standard-bearer was the unit's banker. In AD 89, Domitian limited the amount each man could keep in his legion bank to 1,000 sesterces, after a rebel governor used funds from his legions' banks in an abortive rebellion against him. [Suet., XII, 7]

A soldier who fought bravely could have his pay increased by 50 per cent or doubled for the rest of his career, and accordingly gained the titles of *sesquipliciarus* or *duplicarius*. Men with these awards were represented separately from the other rank and file when units submitted their strength reports to area headquarters, immediately following the optios and centurions on the lists. Men of duplicarius status proudly made reference to it on their tombstones.

To gain popularity with the legions, the emperor Caracalla (AD 211–217), 'who was fond of spending money on the soldiers', increased legionary pay and introduced various exemptions from duty for legionaries. [Dio, LXXVIII, 9] Cassius Dio, a senator at the time, complained that the salary increase would add 280 million sesterces to the cost of maintaining the legions. [Dio, LXXIX, 36] In AD 218, Caracalla's successor Macrinus announced that the pay increase would only apply to serving legionaries and that new recruits would from that time forward be paid at the same rate as had applied during the reign of Caracalla's father, Septimius Severus. This only hastened Macrinus' overthrow that same year. [Ibid.]

VII. COMPARATIVE BUYING POWER OF A LEGIONARY'S INCOME (First–Second Centuries AD)

Item	Amount (In sesterces, [HS])	Source
Annual salary, legionary (from reign of Domitian)	1,200	Suetonius [*Twelve Caesars*]
Legionary's retirement bonus	12,000	Dio [*Histories*]
Annual salary, centurion	20,000	Dudley [*RaiB*]
Annual salary, chief centurion	100,000	Dudley [*RaiB*]
Annual salary, procurator	60,000–100,000	Radice*
Annual salary, senior proconsul, Prefect of Egypt, and senior legate	400,000	Radice*
Praetorian guardsman's retirement bonus	20,000	Dio [*Histories*]
Value, small farm	100,000	Pliny [*Letters*]
Purchase price, large Italian estate	3 million	Pliny [*Letters*]
Permissible fee for defence advocate in a major court case	10,000	Pliny [*Letters*]
Cost of banquet thrown by the emperor Vitellius (AD 69)	400,000	Suetonius [*Twelve Caesars*]
Estimated fortune of writer and senator Pliny the Younger	15–20 million	Pliny [*Letters*]
Estimated fortune of Nero's chief secretary Seneca (AD 60)	300 million	Tacitus [*Annals*]
Entry requirement, Equestrian Order – personal net worth	400,000	Dio [*Histories*]
Entry requirement, Senatorial Order – personal net worth	1.2 million	Dio [*Histories*]
State price for grain, per peck (one fourth of a bushel)	3	Tacitus [*Annals*]
Daily cash dole (*sportula*) to clients	6¼	Juvenal [*Satires*]
Cost of admission to public baths	¹/₁₆	Juvenal [*Satires*]
Purchase price of the latest book by the author Martial	20	Martial [*Epigrams*]

*Betty Radice, editor and translator, in notes to *The Letters of the Younger Pliny*, Penguin Books, 1963.

VIII. MILITARY DECORATIONS AND AWARDS

Legionaries who distinguished themselves in battle could expect not only monetary rewards. At an assembly following a victorious battle, soldiers would be called forward by their general. A thorough written record was maintained on every man in every unit, with promotions, transfers, citations, reprimands and punishments all studiously noted down by the man's optio, the second-in-command of his century. The general would read the legionary's previous citations aloud, then praise the soldier publicly for his latest act of gallantry, promoting him and often giving him a lump sum cash award or putting him on double pay, before presenting him with decorations for valour, to the applause of the men of his legion. Polybius recorded these awards, which continued to be presented for hundreds of years: [Poly., VI, 39]

> **THE SPEAR:** for wounding an enemy in a skirmish or other action where it was not necessary to engage in single combat and therefore expose himself to danger. Literally 'the Ancient Unadorned Spear', a silver, later golden, token. No award was made if the wound was inflicted in the course of a pitched battle, as the soldier was then acting under orders to expose himself to danger. The emperor Trajan appears to be presenting a spear to a soldier in a scene on Trajan's Column.
>
> **THE SILVER CUP:** for killing and stripping an enemy in a skirmish or other action where it was not necessary to engage in single combat. For the same deed, a cavalryman received a decoration to place on his horse's harness.
>
> **THE SILVER STANDARD:** for valour in battle. First awarded in the first century AD.
>
> **THE TORQUE AND AMULAE:** for valour in battle. A golden necklace and wrist bracelets. Frequently won by centurions and cavalrymen.
>
> **THE GOLD CROWN:** for outstanding bravery in battle.

This memorial to a Roman soldier named Voconius at Merida in Spain, a military colony established by Augustus, depicts the soldier's military decorations – a pair of torques and amulae.

THE MURAL CROWN: awarded to the first Roman soldier over an enemy city wall in an assault. Crenallated, and of gold.

THE NAVAL CROWN: for outstanding bravery in a sea battle. A golden crown decorated with ships' beaks.

THE CROWN OF VALOUR: awarded to the first Roman soldier to cross the ramparts of an enemy camp in an assault.

THE CIVIC CROWN: awarded to the first man to scale an enemy wall. Made from oak leaves, the Civic Crown was also awarded for saving the life of a fellow soldier, or shielding him from danger. The man whose life was saved was required to present his saviour with a golden crown, and to honour him as if he were his father for the rest of his days. It was considered to be Rome's highest military decoration, and the holder of the Civic Crown was venerated by Romans and given pride of place in civic parades. Julius Caesar was awarded the Civic Crown when serving as a young tribune in the assault on Mytilene, capital of the Greek island of Lesbos.

Entire units could also receive citations, and these were displayed on their standards.

IX. LEGIONARY UNIFORMS AND EQUIPMENT

In early republican days, each legionary was expected to provide his own uniform, equipment and personal weapons, and to replace them when they were worn out, damaged or lost. After the consul Marius' reforms, the State provided uniforms, arms and equipment to conscripts.

The tunic and personal legionary equipment remained basically unchanged for hundreds of years. By Augustan times, the legionary wore a woollen tunic made of two pieces of cloth sewn together, with openings for the head and arms, and with short sleeves. It came to just above the knees at the front, a little lower at the back. The military tunic was shorter than that worn by civilians. In cold weather, it was not unusual for two tunics to be worn, one over the other. Sometimes more than two were worn – Augustus wore up to four tunics at a time in winter months. [Suet., II, 82]

With no examples surviving to the present day, the colour of the legionary tunic has always been hotly debated. Many historians believe that it was a red berry colour and that this was common to legions and guard units. Some authors argue that legionary tunics were white. Vitruvius, Rome's chief architect during the early decades of the empire, wrote that, of all the natural colours used in dying fabrics and for painting, red and yellow were by far the easiest and cheapest to obtain. [Vitr., *OA*, VII, 1–2]

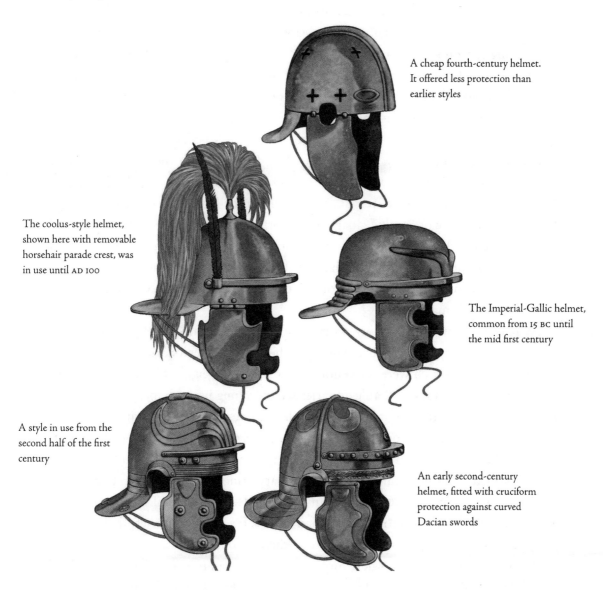

A cheap fourth-century helmet. It offered less protection than earlier styles

The coolus-style helmet, shown here with removable horsehair parade crest, was in use until AD 100

The Imperial-Gallic helmet, common from 15 BC until the mid first century

A style in use from the second half of the first century

An early second-century helmet, fitted with cruciform protection against curved Dacian swords

LEGIONARY HELMETS

Second-century Roman general Arrian described the tunics worn by cavalry during exercises as predominantly a red berry colour, or, in some cases, an orange-brown colour – a product of red. He also described multicoloured cavalry exercise tunics. [Arrian, *TH*, 34] But no tunic described by Arrian was white or natural in colour. Red was also the colour of unit banners, and of legates' ensigns and cloaks.

Tacitus, in describing Vitellius' entry into Rome in July AD 69, noted that marching ahead of the standards in Vitellius' procession were 'the camp-prefects, the tribunes, and the highest-ranked centurions, in white robes'. [Tac., *H*, II, 89] These were the loose ceremonial robes worn by officers when they took part in religious processions. That Tacitus specifically notes they were white indicates that he was differentiating these garments from the non-white tunics worn by the military.

The one colour that legionaries and auxiliaries were least likely to wear was blue. This colour, not unnaturally, was associated by Romans with the sea. Pompey the Great's son Sextus Pompeius believed he had a special association with Neptune, god of the sea, and in the 40s to 30s BC, when admiral of Rome's fleets in the western Mediterranean, he wore a blue cloak to honour Neptune. After Sextus rebelled and was defeated by Marcus Agrippa's fleets, Octavian granted Agrippa the right to use a blue banner. Apart from the men of the 30th Ulpia Legion, whose emblems related to Neptune, if any of Rome's military wore blue in the imperial era, it would have been her sailors and/or marines.

Whatever the weather, and irrespective of the fact that auxiliaries in the Roman army, both infantry and cavalry, wore breeches, Roman legionaries did not begin wearing trousers, which were for centuries considered foreign, until the second century. Some scholars suggest that legionaries wore nothing beneath their tunics, others suggest they wore a form of loin cloth, which was common among civilians.

Over his tunic the legionary could wear a *subarmalis*, a sleeveless padded vest, and over that a cuirass – an armoured vest. Because of their body armour, legionaries were classified as 'heavy infantry'. Early legionary armour took the form of a sleeveless leather jerkin on to which were sown small ringlets of iron mail. Legionaries and most auxiliaries continued to wear the mail cuirass for many centuries; there was no concept of superseding military hardware as there is today.

Early in the first century a new form of armour began to enter service, the *lorica segmentata*, made up of solid metal segments joined by bronze hinges and held together by leather straps, covering torso and shoulders. This segmented legionary armour was the forerunner of the armour worn by mounted knights in the Middle Ages. By AD 75, a simplified version of the segmented infantry armour was in widespread use. Called today the Newstead type, because an example was found in modern times at Newstead in Scotland, it stayed in service for the next 300 years.

On his head, the legionary wore a conical helmet of bronze or iron. There were a number of variations on the evolving 'jockey cap' design, but most had the common features of hinged cheek flaps of metal, tied together under the chin, a horizontal projection at the rear to protect the back of the neck, like a fireman's helmet, and a small brow ridge at the front.

First- and second-century legionary helmets unearthed in modern times have revealed occasional traces of felt inside, suggesting a lining. In the fourth century, the Roman officer Ammianus Marcellinus wrote of 'the cap which one of us wore under his helmet'. This cap was probably made of felt, for Ammianus described how he and two rank and file soldiers with him used the cap 'in the manner of a sponge' to soak up water from a well to quench their thirst in the Mesopotamian desert. [Amm., XIX, 8, 8] By the end of the fourth century, legionaries were wearing 'Pamonian leather caps' beneath their helmets, which, said Vegetius, 'were formerly introduced by the ancients to a different design', indicating the caps beneath helmets had been in common use for a long time. [Vege., *MIR*, 10]

After a legion had been wiped out in AD 86 by the lethally efficient *falx*, the curved, double-handed Dacian sword, which had sliced through helmets of unfortunate Roman troops, legion helmets had cruciform reinforcing strips added over the crown to provide better protection. It was not uncommon for owners of helmets to inscribe their initials on the inside or on the cheek flap. A legionary helmet unearthed at Colchester in Britain had three sets of initials stamped inside it, indicating that helmets passed from owner to owner. [W&D, 4, n. 56] In Syria in AD 54, lax legionaries of the 6th Ferrata and 10th Fretensis legions sold their helmets while still in service. [Tac., *A*, XIII, 35]

During republican times, Rome's heavy-armoured troops, the hastati, wore eagle feathers on their helmets to make themselves seem taller to their enemies. By the time of Julius Caesar, this had become a crest of horsehair on the top of legionary helmets. These crests were worn in battle until the early part of the first century, before being relegated to parade use. The colour of the crest is debatable. Some archaeological discoveries suggest they were dyed yellow. Arrian, governor of Cappadocia in the reign of Hadrian, described yellow helmet crests on the thousands of Roman cavalrymen under his command. [Arr., *TH*, 34] The feathers of the republican hastati were sometimes purple, sometimes black, which possibly evolved into purple or black legionary helmet crests. [Poly., VI, 23]

The helmet was the only item of equipment a legionary was permitted to remove while digging trenches and building fortifications. Helmets were slung around the neck while on the march. The legionary also wore a neck scarf, tied at the throat, originally to prevent his armour chafing his neck. The scarf became fashionable, with auxiliary units quickly adopting them, too. It is possible that different units used different coloured scarves. On his feet the legionary wore heavy-duty hobnailed leather sandals called *caligulae*, which left his toes exposed. At his waist he wore the *cingulum*, an apron of four to six metal strands which by the fourth century was no longer used.

X. THE LEGIONARY'S WEAPONS

The imperial legionary's first-use weapon was the javelin, the *pilum*, of which he would carry two or three, the shorter 5 feet (152 centimetres) in length, the longer, 7 feet (213 centimetres). Primarily thrown, javelins were weighted at the business end and, from Marius' day, were designed to bend once they struck, to prevent the enemy from throwing them back. 'At present they are seldom used by us,' said Vegetius at the end of the fourth century, 'but are the principal weapon of the barbarian heavy-armed foot.' [Vege., *MIR*, I] By Vegetius' day, a lighter spear, with less penetrating power, was used by Roman troops.

This golden sword and scabbard would have been the proud possession of an imperial officer.

The legionary carried a short sword, the *gladius*, its blade 20 inches (50 centimetres) long, double-edged, and with a sharp point for effective jabbing. Spanish steel was preferred, leading to the gladius becoming known as 'the Spanish sword'. It was kept in a scabbard, which was worn on the legionary's right side, in contrast to officers, who wore it on the left.

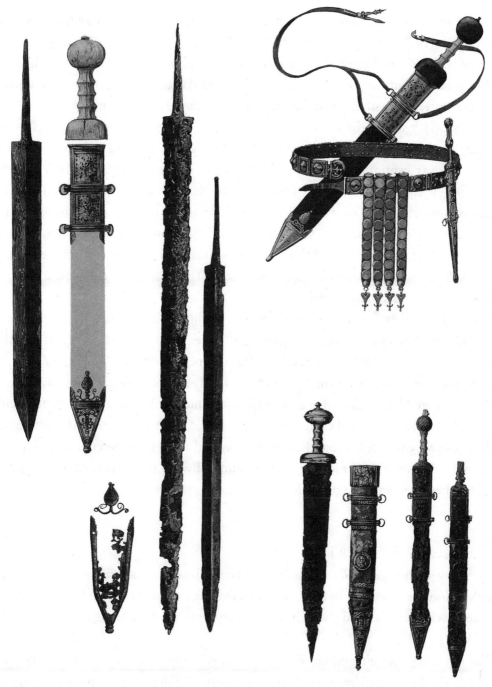

Top right: Roman sword, a gladius, with baldric and dagger belt, mid to late first century AD. Bottom right: an early first-century AD gladius from Rheingoenheim and a sheath from the Rhine; a gladius found at Pompeii, and another now in a museum in Mainz. On the left: other swords found on the Rhine.

By the fourth century, the gladius had been replaced by a longer sword similar to the *spatha* carried by auxiliary cavalry from Augustus' time. The legionary was also equipped with a short dagger, the *pugio*, worn in a scabbard on the left hip, which was still being carried into the fifth century. Sword and dagger scabbards were frequently highly decorated with silver, gold, jet and ceramic inlay, even precious stones.

The legionary shield, the *scutum*, was curved and elongated. Polybius described the legionary shield as convex in shape, with straight sides, 4 feet (121 centimetres) long and 2½ feet (75 centimetres) across. The thickness at the rim was a palm's breadth. It consisted of two layers of wood fastened together with bull's hide glue. The outer surface was covered with canvas and then with smooth calf-skin, glued in place. The edges of the shield were rimmed with iron strips, as a protection against sword blows and wear and tear. The centre of the shield was fixed with an iron or bronze boss, to which the handle was attached on the reverse side. The boss could deflect the blows of swords, javelins and stones. [Poly., VI, 23]

On to the leather surface of the shield was painted the emblem of the legion to which the owner belonged. Vegetius, writing at the end of the fourth century, said that 'every cohort had its shields painted in a manner peculiar to itself'. [Vege., *MIR*, II] While Vegetius was talking in the past tense, several examples suggest that each cohort of the Praetorian Guard may have used different thunderbolt emblems on their shields. The shield was always carried on the left arm in battle, with a strap over the arm taking much of the weight. On the march, it was protected from the elements with a leather cover, and slung over the legionary's left shoulder. By the third century, the legionary shield had become oval, and much less convex.

XI. LEGIONARY TRAINING

First-century Jewish general and historian Flavius Josephus described the training of Rome's legions as bloodless battles, and their battles as bloody drills. 'Every soldier is exercised every day,' he said, 'which is why they bear the fatigue of battles so easily.' [Jos., *JW*, 3, 5, 1]

The legionary's training officer was his *optio*, who ensured that his men trained and exercised. The Roman soldier's sword training involved long hours at wooden posts. He was taught to thrust, not cut, using the sharp point of his sword. 'A stab,' said Vegetius, 'although it penetrates just 2 inches [5 centimetres], is generally fatal.' [Vege., *MIR*, I]

A legionary also learned to march in formation, and to deploy in various infantry manoeuvres. In standard battle formation soldiers would form up in ranks of eight men deep by ten wide, with a gap of 3 feet (1 metre) between each legionary, who, in the opening stage of a battle, would launch first his javelins then draw his sword. Withdrawing auxiliaries could pass through the gaps in the ranks, until, on command, the legionaries closed ranks. In close order, compacted against his nearest comrades, the legionary could link his shield with his neighbour's for increased protection. His century might run to the attack, or steadily advance at the march.

In battle order, the century's centurion was the first man on the left of the first rank. The century's *tesserarius* was last on the left in the rear rank, while the optio stood at the extreme right in the rear rank, from where it was his task to keep the century in order and to prevent desertions. Basic battle formations included the straight line, oblique and crescent. For defence against cavalry, the wedge or a stationary hollow square would be employed, or a partial hollow square with the men on three sides facing outward while the tightly packed formation continued to shuffle forward. The *orbis*, or ring, was a formation of last resort for a surrounded force.

Apart from route marches, legionaries, from the time of the consul Marius, were also trained to run considerable distances carrying full equipment. In addition, the legionary learned defensive and offensive techniques, and to rally round his unit's standard, or any standard in an emergency. The famous *testudo*, or tortoise, involved locked shields over heads and at sides, providing protection from a rain of spears, arrows, stones, etc. The testudo, 'most often square but sometimes rounded or oblong', was primarily used when legions were trying to undermine the walls of enemy fortresses, or to force a gate. [Arr., *TH*, 11] Double testudos are also known, with one group of men standing on the raised shields of a formation beneath them and in turn fixing their shields over their own heads.

XII. LEGIONARY RATIONS AND DIET

Cassius Dio wrote of the diet of legionaries: 'They require kneaded bread and wine and oil.' [Dio, LXII, 5] Legionaries were given a grain ration, which they were expected to grind into flour using each squad's grinding stone. They cooked their own loaves, typically round and cut into eight slices, one for each member of the squad. Legionaries drizzled their bread with olive oil. They also ate meat, but this was considered supplementary to their bread ration. Coffee, tomatoes and bananas were unknown to the Romans, as was sugar; honey was their only sweetener.

The quantity of grain provided for the troops depended on the available supply and the generosity of commanders. In Polybius' day it was half a bushel per legionary a month, and the cost was deducted from the soldier's pay. In imperial times, the legionary's grain ration was free. Much of the general population of Rome at that time was also provided with free grain by the government, although bakers, pastrycooks, and other commercial operators had to pay for it.

Like the upper class, Roman soldiers ate with their fingers. They used their dagger to cut bread and meat. The fork was unknown to all classes. Romans drank wine with their meals, but it was diluted with water; legionaries are rarely recorded drunk in camp. Breakfast for Romans was often just a cup of water. Lunch, *prandium*, was a cold snack at noon, or a piece of bread at the end of the day's march. For legionaries, the day's main meal was in the evening.

By late in the first century, with legions based in permanent winter camps, rations were being acquired from local merchants who themselves sourced food and wine from the far corners of the empire. Some of those foods could be quite exotic, and both legionaries and auxiliaries ate well. Parts of the handwritten labels on amphorae have been found on pottery shards discovered in a fort which housed the cavalry of the Ala Augusta at Carlisle, Roman Luguvalium, in Britain. One had contained the sweet fruit of the doum palm from Egypt. Another reads: 'Old Tangiers tunny, provisions, quality, excellent, top-quality.' Tunny fish (*cordula*) netted in the Straits of Hercules (off Gibraltar) was processed at Tingatitanum, today's Tangiers, being chopped up and packed in its own juice into amphora for shipment. The resultant fish paste was a great delicacy; at the Carlisle base it was probably exclusively consumed by officers. [Tom., *DRA*]

Amphorae containing provisions were also marked with the age of the contents in years, the capacity of the container, and the name of the firm that had produced it – a label found at Colchester named the firm of Proculus and Urbicus. Another label from the very same firm was also found in the ruins of Pompeii in Italy. [Ibid.]

XIII. FURLOUGHS AND FURLOUGH FEES

During the first century, and probably for much of the imperial era, when a legion went into winter quarters each year one legionary in four could take leave. The job of recording leave details fell to each unit's records clerk, who was 'exact in entering the time and limitation of furloughs'. [Vege., *DRM*, III] To receive their leave pass, the enlisted men of each legion had to pay their centurion a furlough fee, which the centurions retained.

Until AD 69, centurions could set the fee at any amount they chose, and this became a source of great complaint from legionaries. Tacitus wrote, 'A demand was then made [to new emperor Otho] that fees for furloughs usually paid to the centurions be abolished. These were paid by the common soldiers as a kind of annual tribute. A fourth part of every century could be scattered on furlough, or even loiter about the camp, provided they paid the fees to the centurions.' The officers had not given any attention to these fees, said Tacitus, and the more money a soldier had, the more his centurion would demand to allow him to go on leave. [Tac., *H*, I, 46]

Otho did not want to alienate the centurions by abolishing furlough fees, a lucrative source of income for them, but at the same time wanted to ensure the loyalty of the enlisted men. So he promised in future to pay to centurions the furlough fees on all legionaries' behalf from his own purse. [Ibid.] Within months, Otho was dead, but his successor as emperor, Vitellius, kept his promise to the rank and file: 'He paid the furlough fees to the centurions from the imperial treasury.' [Tac., *H*, I, 58] 'This was without doubt a salutary reform,' Tacitus observed, 'and was afterwards under good emperors established as a permanent rule of the service.' [Ibid., 46]

Men on furlough often went far afield, and could not easily be recalled in emergencies. [Tac., *A*, XV, 10] It seems that while the men left their helmets, shields, javelins and armour back at base when they went on furlough, they habitually continued to wear their military sandals and travelled armed with their swords on sword-belts wherever they went, even in towns, where civilians were forbidden to go armed. Petronius Arbiter, in his *Satyricon*, written in the time of Nero, has his narrator strap on a sword-belt when staying in a seaside town in Greece. While walking through the town's streets at night, illegally wearing his sword, he was challenged.

'Halt! Who goes there?' a guard demanded. Seeing the sword on his hip, the guard assumed the man must be a legionary on leave, and asked, 'What legion are you from? Who is your centurion?' The guard then noticed that the man was wearing Greek-style white shoes. 'Since when have men in your unit gone on leave in white shoes?' In response, Petronius' narrator lied about both centurion and legion. 'But my face and my confusion proved that I had been caught in a lie,' he went on, 'so he [the guard] ordered me to surrender my arms.' [Petr., 82]

XIV. LEGION MUSICIANS

To relay orders in camp, on the march, and in battle, unarmed musicians were attached to all legions to play the lituus, a trumpet made of wood covered with leather, and the cornu and buccina, which were horns in the shape of a 'C'. Legion musicians wore leather vests over their tunics, and bearskin capes over their helmets. There is no record of them playing music on the march. Their role was exclusively that of signallers.

Legion horn players were unarmed, and wore animal skin capes.

XV. THE STANDARD-BEARER, TESSERARIUS AND OPTIO

Every legion, maniple and century had a standard behind which its men marched, and it was a great honour to be the official bearer of the sacred standard. It was the greatest honour of all to be the *aquilifer*, the man who carried the legion's golden eagle standard, the *aquila*. Ranking above ordinary legionaries, the standard-bearer had much influence with the rank and file and was sometimes involved in councils of war by their generals. Standard-bearers also managed the legion banks.

The *tesserarius* was the man in each century whose task it was to circulate the *tessera*, a wax tablet containing the daily watchword, to sentries in camp, and to all ranks prior to battle.

In the infantry, the *optio* was the deputy to a century's centurion. In the cavalry, he was deputy to a decurion. The equivalent of a sergeant-major today, the

Legion and Praetorian Guard standard bearers are frequently depicted on Trajan's Column, early second century.

optio was responsible for the century's records and training, and in battle was required to keep his century in order – several trumpet calls were directed specifically at optios for this purpose. An optio was a centurion-designate, and when a vacancy arose for a new centurion, an optio would be promoted to fill it.

XVI. THE DECURION

With his title literally and originally relating to the command of ten men, the *decurio* was a junior officer, subordinate to a centurion, who commanded a troop of cavalry in both the legions and auxiliary mounted units, which in turn was commanded by a squadron's most senior decurion. Typically, decurions of auxiliary cavalry had previously served as legionaries and were transferred to the alae.

A second-century decurion, Titus Calidius, joined a legion at the age of 24 and rose to become a decurion with the cavalry squadron of the 15th Apollinaris Legion. He was subsequently transferred, as a senior decurion, to the 1st Alpinorum Cohort, an auxiliary equitata unit based at Carnuntum with the 15th Apollinaris during the reign of Domitian. When Calidius completed his enlistment with the 1st Alpinorum he re-enlisted with the unit, which continued to be based at Carnuntum after the 15th Apollinaris Legion was transferred to the East in AD 113 for Trajan's Parthian War. Calidius went back to the 1st Alpinorum Cohort at the reduced rank of optio of horse. He died at the age of 58, having served in the Roman military for thirty-four years, and was buried at Carnuntum. [Hold., *DRA*, ADRH]

XVII. THE CENTURION

The *centurio* was the key, middle-ranking officer of the Roman army. Julius Caesar considered the centurion the backbone of his army, and knew many of his centurions by name. Apart from some centurions of Equestrian rank during the reign of Augustus, the imperial centurion was an enlisted man like the legionary, promoted from the ranks. One centurion of Equestrian rank was Clivius Priscus, a native of Carecina in Italy, who ended his military career as a first-rank centurion. His son Helvidius Priscus, born around AD 20, became a quaestor, legion commander and praetor.

The gravestone of first-century centurion, Marcus Favonius.

The centurion originally commanded a century of one hundred men. Centurions commanded the centuries, maniples and cohorts of the legion, with each imperial legion having a nominal complement of fifty-nine centurions, across a number of grades. Julius Caesar's reward for one particular centurion who had pleased him was to promote him eight grades. The centurion could be identified – by friend and foe alike – by a transverse crest on his helmet, metal greaves on his shins, and the fact that, like all Roman officers, he wore his sword on the left, unlike legionaries, who wore their swords on the right.

The first-rank centurions, or *primi ordines*, of a legion's 1st cohort, were the most senior in the legion. Promotion came with time and experience, but many centurions never made it to first-rank status. One first-rank centurion in each legion held the title of *primus pilus* – literally 'first spear'. He was chief centurion of the legion, a highly prestigious and well-paid position for which there was always intense competition among centurions. The vastly experienced *primi pili* always received great respect and significant responsibility, not infrequently leading major army detachments.

Promotion up the various centurion grades involved transfer between various legions. One centurion typically served with twelve different legions during his forty-six-year career throughout the empire. Centurions were also detached from legions to serve as district officers in areas where no legions were based, and were also sent to other legions and auxiliary units as training officers. In AD 83, after a centurion and several legionaries were sent to train a new cohort of Usipi German auxiliaries in Britain, the trainees rebelled, killed their trainers, stole ships and sailed to Europe. The mutineers were subsequently apprehended.

Slaves were not permitted to become legionaries, let alone centurions. In AD 93, time-served centurion Claudius Pacatus was living in retirement when he was recognized as a slave who had escaped many years before. Because of Pacatus' distinguished military service, the emperor Domitian spared his life, but he returned him to his original master, to live out the rest of his days as a slave.

On their retirement, centurions were eligible for employment as lictors, the attendants of magistrates. This well-paid and prestigious post, renewed annually, involved walking ahead of the officials, and clearing the way, carrying one of their ceremonial *fasces*, the magistrates' rods and axes of office.

Many centurions had long careers. Titus Flavius Virilis, a centurion with the 9th Hispana Legion, served for forty-five years before he died at Lambaesis in Africa early in the second century while on attachment to the 3rd Augusta Legion; he was 70 years of age. [*ILS*, 2653]

XVIII. THE CAMP-PREFECT

The third-in-command of each legion of the early empire was the *praefectus castrorum*, or camp-prefect. A mature former primus pilus, the camp-prefect was the legion's quartermaster, and commanded major legion detachments. On occasion – in

Varus' army in the Battle of the Teutoburg in AD 9, and in the case of the 2nd Augusta Legion in Britain in AD 60, for example – camp-prefects commanded entire legions.

By the end of the fourth century, the camp-prefect had been abolished, being replaced by a junior tribune.

XIX. THE TRIBUNES

Young men of Equestrian rank 'served as military tribune as a stepping stone to the Senate', said Dio. [Dio, LXVII, 11] In the republican Roman army, a legion's six tribunes had commanded the troops in battle – each one, on rotation, commanding the legion, the other five commanding two cohorts each. But over time this proved unsatisfactory, and in Augustus' remodelled Roman army the command structure changed dramatically.

Each imperial legion still had six tribunes – one broad-stripe tribune or military tribune, five thin-stripe tribunes (the titles referring to the width of the purple stripes on their togas, and possibly also on their tunics). But the tribunes' roles had altered.

From 23 BC, every well-to-do young Equestrian had to serve as a *tribunus angusticlavius*, tribune of the thin stripe. According to Seneca, the chief secretary to Nero, a thin-stripe tribune did 'his military service as the first step on the road to a seat in the Senate'. [Sen., XLVII] The thin-stripe tribune was an officer cadet, serving a six-month military apprenticeship, the *semestri tribunata*, during the annual campaigning season from March to October. Once they turned 18, thin-stripe tribunes became eligible for the semestri tribunata and – provided their assets totalled the qualifying sum of 400,000 sesterces net – were granted membership of the Equestrian Order.

Gnaeus Agricola, for example, when he went to Britain as a thin-striper in AD 60, was 19. Most thin-stripe tribunes served on the staff of a legate, a legion commander. But some thin-stripers, like Agricola, were taken on to the staff of provincial governors, where they had more opportunity to shine. Appointment as a thin-striper under a legate of note, whose commendation would help later career prospects, did not come about by chance. Examples exist of senators writing to legion commander friends and provincial governors, putting forward their relatives or the sons of friends for appointment as thin-stripe tribunes. [Birl., *DRA*, TCEO]

Legates often took their own sons with them to the provinces to serve on their staff, apparently submitting lists of names of young men they would like to accompany them, or to fill vacancies in their province, for the emperor's approval.

The legion in which Romans served out their semestri tribunata was never listed on memorials or in biographies when the careers of men of achievement were later recorded. It was, after all, nothing more than an internship. Conscientious thin-stripers wishing to make an impression on their sponsors and earn commendation would volunteer for special duty. Historian Tacitus' father-in-law Agricola did not waste his time on the staff of the governor of Britain as a 'loose young' thin-stripe tribune enjoying a 'life of gaiety'. Said Tacitus, Agricola did not 'make his thin-stripe status or his inexperience an excuse for idly enjoying himself and continually going on leave'. Instead, 'he acquainted himself with his province and made himself known to the troops. He learned from the experts and chose the best models to follow. He never sought a duty for self-advertisement, and never shirked one through cowardice.' [Tac., *Agr.*, 5] This suggests that many teenage thin-stripe tribunes wasted their semestri tribunata appointments living it up, leading the 'life of gaiety' that Agricola eschewed.

Thin-stripe tribunes had no authority. When Varus' legions were wiped out at the Battle of the Teutoburg in AD 9, the units' most senior officers were their camp-prefects. [Velle., II, CXX] The three legions involved all had junior tribunes serving with them, and these young men were burned to death by the Germans after their capture. [Tac., *A*, I, 61] Apart from staff duties, thin-stripe tribunes could sit on court martials and shared watch command duties in camp, but in battle they held no power of command.

The sixth tribune in each imperial legion was the *tribunus laticlavius*, tribune of the broad stripe. Called a military tribune in official Roman records, to differentiate this position from the civil post of tribune of the plebeians, a broad-stripe tribune was second-in-command of his legion. Senior tribunes wore a richly decorated helmet, moulded armour and wore a white cloak. They were armed with a sword, worn on the left hip.

Broad-stripers frequently found themselves leading their unit. Some legions, such as those stationed in Egypt, and also in Judea for a time, were permanently commanded by their senior tribunes. This was because those provinces were governed by prefects, and as the legion commanders in their provinces had to take orders from the governors, they could not outrank them. There are numerous examples of legions

A rare depiction of a tribune on a second-century relief. His moulded cuirass was reserved for officers of Equestrian and Senatorial rank; centurions wore the same armour as the rank and file. Were this officer a legate, he would be girdled by a cincticulus, tied in a bow at the front, insignia of rank of legion and army commanders.

elsewhere being led on the march and into battle by their broad-stripe tribunes.

To be promoted to the broad-stripe tribunate, an Equestrian officer had to serve out the first two steps of the three-step promotional ladder formalized by the emperor Claudius (AD 41–54), first as a prefect of auxiliary infantry, then as a more prestigious prefect of auxiliary cavalry, then as a broad-stripe tribune. [Suet., v, 25] A broad-stripe tribune was not yet a senator, but his appointment to the tribunate put him on the list for promotion to the senatorial order at the emperor's pleasure. Broad-stripe tribunes usually served with a legion for three to five years, with passage through the entire three-step promotional process frequently taking nine or ten years, although an outstanding senatorial candidate could be appointed to the Senate at the age of 25.

Claudius realized that, with just twenty-seven legions in his day, there were only twenty-seven military tribunates to fill every three years or so, limiting the number of annual vacancies. With the military tribunate becoming a promotional bottleneck, Claudius introduced the annual appointment of *supernumerary* military tribunes, to push larger numbers of qualified young men through to the Senate. [Ibid.] These supernumerary tribunes did not serve with the legions, but were found other duties. In AD 68–69, Agricola fell into this category, serving out his military tribunate in Italy raising recruits. By AD 71 he had been promoted to a legion command.

Occasionally, broad-stripe tribunes of the early empire went from being second-in-command of legions to being in command of auxiliary cavalry units, an apparently backward step. These seem to have been special battlefield appointments, such as that of Gaius Minicius, who was transferred from the 6th Victrix Legion to command of the 1st Wing of the Singularian Horse in AD 70 during the Civilis Revolt. [*See page 347.*]

Promotion to legion command was neither automatic nor necessarily swift. The future emperor Hadrian, while he was building his military career between AD 95 and 105, spent ten years as a prefect and tribune, commanding various auxiliary units and then being promoted to second-in-command of a legion, the 5th Macedonica, before gaining command of the 1st Minervia Legion.

In around AD 85, Pliny the Younger served as a tribune with the 3rd Gallica Legion at Raphanaea on the Euphrates in southern Syria, where, on the orders of the province's governor, he conducted an audit of the accounts of the cavalry and infantry cohorts attached to his legion (in several cases finding, 'a great deal of shocking rapacity and deliberate inaccuracy'). [Pliny, VII, 31]

By the second half of the second century, military tribunes were increasingly appointed to the command of auxiliary units, probably because of the growing number of supernumerary tribune appointments. For instance, Pertinax, a future emperor, served as a tribune of cavalry on his way to becoming a successful general. [Dio, LXXIV, 3]

XX. THE PREFECT

After his junior tribuneship, a young Equestrian officer gained the rank of prefect and was appointed to command an auxiliary cohort – either an infantry unit or an *equitatae* unit which combined infantry and cavalry. After serving for several years, he would be transferred to the command of an equitatae unit or cavalry wing. He still held the rank of prefect, but a prefect of a mounted unit outranked an infantry prefect. A promising candidate could eventually be appointed a tribune of the broad stripe.

XXI. THE QUAESTOR

Every consul and every provincial governor had a quaestor appointed to his staff; Mark Antony initially served as quaestor to Julius Caesar during the Gallic War. The quaestor was a former broad-stripe tribune. In the provinces, a quaestor's responsibilities included military recruitment in his province. He automatically entered the Senate on completion of his term as quaestor.

A junior magistrate, the quaestor was entitled to one fasces and one lictor. The fasces represented the magistrate's power over life and death. Its symbol was an axe-head projecting from a bundle of elm or birch rods tied with a red strap. Rods of birch were used to beat a condemned man; the axe was then used to behead him.

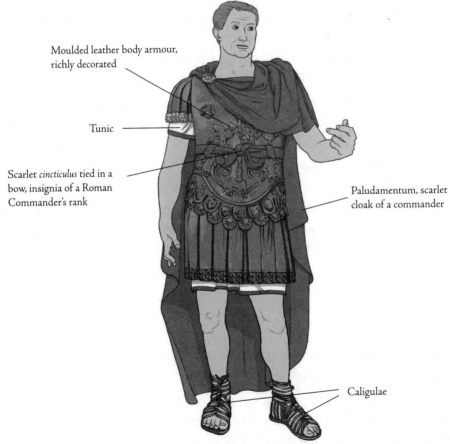

Moulded leather body armour, richly decorated

Tunic

Scarlet *cincticulus* tied in a bow, insignia of a Roman Commander's rank

Paludamentum, scarlet cloak of a commander

Caligulae

THE LEGATE (LEGATUS LEGIONIS)
IMPERIAL LEGION COMMANDER
A senator typically in his early thirties and serving for three to four years.

In 1919, the Fascist Party of Italy took the ancient Roman fasces as its symbol, a word from which the fascist name derived. Benito Mussolini's Italian fascists adopted other imperial Roman symbols such as the eagle and military standards, hoping that some of the old glory would rub off. The fascist name, the eagle and the standards were in turn appropriated by Hitler's National Socialist Party in Germany, the Nazis.

XXII. THE LEGATE

In Augustus' military reforms, the legion commander was the *legatus legionis*, or legate of the legion. A member of the Senatorial order, he was typically in his thirties. The oldest legion legate on record is 62-year-old Manlius Valens, commander of the 1st Italica Legion in AD 68–69; his appointment was the result of a political favour from the emperor Galba.

Augustus set the maximum tour of duty of a legionary legate at two years. Under later emperors this stretched to an average four-year appointment. Tiberius was infamous for leaving men in appointments long term once he had found a place for them, and under him service was longer than usual.

The legate could be distinguished by his richly decorated helmet and body armour, his embroidered scarlet cloak, the *paludamentum*, and his *cincticulus*, a scarlet waistband tied in a bow at his waist. He was entitled to five fasces and five lictors.

By AD 268, the emperor Gallienus had decreed that senators could no longer hold legion commands, and by the end of the third century all legions were being commanded by Equestrian prefects, who then outranked tribunes. [Amm., v, 33]

XXIII. THE PRAETOR

The praetor was a senior Roman magistrate. From the middle of the first century, former praetors were increasingly given legion commands. Outranking legion legates, they were entitled to six fasces and lictors. Both Vespasian and his brother Sabinus held praetor rank when they commanded legions in the AD 43 invasion of Britain.

After AD 268, under the decree of Galienus, praetors no longer held commands.

Propraetor was the title given to governors of imperial Roman provinces – as opposed to proconsul, the title given to 'unarmed' senatorial provinces, whose governors were appointed by the Senate.

XXIV. SENIOR OFFICER RANK DISTINCTIONS
Early Imperial Roman Army

RANK	FASCES AND LICTORS	INSIGNIA
Military Tribune	0	White cloak
Quaestor	1	White cloak
Legatus Legionis	5	Scarlet cloak, waistband and standard
Praetor	6	Same as Legatus
Consul/ex-Consul	12	Purple cloak and standard
Emperor	12–24*	Varied

* Most emperors used 12, although Domitian used 24, as did dictators during the Republic.

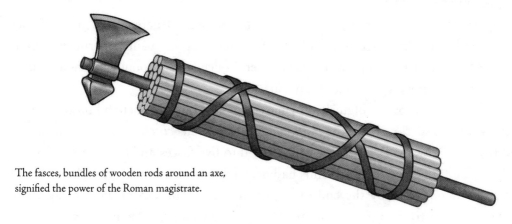

The fasces, bundles of wooden rods around an axe,
signified the power of the Roman magistrate.

XXV. SENIOR OFFICERS OF THE LATE EMPIRE
Prefects, dukes and counts take command

During the reign of co-emperor Diocletian (AD 285–305), Rome's original provinces were divided into more than a hundred smaller provinces, each with their own governor and military commander. Between AD 312 and 337 Constantine the Great took this reorganization further.

With prefects commanding legions, senior tribunes continued to be second-in-command of legions, on the emperor's direct appointment. A 'second tribune' replaced the old enlisted rank of camp-prefect as third-in-command of a legion, and was given the appointment on merit after lengthy service. [Vege., II]

Thin-stripe tribunes were replaced as officer cadets by the *candidati militares*, the military candidates. Under Constantine, this officer training corps comprised two cohorts attached to the emperor's bodyguard. Wearing white tunics and cloaks, *candidatores*, as they were called, were all young men chosen for their height and good looks. Candidati service prepared suitable trainee officers for promotion to tribune and unit commands. On several occasions in the fourth century, the candidates militares went into battle with their emperors, serving as independent fighting units within the imperial bodyguard.

The fourth-century provincial governor was a civilian. Separate provincial military commanders held the rank of *dux*, or 'leader', the latter-day duke. The duke's superior was a regional commander whose authority might extend across several provinces, or even in some cases the entire east or west of the empire, holding the rank of *comes*, literally meaning 'companion' of the emperor, the latter-day count. Counts also had charge of areas of civil administration. Military *comites* also commanded the household guard. In the late fourth century there were always two military counts and thirteen dukes in the west of the Roman Empire, while in the east there were four military counts and twelve dukes.

Both duke and count were distinguished when in armour by a golden *cincticulus*, the general's waistband, as opposed to the scarlet cincticulus of legion legates of old. The duke and count received generous salaries as well as allowances that provided each with 190 personal servants and 158 personal horses. In place of the two praetorian prefects, Constantine introduced the posts of master of

Stilicho, with the rank of count, commanded both the infantry and cavalry arms of the Roman army in the fourth–fifth century.

infantry and master of horse as the empire's supreme military commanders. The post of praetorian prefect was retained, but in a civil administrative role, with several stationed throughout the empire as financial auditors reporting directly to their emperor. [Gibb., XVII]

Many fourth- and fifth-century Roman commanders had foreign blood, among them the counts Silvanus and Lutto, both Franks; Magnentius, a German; Ursicinus, who was probably an Alemanni German; and Stilicho, one of whose parents was a Vandal. The father of Count Bragatio, Master of Horse under Constantius II, was a Frank. Mallobaudes, who was a tribune with the *armaturae*, a heavy-armoured element of the Roman household cavalry in the fourth century, was a Frank by birth, and went on to become king of the Franks. Victor, Master of Horse under the emperor Valens, was a Sarmatian.

XXVI. AUXILIARIES

The auxiliary was a foreign soldier who did not originally hold Roman citizenship. Most provinces and a number of allied states supplied men to fill auxiliary units of the Roman army. Some auxiliary units lived and fought alongside particular legions; others operated independently. In the AD 60s, for example, eight cohorts of Batavian light infantry were partnered with the 14th Gemina Legion.

At least two wings of auxiliary cavalry would also march with a specific legion, so that a legion, with its auxiliary support, would typically take the field with around 5,200 legionaries and a similar number of auxiliaries, creating a fighting force of 10,000 men. In the first century, it was assumed that a legion would always march with its regular auxiliary support units – Tacitus, referring to reinforcements received by Domitius Corbulo in the East in AD 54, described the arrival of 'a legion from Germany with its auxiliary cavalry and light infantry'. [Tac., *A*, XIII, 35]

Independent auxiliary units provided the only military presence in so-called 'unarmed' provinces – Mauretania in North Africa, for instance, was for many years only garrisoned by auxiliaries.

Although often armed in a similar manner to legionaries, auxiliaries wore breeches, sported light ringmail armour, and were referred to as 'light infantry'. Specialist units such as archers, and slingers firing stones and lead shot, were always auxiliaries. Syria provided the best bowmen, while Crete and Spain's Balearic Isles were famous for their slingers. Each legion had a small cavalry component of 128 men, as scouts and couriers, but auxiliaries made up all the Roman army's independent cavalry units. Germans, and in particular Batavians, were the most valued cavalry.

The auxiliary was paid just one third of the salary of the legionary; 300 sesterces a year until the reign of Commodus, when it increased to 400 sesterces. [Starr, v. 1]

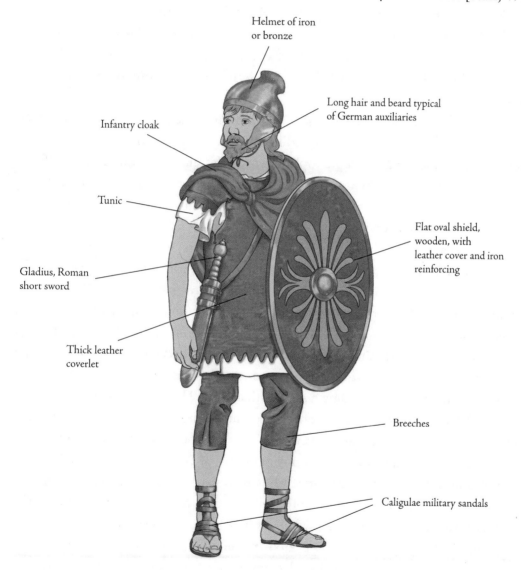

Helmet of iron or bronze

Long hair and beard typical of German auxiliaries

Infantry cloak

Tunic

Flat oval shield, wooden, with leather cover and iron reinforcing

Gladius, Roman short sword

Thick leather coverlet

Breeches

Caligulae military sandals

AUXILIARY
LIGHT INFANTRY SOLDIER
Early second century (taken from Trajan's column).

The auxiliary also served for longer – twenty-five years, as opposed to the legionary's sixteen- and later twenty-year enlistment (plus Evocati service). Once discharged, auxiliaries could not be recalled. They did not receive a retirement bonus, but both auxiliaries and seamen received an enlistment bonus, the *viaticum*, on joining the service, of 300 sesterces. [Ibid.]

From Britain to Switzerland, and from the Balkans to North Africa, tribes were responsible for supplying recruits for their particular ethnic auxiliary units, although there were occasional exceptions. Tiberius decreed that new recruits to the Thracian Horse would come from outside Thrace, much to the aggravation of the proud men of the existing Thracian Horse.

Copies of every individual patent of citizenship issued to discharged auxiliary soldiers were kept at the Capitoline Hill complex at Rome in the Temple of the Good Faith of the Roman People to its Friends. The auxiliary prized his certificate of citizenship; some had themselves depicted on their tombstones holding it. In AD 212, Commodus made Roman citizenship universal, eliminating citizenship as an incentive for auxiliary service.

A typical auxiliary who served his twenty-five years and gained his citizenship was Gemellus from Pannonia, who joined up in AD 97 during the reign of Nerva, and was granted his citizenship on 17 July AD 122 in the reign of Hadrian. Just as a legionary could be transferred between the legions with promotion, auxiliaries moved between different units. When Gemellus received his honourable discharge, he was a decurion with the 1st Pannonian Cohort. His career had seen him work his way from 7th cohort to 1st, serving in units from the Balkans, France, Holland, Spain, Switzerland and Greece, including a stint with the 7th Thracian Cohort in Britain.

Even after they obtained their citizenship, auxiliaries frequently signed up for a new enlistment. Lucius Vitellius Tancinus, a cavalry trooper of the Vettonian Wing, born at Caurium in Spain, joined the army at the age of 20, served his twenty-five-year enlistment in Britain, obtained his citizenship, then signed on for another term. A year later, at the age of 46, he died, probably seeking a cure for whatever ailed him at the Temple of Aquae Sulis in Bath, the waters of which had legendary healing powers.

During most of the imperial era, auxiliary units were commanded by prefects, always members of the Equestrian Order, and frequently young gentlemen of Rome. But in some cases, auxiliary units were commanded by nobles from their own tribe. These ethnic prefects were rarely permitted to rise above prefect rank.

A BRITISH AUXILIARY EARNS EARLY RETIREMENT
The reward for brave service for Rome

On 10 August AD 110, Novanticus, a foot soldier born and raised in the town of Ratae, modern-day Leicester in England, was standing at assembly in a Roman army camp at Darnithethis in recently conquered Dacia. Novanticus was a Celtic Briton. He and some 1,000 other young Celts had joined the Roman army in the spring of AD 98, enrolled by the recently enthroned emperor Trajan in a new auxiliary light infantry unit honoured with the emperor's family name: the *Cohors I Brittonum Ulpia*, or 1st Brittonum Ulpian Cohort.

Three years later, the 1st Brittonum had been one of many units in the 100,000-man Roman army that had invaded Dacia. Novanticus and his British comrades had fought so fiercely and so bravely in the bitterly contested battles in the mountains and passes of Dacia, that, four years after the country had been conquered, the emperor granted all the surviving members of the unit honourable discharges, thirteen years before their twenty-five-year enlistments were due to expire.

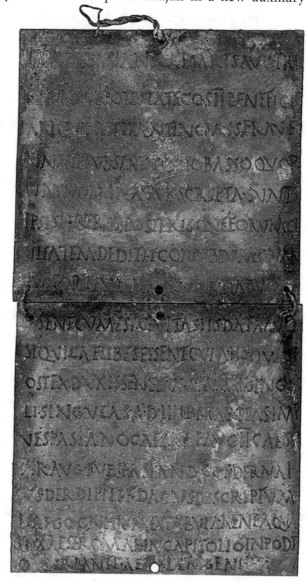

This diploma gives Dernaius Derdipili an honourable discharge from the navy of Emperor Vespasian, Roman citizenship for himself and his descendants, and the right of legal marriage. It is also one of the very few diplomas with the original string and hinge wires preserved. [Translation: *Fleet diploma given by Emperor Vespasian to the veteran sailor Dernaius Derdipili of Thrace after 26 years of service in the Ravenna fleet under the command of Sextus Lucilius Bassus.*]

At assembly, Novanticus presented himself before his commanding officer and was handed a set of bronze sheets just large enough to fit in one hand. This was the Briton's discharge certificate, a copy of which would go to Rome to be displayed with hundreds of thousands of others. With discharge, Novanticus received the prize of Roman citizenship. With citizenship, he could take a multipart Roman name. Novanticus chose a name that honoured the emperor he had loyally served for the past twelve years.

'To the foot soldier Marcus Ulpius Novanticus, son of Adcobrovatus, of Ratae,' the commander read, 'for loyal and faithful service in the Dacian campaigns, before the completion of military service.' [*Discharge certificate of Marcus Ulpius Novanticus, British Museum*]

Marcus Ulpius Novanticus would return home to Britain to enjoy the fruits of his military service and raise a family. Nearly 2,000 years later, his bronze discharge certificate would emerge from the British earth to tell of his part in the Roman war machine.

XXVII. THE USE OF MULTIPART NAMES BY ROMAN AUXILIARIES AND SAILORS

Until AD 212, when Caracalla introduced universal Roman citizenship, auxiliaries, marines and seamen in the Roman navy were not Roman citizens. Non-citizens, so-called *peregrines*, traditionally only used a single name – Genialus, for example. A Latin multipart name such as Gaius Julius Genialus was the preserve of those with the Latin franchise. Accordingly, students of Roman history, from the famous nineteenth-century German scholar Theodor Mommsen onwards, came to assume that anyone recorded with a multipart name had to be a Roman citizen. But, as Professor Chester Starr and others point out, non-citizens serving in the Roman military not infrequently used Latin names, and consequently the legal status of a Roman soldier or sailor cannot always be ascertained from their name. [Starr, v. 1]

Among other examples, Starr, quoting three other eminent scholars, cites the cases of Isidorus and Neon, two non-citizen Egyptian recruits to the 1st Cohort Lusitanorum Praetoria who immediately changed their names to Julius Martialis and Lucius Julius Apollinaris on enrolling. Octavius Valens, an Alexandrine recruit to the same unit, could not have possessed Latin rights either, despite using a Latin name. [Ibid.]

Claudius attempted to stamp out this practice, forbidding peregrines to adopt

Roman family names. But under later emperors the practice revived, and, as Starr notes, auxiliaries came to take on Latin names 'at their pleasure'. [Ibid.] Until the reign of Nero, auxiliaries recruited into the German Guard (the imperial bodyguard) took Greek or Latin names, or cobbled Latin names to their native names on joining. [Speid., 4] During Nero's reign, numerous serving members of the German Guard bore tri-part names which included their native name and 'Tiberius Claudius'. [Ibid.] This was in honour of Nero's predecessor Claudius, in whose reign these men would have joined the unit.

In the reign of Trajan, auxiliary troopers of the Augustan Singularian Horse, the household cavalry, routinely added the names Marcus Ulpius to their own immediately on joining. This would always mark them as men who served the emperor. Likewise, in the reign of Hadrian, when recruits joined this same unit, many took the names of that emperor, Publius Aelius. [Ibid.]

By the second century, the practice of non-citizens using multi-part Latin names was not only commonplace but was accepted at the highest levels, as is made clear by a *c.* AD 106 letter of Pliny the Younger to Trajan, in which he wrote, 'I pray you further to grant full Roman citizenship to Lucius Satrius Abascantus, Publius Caesius Phosphorus and Pancharia Soteris'. [Pliny, x, 11]

Latin names were in extensive use by men serving in second-century auxiliary units despite the fact they had yet to gain Roman citizenship. This is plain to see in an AD 117 report from the 1st Lusitanorum Cohort in Egypt. The report details the receipt of new recruits from the province of Asia and their distribution to various centuries within this auxiliary cohort. The names of the standard-bearers of those auxiliary centuries are all either double- or triple-barrelled. [Tom., *DRA*]

The few surviving records of complete careers of centurions and decurions who served in auxiliary units reveal that those men were Roman citizens, having started out as legionaries before being promoted and transferred to auxiliary units. Yet a ration report from the cavalry wing stationed at Luguvalium in Britain, in the late first or early second century, refers to most of the decurions who commanded the sixteen troops of cavalry at the fort by single name. But all these were nicknames, among them: Agilis (Nimble), Docilis (Docile), Gentilis (Kinsman), Mansuetus (Gentle), Martialis (Warlike), Peculiaris (Special Friend), and Sollemnis (Solemn).

An example of a peregrine who adopted a multipart Latin name as soon as he joined the Roman navy is second-century Egyptian seaman Apion, who wrote home to his family in Egypt to tell them that he had arrived safely at the fleet base at Misenum on Italy's west coast and joined the crew of the warship *Athenonike*. Almost as an aside, he finished his letter with, 'My name is now Antonius Maximus'. [Starr, v, 1]

XXVIII. NUMERI

From the second century, units made up of foreign troops called *numeri* – literally 'numbers' – served with the Roman army as frontier guards, supplied by northern neighbours including the Sarmatians and Germans. Numeri was a generic title for a unit that was not of standard size or structure. No information exists about them. More than twenty numeri units served in Britain alone. [Hold., *RAB*, Indices]

XXIX. MARINES AND SAILORS

Marines served with the two principal Roman battle fleets, at Misenum near Naples, and at Ravenna on the northeast coast, on the Adriatic, as well as with the lesser

Roman officers and marines ready to storm aboard an opposition ship. The ship's oarsmen, out of sight below deck, were paid seamen, not slaves, and were trained to also join shipboard fighting.

fleets around the empire. Marine cohorts also acted as firefighters at major ports such as Ostia and Misenum.

Always non-citizens, and frequently former slaves, marines and sailors were considered inferior to both the legionary and the auxiliary. The marine, the *miles classicus,* was paid less than the legionary and served longer, for twenty-six years. Seamen operating the oars and sails of Rome's warships served under identical conditions to marines, and also received weapons training, to allow them to repel boarders and to act as boarders. Both marines and seamen were organized into centuries, under centurions, aboard their vessels. A libernium, the smallest Roman war galley, typically had a crew of 160 seamen and forty marines.

Marines were trained to operate catapults that fired burning missiles from their ships. They were also involved in close-quarters combat, throwing javelins at enemy ships alongside, often from elevated wooden towers erected on deck. And they formed boarding parties to take enemy ships.

· II ·

THE LEGIONS

'Heaven certainly inspired the Romans with the organization of the legion, so superior does it seem to human invention.'

VEGETIUS, *De Re Militari*, FOURTH CENTURY AD

The Roman legion was more than just a collection of armed men. Each was an institution, with a distinct identity, and a history, sometimes of fame, sometimes of shame. The original imperial legions were not numerous - just twenty-five at the death of the first emperor, Augustus, and thirty a century later under Trajan. Many remained in existence for over 400 years. Although, by the time Rome's fall loomed, many of her once feared and revered legions had disappeared or been relegated to border guard duties. Some legions were consistently reliable, some overcame humiliating defeats to claim glory, while others seemed fated to lead lacklustre careers. These are the legions which made Rome great.

I. LEGION ORGANIZATION

'The peculiar strength of the Romans always consisted of the excellent organization of their legions,' said Vegetius. [Vege., II] He was writing in the late fourth century, when the military organization introduced by Augustus more than 400 years before had been so degraded over time as to make the legions of Vegetius' day pale imitations of the imperial originals.

From 30 BC, Augustus took the 6,000-man republican legion, with its ten cohorts of 600 men, and turned it into a unit with nine cohorts of 480 men, and a so-called 'double strength' 1st cohort of 800 men charged with the protection of the legion's commander and eagle standard. To this, Augustus added a legion cavalry squadron of 128 men, making a legion, on paper, amount to 5,248 men, including 59 centurions, plus three senior officers, its legate, its broad-stripe tribune and its camp-prefect. Added to this were five thin-stripe tribune officer cadets.

Cohorts 2 to 10 were broken down into three maniples, each of 160 men, with every maniple made up of two centuries, each now of 80 men as opposed to the 100-man century of the republican legion. The 1st cohort comprised five maniples, or ten centuries.

The smallest sub-unit in the imperial legion was the *contubernium*, or squad, of eight men. These eight men shared the same tent, cooked together, ate together, fought and died together. In 1963, Lieutenant-General Sir Brian Horrocks, a renowned British corps commander during World War II, was to remark that in an average group of ten fighting men, two are leaders, seven follow, and one doesn't want to be there. [Horr., *SSW*] A similar generalization could probably have applied to the men of a legionary contubernium.

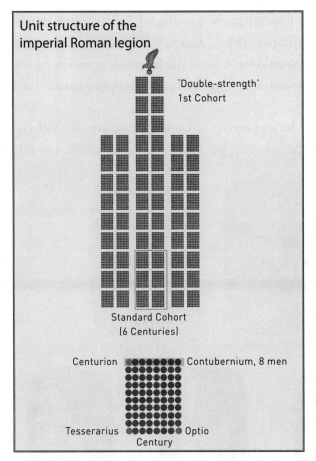

Unit structure of the imperial Roman legion

'Double-strength' 1st Cohort

Standard Cohort (6 Centuries)

Centurion — Contubernium, 8 men

Tesserarius — Optio

Century

Tacitus spoke of 'the military custom by which a soldier chooses his comrade' in his day, indicating that legionaries were encouraged to choose a comrade from their squad who would watch their back in battle and who, if the worse came to the worst, would bury them and ensure that the terms of their will were followed. [Tac., *H*, 1, 18]

II. LAWRENCE KEPPIE'S LEGION NUMBER FORMULA
Explaining the origins of the 5th to 10th Legions

From Livy, we know that in the second century BC, Rome had the 5th, 7th and 8th legions stationed in Spain. We find the 5th and 8th there in 185 BC and the 5th and 7th there in 181 BC. A little earlier, the 11th, 12th and 13th legions had been campaigning in Cisalpine Gaul. [Livy, XXXIX, 30, 12]

Modern legion scholar Dr Lawrence Keppie suggests that, following the series of legion numbers 1 to 4, which were reserved for the consuls, the Senate of the Republic traditionally allocated the legion numbers from west to east across the empire, with legions 5 to 10 in Spain, 11, 12, and 13 in Cisalpine Gaul, and with higher numbers sent to the East, with the 18th Legion, for example, stationed in Cilicia. [Kepp., *MRA*, 2] Much circumstantial evidence supports this formula.

On the basis of the Keppie formula, it is highly likely that when Julius Caesar took up the post of governor of Baetica, or Further Spain, in 61 BC, the 5th, 7th and 8th legions were still based in Rome's then two Spanish provinces, along with a 6th and a 9th. Plutarch says that there were already two legions based in Baetica

that spring, when Caesar arrived in Corduba, the provincial capital, and immediately raised a new legion in the province. [Plut., *Caesar*] Following the Keppie
formula, it is clear that this new unit would have been the latest incarnation of the
10th Legion. Caesar would not raise the 11th and 12th, in Cisalpine Gaul, until
two years later.

Caesar himself wrote that in 58 BC he was served in Gaul by 'four veteran legions'
– as events were to show, these were the 7th, 8th, 9th and 10th. [Caes., *GW*, I, 24] It

5TH ALAUDAE

5TH MACEDONICA

6TH FERRATA

6TH VICTRIX

7TH CLAUDIA

7TH GEMINA

8TH AUGUSTA

9TH HISPANA

10TH FRETENSIS

10TH GEMINA

is probable that he had asked the Senate to give him the three that had served under him in Baetica two years earlier, plus another Spanish-based legion. Caesar says that the Senate soon returned the legion complement in Spain to six. [Caes., *CW*, I, 85] The Keppie formula suggests that the 5th and 6th legions were left behind in Spain when the 7th, 8th, 9th and 10th joined Caesar for his Gallic campaigns.

Later events point to the Senate sending the 2nd, 3rd and 4th to the Iberian peninsula to replace the four legions given to Caesar, together with another unnamed Italian legion, possibly the Martia, while retaining the 1st Legion in Italy. We know that the 2nd Legion was definitely one of those replacement legions sent to Spain by the Senate. [*Alex. W.*, I, 53] These six legions in Spain were under the overall control of Pompey the Great, who at that time governed Spain from Rome, and by 52 BC Pompey had loaned the 6th Legion to Caesar for use in Gaul. By 50 BC, Pompey had recalled the 6th Legion to Spain. [*See page 138*]

There are additional clues that support Keppie's formula. Caesar tells us that in the summer of 49 BC, after he had accepted the surrender of Pompey's five republican legions in Nearer Spain, he sent some of their troops to the south of France, to be discharged once they reached the River Var. He wrote that a third of the surrendered troops, 'those who had homes and possessions in Spain', were discharged at once and allowed to go home. [Caes., *CW*, I, 86] If the men of the 5th and 6th legions were indeed among those surrendered troops, as the Keppie formula would suggest, they had been stationed in Spain for years, and possibly recruited there.

Following the surrender of the two republican legions remaining in Baetica in 49 BC, Caesar left Quintus Cassius Longinus in charge there. The following year, Cassius 'enrolled a new legion, the 5th' at Cordoba. [*Alex. W.*, IV, 50] Why would Cassius choose to give the number 5 to the new legion? Earlier, at the beginning of 49 BC, before the surrender of republican forces in Spain, Pompey's governor in Baetica, Varro, had also raised a new legion in the province, but he had never given it a number; it was known, and continued to be known, even after it defected to Caesar, as the Native or Home-Bred Legion.

At the time the Home-Bred Legion was raised, none of the numbers of the senatorial series normally allocated to legions stationed in Spain (according to the Keppie formula) was vacant – the legion numbers 5 to 10 had all been allocated to serving legions. By the following year, the republican 5th Legion no longer existed, having surrendered to Caesar in eastern Spain. Cassius was therefore free to use one of the numbers of the surrendered legions. Because the 5th had previously been raised in Baetica, and because 5 was the first number in the Senate-approved Spanish series, Cassius was able to use that, creating the new 5th Legion.

It would seem that the numbering sequence identified by Keppie was retained in the imperial era, for in AD 68, when Galba, governor of Nearer Spain, raised a new legion in his province to support his tilt at Nero's throne, he called it the 7th Legion, even though a 7th Legion, the 7th Claudia, already existed. No good reason for his choosing of the number 7 has been advanced by ancient or modern authors. Under the Keppie formula, it would have been perfectly logical to allocate the number 7 to a legion raised in Nearer Spain, the province traditionally involved with the 7th Legion and possibly by AD 68 still an ongoing recruiting ground for the existing 7th Claudia.

There is one more intriguing linking aspect that also lends credence to Keppie's theory that the 5th to 10th legions were traditionally stationed in Spain in the late republican era – the bull emblem. Ever since the nineteenth century, authors have declared that every legion raised by Julius Caesar used a bull emblem. This is not correct. Caesar himself never used the bull as an emblem, and only a fraction of the legions associated with him did so.

Only a 3rd, as well as the 5th, 6th, 7th, 8th, 9th and 10th legions used the bull emblem, and all were stationed in Spain in the republican era. While the 5th Alaudae Legion took Caesar's elephant symbol following the 46 BC Battle of Thapsus – this was for defeating King Juba's elephants – an imperial 5th Legion, the Macedonica, would use the bull emblem. It is probable that the 5th Alaudae had used the bull symbol prior to Thapsus. Conversely, no legion with a number above 10 is ever known to have used the bull as its emblem. And Caesar raised many legions with numbers above 10.

Finally, another interesting fact could be seen as one more brick in the foundation supporting the Keppie formula. After the Cantabrian War had been concluded in 19 BC, and the large number of legions involved in that conflict had been withdrawn from Spain for service in other provinces, the only legions stationed permanently in Spain for the next 300 years of the imperial era were a 4th, a 6th, a 7th, and finally, a 10th. No legion with a number above 10 was ever stationed there. This may be purely coincidence, but if it is, it is a fantastic one. It is more likely that the 5 to 10 Spanish policy identified by Keppie continued to be deliberately adhered to for hundreds of years under the emperors.

III. THE LEGION CAMP

Augustus required that permanent winter camps be established for every legion in the province in which they were based, with a maximum of two legions per camp. The legions traditionally went into camp when the campaigning season officially ended on 19 October with a ceremony at Rome's Temple of Mars. Originally built of timber, the winter camps became permanent bases built in stone. Spreading over many acres, they included troop quarters, a headquarters complex, bathhouses, granaries and a hospital. Typically, in the permanent camp of the 2nd Augusta Legion at Exeter, each barrack building accommodated a century of eighty men, with a bunk-room for each of the century's ten squads, a room each for the centurion and the optio, and a large mess and equipment storage room.

When on the march, legions built a fortified marching camp at the end of every day, marching in the morning and digging and building in the afternoon. These over-

The permanent camp erected by the 10th Gemina Legion at the former Batavian capital, Noviomagus, today's Nijmegen, following the Civilis Revolt.

night camps, while only temporary, were expected to provide 'all the strength and conveniences of a fortified city'. [Vege., II] Camp construction was carried out by the legionaries, who were as handy with a *dolabra* (pick) and shovel for creating camps and siege works as they were with a javelin and sword. 'Domitius Corbulo used to say that the dolabra was the weapon with which to beat the enemy,' wrote Corbulo's fellow first-century general, Frontinus. [Front., *Strat.*, IV, VII, 2]

When it moved on, the legion literally broke camp, burning what it could not carry. As part of his equipment, each legionary carried two stakes, which he collected as the legion was about to march and handed in at the next campsite; these stakes lined the top of the palisade that surrounded the camp.

'One simple formula for a camp is employed,' said Polybius, 'which is adopted at all times and in all places.' [Poly., VI, 26] Josephus described how, on campaign in Judea, at the head of Vespasian's column with the road-building party marched ten men from each century of the advance legion whose job it was to mark out each new marching camp to this prescribed formula.

A hilltop campsite was preferred. Once this was levelled, the camp was drawn up, starting with the *praetorium*, the general's headquarters, laid out to exact proportions. A white flag denoted its location. A grid pattern of streets and tent lines was drawn from it, with purple flags and spears denoting the location of officers' tents and those of cohorts and maniples. When the army arrived a little later, troops always entered via the main gate, and knew exactly where to pitch their tents and set up the rest of the camp.

Before they erected or struck their own tents, a detail attended to the tents of legate and tribunes. All officers had tents to themselves. Legionaries slept in eight-man tents originally made of pieces of leather stitched together, with straight sides and gable roofs. Canvas tents became the norm by the second half of the first century. In front of the tribunes' tents there was an assembly area, with a tribunal, or reviewing stand, built from turf.

Marching camp walls were 10 to 12 feet (3 to 4 metres) high, made of

The dolabra, scythe and field knife were tools carried by every Roman legionary.

bricks of turf, while the ditch on the far side which provided the earth for the walls averaged 12 feet (4 metres) deep and 3 feet (1 metre) across, but this varied according

Marching camps, although only temporary, took on the appearance of permanent camps. This camp at Alesia in 54 BC was intended as a short-term camp for the duration of Caesar's siege of the rebel Gallic headquarters.

to individual commanders. A clear space of 200 feet (60 metres) was left between tent line and camp walls to prevent burning arrows or firebrands reaching the tents from outside. Plunder, cattle and prisoners were kept in this open space.

Once wooden gates and towers were in place, the legion's catapults were installed along the walls. There were four camp gates, one in each wall, wide enough to allow troops to pass through ten men abreast. The main entrance, called the Decuman Gate, faced away from the enemy. On the opposite side of the camp, the Praetorian Gate, near the praetorium, faced the enemy. No man, not even a general or a king, was permitted to ride within a camp, as it was apparently considered to bring bad luck. When two young men, probably junior tribunes, rode through his camp just prior to Drusus Caesar's death in 9 BC, it was seen as an evil omen. [Dio, LV, 1]

While camp construction was being carried out by part of the legion, a guard cohort stood sentry duty and other details went out gathering wood, water and food with the auxiliaries. Once construction was completed and detachments had reported back in, the legionaries assembled in their maniples, then were dismissed, cohort by cohort, departing for their quarters in disciplined silence.

Each maniple drew lots to allocate sentry duty, which was broken down into four watches, each of three hours' duration, during the twelve Roman hours of the night, the time being calculated using water clocks. Eight sentries, four in front and four behind, were posted at the tent of the duty tribune, changing with each new watch. Three sentries were also posted outside the praetorium, and two outside the tent of any other general present in camp. Every maniple and cavalry squadron posted a guard at its own quarters, ten sentries were posted at each camp gate, and others manned the wall and guard towers. [Poly., VI, 35–7] During the day, a guard picket was posted outside the camp.

The job of patrolling camp sentries at night fell to the cavalry. The senior decurion of the legion's cavalry unit delegated four troopers to patrol the sentries during the four night watches, one for each, to ensure all were present and awake. [Ibid.] This system of watches and roundsmen, as described by Polybius in the second century BC, was still in use 550 years later. [Vege., III]

IV. WATCHWORDS AND TRUMPET CALLS

A new watchword was issued at sunset every day by the most senior officer in camp, and anyone approaching the camp at night would be challenged for the watchword. The tribune of the watch had to pass on the new watchword to each tesserarius for distribution to the guard posts for the coming twenty-four hours. Watchwords also applied in Rome, where they were issued by the emperor, or, in his absence, by a consul. Nero once chose 'The best of mothers'. Claudius often gave quotes from Homer.

Legionaries' daily lives were dictated by trumpet calls. 'All guards are mounted by the sound of a lituus and relieved by the sound of a cornu,' said Vegetius. [Vege., III] Legionaries rose and went to bed to the sound of trumpet calls. When 'Prepare to march' was sounded for the first time in camp, legionaries struck their tents and those of their officers, then assembled the baggage and stood by it. At the second trumpeting of 'Prepare to march', the baggage train was loaded. When the call was sounded a third time, the first maniples in the order of march led off out of the camp gate. [Jos., JW, 3, 5, 4]

There was a long list of trumpet calls that legionaries had to recognize and to which they had to promptly react on the battlefield. According to Arrian, battle signals included: 'Forward march', 'Turn right', 'Turn left', 'Wheel right', 'Unfold', 'Reform', 'Reform straight', 'Double up by depth', 'Return to formation', 'Spears up', 'Spears down', 'Optio straighten century', 'Optio maintain intervals'. [Arr., *TH*, 31–2]

V. ON THE MARCH

On the march, legionaries proceeded in 'marching order', each man with a helmet slung around his neck, covered shield on his left arm, and baggage pole over his right shoulder. From the pole were suspended his rolled woollen cloak, bedroll, rations, dolabra, sickle, turf-cutter, wicker basket for earth-moving, mess tin and a water bucket which also served as a kettle, helmet crest and personal items such as decorations. Javelins and camp palisade stakes were strapped to the pole. Heavier items such as tents and millstones were carried on the pack mule allotted to each squad.

The order of march was frequently determined by units drawing lots. Josephus described the order of march of Vespasian's army. Auxiliary light infantry and archers went first, to reconnoitre. Then came the army's first legion, accompanied by heavy cavalry. The surveying party followed, together with a large body of legionaries assigned to road building and levelling the next campsite. Behind them came wagons carrying the personal baggage of the commander and senior officers, with a strong cavalry escort. [Jos., *JW*, 3, 6, 2]

Vespasian himself came next, with the cream of his auxiliary cavalry and hand-picked legionaries, plus auxiliary spearmen of the general's bodyguard. They were followed by troops of legion cavalry, then the main baggage train, carrying artillery and siege equipment. Then came the other generals, camp-prefects and tribunes, with a bodyguard, followed by a legion's standards surrounding the eagle, preceding the men of the legion, who marched six abreast in their centuries with their centurions. Then came the next legion, and the next. The non-combatants followed, with the rest of the baggage train, pack mules, and other beasts. Last of all came allied troops and a rearguard of legionaries and auxiliary cavalry.

Marching legions covered 18 to 20 miles (29 to 32 kilometres) a day. More than 30 miles (48 kilometres) in a day, achieved by an army of Vitellius in Italy during the AD 69 war of succession, was considered praiseworthy. A column's speed was dictated by the speed of the baggage train.

VI. BAGGAGE TRAINS AND NON-COMBATANTS

The Romans called the baggage train the *impedimentum*, from which we derive the word impediment, meaning obstruction. And, if not carefully managed, a baggage train could indeed impede the march. A wise commander had to guard against losing his baggage. Mark Antony, marching into Armenia and Media in 36 BC, grew impatient with his trundling baggage train and left it to follow him at its own pace, hurrying forward with his legions. The Parthians and Medes circled around behind Antony and wiped out the train's defenders, seizing the train and depriving Antony of most of his food and ammunition.

One pack mule was assigned to every squad of a legion, requiring 650 mules for a full-strength legion. The mules were managed by civilian muleteers. A legion baggage train might involve a hundred carts, pulled by mules or oxen and also managed by non-combatants. These carried heavy supplies, artillery, siege equipment, building materials, ammunition, and officers' dining plate and camp furniture.

Arrian, in the second century, said that Roman commanders were familiar with five set ways of assigning the baggage train in a marching column, all designed to provide maximum protection. Where the army was advancing towards the enemy, he said, it was necessary for the baggage train to follow the legions. When withdrawing from enemy territory, the baggage train went ahead. On an advance where an enemy attack was feared on one flank, the baggage train was placed on the opposite flank. Where neither flank was considered secure, the baggage train advanced in the midst of the legions. [Arr., *TH*, 30]

A vast body of camp followers inevitably trailed the legions: merchants, prostitutes, de facto legionary families. There were also the slaves of the officers, who took part in arms training and drills with their masters. Said Tacitus, 'of all slaves, the slaves of soldiers are the most unruly'. [Tac., *H*, II, 87] The number of non-combatants with an army frequently equalled it in number; when 40,000 Roman soldiers sacked the Italian city of Cremona in AD 69, they were joined by an even larger number of non-combatants. [Tac., *H*, III, 33]

VII. ARTILLERY AND SIEGE EQUIPMENT

Each legion of the early empire was equipped with one stone-throwing *ballista* per cohort and one metal dart and spear-firing *scorpio* per century. The single-armed catapult of the *onager* or 'wild ass' type – so named because of its massive kick – was employed from 200 BC and was still employed in AD 363, when Ammianus Marcellinus saw it in action. 'A round stone is placed in the sling and four young men on each side turn back the bar with which the ropes are connected and bend the pole almost flat. Then finally the master [gunner], standing above, strikes out the pole-bolt' with a hammer. [Amm., II, xxiii, 4–6] This released the tensioned firing pole, which sprang forward and launched the missile.

Catapults had a great effect on the morale of both attackers and defenders. All authorities wrote of the enormous noise made by catapults when they fired, and of the terrifying sound made by catapult balls and spears on their way to the target. The normal operating range of legion artillery was 400 yards (365 metres) or less. Catapult stones were used to batter down fortified defences and eliminate defenders on walls and in towers. A number of scorpio darts have been found at siege sites in modern times, usually with pyramid-shaped heads and three flights made of wood or leather.

The Roman engineer Vitruvius wrote that the Roman military used the following weights for their rounded ballista balls: 2lbs, 4lbs, 6lbs, 10lbs, 20lbs, 40lbs, 60lbs, 80lbs, 120lbs, 160lbs, 180lbs, 200lbs, 210lbs and a massive 360lbs; a range of 0.9 to 163 kilos. [Vitr., *OA*, x, 3] One of the larger balls was nicknamed the 'wagon stone', perhaps because it took a wagon to carry it. [Arr., *TH*, 11] Trajan's Column shows catapult balls packed in a crate, like apples, in which they were delivered to the firing line from the stone-quarries where they originated. The *cheiroballistra* was an improved ballista; in service by AD 100, it used a metal frame. Light, sturdy and accurate, it was often mounted on a cart for mobility.

Four legions involved in the AD 70 Siege of Jerusalem employed more than 200 catapults between them. The 10th Legion built a veritable monster of a ballista for this siege. Josephus records that the balls fired against both Jotapata and Jerusalem weighed around 60lbs (27 kilos) and travelled more than 440 yards (400 metres). To make spotting difficult for the Jewish defenders, Roman artillerymen coated their white ballista stones with black pitch. Incendiaries were also used: stones and arrows dipped in pitch, sulphur and naphtha, and set alight. [Jos., *JW*, 5, 6, 3]

Earth mounds were built for the artillery, to gain elevation over the heads of the infantry. To determine range, Roman artillerymen tossed lead weights on lengths of string to enemy walls, and measured back. As a result of this practice, Roman artillery achieved remarkable and frightening accuracy. At the AD 67 Siege of Jotapata, where Josephus commanded, a single spear from a scorpion ran through a row of men. A ballista stone took the head off a Jewish defender standing near Josephus; the man's head was found 660 yards (600 metres) away. [Jos., *JW*, 3, 7, 23]

Ammianus described how, in around AD 363, Roman forces used 'fire darts' that had been hollowed out and filled with incendiary material: 'oil of general use' mixed with 'a certain herb', which was allowed to stand and thicken 'until it gets magic power'. [Amm., II, xxiii, 5, 38] The fourth-century fire-arrow had to be fired slowly, 'from a loosened bow,' said Ammianus, 'for it is extinguished by swift flight'. But once it landed, it burned persistently. 'If one tries to put it out with water he makes it burn the more fiercely, and it can be extinguished in no other way than by throwing dust on it.' [Ibid., 37] As for the 'Greek fire' type of incendiary depicted in the feature film

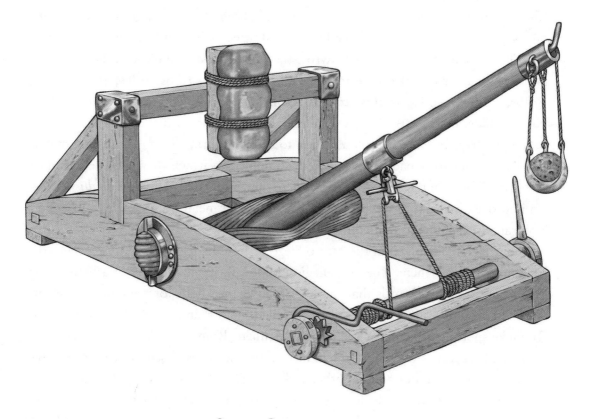

ONAGER CATAPULT

The basic stone-throwing catapult in use for centuries by the Roman military, equipped every legion.

Gladiator (based on events of AD 180), this was not developed until the seventh century.

Legionaries were also trained to build wooden siege 'engines' for use when fortresses and cities were assaulted. Mantlets, wooden sheds on wheels, were frequently used to provide cover for battering rams. Other war machines, such as a sling used in the defence of Old Camp in AD 69–70, depended on the ingenuity of individual legions. Siege towers on wheels were common, each with several levels on which artillery was mounted. Elaborate measures to fireproof these towers were not always successful. Siege towers were prominent in the Roman assaults on Jerusalem and Masada in the First Jewish Revolt and in the Siege of Sarmizegethusa during the Second Dacian War.

Caracalla, for his AD 217 eastern campaign, had two massive siege engines built in Europe which were dismantled and shipped to Syria. Caracalla was assassinated during the campaign, and there is no record of his super siege engines being deployed. By the AD 359 Persian Siege of Amida, Rome's enemies had turned her technology against her, employing siege machinery built by Roman prisoners.

By the fourth century, legions were no longer building their own artillery or siege equipment. Nineteen cities in the Roman east and fifteen in the west possessed large government arms workshops by that time, which manufactured catapults and other weapons, armour and siege machinery. Their output was deposited in arsenals in the manufacturing cities and distributed to the military as required. [Gibb., XVII] As a result, legionaries lost the skills that had previously ensured Rome's legions were, in a great many respects, self-sufficient.

VIII. LEGION, PRAETORIAN GUARD AND AUXILIARY STANDARDS

'The army must become accustomed to receiving commands sharply,' said second-century general Arrian, 'some by voice, some by visible signals, and some by trumpet.' [Arr., *TH*, 27]

Originally, the Roman military standard was merely a pole around which hay was wound, used as a visual rallying point for soldiers in battle and as a method of signalling commanders' orders. The republican consul Marius made the eagle, a bird sacred to Jupiter, sole symbol of the legion. Previously, wolves, bears, horses, minotaurs and eagles had all been used. The eagle standard of the legion, the aquila, initially silver,

A legion aquila standard flanked by those of maniples.

later gold, was a religious as well as a practical symbol endowed with huge mystical significance for Romans. The recovery of 'eagles' lost to the enemy was a celebrated event which added lustre to the reputations of generals responsible.

The eagle standard was considered, said Dio, to be 'a small shrine'. It led the legion's 1st Cohort, whose job it was to defend it, and always remained with the legion commander. 'It is never moved from the winter quarters unless the entire army takes the field,' said Dio. 'One man carries it on a long shaft which terminates in a sharp spike so that it can be set firmly in the ground.' [Dio, XL, 18] Long after the fall of the Roman Empire, the eagle which had symbolized her greatness would be taken up as a national symbol by countries such as Germany, Russia, Poland and the USA, and used by the Roman Catholic Church.

Each maniple of the legion also had its own standard. The manipular standard had a raised hand on top – *manipulus* means 'a handful'. Each imperial standard bore an *imago*, a small round ceramic portrait of the ruling emperor, and frequently of the empress of the day and other exalted personages. Legion standards also bore the unit emblem, a symbol representative of its zodiacal birth sign, plus devices depicting bravery decorations awarded to the unit, and symbolic grass tufts.

On the march and in formal processions, the standards preceded the troops, bunched together. The legion's standards were planted at the centre of both winter and marching camps, and even the ground they occupied was considered sacred. They formed part of an altar that included statues of the emperor. Placed outside the standard-bearer's quarters, it was illuminated at night by burning torches.

The Praetorian Guard used the image of Victoria, winged goddess of victory, on their standards. Auxiliary cohorts and alae used animals on their standards, including the boar and lion. Prior to the commencement of military campaigning every year, a religious ceremony called the *lustratio exercitus*, or lustration exercise, was performed, where Roman military standards were purified, dressed with garlands and sprinkled with perfumed oil, and animal sacrifices performed. Traditionally this took place in Rome between 19 and 23 March, but in the field could be performed at other times.

Roman standards were focal points for the attacking enemy, who particularly went after the golden aquila. To lose its eagle was the single greatest disgrace for a legion. The 5th Alaudae, 12th Fulminata and 21st Rapax legions all suffered this fate.

IX. THE VEXILLUM

Detachments from a legion marched under a *vexillum*, a square cloth banner, bearing the unit's number and title. Such detachments were called vexillations. A remnant of a vexillum found in Egypt was made of coarse linen, dyed scarlet. It has a decorative fringe at the bottom and a hem at the top to receive the transverse bar that held it. This vexillum carries an image in gold of Victoria, goddess of victory, standing on a globe. It may have been related to the Praetorian Guard and a visit to Egypt by an emperor such as Hadrian or Septimius Severus. [Web., 3]

Reconstruction of a Roman vexillum with the boar emblem of the 20th Legion.

X. THE DRACO, OR DRAGON STANDARD

Following the Dacian Wars of AD 101–106, Roman cavalry units increasingly adopted the Dacian-style dragon standard. The *signum draconis*, or 'draco', consisted of a wood or bronze dragon's head on a pole, from which draped a long 'body' made

The Dacian trophies from Trajan's victories in Dacia shown here include armour, weapons, horns, and the draco, the dragon standard which came to be adopted by Roman cavalry units.

of several lengths of dyed cloth sewn together. As the draco's bearer galloped along, the body filled with air and trailed behind him, to great visual effect. A device in the dragon's mouth made it howl as the wind passed through it. Arrian indicates that by the first half of the second century, the draco was used by all Roman mounted units.

XI. THE COMMANDER'S STANDARD

Each Roman army commander had his own standard. In the early imperial era standards were large square banners with purple letters on them identifying the army and its commander-in-chief.

In camp, the general's standard remained in his praetorium. When there was disturbance in Germanicus Caesar's camp at Cologne in AD 14, rebellious troops forced their way into his praetorium and forced him to give up his standard to them. [Tac., A, I, 39] When a general raised his standard in camp, this was the signal to prepare for battle. It therefore needed to be large enough to be seen from a distance.

On the march, the general's standard could be fixed to a packhorse. Famously, the horse carrying the standard of Caesennius Paetus bolted while his army was crossing the Euphrates river in AD 62. It was seen as a bad omen at the time, for Crassus' standard had reportedly blown into the river when he was crossing the Euphrates in 53 BC on his way to disaster at Carrhae. The AD 62 incident presaged the humiliating retreat of Paetus' army from Armenia months later. [Dio, XL, 18]

By the fourth century, the draco, of the appropriate scarlet or purple colour, had also been adopted by field commanders as their personal standard. Ammianus tells of how, in AD 357, Roman general and future emperor Julian, nephew of Constantine the Great, used 'the purple dragon standard, fitted to the top of a very long spear and stretching out' behind the standard-bearer as Julian rode to battle. [Amm., XVI, 12, 39]

XII. LEGION EMBLEMS AND BIRTH SIGNS
Caesar's bulls, and other myths

Every legion and auxiliary unit had its own unique emblem, as did the Praetorian Guard. These emblems appeared on the shields of each soldier. With Roman soldiers all wearing the same uniform and using similar equipment, the only way to distinguish one unit from another was by the emblems on their shields. In the night phase of the Battle of Cremona in AD 69, two enterprising soldiers from Vespasian's army took up the shields of dead opponents emblazoned with the emblem of a Vitellianist legion and, thus disguised, were able to make their way unchallenged through enemy ranks on to a causeway, and sabotage a massive catapult being operated by a Vitellian legion. [Tac., *H*, III, 23]

The most frequently used symbols for imperial legions were animals or birds, especially those with religious significance to the Romans, such as the eagle, bull, stork, and lion. Some legions used representations from Greco-Roman mythology – Pegasus, the centaur, Mars' thunderbolt, and Neptune's trident.

The Celts used the boar symbol to ward off evil, and the boar appears on Celtic helmet crests and shield decorations. Cisalpine Gaul in northern Italy, which was made a province of Rome in 220 BC, was populated by Celtic tribes. Even after Rome officially incorporated Cisalpine Gaul into Italy in 42 BC some Celtic customs lingered. Several legions raised in Italy used the boar as their symbol, the 1st Italica and 20th Valeria Victrix among them. Likewise, the centaur, associated with Thessally in Greece where it is said to have resided, made it a natural emblem for three legions raised in Macedonia and Thrace at the end of the second century – the 1st, 2nd and 3rd Parthica legions.

As mentioned above (*see page 64*), it has frequently, but erroneously, been written that all legions raised by Julius Caesar carried the bull emblem. It has also been claimed that those which used Capricorn's sea-goat as an emblem were raised or reorganized by Octavian. Neither assertion is supported by the facts. Of the legions that can be linked to Caesar, the majority actually carried emblems other than the bull. For example, of four legions known to have been raised by Caesar in Italy in 58–56 BC, the 11th to the 14th, not one used the bull emblem.

Conversely, Keppie notes that at least three of Octavian's legions which, in his words, *did not* derive from Caesar, did use the bull emblem. [Kepp., *CVSI*, N35, 2.2] Of those legions that did use the bull emblem, none had a numeral higher than

Bull emblem on a boss from a legion shield.

10. Yet Caesar raised many legions which carried numbers higher than 10. In fact, he raised as many as forty legions. Caesar himself never used the bull emblem; his personal motif was the elephant.

In reality, the common denominator linking legions that used the bull emblem was not Caesar, but Spain. As mentioned earlier, Keppie suggests the strong possibility that republican Rome stationed legions numbered up to 10 in Spain for hundreds of years. Legions 5 to 10 seem to have been raised there subsequently.

Even today the bull is a symbol immediately associated with Spain, where bullfighting has ancient roots. Both the Romans and the Carthaginians before them marvelled that the native Celtiberean people of Spain had a tradition of fighting bulls; in those ancient contests in Baetica, bulls were given the death blow with a spear or axe. [Bon., *B&B*]

In both the late Republic and early imperial era, the bull emblem was used by every legion numbered 4 to 10 except one; the 5th Alaudae, which adopted the elephant after Thapsus, may have used the bull prior to that. Only one other legion, the 3rd Gallica, is known to have used the bull emblem. This is possibly because the republican 3rd Legion served under Pompey in Spain between 59 and 49 BC. The 4th Flavia, which replaced the 4th Macedonica, took the Flavian lion emblem.

It is likewise frequently written that all legions that used the sea-goat emblem of Capricorn were raised by or at least associated with Octavian/Augustus. This is another myth. Legions created long after the reign of Augustus, units such as the 22nd Primigeneia (raised by Caligula), 1st Italica (Nero), 1st Adiutrix and 2nd Adiutrix (Galba/Vittelius/Vespasian), 30th Ulpia (Trajan), and 2nd Italica (Marcus Aurelius), used the Capricorn symbol, but this is because Capricorn was the zodiacal birth sign of the legions in question. All legions displayed the sign linked to the time of their foundation. Capricorn, falling in the midwinter period, when many legions were raised in time for service starting in the upcoming spring, was the most commonly adopted of the twelve birth signs, and seems to have been considered lucky.

It is true that the standards of a number of the legions in Octavian's standing army from 30 BC carried the Capricorn emblem as their birth sign. These same legions also carried separate unit emblems. For example, the 2nd Augusta Legion used Pegasus, the flying horse, as its emblem and Capricorn as its birth sign. Both the 4th Macedonica and 4th Scythica legions used the bull emblem and the Capricorn birth sign. The 20th Valeria Victrix used the boar emblem and the Capricorn birth sign. And so on.

Many modern authors have also written that from the second century the thunderbolt symbol was standardized as the emblem of all the legions, but available evidence contradicts this. The thunderbolt assertion has been based on the fact that all the legion and Praetorian Guard shields depicted on Trajan's Column, which was dedicated in AD 113, display thunderbolt symbols of one design or another. This is more accidental than historical, for apart from the Praetorian Guard, only four citizen units can be proved to have used the thunderbolt as an emblem during the imperial era – the 11th Claudia, the 12th Fulminata, the 14th Gemina Martia Victrix and the 30th Ulpia legions.

Why, then, does Trajan's Column show a profusion of thunderbolt shield emblems? It is probable that men of the Praetorian Guard, the only citizen unit stationed at the capital, modelled for the Greek artisans responsible for the images on Trajan's Column when these were crafted in Rome between AD 106 and 113. The artisans would have had no idea of Roman military culture, or the corporate nature of legion emblems. They would have crafted the shield emblems being carried by their models. Consequently it is the Praetorian thunderbolt emblem in several differing cohort designs that ended up on *all* the scutums depicted on the column. There is evidence to suggest that each cohort of the Praetorian Guard used a different variant of the thunderbolt emblem. [*See page 410.*]

The Praetorian Guard was one of only a handful of units to use the thunderbolt emblem.

The Notitia Dignitatum of the fifth century depicts the shield designs of a great many legions and auxiliary units; not one used the thunderbolt emblem. It could be expected that, by the time of the Notitia Dignitatum, Christian symbols had replaced the old legion emblems

This relief from the principia of the legion base at Mainz shows a centurion of Legio XIIII Gemina Martia Victrix, which was stationed there for much of the first century. On his shield can clearly be seen the legion's emblem of eagle wings and lightning bolts, an emblem normally associated with the Praetorian Guard and which was probably granted to the 14th following its defeat of Boudicca's rebels in Britain.

of pagan Rome, for Christianity had by that time been the official Roman religion for close to a century. Surprisingly, there are very few crosses on Notitia Dignitatum shields, and not one shield used the 'XP' [⚹] Christian symbol that Constantine the Great is said to have had his men paint on their shields. The only identifiably Christian emblem, a pair of angels, appears on the shields of the two bodyguard units of the Eastern (but not the Western) Emperor, the Equites Domestici and the Pedites Domestici, the Household Cavalry and Household Foot. [Berg., *IND*]

An emblem that did feature on many legion and auxiliary shields in the Notitia Dignitatum was the wheel of the pagan goddess Fortune. Ammianus Marcellinus, writing at the end of the fourth century, pointed out the significance that the wheel of Fortune still held for the Roman military when he described 'Fortune's rapid wheel, which is always interchanging adversity and prosperity', and associated it with the war goddess Bellona. [Amm., XXXI, 1, 1]

By the fifth century the 5th Macedonia's bull had been replaced by a rosette. [Berg., *IND*] The rosette was a martial symbol also associated with war goddess Bellona, and had been used extensively as a decoration on shields and legionary gravestones from early in the imperial period. It might be argued that the thunderbolt had been discarded because it represented a pagan god, yet, as can be seen from the above, the wheel of Fortune and the rosette, which also represented pagan gods, were in use in Christian times.

By the fifth century, numerous imperial legions had replaced their original emblems. The 3rd Augusta Legion, for example, was using a plain circular design. The two imperial 7th legions had survived; one using a ten-pointed star, another, a nine-spoked wheel of Fortune. The 1st Italica Legion had replaced its boar emblem with a circular motif, while the 2nd Italica was using a four-spoked wheel. Yet the 13th Gemina Legion of the fifth century was still using the lion as its emblem, just as it had done since the reign of Augustus. [Ibid.]

XIII. THE TRIUMPH

For a Roman general, the supreme accolades were the Triumph and the title *imperator*. In republican times the latter was accorded a victorious general by his troops. The emperors took this award for themselves, on a vote of the Senate, for victories in battles where they or their generals had commanded. At the start of all their letters, emperors proudly listed the number of times they had been hailed imperator; it is from this word that the title 'emperor' evolved.

Triumphs were awarded by a vote of the Senate for a major victory over foreign enemies. In the Republic, Triumphs could only be celebrated by generals of consular rank. Under the emperors, Triumphs became reserved for members of the imperial family. The Triumph took the form of a procession through the streets of Rome, which were lined by cheering crowds for the occasion, with all the senators of Rome wearing their togas with purple borders as required by Augustan decree.

The general celebrating the Triumph rode in a golden chariot, a *quadriga*, which was kept reverently at a temple, drawn by four white horses and decorated with branches of laurel, the symbol of victory. Revered young general Germanicus Caesar won the hearts of Romans when, on 26 May AD 17, he took his five young children with him in his quadriga when he celebrated his Triumph for victories in Germany.

The triumphant wore the *ornamenta triumphalia* – triumphal decorations of a wreath of bay leaves (a symbol of purification), a vest decorated with the golden palm motif (a victory symbol), and a gold-embroidered purple cloak. The general

The procession of the Roman Triumph of the emperor Septimius Severus, accompanied by his sons Caracalla and Geta.

held a laurel branch in one hand. An ivory sceptre topped with a golden eagle frequently formed part of the *ornamenta*. In addition, the general was awarded a statue in the Forum, and a large cash prize, with which he was expected to erect a public monument such as a triumphal arch; most surviving Roman arches relate to a Triumph.

The Gate of Triumph, a special gate in Rome's Servian walls, was only opened to allow the triumphal procession to pass through, and for emperors' funerals. Trumpet fanfares heralded the approach of the triumphant general. Then came wagons loaded with the spoils from the general's campaign, followed by elaborate wheeled dioramas, like portable stage sets, illustrating to the public where and how the general had obtained his victory. Behind these came white oxen with gilded horns and other animals to be sacrificed. Prisoners taken during the campaign tramped along in chains, jeered by the crowd. For the Triumph celebrated by Vespasian and Titus in AD 71 for putting down the Jewish Revolt, 700 Jewish prisoners, 'selected out of the rest as being eminently tall and handsome', were shipped to Rome. [Jos., *JW*, 7, 5, 3]

Some prisoners were later sold into slavery, others sent to fight in the amphi-

theatre. Enemy leaders had a mixed fate. Following his appearance in a Claudian Triumph, Britain's King Caratacus was allowed to live in Rome with his family for the rest of his days. More typically, enemies such as Simon Gioras, a leader of the Jewish Revolt, were garrotted to death inside the Mamertine Prison at the foot of the Capitoline Mount, at the end of the parade.

Behind his prisoners came the general in his chariot, and behind him came musicians and representative cohorts from his victorious legions. Their standards held high, the legionaries marched proudly, alternately cheering their triumphant general and singing irreverent songs about him, as tradition permitted. On reaching the Capitoline Temple, the general laid his laurel branch on the knees of the statue of Jupiter and, with the help of waiting priests, performed ritual sacrifices. A cheer would go up from the crowd when it was signalled that the enemy leader had been garrotted. After this came the triumphal banquet, sometimes lasting for days.

The Ovation was a lesser form of Triumph in which the general being honoured rode on horseback in the procession. Generals whose deeds were deserving of a Triumph but were not members of the imperial family were awarded Triumphal Decorations, the trappings of a Triumph without the street parade.

XIV. UNIT HISTORIES
Rome's imperial legions and guard units

IST ADIUTRIX LEGION

LEGIO I ADIUTRIX   *1st Supporter Legion*

EMBLEM:	Pegasus.
BIRTH SIGN:	Capricorn.
FOUNDATION:	AD 68, to serve new emperor Galba.
RECRUITMENT AREA:	Initially, Gallia Narbonensis and Italy.
POSTINGS:	Misenum, Spain, Mogontiacum, Sirmium, Brigetio, Dacia, Parthia, Brigetio.
BATTLE HONOURS:	Battle of Old Camp, AD 70. Trajan's Dacian Wars, AD 101–106. Trajan's Parthian Campaign, AD 114–116. Marcus Aurelius' German Wars AD 161–180.
NOTABLE COMMANDER:	Publius Helvius Pertinax, future emperor.

BLOODED AT ROME, TESTED ON THE DANUBE
Thrown together during the war of succession, fighting on Otho's losing side before making a name for itself under Trajan, it would be one of Stilicho's legions in the last desperate battles before the fifth-century fall of Rome.

A legion with surprising beginnings
In the late spring of AD 68, in a desperate bid to keep his throne, the 30-year-old emperor Nero raised a new legion, taking the unprecedented step of enlisting sailors from the Roman battle fleet based at Misenum, on the east coast of Italy, for legionary service. But the sailors could not save him; or would not. With both the Praetorian Guard and his German Guard bodyguard deserting him, and with the Senate declaring him an enemy of the state and sending troops to arrest him, on 9 June Nero apparently committed suicide. The Senate had already recognized the claim to the throne of 70-year-old Sulpicius Galba, governor of the province of Nearer Spain, and that autumn Galba came marching to Rome from Spain, attended by an entourage

which included a new 7th Legion he had raised there, and a large body of cavalry.

In the meantime, Nero's legion of seamen had sat stubbornly in Rome awaiting developments. With no quarters, they slept wherever they could around the city. At the time, Rome was crowded with legion detachments summoned to Rome by Nero during the last gasps of his reign; those troops, including men from the 11th Claudia and 15th Apollinaris legions, had resorted to sleeping in temples and public buildings. [Tac., *H*, I, 31] The seamen from Misenum had not been presented with an eagle and standards to signify that their legion was officially constituted, but they were determined to gain recognition of their unit; with that recognition would come a grant of Roman citizenship to each of them.

At this time, seamen and marines serving in Rome's navy were not citizens. Neither were they slaves. Contrary to the erroneous picture painted by nineteenth-century authors, Rome's sailors of this era were salaried free men who possessed neither Latin status nor Roman citizenship. [Starr, III, 3, and V, I] Once the much valued prize of citizenship had been dangled before them by Nero, the seamen from Misenum were determined to win it from the new emperor Galba. Consequently, when news reached Rome in October AD 68 that Galba and his column from Spain were approaching, the 5,000 sailors of the new legion went flooding out of the city gates, joining the thousands of civilians gathered there to greet him.

Three miles (4.8 kilometres) north of Rome, this 'disorderly rabble of the seamen', as Plutarch described them, 'those whom Nero had made soldiers, forming them into a legion', crowded around Galba and loudly demanded 'to have their commission confirmed'. [Plut., *Galba*] Preventing the emperor from being seen or heard by the crowds lining the route into the city, the ex-sailors 'tumultuously pressed him, shouting loudly to have colours for their legion and quarters assigned to them'. [Ibid.] Galba tried to put them off, saying he would consider the matter later, and rode on.

But the seamen were not satisfied with this response, 'which they interpreted as a denial' of their request. [Ibid.] Growing 'more insolent and mutinous' and 'some with drawn swords in their hands', they continued to follow him, yelling their demands. [Ibid.] The sight of the sailors' drawn swords frightened Galba, and as the column approached the Milvian Bridge over the Tiber river he 'ordered the cavalry to ride over them'. [Ibid.] The seamen, the vast majority of whom were unarmed, 'were soon routed' by the cavalry. Not a man stood his ground, 'and many of them were killed, both there and in the pursuit' as they tried to flee back to the city. [Ibid.]

According to Tacitus, the affair resulted in 'the slaughter of thousands of un-armed soldiers' of the unofficial legion by Galba's cavalry. [Tac., *H*, 1, 6] Cassius Dio, writing of the event more than 150 years later, estimated that 'about 7,000 perished on the spot, and the survivors were later decimated', with one in ten executed. [Dio, LXIII, 3] But 7,000 was certainly an exaggerated figure; an imperial legion only numbered a little over 5,200 men. And there is no other record of the decimation.

Word of Galba's cold-blooded act of brutality against his own men at the Milvian Bridge soon spread around the empire, and did nothing to endear their new emperor to the Romans. The event was so impressed on the mind of Plutarch, who was at the time a young man in his twenties, and that of fellow historian Tacitus, then in his early teens, that both would observe that this was a bad omen for the new emperor's reign 'that Galba should make his first entry [to Rome] through so much blood and among dead bodies'. [Plut., *Galba*] Despite this lethal treatment, the surviving seamen hardened their resolve to gain recognition. The legion 'which Nero had levied from the fleet' still remained in the congested capital, albeit in custody, and significantly reduced in numbers. [Tac., *H*, 1, 6, 87]

This legion's tortured beginnings were now about to take another turn. Tacitus wrote that, several months later, the city of Vienna 'had recently raised legions for Galba'. [Tac., *H*, 1., 65] This was not today's Vienna in Austria, but present-day Vienna, in southern France. Roman Vienna was a leading city of the province of Narbon Gaul, through which Galba had passed on his march from Spain to Rome. [Plut., *Galba*] Situated on the south bank of the Rhône, Vienne, the capital of the powerful Allobroges tribe in Celtic times, had become one of the wealthiest cities in Gaul, even advertising its wealth with an inscription above the city gates, 'VIEN FLOR FELIX', which declared that Vienna was rich and flourishing. Such riches, and such boasts, could only attract the avaricious attention of neighbours who coveted 'the gold of the men of Vienna'. [Tac., *H*, 11, 29] And so it was to prove.

From AD 67 to AD 69, Vienna and the neighbouring city of Lugdunum, today's Lyon, were in a state of 'perpetual feud'. [Tac., *H*, 1, 65] Rivalry between the two went back as far the first century BC, when Vienna had expelled Roman colonists, who had subsequently been taken in by Lugdunum. When Gallic governor Vindex rose in revolt against Nero in AD 67, Lugdunum immediately threw its support behind Vindex, while Vienna retained its loyalty to Nero. During this period, Vienna had even sent armed men to raid Lugdunum. To keep the peace following the Vindex

A coin minted for the 1st Adiutrix Legion during the reign of Gallienus (ruled AD 253–268), showing its Capricorn birth sign.

Revolt, Nero's Palatium stationed the new 1st Italica Legion in Lugdunum, supporting the 18th Cohort of Rome's City Guard, which was there to guard Lugdunum's imperial mint. In an ironic twist, Lugdunum had then switched its support to Nero, and Vienna to Galba.

According to Tacitus, the people of Lugdunum now 'began to work on the passions of individual soldiers, and to goad them into destroying Vienna'. [Ibid.] Tacitus says that in trying to coerce the 1st Italica legionaries into attacking Vienna, the people of Lugdunum claimed that while their city had begun as a colony of Roman legion veterans, the people of Vienna were foreigners. This potential threat, of an attack by the 1st Italica Legion, appears to have spurred the people of Vienna to come up with a novel solution, the formation of the first of their 'legions for Galba' mentioned by Tacitus, levying young men locally.

Vienna's first objective was the creation of a force to protect their city from attacks sponsored by Lugdunum, but the elders of Vienna would claim that they were merely creating legions in support of the nearby 1st Legion, the Italica, out of loyalty to their new emperor. Hence, the name taken by this, the first of Vienna's new legions for Galba, was the 1st Adiutrix, or 1st Supporter Legion; literally, the legion in support of the 1st. Several months later, as Galba passed through their province on his way to Rome, the Viennase would have presented him with their new legion – a unit with perhaps a name but without an eagle, standards, or official standing – and Galba would have added Vienna's recruits to his train as he marched on.

On 22 December, apparently in a Saturnalia Festival act of clemency connected with his birthday, which was just two days away, Galba released some of the imprisoned seamen who had survived the massacre in October outside the city, discharging from military service those considered too old or too unfit to be of further use to the State. [Starr, VIII] The discharge diplomas issued to these men show that up to that point they had not received the Roman citizenship promised by Nero. Meanwhile, the remaining seamen from the Milvian Bridge massacre continued to languish in prison.

At this same time, Galba conveyed eagle and standards to the new legion, officially commissioning it into service as the 1st Adiutrix Legion. [Ibid.] That the legion was officially constituted by Galba, not Nero, is confirmed by Cassius Dio. [Dio, LV, 24] The 22 December timing of this formal presentation ceremony meant that from this time forward the legion would display the astrological birth sign of Capricorn.

Meanwhile, the remaining seamen of Nero's legion enlistment were still imprisoned. [Tac., H, I, 87] So who was filling the legion's ranks? It would seem that it was Vienna's citizen recruits. Twenty-four days later, on 15 January AD 69, Galba was assassinated in Rome by a disaffected soldier of the 15th Apollinaris Legion. The Praetorian Guard at once hailed as their new emperor Otho, the former governor of Lusitania, who had marched to Rome with Galba the previous autumn. The Senate endorsed their choice.

Knowing how unpopular Galba had become with the military, one of Otho's first acts was to win the loyalty of the fleet at Misenum. Tacitus records how Otho achieved this: Otho 'enrolled in the ranks of the legion the survivors of the slaughter at the Milvian Bridge, who had been retained in custody by the stern policy of Galba'. [Tac., H, I, 87] That is, Otho added to the already existing 1st Adiutrix Legion the sailors he now released from custody. On being taken into the legion and joining the Viennase recruits, these seamen would be granted the Roman citizenship for which they had hungered. This diverse mix produced 1st Adiutrix soldiers who were, according to Plutarch, 'strong and bold'. [Plut., Otho] As for the rest of the sailors of the fleet at Misenum, to them Otho 'held out hopes of a more honourable service in future'; they, too, might aspire to citizenship eventually. [Ibid.]

With the unit's official commissioning by Galba, the name of the 1st Adiutrix Legion was formalized, as was its emblem, Pegasus the flying horse. In mythology, Pegasus was the son of Neptune, god of the sea, which would seemingly make the flying horse an appropriate symbol for a legion whose first recruits had come from the navy. Yet, as Starr points out, the seamen of Rome's battle fleets showed no inclination to worship Neptune. [Starr, IV, 2] Neither did they worship Castor and Pollux, the patron deities of merchant sailors. In fact, the men of the fleet at Misenum venerated Isis, the patron goddess of sailors in Hellenistic times, who was believed to control the weather. [Ibid.]

Another new legion to adopt the Pegasus emblem, the 2nd Adiutrix, was raised the following year. This unit would also have a connection with both Vienna and the Roman navy. Apart from these two units, only one other imperial Roman legion is known to have employed the Pegasus emblem, and that was the 2nd Augusta Legion – a long-established and renowned unit known to use Gallia Narbonensis, a maritime province, as a recruiting ground. It may be that, rather than as a symbol of veneration of Neptune, both Adiutrix legions instead took Pegasus as their emblem in emulation of the 2nd Augusta, the 'home' legion of Narbon Gaul, where they began life.

The 1st Adiutrix Legion spent that winter at Misenum, using the fleet's quarters. Less than two months after the seamen officially joined the unit, the legion was ordered to prepare to march; its first battle was just weeks away. Ironically, the 1st Adiutrix faced the 1st Italica Legion, which it had been founded by Vienna to counter, in its first battle in April AD 69. It fought for Otho against Vitellius' army at the First Battle of Bedriacum in northern Italy. Otho's army lost; the 1st Adiutrix surrendered, after which Vitellius sent it to Spain.

In AD 70, the new emperor Vespasian transferred the 1st Adiutrix from Spain to Mogontiacum on the Rhine. Domitian stationed it in Pannonia. By the reign of Nerva it was at Brigetio, on the Danube. From there it took part in both of Trajan's Dacian Wars, after which Trajan took it to the East for his Parthian campaign. From the reign of Hadrian the legion was back at Brigetio in Lower Pannonia, where it remained for the next 200 years defending the Danube.

In AD 193 the legion joined the march to Rome by the Pannonian legions that installed Septimius Severus on the throne after the Praetorian Guard murdered the popular soldier emperor Pertinax.

The Notitia Dignitatum shows the legion still in existence early in the fifth century, as part of the army of the Eastern Roman emperor, and stationed in the centre of modern-day Hungary under the command of the Duke of Valeriae Ripensis.

1ST GERMANICA LEGION

LEGIO I GERMANICA   *Germanicus' 1st Legion*

OTHER TITLES:	Augusta; withdrawn 19 BC.
EMBLEM:	Possibly Pompey's lion with sword in paw symbol.
BIRTH SIGN:	Capricorn (probably).
FOUNDATION:	Stemmed from Pompey the Great's most elite legion.
RECRUITMENT AREA:	Originally Italy. Later Spain.
IMPERIAL POSTINGS:	Hispania, Gallia, Colonia Agrippinensis, Bonna.
BATTLE HONOURS:	Cantabrian War, 29–20 BC.
	Tiberius' German campaigns, 15–5 BC.
	Battle of Idistavisus, AD 15.
	Battle of the Angrivar Barrier, AD 15.
	Battle of Long Bridges, AD 15.
	First Battle of Bedriacum, AD 69.
	Battle of Old Camp, AD 70.

A PROUD LEGION DISGRACED

Descendant of Pompey the Great's most elite unit, winning and losing the 'Augusta' title in short order, it gained fame and the new 'Germanica' title fighting Arminius' Germans for Germanicus, only to turn traitor and be abolished in disgrace.

The 1st was Pompey the Great's most elite and loyal legion, fighting against Caesar in the major civil war battles at Pharsalus, Thapsus and Munda. The imperial 1st Legion of Augustus is likely to have been the direct descendant of Pompey's 1st. From 29 BC, the 1st Legion fought in the Cantabrian War in Spain, and in around 25 BC the emperor granted it the title 'Augusta' in recognition of its meritorious service. But in 19 BC, after the war flared up again in the Cantabrian Mountains, Marcus Agrippa stripped the legion of its title, for cowardice. It was transferred to Gaul the same year.

By AD 9, the legion was based at the future Colonia Agrippinensis (Cologne) on the Rhine with the 5th Alaudae, as part of the army of the Lower Rhine. In AD 14, it participated in the Rhine mutiny, before taking part in Germanicus Caesar's campaigns in Germany. In the AD 15 Battle of Long Bridges against Arminius and the German tribes, the legion saved army commander Aulus Caecina at a critical juncture. Following this, the legion took to using the honorific 'Germanica'. As none of the other seven legions which fought in these German campaigns adopted the Germanica title, it is likely that the title was bestowed on the 1st by Germanicus for the unit's spirited performance at Long Bridges.

On 1 January AD 69, the legions on the Rhine were called upon to make the annual oath to the emperor – in this case Galba, who had taken the throne by force the previous summer. But at Cologne, 'the soldiers of the 1st and 5th were so mutinous,' said Tacitus, 'that some of them threw stones at the images of Galba.' [Tac., *H*, I, 55] Fabius Valens, the commander of the 1st Germanica Legion, subsequently led the movement which saw the legions all along the Rhine soon hailing Vitellius, commander of the army of the Upper Rhine, as their emperor, in opposition to Galba.

After Galba was assassinated and replaced by Otho as emperor, several cohorts of the 1st Germanica marched to Italy with Valens to overthrow him. Meanwhile, the legion's other cohorts remained on the Rhine. The cohorts of the 1st in Italy were in Vitellius' victorious army, which defeated Otho's army at Bedriacum in April AD 69. But in the autumn the legion's cohorts on the Rhine were caught up in the Civilis Revolt and by early the following year had surrendered to the rebels. Meanwhile, the cohorts in Italy had been defeated at Bedriacum and Cremona by Vespasian's legions.

In AD 70, as Petilius Cerialis' army pushed up the Rhine, driving Civilis' rebels ahead of it, the 1st Legion's Rhine cohorts there defected back to Vespasian and took part in the defeat of the rebels at the Battle of Old Camp. But this did not satisfy Vespasian; disgusted that a Roman legion could murder its generals and surrender to rebels (*see later chapter on the Civilis Revolt for full details*), he disbanded the 1st Germanica that same year.

IST ITALICA LEGION

LEGIO ITALICA   *1st Italian Legion*

INFORMAL TITLE:	Phalanx of Alexander.
EMBLEM:	Boar.
BIRTH SIGN:	Capricorn.
FOUNDATION:	AD 66, by Nero.
RECRUITMENT AREA:	Italy.
POSTINGS:	Gallia Cisalpina, Lugdunensis, Novae, Dacia, Novae
BATTLE HONOURS:	Battle of Bedriacum, AD 69. Dacian Wars, AD 101–106. Marcus Aurelius' German Wars, AD 167–175.

AN ITALIAN LEGION DEVOURED BY THE INVADERS

Created by Nero for his later aborted invasion of Parthia, the first legion raised in Italy proper in a century, successful in its first battle, defeated in its second, it would fight losing battles to fend off the Germans, Sarmatians, Goths and Huns.

'Nero organized the 1st Legion called the Italica,' said Dio. [Dio, LV, 23] Nero had plans to launch two simultaneous military operations, which, if they had gone ahead, might have changed history. One was to be a push south into 'Ethiopia' from Egypt, the other, the invasion of Parthia, which Julius Caesar had been planning at the time of his death. The 1st Italica Legion was raised in AD 66 for the latter, the first legion founded and recruited in Italy for a hundred years. Nero specified that the legion's recruits were all to be 6 (Roman) feet tall, and equipped in the manner of a Macedonian phalanx.

With the Parthian operation aborted because of the Jewish Revolt, the 1st Italica was sent to Lugdunum in Gaul in AD 67 to keep order in the wake of the Vindex Revolt. The unit swore loyalty to Vitellius in AD 69, and first saw action for him as victors in the First Battle of Bedriacum. Subsequently posted to Novae in Moesia,

A third-century coin minted for the 1st Italica Legion, showing its boar emblem.

the legion remained based there, apart from service in Dacia during Trajan's Dacian Wars, until the fourth century.

In AD 471, long after the 1st Italica Legion had departed, Novae became the headquarters of Theodoric, the Christian king of the Ostrogoths, who had been driven out of the Ukraine by the Huns. In 489, Theodoric led his Ostrogoth army into Italy, and with the support of the Visigoths defeated the forces of Oadacer, its Christian barbarian ruler. Theodoric made himself king of Italy, with his capital at Ravenna. 'Military service for the Romans he kept on the same footing as under the emperors.' [Vale., 12, 60] But this was an Ostrogoth army, all of Italy having been occupied. The power of Rome, like her 1st Italica Legion, had disappeared.

IST MINERVIA LEGION

LEGIO I MINERVIA   *1st Minerva Legion*

EMBLEM:	Probably a Gorgon's head, a symbol connected with Minerva and used by Domitian on his armour.
BIRTH SIGN:	Aries (Ram).
FOUNDATION:	AD 82, by Domitian.
RECRUITMENT AREA:	The provinces.
POSTINGS:	Bonna, Moesia, Dacia, Bonna, Syria, Bonna, Lugdunum, Bonna.
BATTLE HONOURS:	Domitian's Chattian campaign, AD 83. Dacian Wars, AD 101–106. Parthian War, AD 161–166. Marcus Aurelius' Danube Campaigns, AD 167–175. Battle of Lugdunum, AD 197.
NOTABLE COMMANDER:	Publius Aelius Hadrianus, future emperor Hadrian.

DOMITIAN'S DARLINGS FACE ALARIC'S VISIGOTHS

Raised by Domitian for his Chattian War, it fought the Dacians for Domitian and Trajan, then went east for Marcus Aurelius' second-century campaigns against the Parthians, returning to the Rhine to stem the flow of invaders.

Domitian had a thirst for military glory, which he gained from his AD 83 campaign against the Chatti tribe of Germany, then a Roman ally. In AD 82 he raised a new legion for the campaign, naming it after his favourite deity, the goddess Minerva, and stationing it at Bonna on the Rhine, opposite the Chattian homeland, prior to his surprise attack the following year.

Posted to Moesia by Trajan, the 1st Minervia took part in his Dacian Wars before returning to Bonna. Marcus Aurelius transferred the legion east for his AD 161–166 operations. It was back at Bonna in AD 167.

A coin minted for the 1st Minervia Legion displays the legion's ram birth symbol, the sign of Aries.

Fighting for Septimius Severus in the civil wars that broke out after he took the throne in AD 193, the legion played a leading role in Severus' victory against Albinus at the Battle of Lugdunum in Gaul four years later. From AD 198 to 211, the 1st Minervia was stationed at Lugdunum. It served there as an occupying force, for the people of Lugdunum had supported Albinus against Severus and would have received harsh treatment from the Minervians. The city never regained its former importance. [Pelle., *HdL*]

The legion returned to Bonna after its Gallic posting. In AD 401 it was withdrawn from the Rhine for Stilicho's defence of Italy. Despite Stilicho's success, the 1st Minervia never returned to the Rhine, and seems to have been destroyed fighting Alaric's Visigoths following Stilicho's death.

IST PARTHICA LEGION

LEGIO I PARTHICA   *1st Legion of Parthia*

EMBLEM:	Centaur.
BIRTH SIGN:	Probably Capricorn.
FOUNDATION:	AD 197, by Septimius Severus.
RECRUITMENT AREA:	Macedonia and Thrace.
POSTINGS:	Parthia, Singara, Constantia.
BATTLE HONOURS:	Severus' eastern campaigns, AD 197–201.

CREATED TO FIGHT THE PARTHIANS, DOOMED TO FALL TO THE PERSIANS

Raised by Septimius Severus for his eastern campaigns against the Parthians, which brought Mesopotamia into Rome's empire and brought the plague back to Europe, this legion would go down fighting the Persians at Singara as Roman power eroded.

The 1st Parthica was one of three legions recruited by Septimius Severus in Macedonia and Thrace in AD 197, for his Parthian campaign. [Cow., *RL 161–284*]

The Parthian campaign initially went well, and the 1st Parthica joined in the looting of Ctesiphon in AD 198. But the succeeding years were characterized by hot marches, grinding sieges and a lack of supplies. By AD 201 Severus abandoned the enterprise, leaving the 1st Parthica and 3rd Parthica to garrison Mesopotamia, while he travelled to Egypt before returning to Rome. The 1st Parthica built a base at Singara. There the legion served for more than 150 years, fighting off the Parthians and their Persian successors.

The 1st Parthica's longtime base at Singara fell to King Shapur's Persian coalition in AD 360. The legion, or elements of it, then defended Bezabde, which was subsequently also taken by siege by the Persians. According to Roman officer Ammianus, who fought in this war, all the surviving defenders of Bezabde were led off in chains after the city fell. Yet according to the Notitia Dignitatum, the 1st Parthica was still in existence by the end of the fourth century and stationed at Constantia – Veransehir in present-day Turkey. Either the Notitia was wrong, or its section covering the East was written prior to AD 360, or part of the legion was not present at the fall of Bezabde, or the legion was reformed following that defeat.

2ND ADIUTRIX PIA FIDELIS LEGION

LEGIO II ADIUTRIX-P-F 2ND SUPPORTER LEGION

EMBLEM:	Pegasus.
BIRTH SIGN:	Capricorn.
FOUNDATION:	AD 69. Used by Vitellius, but officially commissioned by Vespasian.
RECRUITMENT AREA:	Originally, Gallia Narbonensis/Italy.
POSTINGS:	Ravenna, Noviomagus, Lindum, Deva, Singidunum, Aquincum, Dacia, Aquincum, Syria, Aquincum.
BATTLE HONOURS:	Battle of Old Camp, AD 70. Conquest of Brigantia, AD 71–74. Agricola's Welsh Conquest, AD 82–84. Trajan's Dacian Wars, AD 101–106. Marcus Aurelius' Parthian Campaign, AD 114–166.
NOTABLE SECOND-IN-COMMAND:	Publius Aelius Hadrianus, future emperor Hadrian, AD 95.

MAKER OF EMPERORS

Raised for Vitellius from marines and Gauls, used by Vespasian against Civilis, with a decade of fighting in Britain before stemming the tide on the Danube, this legion would march on Rome to make Septimius Severus emperor.

One fine day in the summer of AD 70, 5,250 young men of the new 2nd Adiu-trix Legion stood nervously in their centuries beside the River Rhine in armour and helmet, with javelins in one hand and raised shield in the other, waiting for their baptism in battle. To their left and right, the hardened men of other long-established legions also waited silently, rank upon rank. Little more than 500 yards (450 metres) to their front, outside the burnt-out ruins of the Castra Vetera (or Old Camp) legion-ary fortress, tens of thousands of German warriors and rebel Roman auxiliaries were booming out a deep-throated war chant and shaking their weapons at the legionaries.

This legion's first battle would prove to be a Roman victory, but not before the

2nd Adiutrix's eager but untried recruits were extricated from trouble by the famous 14th Gemina Martia Victrix Legion. But where did these recruits come from, and how did they come to be here? Some modern authors state that the 2nd Adiutrix Legion was raised at Ravenna in AD 69 for Vespasian, and that its men were all marines from the Roman fleet based at Ravenna. Yet the facts do not support this. The origins of the 2nd Adiutrix Legion are much more complicated than that.

Officially, *Legio II Adiutrix Pia Fidelis* came into being on 7 March AD 70, by decree of the new emperor Vespasian. [Starr, VIII] But the 2nd Adiutrix Legion had travelled an irregular path to reach that point. The most intriguing aspect of the title bestowed by Vespasian on the legion was the 'Pia Fidelis'. The last time that a legion had been granted this honorific suffix had been thirty-eight years before, when the emperor Claudius named both the 7th Legion and the 11th Legion *Claudia Pia Fidelis* for putting down an attempted revolt against him by the governor of Dalmatia, Camillus Scribonianus. Over the next few centuries, other emperors would also grant the 'Pia Fidelis' honorific, but to existing legions (and even to a fleet).

Against precedent, could this supposedly new legion, the 2nd Adiutrix, have truly received such recognition from Vespasian in AD 70, at the supposed time of its creation? The very grant of 'Pia Fidelis' suggests that the 2nd Adiutrix was already in existence. Later this same year, Vespasian would abolish several legions that had surrendered to the enemy during the Civilis Revolt. In their place he was to raise two new legions, bestowing his family name of Flavia on both – the 4th Flavia and 16th Flavia legions. If the 2nd Adiutrix Legion was indeed a new Vespasianist unit, why was it not called the 2nd Flavia?

The fact is that in March AD 70, the 2nd Adiutrix was not a new legion and, according to numismatic evidence, was in existence in AD 69. That the legion proudly carried the birth sign of Capricorn throughout its career signals that it was established at some time between 22 December and 19 January – but in which year?

Invariably, the grant of 'Pia Fidelis' was given by emperors in recognition of a unit's support for their successful bid for, or defence of, the throne. Could this legion have helped Vespasian to win his throne? And if so, how? The reliable Roman historian Tacitus wrote

A coin of the 2nd Adiutrix Legion showing the unit's emblem, Pegasus the flying horse.

that the city of Vienna in Narbon Gaul, the Roman Vienna, 'raised legions for Galba'. [Tac., *H*, 1, 65] One of those legions can be identified as the 1st Adiutrix Legion, raised in AD 68. [*See page 87*] The indications are that a second unit with a Viennase connection was this second Adiutrix Legion, and that it was raised for Galba. In which case the 2nd Adiutrix could have been raised no later than 19 January AD 69.

Vienna and the neighbouring city of Lugdunum had supported opposite sides in the Vindex Revolt of AD 67, and Tacitus writes that well into AD 69 the city of Vienna was under threat from Lugdunum as a result of that enmity. [Tac., *H*, 1, 67] The evidence points to the Viennase raising the 1st Adiutrix Legion as a 'supporter' of the 1st Italica Legion, which was then stationed in Lugdunum, in order to defend Vienna against an attack – which the people of Lugdunum were urging the 1st Italica to launch.

After Galba took the 1st Adiutrix recruits to Italy with him, it seems that the elders of Vienna sent recruiting officers throughout Narbon Gaul to enlist young men from farms, villages and towns for their second legion. Once again, to give legitimacy to their action, the Viennase would have claimed to be raising a legion for the emperor.

Having already created the 1st Adiutrix Legion as a 'supporter' of the 1st Italica Legion, the Viennase would have settled on the title 2nd Adiutrix for their second creation. Another factor may have influenced this: Narbon Gaul was a recruiting ground of the 2nd Augusta Legion. When, in AD 67, Galba had raised a new legion in the Spanish recruiting grounds of the 7th Claudia Legion, he had called the new unit his 7th Legion. Similarly, a legion raised in the home territory of the 2nd Augusta is likely to have also become a 2nd. Support for this latter connection comes from the emblem adopted by the 2nd Adiutrix. The emblem of the 2nd Augusta was Pegasus the flying horse; it was in fact the only imperial Roman legion known to use the Pegasus emblem up to that time. Pegasus was the emblem adopted by both the 1st Adiutrix and 2nd Adiutrix legions.

But if the 2nd Adiutrix did indeed originate in Narbon Gaul in January AD 69, for Galba, how did it end up being commissioned by Vespasian fourteen months later? Tacitus records that, by early spring, the 1st Italica Legion had received orders to withdraw from Lugdunum and march to link up with Vitellius' army in Italy. On its way to the Graian Alps, the legion had to cross the Rhône and pass the city of Vienna. When they reached Vienna, said Tacitus, the men of the 1st Italica, inspired by the people of Lugdunum, were all for looting the city. In the end, the 1st Italica's elderly commander, Manlius Valens, was paid a small fortune by the Viennase to spare their city, and he distributed 300 sesterces, four months' pay, to each of his legionaries. [Tac., *H*, I, 66]

Vienna was spared, but was required to hand over all its arms to the 1st Italica. Valens and the enriched 1st Italica marched on, crossed the Alps, and joined the army of Vitellius in Italy, leaving the Viennase and their latest recruits without weapons. [Ibid.]

In the opening campaign of the short war waged in March and April between Vitellius and Otho, the latter sent part of Misenum's battle fleet ranging up Italy's west coast, carrying armed 'levies from the fleet' and several Praetorian Guard cohorts, with orders to blockade Narbon Gaul and prevent reinforcements from reaching Vitellius' forces in Italy. [Tac., *H*, II, 14] At the same time, Otho sent Praetorian and City Guard cohorts from Rome to the Graian Alps with orders to enter Narbon Gaul overland and link up with the fleet.

Otho's overland push was slowed when pro-Vitellius towns in the Alps resisted the passage of his troops. Meanwhile, a battle was looming on the Gallic coast, near the port city of Forum Julii, today's Frejus. Otho's warships landed Praetorian guardsmen, who occupied level ground a little inland, between the sea and the hills. Armed seamen were also put ashore and took up positions on the hill slopes. In addition, says Tacitus, the seamen onshore were joined by many locals, so that they 'had a number of rustics among their ranks'. 'Rustics' was a Roman term for unsophisticated country people. [Tac., *H*, II, 14]

Where did these numerous rustics come from in sudden support of Otho's forces? Were they perhaps Vienna's latest levy of raw recruits, sent south by the city fathers to link with Otho's fleet, despite having been deprived of their arms by Vitellius' 1st Italica months before? Tacitus was to note that they had no formal arms, and in the battle that ensued they resorted to pelting the other side with stones, proving to be 'skilful throwers'. Supported by the catapults of their warships, which came close inshore behind the opposition forces, Otho's fighters twice bloodily defeated the cohorts of experienced auxiliary infantry and cavalry thrown at them by one of Vitellius' generals. [Ibid.]

East of Forum Julii, the defeated survivors from Vitellius' force retreated, leaving Otho's troops in control of the southeastern coast of Narbon Gaul and the route across the Graian Alps. But this victory did not materially affect Otho's cause, for on 15 April, at Bedriacum in central northern Italy, his main army was defeated by Vitellius' army. The following day, at Brixellum, Otho committed suicide, leaving Vitellius – for the moment at least – the undisputed new emperor.

Tacitus wrote that, despite Narbon Gaul having vowed allegiance to him, Vitellius had doubts about the loyalty of Vienna. Perhaps he had heard rumours that rustic levies raised by the city had participated in the actions that had repulsed his troops outside Forum Julii. When Vitellius sent Otho's 14th Gemina Martia Victrix Legion back to its old station in Britain following the surrender at Bedriacum, its orders required the legion, whose loyalty Vitellius suspected, to 'pass over the Graian Alps and then take that line of road by which they would avoid passing Vienna, for the inhabitants of that place were also suspected'. After the men of the 14th had crossed the mountains, says Tacitus, 'the most mutinous among them were for carrying their standards to Vienna'. [Tac., *H*, II, 66]

Despite this, the 14th Gemina Martia Victrix Legion followed orders, and returned to Britain. But, clearly, Vienna was seen as a city opposed to Vitellius. Meanwhile, Vitellius ordered Otho's Praetorian Guard to lay down their weapons. At first, he distributed these disarmed cohorts throughout northern Italy, then within weeks, summarily discharged them without benefits, replacing them with a new Praetorian Guard created from men from his legions.

In July, legions in the East hailed their commanding general Vespasian emperor, in opposition to Vitellius. An army led by the governor of Syria began a long march to Rome to topple Vitellius. Before the summer was over, troops from legions on the Danube and in the Balkans also declared for Vespasian, and they too set off to march to Italy to dethrone Vitellius. Meanwhile, at Forum Julii, one of Otho's defeated generals, Suetonius Paulinus, who had once been a tribune in the Praetorian Guard, also took up Vespasian's cause. Paulinus, a native of Forum Julii, had been allowed to go home after Vitellius took power. Now, he 'collected all the troops who, having been disbanded by Vitellius, were now spontaneously taking up arms'. [Tac., *H*, III, 43] These included former Praetorian guardsmen, who respected the reputation of a man who had put down the Boudiccan Revolt in Britain and who had himself once been a tribune in the Praetorian Guard.

It is possible that a legion of rustic recruits raised by the anti-Vitellius city of Vienna also numbered among those who now flocked to Paulinus' banner and were rearmed by the people of Forum Julii to fight for Vespasian. Some of Paulinus' men, possibly Vienna's rustics, then took over Forum Julii, making it the first city in the west to raise the banner of Vespasian. Leaving these men to hold Forum Julii, the ex-Praetorians marched across the Alps to link up with forces advancing into Italy for Vespasian from Pannonia. In October, these guardsmen, once more in their Praetorian cohorts, would help defeat the Vitellianist forces at Bedriacum and Cremona. On 20 December, Vespasian's army fought its way into Rome, and Vitellius was executed. The following day, the Roman Senate declared Vespasian emperor.

The 2nd Adiutrix Legion first appears in a classical text three months later. Tacitus tells of three existing legions and 'the 2nd, which consisted of new levies', being marched into Gaul from northern Italy in the spring of AD 70. These legions were on their way to counter the Civilis Revolt on the Rhine. [Tac., *H*, IV, 68]

Numismatic evidence suggests that the 2nd Adiutrix spent the winter of AD 69–70 at the naval city of Ravenna. Then, in late AD 69, Tacitus commented that marines from the Ravenna fleet were being taken into the army of Vespasian at that time. Taken together, the numismatic evidence and Tacitus' comment gave rise to the later incorrect assumption by some historians that the 2nd Adiutrix Legion must have been recruited entirely from the Ravenna Fleet.

Tacitus in fact wrote that, following the Second Battle of Bedriacum in October AD 69, as the Ravenna Fleet deserted Vitellius' cause and vowed allegiance to Vespasian, the 11th Claudia Legion came marching into northeastern Italy from its station in Dalmatia to join Vespasian's victorious army. In describing the arrival of the 11th Claudia, Tacitus added that 'a recent levy of 6,000 Dalmatians was attached to the legion'. [Tac., *H*, III, 50] These Dalmatian levies were nominally commanded by an ex-consul, Pompeius Silvanus, who had apparently been in charge of the draft in Dalmatia; but, said Tacitus, these recruits were, in reality, under the control of the 11th Claudia Legion's legate, Annius Bassus. [Ibid.]

'To these forces,' says Tacitus, referring to the 11th Claudia and the Dalmatian levies, 'were added the best of the marines of the Ravenna Fleet, who demanded permission to serve in the legions.' [Ibid.] To replace these marines, the crews of the ships deprived of these seagoing soldiers 'were made up by the Dalmatians'. [Ibid.] To be assigned to the fleet, the Dalmatian levies were not Roman citizens, for citizens did not at that time serve as sailors or marines.

Tacitus' text has been taken by some historians to mean that there was a straight swap of some 5,200 non-citizen marines for 5,200 Dalmatian levies, to fill the new

2nd Adiutrix Legion. This is highly improbable. A few marines might be granted Roman citizenship to enable them to serve in a legion, but granting citizenship to 5,200 men to equip a legion entirely was unheard of in imperial times.

More importantly, there were nowhere near that many marines serving with the Ravenna Fleet, or with any other Roman fleet for that matter. Roman naval authority Professor Starr has calculated that in AD 69 the Misenum Fleet, Rome's largest, would have consisted of a little over 10,000 sailors and marines, with fewer serving with the Ravenna Fleet. [Starr, II, 1 and 2] On every Roman warship the rowers, deck hands and officers vastly outnumbered marines. A liburnium with a crew of some 200 men might only include 15 dedicated marines, with a maximum of 40 or so when going into battle. So, out of a fleet complement of 8,000 men, perhaps 1,200 were marines, meaning that, at most, there would have been no more than 1,500 marines at Ravenna. And Tacitus says that only the 'best' from these marines were taken into Vespasian's forces, indicating that perhaps several hundred men were involved. Note also that Tacitus wrote that these marines demanded to be allowed to serve in 'the legions', plural, not in 'the legion'.

Four months later, in March AD 70, the 2nd Adiutrix was in Italy and receiving the grant of the 2nd Adiutrix Pia Fidelis title in the name of Vespasian. As surviving discharge diplomas prove, at the same time that the 2nd Adiutrix received its formal title, all those marines serving with the new unit who had been in the Roman navy for twenty years or more were now granted an honourable discharge, as much as six years in advance of their normal discharge dates. In addition, those marines in the 2nd Adiutrix, who were considered 'useless for war' because of age or infirmities, were excused from further military service and also received their honourable discharges, even if they had served less than twenty years. [Starr, VIII]

In this way, the number of marines who had been with the 2nd Adiutrix for the past few months was whittled down to leave only the youngest and fittest in the legion's ranks. This left several thousand other men in the legion. Were they Dalmatians, from among the 6,000 levies brought to Italy with the 11th Claudia Legion? Or were the majority of them the rustic Viennase recruits who had been marching as the 2nd Adiutrix Legion for the past fourteen months and had occupied and held Forum Julii for Vespasian? And was it the activities of the 2nd Adiutrix in and around Forum Julii that caused the 2nd Adiutrix Legion to be granted the honorific of 'Pia Fidelis'?

So grateful was Vespasian to the two battle fleets for supporting him during the war that he granted both the title 'Praetoria', and granted mass discharges to many men of both fleets. [Ibid.] This he was able to do because he could replace these men from the levy of 6,000 Dalmatians brought to Italy by the 11th Claudia Legion.

If Vienna did indeed supply many of the troops who made up the 2nd Adiutrix Legion, and with Vespasian granting that legion the Pia Fidelis honorific, the city of Vienna might be expected to have also received an indication of his gratitude in the form of some Flavian title or honour. Yet no records exist of honours granted to Vienna during this or any other imperial reign. But around this time – no exact date can be attributed – the emperor did give Vienna permission to build a circus for chariot-racing.

This was a great honour, for chariot-racing was strictly regulated by the emperors. At the commencement of Augustus' reign, only Rome was allowed to stage the hugely popular chariot races, which accounts for the vast spectator capacity of more than 200,000 of the Circus Maximus in the capital. Eventually, fifty cities throughout the Roman world were granted the privilege of building circuses and staging chariot races. These not only gave a city status, but attracted vast crowds from near and far on race days, giving any city with a circus a major financial boost, its inns, taverns, shops and brothels all benefiting.

Few cities in Gaul apart from Vienna were permitted to build circuses. The others so honoured included Lugdunum, Arelate (Arles), and Mediolandum Santorum (Saintes). Precisely when these other Gallic cities built their circuses is unclear. Possibly, Vienna's circus was the first in Gaul. Even if it were not, the city seems have earned its circus as a reward; quite possibly for being Vespasian's champion.

There is other evidence to support the argument that the majority of the men of this first enlistment of the 2nd Adiutrix Legion had indeed been raised by Vienna in Narbon Gaul. That proof was found in Chester, the Roman town of Deva, in Britain. Having taken part in the grinding skirmishes and bloody battles on the Rhine that finally terminated the Civilis Revolt by the winter of AD 70, the 2nd Adiutrix Legion crossed the English Channel the following spring to serve in Britain. The unit's main base for the next decade or so would be Lindum, today's Lincoln. Later it would fully relocate to Deva.

Archaeologists believe that a detachment from the 2nd Adiutrix may have joined elements of the 20th Legion (later the 20th Valeria Victrix) at Chester as early as AD 71. By AD 69 the 20th had moved its headquarters from Deva to Viroconium, today's Wroxeter, then the fourth largest town in Britain, but elements of the 20th remained at Deva for the next two decades until the entire unit relocated in AD 88. They were joined at Deva in AD 71 by cohorts of the 2nd Adiutrix.

This is substantiated by the fact that gravestones have been found at Chester of men of the inaugural enlistment of the 2nd Adiutrix Legion. Fourteen in all, these gravestones originated some time between AD 71 and AD 87. In the same area, fifteen gravestones of men of the 20th Legion, dating from between AD 69 and 117, were located. The details on those 1,900-year-old slabs of stone have been tabulated by the Chester Archaeological Society, and allow us to study the origin of each man. [CAS]

Of the fourteen identifiable 2nd Adiutrix legionaries in this sample, one had indeed been born in the province of Narbon Gaul, at Forum Julii. Another was born at Lugdunum, in Gallia Lugdunensis, just 20 miles (32 kilometres) north of Vienna. Roman tombstones recorded where legionaries were born, not where they were recruited, so it is possible that this man had been in Narbon Gaul at the time of the levy for the 2nd Adiutrix; or, attracted by an enrolment bonus, he went south to join up. A 15th legionary tombstone shows a man from either the 2nd Adiutrix or 20th who was also from Forum Julii. If he is counted as a 2nd Adiutrix soldier, then three of fifteen men, or 20 per cent of the sample, can be linked to Narbon Gaul recruitment. These men would not have been former sailors or marines from the Misenum or Ravenna fleets, for, as Starr has pointed out, based on the records no sailors serving with those fleets ever came from Narbon Gaul. [Starr, v, 1]

Just the same, 20 per cent is not strong evidence that the 2nd Adiutrix Legion's initial recruitment was in Narbon Gaul. Interestingly, two of the remaining 2nd Adiutrix men commemorated at Deva were from Dalmatia, suggesting that they may have come from the Dalmatian levy brought to Italy with the 11th Claudia Legion, or were ex-marines from the Ravenna Fleet. But before the gravestone evidence is dismissed, another intriguing factor comes into play. For, about the time the 2nd Adiutrix Legion marched into Britain in AD 71, the 20th Legion received a new commander, after that legion had been slow to transfer its allegiance to new emperor Vespasian. The 20th's latest commander was Gnaeus Agricola, father-in-law of historian Tacitus.

The 20th was then so unruly, Tacitus wrote, that even the governors of Britain had been afraid of it, and Agricola had been sent 'not merely to take over command but also to mete out punishment, [and take] disciplinary measures'. [Tac., *Agr.*, 7] A logical disciplinary step for Agricola would have been the transfer of leading troublemakers from the 20th to the newly arrived 2nd Adiutrix, which had proved its loyalty to Vespasian during the Rhine campaign. At the same time, Agricola could have filled the places of transferred 20th Legion men with legionaries from the 2nd Adiutrix in a straight swap.

Deva gravestones support this possibility. Of fourteen 20th Legion men recorded during this period, three came from that legion's traditional recruiting ground of northern Italy, and one from the East; by AD 14, the 20th was routinely receiving recruits from Syria. [Tac., *A*, I, 42] Here is a revealing fact: two of the 20th's legionaries came from Vienna, a third was a native of Arelate in Narbon Gaul. Another came from neighbouring Lugdunum, and yet another was from that same province.

In addition, three 20th Legion men were Dalmatians, all three coming from the very same town, Celea – as did one of the 2nd Adiutrix's previously mentioned Dalmatians. And, one of the memorialized 20th Legion men from northern Italy had gone home to Ravenna on retiring from the legion, which suggests that he may have been one of the Ravenna marines taken into Vespasian's army with the Dalmatians. The numbers involved would seem to rule out coincidence.

In total, then, 36 per cent of these 20th Legion men buried at Chester are likely to have been recruited into the 2nd Adiutrix in Narbon Gaul and subsequently transferred into the 20th Valeria Victrix; 22 per cent are likely to have been Dalmatian levies originally allocated to the 2nd Adiutrix; and one of the fourteen 20th Legion men had possibly been a Ravenna marine also assigned to the 2nd Adiutrix. Conversely, two men from northern Italy and six from the East on the 2nd Adiutrix gravestones were likely to have been transferred from the 20th. This evidence, while not conclusive, is nonetheless compelling. It points to a strong link between Roman Vienna and the first enlistment of the 2nd Adiutrix Legion.

After the 2nd Adiutrix arrived in Britain it took part in Petilius Cerialis' invasion of the kingdom of the Celtic Brigante tribe, today's Yorkshire, 'which is said to be the most populous of the entire province of Britain', wrote Tacitus. 'After a series of battles, some of them by no means bloodless, Petilius had overrun, if not actually conquered, the major part of their territory.' [Tac., *Agr.*, 17] That conquest fell to future governors of Britain. The next governor, Julius Frontinus, 'subdued by force of arms', including the arms of the 2nd Adiutrix, 'the strong and warlike nation of the Silures', in Wales. 'After a hard struggle, not only against the valour of his enemy, but against the difficulties of the terrain,' Frontinus and his legions completed the conquest of Wales for Rome. [Ibid.]

The 2nd Adiutrix Legion would also have taken part in Agricola's campaigns, which advanced Rome's occupation of Britain well into Scotland by AD 84. With the end of the enlistments of many of these initial men of the legion coming up in AD 88–89, the 2nd Adiutrix was transferred out of Britain in AD 87, and sent to Singidunum, today's Belgrade.

From there, the legion, bolstered with a new enlistment of recruits, joined Domitian's campaigns against the Dacians and the Alemanni which ended in humiliating defeats and withdrawals for the Romans. By the time of Domitian's AD 89 peace agreements with his northern adversaries, the 2nd Adiutrix had made its base Aquincum, the modern-day Hungarian capital Budapest on the Danube, in the province of Lower Pannonia.

Sent to the East by Marcus Aurelius along with the 1st Minervia from Bonna, the legion participated in his AD 161–166 campaigns against the Parthians before returning to Aquincum. From there, in AD 193, it marched to Rome with fellow Pannonian legions, including the 1st Adiutrix, to install their governor Septimius Severus on the throne. The legion was still in Hungary by the beginning of the fifth century at the time of the writing of the Notitia Dignitatum.

2ND AUGUSTA LEGION

LEGIO II AUGUSTA   *2nd Augustan Legion*

EMBLEM:	Pegasus.
BIRTH SIGN:	Capricorn.
FOUNDATION:	In Italy, by Pompey the Great, for service in Spain.
RECRUITMENT AREA:	Originally, northern Italy.
POSTINGS:	Nearer Spain, Lower Germany, Argentoratum, Britain, Isca Dumnoniorum, Glevum, Isca, Carpow, Richborough.
BATTLE HONOURS:	Cantabrian War, 29–19 BC. Germanicus' German campaigns, AD 14–16. Invasion of Britain, AD 43. Conquest of Wales, AD 80.
FAMOUS COMMANDERS:	Publius Vitellius (the uncle of the future emperor Vitellius), AD 14–16. Titus Vespasianus (the future emperor Vespasian), AD 42–47.

CONQUERING THE BRITONS WITH VESPASIAN

Made famous by its commander Vespasian in the invasion of Britain, winning more than thirty battles against King Caratacus and the Celts, disgraced during Boudicca's Revolt, it would spend many years in Wales stamping out Welsh resistance to Roman rule.

The republican 2nd Legion fought for Pompey in Spain early in the Civil War, surrendered to Caesar in 49 BC, then defected back to the senatorial side and fought for Pompey's sons until the defeat at Munda in 45 BC, after which it would have again been folded into Caesar's army. By AD 30, it was part of Augustus' standing army and marching into northern Spain to take part in the Cantabrian Wars. For its service in this conflict the legion gained the 'Augusta' honorific from Augustus.

By AD 9 the legion was on the Rhine, and five years later, commanded by Publius Vitellius, uncle of future emperor Aulus Vitellius, it was playing a leading role in Germanicus Caesar's German campaigns. In AD 17, with Germanicus' recall from the Rhine, the legion was transferred to Argentoratum, today's Strasbourg.

A distance slab erected by the 2nd Augusta Legion.
Its Pegasus emblem appears at the bottom.

In AD 43, it was one of four legions that took part in Claudius' invasion of Britain. Under the command of the future emperor Vespasian, then a praetor, the 2nd Augusta drove along the south coast of England in a blisteringly efficient drive that overran all opposition, fighting thirty battles, storming twenty Celtic towns, and occupying the Isle of Wight.

The 2nd Augusta halted its advance at Isca Dumnoniorum, capital of the Dunmoni tribe, today's Exeter. There, it built a 42-acre (17-hectare) permanent camp which became its base for several decades. The legion was there in AD 60 at the time of the Boudiccan Revolt, when its camp-prefect famously ignored orders to march the legion to the support of the province's governor, Suetonius Paulinus; the legion's disgraced camp-prefect later committed suicide.

In AD 67, elements of the legion transferred to Glevum, today's Gloucester. Eight years later, the entire legion moved to Isca, modern Caerleon, in Wales, at which time the Exeter base was entirely abandoned. Between AD 122 and 136, 2nd Augusta vexillations participated in the construction of Hadrian's Wall across northern Britain.

By AD 290, the 2nd Augusta had systematically dismantled its base at Isca in Wales and transferred to Carpow in Scotland, where it was needed to deal with the invading Picts and Scots. By around AD 390, the legion was located at Richborough in Kent. But the unit had been greatly reduced; its base at Richborough was only a tenth of the size it had occupied at Isca, and this unit – renowned for its exploits under Augustus, Germanicus and Vespasian – ended its days reduced to a small frontier guard unit under the command of the Count of the Saxon Shore.

2ND ITALICA LEGION

LEGIO II ITALICA   *2nd Italian Legion*

EMBLEM:	She-wolf and twins.
BIRTH SIGN:	Capricorn.
FOUNDATION:	In Italy, by Marcus Aurelius, c. AD 165.
RECRUITMENT AREA:	Originally Italy.
POSTINGS:	Aquileia, Locica, Albing, Lauriacum.
BATTLE HONOURS:	Relief of Aquileia, AD 169.
	Marcus Aurelius' German Wars, AD 165–175.

FIGHTING FOR SURVIVAL, NOT GLORY

Raised by Marcus Aurelius in Italy for his wars against the Germans, it would spend its career fighting on the Danube.

As indicated by its Capricorn birth sign and numismatic evidence, the 2nd Italica Legion was founded in Italy by Marcus Aurelius during the winter of AD 164–165, when German tribes were storming across the Danube into Pannonia, Dalmatia and even into northern Italy. The legion's emblem, the she-wolf and twins, reflects the fact that it was born at the same time and in the same place as its brother unit the 3rd Italica.

The 2nd Italica was first based at Aquileia in northeastern Italy, where it was to be joined by the 3rd Italica in resisting a German siege. In the subsequent years of hectic battles against German tribes from north of the Danube, the 2nd Italica was regularly on the move. It was at Locica in Dalmatia, near today's Celje in Slovenia, until AD 172, before being moved to Albing in the province of Noricum. By AD 205, in the reign of Septimius Severus, it had relocated within Noricum to Lauriacum, modern-day Lorch in Austria, having left its base at Albing unfinished.

There at Lauriacum the 2nd Italica stayed for the next century, forever fighting barbarian invasion. By the time of the Notitia Dignitatum, sporting a four-spoked wheel as its emblem, the 2nd Italica had become one of thirty-two comitatense legions. Under the overall command of the Duke of Pannonia and Noricum Ripensis, it had been split into three sub-units, each commanded by a prefect. Soon it would be overwhelmed by the Goths, the Sarmatians and the Huns.

2ND PARTHICA LEGION

LEGIO II PARTHICA   *2nd Parthian Legion*

EMBLEM:	Centaur.
BIRTH SIGN:	Capricorn (probably).
FOUNDATION:	By Septimius Severus, AD 197.
RECRUITMENT AREA:	Originally, Macedonia and Thrace.
POSTINGS:	Parthia, Alba, Apamea, Parthia, Alba, Bezabde, Mesopotamia.
BATTLE HONOURS:	Severus' Parthian campaign, AD 197–201. Caracalla's Parthian campaign, AD 215–218. Battle of Nisibis, AD 217.

SEVERUS' GUARDIANS, MAXIMINUS' ASSASSINS

Raised for Severus' Parthian campaigns, the first imperial legion based permanently in Italy, it would be banished to the East by Constantine the Great, where it would hold 100,000 Persians at bay for seventy-three days at Amida in its last great battle.

Rome's legions suffered extensive casualties in Marcus Aurelius' wars against the Germans along the Danube and against the Parthians in the East. So Septimius Severus raised three new legions for his invasion of Parthia in AD 195. Their recruiting grounds were in Macedonia and Thrace, and all took the centaur as their emblem.

Severus' Parthian campaigns, although they resulted in the storming of the Parthian capital of Ctesiphon, achieved little. Severus returned to Rome after sightseeing in Egypt, leaving the 1st Parthica and 3rd Parthica legions to garrison Mesopotamia. He took the 2nd Parthica back to Italy with him. Severus had replaced the previous Praetorian Guard with men from the legions, after the previous Praetorians had murdered Pertinax and Julianus, his predecessors. But still he did not feel secure at the capital without a force, ready to hand, on which he could depend. Insurance, if you will. The 2nd Parthica Legion, having performed loyally and bravely for Severus against the Parthians, was chosen for this role.

The 2nd Parthica became the first imperial legion to be permanently based in Italy. Severus located it at Alba Longa, just 12 miles south of Rome, less than three hours' march away if he needed them urgently. The base of the 2nd Parthica Legion at Alba was built by the legion on the Via Appia, beside a large villa that had been erected by Domitian late in the first century.

The Rotonda, a circular nymphaeum that was part of Domitian's villa, was converted into a bathhouse for the officers of the legion, and incorporated into the legion complex. While most of the legion base has all but disappeared, the bathhouse building has survived to the present day as the church of St Maria della Rotonda.

A larger baths complex, the Baths of Cellomaio, was built for the legion's rank and file by Severus' son and successor Caracalla. It stood just across the road from the camp's main gate. For the entertainment of legionaries,

The base of the 2nd Parthica Legion at Albano, 12 miles south of Rome. For opposing him, Constantine the Great banished the legion to the East, and gave its Albano base to the Christian Church.

locals and visiting members of the imperial court, an amphitheatre capable of seating 16,000 spectators was built into a rocky hillside just to the north of the base.

The commander of the 2nd Parthica in AD 217 was Aelius Decius Triccianus, who ran the legion with a firm hand. Triccianus had started his military career as a common soldier with a legion in Pannonia, where his duties had included acting as sentry at the door of the provincial governor. By AD 218, the emperor Macrinus had appointed Triccianus governor of Pannonia, enabling him to return to the palace that he had once guarded, this time as its gubernatorial occupant. [Dio, LXXX, 5]

Either the entire legion or elements from it were soon sent back to the East. Gravestones of men of the 2nd Parthica Legion and their family members found at Apamea show that cohorts of the legion used that city as their winter quarters over an extended period. One such gravestone was erected by 2nd Parthica centurion Probius Sanctus for his 'incomparable' 28-year-old wife. [AE 1993, 1597]

Shipped to Syria for Caracalla's eastern campaign, cohorts of the legion took part in the Battle of Nisibis against the Persians in AD 217. These 2nd Parthica troops remained in Apamea following Caracalla's murder; it was there that his successor Macrinus found them in the summer of AD 218. The legionaries, and their family members, returned to the Alban Mount.

In AD 238, the 2nd Parthica was in Pannonia. Having campaigned with the emperor Maximinus against the Germans and Sarmatians, the legion was preparing to go against the Goths. When news reached Pannonia that the Senate had dethroned Maximinus and recognized Gordian I, governor of Africa, and his son Gordian II as co-emperors, after leading citizens of Africa had declared that pair emperors, Maximinus led his legions, including the 2nd Parthica, into Italy to reassert his control. Meanwhile, in Africa, the resident 3rd Augusta Legion, which remained loyal to Maximinus, killed Gordian II and forced Gordian I to commit suicide. In response, the Senate proclaimed two senators as co-emperors in opposition to Maximinus: Pupienus Maximus and Balbinus. After Maximinus arrived outside Aquileia, which opposed him, he began a siege of that city.

The 2nd Parthica Legion had lost faith in their emperor, and its troops were fearful for their loved ones at Alba, in senatorial territory. During a break in the fighting outside Aquileia, men from the 2nd Parthica combined with Praetorian guardsmen to murder Maximinus and his son Maximus, then killed the prefect of the Praetorian Guard and the emperor's closest advisers. Soon, the Praetorian Guard murdered both Pupienus and Balbinus, and Gordian I's teenage grandson Gordian III came to throne. The 2nd Parthica returned to Alba, honoured by the new emperor.

The 2nd Parthica also remained loyal to the co-emperor Maxentius, Constantine the Great's brother-in-law. When, in AD 312, Constantine marched into Italy with 40,000 men to dethrone Maxentius, the 2nd Parthica formed up for Maxentius at the Milvian Bridge just north of Rome, where Maxentius was defeated in the battle and drowned in the Tiber. Constantine, victorious, abolished both the Praetorian Guard and the Singularian Horse household cavalry, because they had fought for Maxentius, but he did not abolish the 2nd Parthica Legion; instead he shipped the unit to the farthest reaches of the empire. From that time forward, the 2nd Parthica was based in Mesopotamia, facing the Persian threat. Constantine gave the legion's base at Alba to the Christian Church, together with the civilian *vicus* that had grown outside it. Many displaced family members would have trailed after the legion to their new base.

The legion later transferred to the hill town of Bezabde (today's Cizre in Turkey), beside the Tigris, still in Mesopotamia. According to the historian Ammianus, who was familiar with the unit, the 2nd Parthica Legion was destroyed in AD 360 when King Shapur led a siege of Bezabde which overran the city. The 2nd Flavia and 2nd Armeniaca legions were wiped out in the same battle. The majority of the men of the 2nd Parthica Legion were taken prisoner and became slaves of the Persians.

According to the Notitia Dignitatum, both the 1st Parthica and 2nd Parthica legions were garrisoned in Mesopotamia under the Duke of Mesopotamia, with the 2nd Parthica based at Cefae in the late fourth century. But not only had both legions apparently been destroyed by that time, but Mesopotamia had not been a Roman province for many years, having been surrendered to the Parthians by the emperor Jovian in AD 363.

2ND TRAIANA LEGION

LEGIO II TRAIANA   *Trajan's 2nd Legion*

EMBLEM:	Hercules' hammer and lightning bolt.
BIRTH SIGN:	Aries.
FOUNDATION:	By Trajan, c. 105 AD.
RECRUITMENT AREA:	Originally, probably German provinces.
POSTINGS:	Laodicea, Nicopolis.
BATTLE HONOURS:	Trajan's Parthian campaign, AD 111–114.
	Defence of Alexandria, AD 172–173.

A LIFE IN EGYPT
Raised by Trajan, taking his name, this legion fought under him against the Parthians and took their capital.

In the preparations for his second invasion of Dacia, Trajan gave orders for two new legions to be levied. One would support the Dacian operation, the other sent to the East in preparation for Trajan's planned Parthian incursion.

The 2nd Traiana Legion, named after Trajan, was one of those two legions; the other was the 30th Ulpia. There is no record of why Trajan gave it the number 2, but it is likely that it was raised in the recruiting grounds of an existing 2nd Legion, which were probably then in the Rhine provinces – Hercules, patron deity of the legion, was, in the Germanic form of Donar, a revered war god among Germans.

Shipped to Syria, the 2nd Traiana was located at the port city of Laodicea in AD 105. From there it moved south to Egypt, making its base at Nicopolis, not far from Alexandria. There the legion remained, possibly contributing a vexillation to operations in Judea during the Second Jewish Revolt of AD 132–135.

In AD 172, Bucoli herdsmen from the Nile Delta rose in revolt under the leadership of an Egyptian priest named Isodorus. After defeating an auxiliary force sent to deal with them, the Bucoli laid siege to Alexandria, which would have been defended by the 2nd Traiana Legion. The siege was only lifted in the new year, and the revolt put down, when Avidius Cassius, governor of Syria, came marching down from Syria with a relief force.

Presumably, the 2nd Traiana sided with Queen Zenobia of Palmyra in AD 269 when she seized Egypt, for there is no record of it fighting her. Early in the fifth century the 2nd Traiana was one of six legions based in Egypt, according to the Notitia Dignitatum, answerable to the Duke of Thebes. After the fall of the Western Roman Empire it would have been absorbed into the army of the Byzantine emperors.

3RD AUGUSTA LEGION

LEGIO III AUGUSTA   *Augustus' 3rd Legion*

EMBLEM:	Lion, on first-century numismatic evidence. (Pegasus also suggested, but not proven.)
BIRTH SIGN:	Capricorn.
ORIGIN OF TITLE:	Granted by Augustus, c. 19 BC.
FOUNDATION:	Probably raised by Octavian.
RECRUITMENT AREA:	Originally, Cisalpine Gaul. Later, North Africa.
POSTINGS:	Africa, Ammaedra, Tebessa, Lambaesis.
BATTLE HONOURS:	Tacfarinas' Revolt, AD 17–23. Battle of Carthage, AD 238.
DISBANDED:	AD 238. Reformed, AD 253.
NOTABLE COMMANDER:	Marcus Aurelius Probus, future emperor (AD 276–282).

GUARDIANS OF NORTH AFRICA

From putting down the long-lasting Tacfarinas' Revolt in Tunisia for Tiberius to paying the price for loyalty to Maximinus, for hundreds of years it was Rome's only legion in North Africa.

The 3rd Legion that arrived in the province of Africa in 30 BC may have descended from Pompey the Great's 3rd Legion. It served Octavian during the war against Antony and Cleopatra.

Some time between 27 BC, when Octavian took the title of Augustus, and his death in AD 14, the 3rd Legion was granted the title 'Augusta' by the emperor. After a campaign against desert tribes in 19 BC, the governor of Africa, Cornelius Balbus, was awarded a Triumph by the Senate. It has been suggested, with some merit, that this was when and why the 3rd Augusta Legion was given its title. [Kepp., *MRA*, 5] It was perhaps not coincidental that 19 BC was the year of the final termination of the Cantabrian Wars in Spain, during which four legions all received the title of Augusta. It was also in 19 BC that one of those legions had its Augusta title removed, for cowardice.

The 3rd Augusta Legion's finest hour came with its termination of the AD 17–23 Tacfarinas' Revolt in Africa. In AD 75, the legion was transferred by Vespasian to Tebessa, known today as Timgad, where the men of the legion then built a handsome town astride the road to their old base at Lambaesis, laid out in military grid pattern. The legion would continue to labour on the city's major building projects for another half century.

In AD 238, leading citizens in the province of Africa rebelled against the emperor Maximinus, declaring the province's governor Gordian I and his son Gordian II co-emperors in opposition to Maximinus. But the resident 3rd Augusta remained loyal to Maximinus and defeated the usurpers' army of raw levies in a one-sided battle outside Carthage, when Gordian II was among the many killed. On learning of his son's death, Gordian I committed suicide.

But the Senate, which despised Maximinus, declared two of their members, Pupienus Maximus and Balbinus, co-emperors. Maximinus, in Pannonia and about to go to war with the Goths, turned his army around and marched into Italy. But as he was besieging Aquileia, which was held by forces loyal to the Senate, his own troops murdered him in his camp.

With Maximinus dead, the Praetorian Guard murdered Pupienus and Balbinus, allowing Gordian I's 13-year-old grandson to become the next emperor, Gordian III. Because the 3rd Augusta Legion had remained loyal to their emperor, Maximinus, and had been responsible for the deaths of his grandfather and uncle, Gordian III ordered the 3rd Augusta Legion abolished. Its troops were dispersed around other units.

Fifteen years later, in AD 253, a year when there were three emperors, the 3rd Augusta Legion was reformed, apparently by Valerian, with Sattonius Jucundus as its chief centurion, Sattonius having previously served with the legion prior to its disbanding. [ILS, 2296]

With Africa in a peaceable state, vexillations from the 3rd Augusta frequently served in Europe in the decades that followed. One such detachment was stationed in Macedonia and saw action against the Goths. [AE 1934, 193] The legion was eventually withdrawn from Africa. Numbered among the comitatense legions under the command of the Master of Foot, its men recruited in Gaul, the legion was part of the army sent by Stilicho in AD 395 to put down Africa's rebel governor, Gildo.

3RD CYRENAICA LEGION

LEGIO III CYRENAICA *3rd Cyrenaican Legion*

EMBLEM:	Ammon/Jupiter (probably).
BIRTH SIGN:	Capricorn (possibly).
FOUNDATION:	Probably by Mark Antony, c. 36 BC.
RECRUITMENT AREA:	Originally, province of Cyrenaica.
POSTINGS:	Egypt, Judea, Bostra, Judea, Bostra.
BATTLE HONOURS:	Siege of Jerusalem, AD 70.
	Trajan's Parthian campaign, AD 114–116.
	Second Jewish Revolt, AD 132–135.

FROM EGYPT'S QUIET
TO THE THICK OF CONFLICT

A resident legion of Egypt for many years, it occupied and created the new province of Arabia, then slugged through the Second Jewish War, which resulted in all Jews being banned from within sight of Jerusalem.

The 3rd Cyrenaica Legion is known to have fought for Mark Antony, who, as its title implies, probably raised it in Cyrenaica in North Africa, which came under Antony's control during the Second Triumvirate. It surrendered to Octavian at Actium in 31 BC, and the following year became one of Augustus' twenty-eight standing legions, posted to Egypt.

Neither the emblem nor the birth sign of the 3rd Cyrenaica is recorded, but the men of the legion were known to venerate the Cyrenaican god known in Egypt as Ammon, and which the Romans depicted as Jupiter with horns; it is possible that the 3rd Cyrenaica Legion bore this officially recognized manifestation as its emblem.

Based at Alexandria, the legion put down Jewish rioting in that city in the first century and contributed cohorts to Titus' AD 70 Siege of Jerusalem. In AD 106 the legion departed its longtime base at Alexandria, joined a task force led by Aulus Cornelius Palma, governor of Syria, and invaded the old kingdom of Nabataea. On the orders of the emperor Trajan, Palma carved out the new Roman province Arabia

Petraea. At Bostra, the 3rd Cyrenaica built itself a new base.

Between AD 114 and 116, the legion took part in Trajan's campaign in Mesopotamia and Parthia, before returning to its Bostra base. Between AD 132 and 135 it took part in Julius Severus' grinding operations in Judea that put down the Second Jewish Revolt. The legion continued to be based at Bostra for the next few hundred years, regularly fighting the Persians, with mixed fortunes.

By the end of the fourth century, the 3rd Cyrenaica was still in Arabia, accompanied by the 4th Martia Legion, a relatively new creation, plus twelve mounted units and five auxiliary cohorts.

3RD GALLICA LEGION

LEGIO III GALLICA   *3rd Gallic Legion*

EMBLEM:	Three bulls.
BIRTH SIGN:	Capricorn.
FOUNDATION:	Reformed by Julius Caesar in Gaul in 49 BC; based on Pompey's 3rd Legion.
RECRUITMENT AREA:	Originally, Gaul. Under Mark Antony, changed to Syria.
POSTINGS:	Emesa, Apamea, Cappadocia, Armenia, Judea, Moesia, Rome/Capua, Raphanaea, Judea, Danaba.
BATTLE HONOURS:	Corbulo's First Armenian Campaign, AD 58–60. Corbulo's Second Armenian Campaign, AD 62. First Jewish Revolt, AD 66–67. Defeat of the Roxolani Sarmatians, AD 68. Second Battle of Bedriacum, AD 69. Battle of Cremona, AD 69. Battle of Rome, AD 69. Second Jewish Revolt, AD 132–135.

VESPASIAN'S TERRORS

One of Mark Antony's legions, it was subsequently badly mauled in the First Jewish Revolt before single-handedly crushing 9,000 Sarmatian cavalry in Moesia, this feared legion led the way into Italy to defeat Vitellius and make its former general Vespasian emperor.

> '*Under Marcus Antonius they had defeated the Parthians, under Corbulo the Armenians, and had lately discomforted the Sarmatians.*'
> (TACITUS, *Histories*, III, 24)

The emblem of three bulls depicted on the coins of the 3rd Gallica Legion reflects the fact that this was the second 3rd Legion in existence at or shortly after the time that it was reformed by Caesar in 49 BC. As Caesar himself wrote, the other 3rd Legion was marching for Pompey the Great in Greece at the time, and it fought against Caesar at Pharsalus. [Caes., *CW*, III, 88] This legion's Gallica title may have been given to it by Caesar to differentiate it from Pompey's 3rd and also to reflect the fact that it had been raised in Gaul. The original 3rd, having served Pompey in Spain, almost certainly carried the bull emblem.

The 3rd Gallica was one of the Caesarian legions that Mark Antony took to the East during the Second Triumvirate. There, it distinguished itself in Antony's army during his disastrous 36 BC campaign in Media. Prior to this campaign Antony filled several of his legions with Syrian recruits, and for at least the next hundred years the ranks of 3rd Gallica Legion were occupied by Syrians, most of whom, if not all, were followers of the eastern sun god Baal, or Elagabalus.

Once Octavian absorbed the 3rd Gallica into his new standing army in 30 BC, the legion was made part of the Syria station. The coins of its wages were minted alternatively at Emesa, home of the shrine of Baal, and Apamea.

There was then a convention that legions were not stationed where they were recruited, and later indications put the legion in Judea, a sub-province of Syria. In Judea, the legion was not permitted to circulate coins bearing images of the emperor, nor raise their standards, because of the Jewish prohibition of graven images. And because the governor of Judea was only of Equestrian status, the legion was commanded by their tribune, an Equestrian, in the same way that only Equestrian officers were permitted in Egypt. At one time the 3rd Gallica's senior tribune was an officer named Celer, who was put to death for defrauding the Jews of Judea. [Jos., *JA*, 20, 6, 2–3]

By the spring of AD 58, a six-cohort 3rd Gallica vexillation had marched up to Cappadocia under the legion's camp-prefect, Capito, and took part in Corbulo's lightning campaign in Armenia. In AD 62, another vexillation participated in Corbulo's second Armenian campaign.

When the Jewish Revolt erupted in Judea in AD 66, three of the 3rd Gallica's cohorts were surprised at the outset and were wiped out. The legion's remaining cohorts took part in Vespasian's AD 67 counter-offensive in Galilee. But, despite the enthusiasm of its vengeful legionaries, the legion suffered so many losses by the end of the summer that the Palatium transferred it across the Roman world to Moesia, on the Danube, where it arrived in AD 68.

In early AD 69, just as the winter in Moesia was coming to an end, the depleted legion was called out to counter an invasion of the province by 9,000 heavily armoured Sarmatian cavalrymen from the Roxolani tribe. In a surprise attack on an icy day, the men of the 3rd Gallica killed the Roxolani to a man, with minimal casualties of their own. For their victory, the legion's legate was awarded Triumphal Decorations by the emperor Otho.

In the late summer of AD 69, the men of the 3rd Gallica learned that their former commander-in-chief in Judea, Vespasian, had been hailed emperor by the legions of the East. This was in opposition to the incumbent, Vitellius, who had overthrown Otho. The legion then swore for Vespasian and convinced the other legions of Moesia, Pannonia and Dalmatia to do the same. In September, a delegation from the legion, led by it chief centurion, Attius Varus, attended a war conference held at Poetovio, the headquarters of the 13th Gemina Legion, in Pannonia.

The legate of the 7th Galbiana Legion, Marcus Antonius Primus, then declared that he would march on Italy to dethrone Vitellius with just the few auxiliaries he had with him. When the other generals at the meeting failed to support Primus, Centurion Varus and the men of the 3rd Gallica with him immediately gave him their allegiance and support.

With Centurion Varus as his deputy and just Varus' men of the 3rd Gallica and his auxiliaries, Primus marched into Italy where they were soon joined by the remainder of the 3rd Gallica and the other legions of Moesia and Pannonia. Primus' army defeated the forces of Vitellius, first at Bedriacum and then at Cremona, with the 3rd Gallica at the forefront. At Cremona, 'the 3rd broke down the gate with axes and swords. All authors agree that Gaius Volusius, a soldier of the 3rd Legion, entered first. Beating down all who opposed him, he mounted the rampart, waved his hand, and shouted aloud that the camp was taken.' [Tac., *H*, III, 29]

The 3rd Gallica then marched on Rome and stormed into the city. After helping to bring down Vitellius, they then set about looting the homes of his supporters. When Vespasian's deputy Mucianus arrived at Rome, he ordered the rapacious 3rd Gallica to spend the winter at Capua, to remove them from the capital. Capua was not only wealthy, but had supported Vitellius to the end, so the men of the 3rd Gallica had no reservations about systematically looting the town over the winter.

Varus, the legion's chief centurion, was rewarded for his part in the defeat of Vitellius with a praetorship, but he was soon sidelined, and in the spring of AD 70 his former legion was sent back to the East, where it could no longer influence events. The legion's new station was remote Raphanaea, on the Euphrates river, in southern Syria.

The 3rd Gallica took part in the Roman counter-offensive in Judea during the Second Jewish Revolt of AD 132–135. It was back at Raphanaea during the reign of Marcus Aurelius. During the reign of Septimius Severus the legion's province was Syria Phoenicia, and the legion would have taken part in Aurelian's AD 273 campaign to take back the East from the rebel queen of Palmyra, Zenobia.

By the reign of Diocletian, the 3rd Gallica's base was at Danaba, between Damascus and Palmyra. In the reign of Theodosius I, the legion was still at Danaba, along with the 1st Illyricorum Legion, a unit which dated from the late third century.

During the legion's heyday, in that short period between AD 67 and AD 70, few legionaries were more feared, by both friend and foe, than the wild, sun-worshipping Syrians of the 3rd Gallica.

3RD ITALICA LEGION

LEGIO III ITALICA   *3rd Italian Legion*

EMBLEM:	Stork.
BIRTH SIGN:	Capricorn (probably).
FOUNDATION:	AD 165, by Marcus Aurelius, for the Marcomani Wars.
RECRUITMENT AREA:	Originally Italy.
POSTINGS:	Aquileia, Eining, Castra Regina.
BATTLE HONOURS:	Marcus Aurelius' Marcomani Wars, AD 165–175.

MARCUS AURELIUS' STORKS

The second of two legions raised in Italy in AD 165 by Marcus Aurelius for his Danube wars, it was in action immediately.

Marcus Aurelius' newly raised 3rd Italica Legion was fighting the Alemanni and Quadi Germans from the moment it reached the battlefront. Its first enlistment was enrolled in Italy in AD 165 along with that of the 2nd Italica.

The 3rd Italica's emblem of a stork, unique among legion emblems, may have referred to its new birth, but it could also have referred to the region in Italy where it was born. Puglia, for instance, was a famous nesting place of the stork in ancient times; the commune of Cerignola still uses the stork as its emblem to this day.

The 3rd Italica was initially stationed at Aquileia in northeast Italy with the 2nd Italica. It was at Eining in Austria by AD 172, then moved to Castra Regina in Raetia, today's Bavarian city of Regensburg. Construction of the Castra Regina legion camp began beside the Danube in AD 179, when numismatic evidence puts the 3rd Italica Legion in residence.

By the end of the fourth century the unit was a comitatense legion under the command of the Master of Foot.

3RD PARTHICA LEGION

LEGIO III PARTHICA   *3rd Parthian Legion*

EMBLEM:	Centaur.
BIRTH SIGN:	Capricorn (probably).
FOUNDATION:	c. AD 197, by Septimius Severus, for his Parthian campaign.
RECRUITMENT AREA:	Originally Thrace/Macedonia.
POSTINGS:	Parthia, Rhesana.
BATTLE HONOURS:	Septimius Severus' Parthian campaign, AD 197–201.

FODDER FOR THE PERSIANS

Raised by Septimius Severus for service against the Parthians, and by AD 197 based in newly occupied Mesopotamia, where it would spend its later career fighting the Persians.

Together with the 1st and 2nd Parthica legions, the 3rd Parthica was raised in Thrace and Macedonia by Septimius Severus for his Parthian campaigns of AD 197–201. After overcoming Parthian resistance and taking Edessa, capital of the kingdom of Osroene, a Parthian ally, and capturing the king, Abgar, Severus' legions marched down the Tigris and stormed and looted the Parthian capital, Ctesiphon.

During these operations, the European recruits of the three Parthica legions regularly outperformed the men of the legions based in the East. But after a prolonged, bloody, and ultimately unsuccessful siege of the rich desert city of Hatra, even they had reached their limit and were on the point of mutiny. Severus gave up the siege and withdrew, leaving the 1st Parthica and 3rd Parthica legions to garrison Mesopotamia.

The 3rd Parthica Legion made its base at Rhesana, today's Ra's al-Ayn in Syria, midway between Nisibis and Carrhae. During the fourth-century campaigns of Persia's conquering king Shapur II, the 3rd Parthica's Rhesana base fell to the Persians. The 3rd Parthica Legion disappeared, apparently destroyed during the fall of Rhesana.

By the end of the fourth century, a 4th Parthica Legion was in existence. Raised during the third century, it was stationed at Circesio, today's Aba Serae in Iraq, under the command of the Duke of Osroene. Based at Beroea (Aleppo), in Syria, this unit later probably formed part of the Byzantine army.

4TH MACEDONICA LEGION

LEGIO IIII MACEDONICA *4th Legion of Macedonia*

EMBLEM:	Bull.
BIRTH SIGN:	Capricorn.
FOUNDATION:	By Pompey the Great (probably).
RECRUITMENT AREA:	Originally Spain or Italy.
POSTINGS:	Juliobriga, Mogontiacum.

FROM FAME AT PHILIPPI
TO IGNOMINY ON THE RHINE

The 4th Macedonica survived the Battle of Philippi, spent time in Spain before transfer to the Rhine, valiantly fought Arminius under Germanicus, only to disgrace itself in the Civilis Revolt and be disbanded by Vespasian and reformed as the 4th Flavia.

The 4th Legion was carrying the 'Macedonica' title very early in the imperial era; '4th Macedonica' appears on the tombstones of centurion Lucius Blattius and another, unnamed soldier, who settled at Este in Italy some time before 14 BC. [Kepp., *CVSI*, Syl. 24 and 25] It is probable that the legion appropriated its title following the first Battle of Philippi, in Macedonia, in 42 BC, where it fought on the left wing of Mark Antony's army and took very heavy casualties. Opposing general Marcus Brutus congratulated his troops for having 'completely destroyed their famed 4th Legion' in the battle. [App., IV, 117] But the unit survived to be rebuilt.

Under Octavian/Augustus, the legion was posted to Nearer Spain. Its base was at Juliobriga, modern Retorillo, where it remained until AD 43, when Claudius transferred it to Mogontiacum on the Upper Rhine, replacing the 14th Gemina, which was assigned to the invasion of Britain.

In January AD 69, the 4th Macedonica led the movement which resulted in the legions of the army of the Upper Rhine declaring their general Vitellius emperor, in opposition to Galba and then Otho. [Tac., *H*, I, 55] The legion subsequently sent several cohorts to Italy, which fought for Vitellius at the Second Battle of Bedriacum and Battle of Cremona against Vespasian's troops. They lost, and surrendered. The 4th Macedonica cohorts remaining on the Rhine became embroiled in the Civilis Revolt later that year, and surrendered to the rebels early in AD 70.

Vespasian, the new emperor, was so disgusted with the 4th Macedonica's involvement with Civilis and his rebels that he abolished the legion.

4TH FLAVIA FELIX LEGION

LEGIO IIII FLAVIA-F   *4th Fortunate Flavian Legion*

EMBLEM:	Lion.
BIRTH SIGN:	Capricorn (probably).
FOUNDATION:	Founded by Vespasian in AD 70 to replace the abolished 4th Macedonica.
RECRUITMENT AREA:	Originally, possibly Dalmatia.
POSTINGS:	Burnum, Singidunum, Dacia, Singidunum.
BATTLE HONOURS	Trajan's Dacian Wars, AD 101–106.

BECOMING VESPASIAN'S LIONS

Fighting stoutly under Germanicus only to disgrace itself in the Civilis Revolt, a legion that was disbanded by Vespasian, who reformed it as the 16th Flavia, and sent it to the East.

After the disbanding of the disgraced 4th Macedonica Legion in AD 70, Vespasian reformed the unit as the 4th Flavia Felix Legion, giving the unit his family name of Flavia and the emblem of a lion, a symbol associated with Vespasian's favourite deity, Hercules. The 'Felix' title, denoting imperial favour, was also applied by emperors to various military colonies founded by them.

With much to prove in the wake of the shaming performance of the 4th Macedonica during the Civilis Revolt, the new 4th Flavia Felix Legion marched to Burnum, capital of the province of Dalmatia, where it had taken up residence by the end of AD 70.

By AD 85 the legion had been transferred to Moesia. Its base was at Singidunum, modern Belgrade in Serbia, at the confluence of the Danube and Sava rivers. The 4th Flavia would have been involved in the fighting with the Alemanni Germans and Dacians in Moesia and Pannonia during the reign of Domitian, and during the reign of Trajan it took part in his invasions of Dacia which ultimately made the kingdom a province of Rome.

The legion continued to be based at Singidunum for the next 200 years, after which it disappeared from history.

4TH SCYTHICA LEGION

LEGIO IIII SCYTHICA   *4th Scythian Legion*

EMBLEM:	Bull.
BIRTH SIGN:	Capricorn.
ORIGIN OF TITLE:	Adopted after defeating the Bastarnae, a Scythian tribe, 29 BC.
FOUNDATION:	Stems from a late republican legion of Pompey the Great.
RECRUITMENT AREA:	Originally Italy, then Spain.
POSTINGS:	Macedonia, Moesia, Zeugma, Balkis, Zeugma, Sura.
BATTLE HONOURS:	Defeat of the Bastarnae, 29 BC. Jewish Revolt, AD 66. Trajan's Eastern Campaigns, AD 114–116.
NOTABLE COMMANDER:	Septimius Severus, future emperor, AD 181–183.

EARLY SUCCESS PROVES HARD TO EMULATE

Winning its title against Scythian invaders of Moesia and Macedonia early in Augustus' reign, it would become a bulwark of the Euphrates defence line.

Legions with the number IIII were traditionally raised in Italy. By the time of Pompey the Great this legion was stationed in Spain. It seems to have fought for Pompey against Caesar in eastern Spain, and surrendered to Caesar there in 49 BC. Cohorts of the legion are believed to have then escaped to Greece with Afranius (some of the 'Spanish cohorts' referred to at Pharsalus by Caesar), then escaped after Pharsalus to North Africa, where the depleted legion is known to have taken part at the Battle of Thapsus – with its ranks augmented by slave recruits, to the disgust of the legionaries – finally surrendering after the defeat of republican forces there.

Octavian subsequently raised a new 4th Legion, probably using some of Pompey's former men as its core. There were 4th legions in the armies of both Octavian and Antony at the time of the 31 BC Battle of Actium, and in 30 BC Octavian posted Antony's former legion, now calling itself the 4th Macedonica, to Spain, while he sent the second 4th Legion to Macedonia, where it would be joined by the 5th and 10th legions.

In Macedonia and Moesia in 29 BC, under the province's ambitious new governor, Marcus Licinius Crassus (the grandson of Crassus the triumvir who had perished with his army at Carrhae in 53 BC), the legion destroyed the invading Bastarnae, a Scythian tribe, during a series of battles. For this comprehensive victory, Crassus was voted a Triumph by the Senate, and Octavian was hailed imperator. Officially, or unofficially, the 4th Legion adopted the title 4th Scythica following its defeat of these Scythians, by which title it was known for the rest of its days.

By AD 9 the legion was stationed in Moesia, and over the next half century it moved between Moesia and Macedonia. By AD 62, the 4th Scythica Legion had been shipped to Syria, to take part in the push into Armenia by Caesennius Paetus. The legion landed at Laodicea, and, commanded by Funisulanus Vettonianus, was led into Armenia by Paetus, together with the 12th Fulminata Legion.

Several forts were taken, 'and some glory as well as plunder' gained. [Tac., *A*, xv, 8] But the dilatory Paetus allowed his camp at Rhandeia in Armenia to be surrounded and besieged by the army of the Parthian king Vologases. Months later, with his starving troops reluctant to go on the offensive, Paetus agreed to humiliating terms, then led his bedraggled legions from Armenia, leaving behind their baggage and heavy equipment for the enemy.

Rome did not forgive this poor performance. The 4th Scythica was posted to remote Zeugma on the Euphrates, today's Balkis in Syria. There it would remain for hundreds of years. In AD 66, following the outbreak of the Jewish Revolt, the legion contributed several cohorts to the army led to Jerusalem by Cestius Gallus, which subsequently retreated all the way to Caesarea. Again the 4th Scythica was associated with defeat, and the subsequent Roman commanders against the Jews, Vespasian and then his son Titus, ignored the legion when selecting units for the counter-offensives that finally terminated the revolt.

The legion also contributed cohorts to the Roman operations that put down the Second Jewish Revolt of AD 132–135. In AD 218, a centurion of the 4th Scythica captured the 10-year-old son of the deposed emperor Macrinus when the boy arrived at Zeugma en route to seeking asylum with the Parthians following the defeat of his father by Elagabalus.

By the late fourth century, the 4th Scythica legion was shown in the Notitia Dignitatum still based in Syria, but at Sura.

5TH ALAUDAE LEGION

LEGIO V ALAUDAE   *5th Crested Larks Legion*

EMBLEM:	Elephants.
BIRTH SIGN:	Cancer (possibly).
FOUNDATION:	The 5th Legion was founded for Julius Caesar in 48 BC in Spain. Alaudae auxiliaries were raised in Transalpine Gaul in 52 BC, formed into a legion by 43 BC, and later folded into the 5th.
RECRUITMENT AREA:	The 5th originally in Further Spain; the Alaudae originally in Transalpine Gaul.
POSTINGS:	Hispania Tarraconensis, Germania, Vetera, Dacia.
BATTLE HONOURS:	Germanicus' German campaigns, AD 14–16.
A HISTORY OF DISASTER:	Lost its eagle to the Germans in 16 BC. Wiped out by the Dacians in AD 86.

FATED TO FAIL

From favour under Julius Caesar and carrying the elephant emblem for its victory at Thapsus, it would lose its eagle on the Rhine in 15 BC and be wiped out by the Dacians during Domitian's reign.

In 185 BC, the Roman Republic had a 5th Legion serving in Spain [Livy, XXXIX, 30, 12] where Keppie suggests legions 5 to 10 were always stationed. [Kepp., *MRA*, 2] In all probability a 5th legion was one of the unidentified Pompeian legions that surrendered to Caesar in Nearer Spain in 49 BC. In the following year, on Caesar's orders, his governor of Further Spain, Quintus Cassius Longinus, 'enrolled a new legion, the 5th' [Caes., *CW*, IV, 50], the new legion seemingly being enrolled in the recruiting grounds of Pompey's disbanded 5th.

    This 5th Legion was subsequently shipped to North Africa to take part in Caesar's campaign against the republican forces there, and at the Battle of Thapsus on 6 April 46 BC, the legionaries of the 5th, split over the two wings of Caesar's army, took on and turned the sixty war elephants of King Juba of Numidia. According to Appian, the men of the 5th had asked to be pitted against the elephants. 'As a result, this legion bears elephants on its standards even now.' [App., II, 96]

As for the 'Alaudae' background of the legion, two years after the 5th Legion's participation in the last great battle of the Civil War, Munda, and a year after the murder of Caesar in Rome, Mark Antony was making a play for power in Italy. His troops were ranging the countryside looking for supporters of the 'Liberators', Brutus and Cassius. From late 44 BC to early 43 BC, Marcus Cicero, famed orator and author, wrote that troops of Antony's Praetorian Guard and 'the Alaudae Legion' were looking for him, on Antony's orders. [Cic., *Phil.*, i. 20, v, 12; XIII, 3, 37; *Att.*, XVI, 8, 2]

Monument at Cologne to Lucius Poblicius, a soldier of the 5th Alaudae Legion, a unit whose career on the Rhine was ill-starred.

Was Cicero referring to the 5th Alaudae Legion? Many modern authors believe so, and suggest that Cicero was merely unfamiliar with the legion's full name. Yet Cicero was a former consul and general who had led legions in battle and had been voted a Triumph; he had an intimate knowledge of the Roman military. Had the legion that was looking for him been called the 5th Alaudae, Cicero would surely have identified it as such.

Available evidence suggests that in 43 BC the 5th and the Alaudae were two separate legions. Suetonius wrote that during the Gallic War Caesar raised a legion in Transalpine Gaul 'called the Alaudae, Gallic for "The Crested Lark", which he trained and equipped in Roman style. Later, he made every Alaudae legionary a full citizen'. [Suet., 1, 24] Caesar himself only wrote of raising twenty-two cohorts of auxiliaries in Transalpine Gaul. Raising a legion of non-citizens was then illegal. There is no mention of this Alaudae Legion during the Civil War, so perhaps the men of the Alaudae were originally among these auxiliaries, helping to keep the peace in Gaul during the Civil War.

At some point during the years 45 BC to 30 BC, the 5th Legion and Alaudae auxiliaries merged to form the 5th Alaudae Legion. The combination of a number and a name in a legion's title was, prior to this, unheard of. It was only after Caesar's death that it became widespread.

The general who created this combined legion may have been Ventidius, who provided Antony with several legions; the 5th Alaudae went on to march for Antony. By 30 BC, the 5th Alaudae was certainly one of the legions retained in Octavian's standing army, and was posted to Spain, where it served during the 29–19 BC Cantabrian Wars. By 17 BC it had been transferred to the Rhine.

In 16 BC, under the governor of Lower Germany, Marcus Lollius, the 5th Alaudae Legion collided with invading Germans of the Sugambri, Usipetes and Tencteri tribes, west of the Rhine. The three tribes had swept across the river, repulsed a cavalry force sent by Lollius to intercept them, then surprised the 5th Alaudae as Lollius was advancing them. In the fierce fighting that followed, the legion was deprived of its eagle by the Germans. Lollius and the 5th Alaudae's survivors fell back, but when the Germans heard that Augustus himself was in Gaul and hurrying towards them with a large army, they withdrew across the river, subsequently sealing a peace with the emperor by providing hostages. But the damage had been done to the 5th Alaudae Legion's reputation; the stain of losing its eagle would remain with it for ever.

By AD 14, the unit was stationed at Vetera with the other three legions of the army of the Lower Rhine, and took part in the victorious battles of Germanicus Caesar's AD 14–16 campaigns in Germany. In AD 28, under the governor of Lower Germany, Lucius Apronius, the 5th Alaudae was victorious in battle in a campaign against the Frisii in which 1,300 auxiliaries died: 'The soldiers of the 5th sprang forward, drove back the enemy in a fierce encounter, and saved our cohorts and cavalry.' [Tac., *A*, IV, 73]

The legion remained at Vetera until AD 69, when some of its cohorts went to Italy for Vitellius. Those that remained at Vetera were savaged in Civilis' rebellion and the legion was almost exterminated. From AD 70, the legion probably served in Pannonia and Moesia. In AD 86, it was almost certainly the legion wiped out in Dacia with Praetorian Prefect Fuscus. It was never again mentioned in Roman records, and never reformed.

5TH MACEDONICA LEGION

LEGIO V MACEDONICA   *5th Legion of Macedonia*

ORIGIN OF TITLE:	Apparently for meritorious service in Macedonia in 30 BC–AD 6.
EMBLEM:	Bull.
BIRTH SIGN:	Not known.
FOUNDATION:	By Octavian, prior to 42 BC.
RECRUITMENT AREA:	Initially, probably Spain. Under Nero, it became Moesia.
POSTINGS:	Macedonia, Oescus, Pontus, Armenia, Judea, Jerusalem, Egypt, Oescus, Dacia, Troesmis, Syria, Potaissa, Oescus.
BATTLE HONOURS:	Macedonian campaigns, 30 BC–AD 6. Corbulo's Second Armenian campaign, AD 62. Jewish Revolt, AD 66–71. Trajan's Second Dacian War, AD 105–106. Second Jewish Revolt, AD 134–135. Marcus Aurelius' Eastern campaign, AD 161–166.
NOTABLE SECOND-IN-COMMAND:	
	Publius Aelius Hadrianus, future emperor, AD 96.

THE WELL-TRAVELLED FIFTH

Gaining its title in Macedonia, fighting in Armenia for Corbulo, it put down the First Jewish Revolt in Judea and besieged Jerusalem, then came back to Europe to serve in Trajan's Dacian Wars, before marching in the East again under Marcus Aurelius.

Few imperial legions changed bases as frequently as the 5th Macedonica. Stemming from Octavian's 5th Legion of the triumviral period, it served in Macedonia from 30 BC to AD 6, and seems to have gained its title from service in that turbulent province, quite probably during the same battles that earned the 4th its Scythica title.

The 5th Macedonica was subsequently based in Moesia, at Oescus, today's Gigen in Hungary. By AD 62, having just filled its empty ranks with a new enlistment of Moesian recruits, the legion was transferred by Nero's Palatium to the East, to take part in the next Armenian campaign. [Tac., *A*, xv, 6]

Shipped across the Black Sea from the Danube by Rome's Pontic Fleet, it was left in Pontus by the commander-in-chief of the Armenian operation, the over-confident Caesennius Paetus, who embarked on the operations with just two legions. After Paetus and his troops were forced by the Parthians to withdraw, the 5th Macedonica was summoned by Domitius Corbulo for his operation in the region, with Corbulo's impetuous young son-in-law, Vinianus Annius, as its commander.

The legion was subsequently transferred to Alexandria in Egypt. From there it joined Titus for the successful but bloody AD 70 Siege of Jerusalem, which ended the main phase of the First Jewish Revolt. By AD 71, the legion was back at Oescus in Moesia. While based there it fared badly attempting to counter a raid by King Decebalus of Dacia, in which the provincial governor was killed. The 5th Macedonica had its revenge in Trajan's Dacian Wars of AD 101–106, after which the legion returned to Moesia, to be based at Troesmis, modern-day Turcoaia in Romania.

By the spring of AD 135, the legion, or a large vexillation from it, had been shipped from Moesia to Palestine for the last stage of the Second Jewish Revolt. It took part in the successful Siege of Bethar, headquarters of resistance leader Shimeon bar-Kokhba, in the spring and summer of that year. [Yadin, 13] Once Bar-Kokhba was eliminated and the revolt quashed, the 5th Macedonica men returned to their home base in Moesia.

Between AD 161 and 166, the legion took part in Marcus Aurelius' eastern campaigns. On its return to Europe, the legion was stationed in Dacia, at Potaissa in the mountainous north. In AD 274, when Dacia was surrendered to the barbarian tribes, the 5th Macedonica was withdrawn south of the Danube, returning to its former station at Oescus.

By the end of the fourth century the legion had been split up. One part was still in Moesia, with its cohorts divided between four different locations as border defence units. Another part of the 5th Macedonica Legion was stationed in Egypt, along with three other legions and a large number of auxiliary units. [Not. Dig.]

6TH FERRATA LEGION

LEGIO VI FERRATA   *6th Ironclad Legion*

ORIGIN OF TITLE:	Apparently adopted after surviving the Civil War, first against Caesar, later for him.
EMBLEM:	Bull.
BIRTH SIGN:	Gemini (she-wolf and twins).
FOUNDATION:	Originating as Pompey the Great's 6th Legion in Spain.
RECRUITMENT AREA:	Originally Italy, later Spain.
POSTINGS:	Laodicea, Raphanaea, Rome, Arabia, Judea, Legio (Caparcotna), Africa, Mesopotamia, Arabia, Legio (Caparcotna), Arabia, Legio (Caparcotna).
BATTLE HONOURS:	Corbulo's First Armenian campaign, AD 54–58. Corbulo's Second Armenian campaign, AD 62. The March on Rome, AD 69. Defeat of the Sarmatians, Moesia, AD 69. Conquest of Commagene, AD 73. Trajan's Eastern campaign, AD 114–116. Second Jewish Revolt, AD 132–135.

CAESAR'S IRONCLADS

Famous as Caesar's 'Ironclads', a legion that spent most of its career in Syria, it marched to Rome to make Vespasian emperor, fought in the last battles of the Civilis Revolt, then, based in Galilee, took the brunt of the Second Jewish Revolt.

The 6th Legion was one of six legions stationed in Spain under the control of Pompey the Great while Caesar was conquering Gaul. During the Gallic War, Pompey loaned the 6th to Caesar for service in Gaul; Cato the Younger protested: 'He sent Caesar a force of 6,000 men into Gaul, which Caesar never asked the [Senate] for, nor had Pompey obtained their consent to give.' [Plut., *Cato*] This was several years before the incident when Caesar and Pompey each contributed a legion to a later aborted mission to the East, after which Caesar's legion, the 15th, was handed over to Pompey, along with Pompey's unit, which in that instance was the 1st Legion.

Because the 6th Legion was Pompey's, Caesar relegated it to mostly rear echelon duties. Pompey took it back by 50 BC as tensions rose between Caesar and the Senate, finally erupting into the civil war initiated by Caesar in 49 BC. The 6th was one of the republican legions that surrendered to Caesar in Spain in 49 BC, but apparently, along with cohorts of the surrendered 4th Legion, escaped from Spain with Pompey's generals Afranius and Petreius and joined Pompey in Greece. Seven combined cohorts from these two legions, 'the Spanish cohorts, which, as we have said, were brought over by Afranius', in Caesar's own words, fought for Pompey in the 48 BC Battle of Pharsalus. [Caes., CW, III, 88]

Following the republican army's defeat at Pharsalus, cohorts of both the 4th and 6th were among 18,000 Pompeian troops who escaped to North Africa to fight on, leaving just under 1,000 men of the 6th Legion among the troops who surrendered to Caesar. When Caesar's own men at Pharsalus refused to fight on, he sent them back to Italy with Mark Antony, and negotiated a deal with the men of the 6th. They signed up to march for Caesar, becoming the core of the Caesarian army which conquered the Egyptians then overcame Pharnaces' chariots at the Battle of Zela in Pontus. Finally, the 6th took part in Caesar's defeat of Pompey's sons in Spain. No wonder they called themselves the 'ironclads'; in surviving, and winning, against enormous odds, they would have thought themselves impregnable.

Meanwhile, the remaining men of Pompey's 6th Legion fought on the losing side at Thapsus in North Africa. This second 6th Legion would be fighting for Octavian by 31 BC and eventually became the 6th Victrix.

Following Caesar's assassination, the 6th Ferrata Legion marched for Antony until the Actium defeat, then became part of Octavian's standing army. Octavian sent it to Syria following the death of Antony, and it was based at Raphanaea in southern Syria for much of the next one and a half centuries.

In AD 66, the legion contributed four cohorts to Gallus' disastrous march to and from Jerusalem after the outbreak of the Jewish Revolt. Three years later, the legion marched on Italy with Licinius

The she-wolf and the twins Romulus and Remus, one of the emblems of the 6th Ferrata Legion.

Mucianus, governor of Syria, plus auxiliaries and 13,000 recalled Evocati militia-men, to dethrone Vitellius and install Vespasian. On the march, news was received that Sarmatian raiders had stormed into Moesia and overrun several auxiliary forts. Mucianus swung north towards the Danube and, taking the raiders by surprise, the 6th Ferrata destroyed the Sarmatians.

In AD 70, the legion marched all the way from Rome back to its Syrian base. The legion participated in Trajan's AD 111–116 Parthian campaign, after which it was based at Caparcotna in Galilee. Archaeological evidence puts the legion at Capar-cotna in AD 117 at the time of the Jewish uprisings in Egypt and Cyrenaica and on Cyprus. The Caparcotna fortress built by the legion was situated not far from the entrance to the Wadi Ara pass, 25 miles (38.6 kilometres) from Gadara and 15 miles (24 kilometres) from Nazareth.

By AD 119, the legion was in Arabia, but by AD 120 was back at Caparcotna, which then took the name Legio, until it was renamed Maximianus, apparently after the emperor Maximianus Galerius (reigned AD 305–311). The legion was based there for the remainder of its known career.

6TH VICTRIX LEGION

LEGIO VI VICTRIX *6th Victorious Legion*

ORIGIN OF TITLE:	Apparently granted by Augustus.
EMBLEM:	Bull (probably).
BIRTH SIGN:	Gemini (probably).
FOUNDATION:	Based on the remnants of Pompey's 6th.
RECRUITMENT AREA:	Probably Italy and Spain.
POSTINGS:	Hispania Tarraconensis, the Rhine, Novaesium, Vetera, Eburacum.
BATTLE HONOURS:	Battle of Old Camp, AD 70.

THE VICTORIOUS SIXTH

Fighting Augustus' Cantabrian War, this unit garrisoned Spain, then helped put down the Civilis Revolt before being sent to Britain in AD 122 after the disappearance of the 9th Hispana Legion. It was the last legion to leave Britain.

Like the 6th Ferrata, originating from the republican 6th Legion that had marched for Pompey the Great, this legion was under Octavian's control by the 42 BC Battles of Philippi. As part of Octavian's new standing army, this second 6th served in the Cantabrian Wars in Spain from 29 BC, during which it may have gained its Victrix title.

Stationed in Nearer Spain until AD 70, the legion supported the grab for imperial power by its province's governor, Galba, and would have supplied centurions for the new 7th Legion raised by Galba in eastern Spain for his march on Rome. In AD 70, the 6th Victrix marched to the Rhine to join Petilius Cerialis in putting down the Civilis Revolt. It was thereafter stationed in Lower Germany at Novaesium, modern-day Neuss.

The legion transferred to Vetera during the Dacian Wars, during which the Rhine legions were reduced to provide units for Trajan's Dacian invasions. It was still at Vetera in AD 122, when it was ordered to transfer urgently to Britain to replace the destroyed 9th Hispana Legion. [*See page 421–8.*]

The 6th Victrix was subsequently based at Eburacum, today's York, for almost 300 years. In 401, the legion was ordered by Stilicho, Master of Combined Forces, to join him in Italy for the last-ditch defence of Italy against Alaric and his Visigoths. The last legion to leave Britain, it never returned. It seems to have been destroyed in the battles leading up to Alaric's sacking of Rome in the year 410.

7TH CLAUDIA LEGION

LEGIO VII CLAUDIA PIA FIDELIS
Claudius' Loyal and Patriotic 7th Legion

ORIGIN OF TITLE:	Granted by Claudius in AD 42 for terminating the Scribonianus Revolt.
EMBLEM:	Bull.
BIRTH SIGN:	Leo.
FOUNDATION:	Raised c. 55 BC by Pompey the Great.
RECRUITMENT AREA:	Initially Spain. By the late first century BC, Asia Minor. [Kepp., *MRA*]
IMPERIAL POSTINGS:	Galatia, Tilurium, Moesia, Rome, Viminacium, Dacia, Viminacium.
BATTLE HONOURS:	Pannonian War, AD 6–9. Second Battle of Bedriacum, AD 69. Battle of Cremona, AD 69. Battle of Rome, AD 69. Battle of Tapae, AD 88. Trajan's Dacian Wars, AD 101–106.

CAESAR'S SEVENTH BECOMES CLAUDIUS' SEVENTH

Rewarded by Claudius for putting down a rebellion against him, this legion participated in a rare decisive victory against the Dacians under Domitian before invading Dacia itself under Trajan.

A 7th Legion was known to be serving the Roman Republic in Spain in 181 BC [Livy, XXXIX 30, 12], and 7th legions were stationed in Spain right up to the time the 7th served under Caesar in Gaul. During the conquest of Gaul, the 7th Legion served under Publius Crassus, son of Crassus the triumvir, both of whom would be killed by the Parthians at Carrhae. Under young Crassus, the 7th Legion single-handedly took all of Aquitania for Rome. In 52 BC, under Caesar's deputy Titus Atius Labienus, the 7th was one of four legions that defeated a large Gallic army led by the chieftain Camulogenus, at Grenelle beside the Seine, not far from the site of Paris. Caesar considered the 7th one of his best legions, and took it on both his expeditions to Britain.

Caesar's 7th served Octavian at the time of the Battle of Actium, after which he stationed it in Galatia. It was one of five legions rushed from the East to Pannonia in AD 6 after the outbreak of the Pannonian War. Despite the fact that Velleius says that Tiberius afterwards sent all these legions back to the East, by the end of the war in AD 9 the 7th Legion was stationed in Dalmatia at Tilurium, today's Gardun in Croatia. It remained there through the mutiny of AD 14, until transferred to Moesia many years later.

In AD 42, Claudius had only been on the throne for a little over a year when Furius Camillus Scribonianus, governor of Dalmatia, ordered the two legions of his province, the 7th and the 11th, to prepare to march on Rome to depose Claudius. Five days later, men of the 7th and 11th killed Scribonianus and the officers support-ing his rebellion. In his gratitude, Claudius bestowed the titles *Claudia Pia Fidelis* on the two loyal legions: 'Claudius' Loyal and Patriotic'. Nonetheless, the authoritarian general sent to take over in Dalmatia executed the soldiers who had killed their own officers, as an example, even though they had done so in support of the emperor. The 7th Claudia Pia Fidelis was immediately transferred to Moesia.

By AD 69, Tettius Julianus was commanding the 7th Claudia, as it was now com-monly known. The governor of Moesia, taking advantage of the upheaval caused by the war of succession that year, sent a centurion to kill Julianus to settle an old personal feud. Julianus escaped to the mountains. Following the war, rivals in the Senate accused Julianus of deserting his legion when he had gone into hiding, and the House had withdrawn his praetorship. Once Vespasian arrived at Rome and learned the facts, Julianus' rank was restored.

Meanwhile, Julianus' legion, led in his absence by its senior tribune, swore for Vespasian in AD 69 and fought under Vespasian's general Primus at Bedriacum and Cremona later that year, playing a leading role in defeating the Vitellianist forces: 'The fiercest struggle was maintained by the 3rd [Gallica] and 7th Legions.' [Tac., *H*, III, 29] The 7th was subsequently in the army that fought its way into Rome to make Vespasian emperor.

Vespasian posted the legion back to Viminacium in Moesia (now Kostolac, in Serbia). In AD 88–89, during Domitian's otherwise disastrous war with the Dacians, Tettius Julianus had his opportunity to repay the faith shown in him by Domitian's father by leading a Roman army to a bloody victory over Dacian forces at Tapae in central Dacia. The gravestone of Tiberius Claudia Maximus (then a standard-bearer in the 7th Claudia's mounted squadron, who was later decorated by Domitian) reveals that the legion was one of Julianus' units in this campaign. [*AE* 1969/70, 583]

On this war's conclusion, with a treaty which strongly favoured the Dacians, Domitian divided Moesia into two provinces, Upper and Lower Moesia. The 7th Claudia was stationed in Upper Moesia, the western part of the old province.

The 7th Claudia took part in Trajan's two Dacian Wars of AD 101–102 and 105–106 which finally conquered Decebalus and brought Dacia into the empire. From its long-term base at Viminacium, the legion would also have been involved in the gruelling wars against the Germans, waged by Marcus Aurelius along the Danube, which occupied most of his reign between AD 161 and 180.

With the surrender of Dacia by Aurelian in AD 274, the 7th Claudia remained at Viminacium, in what became reclassified as Upper Dacia, although it was below the Danube. The legion was still based in this region at the end of the fourth century, at Cuppis. [Not. Dig.] It had apparently by that time spawned two more 7th Legions, the 7th Seniors and 7th Juniors. If they survived the fall of the Western Roman Empire in the fifth century, these units would all have been incorporated into the Byzantine army.

7TH GEMINA LEGION

LEGIO VII GEMINA   *The Twinned 7th Legion*

ORIGIN OF TITLE:	Through combination with another legion.
EMBLEM:	Bull.
BIRTH SIGN:	Gemini – she-wolf and twins (probably).
FOUNDATION:	Founded in AD 68 by Galba.
RECRUITMENT AREA:	Initially eastern Spain.
POSTINGS:	Rome, Carnuntum, Legio (Hispania).
BATTLE HONOURS:	Second Battle of Bedriacum, AD 69.
	Battle of Cremona, AD 69.
	Battle of Rome, AD 69.
NOTABLE COMMANDER:	Marcus Ulpius Traianus (later Emperor Trajan).

GALBA'S SEVENTH

Formed by Galba in Spain, this unit marched to Rome to overthrow Nero, then led the way under Primus to make Vespasian emperor. It became the home legion of Spain.

For his tilt at Nero's throne, Sulpicius Galba raised this legion in his province of Hispania Tarraconensis, or Nearer Spain, in the summer of AD 68. The legion apparently took the number VII because it was raised in the traditional Spanish recruiting grounds of the 7th Claudia Legion. Known as the 7th Hispana and 7th Galbiana, or Galba's 7th Legion, for the next two years, the new legion escorted Galba to Rome. He then sent the unit to Carnuntum in Pannonia under the command of Marcus Antonius Primus, an ambitious general once convicted for fraud, who, after the death of both Galba and Otho, led the army of Vespasian that marched into Italy to dethrone Vitellius.

The 7th Galbiana fought alongside the 7th Claudia Legion in Primus' army in the AD 69 Second Battle of Bedriacum. Following that victory, the legion played a leading role in the capture of Cremona, where it 'attacked the ramparts in wedge formation, endeavouring to force an entrance'. [Tac., *H*, III, 29] The legion also helped take Rome and install Vespasian as emperor. It appears to have suffered heavy casualties in these battles, for in AD 70 Vespasian combined it with another – apparently the

18th Legion, which had been reformed by Nero and had several cohorts on the Rhine at the time of the Civilis Revolt – to create the 7th Gemina Legion.

As the 7th Gemina, and at full strength, the legion returned to Carnuntum. In AD 74, Vespasian transferred it to Spain. The base that it created in northern Spain would sponsor a civilian *vicus*, which, as the base of a legion, was called Legio; it grew into the modern city of Leon. The 7th Gemina was still there in around AD 230 during the reign of Severus Alexander when Cassius Dio made a survey of legion dispositions.

There is no firm evidence of the legion's existence after the third century. The Franks invaded Spain during that century, destroying Tarraco, the capital of Nearer Spain. The Notitia Dignitatum lists a prefect of the 7th Gemina Legion stationed at Leon at the end of the fourth century, yet the legion itself is listed under the command of the Master of the Military for the Orient, without a station. This and other discrepancies in the Notitia suggest that some of that document's listings were either more notional than actual or were of an earlier date than some other listings.

8TH AUGUSTA LEGION

LEGIO VIII AUGUSTA   *Augustus' 8th Legion*

ORIGIN OF TITLE:	Awarded by Augustus for meritorious service in the Cantabrian Wars.
EMBLEM:	Bull.
BIRTH SIGN:	Capricorn (probably).
FOUNDATION:	A republican legion taken over by Caesar.
RECRUITMENT AREA:	Initially Italy, later Spain.
POSTINGS:	Hispania, Poetovio, Novae, Argentoratum.
BATTLE HONOURS:	Cantabrian War, 29–19 BC Second Battle of Bedriacum, AD 69. Battle of Cremona, AD 69. Battle of Rome, AD 69.

THE WORKADAY EIGHTH

Heroes in the Cantabrian and Pannonian Wars for Augustus, this legion fought for Vespasian against Vitellius and Civilis and was on the front line against the Alemanni and the Franks.

The 8th was a hardworking legion that was reliable if unspectacular. Stemming from the republican 8th Legion which served Caesar in the Gallic War and the Civil War, the 8th saw service in Augustus' Cantabrian Wars (as a result of which it almost certainly gained its Augusta title), then in the Pannonian War. Thereafter it was stationed at Poetovio in Pannonia until the reign of Claudius.

The discovery of an 8th Legion shield boss in an English river led some historians to postulate that the unit was involved in the invasion of Britain, but there is no evidence of this. The shield boss may have belonged to a soldier on temporary assignment to a unit in Britain, a common occurrence.

By AD 45 the legion was based at Novae in Moesia. In AD 69 the 8th Augusta marched for Otho, then, after his death, swore for Vespasian, and fought in the Italian battles that made him emperor. In AD 70, it joined the army that terminated the Civilis Revolt on the Rhine, after which it was stationed at Argentoratum on the

Upper Rhine, where it served for 300 years fighting Germans, Sarmatians and Goths. By AD 371 the legion had relocated to Zurzach in Switzerland.

The Octovani Legion shown on the Notitia Dignitatum, late in the fourth century, as one of the twelve palatine legions under the Master of Foot, may have stemmed from the 8th Augusta.

9TH HISPANA LEGION

LEGIO IX HISPANA   *Spain's 9th Legion*

ORIGIN OF TITLE:	Awarded by Augustus for meritorious service in the Cantabrian Wars.
EMBLEM:	Bull (probably).
BIRTH SIGN:	Capricorn (probably).
FOUNDATION:	Probably founded by Pompey the Great, c. 55 BC.
RECRUITMENT AREA:	Initially Spain.
POSTINGS:	Hispania, Siscia, Pannonia, Britannia, Lindum, Britannia.
BATTLE HONOURS:	Cantabrian War, 29–19 BC. Tacfarinas' Revolt, AD 19–21. Invasion of Britain, AD 43. Agricola's British campaigns, AD 77–84. Domitian's German campaign, AD 83. Battle of Mons Graupius, AD 84.

THE LEGION THAT DISAPPEARED

A legion that was decimated by Julius Caesar, savaged in Boudicca's revolt in Britain, yet was victorious for Agricola in Scotland. It then famously disappeared from the face of the earth; an old answer to the mystery of where and when is supported by surprising evidence.

Some time after AD 120, the 9th Hispana Legion disappeared from the face of the earth, with no explanation given in any classical text or on any inscription. Early twentieth-century historians came to believe that the legion, the last known posting of which was northern Britain, had been wiped out by Caledonian tribes in Scotland in around AD 122. Later theories had the legion being destroyed in Judea during the Second Jewish Revolt of AD 132–135, or in Armenia in AD 161 at the start of the reign of Marcus Aurelius. As detailed on pages 421–8, the preponderance of evidence today points back to the original hypothesis, that of annihilation at the hands of the Caledonians in AD 122.

The republican 9th Legion served under Caesar, most likely during his 61 BC posting as governor of Further Spain then most definitely during the Gallic War and the Civil War. At the beginning of the imperial era it served in Augustus' Cantabrian Wars in Spain, from which it derived its title, and subsequently in the Pannonian War, after which it was based at Siscia in Pannonia.

In AD 43 the 9th Hispana was one of the four legions in Claudius' invasion of Britain, after which it was stationed at Lindum, today's Lincoln. In AD 60, four cohorts of the legion were led by its rash young commander, Petilius Cerialis, into an ambush by Boudicca's rebel Britons. The cohorts were wiped out, but Cerialis and some cavalry survived. Unusually, in AD 61, the Palatium transferred 2,000 men from a legion on the Rhine – apparently the 21st Rapax at Vindonissa – to the 9th Hispana, to replace the lost cohorts and bring the legion up to strength at a time when rebellion still simmered in southern Britain.

The 9th Hispana later transferred north to Eburacum (York), and, after AD 108, further north again to Carlisle, where it remained until its disappearance.

IOTH FRETENSIS LEGION

LEGIO X FRETENSIS   *10th Legion of the Strait*

ORIGIN OF TITLE:	Refers to a naval engagement prior to the imperial era.
EMBLEMS:	Bull, warship and dolphin.
BIRTH SIGN:	Taurus (possibly).
FOUNDATION:	Disputed. Long thought to be a legion created by Octavian prior to 42 BC. A more modern interpretation makes it Julius Caesar's original 10th, founded by him in 61 BC.
RECRUITMENT AREA:	Originally Further Spain.
POSTINGS:	Macedonia, Syria, Cyrrhus, Judea, Masada, Jerusalem, Judea, Aela.
BATTLE HONOURS:	Macedonian conflict, 19 BC–AD 2. Corbulo's First Armenian campaign, AD 52–54. Corbulo's Second Armenian campaign, AD 62. Jewish Revolt, AD 66–71. Second Jewish Revolt, AD 132–135.
NOTABLE COMMANDER:	Marcus Ulpius Traianus, father of the future emperor Trajan.

THE FAMOUS TENTH, OR NOT THE FAMOUS TENTH?

For centuries historians were convinced that this was not Julius Caesar's famous 10th, but a new perspective suggests that it was. Rampaging through Armenia and unstoppable at Jerusalem and Masada, it was almost wiped out in the Second Jewish Revolt.

The 10th Legion which served Caesar during the Gallic War and much of the Civil War of 49–45 BC was the most famous legion of its day. Raised by Caesar in person, the 10th Legion swiftly became his favourite unit. 'Caesar placed the highest confidence in this legion for its bravery,' Caesar himself wrote of the 10th in 58 BC, only months after he began campaigning in Gaul. [Caes., *GW*, I, 40]

Caesar said that the men of the 10th commissioned their military tribunes to thank him for his high opinion of them, and to assure him that they were ready to take the field at any moment. [Ibid., 41] Over the next fourteen years the 10th served on the prestigious but dangerous extreme right of his battle lines and helped him achieve his greatest victories.

Of the loyalty of the 10th, Caesar had no doubt, and he told the legion that it should serve as his bodyguard. [Ibid., 40] This led to a celebrated event. When, in that same year, 58 BC, Caesar agreed to a parley with a German king, Ariovistus, and the king stipulated that both leaders should only bring a mounted escort to the meeting, Caesar grew suspicious of his own allied Gallic cavalry. Telling the cavalrymen to dismount, Caesar gave their horses to the infantrymen of the 10th, on whose devotion he felt he could rely absolutely. [Ibid., 42]

In response to this, one of the legionaries of the 10th remarked, no doubt with a grin, 'Caesar is being better than his word. He promised to make the 10th his bodyguard, and now he's making Equestrians of us!' [Ibid.] The Equestrians that the soldier was referring to were the Equestrian Order. In modern times, this remark has sponsored much debate among historians about the identity of Caesar's 10th Legion, for there were two 10th legions during the imperial era, the 10th Fretensis and the 10th Gemina. One of them was the direct descendant of Caesar's 10th. But which one?

German historian Theodor Mommsen claimed that the 10th Fretensis could not have been Caesar's original 10th Legion, and his claim stood on two apparently firm hypotheses. The first related to the title 'Fretensis'. This term, which literally means 'of the strait', had puzzled scholars for centuries. Mommsen proposed that the title derived from fretum Siciliense, the Strait of Sicily, which we know as the Strait of Messina, that narrow stretch of water between the toe of Italy and the island of Sicily. This 10th

In the reign of Trajan work was carried out on this aqueduct to Caesarea in Judea by a vexillation of the 10th Fretensis Legion.

Fretensis Legion, said Mommsen, must have been a new creation of Octavian that fought for him during his epic sea battles against Sextus Pompey off the coast of Sicily in 36 BC, while the original 10th served under Mark Antony in the East.

During these Sicilian sea battles, Octavian's deputy Marcus Agrippa put large numbers of men from Octavian's legions aboard ships of his fleet, and it was these men, fighting as marines, who won the Battles of Mylae and Naucholus for Octavian. Whilst a 1st Legion and a 13th Legion are mentioned by classical historian Appian as

MOMMSEN DISCREDITED

German historian Professor Theodor Mommsen, winner of the 1902 Nobel Prize for Literature for his *History of Rome*, wrote in the nineteenth century that Caesar's 10th Legion became the imperial era's 10th Gemina Legion. Ever since, most historians and authors have followed this line. However, Mommsen is not the only Nobel Prize winner whose work, subsequent to their award, has been found to be flawed, and since his death in 1903 a number of Mommsen's conclusions and interpretations regarding Rome's military have been questioned, challenged, or totally disproved by scholarly research and modern archaeological finds.

Dr Lawrence Keppie, for example, says that the old theories of Mommsen cannot be entertained when it comes to how and when the Augustan legions were created; Mommsen had said that Augustus retained eighteen legions after Actium, created eight more in AD 6 and a further two in AD 9. This theory has been totally discredited by more recent scholarship. [Kepp., MRA, 5]

Similarly, Dr Robert O. Fink, in the *American Journal of Philology* [Vol. 63, No. 1, 1942, pp. 61–71], in discussing Mommsen's interpretation of a papyrus about troop movements within the Cohors I Augusta Lusitanorum, was highly critical of Mommsen's work, showing that it was 'certainly wrong', 'mistaken' and 'not consistent' on various points. He also discounted as 'absurd' one of Mommsen's suppositions, and railed against 'Mommsen's wholly unnatural assumption' on another point.

Professor Chester Starr has shown how Mommsen was wrong time and time again in his conclusions about Rome's navy. [*See below*] Similarly, there is a more credible scenario for the maritime origin of the 10th Fretensis Legion's title than the one proposed by Mommsen, one that discredits his theory that the 10th Gemina Legion was Caesar's original 10th.

being in the general area at the time, none of the legions that Agrippa used to achieve his naval victories for Octavian was ever identified by classical texts or inscriptions.

Mommsen, noting that the 10th Fretensis Legion showed warships on the coins minted for the legion, concluded that the 10th Fretensis had been one of those legions that took part in Agrippa's naval victories against Sextus Pompey and had appropriated the title Fretensis to commemorate that fact. It is generally accepted by historians that Caesar's original 10th Legion joined Mark Antony in late 44 BC and continued to serve him until the 31 BC Battle of Actium. Therefore, went the Mommsen argument, if the 10th Fretensis fought for Octavian off Sicily in 36 BC, there was no way it could have then ended up in Antony's army at Actium by 31 BC; with relations between Octavian and Antony souring from 36 BC, there was neither the will on Octavian's part to send Antony troops nor an opportunity for the 10th Fretensis Legion to have gone from Italy to the East to join Antony. Consequently, so went the Mommsen theory, the 10th Gemina legion created by Augustus in 30 BC from Antony's 10th must have been the direct descendant of Caesar's 10th – not the 10th Fretensis.

In support of Mommsen's conclusion he, and others, have pointed to Italian gravestones from some time after 41 BC for men who had served in a 'Legio X Equestris'. The 'Equestris' in these inscriptions, some said, was a reference to the occasion in 58 BC when Caesar mounted men of his 10th Legion as his bodyguard – the Equestrians of the legionary's quip. This, the argument goes, definitely made these men veterans of Caesar's original 10th.

Mommsen's theory was said to be supported by an inscription on an altar at Rome, dating from after 2 BC, dedicated by centurions and other ranks of the 'Legio X Gemina Equestris'. According to the Mommsen 'school', this inscription made the 10th Gemina Legion and the 10th Equestris Legion one and the same; accordingly, the 10th Gemina Legion was Caesar's 10th Legion, and, conversely, the 10th Fretensis was not.

This all makes sense until each skein of the argument is tested for strength; the argument then begins to fall apart. Keppie points out that the unique altar reference to 'Legio X Gemina Equestris' makes this the only legion of the Civil War era to have been given two titles in the one inscription. [Kepp. *CVSI*, 2.2, n. 44] Secondly, this inscription is the only one ever found that links the 10th Gemina and the otherwise unknown 10th 'Equestris' Legion. Thirdly, the date of this lone inscription at Rome is at least forty-two years after the death of Caesar, and possibly somewhat later, putting it at long remove from Caesar.

Then there is the term Equestris itself. It was only assumed in modern times that the term applied to Caesar and the brief incident relating to men of his 10th on horseback. No classical author, including Caesar himself, ever wrote that men of the 10th Legion subsequently adopted the title Equestris.

Next, we have the '10th Gemina Equestris' inscription at Rome. It is pure assumption that the 'Equestris' reference relates back to Caesar's legion. Keppie, in fact, remarks that the wording of this inscription is curious and may not yet have been correctly interpreted in every respect. [Kepp., *CVSI*, 2.2, n. 41]

Why were these legionaries in Rome to dedicate the altar? There is no occasion on record in the late first century BC or early first century AD when the entire 10th Gemina Legion, which was based in Spain throughout this period, was in Rome. Apart from civil wars much later, or the rare occasion early in the reign of Tiberius when the 9th Hispana Legion passed by Rome on its way to southern Italy from Pannonia for a special posting in Africa, the legions did not go near Rome. In fact, there is no record of the 10th Gemina Legion visiting Rome at any time during its long history, even during civil wars.

The 'Equestris' inscription undoubtedly related to men on horseback. But it is possible that the soldiers of the 'Legion X Gemina Equestris' referred to in the Rome inscription were a detachment from the 10th Gemina's mounted squadron – its equites legionis – led by centurions of the legion, sent to represent their legion at the capital for a special ceremony, such as the dedication of the Alter of Peace or the funeral of Drusus Caesar.

Then there is the origin of the title of the 10th Fretensis Legion. Professor Starr, a leading authority on the imperial Roman navy, has shown that Theodor Mommsen 'was completely wrong', and repeatedly so, with some of his conclusions about ancient Roman maritime matters. [Starr, III.2, III.3, V.1] Similarly, it may well be that Mommsen's assertion that the word Fretensis meant the Strait of Messina is also completely wrong, for the following reasons.

No ancient source, be it a book or inscription, puts a 10th Legion aboard Agrippa's ships at the Battles of Mylae and Naucholus. Even if a 10th Legion did take part in those battles, why would it, and only it, assume the title Fretensis following the battle, when a number of other legions also took part yet did not assume a title referring to the battles? More importantly, the Mylae and Naucholus battles were not fought in a strait. They took place off the north coast of Sicily, some distance from the Strait of Messina.

Where, then, could the Fretensis title have originated? What other strait could be connected with a 10th Legion? Caesar himself offers the answer – the Otranto Strait. In his memoir about the Civil War, Caesar tells how he and Mark Antony shipped twelve legions from Brundisium, today's Brindisi, in southeastern Italy, to the Epirus region on the west coast of Greece to take on the senatorial army led by Pompey. To reach Epirus, those legions had to cross the Otranto Strait. Caesar identifies his 10th Legion as one of the legions he took to Epirus, via the Strait, and he writes of how the 10th subsequently formed up in its usual position on his extreme right at the 48 BC Battle of Pharsalus.

But Caesar's troops were transported by sail-powered merchant ships, while the coins of the 10th Fretensis show oar-powered warships. Caesar also offers an explanation for that, an explanation involving a battle in the Otranto Strait. He writes that, because of a lack of shipping, on 4 January 48 BC he took seven legions with him in a first wave to Epirus, leaving Antony and the five other legions allocated to the campaign back at Brundisium along with his cavalry. Those units had to wait for Caesar's ships to return to collect them for a second landing. [Caes., CW, III, 5]

Caesar says that the legionaries left with Antony comprised three of his veteran legions, which had taken part in the campaign in Spain, plus two newly recruited units, and auxiliary cavalry. [Ibid., 29] It might be assumed that Caesar took his best veteran legions with him in ferrying the first wave of across the strait, but two of those veteran legions, the 7th and 9th, had rebelled in Mark Antony's camp at Placentia in central Italy some months before, demanding their overdue discharges, and Caesar had resorted to decimating the 9th to restore order. The 10th Legion, meanwhile, would soon be siding with the 7th and 9th when they again mutinied, and by the time of Caesar's amphibious invasion of Greece it is quite possible that he left these three increasingly troublesome units in Brundisium and gave Antony the task of bringing them along in the next wave of the invasion.

Further, we have a remark from Appian about the 10th Legion in 43 BC, when he noted that the 10th had been 'led in the past by Antony'. [App., III, 83] There is no occasion on record prior to this when Antony could have led the 10th Legion. It must have been one of the three veteran legions under his command at Brundisium in 49–48 BC.

To prevent Antony from convoying the remainder of Caesar's troops across the strait, senatorial admiral Lucius Libo set sail from the west coast of Greece with a fleet of fifty warships laden with marines, infantry and archers, and sailed to Brundisium. Libo landed his troops on an island opposite Brundisium's harbour, out in the Otranto Strait. Dislodging the Caesarian troops who were holding the island, Libo's force captured several of Antony's transport ships and caused panic in Antony's ranks. No merchant ship subsequently dared to leave Brundisium's harbour.

Antony, boxed in, set out to recover the island and reopen the strait in order to reinforce Caesar, who was sending increasingly impatient letters ordering him to cross the strait without delay with his remaining troops. To do this, Antony fitted sixty ships' boats with protective wicker coverings and screens, then put hand-picked legionaries aboard them. Antony had just two oar-powered warships at his disposal, a pair of triremes he had built at Brundisium, and on to these he also packed troops from one or more of his veteran legions. Now, Antony was ready to launch an attack on Libo.

Antony's two triremes came out of the harbour, entered the strait, and slowly approached the island, as if their recently recruited rowers were being exercised. The veteran legionaries on board were meanwhile keeping low. As Antony had hoped, Libo dispatched five large quadriremes from the island to attack the triremes. 'When these came near our ships,' Caesar was to write, 'our veterans began withdrawing toward the harbour.' [Caes., CW, III, 24] As Libo's five warships closed on Antony's triremes, Antony gave a signal and the sixty smaller vessels came rowing on to the scene from all directions.

The veteran troops on board the triremes now emerged from hiding and launched their javelins at the vessels alongside, while the sixty smaller boats swarmed around the five large warships like angry bees. Antony's veteran troops boarded the nearest quadrireme and captured it together with all its rowers and marines. The remaining quadriremes fled. It was, said Caesar, a 'shameful rout' for Libo's senatorial forces. [Ibid.] Following this defeat, Libo abandoned the island and his blockade of Brundisium, and withdrew to Greece. Through the fighting skill of the veteran Caesarian legions left with Antony, the Strait of Otranto was reopened, and Antony was able to transport his five legions and Caesar's cavalry across the water to Greece. Had these reinforcements not reached Caesar, he would have faced disaster.

Were the men of the 10th Legion at the forefront of this action on water? Was it men from the veteran 10th who were on Antony's two triremes and led the way to victory that day, or who manned the sixty small boats, or both? Such a scenario is more than likely: a naval action in a strait, in which it can be postulated with a high degree of probability that Caesar's 10th Legion took a leading part – unlike the Strait of Messina scenario – gives us a very likely reason for Caesar's 10th Legion to take the honorific title of Fretensis. If we accept this scenario, which is much stronger than that involving the Strait of Messina, then the later 10th Fretensis Legion was without doubt Caesar's original 10th Legion, and the 10th Gemina Legion was not.

It is highly probable that Caesar raised this legion in Further Spain when he governed the province. Legions numbered 5 to 10 were traditionally stationed in Spain, which had been Roman territory ever since the Carthaginians were expelled in 206 BC. Roman praetors had been governing Baetica since 191 BC, and the recruitment of legionaries in Spain was certainly being undertaken by 50 BC, and probably somewhat earlier, with six legions permanently stationed in Spain under Pompey's control while Caesar was campaigning in Gaul. Plutarch wrote that, as soon as Caesar arrived in Corduba in 61 BC, 'he got together ten new cohorts of foot in addition to the twenty which were there before'. [Plut., *Caesar*] These ten cohorts of foot became the new 10th Legion. Furthermore, Appian, talking about the 10th Legion specifically in 43 BC, noted that it had been previously 'recruited from non-Italians'. [App., III, 83]

This 10th Legion then – raised in Spain, seeing service under Caesar, and appropriating the Fretensis title for itself after the Otranto Strait battle – was inherited by Octavian, who, after Mark Antony's death in 30 BC, stationed the unit for a time in Macedonia. [*AE* 1936, 18] Within two decades it had been transferred to the East, where, in 4 BC, following the death of Herod the Great, king of Judea, the legion was cut off at Jerusalem by rioting Jews. It had to be rescued by a Roman force led south by the governor of Syria, Quintilius Varus, who was later to be made famous by the Teutoburg disaster.

By the time that Germanicus Caesar arrived in Syria as Roman commander-in-chief for the East at the end of AD 17, the 10th Fretensis Legion was stationed at Cyrrhus in Syria, not far from Antioch. The legion took part in both Corbulo's Armenian campaigns and, in an AD 62 battle at the Euphrates, helped throw back a Parthian attempt to invade Syria; but only after its by then undisciplined legionaries had been toughened up by several years of intense training by Corbulo.

The legion provided four cohorts for Gallus' failed AD 66 counter-offensive against the Jewish rebels in Judea, while the entire legion took part in Vespasian's

Judean operations the following year, before marching down the Jordan river and taking Jericho. In AD 70, the legion was one of the four that besieged and captured Jerusalem. Titus then stationed the unit at Jerusalem, as Judea's 'home' legion, where it built a base for itself amid the rubble. Between AD 71 and 73, the 10th Fretensis overran the last strongholds of Jewish resistance south of Jerusalem, the fortresses of Machaerus and Masada.

In the early stages of the AD 132–135 Second Jewish Revolt, the 10th Fretensis Legion suffered extremely high casualties, with the cohorts stationed at Jerusalem apparently being wiped out. Hadrian was therefore forced to transfer Egyptian sailors from the Misene Fleet to the legion, granting them citizenship, to swiftly bolster the 10th's ranks. This discharge from the navy, granting of citizenship and transfer into the ranks of a legion was so unprecedented that on the discharge diplomas of the sailors involved it was recorded as being *ex indulgentia divi Hadriani* – 'From the kindness of the Divine Hadrian'. [Starr, V, I]

Some historians came to believe that the 10th Fretensis adopted the wild boar as its emblem after the First Jewish Revolt because the image of a pig was raised by Hadrian at Jerusalem, where the legion was based. But Eusebius, Bishop of Caesarea during the time of Constantine the Great, pointed out that Hadrian placed a marble idol of a domestic pig, not a boar, over Jerusalem's Bethlehem gate, for the purpose of 'signifying the subjugation of the Jews to Roman authority'. [Eus., *Chron.*, HY 20] The Jewish faith, of course, both forbade the eating of the meat of the pig and the display at Jerusalem, their holy city, of graven images of any kind. So, this use of the pig emblem over the city gate was contrived by Hadrian as a double insult to the Jews. Consequently, coins of the 10th Fretensis which later showed a pig image – not the running boar used by other legions as an emblem – refer to the city of Jerusalem, not to the legion stationed there. When the 10th Fretensis later transferred to Arabia it was no longer associated with the pig symbol of Jerusalem.

The legion was still based at Jerusalem by AD 230, but later that century it was transferred to the remote Red Sea town of Aela, today's Elat in Israel, which came to be under the control of the Duke of Palestine in the fourth century. It was there that the legion was last heard of. [Not. Dig.] The 10th, Julius Caesar's most famous legion, whose Fretensis title seems never to have been officially bestowed, had proved to be a solid performer throughout its career, and earned more than its share of glory.

10TH GEMINA LEGION

LEGIO X GEMINA *Twinned 10th Legion*

ORIGIN OF TITLE:	After its combination with another legion by Octavian, c. 30 BC.
EMBLEM:	Bull.
BIRTH SIGN:	Capricorn (probably).
FOUNDATION:	By Octavian, 30 BC or earlier.
RECRUITMENT AREA:	Unknown.
POSTINGS:	Petavonium, Carnuntum, the Rhine, Batavia, Noviomagus, Aquincum, Dacia, Vindobonna.
BATTLE HONOURS:	Cantabrian War, 29–19 BC. Battle of Old Camp, AD 69. Trajan's First Dacian War, AD 101–103. Trajan's Second Dacian War, AD 105–106. Aurelian's Defeat of Queen Zenobia, AD 272–273. Aurelian's Egyptian campaign, AD 273.
NOTABLE COMMANDER:	Marcus Aurelius Probus, future emperor, AD 272–275.

THE QUIET CAREER OF THE TWINNED TENTH

A reliable legion thrown into many of Rome's major imperial conflicts – the Cantabrian War, the Civilis Revolt, Trajan's Dacian Wars and the defence of the Danube.

Theodor Mommsen wrote that the 10th Gemina Legion was the direct descendant of Julius Caesar's famed 10th Legion, and for over a hundred years his claim has been accepted as fact by many historians. As demonstrated in the preceding history of the 10th Fretensis Legion, Mommsen was almost certainly wrong and the 10th Fretensis is more likely to have been Caesar's 10th, having acquired its Fretensis title while in Caesar's army in the winter of 49/48 BC by fighting a battle on water to reopen the vital Otranto Strait between Italy and Epirus.

The 10th Gemina Legion of the imperial era was created by the merger of two existing legions by Octavian, following the defeat of Mark Antony and Cleopatra at the 31 BC Battle of Actium, one of them an existing 10th Legion from either Octavian's army or Antony's. In 30 BC, the 10th Gemina Legion arrived in Nearer Spain. In the following year it formed part of Octavian's army, which fought the bitter ten-year Cantabrian Wars to clear the Cantabrian Mountains in the north of Spain of hostile tribes. The legion was susequently based in Spain at Petavonium, today's Rosinos de Vidriales.

In the AD 60s, the 10th Gemina Legion, like the 14th Gemina Martia Victrix, was transferred to Carnuntum in Pannonia in preparation for Nero's invasion of Parthia, but with the outbreak of the Jewish Revolt in Judea in AD 66 it was returned to Spain. In AD 70, the legion marched from Spain to the Rhine to take part in the final stages of Petilius Cerialis' campaign to put down the Civilis Revolt. In one of the last battles of that revolt, rebels killed the camp-prefect and five first-rank centurions of the 10th Gemina. The legion was thereafter based at the Batavian capital, Nijmegen, where it built a new stone fortress.

The legion transferred to Aquincum on the Danube in the spring of AD 101, and from there took part in both Dacian Wars for Trajan. Following the annexation of Dacia in AD 106, the 10th Gemina re-mained in Dacia for the following twelve years. In AD 118 it left Dacia for the Pannonian base at Vindobonna, today's Vienna in Austria. It was still there when the emperor Marcus Aurelius died in the city in AD 180, and also when Cassius Dio listed legion locations half a century later. In the fourth century, the legion was still in existence, and still in Pan-nonia, but split into two border guard elements, each commanded by a prefect and at different locations. [Not. Dig.]

The 10th Gemina Legion was not, it now seems, Julius Caesar's original 10th Legion.

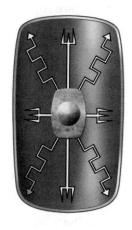

11TH CLAUDIA LEGION

LEGIO II GLAUDIA-P-F   *Claudius' Loyal and Patriotic 11th Legion*

ORIGIN OF TITLE:	Awarded by Claudius for helping put down the Scribonianus Revolt, AD 42.
EMBLEM:	Neptune's trident and thunderbolts.
BIRTH SIGN:	Gemini (she-wolf and twins).
FOUNDATION:	58 BC, by Julius Caesar.
RECRUITMENT AREA:	Originally Cisalpine Gaul.
IMPERIAL POSTINGS:	Gaul, Illyria, Burnum, the Rhine, Batavia, Vindonissa, Brigetio, Oescus, Durosturum, Dacia, Durosturum.
BATTLE HONOURS:	Pannonian War, AD 6–9. Battle of Rome, AD 69. Trajan's Second Dacian War, AD 105–106. Second Jewish Revolt, AD 134–135.

THE LATE ELEVENTH

Raised by Caesar, a legion that was victorious in the grinding Pannonian and Dacian Wars, and gained its title for preventing an internal revolt against Claudius in Dalmatia.

The first legion raised for Julius Caesar in Italy for his Gallic campaigns, the 11th Legion, became part of Octavian's standing army in 30 BC and was posted to Dalmatia. It would have served there throughout the Pannonian War, and was stationed at Burnum, the Dalmatian capital, during the mutiny of AD 14 and into the reign of Claudius.

When Scribonianus, governor of Dalmatia, attempted to revolt against Claudius in AD 42, the legion initially went along with the uprising, but after five days, men of the 11th and the 7th killed Scribonianus and those of his officers who supported him, terminating the revolt. Claudius rewarded both legions with the title 'Claudius' Loyal and Patriotic'. The legion would be known as the 11th Claudia for centuries to come.

In AD 69 the men of the 11th Claudia swore allegiance to Otho, and were marching from Burnum to his support when they learned they were too late; Otho was dead, and Vitellius was emperor. Soon after returning to Burnum the legion swore

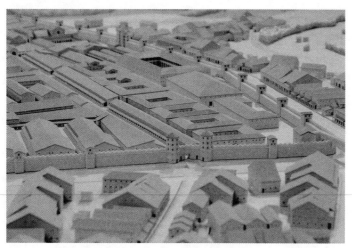

Western gate of the legion base at Vindonissa, today's Windisch in Switzerland. Through the reigns of Vespasian to Trajan, Vindonissa was home to the 11th Claudia Legion.

for Vespasian, but when other legions marched into Italy to do battle with Vitellius' legions, the 11th hesitated. Only when Marcus Antonius Primus and his army had defeated Vitellius' troops at Bedriacum and Cremona did the 11th Claudia arrive, joining the march on Rome that ended in the death of Vitellius and elevation of Vespasian in December of that year.

In AD 70, Vespasian posted the legion to Vindonissa on the Upper Rhine, to replace units disgraced in the Civilis Revolt. It remained there until transferred to Brigetio on the Danube in AD 101, where it remained during the First Dacian War. It took part in the second war in Dacia, and at the war's end spent time in Oescus and Durosturum. The latter, today's Silistra in Bulgaria, became its permanent base.

The legion, or a vexillation of several of its cohorts, was briefly transferred from Moesia to Palestine to take part in the final stage of Sextus Julius Severus' offensive against the Jewish rebels led by Shimeon bar-Kokhba. An inscription records the legion's presence at the AD 135 siege of Bar-Kokhba's fortress at Bethar, just south of Jerusalem. [Yadin, 13]

The 11th Claudia Legion remained at Durosturum for the next 200 years, but by the time of the Notitia Dignitatum in the late fourth century it had ceased to exist. Part of an 11th Legion, a comitatense legion, was then shown in Spain, with another in the East, these possibly having descended from the 11th Claudia.

12TH FULMINATA LEGION

LEGIO XII FULMINATA   *Thundering 12th Legion*

ORIGIN OF TITLE:	Adopted unofficially in early imperial period. Officially conferred by Marcus Aurelius, AD 174.
EMBLEM:	Mars' thunderbolt.
BIRTH SIGN:	Capricorn (probably).
FOUNDATION:	58 BC, by Julius Caesar.
RECRUITMENT AREA:	Originally Cisalpine Gaul.
IMPERIAL POSTINGS:	Egypt, Syria, Raphanaea, Laodicea, Jerusalem, Judea, Melitene, the Danube, Melitene.
BATTLE HONOURS:	Siege of Jerusalem, AD 70. Trajan's Eastern campaign, AD 114–116. Defeat of the Alans, AD 135. Defeat of the Quadi, AD 174.

MARCUS AURELIUS' THUNDERERS

Famous as the 'Thunderer', a legion that lost its eagle in the First Jewish Revolt but was successful when given a second chance, living up to its name under Marcus Aurelius by winning a battle in a thunderstorm.

The second legion raised in Italy for Julius Caesar in 58 BC, the 12th Legion, served him throughout his Gallic campaigns and the Civil War. Both Octavian and Antony had a 12th legion, with Antony's differentiating itself with the title Antiqua, meaning both 'old' and 'former', which suggests that this was Caesar's original. Meanwhile, Octavian's 12th Legion took the title Paterna; this can mean 'father's', referring to Caesar, but it can also mean 'native', implying Italian enrolment.

One of the two units became the sole 12th Legion in Octavian's new standing army. At what point it acquired its thunderbolt title and emblem is unclear, but it was using both in the first century. Octavian initially posted the unit to Egypt with two other legions. It was in Syria in AD 14, and based at Raphanaea with the 6th Ferrata during the reign of Claudius.

In AD 62, commanded by Calavius Sabinus, the legion was summoned to Cappadocia to take part in Paetus' disastrous Armenian campaign. It seems that many of the legionaries were nearing the end of their twenty-year enlistment and the legion was well under strength as a result, for Tacitus noted that it was suffering from 'numerical feebleness' at that time. [Tac., *A*, xv, 8–10] The men of the legion showed little interest in engaging the Parthians, and their retreat from Armenia did nothing for the unit's reputation.

The 12th Fulminata's lack of numbers would explain why, four years later, it was the only almost complete legion in Gallus' AD 66 march to Jerusalem after the outbreak of the Jewish Revolt. In the bloody retreat to Caesarea the legion lost a number of men but, more importantly, it lost its eagle to the hounding Jewish partisans. It would take a long time for the stain of that loss to fade.

Vespasian refused to use the legion in his operations against the Jews but, with its ranks apparently recently replenished with a new enlistment, Titus employed it in AD 70 as one of his four complete legions in the Siege of Jerusalem. The 12th Fulminata operated under the command of its tribune throughout this period, legates perhaps refusing to lead a legion that had lost its eagle. Vespasian annexed the kingdom of Cappadocia in AD 71, making it a new Roman province, and following the 12th's sound performance in the Jerusalem siege it was posted there as home legion, making its new base at Melitene.

The 12th Fulminata remained at Melitene for the next 300 years, during which it regained its reputation. In AD 135 it took part in Arrian's successful campaign against the invading Alans in Lesser Armenia. Several decades later, its eastern stay was interrupted by Marcus Aurelius' Danube wars against the Alemanni and Quadi Germans, for which it was transferred to the Danube. In a battle in a thunderstorm in AD 174, it won a key battle for Marcus, for which it was officially awarded the thunderbolt emblem and title.

The Notitia Dignitatum placed the legion in Armenia in the late fourth century with the 15th Apollinaris, the legion with which it had beaten the Alans in AD 135. Both legions, reduced to border guard units, would have been absorbed into the Byzantine army the following century.

13TH GEMINA LEGION

LEGIO XIII GEMINA   *Twinned 13th Legion*

ORIGIN OF TITLE:	Caesar's 13th was combined with another legion by Octavian.
EMBLEM:	Lion.
BIRTH SIGN:	Capricorn (probably).
FOUNDATION:	58 BC, by Julius Caesar.
RECRUITMENT AREA:	Originally Cisalpine Gaul.
IMPERIAL POSTINGS:	Illyricum, the Rhine, Raetia, Pannonia, the Rhine, Vindonissa, Poetovio, the Rhine, Poetovio, Dacia, Sarmizegethusa, Apulum, Ratiara, Sirmium.
BATTLE HONOURS:	Drusus' German campaigns, 20–15 BC.
	Tiberius' Raetian campaign, 15 BC.
	Pannonian War, AD 6–9.
	Germanicus' German campaigns, AD 14–16.
	Battle of Idistavisus, AD 15.
	Battle of the Angrivar Barrier, AD 15.
	Second Battle of Bedriacum, AD 69.
	Battle of Cremona, AD 69.
	Battle of Rome, AD 69.
	Trajan's First Dacian War, AD 101–102.
	Trajan's Second Dacian War, AD 105–106.

ALWAYS AT THE FOREFRONT

A legion that once marched for Caesar, then fought for Germanicus in Germany, lost and won in the AD 69 war of succession, then stormed the Dacian capital for Trajan.

A 13th Legion is on record as early as 205 BC. [Livy, XXIX, 2, 9] Both Octavian and Antony had 13th legions in their armies, one being the direct descendant of Julius Caesar's 13th, the legion that crossed the Rubicon with Caesar in January 49 BC and helped him change Roman history. Octavian created a new 13th Gemina Legion in 30 BC by combining two existing legions, one of them a 13th; it is possible that both were previous 13ths.

The 13th Gemina Legion was in Raetia by 15 BC, and on the Rhine in the wake of the Varus disaster in AD 9. Based at Vindonissa on the Upper Rhine five years later, it served in Germanicus' victorious German campaigns. By AD 46 it was stationed at

Poetovio in Pannonia. The legion marched for Otho in April AD 69, and gave way to Vitellius' troops in the First Battle of Bedriacum in Italy. Both sides despised the legion for its lack of backbone, and after the defeat of Otho's army the surrendered 13th Gemina was put to work building wooden amphitheatres at Cremona and Bononia, where Vitellius' generals would celebrate their victory.

The 13th was then sent back to Poetovio. It was at the 13th's Poetovio headquarters that generals met in the late summer of AD 69 to discuss an invasion of Italy to dethrone Vitellius and enthrone Vespasian. The legion subsequently had its revenge over Vitellius' troops at the Second Battle of Bedriacum, the Battle of Cremona, and the Battle of Rome. During this period, the 13th Gemina's senior tribune was the father of the later author Suetonius, who was himself born that same year.

Back at Poetovio following the Civilis Revolt, the legion remained in Pannonia until being transferred to Vindonissa in the year AD 97. Between AD 101 and 106 it took part in Trajan's Dacian Wars, and once Dacia was conquered, set up a base at Apulum in the new province. It would frequently have been in action against German, Sarmatian and Goth tribes thereafter.

A Roman military colony was established by Trajan at Sarmizegethusa in Dacia and settled by retiring veterans of the 13th Gemina. Another military colony was created at the Dacian town of Orsova, modern-day Tsierna. The descendants of these legion veterans would have fled Dacia when Aurelian gave up the province in AD 274, joining a refugee column that trailed the 13th Gemina as it abandoned Apulum and relocated south of the Danube. The legion's new Moesian base was at Ratiara, the village of Archar in today's Bulgaria.

By AD 395 the legion had been split; part was based at Ratiara, part in faraway Egypt. [Not. Dig.]

14TH GEMINA MARTIA VICTRIX LEGION

LEGIO XIIII G-M-V   *Mars' Victorious Twinned 14th.*

EMBLEM:	Eagle's wings and thunderbolts.
BIRTH SIGN:	Capricorn.
ORIGIN OF TITLE:	Gemina from combination with existing legion, 30 BC. Remainder disputed.
FOUNDATION:	57 BC, by Julius Caesar.
RECRUITMENT AREA:	Originally Cisalpine Gaul.
IMPERIAL POSTINGS:	Illyricum, Mogontiacum, Viroconium, Lugdunensis, Mogontiacum, Vindobonna, Dacia, Carnuntum.
BATTLE HONOURS:	Pannonian War, AD 6–9. Invasion of Britain, AD 43. Invasion of Anglesey, Britain, AD 60. Boudicca's Revolt, Britain, AD 60–61. Battle of Bedriacum, Italy, AD 69. Battle of Old Camp, Germany, AD 70. Trajan's Dacian Campaigns, AD 101–102 and 105–106. Quadi, Iazyge and Marcomanni Wars of Marcus Aurelius, AD 161–180.

CONQUERORS OF BRITAIN, NERO'S MOST VALUABLE

The most famous legion of the first century, invading Britain for Claudius and defeating Boudicca and her 230,000 British rebels in AD 60. Its name alone enough to unnerve opponents, it went on to fight in Dacia and defend the Danube line.

> 'Close up the ranks, and having discharged
> your javelins, then with shields and swords
> continue the work of bloodshed and destruction.'
>
> (SUETONIUS PAULINUS TO 14TH GEMINA PRIOR TO THE AD 60 BATTLE
> WITH BOUDICCA'S BRITONS. TACITUS, *Annals*, XIV, 36)

In the second half of the first century, the 14th Gemina Martia Victrix Legion had such a formidable reputation that even the suggestion that it was about to engage in a conflict was enough to cause the opposition to panic. [Tac., *H*, II, 68]

In 30 BC, Caesar's original 14th Legion was combined by Octavian with another, creating the 14th Gemina. Some modern-day authors believe that the 14th was later granted its additional 'Martia Victrix' titles by Nero for its defeat of Boudicca's army of rebel Britons in AD 60–61. There is no proof of this. In fact, it is possible that the Victrix title was granted before AD 49, the year the first Roman military colony in Britain was established by the emperor Claudius at Colchester (Roman Camulodunum) in the east of England.

Military colonies traditionally included the name of the legion settling it, as part of their titles. Arelate, today's Arles in the south of France, for instance, was set up for men of the 6th Legion, and this was reflected in the colony's official name: Colonia Julia Paterna Arelatensum Sextanorum, or Julius' Paternal Colony of the Sixth at Arelate. Camulodunum was named Colonia Claudia Victricensis: Claudius' Colony of the Victors. This did not refer to the legion that had previously occupied the city, the 20th Valeria Victrix, because, as Dr R. S. O. Tomlin has pointed out, the use by the 20th Legion of the Valeria Victrix title is not recorded before AD 90. [Tom., *DRA,* DRAC] This suggests that 'the Victors' refers to settlers from the 14th Gemina Martia Victrix, a legion which would have retired a number of its veterans around AD 50 after they had completed their twenty-year enlistments.

The legion was indeed rewarded by Nero after defeating Boudicca's rebels against odds of up to twenty-three to one; he declared the men of the 14th his 'most valuable troops'. And it is likely that the legion was also given the right to assume the thunderbolt and eagle's wings emblem of the Praetorian Guard. Additionally, Roman general Petilius Cerialis called the men of the 14th Gemina Martia Victrix 'Conquerors of Britain'. [Tac., *H*, v, 16]

That AD 60 victory over Boudicca represented a spectacular career turnaround. In 54 BC, the four-year-old legion was wiped out by the Eburone tribe of Belgium. The following year, the reformed legion lost 2,000 men in a battle with mounted German tribesmen. Following Caesar's death, both Octavian and Antony had 14th legions, and it is possible the two were combined to create the new 14th Gemina of 30 BC.

The legion fought in the Pannonian War, and stoutly served Germanicus in Germany in AD 14–16. By AD 43, its reputation had been rehabilitated to the point that it was one of four legions chosen to invade Britain for Claudius. It was stationed in Britain thereafter.

In the spring of AD 60 the legion conquered the Welsh island of Anglesey, only to be recalled to confront the rampaging rebel Celts, and to deliver Boudicca her famous defeat on Watling Street. By AD 67 Nero had transferred the 14th Gemina Martia Victrix to Carnuntum in Pannonia as part of the build-up for his planned offensive against the Parthians. Two years later, the legion's veteran cohorts marched down from Pannonia to fight for Otho at the First Battle of Bedriacum. Although Otho's army surrendered, the 14th Gemina stubbornly declared itself undefeated. Vitellius sent the unit back to its old base at Viroconium, today's village of Wroxeter, in Britain. The following year, the new emperor Vespasian ordered the legion to the Rhine to join Cerialis' operations against Civilis and the Germans on the Rhine, and the legion played a critical role in Cerialis' victory at Old Camp.

The 14th Gemina Martia Victrix was subsequently stationed at Mainz on the Rhine. By AD 92 the legion had built a new base at Mursia in Pannonia. Between AD 100 and 114 it was based at Vindobonna before spending several years in Dacia. By AD 117 the legion was back at Carnuntum, where it remained for the remainder of its career. By AD 230 the Martia Victrix portion of the legion's title had fallen into disuse.

In the fourth century, the men of the once famous 14th Gemina Legion had been relegated to the role of marines on the Danube. Serving on light liburnian galleys, one element was still stationed at Carnuntum; the other came under the Master of the Military for the Dacia region. It was a sad end for a once famous legion. [Not. Dig.]

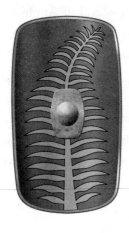

15TH APOLLINARIS LEGION

LEGIO XV APOLLINARIS   *Apollo's 15th Legion*

ORIGIN OF TITLE:	Possibly because Apollo was the patron deity of Emperor Augustus.
EMBLEM:	Originally, possibly a griffin. By the third century a palm branch, the symbol of victory.
BIRTH SIGN:	Capricorn (probably).
FOUNDATION:	54 BC, by Julius Caesar.
RECRUITMENT AREA:	Originally Cisalpine Gaul.
IMPERIAL POSTINGS:	Illyricum, Emonia, Carnuntum, Syria, Judea, Carnuntum, Dacia, Carnuntum, Parthia, Satala.
BATTLE HONOURS:	Pannonian War, AD 6–9. Corbulo's Second Armenian campaign, AD 62. First Jewish Revolt, AD 67–71. Siege of Jerusalem, AD 70. Trajan's Dacian Wars, AD 101–106. Trajan's Parthian campaign, AD 114–116. Arrian's Defeat of the Alans, AD 135.

THE TRAVELLING FIFTEENTH

A veteran of the Pannonian War, mediator in the Illyricum Mutiny of AD 14, victorious in Armenia under Corbulo, in Judea under Vespasian and Titus, in Dacia under Trajan, and against the Alans in the East under Arrian, this was a legion which made history.

Both Antony and Octavian employed 15th legions, but the fact that the imperial 15th incorporated Apollo, favourite deity of Octavian, into its title, suggests that it was his legion which he retained in his new standing army.

The 15th Apollinaris was one of fifteen legions that served in the Pannonian War. It was stationed in Pannonia following the war, initially at Emonia, and by AD 14 at Carnuntum, where it remained for many years, undertaking major building activity in AD 50. In AD 62 the legion was transferred by Nero to the East for operations in Armenia, after which it was stationed in Egypt. Titus then led the 15th Apollinaris from Egypt to Judea for his father's operations against the Jewish rebels, where it was one of the four legions that conducted Titus' siege of Jerusalem in AD 70.

The 15th Apollinaris was then sent back to Europe and its old base at Carnuntum, from where it took part in Trajan's Dacian Wars. When Trajan went east for his AD 114–116 Parthian operations, the 15th Apollinaris went too. In AD 117 the legion took over the 16th Flavia's base at Satala in northern Cappadocia, today's Sadak in Turkey, which became its home for decades thereafter. In AD 135 the legion joined the 12th Fulminata in ejecting the Alans from Lesser Armenia for Arrian, the palm branch emblem shown on coins of the legion in the East possibly being a reflection of that victory.

The legion would have been deeply involved in the Persian Wars of the fourth century, but, unlike many Roman units destroyed by the Persians, the 15th Apollinaris Legion survived, intact, and was still at its Satala base at the end of that century. [Not. Dig.]

15TH PRIMIGENEIA LEGION

LEGIO XV PRIMIGENEIA *15th First-born Legion*

ORIGIN OF TITLE:	Named for the goddess Fortuna Primigeneia.
EMBLEM:	Wheel of Fortune (probably).
BIRTH SIGN:	Capricorn (probably). The 22nd Primigeneia, raised at the same time, used Capricorn.
FOUNDATION:	AD 39, by Caligula.
RECRUITMENT AREA:	Probably the traditional recruiting grounds of the existing 15th Apollinaris.
IMPERIAL POSTINGS:	Mogontiacum, Vetera.

NOT FORTUNE'S FAVOURITE

Founded by Caligula for his farcical invasion of Britain, when he had his troops fire into the English Channel and collect seashells as war trophies, this legion was renamed by Claudius and abolished by Vespasian.

This legion was apparently raised by Caligula for his planned but never executed invasion of Britain. It was named after Fortuna Primigeneia, goddess of Fortune. This was the favourite deity of Claudius, Caligula's uncle and successor in AD 41, so it is not impossible that Claudius actually named both this and the 22nd Primigeneia. This legion is likely to have taken the number 15 because it was raised in the traditional recruiting grounds of the existing 15th Legion, the Apollinaris.

Based at Mainz on the Upper Rhine after Caligula's aborted British operation, by AD 46 it had moved to Vetera on the Lower Rhine. There, in AD 69–70, the legion became embroiled in the protracted defence of Vetera, or Old Camp as it was known, with thousands of its men killed by the rebels.

The shattered 15th Primigeneia Legion was abolished by the new emperor Vespasian, once the Civilis Revolt was terminated in the autumn of AD 70.

16TH GALLICA LEGION

LEGIO XVI GALLICA   *16th Legion of Gaul*

EMBLEM:	Boar (probably).
BIRTH SIGN:	Probably Capricorn.
FOUNDATION:	In 49 BC, by Julius Caesar.
RECRUITMENT AREA:	Gaul.
IMPERIAL POSTINGS:	The Rhine, Mogontiacum, Novaesium.
ABOLISHED:	AD 70, by Vespasian, for surrendering to Civilis.

PAYING THE PRICE OF DISLOYALTY

Fighting stoutly under Germanicus only to disgrace itself in the Civilis Revolt, a legion that was disbanded by Vespasian, who reformed it as the 16th Flavia, and sent it to the East.

Raised in Gaul, the 16th Gallica Legion was serving under Drusus Caesar on the Rhine in 16 BC, where it remained throughout its short career. Based at Mainz, it marched for Drusus' son Germanicus Caesar in his German campaigns of AD 14–16.

In the reign of Nero the legion was transferred to Novaesium on the Lower Rhine. There, in January AD 69, it joined its fellow Rhine legions in hailing Vitellius emperor, and soon after sent several of its cohorts to Italy to help defeat Otho and install Vitellius on the throne.

The remaining 16th Gallica cohorts became caught up in the Civilis Revolt, ultimately deserting their young general Herrenius Gallus, surrendering to the rebels and allowing Gallus to be executed in the spring of AD 70. For these two crimes, the new emperor Vespasian abolished the legion in that same year. He reformed it as the 16th Flavia Legion.

16TH FLAVIA FIRMA

LEGIO XVI FLAVIA-F *16th Steadfast Flavian Legion*

ORIGIN OF TITLE:	Named in honour of first emperor of the Flavian family, Vespasian.
EMBLEM:	Lion.
BIRTH SIGN:	Unknown.
FOUNDATION:	By Vespasian, from vestiges of the disgraced 16th Gallica Legion.
RECRUITMENT AREA:	Unknown.
IMPERIAL POSTINGS:	Satala, Parthia, Samosata, Oescus.
BATTLE HONOURS:	Trajan's Parthian campaign, AD 114–116.

VESPASIAN'S OWN

Formed in AD 70 to replace the disgraced and abolished 16th Gallica Legion, the 16th Flavia took Vespasian's family name and the emblem of the lion, which was associated with Vespasian's favourite deity, Hercules.

With the shameful history of the 16th Gallica to remind it of what it must avoid, the 16th Flavia set off for a new career in the East. Its first permanent base was at Satala in the new province of Cappadocia. From there it joined the emperor Trajan's AD 114–116 Parthian campaign, after which, licking its wounds, it moved to a new base in Armenia, Samosata, today's Samsat in Turkey.

By the reign of Septimius Severus the 16th Flavia had relocated to Syria, where it was still based, at Oescus, late in the fourth century. [Not. Dig.]

17TH, 18TH AND 19TH LEGIONS

LEGIO XVII

LEGIO XVIII

LEGION XIX

EMBLEM:	Boar (probably).
BIRTH SIGN:	Probably Capricorn.
FOUNDATION:	In 49 BC, by Julius Caesar.
RECRUITMENT AREA:	Italy (probably).
IMPERIAL POSTINGS:	Aquitania, Raetia, Novaesium.
BATTLE HONOURS:	Agrippa's Aquitanian campaign, c. 20 BC. Tiberius' Raetian campaign, 15 BC.
WIPED OUT:	Battle of the Teutoburg Forest, AD 9.

THE SHARED FATE OF VARUS' LOST LEGIONS

Ill-starred legions wiped out with Varus in the Teutoburg Forest in AD *9 by Arminius and the German tribes. Only the 18th was ever reformed, by Nero, but it performed so badly that it was soon folded into another legion by Vespasian.*

Three legions raised at the same time and in similar recruiting grounds, the 17th, 18th and 19th, served under Drusus and Tiberius in their German campaigns. When Tiberius hurried off to Pannonia to deal with the uprising there and in Dalmatia, he left the trio on the Lower Rhine, under the command of the governor, Quintilius Varus.

In the summer of AD 9, Varus led all three legions through the homelands of tribes east of the Rhine that had signed peace treaties with Rome. In September, as Varus was leading his army back to the Rhine, he was lured north, to the Teutoburg Forest, where Arminius, a young Cheruscan prince and prefect of Roman auxiliaries, led an ambush by German tribes that wiped out Varus and his three legions, none of which was commanded at the time by either a legate or a senior tribune.

Germanicus Caesar led a series of campaigns in Germany between AD 14 and 16 in which German tribes were defeated in several battles, but Arminius, or Hermann

An iron catapult bolt used by the ill-fated 19th Legion.

as he became known in Germany, evaded both death and capture, although his pregnant wife was taken prisoner by the Romans and his son was born and raised in captivity. Germanicus was able to retrieve two of the lost eagles of Varus' three legions. The third would be recovered from the Cauchi tribe in Germany in AD 41 by a Roman army led by Publius Gabinius, who was granted the title Cauchius by the emperor Claudius for the eagle's return – such was the importance to the Romans of recovered legion eagle standards.

Augustus retired the numbers of the three destroyed legions and never replaced them. But in the reign of Nero, a curious thing happened. Apparently, for one of his planned campaigns in Parthia or Ethiopia, Nero raised a new 18th Legion. Why he gave it the number 18, which must have been considered unlucky by Roman soldiers after what happened to the original 18th in the Teutoburg Forest, is a mystery. In both his *Annals* and *Histories*, Tacitus makes numerous references to this new 18th Legion, which in AD 69 was one of the four legions of the army of the Upper Rhine.

The new 18th was quick to vow allegiance to Vitellius in January that year, but did not send troops to Italy to overthrow Otho as did all the other legions stationed on the Rhine. This was probably because only six of its cohorts were on the Rhine; the remaining four cohorts were in the East. Tacitus wrote that, along with several cohorts of the 3rd Cyrenaica Legion, troops of the 18th Legion were withdrawn from Alexandria by Titus, for his siege of Jerusalem. [Tac., *H*, V, 1] Josephus also referred to these cohorts from two legions that had been at Alexandria; during the Jerusalem siege they were under of the command of the tribune Eternius Fronto. [Jos., *JW*, 6, 4, 3]

How these men of the new 18th Legion came to be in Egypt is explained by another passage in Tacitus, which speaks of 2,000 legion recruits from Libya being stranded in Alexandria in AD 66 by the outbreak of the Jewish Revolt in Judea. These recruits, raised to make up four cohorts of the 18th Legion, remained in

Alexandria until summoned to Judea by Titus to join his AD 70 assault on Jerusalem.

Once Vespasian came to power, the 18th Legion ceased to be. Its six cohorts on the Rhine had surrendered to the rebels during the Civilis Revolt, but at least its cohorts in Judea had done nothing untoward, so it is likely that the men of the 18th were folded into Galba's 7th to create the 7th Gemina Legion.

Following the Varus disaster and the loss of the 17th, 18th and 19th legions in AD 9, three consecutively numbered legions would never again be permitted by the highly superstitious Romans to serve in the same force.

20TH VALERIA VICTRIX LEGION

LEGIO XXV-V   *20th Valorous and Victorious Legion*

ORIGIN OF TITLE:	Uncertain. Use not attested before AD 90.
EMBLEM:	Boar.
BIRTH SIGN:	Capricorn.
FOUNDATION:	In 49 BC, by Julius Caesar.
RECRUITMENT AREA:	Initially Italy. Later Syria.
IMPERIAL POSTINGS:	Hispania Tarraconensis, Illyria, Burnum, Cologne, Neuss, Camulodunum, Glevum, Viroconium, Deva, Luguvalium.
BATTLE HONOURS:	Cantabrian War, 29–19 BC. Pannonian War, AD 6–9. Germanicus' German campaigns, AD 14–16. Battle of Idistavisus, AD 16. Battle of the Angrivar Barrier, AD 16. Invasion of Britain, AD 43. Boudicca's Revolt, AD 60–61.

THE POWERFUL CONQUERORS

The 'brave and victorious' 20th served under Germanicus in the Panonnian War, then joined him on the Rhine. It took part in the invasion of Britain and was one of the last legions to leave Britain.

Many authors have assumed that the title Valeria Victrix, or Powerful Conquerors, was granted to the 20th Legion in AD 60–61 as a reward for the legion's participation in the defeat of Boudicca and her rebel army in Britain. No ancient text or inscription supports this theory, and in fact the use of Valeria Victrix in the legion's title is not attested before AD 90. [Tom., *DRA*, DRAC]

Furthermore, 3,000 20th Legion men at most took part in the AD 60 Battle on Watling Street, and Tacitus described them as 'veterans'; these were apparently members of the Evocati militia, recently retired, and called out under their old 20th Legion standards in the emergency. [Tac., *A*, XIV, 34]

Another theory has the Valeria Victrix title awarded to the 20th Legion for participation in Agricola's victory over the Caledonians at Mons Graupius in AD 84. The 9th Hispana Legion was identified by Tacitus at the forefront of that campaign; the 20th was not mentioned. Had the 20th received such an award after Mons Graupius, the 9th could be expected to have received the same, which it did not.

The one campaign where the 20th Legion is known to have played a leading role was the Pannonian War of AD 6–9. Germanicus Caesar, who had led the legion during that war, said to it five years later: 'You men of the 20th, who have shared with me so many battles and have been enriched with so many rewards.' [Tacitus, *A*, 1, 42] This indicates that it may have received the Victrix award for Pannonian War service.

The original 20th was a reliable legion stemming from Caesar's mass civil war enlistments in Italy. Another comment from Germanicus indicates that the legion was receiving recruits from Syria by AD 14. [Ibid.] Gravestones in Britain show that by later that century there were indeed a number of men from the East serving in the ranks of the 20th Legion.

One of the legions involved in the AD 43 invasion of Britain, the 20th thereafter took part in all the campaigns that saw Roman occupation spread west and north. During the AD 68–69 war of succession, the legion became unruly and it took its new commander, Gnaeus Agricola, to discipline it in AD 71, apparently by transferring troublemakers from the 20th to the newly arrived 2nd Adiutrix Legion. [*See pages 105–107*]

Surviving records of the 20th even include such day-to-day snippets as the fact that on 7 November AD 83, Quintus Cassius Secundus, a legionary serving in the 20th Legion century commanded by the centurion Calvius Priscus, wrote an IOU to a comrade in his unit, Gaius Geminius Mansuetus, for 100 denari, or 400 sesterces. [Tom., *DRA, DRAC*]

An antefix, a roof tile, from a barracks building in Britain occupied by the 20th Legion, showing the legion's boar emblem.

In around AD 213, the second-in-command of the 20th Valeria Victrix Legion, military tribune Marcus Aurelius Syrio, from the town of Ulpia Nicopolis in the province of Thrace, dedicated an altar at the legion's Luguvalium (Carlisle) base to Jupiter Best and Greatest, and to Juno, Minerva, Mars and Victoria. Syrio had previously served with the Praetorian Guard. [Tom., *DRA*]

By AD 230, with elements of the legion at both Eburacum and Luguvalium, Cassius Dio wrote that the legionaries of the 20th Valeria Victrix were 'by no means called Valerians by all, and do not use that name any longer'. [Dio, LV, 23] The 20th Victrix Legion was withdrawn from Britain before the end of the fourth century, and was not replaced. It seems to have been destroyed in the battles with the invaders from east of the Rhine such as the Franks and Vandals.

21ST RAPAX LEGION

LEGIO XXI RAPAX   *The Rapacious 21st Legion*

ORIGIN OF TITLE:	Not known.
EMBLEM:	Boar (probably).
BIRTH SIGN:	Capricorn.
FOUNDATION:	49 BC, by Julius Caesar.
RECRUITMENT AREA:	Originally Gaul. Later Syria.
IMPERIAL POSTINGS:	Gallia Transalpina, Raetia, Pannonia, Vetera, Vindonissa, Bonna, Mogontiacum, the Danube.
BATTLE HONOURS:	Tiberius' Raetian campaign, 15 BC.
	Pannonian War, AD 6–9.
	Germanicus' German campaigns, AD 14–16.
	Battle of Idistavisus, AD 16.
	Battle of the Angrivar Barrier, AD 16.
	First Battle of Bedriacum, AD 69.
	Battle of Rigodulum, AD 70.
	Battle of Augusta Trevorum, AD 70.
	Battle of Old Camp, AD 70.
INGLORIOUS FATE:	Wiped out on the Danube during the reign of Domitian.

A CORPS OF OLD AND DISTINGUISHED RENOWN

After serving Germanicus in Germany, this legion fought for Vitellius in the war of succession, then, under Vespasian, was Cerialis' lead legion when he put down the Civilis Revolt, only to be wiped out by the Dacians in the reign of Domitian.

It is possible that the famed Roman historian Tacitus commanded the 21st Rapax Legion between AD 89 and 92, departing from the unit shortly before it met its bloody end.

Tacitus served as a consul in AD 97. To reach that elevated position he had to have previously commanded a legion. Away from Rome from AD 89, when he was 34 years old, he was back in the capital in AD 93; this would correspond with the period when Tacitus was of praetor rank and eligible for legion command, legion commands being typically of three to four years' duration. Later writing in his *Histories*, which he commenced in around AD 99, Tacitus described the 21st Rapax Legion as 'a corps of old and distinguished renown'. This was the most effusive he would be about any of Rome's legions, and suggests a certain affection born of familiarity. [Tac., *H*, II, 43]

This legion stemmed from the late republican period. Caesar raised a 21st Legion. Antony certainly had a 21st, and this may have been the unit that Octavian retained in his standing army from 30 BC. Early in Augustus' reign the legion served in Raetia. It was stationed on the Lower Rhine, at Vetera, by AD 9, and from there it took part in Germanicus' German campaigns of AD 14–16. By AD 47 the 21st had transferred to Vindonissa, today's Windisch in Switzerland.

Fourteen years later, it seems that the legion gave up four cohorts of newly arrived recruits which were urgently transferred to Britain to make up for 2,000 men of the 9th Hispana Legion wiped out in Boudicca's revolt. These men were never returned or replaced, leaving the 21st four cohorts down for the remainder of that enlistment period. This explains why it was the only legion not to leave cohorts on the Rhine when it marched with Vitellius' other legions to Italy to overthrow Otho in the spring of AD 69.

The 21st marched for Italy with its commander, the flamboyant Alienus Caecina, who wore colourful attire and included his wife in his column, complete with her own cavalry escort. Before it left Raetia, the 21st lived up to its Rapax title, which means rapacious, or greedy, by looting the Helvetian districts it passed through. It helped Caecina and his colleague Fabius Valens win the First Battle of Bedriacum, overrunning the opposing 1st Adiutrix Legion and killing its legate after the Adiutrix had initially carried off the Rapax's eagle.

By the time of the Second Battle of Bedriacum, Caecina had attempted to defect to Vespasian; the 21st Rapax fought without its commander, and lost. The legion's sound reputation meant that following the Vitellianist surrender at Cremona, Vespasian's general Primus kept the legion intact in a camp in northern Italy. When Petilius Cerialis, Vespasian's cousin, was given the task of leading the advance element of an army that would suppress the Civilis Revolt, it was the Rapax he chose to lead to the Rhine.

Despite being four cohorts down and suffering casualties in the war of succession, the outnumbered 21st Rapax proceeded to win battles for Cerialis at Rigodulum on the Moselle river, then at Trier, and was one of the legions that delivered the final major defeat to Civilis at Old Camp late in the summer of AD 70.

For the next twelve years the legion remained on the Rhine, stationed at Bonna, and receiving new recruits during this period to bring it back up to full strength. In AD 82 Domitian moved the 21st Rapax up the Rhine to Mogontiacum for his Chattian War the following year, after which the legion remained at Mogontiacum until AD 92. That year, the legion was called to the Danube to help stem an invasion by an army of mounted Sarmatians.

The exact details of this encounter with the Sarmatians have not come down to us, but it ended with the 21st Rapax being destroyed. Writing during the reign of Domitian – during which the 5th Alaudae Legion was also wiped out – Tacitus was to rage, 'One after another, armies were lost in Moesia and Dacia, in Germany and Pannonia, through the rash folly or cowardice of their generals. One after another, experienced officers were defeated in fortified position and captured with all their troops.' [Tac., *A*, 41]

It seems that in AD 92 the men of the 21st Rapax Legion, one of Rome's most celebrated legions only a few decades before, were led off in chains to the mountains beyond the Danube, to a life of slavery. The legion was never reformed.

22ND DEIOTARIANA LEGION

LEGIO XXII DEIOTARIANA *22nd Legion of Deiotarus*

ORIGIN OF TITLE:	Formed from the remnants of two legions of King Deiotarus of Armenia Minor, which originally fought for Julius Caesar.
EMBLEM:	Eagle (probably); an emblem used by Deiotarus on his coinage.
BIRTH SIGN:	Not known.
FOUNDATION:	Inherited by Antony from Caesar, retained by Octavian, who gave it the number XXII.
RECRUITMENT AREA:	Originally Armenia Minor.
IMPERIAL POSTINGS:	Alexandria, Judea, Caesarea Mazaka, Elegeia.
BATTLE HONOURS:	Trajan's Parthian campaign, AD 114–116 (probably).
FATE:	Wiped out by the Parthians in Armenia, AD 161.

THE ROCK OF EGYPT SHATTERED IN ARMENIA

Named after the king who raised it, this legion served continuously in Egypt for a century and a half before being wiped out in Armenia by the Parthians early in the reign of Marcus Aurelius.

In 47 BC, while Julius Caesar was locked in combat with local forces in Egypt, a Roman army led by one of his deputies, Gnaeus Domitius Calvinus, was defeated in a battle at Nicopolis in Armenia Minor by King Pharnaces, ruler of the Bosporan kingdom and son of Mithradates the Great, one of Rome's greatest adversaries. Fighting in the Nicopolis battle alongside Roman troops were two legions raised locally by the king of Armenia Minor, Deiotarus. Both units, which had been equipped and trained in Roman style, suffered heavy casualties in that battle. However, the remnants survived to combine into a single legion which subsequently fought for Caesar himself when he took on and defeated Pharnaces the following year at Zela in Pontus. It seems that this legion of Deiotarus' subsequently came into Antony's army, and formed the nucleus of the 22nd Deiotariana Legion retained by Octavian and sent to Egypt in 30 BC.

The legion continued to serve there in Egypt for the next century and a half. It would have taken part in the 23 BC Roman penetration of Ethiopia, but otherwise had a relatively peaceful career. It is last attested to in Egypt in AD 99. After that, the legion disappeared, from Egypt and from the historical record, and it is likely that this was the legion known to have been wiped out by the Parthians in Armenia in AD 161. It was never reformed.

22ND PRIMIGENEIA PIA FIDELIS LEGION

LEGIO XXII PRIMIGENEIA-P-F
22nd Loyal and Faithful First-born Legion

ORIGIN OF TITLE:	Named for the goddess Fortuna Primigeneia.
EMBLEM:	Eagle.
BIRTH SIGN:	Capricorn.
FOUNDATION:	AD 39, by Caligula.
RECRUITMENT AREA:	Probably the East.
IMPERIAL POSTINGS:	Mogontiacum, Rome (vexillation), Vetera, Mogontiacum.
BATTLE HONOURS:	First Battle of Bedriacum, AD 69.
NOTABLE SECOND-IN-COMMAND:	
	Publius Aelius Hadrianus, future emperor Hadrian, AD 97.

MAINZ'S LEGION

Like the 15th Primigeneia, raised by Caligula for the British campaign that never took place, this legion served solidly on the Rhine for centuries, only blemishing its record once when it surrendered to Civilis.

The 22nd Primigeneia had just two permanent bases throughout its career. It was founded by Caligula in AD 39, probably recruited in the eastern recruiting grounds of the existing 22nd Deiotariana Legion, the eagle emblem of which it also adopted. The 22nd Primigeneia was possibly given its title by the next emperor, Claudius, for Fortuna was his patron deity.

The legion was based at Mogontiacum (Mainz), for the next thirty years, sending troops to Italy to help install their commander-in-chief, Vitellius, as emperor. Those cohorts of the 22nd Primigeneia that remained on the Rhine surrendered to Civilis and his rebels in AD 70. Vespasian subsequently transferred them down the Rhine to Vetera, where, for their penance, they built a new base to replace the one destroyed by the rebels.

The legion would have been involved in Domitian's AD 83 Chattian War east of the Rhine. Ten years later, the unit returned to Mogontiacum, to fill the gap left by

A relief from Mainz (Mogontiacum) showing legionaires of the 22nd Primigeneia in close combat order.

the 21st Rapax, which had been destroyed by the Sarmatians. It was still there, by then in company with the 1st Minervia Legion, at the end of the fourth century, under the command of the Duke of Mainz.

In AD 402, both legions were summoned to Italy by Stilicho for a last-ditch effort against Alaric and his Visigoth invaders. The legion appears to have never returned to the Rhine frontier, which was finally abandoned by the Roman military shortly after. Stilicho was executed by a jealous emperor in AD 408. The 22nd Primigeneia probably perished in the battles which preceded the fall of Rome in AD 410.

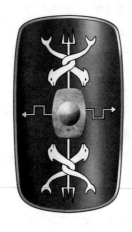

30TH ULPIA LEGION

LEGIO XXX ULPIA   *30th Ulpian Legion*

ORIGIN OF TITLE:	Family name of Emperor Trajan.
EMBLEM:	Neptune's trident, dolphin and thunderbolts.
BIRTH SIGN:	Capricorn.
FOUNDATION:	AD 103, for Trajan's second Dacian campaign.
RECRUITMENT AREA:	Not known.
IMPERIAL POSTINGS:	Brigetio, Dacia, Noviomagus, Vetera, Amida.
BATTLE HONOURS:	Second Dacian War, AD 105–106.

NEPTUNE'S OWN

Second of two legions raised by Trajan prior to the Dacian Wars, it would eventually fall victim to the Persians in Mesopotamia.

The 30th Ulpia Legion was raised by Trajan for his second Dacian War. Stationed on the Danube at Brigetio in AD 103, it marched into Dacia two years later. Taking Trajan's family name, Ulpius, the unit also embraced his favourite deity, Neptune, using Neptune's symbols of trident and dolphins in their emblem. It is likely that the legion also used the colour associated with Neptune, dark blue, certainly on their shields, and perhaps in other ways such as neck scarves. Its number derived from the fact that it was Trajan's thirtieth legion.

Following the Second Dacian War the legion was stationed at Noviomagus, to-day's Nijmegen, on the Lower Rhine. In AD 120, it was relocated to nearby Vetera. There it remained until the fourth century, when it was transferred across the Roman world to take part in campaigns in the East.

The 30th Ulpia was one of seven legions which defended the city of Amida in Mesopotamia from attack by a Persian army of 100,000 men in AD 359. After a bloody siege lasting seventy-three days and which cost the attackers 30,000 casualties, the Persians took the city. Like men of the other six legions defending the city, those legionaries of the 30th Ulpia who survived the fighting became captives of the Syrians. [Amm., XVIII, 9; XIX, 1–9]

There at Amida, in AD 359, Trajan's 30th Ulpia Legion ceased to be.

PRAETORIAN GUARD

COHORS PRAETORIA

EMBLEM:	Eagle and thunderbolt.
STANDARD:	Victoria, goddess of victory.
HEADQUARTERS:	Castra Praetoria, Rome.
FOUNDED:	Sixth century BC.

IMPERIAL BODYGUARD AND POLITICAL POLICE
Rome's political police, together with the CITY GUARD and the VIGILES (Night Watch), responsible for policing and protecting Rome.

The Praetorian Cohorts were created at the formation of the Roman Republic in 509 BC, charged with protecting the praetor, the most senior elected Roman official before the post was superseded by that of consul, and the city of Rome. By early in the first century BC, the Praetorians were no longer being used. In 44 BC, following the assassination of Julius Caesar, Mark Antony revived the unit as his personal bodyguard, with an initial strength of 6,000 former legion men. Following the 30 BC defeat of Antony and Cleopatra, Octavian retained the Praetorians in the role of criminal and political police at Rome. The role of close imperial bodyguard was, until AD 69, filled by the German Guard.

The elite Praetorian Guard enjoyed the most prestige and the highest pay of any unit in the Roman army. For hundreds of years they were the only regular army unit permitted by law to be stationed in Italy. Under Augustus, their recruiting grounds were Etruria, Umbria, Latium and the old legion colonies in Italy. By the time that Septimius Severus came to the throne at the end of the second century, Prateorian recruitment had expanded to take in Spain, Macedonia and Noricum.

Because they usually only served in military campaigns when the emperor was present, which was rare, Praetorians had less opportunities for booty than legionaries. In recompense, Augustus paid his Praetorians twice as much as legionaries;

Tiberius increased it to three times as much. Praetorians also received a larger retirement bonus – 20,000 sesterces, as opposed to 12,000 for legionaries.

Augustus ordained that the power of overall Praetorian command be split between two prefects. Some later emperors used a single Praetorian prefect, whose powerful post became like that of a latter-day minister for war. The emperors presented each new Praetorian prefect with a sword to symbolize the Praetorians' right to bear arms in the capital, for it was illegal for civilians to be armed in the city. When Trajan presented the sword to his new Praetorian prefect Saburanus in AD 110, he unsheathed the weapon, held up the blade to Saburanus, and said: 'Take this sword in order that, if I rule well, you may use it for me, but if badly, against me.' [Dio, LXVIII, 16]

This relief, held by the Louvre Museum in Paris, is said to identify second-century men of the Praetorian Guard in parade dress. The style of cingulum being worn by two men, and the beards and moustaches on three men, combine to date the relief to the second century. And each man is certainly wearing parade dress. The shield designs, all slightly different but each on the thunderbolt theme, are similar to that on shields on Trajan's Column associated with the Praetorian Guard. Yet the eagle standard is anomalous; the Praetorians did not use the aquila – winged Victory adorned their standard. Nonetheless, it is possible that these men, a senatorial officer, tribune and rank and file, represent four different cohorts of the Praetorian Guard.

Troops stationed at Rome normally did duty 'half-armed', with their shields and javelins kept at the Praetorian barracks. That massive fortified building, the *Castra Praetoria*, or Praetorian Camp, was erected in AD 23 on the northeastern outskirts of Rome beyond the old city walls, by the notorious prefect Lucius Aelius Sejanus. Prior to that, the Praetorians had been quartered at several barracks around Rome.

In that same year, a former soldier of the Praetorian Guard, Titus Curtisius, attempted to motivate a revolt of slaves at Brundisium in southern Italy. A contingent of marines quickly rounded up the chief troublemakers, including Curtisius, and Tiberius dispatched a party of Praetorians under their tribune Staius to Brundisium to take charge of the prisoner. Titus Curtisius, one-time soldier of the Praetorian Guard, was subsequently marched up to Rome in chains by his former comrades. His punishment was to be sold into slavery at the capital. [Tac., *A*, IV, 27]

While former centurions sometimes rose to command the Praetorians, the post could also be held by former generals, such as Vespasian's son and successor, Titus. One of the most famously industrious commanders of the Guard was Quintus Marcius Turbo, Praetorian prefect during Hadrian's reign, who always worked into the early hours of the morning. When, in AD 136, the emperor urged him to take life a little more easily, Turbo replied, paraphrasing Vespasian, that the prefect of the Guard should die on his feet. [Dio, LXIX, 18]

The Praetorian Guard provided a cohort to keep order at the circus on chariot-racing days and during public spectacles, at the amphitheatre during spectacles, and at the theatre during musical and dramatic performances. On one occasion during a riot at a theatre in the capital in the first century, a Praetorian centurion and several guardsmen were killed and their tribune injured.

The Praetorian Guard operated the city prison, and carried out death sentences imposed by the emperor and Senate. A typical execution assignment took place in AD 66 when Nero sent a centurion and Praetorian detachment to northwest Italy to execute Marius Ostorius Scapula, who had won the Civic Crown in Britain as a young cavalry prefect twenty years before. He had been found guilty of conspiring to murder the emperor. As was the case with all men, and women, executed by the Praetorians, Ostorius' head was exhibited at Rome, either in the Forum or at the Gemonian Stairs.

In AD 10, Augustus formed the **CITY GUARD**, or City Cohorts, to serve as Rome's daytime policemen and city gate sentinels. City Guard troops, former slaves, were paid substantially less than Praetorians. Under Augustus there were nine Praetorian cohorts, each of 1,000 men commanded by a tribune, numbered 1 to 9, and three City Guard cohorts, numbered 10 to 12, also commanded by tribunes. Tiberius added a 13th City Guard cohort. The City Guard answered to the City Prefect, who was frequently a senator of high rank. Flavius Sabinus, brother of the later emperor Vespasian, was City Prefect for twelve years under Nero, and was so respected for the way he discharged his responsibilities that two of Nero's immediate successors recalled him to the post.

Caligula added three more Praetorian cohorts. By Nero's reign, there were fourteen Praetorian cohorts and four City Guard cohorts, the latter with 1,500 men each. The cohorts were numbered 1 to 18, with the last four being City Guard cohorts. One City Guard cohort was stationed at Lugdunum in Gaul to guard the imperial mint there.

After coming to power in AD 69, Vitellius disbanded the existing Praetorian and City Guard units and replaced them with 20,000 men from his Rhine legions. The sacked guardsmen joined the army of Vitellius' rival Vespasian, and helped dethrone Vitellius. Vespasian's new Praetorian and City Guard units consisted of 7,000 men in fourteen cohorts. By the reign of Alexander Severus, 150 years later, the Praetorian Guard numbered 10,000 men.

Centurions could be transferred to the Guard cohorts from the legions and promoted from within Guard ranks. The twelve-year enlistment period for members of the Praetorian Guard instituted by Mark Antony in 44 BC was increased to sixteen years by Augustus.

The Praetorian Guard served in Augustus' Cantabrian War, one of Germanicus Caesar's German campaigns, in Trajan's Dacian Wars. and in third-century eastern campaigns. By AD 218, the segmented armour worn by the Praetorian Guard at the beginning of the second century, as seen on Trajan's Column, had been replaced by scale-armour. Even this they cast off to fight for the short-lived emperor Macrinus, their former prefect, who thought they would be 'lighter for battle' without their armour. In this battle, near Antioch in Syria, Macrinus' unarmoured Praetorians were defeated by the armoured Syrian legions fighting for Elagabalus. [Dio, LXXIX, 37]

The **COHORTES VIGILIS**, literally 'cohorts that stay awake' – called the Night Watch by latter-day authors – were formed by Augustus in AD 6. Commonly known as the Vigiles, they served as both a night-time police force and fire brigade. Augustus had intended them as a temporary measure, but they proved so useful he retained them. Augustus' Vigiles were freedmen.

This gold aureus issued by Claudius depicts the Castra Praetoria, the headquarters of the Praetorian Guard at Rome.

Later, they also came from other classes of society. They were paid from the public treasury. Augustus divided Rome into fourteen administrative *regios* or precincts, and each of the seven Vigile cohorts covered two *regios* and was quartered in barracks in one of their precincts. Like the City Guard, the Vigiles came under the command of the City Prefect.

Prior to the formation of the Vigiles, the wealthier inhabitants of Rome employed night watchmen to patrol their blocks, carrying bells to warn of fire. Rome's Vigiles were also traffic police, for under a law of Julius Caesar most wheeled traffic could only use Rome's streets at night. Hence imperial Rome's reputation as the city which never slept. Vigiles never left the capital, and were inferior in quality and status to both Praetorian and City Guard troops. They nonetheless made the overthrow of Sejanus possible, and made a failed attempt to hold the Capitoline complex with Vespasian's brother Sabinus in the last days of the reign of Vitellius.

Apart from the lionskin capes of their standard-bearers – as opposed to the bearskin capes of legionary standard-bearers – their different standards and shield emblem, and a slightly more rounded shield than the legionary shield, the Praetorians and City Guards could not be distinguished from legionaries.

The Praetorian Guard was reorganized by Septimius Severus at the start of his reign in AD 193. Cassius Dio, a senator at the time, scoffed that prior to Severus' reforms 'the Praetorians did nothing worthy of their name and of their promise, for they had learned to live delicately'. [Dio, LXXIV, 16] Previously, Praetorian recruits had come straight from civilian life. But because the Praetorians had murdered his predecessor Pertinax, Severus 'ordered that any [Praetorian] vacancies should be filled from all the legions'. Dio said that Severus' motive was 'the idea that he should thus have guards with a better knowledge of the soldier's duties', because they had already undergone military training and service. This new practice, said Dio, made transfer to the Praetorian Guard 'a kind of prize for those who proved brave in war'. [Dio, LXXV, 2]

When Diocletian became co-emperor in AD 285, he disbanded the Praetorian and City Guards, replacing them as Rome's guardians with two legions from the Balkans, with a total strength of 10,000 men who earned the same pay as other legionaries. Diocletian had taken the title Jove, and his co-emperor Maximianus the title Hercules, and their two new city legions became the Jovia and the Herculiana. Both units took the eagle as their emblem, one with wings raised, the other with wings lowered.

Maxentius, emperor from AD 306, reformed the Praetorian Guard, sending the Jovia and Herculiana legions to the frontiers. Maxentius' Praetorian Guard fought for him against his brother-in-law Constantine the Great at the AD 312 Battle of the Milvian Bridge just outside Rome. After winning the battle, Constantine abolished the Praetorian Guard; its surviving members were not permitted within 100 miles (160 kilometres) of Rome. Constantine left Rome without a dedicated military force; the Praetorian Guard was never reformed. Praetorian prefects, who in the past had wielded enormous power, continued to be appointed, but merely as financial administrators.

THE IMPERIAL SINGULARIAN HORSE

EQUITUM SINGULARIUM AUGUSTI

EMBLEM:	Scorpion.
HEADQUARTERS:	Castra Equitum Singularium, Rome.
FOUNDED:	AD 69 by Vitellius. First saw action for Vespasian, AD 70.
GRANTED AUGUSTI TITLE:	By Trajan.

XV. THE EMPERORS' HOUSEHOLD CAVALRY

The imperial household cavalry, the mounted equivalent of the Praetorian Guard.

This elite unit served as the mounted equivalent of the Praetorian Guard from the first century to the fourth century. The original *Equitum singularium,* or Singularian Horse, was an elite auxiliary cavalry unit created in the summer of AD 69 by the emperor Vitellius to replace the Praetorian Horse when he disbanded Otho's Praetorian Guard.

Hand-picked German cavalrymen, these inaugural Singularians surrendered to Vespasian's forces in central Italy in December AD 69. The unit's first service for Vespasian was in early AD 70, against Civilis' rebels on the Rhine. Tacitus wrote that after Vespasian's general Cerialis and his spearhead arrived on the Rhine, 'they were joined by the Singularian Horse, which had been raised some time before by Vitellius and had afterwards gone over to the side of Vespasian'. [Tac., *H*, IV, 70]

The first commander of the Singularian Horse was Briganticus, a Batavian and nephew of Civilis. Briganticus died while fighting his uncle's forces on the Lower Rhine in the late summer of AD 70. Thirty years later, under Trajan, the unit gained the honorific *Augusti*, signifying that it served the emperor. The unit was thought to use a hexagonal, German-style shield bearing the motif of four scorpions. [Warry, *WCW*] The scorpion emblem possibly related to the Greek legend where a scorpion caused the horses of the Sun to bolt when the Sun's chariot was being driven for a day by the inexperienced youth Phaeton.

In AD 70 the unit consisted of two wings, each of 500 men. Trajan increased the Singularians to 1,000 men. Septimius Severus doubled the unit again in AD 193 to 2,000 troopers. The Singularian Horse barracks and stables complex, the *Castra equitum singularium*, stood on the capital's eastern outskirts, beyond the old city walls and below the Esquiline Hill. In republican times Roman horsemen had exercised in the Esquiline Fields. The Singularians' AD 193 expansion saw them with two adjacent barracks, 'old fort' and 'new fort'.

The unit was disbanded in AD 312 by Constantine the Great, for siding with Maxentius and opposing him. Constantine also had the Singularian barracks levelled and the unit's graveyard demolished.

The gravestone of Singularian Horse decurion Marius Alexander of the Vitalis turma, or squadron, at Rome. Originally from Syria, he served under several emperors.

XVI. THE IMPERIAL BODYGUARD
The German Guard and its successors

Confused with the separate Praetorian Guard by some modern authors, the *Germani Corporis Custodes*, literally the German Body Guard, served as the personal bodyguard of Rome's first seven emperors. Variously called 'the Bodyguard', 'the German Cohorts', 'the Imperial Guard' and 'the German Guard' in classical and later historical texts, this was an elite infantry unit made up of hand-picked German auxiliaries. According to Josephus, it was a unit of legion strength. [Jos., *JA*, 19, 1, 15]

On their gravestones, several men of the German Guard referred to themselves as *Caesaris Augusti corporis custos*, to let the world know they had served as the emperor's bodyguard, but the *Augusti* title, carried by the Singularian Horse from the second century, was never officially applied to the German Guard. [Speid., 1]

That the German guardsmen were primarily foot soldiers was made clear by Tacitus and Suetonius, speaking of their 'cohorts', a designation that only applied to infantry or equitata units. [Tac., *H*, III, 69; Suet., II, 49] Josephus wrote, 'These Germans were Gaius' [Caligula's] guard, and carried the name of the country whence they were chosen, and composed the Celtic legion'. [Jos., *JA*, 19, 1, 15] Arrian also described Germans serving in the Roman army as 'Celts', in his case referring to men of the 1st Germanorum miliariae equitata cohort. [Arr., *EAA*, 2] Being the equivalent of a legion, like all legions the German Guard probably included a mounted squadron, explaining why the tombstone of a member of the unit accorded him the rank of decurion.

Suetonius says that Augustus only allowed three cohorts of the German Guard to be on duty at Rome at any one time; the other cohorts, he said, were quartered on rotation in towns near Rome. [Suet., II, 49] In AD 69, the German Guard was using the Hall of Liberty as their quarters at Rome. [Tac., *H*, I, 31] Previously, they had used a fort west of the Tiber, just inside the Servian Wall, which may have been demolished by Galba in AD 68. [Speid., 6, 7] German Guard troops were not Roman citizens. They wore breeches, were tall, muscular, and bearded, and their armaments were the long German spear, a dagger, and a long sword with a blunt, rounded end. Their shield was large, flat and oval. They were commanded by an officer of prefect rank; Caligula's German Guard prefect was a former gladiator.

In AD 41, men of the German Guard hailed Claudius emperor after the assassination of Caligula, and this led to Claudius taking the throne. During the war of succession, the German Guard was dissolved by Galba but reformed by Otho, and was with Otho at Brixium when he committed suicide. Serving Vitellius, three cohorts of the German Guard stormed and burned the Capitol in December AD 69, executing Vespasian's brother Sabinus, before fighting to the death in the 20 December Battle for Rome. Vespasian abolished the German Guard, making the Praetorians his bodyguard.

Later emperors created a variety of bodyguard units. In *c.* AD 350, the personal bodyguard of Constantius II was provided by the *Protectores Domestici*, or Household Protectors. The future historian Ammianus Marcellinus served as a junior officer with this unit, which was based at Mediolanum (Milan) in Italy, Constantius' imperial capital.

A silver plate of AD 388 found at Badojoz in Spain depicts the Spanish-born emperor Theodosius I with his heirs Valentian II and Ariadius, plus a bodyguard from two different units. The tall, clean-shaven spearmen of the bodyguard are shown

The emperor Theodosius I, with men of his bodyguard, AD 388.

carrying very large oval shields and lances, and wearing boots and neck torques. One of the two shield designs of the soldiers of the bodyguard appears on the Notitia Dignitatum thirty years later, and is of the Lanciarii Galliciani Honoriani, or the Honorary Gallaecian Lancers, a Spanish unit which was attached to the central command of the Master of Foot.

According to the Notitia Dignitatum, by early in the fifth century the imperial bodyguards of both the emperors of the east and west were the Domestici Pedites and Domestici Equites, the Household Foot and Household Cavalry.

XVII. LEGIONS OF THE LATE EMPIRE

Numerous new legions were raised by various emperors from the third century. Some of these were split off from existing legions, others were new creations and took the names of the emperors who founded them. Little is known about any of these Late Empire units.

The emperor Diocletian, during his reign (AD 285–305), significantly reorganized the Roman military and increased the pay of the troops in an attempt to keep pace with the galloping inflation of the era. Successor Constantine the Great took Diocletian's reforms even further, and by the end of the fourth century the Roman army was made up, on paper at least, of 132 legions and hundreds of auxiliary and allied numeri units. [Gibb., XVII]

The legions listed in the Notitia Dignitatum at the end of the fourth century were Palatine and Comitatense legions. The former, just two dozen of them, were the elite legions, whose men were paid more than other legionaries and enjoyed other privileges. In the early years of Constantine's reign these legions, slimmed down from the size they had enjoyed even during Diocletian's reign, were no longer housed in their own permanent camps throughout the empire. Withdrawn from the frontiers, they were billeted in the major cities of the provinces, at those cities' expense, and on

'Jockey' style helmet. Within another decade it would have cruciform protection added.

Neck scarf

Lorica Segmentata. Segmented metal armour

Legionary tunic

Leather-covered wooden shield, bearing the emblem of each soldier's unit.

Pilum, weighted javelin

Gladius, Roman short-sword

Cingulum, metal apron

Metal boss

Metal reinforcing

Calligulae; Roman military sandals

ROMAN LEGIONARY AD 75

unfriendly terms with the local populations, becoming idle and undisciplined. This 'innovation', according to Gibbon, 'prepared the ruin of the empire'. [Ibid.]

Another innovation during the reign of Constantine was also, in the opinion of Gibbon, to spell the doom of the Roman military. 'The introduction of barbarians into the Roman armies became every day more universal,' he wrote. Constantine, late in his reign, allowed 300,000 Sarmatians to settle in Pannonia, Thrace, Macedonia, and even in Italy. These new settlers furnished recruits for the Roman army who would join Goths, Scythians, and Germans who not long before had been at war with Rome. These men 'were enrolled not only in the auxiliaries of their respective nations, but in the legions themselves, and among the most distinguished of the Palatine troops'. [Gibb., XVII]

The majority of the thirty legions of Trajan's day still existed in around AD 400, but as Comitatense legions and border guard units, sometimes having been broken up into several smaller units. In this way, the 6th Victrix was, until Stilicho withdrew it for service in Italy in AD 401–402, still stationed in northern Britain; the 2nd Traina and 13th Gemina were stationed in Egypt; and the 3rd Gallica in Phoenicia. All would be either swallowed up in barbarian invasions or find their way into the Byzantine army.

XVIII. CAVALRY

Each legion had its own cavalry squadron of 128 mounted legionaries, used for scouting and courier work. All other cavalry units in the Roman army were composed of auxiliaries.

The smallest cavalry unit was the *decuria*, originally of ten, later of eight troopers. The largest cavalry unit was the *ala*, or wing, so named because the cavalry was allocated to the wings of a battle line. The *ala quingenaria*, of 512 men, consisted of sixteen *turmae*, or troops, of 32 men, with each *turma* made up of four *decuriae*. The turmae were divided over four squadrons of 128 men. [Vege., *DRM*, II] Larger *alae miliaria* consisted of twenty-four turmae, with a total of 768 officers and men. Early imperial legions always had two cavalry alae associated with them: 'He picked up the other two legions and the four wings of horse attached to them and marched to Ptolemais,' wrote Josephus, of the governor of Syria in 4 BC. [Jos., *JW*, II, 5.1]

Roman cavalry horses were not shod, and their riders did not use stirrups. The

First-century cavalry decurion Titus Calidius Severus proudly displayed his best horse, his armour, greaves, and helmet on his gravestone.

Roman cavalry saddle, with two horns front and back, made for a remarkably stable riding and throwing platform. Cavalrymen wore a helmet, mail vest, and breeches.

The principal cavalry weapon was a light spear, the *lancea*, which could be thrown or thrust. Roman cavalry also used smaller javelins, or darts, which were thrown overarm and were kept in a quiver attached to the saddle, with as many as twenty-four per quiver. The cavalryman's sword, the *spatha*, was longer than that of the infantryman. His shield was flat, and oval.

While Numidian cavalrymen in the Roman army were famed for their ability to ride bareback and even without bridles, it was Batavian cavalrymen from the lowlands of Holland who became the most valued to Rome. With his homeland often flooded, the Batavian developed the ability to swim his horse across rivers with full equipment and then immediately go into action. They proved particularly successful in operations in Britain.

Battle experience showed that cavalry without infantry support could be vulnerable, so the Roman army also developed mixed cohorts of both auxiliary infantry and

The discharge and citizenship diploma of Gemellus Braecius, a Pannonian auxiliary cavalryman who served in the Ala I Pannior, a unit raised in AD 97 by the emperor Nerva.

cavalry. These *cohortes equitatae* were both quingenaria and miliaria in size.

By the second century, specialist lancer units were also deployed, to move in close among the enemy and wreak havoc with lances which they kept close to their horses' flanks for added strength and impact. In AD 135, Arrian reserved his lancers for the chase once the enemy had been forced by the infantry to retreat. [Arr., *TH*, 43]

With chariot-racing obsessing even a number of emperors, Rome's chariot-racing corporations operated vast stud farms throughout the empire. They had tens of thousands of employees and even more horses, and always had first call on the best animals, ahead of the army.

XIX. CAVALRY EVOLUTIONS

To keep their skills honed, Rome's cavalrymen took part in mass exercises, or 'cavalry evolutions'. [Tac., *A*, 11, 55] Under laws promulgated by both Augustus and Hadrian, all Roman cavalry units were required to carry out route marches and training evolutions three times every month to sharpen their skills. Route marches were of 20 miles (32 kilometres), in full equipment, on the flat, on broken ground and in mountainous territory. Cavalry evolutions included the pursuit, and the retreat, followed by a 180-degree wheel-about and counter-charge. [Vege., 1]

Cavalry alae often performed day-long evolutions watched by an audience of the provincial governor and invited guests. Flavius Arrianus – Arrian as we know him – governor of Cappadocia during the reign of Hadrian, in AD 137 wrote a detailed description of these cavalry 'games'. [Arr., *TH*, 34–44] The senior and most exceptional horsemen wore gold-plated bronze face masks, moulded to the shape of their faces, with just slits at the eyes through which to see. The purpose of these eye-catching masks, said Arrian, was to single out the riders for audience attention during the exercises. [Ibid.]

To Arrian's mind, precision riding was all well and good – and he trained his cavalry to execute very complex unfolding drills. But to him, accurate missile throwing was the most important skill his troopers could possess. 'I would acknowledge the turma which proves most suitable in javelin-throwing as truly trained for war service,' he said. [Ibid., 42]

XX. CAVALRY OF THE LATE EMPIRE

By the fourth century, while maintaining light cavalry in the mode of the original Roman auxiliary cavalry, the Roman army had also copied the cavalry styles of its chief opponents, in particular the Persians, by creating units of horse archers, and of heavy cavalry in which both horse and rider wore armour.

Of the heavy armoured cavalry, the cataphracts and their mounts wore iron mail armour. The *clibanarii* wore heavy segmented armour from head to foot, including metal face masks fitted to their helmets which entirely covered their faces. Their title came from the Greek word meaning 'oven', which no doubt described how it must have felt inside these suits of armour which presaged the armour of the knights of the Middle Ages.

Late Roman historian Ammianus saw clibanarii entering Rome in AD 357 as part of the escort of the emperor Constantius: 'Fully armoured cavalry, whom they call clibanarii, all masked and equipped with protecting breastplates and girt with iron belts, so that you might have thought them statues polished by the hand of Paraxites, not men. Thin circles of iron plates, fitted to the curves of their bodies, completely covered their limbs, so that whichever way they moved their limbs, their garment fitted.' [Amm., XVI, 10, 8]

Rome's Clibinarii cavalrymen of the fourth century and their steeds were heavily armoured. Their helmets were even known to cover their faces completely, making them the forerunners of medieval knights.

FORTH-CENTURY ROMAN HEAVY CAVALRY TROOPER OF THE LATE EMPIRE

XXI. CAMELS AND WAR ELEPHANTS

The Roman army fielded several auxiliary camel wings, the *alae dromedarii*. Corbulo used a camel column to carry his grain supply when he went to the relief of Paetus and his troops trapped in Armenia in AD 62. Trajan raised a second camel wing for his AD 114–116 campaign against the Parthians. By AD 135, the 1st Dromedarium Ala was serving in Arabia, while Trajan's unit, the 1st Ulpia Dromedarium Ala, a miliaria or 'thousand-strong' unit, was based in Syria. [Hold., *DRA*, ADITROH] Records show that an equitata auxiliary cohort serving in Egypt early in the second century contained, in addition to infantry and horsemen, several camel riders.

For hundreds of years, from Hannibal to Shapur, Rome's military faced war elephants, but never successfully employed them itself.

Sixty-four trained war elephants were captured by Caesar from King Juba in Tunisia in 46 BC. Taken to Italy, they were used for Triumphs and spectacles. Some authors have speculated that the Roman army's Ala Indiana, which served in Britain, was an elephant wing, because the term 'Indian' was applied by Romans to the mahouts who rode elephants. In fact, the Ala Indiana Gallorum was an ordinary cavalry wing which was raised in Gaul in AD 21 and took its name from its founder, Julius Indus, a Treveran noble. [Hold., *RAB*, 2; App.]

In the first century, a troop of elephants was maintained at Laurentum, just outside Rome, for use in spectacles. All were tusked males; female elephants instinctively ran from bull elephants. In AD 43, the Laurentum troop was put on standby for Claudius' invasion of Britain, against British chariots, but there is no evidence that they ever crossed the Channel. Marshy conditions and numerous river crossings precluded their use in Britain.

In AD 193, elephants were brought to Rome from Laurentum by the emperor Julianus, to take part in his defence against the legions of Septimius Severus, who was marching from Pannonia to claim the throne. But the whole affair became such a shambles that it brought Dio and fellow senators to laughter. 'The elephants found their towers burdensome' and threw them off, he said. '[They] would not even carry their drivers any longer, but threw them off, too.' [Dio, LXIV, 16] Severus' son and successor

Caracalla, who reigned between AD 211 and 217, formed an elephant corps for his Parthian campaign, in the course of which he was assassinated in Mesopotamia by his own troops.

During the fourth century, the Persians used war elephants against Roman troops in the East, but there is no record of the Roman military ever having any success with elephants in battle.

XXII. THE EVOCATI

In times of emergency, retired legionaries could be recalled from their homes to serve behind their old standards – which they appear to have taken into retirement with them. This militia, called the Evocati, was controlled by the governor of each province. Paulinus used Evocati to help him defeat Boudicca in Britain in AD 60. Nero sent Evocati to Egypt in AD 66 for an invasion of Ethiopia that had to be aborted because of the Jewish Revolt. Mucianus, the governor of Syria, set off for Italy in AD 69 to depose the emperor Vitellius with an army which included 13,000 Evocati from the East. Vitellius fielded Evocati from Britain and the Rhine when his army opposed Vespasian's army.

Historian Tacitus was to say that in AD 59 most of the legionaries discharged that year 'scattered themselves in the provinces where they had completed their military service'. He complained that 'whole legions were no longer transplanted, as in former days, with tribunes and centurions and soldiers of every grade' to create new colonies 'so as to form a state by their unity and mutual attachment', with the result, he lamented, that the latest discharges 'became a mere crowd rather than a colony'. [Tac., A, XIV, 27]

The Evocati were still in existence by around AD 230, in the time of Cassius Dio, who said that 'they constitute even now a special corps, and carry rods, like the centurions'. He added, 'I cannot, however, give their exact number'. [Dio, LV, 24]

XXIII. THE PALATIUM
Rome's central command

The Palatium was the name for the residence of the Roman emperors on the Palatine Hill at Rome, and from it today's word 'palace' has derived. Augustus was the first emperor to make his home on the Palatine Hill, and his was the first Palatium. Numerous members of the family of the Caesars also built residences there, all of which were interconnected. As Josephus said: 'While the edifice was one, it was built in several parts by those persons who were emperors.' [Jos., *JA*, 19, 1,15]

In the first century, Tiberius, Caligula and Nero all built separate palaces on the hill, with Nero famously creating his vast Golden House below it. Domitian substantially remodelled and extended Augustus' original palace, which had become known as the Old Palatium. Domitian's Palatium even included a private chariot-racing stadium. Various members of the imperial family used the palaces on the hill as their private apartments; Marcus Aurelius was offered Tiberius' old palace by his adoptive father the emperor Antoninus Pius, for example.

More than just a residence, the Palatium was also the civil and military administrative hub of the Roman Empire – in effect a combined White House and Pentagon. With a large staff of freedmen clerks and secretaries, the Palatium managed the military and civil appointments and legion movements ordered by the emperor. The leading members of the Palatium staff in the first century were the chief secretary, the secretary for finances, the secretary for petitions and the correspondence secretary, whose 'outward' department became known as the Sardonychis – the name of the emperor's seal affixed to all outgoing mail.

From the fourth century, once various emperors began using Milan and Ravenna as their capitals, Rome's Palatium fell into disuse. In AD 403, the poet Claudian would rejoice that the young emperor Honorius ventured to Rome and spent a little time at the Palatium. Seven years later, Rome and her sprawling Palatium were sacked by the Visigoths.

· III ·

THE BATTLES

'The announcer stands at the general's right hand, and asks them three times, whether they are ready to go out to war or not. To which they reply as often, with a loud and enthusiastic voice, saying, "We are ready!"'

JOSEPHUS, WITNESSING AN ASSEMBLY OF
VESPASIAN'S LEGIONS.
The Jewish War, 3, 5, 4

Crushing victories, and devastating defeats. The fate of the campaigns of Rome's legions determined the fate of her empire. In the first century, military successes such as the invasion of Britain and reduction of Jerusalem far outweighed occasional and temporary reverses such as Arminius' destruction of Varus' legions in the Teutoburg Forest and the Jewish Revolt. Trajan likewise turned the martial disasters of Domitian's reign into victory in Dacia in the second century. Yet, after Trajan, Rome was forever on the defensive. Her wars became longer, her defeats more frequent, her victories more hard-won. The stories of the legions' battles chronicle the very rise and fall of imperial Rome.

29 BC
I. ROUTING THE SCYTHIANS
The 4th Legion earns a title

In 30 BC, as Octavian, sole ruler of the Roman world following the defeat of Mark Antony and Cleopatra that year, distributed the twenty-eight legions of his new standing army, he sent one of his two 4th legions to Macedonia.

The following spring, a new Roman governor arrived to take charge in Macedonia. Marcus Licinius Crassus, a consul in 30 BC, and grandson of Crassus the triumvir who had perished leading his army to disaster at Carrhae in 53 BC, had supported Antony during the civil war. His Macedonian appointment was an opportunity to impress Octavian with his loyalty and ability. He planned to do that by carrying out a military campaign using the recently deployed units of his new command, one of which was the 4th Legion.

From their northern homeland between the Vistula river and the Carpathian Mountains, King Deldo and his Bastarnae tribe had pushed over the mountains, crossed the Danube, and were threatening Thrace and Macedonia. As Cassius Dio reports: 'The Bastarnae … who are properly classed as Scythians, had at this time crossed the Ister [River Danube] and subdued the part of Moesia opposite them.' [Dio, LI, 23] Initially the Romans did not react, but when the Bastarnae 'overran the part of Thrace belonging to the Dentheletic, which was under treaty with the Romans, then Crassus, partly to defend Sitas, king of the Dentheleti, who was blind, but chiefly out of fear for Macedonia, went out to meet them'. [Ibid.]

The Bastarnae, sometimes also called the Peucini in Roman literature, 'were like Germans in their language, manner of life and mode of settlement', according to Tacitus. They generally lived in squalor, Tacitus said. Their nobles were lazy and the people had the 'repulsive appearance of the Sarmatians' – the slanted eyes typically noted of Scythians. [Tac., *Germ.*, 46] To meet the invaders, Crassus led an army almost certainly made up of the 4th and 5th legions, with the 10th Fretensis Legion possibly also involved; another former Antonian legion, it was stationed in Macedonia some time after the end of the Civil War, but precisely when it arrived in the province is not recorded.

As Crassus' well-drilled legions approached the Bastarnae in full battle array, the invaders retreated out of Thrace in panic. Crassus pursued them into Moesia. There, when his advance guard was assaulting a fortress, local Moesian warriors attacked the Roman besiegers, forcing them to give ground. But when Crassus came up with the bulk of his army, 'he hurled the enemy back and besieged and destroyed the place'. [Dio, LI, 23]

The Bastarnae, meanwhile, had regrouped at the Cedrus (Tzibritza) river, and 'after conquering the Moesians, Crassus set out after them also'. [Dio, LI, 24] Bastarnae envoys came to Crassus, who plied the Scythians with wine and made them drunk, 'so that he learned all their plans. For the whole Scythian race is insatiable in the use of wine and quickly become sodden with it,' according to Dio. [Ibid.] Armed with this intelligence, the Roman general moved his army towards the encamped Bastarnae, quietly taking up positions in a forest in the night, at the same time posting scouts beyond it.

'When the Bastarnae, believing the scouts to be all alone, rushed to attack them and pursued them as they retreated into the thick of the forest, [Crassus] destroyed many on the spot and many more in the rout that followed.' The Bastarnae were hindered by their wagons in the rear, and were anxious for the safety of their wives and children in those wagons. In the chaos, Crassus personally slew Deldo, the Bastarnae king. [Ibid.]

Some of the remaining Bastarnae took refuge in a grove, which Crassus' legionaries surrounded and set alight, burning the Scythians to death. Other survivors retreated to a riverside fort, which Crassus' troops quickly overran. Many of the fort's Bastarnae occupants committed suicide by jumping into the Danube; the remainder were made prisoners, to become slaves or die fighting in the Roman arena.

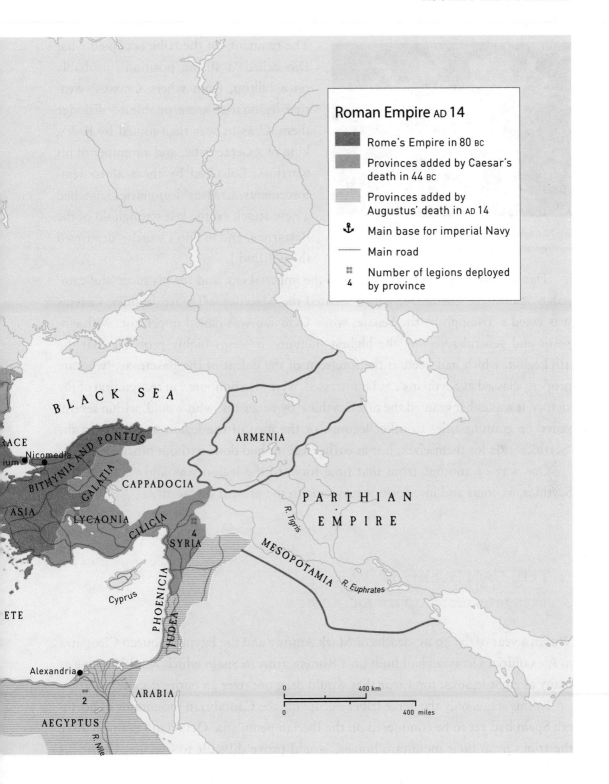

Roman Empire AD 14

- Rome's Empire in 80 BC
- Provinces added by Caesar's death in 44 BC
- Provinces added by Augustus' death in AD 14
- ⚓ Main base for imperial Navy
- Main road
- ⊞ Number of legions deployed by province
4

BLACK SEA

ARMENIA

RACE

Nicomedia

ium

BITHYNIA AND PONTUS

GALATIA

CAPPADOCIA

ASIA

LYCAONIA

CILICIA

SYRIA

4

PARTHIAN
EMPIRE

R. Tigris

Cyprus

PHOENICIA

MESOPOTAMIA

R. Euphrates

ETE

JUDEA

Alexandria

ARABIA

0   400 km

0   400 miles

2

AEGYPTUS

R. Nile

Scythian fighters such as these shown on a gold ornament were typically armed with bows and arrows.

The remnants of the tribe occupied what Dio called 'a strong position', probably on a hilltop, from where Crassus' wearied legionaries were unable to dislodge them. Crassus was then joined by Roles, king of a Getae tribe, and a number of his warriors. Bolstered by these allied reinforcements, Crassus' legionaries launched a new attack on the last stronghold of the Bastarnae, and in Dio's words, 'destroyed them'. [Ibid.]

This was Rome's first major battle of the imperial era, and for his successful campaign against the Bastarnae, which secured the Macedonia/Thrace frontier, Crassus was voted a Triumph by the Senate, while Octavian was hailed imperator. With emperor and general receiving the highest honours, it seems highly probable that the 4th Legion, which had been at the forefront of the defeat of the Bastarnae, 'who are properly classed as Scythians', as Dio stressed, were also honoured in recognition of the victory. It was either granted the title 'Scythica' by Augustus, who would, within several years, be granting titles to other legions, or the men of the legion appropriated the 'Scythica' title for themselves, just as earlier legions had done without official blessing.

One way or another, from that time forward the legion was known as the 4th Scythica, as coins and inscriptions surviving to the present day testify.

29–25 BC
II. THE CANTABRIAN WAR
Securing northern Spain for Rome

Within a year of the 30 BC deaths of Mark Antony and the Egyptian queen Cleopatra in Alexandria, Octavian had built up a Roman army in Spain which would involve as many as eight legions, for a war that would drag out over an entire decade.

By this stage, only the fierce tribes occupying the Cantabrian mountains of northern Spain had yet to be conquered on the Iberian peninsula. Octavian's plan, to drive the tribes from their mountain homes, would prove difficult to execute. Under his generals Gaius Antistius and Titus Carisius, the legionaries and auxiliaries involved in the Cantabrian campaign set up three bases, in the East at Segisima, modern Santander; at Asturica (Asturias), covering the central region; and at Bracara Augusta (Galicia), in the west. Numismatic evidence reveals that the legions that served in Spain at one time or another during the period of the war were the 1st, the 2nd (later the 2nd Augusta), the 4th Macedonica, the 5th Alaudae, a 6th (the later 6th Victrix), the 9th Hispana, the 10th Gemina and the 20th.

In the spring of 29 BC, the legions moved up into the Cantabrian mountains. The next four summers involved costly attempts to dislodge the outnumbered Spanish tribesmen from mountain hideouts. These were 'heavy campaigns conducted with varied success', said Velleius Paterculus, who served as an officer in the Roman army later in the reign of Octavian/Augustus. [Velle., II, xc]

In 25 BC, the 37-year-old emperor arrived in Spain to take personal charge of the frustrating war, bringing a large part of the Praetorian Guard with him. Two years earlier, the Senate had bestowed the title Augustus, meaning 'revered', on Octavian, and it was by the name of Augustus that the emperor was known from this time forward. With his army reinforced by the Praetorians, Augustus launched a fresh campaign against the Asturians and the Cantabri.

'But these peoples would neither yield to him – because they were confident on account of their strongholds – nor would they come to close quarters because of their inferior numbers,' according to Dio. Because their primary weapon was the javelin, said Dio, the tribesmen were at their most effective at a distance, letting fly and then

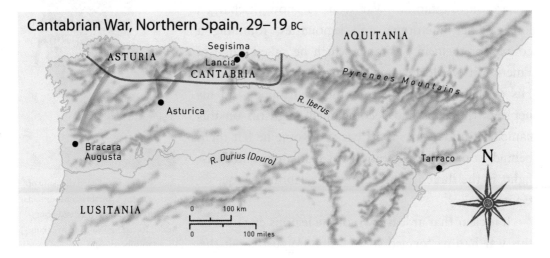

Cantabrian War, Northern Spain, 29–19 BC

running away. [Dio, LIII, 25] It was only when the legions forced the Spanish into close combat that the legionaries' swords brought them success.

As spring turned to summer, the rapid victory that Augustus had anticipated had not come about. The well-led tribesmen always sought to claim the higher ground, and, as Augustus came up with his legions, were constantly 'lying in ambush for him in valleys and woods'. [Ibid.] Dio said that the sickly Augustus was greatly embarrassed by his lack of success, and, falling ill 'from over-exertion and anxiety', he retired from the campaign and withdrew to Tarraco, capital of Nearer Spain, remaining there in poor health as his generals continued the war. [Ibid.]

Gaius Antistius now managed to overcome the Spanish, not because he was a better general than Augustus, said Dio, but because the tribesmen 'felt contempt for him'. [Ibid.] Made over-confident by the news that the Roman emperor had withdrawn from the fray, and assuming that Antistius would be even easier to dismiss, the Cantabrians made the mistake of meeting the Romans in a set-piece battle, which they lost. Soon after, the legions under Augustus' other general, Titus Carisius, succeeded in taking Lancia, principal mountain fortress of the Asturians, after the tribe had abandoned it, and 'also won over many other places'. [Ibid.]

By summer's end, with thousands of Cantabrian and Asturian prisoners being led away into slavery and the tribal leaders suing for peace, Augustus was able to declare the Cantabrian War won. He now discharged long-serving Praetorians and legionaries, founding a colony for them in Lusitania which he called Augusta Emerita; it would become the modern city of Merida. His teenage stepson Tiberius, then a tribune, and his nephew Marcellus had accompanied Augustus on this campaign, and as he set off back to Rome he left them behind to organize exhibitions of gladiators and beast fights in the three legion camps, to celebrate victory in Cantabria.

It is clear that at least two of the legions engaged in this war had performed so well that Augustus felt the

Augustus personally led the early offensive in the Cantabrian Mountains, but stiff tribal resistance and poor health forced him to hand over command to subordinates.

need to honour them. They had perhaps marched with the emperor himself during the campaign. These two, the 1st and the 2nd, received the emperor's own new honorific, becoming the 1st Augusta and 2nd Augusta legions.

Two other legions were to receive the Augusta title under Augustus, the 3rd Augusta and the 8th Augusta. There is no record of either legion serving in Spain, during the Cantabrian War or at any other time. The 3rd Augusta was based in North Africa, and it is likely that it earned its Augusta title there in a 19 BC campaign. The 8th Augusta's location during this period is uncertain.

But the fighting in Spain was not yet over. Hardly had Augustus departed from Spain than Lucius Aemilius, the governor left in charge by him, received envoys from the Cantabrians and Asturians who said that the tribes wished to present his army with grain and other things, and asked him to send a large number of men to bring back the gifts. Aemilius, suspecting nothing, accordingly sent 'a considerable number of soldiers' into the mountains. These Roman troops were ambushed and overpowered by the tribes and made prisoners. Led away to various places in the mountains, the captive legionaries were all eventually executed.

Aemilius reacted by ordering total war on the tribes. As a result, 'their country was devastated,' said Dio. A number of forts were burned, and every Spanish fighting man taken alive had his hands cuts off. 'They were quickly subdued.' [Dio, LXIII, 29] The war was now over. When Augustus returned to Rome, to signify that his empire was once again at peace he closed the gates of the ancient Arch of Janus, which stood in the Forum.

The Roman world had been pacified – but not for long.

22 BC
III. ROME INVADES ETHIOPIA
Penetrating Africa

Candace, ruler of the African Kingdom of Kush, in what the Romans called Ethiopia but what today is known as the Sudan, had apparently heard that the Roman emperor Augustus was engaged in a war in faraway Spain. Some 650 years before this, the kings of Kush had ruled Egypt, with their capital, Napata, becoming the religious centre of the Egyptian world. The ambitious Candace, thinking that Egypt's Roman

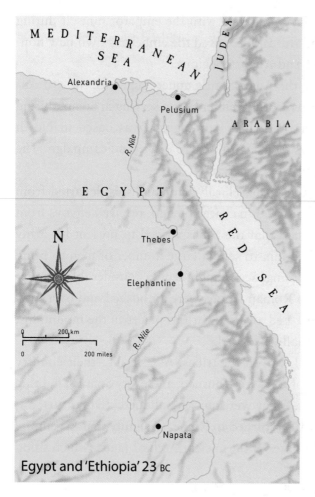

Egypt and 'Ethiopia' 23 BC

rulers would be distracted by their war in Spain, and also learning that two years earlier the Roman legions based in Egypt had lost many men to sunstroke during a disastrous expedition to Arabia, marched a Kushite army along the Nile and entered Egypt.

'Ravaging everything they encountered', the Kushite army advanced to the southernmost Egyptian city, Elephantine, site of an ancient fortress on an island in the Nile. [Dio, LIV, 5] News of this incursion reached the Alexandria-based Prefect of Egypt, Publius Petronius. [Pliny the Elder, *NH*, VI, 181. Cassius Dio, writing two centuries later, called the prefect *Gaius* Petronius: LIV, 5.] At that time, there were three legions stationed in Egypt, the 3rd Cyrenaica, 12th Fulminata and 22nd Deiotariana. All of them were led by their senior tribunes, for a law of Augustus required that no member of the Senatorial Order enter Egypt, let alone hold a command there. Petronius quickly put together an army from the legions and auxiliary units in the province, then marched south to counter Candace.

'Hoping to make good their escape', the Kushites hastily withdrew as the Roman army approached Elephantine. [Dio, LIV, 5] Petronius' troops overtook the invaders on the road south, where they routed the Kushite force. Candace himself escaped with part of his army and fled for his capital. Petronius, seeing the opportunity for further glory, led his army after the fleeing enemy, and was drawn down the Nile. Storming one Kushite city after another, Petronius left a Roman garrison at one of them and pushed on to famed Napata.

Built on a hill called the Barkol, Napata was then 700 years old. The Barkol had been considered by the ancient Egyptians to be the home of their god Ammon. Around the bottom of the hill stood a number of Egyptian temples. The Roman army stormed the city's wall and took Napata with ease. Petronius then ordered that the city be destroyed, and the buildings of Napata, including the handsome temples, were razed to the ground.

Leaving a garrison at the ruined city, Petronius marched on, heading south into the desert. Soon, lack of water and heatstroke affected his troops, who were clad in their helmets and armour. 'Finding himself unable to advance farther on account of the sand and the heat', the Roman commander eventually turned his army around. [Ibid.]

Candace had meanwhile reformed his army, and attacked Petronius' garrisons; it took the return of Petronius' army to rescue them. Petronius then 'compelled Candace to make terms with him', before he withdrew to Egypt with his troops and baggage train weighed down with booty. His legions returned to their bases. This was to be one of the few Roman armies to penetrate Africa south of Egypt in all of Roman history.

19 BC
IV. SECOND CANTABRIAN WAR
Treachery and dishonour in Spain

With Augustus on an extended tour of the East, his long-time close friend and deputy Marcus Agrippa was sent to govern Gaul and respond to recent raids from across the Rhine by German tribes. Agrippa was just a year older than Augustus. They had been at school together in Apollonia in Greece in March 44 BC when word reached them that Augustus' great-uncle Julius Caesar had been murdered in Rome. The pair had immediately set off for Italy, to forge a partnership that was unique in Roman history, for Agrippa was the most loyal of deputies and never once showed any interest in seeking supreme power for himself.

Agrippa had 'put a stop to those troubles' affecting the Gauls when word arrived that the Cantabrians had risen in revolt in northern Spain. [Dio, LIV, 11] A number of men of the Cantabri tribe who had been sold into slavery in Spain had apparently secretly concerted a plan for revolt. All at once they rose up, murdered their masters and escaped to their homeland. Back in the mountains, the fugitives convinced many of their countrymen to join them in a revolution against Rome. The rebels quickly seized several mountain towns, walled them in, and challenged the Roman army to attempt to dislodge them.

Hurrying over the Pyrenees from Gaul, Marcus Agrippa took charge of operations against the rebels. But he soon encountered problems with his own men. 'Not a few of them were too old and were exhausted by the continual wars,' said Dio. Many of Agrippa's troops refused to obey orders to go into the mountains, expecting certain ambush and 'fearing the Cantabri as men hard to subdue'. [Dio, LIV, 11] Partly by disciplining them and partly by exhorting them, the general was able to motivate his legionaries and the operation went forward.

The year's campaign was a gruelling one, during which Agrippa 'met with many reverses'. [Ibid.] While the Cantabri had been living among the Romans as slaves they had familiarized themselves with Roman ways, and having once been enslaved for opposing Rome they had no doubt that if captured they would not be spared a second time. This made the leading rebels fearless, even reckless.

By the end of the year, Agrippa had defeated the rebels but at significant cost, 'losing many soldiers'. Other troops, he demoted, 'because they kept being defeated'. [Ibid.] The legions even lost several standards in the fighting, a matter of great dishonour. [*Res Gest.*, V, 29] Agrippa was so dissatisfied with the performance of the entire 1st Augusta Legion that he deprived it of the Augusta title it had so recently been granted by the emperor. [Dio, LIV, 11]

In the end, Agrippa made captives of the entire Cantabri tribe. He executed almost all the males aged 17 to 46, disarmed those men who survived, and by forced migration brought every remaining member of the tribe down from the mountains and settled them on the plains. But so disgusted was he by the poor fighting qualities of some of his troops and the cost of success that Agrippa did not send a formal message to the Senate in Rome claiming a great victory. And when the Senate voted him a Triumph for the campaign, he declined it.

There would be brief unrest among the subjected peoples of northern Spain three years later, which was quickly put down, but by the time Augustus himself revisited Spain in 14 BC, the peninsula was peaceful. The emperor was back in Rome the following year.

16 BC

V. THE 5TH ALAUDAE LOSES ITS EAGLE
Dishonour in Gaul

After spending ten years in northern Spain as one of the legions fighting the Cantabrian War in 19 BC, with the war's conclusion the 5th Alaudae Legion was transferred to the Lower Rhine, to face the tribes of Germany across the great river. There, three years later, the legion suffered one of the greatest humiliations that any legion could experience.

East of the Rhine, Germany's Tencteri tribe and their neighbours, the Usipetes and Sugambri, had seized Romans travelling through their territory and crucified them. Realizing that Rome would send troops to exact reprisals, the tribes decided to take pre-emptive action by launching a raid across the Rhine into Rome's German and Gallic provinces. As a result, the Gauls 'suffered much at the hands of the Germans'. [Dio, LIV, 21]

Marcus Lollius, Rome's governor of Lower Germany, immediately dispatched Roman cavalry to intercept the Germans, then set off from his headquarters at Cologne to meet the marauders with the 5th Alaudae Legion. Marcus, a consul in 21 BC, was guardian of Augustus' grandson Gaius Caesar, and was close to the emperor. He possessed an excellent military reputation after subjugating the Bessi tribe in Thrace and Moesia earlier in his career, and he confidently advanced towards the German invaders without waiting to gather a larger force.

Even in Tacitus' day, a century later, the Tencteri, the leaders of the invasion, had a formidable reputation. 'The Tencteri, besides sharing in the general military distinction [of the German tribes], excel in horsemanship,' Tacitus wrote. [*Germ.*, 32] Children of the Tencteri grew up on horseback, and on a tribesman's death his horses went to his son; not necessarily the eldest son, said Tacitus, but 'the keenest and ablest soldier'. [Ibid.]

The Germans laid an ambush for the auxiliary cavalry sent against them by Lollius, and routed them. Surviving cavalrymen fled back towards Lollius' approaching column, leading the pursuing Germans straight to the Roman infantry. Caught on the march, the 5th Alaudae struggled to fight off the Germans, who homed in on the legion's golden eagle standard. The eagle was wrested away from its defenders, and the legion, its 1st cohort severely mauled, was forced to withdraw.

Lollius retreated, and began assembling a much larger force from the other legions of the army of the Lower Rhine. Augustus, meanwhile, was in Gaul, dealing with civil matters. On hearing of Lollius' reverse he hurried to the Rhine with a substantial force which would have included cohorts of the Praetorian Guard. On hearing that two large Roman armies would soon be converging on them, the trio of German tribes withdrew back across the Rhine with the spoils from their campaign. Their envoys quickly entered into negotiations with Augustus as soon as he arrived at the Rhine, and sealed a peace treaty with him by providing hostages.

In the opinion of later Roman biographer Suetonius, 'Lollius' defeat was ignominious rather than of strategic importance'. [Suet., II, 23] Even so, Lollius' reputation was ruined by the 'disgraceful' loss of a sacred legionary eagle. [Ibid.] Because of that disgrace, other Roman authors would savage him. 'He was a man more eager for money that for honest action,' wrote Velleius Paterculus, an officer who served under Tiberius; 'and of vicious habits.' [Velle., II, XCVII] One of those habits, according to Suetonius, was the spreading of slanders about Tiberius. [Suet., III, 12]

With his official career brought to an abrupt end by this battle, Lollius would spend his later years counselling his ward, Gaius Caesar. As for the 5th Alaudae Legion, it would never shake off the shame of the loss of its eagle, which was nothing short of a 'disaster' according to historian Tacitus. [Tac., A, I, 10]

This military reverse west of the Rhine was a warning which would not be lost on Augustus. The Rhine frontier was much too porous, and the Germans too numerous. If the Germans were allowed to think that they could get away with emulating the Tencteri and their fellow raiders, Rome's northwestern frontier would soon teem with German invaders. Orders were issued for numerous legions to be transferred to the Rhine to create a strong bulwark against further incursions.

15 BC
VI. CONQUERING RAETIA
Drusus and Tiberius combine

Raetia, situated between Gaul and Noricum, corresponds roughly with today's Switzerland. The alpine Raeti tribe 'were overrunning a large part of the territory of Gaul and carrying off plunder even from Italy'. [Dio, LIV, 22] They were even harassing their allies, including the Vindelici of northern Italy, and Romans who travelled though their territory, killing males and making women their captives, even killing babies in the womb if they deduced, by a form of divination, that the unborn babies were male. These activities were 'what was to be expected of nations which had not accepted peace,' said Dio. [Ibid.]

In 15 BC, therefore, Augustus gave Tiberius and Drusus the task of bringing the Raetians into line. The brothers were very different in style. While Tiberius was a cautious commander who let others do the front-line work, Drusus took part in the fighting alongside his troops and would personally 'chase German chieftains across the battlefield, at great risk to his life'. [Suet., v, 1]

The Raetians were 'strong in number and fiercely warlike', according to Velleius. [Velle., II, XCV] Characteristically, 23-year-old Drusus was the first to engage them, leading a force that routed a contingent of Raetians near Tridentum, today's city of Trent. The Raetians withdrew from Italy, but continued to raid Gaul, so Augustus then sent both his stepsons, from different directions at the same time, into Raetia against them.

Both Roman generals divided their armies into several columns which invaded Raetia via separate routes. Twenty-seven-year-old Tiberius, who had seen service in the Cantabrian War in Spain as a teenager, used ships to cross Lake Garda, near Lake Como, catching

Drusus Caesar, brother of Tiberius and father of Germanicus and Claudius. He would die in Germany after falling from his horse while on campaign.

the tribesmen by surprise. [Dio, LIV, 22] As many as twelve legions, involving some 60,000 legionaries, took part in these large-scale Raetian operations. Numismatic evidence suggests that the units involved included the 13th Gemina, 16th Gallica and 21st Rapax, and probably also the 17th, 18th and 19th legions. Units based in Illyricum at this time, the 11th, 15th Apollinaris and 20th, are likely to have also taken part.

Intriguingly, whilst it may be coincidental, the policy cited by Dr Lawrence Keppie whereby legions numbered 11 and above were traditionally posted to this part of the Roman world during the late republican era, seems also to have applied to the postings of Augustus during this period. [Kepp., MRA, 2] Likewise, no legion numbered over 10 is known to have been used by Augustus in the recently completed Cantabrian War in Spain, further endorsing the Keppie formula, whereby only legions numbered 10 and under were used in Spain during the late republican era. [*See page 226.*]

The Raeti, though numerous, were forced to divide their forces to combat the various Roman incursions, and divided, they were conquered. The natives were 'easily overwhelmed', said Dio. [Dio, LIV, 22] The Roman forces also defeated Raetian allies, the Vindelici. This was all accomplished, said Velleius, after the legions stormed many towns and strongholds and fought several pitched battles in the open. While there was much bloodshed among legions' opponents, there was 'more danger than real loss to the Roman army'. [Velle., II, XCV]

Many thousands of tribesmen were captured. Because the Raeti had a large population, the strongest male captives of military age were deported. Those who were left behind were numerous enough to populate the country 'but too few to begin a revolution,' said Dio. [Dio, LIV, 22] In a single campaigning season, Tiberius and Drusus had defeated the two tribes and extended Roman rule into the alps.

9 BC
VII. AT THE ALTAR OF PEACE
A dedication, and a funeral

'When I returned from Spain and Gaul,' Augustus wrote, 'after successful operations in those provinces, the Senate voted the consecration of an altar to Pax Augusta [the Augustan Peace] in the Campus Martius in honour of my return.' That had been in 14 BC. [*Res Gest.*, II, 12]

It took five years to create the *Ara Pacis Augustae*, the Altar to the Augustan Peace. It was formally dedicated on Rome's Field of Mars on 30 January 9 BC. The altar's marble panels show the entire imperial family attending the ceremony. Two months later, following the lustration ceremonies which preceded the year's campaigning season, Drusus and Tiberius rode off to launch their latest military ventures. For Tiberius, it would be a brief campaign in Pannonia. More ambitiously, 29-year-old Drusus, one of the consuls for the year, led fifteen legions deep into Germany.

Confronted by the Chatti and the Suebi, and 'defeating the forces that attacked him only after considerable bloodshed', Drusus marched his legions through the homelands of the Cherusci tribe, crossed the Weser river, and reached the Elbe, 'pillaging everything on his way'. [Dio, LV, 1]

At the height of the summer, Drusus' army was withdrawing towards the Rhine when the young general was thrown from his horse. It seems that Drusus sustained a broken limb, after which gangrene set in. As his army neared the Rhine, Drusus became too ill to be moved. News of his deteriorating condition reached Tiberius in northern Italy, and he rode all the way to the Rhine, crossed it, and after a journey of 400 miles (640 kilometres) found the army still inside Germany with his brother near death. Thirty days after Drusus' fall, he died in Tiberius' arms.

Tiberius walked in front of his brother's cortège all the way to Rome. Legion tribunes and centurions carried the bier as far as the Rhine, then leading men of every city the cortège passed through took turns as pallbearers. At Rome, Drusus' body was laid in state in the Forum. Tiberius delivered one funeral oration there, Augustus another in the Circus Flaminius. [Suet., III, 1]

The Ara Pacis panels show the entire Roman imperial family in 9 BC, including the doomed general Drusus Caesar.

The body was then borne to the Field of Mars. There, in sight of the Altar of Peace, whose dedication Drusus had attended only months before, the popular young prince of Rome was cremated. His remains were deposited in Augustus' own circular mausoleum. It would be another twenty-two years before Augustus joined him.

AD 6–9
VIII. THE PANNONIAN WAR
Four testing years

In the summer of AD 6, the Roman provinces of Pannonia and Dalmatia ran with blood.

The Roman subjugation of the Balkans had been completed by Augustus in 14 BC, with the regions of Pannonia and Dalmatia annexed to Rome. These new provinces covered parts of modern Austria, Hungary, Slovenia, Bosnia, Croatia and Serbia. In AD 5, Augustus' stepson Tiberius withdrew troops then garrisoned in Dalmatia and Pannonia and levied a number of Dalmatian auxiliaries, who joined him on the Danube for a campaign in Germany. Rebellions had broken out in Pannonia several times in past years, with many locals never entirely accepting Roman overlordship. The departure of the troops left a much reduced Roman military presence. In their absence, revolt flared in Pannonia and Dalmatia under two unrelated leaders, both named Bato, and a third native commander, Pennes.

Velleius Paterculus, who served as a Roman commander in this war, wrote that the revolt began in the north with the Pannonians, who brought the Dalmatians into the conflict as their allies. Velleius estimated that there were 800,000 native people in the two provinces, and that of these the rebel leadership would eventually arm 200,000 foot soldiers and 9,000 cavalry. In the north, the Breuci tribe elected their Bato as the chief Pannonian general; his army set its sights on marching on Italy. Pennes took a second Pannonian army east into Rome's province of Macedonia and began plundering. [Velle., *HR*, II, CX, 1–6]

In the south, Bato of Desidiatia initially led a small band of rebels which struck their first blow for the Dalmatians that summer: 'Roman citizens were overpowered, traders were massacred, a large vexillation of auxiliaries, stationed in the region which was most remote from the commander, was massacred to a man.' This success encouraged many more Dalmatians to join the uprising. In the overall rebel war strategy, the Dalmatian army would have the task of defending their own territories, while the Pannonians took the war to Rome elsewhere. [Ibid.]

Cassius Dio, writing two centuries later, said that the governor of Dalmatia, Marcus Valerius Messalinus, had gone to the Rhine to participate in Tiberius' latest German campaign. [Dio, LV, 29] But Velleius Paterculus, who was a participant in this war, wrote that Messalinus had remained in Dalmatia, and, 'at the outbreak of the rebellion, finding himself surrounded by the army of the enemy and supported by only the 20th Legion, and that at half its strength' (because half of its cohorts were serving with Tiberius in Germany) 'he routed and put to flight more than twenty thousand, and for this was honoured with Triumphal Decorations' by Augustus. [Velle., II, CXII, I]

Pannonian rebels laid siege to Sirmium, modern Sremska Mitrovica, not far from present-day Belgrade, a strategically placed city that controlled the Sava Valley. According to Dio – in a story not verified by Velleius – Caecina Severus, governor of the adjacent province of Moesia, quickly marched west with Roman troops, met Bato the Breucian and his troops near the Drava river and defeated them in a stinging battle, taking heavy casualties himself. News of Dacian and Sarmatian raids into Moesia then caused Severus to withdraw to deal with that threat. [Dio, LV, 29] In the south, said Dio, the Dalmatian Bato attacked Salonae, near Split on the Adriatic coast. Salonae resisted the attack, and Bato himself received a head wound from a sling stone, but his troops overran other Roman communities all the way down the coast to Apollonia in Greece. [Ibid.]

With much of the Adriatic coast opposite Italy in rebel hands, there was uproar in Rome. 'Such a panic did this war inspire,' said Velleius, who was in Rome at the time, 'that even the courage of Caesar Augustus, made steady and firm by experience in so many wars, was shaken by fear.' That fear was of an invasion of Italy. [Velle., II, CX, 6] Augustus, who told the Senate that 'the enemy might appear in sight of Rome within ten days', sent urgently to Tiberius to abort his German campaign and march for the Balkans with five legions. [Ibid., CXI, 2]

Augustus also summoned five legions from the East, while at the capital he ordered mass mobilization. From throughout Italy all legion veterans were recalled from retirement to serve behind their Evocati standards. New troops were levied, and wealthy citizens were required to supply many of their freedmen servants to be equipped as soldiers. [Ibid.]

As for Velleius, who was aged around 30 at this point: 'I was now, at the end of my service with the cavalry, quaestor designate.' Velleius, 'even though not yet a senator', was immediately made an imperial legate by Augustus, the equivalent of a modern-day brigadier, and put in charge of the non-citizen recruits raised in this scramble to arms at Rome. The overall command of this force of Evocati and non-citizen troops was given to Augustus' grandson, Germanicus Julius Caesar. Aged just 21, Germanicus, the son of Drusus Caesar, Tiberius' late lamented brother, had already impressed Augustus as a young man of ability.

Led by Germanicus and Velleius, the mixed force marched with all speed from Rome for the Balkans. The fact that the much admired Germanicus was in charge of this motley force had a calming effect on the people of Rome. Meanwhile, from the Danube, Tiberius marched into Pannonia to Siscia, today's Sisak, near Zagreb, with his five legions – apparently the 8th Augusta, 9th Hispana, 14th Gemina Martia Victrix, 15th Apollinaris and the remaining cohorts of the 20th Legion. At Siscia, Tiberius linked up with local commander Messalinus, and with Germanicus and Velleius from Rome.

'What armies of the enemy did we see drawn up for battle in that first year!' Velleius was to recall. Tiberius, with his combined force vastly outnumbered by the rebels, decided to play for time until the five legions arrived from the East. Tiberius, considered by Augustus the 'bravest of men' and 'the most conscientious commander alive', actively evaded an all-out battle, instead harassing smaller enemy columns and blockading rebel supply routes. [Suet., III, 21]

The fact that a large Roman army was in Pannonia was enough to prevent the Pannonians going through with their plan to march on Italy. To do so would have put Roman troops at their backs.

In the new year, two Roman generals of consular rank marched into Pannonia: Aulus Caecina, who had more than twenty years' experience as a soldier, and Silvanus Plautius, who had arrived from the East. They

Germanicus Caesar, charismatic heir to the imperial throne, was hugely popular with the Roman people. He initially made his name during the Pannonian War, later in campaigns against the Germans. In the third century, Romans were still commemorating his birthday on 23 June each year.

came with their five legions, of which only the 7th Legion, which had been in Galatia up to this point, can be identified with some certainty, and were accompanied by a large number of allied troops including Thracian cavalry led by King Rhoemetacles of Thrace. The two Batos, learning of the approach of this Roman column, hurried towards it with their combined armies.

At the Volcae Marshes, west of Mitrovica in the Sava Valley, the rebels surrounded and attacked the camp of the five legions. When the Roman commanders led the legions, auxiliaries and cavalry out to fight, the rebels closed with the Thracian cavalry. 'The king's horsemen were routed,' said Velleius, and 'the cavalry of the allies put to flight.' Auxiliary cohorts turned and ran, 'and the panic extended even to the standards of the legions'. It was 'a disaster that came near being fatal'. [Velle., *HR*, II, CXII, 5–6]

Tribunes and first-rank centurions were killed by rebels swarming around the prized legionary eagles. Legion camp-prefects and prefects of auxiliary cohorts were cut off and surrounded. 'In this crisis the valour of the Roman soldier claimed for itself a greater share of the glory than it left to the generals.' With their men 'shouting encouragement to each other', the legions mounted a charge and 'fell upon the enemy'. The legion charge broke through the rebel line 'and wrested a victory from a desperate situation'. [Ibid.]

After their units had patched up their wounded, Caecina and Plautius pushed on to Siscia and joined Tiberius. There were now, in one Roman camp, 10 legions, in excess of 70 auxiliary cohorts, 14 cavalry wings, more than 10,000 Evocati militiamen, and the so-called 'volunteers', the freedmen of Rome. [Ibid., CXIII, 1] With this force, totalling more than 100,000 men, Tiberius should have been able to confront the largely untrained rebel troops on an equal footing. But Tiberius did a strange thing. After giving the five newly arrived legions a few days to recover, he sent them back to the East, escorting them through rebel territory to see them on their way.

Velleius claimed that Tiberius found the force 'too large to be managed and was not well adapted to effective control'. [Ibid., 2–3] Reading between the lines, this suggests a falling out between Tiberius and the generals who had come from the East. Yet Tiberius did receive more legion reinforcements during the course of the Pannonian War; Suetonius was to say that before the war was over it would involve 'fifteen legions and a correspondingly large force of auxiliaries'. [Suet., III, 16] At the war's end, the 7th Legion, one of the those from the East, was based permanently in Pannonia.

After a particularly severe winter, in the spring of AD 7 Tiberius launched offensive operations exclusively in Pannonia, ignoring Dalmatia for the time being. On campaign, Tiberius himself always rode, and always sat at the dining table in camp rather than lounged on a couch as was the habit of the Roman upper class. [Ibid., CXIV, 3] This was a demanding campaign, with the Roman army driving the Pannonians high into the mountains. But Augustus was not satisfied with its progress. Leaving Rome, the emperor travelled up to Arminium, today's Rimini, on the Adriatic coast, where he based himself in order to be closer to operations.

Now, the Romans had a little luck. The two Batos fell out. Dio writes that the Pannonian Bato had come to suspect the loyalty of his southern allies, and began making surprise visits on the southern Bato's strongholds, taking hostages from among the Dalmatian leaders' families. Seeing this as a grab for power, the Dalmatian Bato ambushed his co-commander – the troops of the Pannonian Bato's bodyguard were killed, and the man himself captured and imprisoned in a Dalmatian fortress. The Dalmatian Bato then had his rival brought before an assembly of his troops, condemned him, and executed him on the spot. [Dio, LV, 34]

With the northern Bato out of the way, Velleius considered the Pannonian campaign as good as won. Sure enough, the summer of AD 8 saw the Pannonians sue for peace. Velleius was present at a riverbank meeting when the Pannonians laid down their arms. Pennes and other Pannonian leaders surrendered to Tiberius, 'prostrating themselves one and all before the commander'. [Velle., 4]

As if the war was won, Augustus recalled Tiberius, who left Marcus Aemilius Lepidus, a consul in AD 6, in charge in Pannonia. With Dalmatia still in rebel hands, the emperor sent young Germanicus there with a strike force which later events indicate included the 20th Legion. In 'regions both wild and difficult', Germanicus overwhelmed the Mazaei tribe and laid siege to a number of Dalmatian towns. [Velle., CXVI, 1]

At one such town, Splonum, which had 'a vast number of defenders', Germanicus tried frontal assaults and siege equipment, but Splonum's high walls were built of timber, turf and stone, which made them impervious to battering rams. A German cavalryman by the name of Pusio then threw a stone at a section of wall, whereupon – to everyone's astonishment – the parapet and the rebel soldier leaning on it fell away, and the Dalmatians manning the wall fled in terror. Fearing that Germanicus had secret powers, the town surrendered. [Dio, LVI, 11]

At Raetinum, rebels set fire to buildings as Germanicus' troops poured in through a breach they had made in the town wall. A number of Roman soldiers were trapped in the flames, dying a fiery death. Only those townspeople who hid in caves survived the inferno. Germanicus' sieges continued unabated. Seretium, a town which Tiberius had previously unsuccessfully besieged, was now stormed by Germanicus and destroyed. 'After this some other places were more easily won.' [Ibid., 12] In the opinion of Velleius, who soldiered beside Germanicus, the young prince 'gave great proof of his valour'. [Velle., CXVI, 1] Just the same, progress was too slow for some at Rome, and Augustus sent Tiberius back to Dalmatia to conclude the campaign as quickly as possible.

Once he returned to the Balkans in the summer of AD 9, Tiberius created three task forces. Lepidus was to advance from the northwest, and Marcus Plautius Silvanus, a consul in 2 BC, from the northeast. Tiberius, with Germanicus as his deputy, would push along the Adriatic coast in pursuit of Bato, who was believed to be near Solonae. The northern advances encountered significant resistance from rebels, who emerged from hilltop strongholds and fought pitched battles; as a consequence, the Perustae tribe and Bato's Desiadate tribe 'were almost entirely exterminated'. [Velle., RH, CXV] In the south, Tiberius had less success. Bato, refusing to fight on Roman terms, withdrew ahead of Tiberius' advance, until he was finally cornered at Andetrium, in the vicinity of today's Split.

Andetrium was located on a rocky mount surrounded by deep ravines filled with rushing streams; not an easy place to assault. As Tiberius surrounded the hill and settled in for a long siege, Dalmatian guerrillas appeared in his rear and harassed his supply columns, reducing his supplies and at times making the Romans themselves feel under siege. But eventually Bato sent an envoy seeking peace terms. Tiberius responded that Bato would have to convince all rebels still holding out throughout Dalmatia to throw down their arms before he would agree to peace, a guarantee Bato was unable to give.

A number of men who had deserted from the Roman army and gone over to the rebels knew that execution awaited them if they surrendered, so they convinced their Dalmatian hosts not to capitulate. In response, Tiberius broke off negotiations and resumed the assault on Andetrium.

As Tiberius watched operations from a seat on an earth platform, Roman troops in a tightly packed square formation went against the front of the town, struggling up a rutted slope as Dalmatians rained missiles down on them. Wagons were brought out from the town, loaded with stones, then propelled down the hill at the oncoming troops. Loose wheels and round wooden chests, which were a local speciality, were rolled down the slope at the easy targets. It was like a giant bowling alley for the Dalmatians, with their projectiles skittling Roman troops. All the while, other Roman forces lining the bottom of the hill noisily cheered on their struggling comrades.

Tiberius sent in reinforcements, and also sent a force around behind the town; the latter climbed a rock face unobserved and fell on defenders outside the front wall, cutting them off from the town. Throwing off their armour, these rebels tried to flee down the slopes, with Roman troops gleefully giving chase. Most were captured. After Bato later slipped out of Andetrium, the townspeople sent out envoys to arrange a surrender.

Germanicus, meanwhile, leading one of two columns dispatched by Tiberius to assault towns still holding out along the Dalmatian coast, laid siege to Arduba, which was built on an elevated position on a river bend. Here, the male rebels were keen to give in, but German deserters and Dalmatian women disagreed, and it was not until the rebels had overpowered the deserters that they were able to send to Germanicus to arrange a surrender. In the meantime, the women set fire to part of the city. Then, rather than surrender, and clutching their children to them, the women flung themselves into the flames or hurled themselves from the city walls into the swirling river below. Germanicus accepted the surrender. On hearing of the fall of Arduba, other communities sent envoys to Germanicus seeking surrender terms.

As town after town fell in this way, Bato ran out of hiding places. He sent his son Sceuas to Tiberius with an offer of surrender, on condition that he and his followers receive full pardons. Tiberius agreed. A few days later Bato was discreetly admitted to the Roman camp at night, kept under guard until the morning, then brought before Tiberius. According to Dio, in the discussions that followed, Bato blamed Rome for the war: 'We are your flocks, yet you didn't send shepherds to look after us, you sent wolves.' [Dio, LVI, 16]

The Pannonian War, which Suetonius was to characterize as 'the most bitterly fought of all foreign wars since Rome defeated Carthage', was at an end. [Suet., III, 16] Bato was pardoned, and given a house at the Italian naval city of Ravenna. He apparently lived out the rest of his life under house arrest at Ravenna. Tiberius was granted a Triumph and the title of imperator by the Senate for terminating the revolt.

Germanicus was made a praetor, and he and all the other Roman generals involved in the campaign were granted Triumphal Decorations.

But even as young Germanicus was rising from his seat in the Senate to formally announce the end of the Pannonian War, Tiberius was hastening to Germany. Rome would soon find out why, and would again be swept by panic – with the news of the Varus disaster.

AD *9*

IX. THE VARUS DISASTER
Annihilation in the Teutoburg

It was September, in the dying days of summer. Strung out for miles, a large Roman military column was moving west towards the River Rhine after spending many months in Germany east of the Rhine. The column was led by the commander of Rome's two armies of the Upper and Lower Rhine, Publius Quintilius Varus. A member of 'a famous rather than a high-born family', according to Velleius Paterculus, a Roman officer who knew him, Varus was in his sixties. [Velle., II, CXVII]

The general's father, Sextus Quintilius Varus, had supported the Liberators, Brutus and Cassius, against Octavian, Antony and Lepidus, and had taken his own life following the defeat of the Liberators at Philippi in 42 BC. No doubt because Varus was related to Augustus by marriage, Augustus had not penalized Varus' career, enabling him to serve as a consul in 13 BC and as governor of Syria the following decade. Varus was, in the words of Velleius, 'a man of character and of good intentions'. [Ibid., CXX]

In Syria, Varus had acted with alacrity to counter a brief Jewish revolt in Jerusalem following the death of King Herod the Great. But now, a dozen years later, Varus had grown lazy and incautious. According to Velleius, who was at that time fighting the Pannonian War with Tiberius and Germanicus, Varus was no conquering general, but was 'a man of mild character and of quiet disposition' who by AD 9 had become 'more accustomed to the leisure of the camp than actual service in war'. [Ibid., CXVII]

Varus had been called out of comfortable retirement in AD 6 for this posting as overall Roman commander on the Rhine. Tiberius had been conducting a campaign in Bohemia against the Suebi Germans when he was forced to suspend those operations hurriedly, in order to lead his legions south to put down the major revolt in Pannonia and Dalmatia that became the gruelling three-year Pannonian War. Tiberius, who, by AD 9 was still damping down the last embers of that revolt, had left Varus three legions on the Lower Rhine and another two on the Upper Rhine, where Varus' nephew Lucius Asprenus was in charge.

This combined force of five legions on the Rhine compared to the twelve to fifteen legions that Tiberius and his brother Drusus had previously commanded here. Tiberius had also taken a large number of auxiliary and allied units away from the Rhine for service in the Pannonian War; Suetonius wrote that 75,000 auxiliaries and allied troops supported the legions fighting in Pannonia and Dalmatia. [Suet., III, 16]

To fill the gaps left by the departure of all these units, the German tribes in alliance with Rome had been expected to provide cohorts of allied German troops to serve under Varus, as their treaties required. Not that a larger force on the Rhine seemed necessary. As a result of the campaigns of Drusus, Tiberius and others, Augustus felt that Germany east of the Rhine was a pacified area. Flourishing Roman trade in eastern Germany seemed to support that belief. Over the three years that Varus had been in charge here, he had led his troops across the Rhine each spring and, after linking up with allied German contingents, had paraded through Germany between the Rhine and the Elbe both to awe and to inspire the locals.

At various German settlements along his route Varus had sat in judgment over local disputes. According to Velleius, Varus 'came to look upon himself as a city praetor administering justice in the Forum, and not as a general in command of an army in the heart of Germany'. Varus was convinced that the German tribes were subjected peoples who wanted to embrace Roman ways and Roman justice. Varus' campaigns in Germany had involved neither fighting nor booty for his legions; instead, according to Velleius, during this past year Varus had 'wasted a summer campaign holding court and observing the proper details of legal procedure'. [Velle., II, CXVII]

Throughout that summer, Varus had been accompanied on his concourse through Germany by local kings and princes, including a prince of the Cherusci tribe who, said Velleius, 'had been associated with us constantly on previous campaigns'. This young prince, who would be known to future generations of Germans as Hermann, had taken the Roman name of Arminius. [Ibid., CXVIII.]

Like his brother Flavus, Arminius served as an officer with the Roman army, being granted Roman citizenship and membership of the Equestrian Order. Flavus, who was apparently fighting for Rome in the Pannonian War at this time, had previously served under Tiberius on the Rhine, receiving numerous Roman bravery decorations. [Tac., *A*, II, 9, 10]

Arminius, this impressive 'young man of noble birth', was 'brave in action and alert in mind' according to Velleius, who would have known Arminius, having served in Tiberius' army on the Rhine as a prefect of auxiliaries and tribune. Velleius said that the young German 'showed in his countenance and in his eyes the fire of the mind within'. [Ibid.] A marble bust of

A bust of Arminius, or Hermann as he was known to the German people, made when he was an officer of allied troops in the Roman army, and before he led the uprising of German tribes against Roman rule.

Arminius has survived from his years among the Romans; it shows a young man, clean-shaven in the Roman fashion but with wavy hair falling over his ears in the German style, and, in support of Velleius' description, intense eyes.

Arminius, in his late twenties, 'served in our camp as a leader of his fellow countrymen,' said Tacitus. [Tac., *A*, II, 10] With the equivalent rank of a Roman prefect, Arminius was the commander of a cohort of allied Cheruscan troops attached to Varus' army. Arminius had become particularly friendly with Varus, and during this summer Arminius and Segimerus, brother of the king of the Chatti tribe, were so close to Varus that they 'were his constant companions and often shared his dinner table'. [Dio, *RH*, LVI, 19]

But at the final feast hosted by Varus before he set off to lead his troops back across the Rhine for the winter, Segestes, king of the Chatti (who had been granted Roman citizenship by Augustus and valued the alliance between Rome and his people), stood up and warned Varus that Arminius and other German tribal leaders were planning an uprising against Rome. This was not the first time that Segestes had warned Varus against Arminius, but this time he was much more specific. Varus, as he had in the past, dismissed the old king's warning. The Roman general, who had come to trust Arminius implicitly, put Segestes' warning, like the rest, down to personal enmity between Segestes and Arminius, for Arminius had eloped with Segestes' daughter

Thusnelda after her father had promised her hand in marriage to another man. [Tac., A, I, 55] To add further to Segestes' fury was the fact that Arminius' father Sigimer had endorsed the subsequent marriage of Arminius and Thusnelda, in doing so failing to respect the objections of the bride's father, his fellow king. [Tac., A, I, 55; Velle., II, CXVIII] These familial events had, to Varus' mind, caused Segestes to invent a conspiracy involving his fine young friend Arminius, and to his peril Varus 'refused to believe the story'. [Velle., II, CXVIII]

Varus would not even listen when Segestes urged Varus to arrest him and all the other German leaders present, including Arminius, and with them in chains question them about this conspiracy to rebel against Rome in contravention of their peace treaties. [Tac., A, I, 55; Velle., Ibid.] Others close to Varus urged him to take heed of Segestes, but, says Cassius Dio, Varus only became impatient, and 'rebuked them for being needlessly excited and slandering his friends'. [Dio, LVI, 19]

Varus' army was now making its way west, aiming to follow a line of Roman forts along the Lippe river. His intention was to cross back into Roman territory by a bridge of boats where the Lippe joined the Rhine at Castra Vetera, today's Xanten in Holland, a journey that would involve a march of around ten days. The allied German troops had already taken their leave of Varus to head for their home territories, and, at the request of the German tribes, Varus had broken up his legions by distributing some of their cohorts to major settlements throughout eastern Germany, to spend the winter with the locals until his return in the spring. [Dio, LVI, 19]

Other Roman detachments had taken up residence for the winter at the forts east of the Rhine. This left Varus with a force that he now led towards the Rhine of the remaining cohorts of his three legions, plus six auxiliary cohorts and three wings of cavalry. [Velle., II, CXVII] The precise identities of these cohorts and wings are not known, but, according to Dio, at least one of the auxiliary cohorts was a unit of archers. [Dio, LVI, 21]

Of Varus' legions, two are known to have been the 18th and the 19th, while the third was almost certainly the 17th. The 17th Legion had served in Aquitania under Tiberius, then had probably taken part in the 15 BC Raetian campaign before making its permanent winter camp at Novaesium on the Rhine, today's Neuss. The 18th Legion had a similar background before it took up residence at the legion fortress at Vetera, while the 19th had served in Gaul with Tiberius before taking part in the Raetian campaign. The 19th's home base was Cologne.

According to Roman historian Tacitus, as Varus was leading his legions back towards the Rhine, those legions were 'unofficered'. [Tac., A, II, 46] That is, they were without their senior officers: legates or broad-stripe tribunes. Tacitus' statement is supported by Velleius, who wrote that, as the column headed towards the Rhine, two of the three legions were led by their camp-prefects, the legions' third-in-command. The third camp-prefect, said Velleius, was in command of a Roman fort east of the Rhine. Accordingly, the cohorts of the third legion in the column were under the command of its chief centurion. [Velle., II, CXIX, CXX]

Neither Velleius nor Tacitus offers an explanation for this highly unusual absence of the legions' senior officers. It is possible that the demands and casualties of the Pannonian War had drawn senior officers away from the Rhine legions; fifteen legions had been embroiled in the gruelling three-year Pannonian struggle. [Suet., III, 16] Alternatively, ahead of his departure from eastern Germany, Varus had possibly allowed his senior officers to leave his column and return to Lower Germany, or even to go home to Rome for the winter.

Of Varus' officers, we know the identity of the prefect of one of the column's three cavalry wings, Vala Numonius, 'an inoffensive and honourable man' according to Velleius, who would have been acquainted with him. There was also a young gentleman of high birth in the column, identified by Velleius as Caldus Caelius. [Velle., II, CXIX] Young Caelius would have been a thin-stripe tribune, an officer cadet, of whom five served with each of the legions.

Of the scores of centurions in the column, the identity of just one has come down to us. Fifty-three-year-old Marcus Caelius, no relation to the junior tribune above, was a first-rank centurion with the 18th Legion who had put in his full term with the Roman army and was serving an extended enlistment. The recipient of numerous bravery awards including two golden torques, Centurion Caelius, a burly, curly-headed man, was a native of today's Bologna in northern Italy.

As Centurion Caelius rode at the head of his 18th Legion men, it is likely that his two servants, Privatus and Thiaminus, walked in the large train of non-combatants that trailed the military column. Thousands of civilians had followed the Roman army as it tramped around Germany that summer. Among them, Dio would write, were 'not a few women and children', the illegal families of legionaries, 'and a large retinue of servants' such as the freedmen of the centurion Caelius. [Dio, LVI, 20]

A number of German leaders escorted Varus as he set out for the Rhine with his army; Arminius was not among them. Segestes was to claim that, following the feast during which Varus had refused to listen to his last warning, the Chattian king had put Arminius in chains, hoping to prevent a rebellion. But the next day Arminius had been freed by his fellow Cheruscans, who in turn put Segestes in chains. [Tac., *A*, I, 58]

Meanwhile, the German leaders riding with Varus were present when urgent news arrived of an uprising among German tribes to the north. Varus immediately turned the column north, to march to the scene of the uprising and put it down. At this point, the German leaders with Varus 'begged to be excused from further attendance, in order, so they claimed, to assemble their allied forces, after which they would quickly come to his aid'. [Dio, LVI, 19] The Germans galloped away. But most had no intention of bringing forces in support of Varus as they had promised; their tribesmen were actually waiting to launch a surprise attack on Varus' army.

King Segestes had spoken the truth. Arminius was planning an uprising of the tribes. 'This young man made of the negligence of the general an opportunity for treachery,' said Velleius, 'sagaciously appreciating that no one could be more swiftly overpowered than the man who fears nothing.' [Velle., II, CVIII] At first, Velleius wrote, Arminius had involved just a few leaders of other tribes. Even among Arminius' own Cherusci tribe there were leading men, such as his uncle Inguiomerus, 'who had long been respected by the Romans', and with whom Arminius did not feel able to broach safely the subject of revolt against Rome. [Tac., *A*, I, 60]

The first German leader to join Arminius, Dio indicates, was Segimerus, brother of Segestes, who would go against the king and bring the majority of the powerful Chatti tribe into the revolt. [Dio, LVI, 19] Once the Chatti had voted to go to war, it became easier for Arminius to draw 'a large number' of other tribes into the plot. [Velle., II, CXVIII] Convincing other tribal leaders that 'the Romans could be crushed' if the Germans acted furtively and in concert, Arminius, knowing that Varus planned to leave Germany in September, set down a date when all the tribes would rise as one. [Ibid.] In the meantime, they were to arm and train their warriors secretly.

On the chosen day, 'the men in each community had put to death the detachments of soldiers for which they had previously asked'. [Dio, LVI, 19] Having disposed of the Roman troops quartered at their settlements, the German warrior bands then set off for a prearranged rendezvous point in Cherusci territory. At the same time, the message was sent to Varus to tell him that an uprising had taken place in the north, to entice him into the carefully planned ambush.

On Arminius' orders, German leaders likely to remain supportive of the Romans were put in chains. One such German was Boiocaulus, a prince of the large Ampsivarii tribe. Later king of the Ampsivarii, Boiocaulus would remain an ally of Rome for over half a century. Probably in his twenties at this time, Boiocaulus is likely to have been serving as a prefect of German auxiliaries with Varus in AD 9. Overpowered by Arminius' henchmen as he rode to raise his warriors in support of Varus following the first report of an uprising, Boiocaulus was held in chains at a German village. Although he was able to escape and cross the Rhine, he arrived in Roman territory too late to give warning of the uprising. The deed had by that time been done, and Roman blood spilt, in abundance. [Tac., A, XIII, 55]

Meanwhile, Varus and his troops were marching unwittingly to meet their doom in a forest which Tacitus called the Teutoburgium. The precise location of the ambush is not revealed by any classical author, but Dio says that through the Germans' trickery Varus was drawn 'far away from the Rhine into the land of the Cherusci, towards the Visurgis', the Weser river. [Dio, LVI, 18] According to Dio, to reach the chosen place of ambush Varus' column had to pass through territory dominated by 'mountains [that] had an uneven surface broken by ravines [where] the trees grew close together and very high'. [Ibid., 20]

Since the 1700s, German historians became convinced that these mountains referred to by Dio were in fact the Weser Hills, for to reach the Weser from the Lippe, Varus' column would have had to cross those hills. In emulation of Tacitus, the forest covering the Weser Hills was given the name of the Teutoburger Wald. Here, heavily wooded limestone and sandstone ridges arc south from the River Ems for 60 miles (96 kilometres). In 1875, in celebration of the AD 9 victory over Varus' legions, the Hermann-Denkmal, a massive statue of Arminius, was raised on top of the Grotenburg hill outside Dortmold, at the southern end of the Weser Hills.

As early as 1716, however, Roman coins were found by German farmers in the vicinity of Kalkreise, at the other, northern end of the Weser Hills. Kalkreise, just to the northeast of the town of Osnabrück, was then considered to be one of many possible locations of the German ambush of Varus' army. [Wells, 3] Then in 1987–88, British Army officer Tony Clunn also discovered numerous Roman artefacts buried at Kalkreise, the discovery of three lead sling bullets convincing German authorities that this was a site connected with the Roman military. This led German archaeologists to conduct a series of major digs at the site which, over ten years, revealed more than 4,000 Roman artefacts, most of them with military connections. [Ibid.]

Ironically, the lead bullets which spurred the German archaeologists may have been German, not Roman. Tacitus, in describing the AD 70 Battle of Old Camp at Vetera, on the eastern bank of the Rhine, wrote of that battle commencing with 'a discharge of stones, leaden balls, and other missiles' unleashed by the Germans and Batavians opposing the Roman army. [Tac., *H*, V, 17] It is possible that, under the direction of Arminius and other Germans who had served in the Roman military, the tribes had, by AD 9, acquired the means and the skills to make and use lead slingshot.

These archaeological discoveries, and the situation of the Kalkreise site – which was on Varus' likely route to the Weser – have convinced many that this was indeed the location of the last stand of Quintilius Varus and his legions. We know that Varus, rather than break up the column, marched north with his entire force, including a large baggage train. Some of the camp followers appear to have left the column to await the legions' return, taking refuge at the Roman forts east of the Rhine. But, Dio wrote, many civilians, including women and children, continued to tag along behind Varus and his troops, either for protection, or in expectation of booty and celebration once the legions put down the 'uprising' that was luring them north. [Dio, LVI, 20] Finds of women's jewellery at the Kalkreise site support this. [Wells, 3]

With a number of their cohorts detached by Varus to winter at German settlements – cohorts that had by this time been massacred by the tribes – Varus' three legions would have numbered around 10,000 men between them. As Velleius reveals, the column also included 1,500 auxiliary cavalry and 3,000 auxiliary light infantry. In textbook fashion, Roman style, this force of some 14,500 men would have been led into the Weser Hills by cavalry and auxiliaries, guided by Germans who had been sent to lead the Roman army into Arminius' trap. Roman road-building parties came next. In the vanguard of the column rode the commander-in-chief himself and his staff and cavalry bodyguard. Two legions probably came next, ahead of Varus' strung-out baggage train, which included as 'many wagons and beasts of burden as in peacetime'. [Ibid.]

Knowing that a lightly protected, fully-laden baggage train heading for the Rhine on its own would have attracted Germans intent on plunder like bears to honey, Varus had refused to detach his train, which would have included some 1,800 pack mules; one for every eight soldiers was the norm. But neither did he lighten it to speed his progress. There would also have been hundreds of two-wheeled carts drawn by mules and oxen, the carts loaded down with the catapults of the three legions, as well as ammunition, tents and millstones, officers' furniture and silver dining plate, and supplies for the march. As finds at the digs at Kalkreise would suggest, the train also carried items as diverse as medical instruments, glass gaming pieces and the small statues of officers' household gods. [Wells, 3]

A cavalry detachment brought up the rear, trailed – with increasing apprehension as they entered the forbidding forest of tall birch, spruce and oak – by the camp followers. The legionaries of the column were in marching order. Their personal effects were suspended from carrying poles over one shoulder: bedrolls, entrenching tools, mess equipment, bravery decorations and rations. Their javelins and two palisade stakes per man were tied to the pack poles. Their shields, wrapped in protective leather covers, were slung over their left shoulder. Their helmets, slung around their necks, rested against their chests. With this sort of load and a long baggage train they would cover 15–18 miles [24–29 kilometres] a day, marching until noon then spending the afternoon building a marching camp for the night and gathering firewood, fodder and water, repeating the process each day.

In the Teutoburg Forest, Arminius and the tense German tribesmen 'came through the densest thickets, as they were acquainted with the pathways', then took up positions in the trees on the hillside, out of sight, and waited. Not all the tribes had answered the call to arms, and some bands that had come to the Weser Hills held back, waiting to see the outcome of Arminius' initial attack. A black sky shrouded the area. Heavy rain, which had begun as a shower that morning, tumbled down on to the warriors and wild winds lashed the treetops. But at least the storm would mask any sound made by the hidden tribesmen and their horses, so that the approaching Romans were not alerted to their presence. [Dio, LVI, 20–21]

Apart from Arminius and his Cherusci, the tribes waiting in the forest included the formidable Chatti, a people of 'hardy bodies, well-knit limbs, fierce appearance, and unusual mental vigour', according to Tacitus. The Chattian contingent was led by Segimerus, who was accompanied by his son. Other Chatti clan leaders also present would have been Catumerus, who was the father-in-law of Arminius' brother Flavus, as well as Arpus and Adgandestrius; all three were future kings of the Chatti. The tribe primarily fought on foot, and always ventured forth well prepared. In addition to weapons, they went to war equipped with entrenching tools and provisions. While other tribes went forth to battle, said Tacitus, 'the Chatti come out for a campaign'. A custom of the Chatti fighting man, copied by some other tribes, was to let his beard grow when he went to war, only trimming it once he had slain an enemy in battle. [Tac., *Germ.*, 30]

The Cauchi were also there. They had been subjected by the massive armies led through Germany by Drusus and Tiberius two decades earlier, but in AD 5, while Tiberius was leading a new campaign in Germany, their young men had again proved troublesome to Rome, until forced to surrender and disarm by Tiberius. These same young men had rearmed, and had come to avenge their past humiliations. Then there were the Bructeri from north of the Lippe, and the Usipetes and the Tubantes, as well as Cheruscan near neighbours and subservient allies, the Fosi. The Marsi tribe, which resided between the Lippe and Ruhr rivers, was there, together with other tribes likely to have sent warriors – the Tencteri, Chamavi, Angrivarii, Sugambri and Mattiaci.

In all, some 30,000 tribesmen were present. The front-line weapon of most German tribes was a 12-foot (3.6-metre) wooden spear. Second-rank men carried the *framea*, the short, metal-tipped spear used for both throwing and jabbing that was common throughout Europe. Some warriors came armed merely with saplings whose ends had been sharpened and then hardened in a fire. Nobles also carried swords, copies of the Roman gladius, and large, blunt-ended broadswords.

All tribes were equipped with flat shields. These were generally made of oak or linden planks, with the poorer warriors using woven wicker shields covered with hide. Shield shapes varied by tribe; the Chatti used a small, square shield, while others carried more substantial rectangular shields as much as 4 feet (1.2 metres) long. All Germans tended to wear a cloak fastened at one shoulder with a brooch or pin. The wealthier tribesmen sported armoured breastplates and helmets, but some were entirely naked beneath their cloaks. And all the waiting Germans were now saturated by the rain.

Varus' men were finding the passage through the hills tough going, 'felling trees, building roads, and bridging places that required it', said Dio. [Dio, LV, 20] The rainstorm only made conditions all the more difficult, separating various parts of the column as the ground became slippery under foot and rainwater washed away earth to expose roots and logs that became obstacles for cartwheels. The wind was so strong that it broke off tree branches, which came tumbling down on to the column. [Ibid.]

Arminius had chosen the location for his ambuscade with care. The narrow defiles and often marshy ground through the Weser Hills prevented cavalry from deploying, while the legions' heavy infantry would not be able to use their normal battlefield formations. As far as the tribes were concerned, too, there was a religious significance to the Teutoburg, with several groves sacred to the German gods situated in the forest. It must have seemed that those gods were smiling on the German enterprise, for the violent storm was in the Germans' favour, making conditions for the Roman column struggling over rain-soaked ground all the more trying and exhausting.

The participating tribes had been allocated their positions along Varus' route by Arminius, and told to await his signal to strike. The column came into sight, and slowly filled the defile opposite Arminius. According to Dio, the storm had broken the column into several straggling parties, so that various units were mixed up with the wagons and the non-combatants. This played right into Arminius' hands. He gave the signal for the assault to begin, and, with a roar, on both sides of the defile, Germans emerged from the trees to pelt the Romans with stones, slingshot and throwing spears, while other tribesmen ran to block both the way forward and the way back.

'At first they [the Germans] hurled their volleys from a distance,' said Dio. As missiles came at them from all directions, the Romans, completely taken by surprise, dumped their shoulder poles – which carried their supplies of javelins – and hurriedly raised shields to defend themselves against missiles. Many Romans were wounded by missiles in these early minutes of the attack. When the Germans found that the Romans were not returning fire with javelins, they moved in to launch their spears at closer range. The Romans, unable to assemble in regular formation, and 'being fewer at every point than their assailants, suffered greatly and could offer no resistance'. [Ibid.]

These were not inferior legions. Velleius Paterculus had served as a prefect of cavalry on campaign in Germany with the 17th, 18th and 19th legions. He considered them 'unexcelled in bravery, the first among Roman armies in discipline, in energy, and in experience in the field'. [Velle., II, CXIX] But for all their discipline, energy and experience, these legions were in desperate straits. Varus ordered a marching camp to be thrown up on the spot. 'After securing a suitable place, so far as that was possible on a wooded mountain', part of the army dug the walls and fosse of a camp while the remaining troops kept the Germans at bay. [Dio, LVI, 21]

At nightfall the tribesmen pulled back, and Varus and his bloodied troops, together with the terrified civilians, spent a sleepless night behind the camp walls.

The bell, stuffed with straw, found at the Kalkreise site, thought to be the location of Varus' last stand.

Varus seems to have been determined to keep pushing forward, convinced that he was needed further to the north. Perhaps the initial report of a German uprising had included the lie that Arminius was trapped, and Varus, unaware that Arminius was in fact leading the attack on him, was determined to save his young friend. He must have thought his attackers that day had been sent to prevent him relieving loyal troops to the north. Varus, a man of honour, was determined to fight his way through the hills and rescue his colleagues, just as he had rescued a legion under siege at Jerusalem a dozen years earlier.

As subsequent events were to indicate, Varus may have met opposition from some of his subordinates at a council of his officers that night, men who wanted to turn around and drive for the Rhine. But Varus would have none of it. He gave orders for most of the carts to be abandoned and burned, with everything that was not absolutely necessary to be left behind. This had the double advantage of reducing the load and of diverting the attention of Germans intent on plundering discarded Roman baggage. [Ibid.] It is probable, too, that Varus ordered the legions to depart before dawn, to surprise the enemy and to give the column a chance to be well on its way before the sun rose, for among the many items unearthed at Kalkreise was a bronze mule-bell, of the kind that hangs around the necks of pack mules even to this day, which was stuffed with straw to prevent it from ringing. [Wells, 3] A general intending to sneak out of his camp before dawn without alerting the enemy would have ensured his muleteers silenced the pack mules' bells.

Certainly Varus' troops were able to escape the hastily dug camp. 'The next day they advanced in a little better order, and even reached open country, although they did not get away without loss' as they pushed through the Germans stationed in their path. [Dio, LVI, 21] Behind them they had left the abandoned carts in flames, and these and the discarded baggage had attracted the attention of most of the tribesmen.

From Dio's narrative it seems that the Romans may have spent a day on the march before building another camp for the night. But once the Germans had gathered up their loot and hidden it away they gave chase, overtaking the Roman column on the third day.

As the column entered thick woodland again, the tribesmen resumed the attack in earnest. This time the Romans energetically defended themselves, only to take the heaviest casualties so far. 'Since they had to form their lines in a narrow space in order that the cavalry and infantry together might run down the enemy,' said Dio, 'they collided frequently with one another and with the trees.' The depleted, savaged army again laboured to build a marching camp for the night. [Ibid.]

Dio says that when the fourth day of the encounter dawned, Varus' exhausted men resumed the march, to be faced with a return of the rain that had made progress so difficult on the first day. Soaked by the downpour, the Roman troops were now buffeted by the wind. So strong was the gale, said Dio, that the Romans were unable to keep their feet, let alone launch their javelins or loose off their arrows. Their waterlogged shields, meanwhile, were almost too heavy to raise. By this time, too, Arminius' original bands had been reinforced by more Germans, 'as many of those who had at first wavered now joined them, largely in the hope of plunder'. Significantly outnumbered, the surviving men of the Roman column again found themselves completely surrounded by the Germans. [Ibid.]

Velleius says that, at the last, the column was 'hemmed in by forests and marshes and ambuscades'. [Velle., II, CXIX] If the Kalkreise site was indeed the location of Varus' last stand, its topography fits Velleius' description, for it combines forest and marsh. To the south rises the 350 feet high [106 metres] Kalkreise Hill. Thickly forested, on this day in September AD 9 the hill would have been seething with German tribesmen using the trees for cover. To the north there is marshland known as the Great Bog. Between the hill and the bog there is a stretch of dry, level ground, in the shape of an hourglass, which is half a mile wide [0.8 of a kilometre] at

A cavalry parade helmet of the kind described by Arrian. This one was found at Kalkreise, near Osnabrück in Germany, the likely site of the Varus disaster.

its narrowest point. Archaeologists say that this piece of land was sandy 2,000 years ago, and it was here that the largest concentration of Roman artefacts was found. [Wells, 3] Varus' army, it would seem, was trapped here between the hill and the marsh as it tried to make its way to the northeast.

At this point, with the way ahead blocked by more tribesmen arriving from the north, Varus gave orders for a new camp to be built on the spot. Some legionaries withdrew from the fighting to commence building a camp wall, which would run along the bottom of the hill to give the Romans some protection from the Germans on the slope.

Some modern authors have surmised that this wall was in fact built by the Germans for offensive purposes, but this is unlikely. The Germans had spent several days pursuing the Romans from the last battle site, and it is improbable that they would have prepared a position several days' march north of the original ambush location, especially when there is no record of them building a wall at the original site. Secondly, it makes no sense for the Germans to build a wall that could prove of more use to the Romans, who were in the open, than to the Germans, who already had the cover of the trees. As before, Varus ordered a marching camp to be erected when further forward progress proved impossible. But the construction work could not have been undertaken in more difficult circumstances.

At this point, one of Varus' cavalry officers decided to try to make a break for the east. Vala Numonius, the prefect of horse, may have argued earlier for an attempted breakout for the Rhine, only to be overruled by his general. Now, Numonius 'tried to reach the Rhine with his squadrons of horse'. In doing so, said Velleius, Numonius 'set a fearful example in that he left the infantry unprotected by the cavalry'. But Numonius and his cavalry did not get far. 'He did not survive those whom he abandoned, for he died in the act of deserting them.' Overwhelmed by mounted Germans and warriors on foot, Numonius and his troopers died some little way to the east of the main battle site. [Velle., II, CXIX]

As the thinning ranks of legionaries assigned to digging hacked out a shallow ditch and threw up a wall 5 feet (1.5 metres) high, 15 feet (4.5 metres) thick at the base, and at least 700 yards (640 metres) long, at the bottom of the hill, a few surviving pack animals were herded up against the earth bank, to take advantage of the slight protection it offered. This was as much of the camp as the embattled legions were able to build. Varus, meanwhile, abandoned by his cavalry and with many of his soldiers dead or wounded, tried to organize the defence. But then he, too, was wounded, apparently by a spear. His bodyguards moved him to another part of the field; perhaps closer to the wall. The Germans either mounted a rush down the slope against the wall, or actively undermined it, for the wall collapsed at one point, burying a pack mule. The mule's skeleton was discovered by archaeologists in the 1990s. [Wells, 3]

With a victorious roar, warriors of the Bructeri tribe carried off the 19th Legion's eagle, leaving its standard-bearer and numerous other 1st cohort defenders piled dead on the field. Before long, the Cauchi and the Marsi seized the eagles of the 17th and 18th legions. The wounded Varus could see that many surviving officers were also wounded. Clearly, the battle was lost. Emulating his father and his grandfather, who had both taken their own lives in times past, 'he ran himself through with his sword'. [Velle., II, CXIX]

It seems that the general's staff then attempted to burn his body so that it did not fall into enemy hands; they were not wholly successful, for a little later his corpse was found to be 'partially burned'. One of the two camp-prefects, Lucius Eggius, now followed his general's example and also committed suicide. [Ibid.]

When news of Varus' death spread among the surviving Roman troops, some officers and enlisted men also took their own lives. Others cast aside their shields and weapons and invited the Germans to kill them, which the tribesmen were happy to do. [Dio, LVI, 22] After the death of the general, and with much of the Roman army fallen, the surviving camp-prefect, Ceionius, proposed to surrender what remained of the army. This was an action despised by Velleius Paterculus, for surrender, in the view of most Romans, was dishonourable. Besides, Velleius could not understand why Ceionius preferred 'to die by torture at the hands of the enemy than in battle'. [Velle., II, CXIX]

Arminius, receiving Ceionius' surrender offer, called on his countrymen to stay their weapons. The command spread, and across the battlefield the fighting came to a halt and the din of battle subsided. Only the groans of the wounded could be heard, as all eyes turned to Arminius. Perhaps several hundred Romans still lived; on Ceionius' command, they threw down their weapons. Heavy chains were brought out by the Germans and the prisoners bound.

The centurions and thin-stripe tribunes were separated from their men, then thrust into the pits which the rank and file had been forced to dig. Realizing that the

Germans planned painful deaths for them, junior tribune Caldus Caelius, 'a young man worthy in every way of a long line of ancestors', according to Velleius, took a section of the chain with which he was bound and crashed it down on his skull with all his might, causing his instant death; with 'both his brains and his blood gushing from the wound'. [Velle., II, CXX]

The son of Segimerus looked down at the body of Quintilius Varus, which had been partly disfigured by the botched attempt to burn it. The general's expensive armour and fittings had been ripped from his corpse, his gold-decorated helmet taken as a souvenir. Tacitus says that the young Chattian insulted the body. [Tac., *A*, 1, 71] Perhaps this was merely with a kick; more gruesomely, perhaps he attacked the general's corpse with a knife and gouged out his eyes; or perhaps it was that time-honoured insult – urinating on the body. A warrior soon stepped up and swung a blade, severing the head from Varus' body. That head was raised on the point of a spear. Tens of thousands of German tribesmen roared their approval.

Arminius was to send Varus' head as a trophy to King Maroboduus of the Marcomanni tribe in Bohemia, which had not participated in the attack on Varus' army. Maroboduus then sent it to Augustus at Rome. Despite the disgrace that attended Varus' defeat, Augustus gave permission for Varus' head to be interred in the family vault outside Rome.

At the battle site, in the immediate wake of his victory, Arminius climbed on to a mound – perhaps the embankment built by the Romans troops. To a tumultuous reception from his warriors, he praised them for their courage, derided the defeated Romans, and spat on the captured Roman eagles and other standards. Heads were chopped from dead Roman officers' bodies and nailed to tree trunks. Junior centurions were crucified in front of their men. Thin-stripe tribunes and first-rank centurions were dragged away to nearby sacred groves. [Tac., *A*, 1, 61]

These groves were clearings in the forest sometimes surrounded by a high palisade. All had a central altar, and some also contained tables where religious feasts took place. In others, sacred white horses were kept. To avoid offending the gods, women and children and foreign speech were banned. Some tribes required their men to wash as an act of purification before entering their groves.

Julius Caesar had written that human sacrifice took place in the sacred groves of some Gallic tribes, with the victims placed inside giant wicker cages in the shape of a man. These cages were suspended over a fiery altar, where the victims were roasted alive. [Caes., *GW*, VI, 16] This, it seems, was how the last remaining officers of the 17th, 18th and 19th legions died – a slow, agonizing death, roasted like game on the spit. It is likely that the 18th Legion's first-rank centurion Caelius would, if he had survived to this point, have been one of those who perished in the flames with his colleagues.

The three legions would have started this campaigning season with fifteen thin-stripers, young officer cadets of 18 and 19 years of age, all of them members of the Equestrian Order and the sons of leading Roman families. Half a century later, the writer and philosopher Lucius Seneca, chief minister to the emperor Nero, was to write to a friend: 'Remember the Varus disaster? Many a man of the most distinguished ancestry, who was doing his military service as the first step on the road to

The Hermannsdenkmal, a massive nineteenth-century statue of Arminius in the Weser Hills near Osnabrück.

a seat in the Senate, was brought low by Fortune.' [Sen., *L*, XLVII]

After celebratory banqueting and thanks to their gods, the victorious Germans moved on. The spoils from the defeated Roman army were borne away, to be divided among the tribes. The eagles and standards of the annihilated legions were hung up in sacred groves across Germany. The legionary prisoners, chained and dragged away, became slaves of the Germans. The naked, butchered dead of three legions were left where they had fallen.

But there was more fighting to be done. For the Romans still occupied forts on German soil east of the Rhine. Tribesmen, buoyed by their victory in the Teutoburg Forest, swarmed west to deal with those invaders also.

AD 9

X. THE STRUGGLE AT FORT ALISO
Holding out against the Germans

Modern-day archaeologists have identified the locations of several Roman forts that existed east of the Rhine in AD 9. Most are on the Lippe river. Roman merchant vessels had used the Lippe to take trade into eastern Germany from west of the Rhine.

From nearest the Rhine to the east, those forts were at or near the present-day towns of Holsterhausen, Haltern, Beckinghausen, Oberaden and Anreppen. Traces of other, smaller Roman forts have been found further inland, at sites including Sparrenburger Egge, near Bielefeld, but these are thought to have been only marching camps. The permanent camps on the Lippe were extensive. The Roman fort at Haltern, for example, dating from around 5 BC, covered 47 acres (23 hectares) and contained facilities for a wing or more of cavalry. [Wells, 5, 11, & Illustr. 16]

Both Velleius and Dio wrote that the German tribes in revolt were able to surprise and overrun every one of those forts but one, apparently reducing them one at a time. Archaeological evidence at these fort sites indicates that Roman occupation indeed ceased in AD 9, with hordes of coins and other valuable material having been swiftly buried on the sites. There were also the bones of two dozen men found in a pit at the Haltern site, apparently tossed in there by the Germans after they took the fort. [Ibid.]

The lone fort holding out against the attacking Germans was named Aliso. Tacitus states that it was one of those on the Lippe, although he doesn't indicate its specific location. An altar in memory of Drusus Caesar had been erected at the fort, and it is possible that it was there that Drusus had died in 9 BC. With many present-day German place-names preserving the first letter or sound of the original Latin name, it is tempting to suspect that Aliso was either the fort at Anreppen or the one at Oberaden – literally, 'Above Aden'. [Velle., *RH*, 11, CX; Tac., *A*, 11, 7]

While no classical author gives the precise location of the Aliso fort, Velleius identifies its commander, Lucius Caedicius, who was camp-prefect of one of the three legions that had by this point been wiped out in the Teutoburg Forest. Fortune had spared camp-prefect Caedicius from the horrors of the Teutoburg, but now he faced his own dice with death. Fort Aliso was besieged by 'an immense force of Germans', says Velleius. [Velle., 11, CXX]

But the tribesmen 'found themselves unable to reduce this fort,' said Dio, 'because they did not understand the conduct of sieges'. Camp-prefect Caedicius received sufficient warning of the revolt to close his fort gates in time. He was also fortunate to have a cohort of archers stationed at the fort, and they 'repeatedly repulsed' the German attackers 'and destroyed large numbers of them'. [Dio, LVI, 22]

The Germans surrounded the fort and settled in to starve the Romans into submission. But this delay worked in Rome's favour. Lucius Asprenas, Varus' nephew and Roman commander on the Upper Rhine, having heard of the uprising, possibly as a result of the warning from Boiocaulus, came rushing down from Upper Germany to Vetera with his two legions. Velleius was full of praise for Asprenas' swift reaction. Asprenas' arrival on the Lower Rhine, he said, strengthened the allegiance of the locals west of the Rhine, 'who were beginning to waver'. [Velle., II, CXX]

Dio says that, after maintaining the siege of Aliso for some weeks, Arminius' warriors came to hear that 'the Romans had posted a guard [Asprenas' legions] at the Rhine and that Tiberius was approaching with an imposing army'. This was enough to frighten off some tribesmen, who pulled out of the siege and returned home. If Arminius had planned to cross the Rhine and invade Gaul – and there is no indication that this was on his agenda – he no longer had the manpower or momentum to mount such an operation. He therefore left a detachment of tribesmen guarding the roads leading to the Rhine at 'a considerable distance' from Fort Aliso, 'hoping to capture the Roman garrison' after it emerged due to 'the failure of their provisions'. [Dio, LVI, 22]

Velleius reported that the garrison at Aliso did indeed end up suffering 'difficulties which want [of supplies] rendered unendurable'. Camp-prefect Caedicius was not only having to supply the troops of his garrison, he had many other mouths to feed, for the fort was also crowded with civilians – women and children associated with the men of the garrison, who had been living near the fort, as well as camp followers who had withdrawn from Varus' column when he had turned north for the Teutoburg several weeks earlier. [Velle., II, CXX]

While they had provisions, Caedicius and his multitude, pent up at Aliso, waited for relief to come from west of the Rhine. But as the weeks passed and the weather became wintry, their provisions dwindled to nothing. Unbeknownst to Caedicius, Asprenas had taken the decision not to cross the Rhine, so no Roman relief force was going to appear on the scene. Caedicius decided to break out and make a run for the Rhine, but his would not be a blind charge west. Following his orders, Caedicius' scouts sneaked from the fort and discreetly observed the Germans camped between Aliso and the Rhine, noting their dispositions and their guard routines. Now Caedicius and his troops 'watched their chance'. That chance, said Dio, came with a stormy night. [Velle., II, CXX; Dio, LVI, 22]

It would have been a bleak November night as the storm raged along the Lippe valley. Knowing the Germans would be keeping under cover, Caedicius and the occupants of Fort Aliso crept from the fort and made their way through the darkness. 'The soldiers were few, the unarmed many.' Caedicius and his troops led the way, prepared to fight if they had to, but hoping to sneak by the tribesmen. Hundreds, and perhaps thousands, of women and children fearfully trailed along behind, shivering in the icy conditions as the storm raged about them, toting everything of value they could carry as they strove to keep up with the soldiers. [Ibid.]

'They succeeded in getting past the foes' first and second outposts,' said Dio. But by the time they reached the third and last outpost, the column was well strung out, and the civilians, cold, exhausted and afraid, had lost contact with the soldiers leading the way. Women and children panicked, and began calling out to the troops to come back for them – calls which the German sentries heard in the night. [Ibid.]

Caedicius and his troops now had to fight their way through the alerted enemy. They cut down the first Germans they encountered, but tribesmen were coming from everywhere behind them. Caedicius had to think fast. He ordered the civilians to drop what they were carrying and run for it. At the same time, he sent his trumpeters ahead and had them sound the signal for his troops to hurry forward at a double-quick march. The Germans, already distracted by the plunder they found discarded by the civilians, thought the trumpets were being sounded by Roman relief units sent by Asprenas, and gave up the pursuit. Some civilians were killed or captured by the Germans, but 'the most hardy' managed to escape, [Ibid.] as did Caedicius and his men, who 'with the sword won their way back to their friends'. [Velle., II, CXX]

At Vetera, Asprenas, learning that Roman fugitives were making their way towards the Rhine, sent troops across to their assistance, and Caedicius and his party accordingly reached the safety of the western bank of the Rhine. [Dio, LVI, 22] Behind them, the Germans destroyed Fort Aliso. This was the final act of Arminius' uprising. It had achieved its objective – there was no longer a Roman military presence east of the Rhine.

AD 9

THE REACTION AT ROME
Panic and grief

The emperor Augustus was devastated by the news of what became known as the Varus disaster when he heard of it in October AD 9. He let his hair grow and failed to shave for months, mourning the lost legions as if they were his children. Suetonius says that he was often heard to cry, 'Quintilius Varus, give me back my legions!' [Suet., II, 23] Eighteenth-century historian Edward Gibbon was to remark: 'Augustus did not receive the melancholy news with all the temper and firmness that might have been expected from his character.' [Gibb., n. I, 1.3]

The immediate dread in Rome was that Arminius and his Germans would flood over the Rhine, sweep down through Gaul, and ravage Italy. Suetonius says the emperor immediately ordered patrols of the city at night to prevent any rising of the populace. He also prolonged the terms of all his provincial governors, so that Rome's allies would have men they knew and trusted in places of power. And, suddenly mistrusting Germans, he temporarily disbanded his bodyguard, the German Guard. [Suet., II, 23; 49]

Augustus also ordered special cohorts of slaves levied at Rome, and sent them to Germany. 'The Roman bank of the Rhine had to be held in force.' Recruited as slaves from the households of well-to-do men and women, these men were officially given their freedom once they joined their cohorts. These special units of freedmen were euphemistically called 'Volunteer' cohorts, because the slave owners were forced to volunteer their services. On Augustus' express orders, the members of these special units were not permitted 'to associate with soldiers of free birth or to carry arms of standard pattern'. [Ibid., 25]

As these Volunteer cohorts marched to the Rhine, six of the legions and numerous auxiliary units that had been fighting in Dalmatia, where the Pannonian War had ended just five days before the Varus disaster in Germany, were heading in the same direction. But under no circumstances would Augustus permit his legions to cross the Rhine. The river was now the empire's borderline.

Augustus did not raise new legion enlistments to replace the Teutoburg dead. He retired the shamed numbers of the destroyed legions, the 17th, 18th and 19th, and

The memorial to Centurion Marcus Caelius of the 18th Legion, and his two freedmen, who perished in the ambush of Varus' legions in Germany. It was erected by Caelius' brother beside the Rhine, with the request that if his bones were ever found they be laid to rest there.

left the Roman army numbering twenty-five legions. The Varus disaster was a stinging blow to Roman pride that ranked with Marcus Crassus' 53 BC defeat at Carrhae. The September day in AD 9 that General Varus' three legions ceased to exist would never be forgotten by Romans. It was as if the defeat, and the loss of the sacred eagles of the legions, scarred the national soul.

At Vetera, a stone monument 54 inches (137 centimetres) high was raised to Centurion Marcus Caelius of the 18th Legion by his brother. The monument, which survives to this day, shows Caelius, looking fierce, adorned with all his military decorations and holding his centurion's vine stick, the symbol of his authority. On either side of Caelius are his two servants, Privatus and Thiaminus. Both carry Caelius' name, indicating that they had become freedmen. In all probability they too perished at the Teutoburg, with thousands of other civilians in Varus' train.

The monument's inscription, after giving the details of the centurion's life, asked that, should Marcus Caelius' bones ever be found, they be deposited there, at the monument. But Caelius' whitening bones lay across the Rhine, on a silent, deserted battlefield in the Teutoburg Forest, indistinguishable from those of thousands of his fellow soldiers who had also been left to rot by the victors of the battle. Caelius' monument and his bones would never be united.

AD 14–15

XI. INVADING GERMANY
Germanicus versus Arminius

Ever since the disaster in the Teutoburg Forest, Romans had thirsted for revenge – for the loss of Varus' three legions, for the loss of Rome's foothold east of the Rhine, and for the loss of Roman prestige which the defeat by Arminius and the German tribes had represented. In AD 14, almost by accident, the Roman military was given the excuse and the opportunity to take that revenge.

Augustus, who had refused to send any more military expeditions across the Rhine following the Varus disaster, died in August AD 14, after reigning since 30 BC. Several years before, Augustus had extended the enlistments of all legionaries from sixteen to twenty years. In the atmosphere of uncertainty that followed the emperor's death, with his stepson Tiberius not immediately claiming the throne, the extended enlistments and numerous other complaints about service conditions sparked discontent that spread through the legions and ignited the mutinies. In the wake of

The circular Mausoleum of Augustus today. In AD 14, when Augustus' remains were interred there, next to those of his stepson Drusus, the mausoleum was topped by a hill planted with cyprus trees.

Augustus' death, mutinies broke out among the three legions stationed in Dalmatia and the eight legions on the Rhine.

The Dalmatian legions were soon brought to heel by Tiberius' son Drusus and Praetorian prefect Sejanus, who led elements of the Praetorian Guard and German Guard to Dalmatia where they executed ringleaders. In command on the Rhine was Drusus' dashing 28-year-old adoptive brother Germanicus Caesar, brother of Claudius, father of Caligula, and the grandfather of Nero. He himself was heir apparent to the Roman throne. Germanicus was collecting taxes in Gaul when his legions mutinied. Hurrying first to the army of the Lower Rhine at the city that became Cologne, he settled their grievances, then did the same with the the army of the Upper Rhine at Mogontiacum (Mainz). But when discontent flared again at Mogontiacum, Germanicus' general Aulus Caecina had loyal legionaries cut the troublemakers to pieces. 'This was destruction rather than remedy,' Germanicus lamented. So, to distract his troops, he launched a lightning campaign east of the Rhine. [Tac., A, 1, 49]

In October, Germanicus led 12,000 men from four legions, twenty-six allied cohorts, and eight wings of cavalry into the territory of the Marsi, between the Lippe and Ruhr rivers. Surprising and wiping out Marsi warriors while they were celebrating their festival of their goddess Tamfana, Germanicus advanced across a broad front for 50 miles (80 kilometres), destroying every village and every living thing in his path. As he turned his army around and marched back towards the Rhine, Germans from the Bructeri, the Tubantes, and the Usipetes tribes overtook him, but were beaten off the Roman column's tail by the 20th Legion, acting as rearguard. A day later, the column crossed back to the western side of the Rhine. The Senate voted Germanicus a Triumph for his success. But he had only just begun.

During the winter of AD 14/15, all eight of Germanicus' Rhine legions prepared for a massive spring offensive in Germany. But when news reached Germanicus that Arminius was clashing with his father-in-law Segestes, king of the Chatti tribe, he seized the opportunity to split the German confederation by striking before the winter had ended. From Mogontiacum, Germanicus led the four AUR (Army of the Upper Rhine) legions and their auxiliary support across the river and into the Chatti homeland. At the same time, Caecina led his four legions of the Lower Rhine army across the Rhine at Vetera, via a bridge of boats.

With this offensive taking the Germans completely by surprise, Germanicus made a rapid advance as far as the River Eder. After burning Mattium, the Chatti capital,

The German Wars AD 6–16

NORTH SEA

CHAUCI

R. Elbe

Zeider Zee

FRISI

AMPSIVARII

ANGRIVARI

Traiectum
(Utrecht)

USIPETES

✕ Angrivar
Barrier
AD 16

✕ Teutoburg
Forest
AD 9

CHERUSCI

BATAVI CANNINEFATES

Noviomagus
(Nijmegen)

Fort Aliso

✕ Idistavisus
AD 16

Vetera
(Xanten) R. Lippe

✕ Long
Bridges
AD 15

Novaesium
(Neuss)

BRUCTERI

R. Weser

N

Cologne

Bonna
(Bonn)

SUGAMBRI

R. Rhine

LOWER
GERMANY

Confluentes
(Coblenz)

CHATTI

Mogontiacum
(Mainz)

GERMANIA

Augusta Treverorum
(Trier)

MARCOMANNI

Dividorum
(Metz)

R. Rhine

R. Neckar

R. Altmuhl

Castra
Regina
(Regensburg)

Argentoratum
(Strasbourg)

R. Danube

0   100 km

0   100 miles

Augusta
Vindelicum
(Augsberg)

he turned for the Rhine. Caecina's army covered his withdrawal, colliding with the Cherusci and Marsi tribes, who hurried down from the north in support of the Chatti.

As Germanicus withdrew, his aid was sought by the son of the Chatti king. Segestes wanted to return to the Roman fold, and offered Thusnelda, his daughter and the pregnant wife of Arminius, as prize. But Segestes was surrounded and besieged by Arminius' Cheruscans at a stronghold in the hills. Germanicus marched to the stronghold and drove off the Cherusci, then was able to return to the western side of the Rhine with the king of the Chatti and Arminius' wife. Thusnelda was sent to Italy and confined at Ravenna. (Her sister-in-law, the Chattian wife of Arminius' brother Flavus, also lived at Ravenna, with her son Italicus.)

Not content with this success, Germanicus launched a full-scale offensive in the summer, involving a three-pronged attack. In the first stage, Germanicus took a fleet of ships from Traiectum, today's Utrecht in Holland, across the Zeider Zee and into the North Sea. He then sailed along the Frisian coast, turning up the River Ems, the Roman Amisia, retracing a route followed by his father Drusus Caesar in 12 BC and Tiberius in AD 5. Meanwhile, Albinovanus Pedo led a diversionary cavalry operation in the Frisian area of Holland and northwest Germany. At the same time, Caecina crossed the Rhine from Vetera yet again, then marched his four army of the Lower Rhine legions northeast, heading for the Ems. All three forces linked up beside the river; Germanicus had brought together close to 80,000 men deep inside German territory.

From here, Germanicus sent Lucius Stertinius with 4,000 cavalry to sweep through the homeland of the Bructeri, routing every German band that stood in their path. In one village, Stertinius' troopers recovered the sacred golden eagle of the 19th Legion taken by the Bructeri during the Teutoburg massacre. At the same time, Germanicus marched the legions to the Teutoburg Forest, site of the Varus disaster, where they found, lying on the ground, the whitening bones of thousands of Roman legionaries. Skulls were nailed to tree trunks. They found the pits where Roman prisoners had been temporarily held, and, in adjacent groves, altars where the junior tribunes and first-rank centurions had been burned alive as offerings to the German gods. There, 'in grief and anger', Germanicus' men buried the bones of Varus' legionaries, with 'not a soldier knowing whether he was interring the remains of a relative or a stranger'. [Tac., A, 1, 62]

Germanicus' legions marched on, linking up with Stertinius and the cavalry and dispersing harassing German bands. On the bank of the Lippe, Germanicus rebuilt Fort Aliso, possibly because it was there that his father had died, and garrisoned it with auxiliaries. On reaching the Ems, Germanicus and the Upper Rhine legions boarded the waiting fleet, and Pedo's cavalry set off to retrace their path via the Frisian coast. Caecina turned for the Rhine with the 1st, 5th Alaudae, 20th and 21st Rapax legions. On Germanicus' orders, Caecina was to follow a long-neglected overland route to the Rhine. It was called Long Bridges.

XII. BATTLE OF LONG BRIDGES
How the 1st Germanica Legion made its name

As the summer of AD 15 ebbed away, Germanicus Caesar was withdrawing his Roman army from Germany after a successful campaign. While Germanicus' division was returning to Holland by sea, and Albinovanus Pedo was leading the cavalry back via Frisia, Aulus Caecina, commanding general of the Army of the Upper Rhine, was leading the 1st, 5th Alaudae, 20th and 21st Rapax legions along the route called Pontem Longus, or Long Bridges.

This causeway had been built through a marshy valley by Lucius Domitius during his campaigns in Germany between 7 BC and AD 1. Long Bridges provided the shortest route to the Rhine, but Germanicus knew this road was narrow and frequently flanked by muddy quagmires, making it an ideal place for an ambush, so in sending Caecina this way he had urged his deputy to make all speed through the region.

Arminius, the long-haired, 33-year-old German leader, also knew all about Long Bridges. When he saw the route that Caecina's four legions were taking, he hurried his Cherusci warriors around the Romans, whose progress was limited to the speed of their baggage train, and occupied the wooded hills around Long Bridges. Caecina reached the valley, and saw the raised roadway stretching towards the west, but on close inspection he found that many of the bridges built by Domitius so many years before had been washed away or were in such bad repair that it would be impossible to send the pack animals or baggage vehicles across them.

It was too late to turn back. Caecina was a general with four decades of military experience. He knew that behind him lay all the massing tribes of Germany, and ahead, the Rhine and safety. Described as 'perfectly fearless' by Tacitus, Caecina divided his force into two groups, one to carry out road and bridgeworks, the other to defend the workers. He built a camp on the road, set up outposts and sent his work parties ahead. [Tac., *A*, 1, 64]

Now Arminius struck. Germans swooped down from the trees in their thousands. This was their home territory; and they negotiated the swampland with ease. They harried the work parties with their massive spears, they attacked the outposts with showers of javelins. The legionaries fought them off all day, slipping in the mud and splashing into the water, struggling under the weight of their armoured mail, cursing, calling for help from comrades when sucking mud or Germans threatened to end their days. Respite finally came when darkness fell and the Germans withdrew to the hills.

But Arminius and his Cheruscans did not waste this time. Through the night they worked, digging in the hills to divert the course of streams so that torrents of water swept down into the valley and washed away the bridgeworks the Romans had laboured to build that day. Next morning, the legionaries had to start from scratch. Under attack again, they rebuilt all day, until Caecina felt he could reach a distant plain between the marsh and the hills. At the end of the day, he gave the order to break camp at dawn and resume the march.

Through the night, the Germans all around them sang guttural songs or let out terrifying shouts to intimidate the Romans. The unsettled legionaries slept fitfully, many rising up and wandering from campfire to campfire to talk with comrades into the early morning hours. Even their general's sleep was troubled; Tacitus says Caecina awoke in a cold sweat after a nightmare in which he'd seen General Varus rising out of the swamps, covered in blood, extending his hand and beckoning to him. [Ibid., 65]

At daybreak, with the army's baggage train in the middle, the 1st Legion took the lead, the 5th Alaudae the right wing, the 21st Rapax the left, and the 20th brought up the rear. For a time, the advance went according to plan. But eventually the legions on the wings tired of floundering through mud and water. Flouting Caecina's orders, the 5th and 21st pressed on ahead to dry land, leaving the column struggling along the road loaded down with wounded, and exposed on the flanks.

Worse still, the hastily improvised bridgeworks proved inadequate. Carts slipped from the road and became trapped in the bog, blocking the way. Legionaries from the 20th in the rear of the column broke ranks and hurried up to try to help heave the carts free, anxious that they were going to be cut off there on the causeway. Centurions in the ranks who had survived the Teutoburg debacle saw that history could well repeat itself, as chaos loomed and invited disaster.

Arminius was watching from the hills. 'Behold, a Varus!' he said to his men, 'and legions entangled in Varus' fate!' [Ibid.]

With a roar, the Germans charged from the tree line. Arminius struck at the middle of the column, where the baggage carts were struggling, knowing that thoughts of plunder would drive his tribesmen on. It would also serve the tactical purposes of the Roman-trained German commander to cut the column at its centre. Roman cavalry attempted to intercept the Germans before they reached the baggage, but, using their long spears, the tribesmen pierced the undersides of the horses. Panicking steeds threw their riders then galloped through the legionary ranks, adding to the confusion.

As Arminius succeeded in splitting the column in two, Gaius Caetronius, legate of the 1st Legion, turned from where he had been leading the column along the causeway, and brought several cohorts of the 1st to the defence of the baggage train. From the other direction, men of the 20th pressed forward from the rear to do the same. The battle raged, on the raised roadway and in the mud and water all around it, with fierce yells, screams of pain, the neighing of horses and the bellowed commands of centurions trying to keep their units intact. The fighting around the golden birds of the 1st and 20th proved the most violent of all, with the eagle-bearers unable to either speed their standards away from danger or plant them in the soggy ground and use their freed hands to defend their eagles.

General Caecina, in the thick of it all, lost his horse from under him, pierced by German javelins, and was thrown to the ground. Before the tribesmen could rush the downed commander, men of the 1st Legion quickly closed ranks around him as, dazed, he dragged himself to his feet. Fighting with grim determination and pride, the men of the 1st fought off the attackers. When Caecina saw more and more Germans turning from the fighting to plunder the baggage carts and pack mules, he gave orders for the baggage to be abandoned.

This was the only reason the 1st and 20th legions reached the 5th Alaudae and 21st Rapax on dry land by nightfall. The latter two legions had spent their time constructively, building a new camp while the others had been fighting for their lives, so they all had protection for the night. But the men who struggled in through the camp gate in the twilight, covered in blood, sweat and mud, and helping their wounded comrades make their way, would have been hugely unimpressed that the other two legions had deserted them. With few rations between them, and with their tents abandoned back at the causeway, they ate food soiled with mud and blood, and slept under the stars as, in the hills, the Germans sang to celebrate the taking of Roman booty that day.

In the middle of the night, there was sudden alarm in the Roman camp. Legionaries ran around crying that Germans were in the camp. Grabbing their weapons, and determined not to be trapped inside the walls, hundreds of men rushed to the camp's decuman gate, which faced away from the Germans, demanding that it be opened. Caecina pushed through the mob, stood in their way, and ordered the men back to their beds, assuring them a horse had merely broken loose and run wild in the camp. When his men would not believe him, he drew his sword and cast determined eyes around the grim faces. The gate, he declared, stayed closed. When the troops persisted, he told them they would only pass over his dead body. [Ibid., 66]

This checked the men long enough for the tribunes and centurions to reach them. The officers were able to convince the men that there were no Germans in the camp, and the legionaries guiltily melted away. Caecina then called a council of war with all his officers, at his praetorium. There, in the early hours of the morning, Caecina discussed a desperate plan. His officers went away determined to make the plan work, and in the darkness, centurions moved among their men, taking aside legionaries who could ride, giving them special instructions.

In the hills, Arminius and his chieftains were also in conference. Arminius counselled letting the Romans leave their camp in the morning and resume the march for the Rhine. Once the legionaries were in the open and clear of the camp, he said, the Cheruscans could wipe them out. But Arminius' uncle Inguiomerus did not want to give the Romans a chance to escape. He was all for attacking their camp at dawn and overrunning it. Other chiefs concurred. So Arminius, outvoted, agreed to lead a dawn attack on the Roman camp. [Ibid., 68]

At daybreak, the Germans swarmed out of the trees and surrounded the camp. Filling in the trench around the camp walls with hurdles woven from tree branches, the Cheruscans crossed the ditch and assailed the walls. The Roman defenders on one wall seemed to be paralysed by fear. Led by Arminius and Inguiomerus, Germans flooded over the ramparts and into the camp, then gleefully headed for the remnants of the baggage train. Now Roman trumpets sounded. The ramparts behind the Germans suddenly filled with legionaries who repelled other tribesmen still trying to climb the wall and enter the camp.

Mounted soldiers suddenly galloped around behind the Germans; all the Roman officers had given up their horses to the fighting men and combined them with their surviving cavalry. The horsemen charged into Arminius and his followers with javelins pumping and swords flailing. Now, the Germans only wanted to escape over the walls. 'Arminius and Inguiomerus fled from the battle, the first unhurt, the other severely wounded,' Tacitus was to write. Some of their men managed to escape the camp with them, but many more died in the trap. [Ibid.]

Now the camp gates opened and the legions came sweeping out in formation against the Germans outside the camp, who were 'slaughtered as long as our fury and the light of day lasted,' said Tacitus. Caecina's legionaries, though suffering from wounds and lack of rations, 'found strength, healing, sustenance, indeed everything, in their victory'. [Ibid.]

First-century tombstone from Bonn on the Rhine of Publius Clodius, a soldier of the 1st 'Germanica' Legion who may well have fought at Long Bridges.

When Caecina's four legions finally reached the Rhine, bloodied, filthy, hungry and exhausted, they came without their baggage and carrying severely wounded comrades on hastily improvised litters. They found Germanicus Caesar's wife Agrippina waiting for them at Vetera's bridge of boats. Agrippina had forbidden the bridge's destruction when, with Caecina's army overdue and feared lost, the Roman commander at Vetera had wanted to dismantle it to prevent Arminius using it. With her 2-year-old son Caligula at her side, Agrippina handed out coins, clothing and medicine to the returning men.

Following this campaign, the 1st Legion adopted the title 'Germanica'. It was the only one of the eight Rhine legions to do so. Without doubt, this was taken by the 1st, or bestowed on it by Germanicus, for repulsing the Germans at Long Bridges, and most particularly for stoutly defending their general Aulus Caecina in that battle.

AD 16
XIII. BATTLE OF IDISTAVISUS
Defeating Arminius

'It was a great victory, and without bloodshed to us.'
TACITUS, *The Annals*, II, 18

It was the summer of AD 16, and Germanicus Caesar had used a fleet of 1,000 newly built ships to return to the heart of Germany in search of Arminius and his German allies. At mid morning, the Roman army came marching down beside the Weser river from where it had camped for the night. With a small force left at the camp to guard the baggage, the legions were marching in battle order.

This time, the Germans were not only ready for Germanicus, but their leader had chosen the location for a decisive battle, and had sent men posing as defectors to lure the Romans into a trap, in the same way that he had lured Varus into a trap seven years before. The chosen place, called Idistavisus by the Romans, was just east of the Weser on a rolling river plain between ranges of low hills. The so-called Great Forest ran along the eastern fringe of the plain, with grassland extending for 2 miles (3.2 kilometres) over low hillocks from the trees to the Weser. Fifty thousand German tribesmen stood waiting on the grass, massed in their tribes and clans, their ranks extending from the forest to the river. [Warry, WCW]

In addition to Arminius and his Cherusci, tribes represented are likely to have included Arpus and his Chatti; Mallovendus and the remnants of the Marsi, plus the Fosi, Usipetes, Tubantes and Bructeri; the Cauchi, who had captured one of Varus' eagles, were probably present, along with young men of the Angrivarii – in defiance of their tribe's latest treaty with Rome; and Tencteri and Mattiaci from the Rhineland opposite Cologne, as well as Langobardi and Ampsivarii from along the Weser and Hunte rivers.

As the Roman army rounded the river bend and met the sight of the waiting German horde, Germanicus, riding in the middle of the column, calmly gave orders for his units to deploy. To the 28,000 men of his eight under-strength legions he had added the 2,000 men of two Praetorian Guard cohorts sent to him from Rome by Tiberius. It was unique for Praetorians to fight in a field army when the emperor was not present. Their presence had more to do with Tiberius' unfounded fear of his adopted son using his legions to topple him from the throne than from a genuine desire to help Germanicus.

In addition, the Roman army of 74,000 men included 30,000 auxiliaries from Gaul, Raetia, Batavia, Spain and Syria, 6,000 men from allied German tribes, and 8,000 cavalry including 2,000 mounted horse archers. One of Germanicus' German auxiliary cohort commanders was none other than Flavus, brother of Arminius. Germanicus was not concerned at seeing the Germans waiting for him – the tribesmen sent to lure him here had confessed that Arminius planned to entrap him, telling of the Germans' location and numbers. [Tac., *A*, 11, 16]

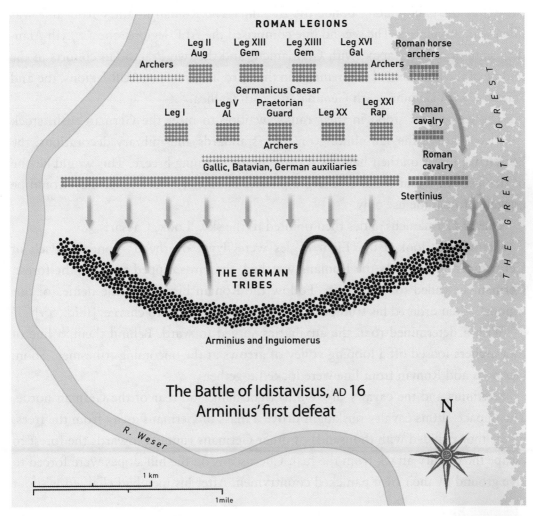

The Battle of Idistavisus, AD 16
Arminius' first defeat

Germanicus was also confident of the morale of his legionaries. In the days leading up to the battle, a German had ridden to the Roman camp ramparts in the night and called out that Arminius would reward every Roman who changed sides, with a German wife, a plot of land, and 100 sesterces a day while the war lasted. Germanicus had heard one of his men yell back, 'Let daylight come, let battle be given! Then we'll *take* your land, and *carry off* your wives!' [Ibid., 13]

As the Roman infantry spread with drilled precision in three battle lines, German tribesmen with massive spears up to 12 feet (3.6 metres) long began spilling down the slopes towards them. Germanicus turned to Lucius Stertinius, and ordered him to execute a prearranged cavalry manoeuvre; the general rode off and led the Roman cavalry at the gallop along beside the tree line. The Roman infantry front line was filled with auxiliaries. The second line comprised the ALR legions: the 1st, 5th Alaudae, 20th and 21st Rapax, with Germanicus and the two Praetorian cohorts in the middle of the line. Behind Germanicus in the third line were the AUR legions, the 2nd Augusta, 13th Gemina, 14th Gemina and 16th Gallica.

The legionaries stood in their ranks, waiting to meet the German rush, stock still, like statues, the sun glinting on their standards and military decorations, the horsehair plumes on their helmets wafting in the morning breeze. This would be one of the last times that legionaries wore plumes in battle; before long, they would be relegated to parade use only.

One of Germanicus' aides then pointed to the sky. 'Look, Caesar!'

Germanicus looked up. Eight eagles were flying overhead – one for each of Germanicus' legions. As the Romans watched, the birds dipped towards the forest. Germanicus called to his troops: 'Follow the Roman birds, the true deities of our legions!', then ordered his trumpeter to signal the front line to charge. [Ibid., 17]

With a determined roar, the auxiliaries surged forward. Behind them, a line of foot archers loosed off a looping volley of arrows at the oncoming tribesmen. Soon, Germans and Roman front line were locked together.

Stertinius and the cavalry drove into right flank and rear of the German horde. The impact of this cavalry onslaught drove a mass of Germans away from the trees, where they collided with thousands of other Germans running towards the forest to escape the cavalry attack from the rear. Cheruscans on the hill slopes were forced to give ground by their own panicked countrymen. After his men had charged without waiting for his orders, Arminius, on horseback, had been forced to join them. In the midst of the fighting, he was soon wounded.

Realizing that the day was already lost, Arminius smeared his face with his own blood to disguise his identity, urged his horse forward, and with his long hair flying, headed towards the Roman left wing, by the trees, which was occupied by Chauci Germans from the North Sea coast. These men had fought alongside Arminius in the Teutoburg, but had since allied themselves with Germanicus. Tacitus was to write: 'Some have said that he was recognized by Chauci serving among the Roman auxiliaries, who let him go.' [Ibid.]

Arminius escaped into the forest, and kept riding, as, behind him, Germanicus sent his legions into the fight. The struggle between 128,000 men went on for hours. 'From nine in the morning until nightfall the enemy were slaughtered,' said Tacitus, 'and ten miles were covered with arms and dead bodies.' Arminius' army was routed. 'It was a great victory, and without bloodshed to us,' Tacitus declared. But Arminius himself was still at large. [Ibid., 18]

AD 16–17
XIV. BATTLE OF THE ANGRIVAR BARRIER
No prisoners, no mercy

After the bloody defeat of Idistavisus, Arminius was determined to have his revenge on Germanicus and his legions. In years past, when the Angrivari tribe was at war with the Cherusci, they had built a massive earth barrier to separate the tribes. The Weser river ran along one side of the Angrivar barrier; marshland extended behind it. A small plain ran from the barrier to forested hills. It was here at the barrier that Arminius planned to defeat Germanicus Caesar.

Word reached Germanicus that Arminius and his allies were regrouping at the barrier and receiving thousands of reinforcements. From a German deserter, Germanicus also learned that Arminius had set another trap for him, hoping to lure the Romans to the barrier. Arminius would be waiting in the forest with cavalry, and would emerge behind Germanicus as he attacked the barrier, to destroy him from the rear. Armed with that intelligence, Germanicus made his own plans. Sending his cavalry to deal with Arminius in the forest, he advanced on the Angrivar barrier in two columns.

While one Roman column made an obvious frontal attack on the barrier in full view of its thousands of German defenders, Germanicus and the second division made their way unnoticed along the hillsides. He then launched a surprise flanking attack against the Germans. But, in the face of determined defence, and devoid of scaling ladders or siege equipment, Germanicus' troops were forced to pull back. After bombarding the barrier with his legions' catapults, keeping the Germans' heads down, Germanicus personally led the next attack, at the head of the Praetorians, removing his helmet so that no one could mistake who he was. The men of eight legions followed close behind their bareheaded general and the Praetorians. On clambering up the barrier they found a 'vast host' of Germans lined up on the far side, commanded by Arminius' uncle Inguiomerus, who, with blood-curdling war cries, surged forward to repulse the Romans.

The intense hand-to-hand combat continued for hours. Germanicus ordered that no prisoners be taken. The situation was equally perilous for both sides. 'Valour was their only hope, victory their only safety,' said Tacitus. 'The Germans were equally brave, but they were beaten by the nature of the fighting and the weapons', for they were too tightly compressed to use their long spears effectively. [Tac., *A*, 1, 21]

Pushed into woods, trapped with their backs to the marsh, the tribesmen were slaughtered. At nightfall, the killing stopped. The Germans had been dislodged from the barrier and butchered in their thousands. Inguiomerus escaped, but took no further part in German resistance. That night, Germanicus was joined by Seius Tubero, commander of the Roman cavalry that had gone after Arminius in the forest. Tubero, a close friend of Tiberius, had certainly prevented Arminius from attacking Germanicus in the rear, but after indecisive fighting had allowed the German cavalry to escape. While the battle at the barrier had been another crushing Roman victory, Arminius had again evaded capture.

The Roman victory was soured when, on the return voyage to Holland, a number of Germanicus' ships were wrecked in a storm. To prove that the legions were still to be reckoned with, Germanicus immediately regrouped his forces and led a new raid across the Rhine, this time returning with another of Varus' lost eagles.

The Senate heaped honours on Germanicus, and the adoring Roman people sang the prince's praises. But Tiberius was unimpressed. When Germanicus asked the emperor for another year to complete the subjugation of the Germans, he recalled him. Germanicus returned to Rome, 'though,' said Tacitus, 'he saw that this was a pretence, and that he was hurried away through jealousy from the glory he had already acquired'. There would be no further Roman expeditions east of the Rhine during the reign of Tiberius. [Ibid., 26]

After Germanicus celebrated his Triumph in Rome in AD 17, Tiberius made him supreme Roman commander in the East, and in Syria, in AD 19, Germanicus, Tiberius' heir apparent as emperor, would die – apparently poisoned, with Tiberius the chief suspect. Ironically, in Germany that same year, Arminius would also die, and also at the hands of his own people. Many hundreds of years later, Arminius, or Hermann, would become the hero of German nationalists.

As for Germanicus Caesar, many modern-day historians consider him a mediocrity. Yet Germanicus would be lamented by the Roman people for generations – as late as the third century, his birthday was still being commemorated on 23 June each year. [Web., *RIA*, 6] Fearless soldier and noble prince, Germanicus was, said Cassius Dio in the third century, 'the bravest of men against the foe' yet 'showed himself most gentle with his countrymen'. [Dio, LVII, 18]

AD 17–23
XV. TACFARINAS' REVOLT
Shame and fame in North Africa

Tacfarinas was a native of Numidia in North Africa who joined the Roman army and served with a Numidian auxiliary unit for a number of years. Some time before AD 17 he deserted and led a roving band of robbers, who plagued travellers and outlying farms in southern Tunisia. Like Robin Hood's merry men, Tacfarinas' band attracted more and more disaffected locals as its successes mounted. With the addition of auxiliary deserters, it grew to the size of a small army.

By AD 17, using the skills he had learned in the Roman military, Tacfarinas had formed his men up behind standards in maniples and cohorts, and equipped and trained them like legionaries. That year, he began leading them against Roman out-

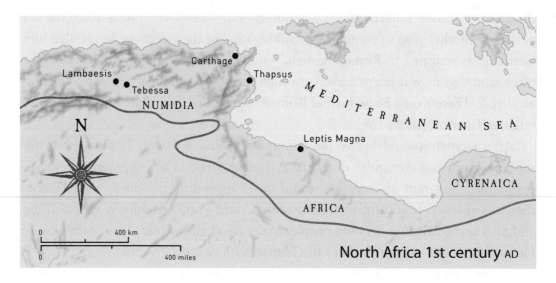

North Africa 1st century AD

posts throughout the province of Africa, which was administered from Carthage on the coast. The site of the original Carthage and Roman Carthage is today a residential suburb of Tunis, capital of Tunisia.

This was not the first time that a former Roman auxiliary had used the skills learned from Rome against her, nor would it be the last. Tacfarinas' little army soon became more than a nuisance to the Roman authorities. The failure of those authorities to halt Tacfarinas' raids on farms, villages and military outposts attracted many more rebel recruits to his force. The fighting men of Tacfarinas' own people, the Musulamian tribe from territory bordering the Sahara Desert, willingly joined his ranks, while those of the neighbouring Ciniphi tribe were compelled to do so by Tacfarinas.

Dark-skinned Moors from neighbouring Morocco also rallied to Tacfarinas; their cavalrymen were famous for riding like the wind without bridles, while their infantry were nimble. The leader of Tacfarinas' Moorish allies was Mazippa, whom Tacfarinas put in charge of his mobile division, made up of cavalry and light infantry. Tacfarinas himself retained command of the heavy infantry. In total, Tacfarinas now commanded a force of up to 30,000 men. Now, he was no mere bandit leader, he was a general, and his partisan army threatened Rome's control over North Africa.

To counter Tacfarinas' army, just a single legion, the 3rd Augusta, was stationed in all of North Africa. Since the beginning of Augustus' reign, the legion had been based at the city of Ammaedra – Haidra, in modern-day Tunisia. This town was well inland, close to the border with Numidia. The legion, together with the auxiliary

units based in the provinces of North Africa, gave the governor of Africa, the proconsul Furius Camillus, little more than 10,000 troops. While Camillus' ancestors had
gained fame as Roman commanders, Camillus himself, said Tacitus, 'was regarded as
an inexperienced soldier'. [Tac., *A*, II, 52]

Despite having no record as a field commander, Camillus combined the 3rd Augusta Legion with all his auxiliaries plus troops from Roman allies in the region, and
marched against Tacfarinas. Knowing that he significantly outnumbered the Romans,
and having trained his men in the Roman style, Tacfarinas possessed the confidence
to meet Camillus in open battle rather than rely on the hit-and-run tactics that had
previously brought him success. Camillus was not an ambitious man, but he was a
loyal servant of Rome and had a steady nerve. [Ibid.] As the two armies formed up on
the flat North African landscape, facing each other, Camillus calmly and deliberately
allocated his units their places, putting the 3rd Augusta Legion in the centre of his
battle line and his light infantry and two cavalry squadrons on the wings.

When the battle began, the Africans charged, but the Roman troops held their
ground. Camillus drew the Numidians into close combat, after which the 3rd Augusta Legion soon overran Tacfarinas' inexperienced and over-confident infantry.
The victory was swift, and appeared complete. But Tacfarinas escaped the battlefield,
and lived to fight another day. Once news of the Camillus' victory reached Rome,
the Senate voted him Triumphal Decorations, which was the next best thing to a
Triumph. But the award was a little premature; Tacfarinas was far from conquered.

Gathering fresh support, Tacfarinas began his raiding again the following year,
so that, by the autumn of AD 19, the Palatium decided to take the unusual step of
sending an additional legion to the African front to help the province's new governor.
That governor was Lucius Apronius, a personal friend of the emperor; Tacitus actually described him as a sycophant of Tiberius. [Tac., *A*, II, 32]

The legions stationed in Africa and Egypt were generally considered to be inferior
to those in Europe, so a 'superior' European-based legion was now given the job of
going to North Africa to complete the task which the local legionaries had not been
able to accomplish. The legion chosen for the job was the 9th Hispana, which had
been based in Pannonia ever since taking part in the Pannonian War of AD 6–9. Led
by their senior tribune and second-in-command, Gaius Fulvius, in December AD 19
the men of the 9th Hispana Legion marched out of their winter quarters at Siscia
and tramped to the city of Aquileia in northeastern Italy. From there they proceeded

down to Rimini, on the Adriatic coast, then down the Aemilian Way and finally the Flaminian Way, the military highway to Rome.

On the march, complete with its long baggage train containing all its artillery, officers' furniture and plate and the other personal belongings of the troops, the legion was overtaken by the party of a senator, Gneius Calpurnius Piso. Until recently the propraetor of Syria, Piso was welcomed into the column, and he and his wife Plancina, son Marcus, and their companions and slaves accompanied the legion over the snow-covered Apennines. The men of the legion were unaware that Piso was in disgrace and on his way to Rome to face a trial in the Senate, accused of the murder of Germanicus Caesar.

After mixing freely with the troops on the march – to the surprise and discomfort of Fulvius and his officers – Piso left the legionary column at Narnia and went by boat along the Narn and then the Tiber to Rome, travelling in style while the legion marched on to the capital. The men of the 9th would have camped on the Field of Mars, then continued their march the next day, passing down the Appian Way to Capua, then joining the Popilian Way for the last stage down the west coast of Italy to the port city of Reggio.

There, they boarded transports which shipped them the short distance across the Strait of Messina to the Sicilian port of Messina. They would have marched along the north coast of Sicily to where another convoy waited at Marsala. Making a short crossing of the Mediterranean to North Africa directly opposite, the 9th landed at Utica early in the year 20. Geological changes over the centuries mean that today Utica is 7 miles (11 kilometres) inland; back then the town was the principal port of the North African provinces, located just a few miles along the coast from Carthage.

The city of Carthage had been levelled by Rome after its capture in 146 BC. Caesar had sent Roman settlers there after his 46 BC victory at Thapsus, but only in the reign of Augustus was the city really reborn, when he established a military colony on the site. It had quickly grown to become the commercial hub of North Africa, and within another century would boast 250,000 inhabitants. At this point in its history it was a pleasant and bustling metropolis with all the adornments of a civilized Roman city, from public baths to theatres, circus to amphitheatre, and, like most military colonies, a grand temple to Jupiter, Juno and Minerva. The city was neither as large nor as influential as Antioch or Alexandria, second and third cities of the empire, but Roman Carthage's leading citizens considered themselves to be just as sophisticated.

The men of the 9th Hispana did not see Carthage. Nor were they posted to the headquarters of the 3rd Augusta at Ammaedra. The 9th Hispana was going even further into the North African wilds. Governor Lucius Apronius split up the cohorts of the 9th Hispana and divided them around forts on the far frontier of the province, under their tribune, camp-prefect and centurions, with many of the emplacements having to be constructed from scratch by the legionaries.

There, in their forts in the blinding African sun, the men of the 9th Hispana Legion gazed unhappily out over the desert wastes to the south. This deployment of troops in isolated outposts, where they sat behind their camp walls, was an invitation to Tacfarinas to do what he did best; to range across the countryside making guerrilla raids. It was an invitation he was soon to take up. By the spring of AD 20, Tacfarinas was intercepting travellers on the roads and plundering and destroying villages.

A cohort of new recruits of the 9th Hispana under an experienced centurion by the name of Decrius set off in pursuit after the raiders struck in their district. But Tacfarinas turned on his pursuers and hemmed in the cohort beside a river in southern Tunisia. Centurion Decrius and his men rapidly built a marching camp beside the river, but the centurion felt that to simply sit behind the walls and allow these natives to besiege his troops was a disgrace to the legion, so he led his nervous youngsters out and lined them up in battle order on the open river plain outside his entrenchments.

Tacfarinas, commanding a much larger force, charged the 480 young legionaries, who buckled under the volleys of Numidian missiles and were forced to give ground. Before long, most of the legionaries, including the cohort's standard-bearers, turned and ran for the camp. Centurion Decrius, disgusted by his men's retreat, stood his ground, yelling to the retreating standard-bearers that they should be ashamed for allowing Roman soldiers to show their backs to the enemy. The centurion was struck time and again by javelins and stones. A missile took out one of his eyes, and he was bleeding from other wounds, but still he held firm as Tacfarinas' men fell on him. He fought them off with his sword, sending Numidians reeling away with savage wounds, but eventually their numbers and his wounds told, and Centurion Decrius fell dead.

The frightened young legionaries of his cohort barricaded themselves inside their camp, with the Numidian horde outside the walls baying for their blood. Before long, Tacfarinas led his men away; they had neither the skills nor the inclination to conduct a siege. Once the coast was clear, the men of the 9th Hispana cohort sent a messenger to their tribune Gaius Fulvius with the news of the attack and to explain the circumstances of the death of their centurion. Tribune Fulvius sent a full report to the governor at Carthage.

Apronius was furious. The governor, by law the only magistrate in the province with the power over life and death, 'flogged to death every tenth man drawn by lot from the disgraced cohort'. [Ibid., III, 21] This was the first recorded instance of decimation in the Roman army since the Civil War. And, ironically, it had been the 9th Legion which was decimated on that last occasion too, by Julius Caesar, in 49 BC. The punishment was duly carried out. Each of the men of the cohort drew a lot. Men who drew the marked tokens were taken from the ranks, stripped, and tied to whipping posts. Some fifty condemned men were then whipped to death.

Tacitus would declare that the decimation had the desired effect on the morale and courage of the rest of the men of 9th Hispana Legion, for shortly after the punishment was meted out Tacfarinas attacked a fort at Thala, to the west, above Lambaessa. This was garrisoned by a veteran cohort of the 9th Hispana, made up entirely of mature, experienced soldiers. And they fought like demons, driving off the vastly superior force. [Ibid.]

During this latest hectic battle, when a legionary of the 9th Hispana by the name of Rufus Helvius saved the life of a fellow soldier, his name was passed on to the governor with a recommendation that he receive an award for his bravery. Governor Apronius duly awarded Helvius the golden torque and silver spear, highly esteemed bravery awards. But the deed had deserved more, and, after Tiberius heard of the decorations conferred by Apronius on Helvius, he added the Civic Crown, Rome's highest gallantry award, at same time writing to tell Apronius, 'without anger', that as proconsul he himself could have bestowed this great honour. [Ibid.]

With the Roman military still confined to their outposts by the unadventurous governor, Tacfarinas continued his raiding. He had learned his lesson after being re-pulsed at Thala. Now, if a legionary cohort gave chase, Tacfarinas sped away without giving battle. Then, when the exhausted legionaries turned around and marched back to their camps, the Numidians hung on their tail and stung their rearguard. This was all most humiliating for the Roman troops, with two legions now being made to look foolish by the rebels. Tacfarinas, said Velleius Paterculus, one of Tiberius' officers, meanwhile 'caused great consternation and grew more formidable every day'. [Velle., II, CXXIX, 3]

Filled with confidence by the success of his tactics and the failure of the fort-bound Romans to trouble him, Tacfarinas, weighed down with booty, advanced towards the Mediterranean coast and set up a fortified camp where his men could enjoy a little rest and recreation. When the governor learned of this, he put together a mobile expeditionary force under the command of his son Caesianus Apronius, then a young prefect with an auxiliary command in the province. This appointment was not unusual. Just as Junius Blaesus, the governor of the 9th Hispana's last province, had his son on his staff, and the disgraced propraetor Piso of Syria, the 9th's companion on the march to Rome the previous winter, had his son Marcus on his staff in the East, governors frequently took along their sons to share their provincial postings when the youths were tribunes and prefects learning their military craft.

With a force of auxiliary cavalry and light infantry, plus 1,000 or so of the younger, fitter legionaries of the 9th Hispana's cohorts, Caesianus Apronius the prefect quickly advanced on Tacfarinas' camp. Young Apronius forced the Numidians to abandon their position, and drove them south, into the desert. For this apparent success, Tiberius awarded the governor Triumphal Decorations. But again, the celebrations were premature.

Most provinces garrisoned by the legions were imperial provinces, with their governors appointed by the emperor. At this time, the governors of the province of Africa were appointed on the vote of the Senate. In fact, Africa was one of the few senatorial provinces where the governor controlled legionary forces. Their commands only covered auxiliary troops as a rule. Being a senatorial province, Africa's governors could only hold their appointment for one year. Together with the governorships of Asia and Syria, Africa was the most highly paid of all the gubernatorial offices, and was always considered a prestigious step for ambitious Romans. Several later emperors would serve there in the early stages of their careers.

By the spring of AD 21 the year-long tour of duty of Lucius Apronius came to an end, and he and his son returned to Rome. But news of an outbreak of further trouble led by Tacfarinas in Africa caused the Senate to ask the emperor to appoint the next governor personally. Apronius' replacement was a familiar face to old hands of the 9th Hispana Legion – Junius Blaesus, who had governed Pannonia, the 9th Hispana's home province, at the time of the AD 14 mutinies. Blaesus was considered 'an experienced soldier of vigorous constitution who would be equal to the war'. [Tac., *A*, III, 32] He was also the uncle of Sejanus, Tiberius' powerful prefect of the Praetorian Guard.

Not long after Blaesus arrived at Carthage, Tacfarinas cheekily sent envoys to the emperor at Rome, demanding a settlement involving land and money for his men and himself in return for peace. If his demands were not met, his envoys told Tiberius, then Tacfarinas would wage interminable war on the Roman forces so that the provinces of North Africa would never know peace. 'Never, it was said, was the emperor so exasperated by an insult to himself and the Roman people as by a deserter and brigand assuming the character of a belligerent.' Even Spartacus, Tiberius said, when ravaging Italy with his slave army ninety-five years before, had never been offered an amnesty by Rome, so a bandit such as Tacfarinas stood no chance of having his demands met. Tiberius instructed Blaesus to offer full pardons to followers of Tacfarinas who laid down their arms, but he was to pursue Tacfarinas himself with all the resources at his disposal. [Ibid., 73]

A number of Numidians did take advantage of the amnesty. But deep in the North African interior, sheltered by the Garamantes tribe, Tacfarinas was able to recruit new followers with promises of booty. Throughout the summer of AD 21, Tacfarinas emerged from hiding and employed his tested guerrilla tactics to great success, preying in particular on the peaceful Leptitani tribe. Dividing his forces into a number of detachments, he would strike at several places at once, then dash away. He would elude pursuit, and then ambush Roman troops sent out after him. The hit-and-run tactics suited the temperament and skills of his nomadic followers, and left the Romans in their static formations at a disadvantage.

Blaesus, a no-nonsense man, decided that enough was enough. With just one year in which to show what he could do, he mounted a major operation to track down and eliminate Tacfarinas. Three columns were put together, comprising the 3rd Augusta Legion, 9th Hispana Legion and auxiliary units. Up to this point, both the 3rd Augusta and 9th Hispana had been commanded by their senior tribunes, but for this latest campaign Cornelius Lentulus Scipio, an able legate of senatorial rank, was sent to Africa to take over the command of the 9th Hispana Legion. He would subsequently become one of the emperor Claudius' most trusted military advisers. Under the newly arrived general, the 9th Hispana formed one of Blaesus' three divisions. Another force, made up of the auxiliaries, was headed by Governor Blaesus' son, a prefect. Blaesus himself would command the third column, comprising the 3rd Augusta Legion.

Each column had a specific task. Lentulus Scipio and the 9th Hispana took the left flank, pushing southeast to end enemy attacks on the Leptitani tribe, which remained loyal to Rome. The 9th Hispana was then to sweep around and cut off Tacfarinas' retreat into friendly Garamantian territory. Prefect Blaesus led the column which took the right flank of the offensive, driving west to protect villages around Cirta (modern Constantine), capital of Numidia, and preventing Tacfarinas' escape to the west. At the same time, Governor Blaesus would be slicing down through the middle of the province with the 3rd Augusta.

With machine-like efficiency, all three forces achieved their objectives then linked up deep inside southern Tunisia. There, Blaesus set up a series of forts, walls and trench lines at prime locations. From these he sent out small detachments under first-rank centurions on search-and-destroy missions. From now on, no matter which direction Tacfarinas' men turned, they found Roman troops in front of them, on their flanks, suddenly appearing behind them. It was an uncomfortable time for the rebels.

No doubt Tacfarinas told his followers to hold on until the Romans withdrew for the winter, as they always did. But as the autumn arrived, Blaesus defied tradition. His troops stayed in the field, and from his forts he sent out lightly equipped flying columns with local guides who knew the desert. Tacfarinas' rebels were forced to scatter across the sandy wastes. As for Tacfarinas himself, he was chased through the wilderness from one group of miserable huts to another. The Roman detachments came back with a number of prisoners, including the brother of Tacfarinas. But Tacfarinas himself again eluded capture.

This success was good enough for Blaesus. In early AD 22, with his term as governor due to end in the spring, he withdrew to Carthage and prepared to hand over to his successor. It was also good enough for the emperor; in addition to the now customary and almost annual award of Triumphal Decorations to the governor of Africa, Tiberius accorded Blaesus the added distinction of being hailed *imperator* for his 'victory'. Now, as the historian Tacitus was to note, there were statues of three ex-governors of Africa standing in Rome bearing the laurel wreath of the Triumphal Decorations for conquering Tacfarinas. Yet Tacfarinas was still at large. [Tac., *A*, IV, 23]

With the award of the exalted title of imperator to Blaesus, Tiberius backed himself into a corner. Questions were asked in the Senate. Why, if Tacfarinas had been dealt with, was the 9th Hispana Legion still in Africa? The emperor had no real answer to this. So, shortly after the newly appointed proconsul of Africa, Publius Dolabella, arrived at Carthage to take up his post, he received a dispatch from the emperor instructing him to send the 9th Hispana back to its 'home' station in Pannonia. Governor Dolabella, said Tacitus, did not dare to retain the legion, 'because he feared the emperor's orders more than the risks of war'. [Ibid.]

Dolabella knew that Tacfarinas was far from subdued. He would have desperately wanted to retain the 9th Hispana for continued operations against the Numidians, doubting his ability to contain Tacfarinas with a reduced army. Just the same, orders went out to the 9th Hispana to prepare to return to the Balkans. In AD 23, as soon as the spring arrived, the 9th Hispana was shipped back across the Mediterranean to Sicily. The men of the legion then retraced their steps of three and a half years before, to their former Pannonian base.

Tacfarinas would not have been able to believe his luck. When he heard of the withdrawal of the 9th Hispana, he spread a rumor around the region that the forces of Rome were in trouble throughout the empire and it would only be a matter of time before they pulled out of North Africa altogether. With this apparent success the bandit genuinely took on the aura of a freedom fighter. More tribesmen flocked to his banner, inspired by the fact that he had already sent one legion back where it came from, and with the hope of throwing Rome out of their homeland.

With his new army, Tacfarinas boldly besieged the town of Thubuscum, but, as before, his followers had no taste for long sieges. Governor Dolabella marched to the rescue of the troops at Thubuscum, and as his column approached, the rebels withdrew. Dolabella, pulling in every Roman legionary, auxiliary, ally and mercenary he could muster, then followed the lead of Blaesus the previous summer and divided his force. He created four columns, commanded by 'his deputies and tribunes', and went looking for the enemy, with 'Dolabella in person directing every operation'. He even sent hand-picked Moorish cavalry marauding parties to cause problems for the rebels in their rear. [Ibid., 24]

Perhaps through an informant, the retreating Numidians were tracked to the partly destroyed fortress of Auzea. Tacfarinas' men did not build marching camps for the night as the legions did. There at Auzea, with the Africans mostly sleeping in the open, as was their custom, they were surprised in a dawn attack by Dolabella's troops. 'With the sound of trumpets and fierce shouts' the Romans surged into the undefended camp in 'close array'. They cut down Numidians and Moors in their thousands as they ran for their weapons and for the horses they had allowed to roam and graze. The rebels, 'without arms, order or plan, were seized, slaughtered or captured like cattle'. [Ibid., 25]

'The word went through the units that all were to aim at securing Tacfarinas', and in the early morning light Tacfarinas was located and surrounded. His son was captured, his bodyguards slain around him. Tacfarinas knew how badly the Romans wanted to take him alive, to drag him through the streets of Rome in a Triumph. But he would not give them that pleasure. Determined to avoid the humiliation of capture, he raised his sword and ran at the Roman troops encircling him. He was felled by a swarm of flying javelins before he could reach his attackers. [Ibid.]

Tacfarinas' revolt died with him. Africa was once more at peace, and the 3rd Augusta Legion was able to stand down from the condition of high alert that it had been in for almost a decade. Governor Dolabella, the man who had succeeded in terminating Tacfarinas and his seven-year uprising, applied to the emperor for the award of Triumphal Decorations, the same honour accorded the three previous governors, none of whom had actually succeeded putting an end to the revolt. Tiberius declined to award Dolabella the Triumphal Decorations his deed deserved. This was because, said Tacitus, the emperor was influenced by his Praetorian prefect Sejanus, who did not want the so-called glory of his uncle Blaesus diminished by Dolabella receiving an award for completing Blaesus' unfinished work, and with a smaller army at that. [Ibid., 26]

The fact that Dolabella failed to receive the award actually increased his fame, said Tacitus, for it was he who brought Tacfarinas' son and surviving lieutenants back to Rome as prisoners and received the plaudits of the people. As for Blaesus, both he and Sejanus would perish within several years after the Praetorian prefect was convicted of plotting to overthrow the emperor. [Ibid.]

AD 42

XVI. SCRIBONIANUS' REVOLT
The Claudian legions make their names

Ever since the Praetorian Guard and German Guard had proclaimed Claudius Caesar, the crippled uncle of Caligula, emperor of Rome in January AD 41, there had been an undercurrent of unrest among leading senators who felt they were better qualified to occupy the throne. One of those men, Annius Vinicianus, had actually been proposed as a potential emperor by fellow senators, following the assassination of Caligula. Claudius had not been in power a year before Vinicianus and a number of his friends formed a plot to overthrow the timid, scholarly emperor whose only claim to the throne, to their mind, was his blood as a member of the Julio-Claudian line.

As Vinicianus had no troops of his own, and with the men of the various Guard units in Rome expected to protect Claudius, the plotters made contact with the governor of the province of Dalmatia, just across the Adriatic Sea from Italy, who they were sure would be in sympathy with them. According to Cassius Dio, that governor, Marcus Furius Camillus Scribonianus, already had his own plans for a revolt, because he too had been spoken of as a potential emperor. [Dio, LX, 15]

A descendant of Pompey the Great, Scribonianus (also variously referred to as both Furius and Camillus by Roman historians) had two legions under his command in Dalmatia. The 7th Legion was based at Tilurium, near modern-day Split in Croatia, while the 11th Legion had its winter quarters at Scribonianus' provincial capital, Burnum, today's Croatian city of Kistanje. In addition to the roughly 10,000 legionaries of the two legions, the province's garrison included a similar number of auxiliaries, giving Scribonianus a force of 20,000 men.

At the beginning of the third week of March AD 42, after hearing from Vinicianus at Rome, Scribonianus called an assembly of his troops and announced that he intended to dethrone Claudius. According to Dio, Scribonianus 'held out the hope' to his troops that he would restore the

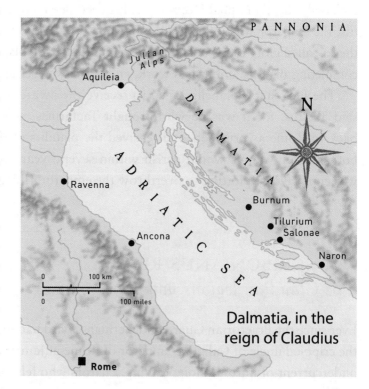

Dalmatia, in the reign of Claudius

Roman Republic, something many Romans still dreamed of ninety years after Julius Caesar launched the rebellion that had brought about its end. On this false promise, Scribonianus ordered his legions to prepare to march on Rome. [Dio, LX, 15]

Meanwhile, Scribonianus sent Claudius an 'impudent, threatening, and insulting letter' which caused the terrified emperor to call a meeting of his chief advisers. At this meeting, Claudius canvassed the prospect of him abdicating and going into retirement. Vinicianus and his supporters were in fact convinced that Claudius would be scared into abdicating once he received this letter from Scribonianus, and a number of leading senators and Equestrians flocked to Vinicianus' cause. But, buttressed by the opinions of his leading freedmen, who were determined that he would not be bullied from office, Claudius did not step down. [Suet., V, 35]

On the other side of the Adriatic, there were a number of soldiers in the ranks of Scribonianus' two legions who were not enamoured with the idea of overthrowing their emperor. Claudius was of the imperial line, he was the brother of the late, revered general Germanicus Caesar, and it had been little more than a year since Claudius had been installed. For many legionaries, the idea of replacing him was repugnant.

Between 19 and 23 March each year, across the empire, the legions removed their sacred golden eagle standards from the shrines where they stood in camp and took them to assembly, where, in front of the legions, priests anointed the eagles with perfumes and dressed them with garlands of flowers, in an ancient ceremony called the lustration exercise. In the third week of March in the camps of the 7th and 11th legions in Dalmatia, word swept through the ranks that when the eagle-bearers had gone to remove their eagles from the ground in their shrines, they would not budge. [Dio, LX, 13]

All Romans were superstitious, legionaries more than most; with their lives frequently on the line, they would always look for omens good and bad to guide them and keep them out of harm's way. This tale of eagles that could not be removed from the ground had an electrifying effect on the men of the two Dalmatian legions. This, to them, signified that they were not meant to march on Rome with Scribonianus, and 'because of a superstitious terror which caused his legions to repent', the revolt crumbled to dust overnight. [Ibid.]

Experienced rank and file soldiers conferred, and, agreeing that they must strike against Scribonianus and his supporters, they sought out the senior officers who backed the governor's seditious scheme and put them to the sword in their quarters. Scribonianus, alerted to the fact that his own legions had turned against him, fled from Burnum to the Adriatic coast, and from there to Issa, today's Croatian island of Vis. Seeing no other option, Scribonianus took his own life there on Issa. From the moment that he had addressed his legions and announced that he was acting against Claudius until the time of his death, Scribonianus' revolt had lasted just five days. [Ibid., 15]

Once word of the swift end of the rebellion reached Rome, several of the conspirators, including Vinicianus, initiator of the plot, followed the lead of Scribonianus and committed suicide. A number of others, both men and women, were rounded up by the Praetorian Guard. Some were tortured for confessions. Senators were tried in the Senate in the presence of Claudius, the prefects of the Guard, and the emperor's freedmen advisers. Convicted, the accused were executed, with their decapitated heads exhibited on the Gemonian Stairs. [Ibid., 16]

One of the conspirators was the senator Caecina Paetus. His wife Arria was 'on very intimate terms' with the empress Messalina, and might herself have escaped punishment for involvement in the plot had she sought Messalina's intervention. But Arria loyally chose to share her husband's fate. Dio tells the story that, with both of them having resolved to die, Arria and Paetus sat in a room of their house at Rome, he with his sword in his hands. But Paetus did not have the courage to go through with the deed. So, Arria took the sword from him and plunged it into her own body. Alive still, she withdrew the blade, saying, as she handed the sword back to her husband for him to follow suit, 'See, Paetus, I feel no pain.' [Ibid.]

Once the manner of the revolt's termination became known, the grateful Claudius sent word to Dalmatia that he was honouring the two legions that had retained their loyalty to him and put an end to the sedition of their officers. That honour took the form of the emperor's name, via the title 'Claudia'. From that time forward, the legions would be known as the 7th Claudia Pia Fidelis, literally meaning 'Claudius' Loyal and Patriotic 7th', and the 11th Claudia Pia Fidelis. [Ibid., 15] As for the soldiers who had acted of their own volition to kill the officers involved in the plot with Scribonianus, all were promoted on Claudius' order. [Suet., VIII, 1]

To ensure that the legions of Dalmatia were restored to order, the Palatium dispatched a senior officer to the province. This was Lucius Otho, father of the future emperor Marcus Otho. Lucius Otho, rumoured to be the illegitimate son of the late emperor Tiberius, had a reputation for being a strict disciplinarian, both when a magistrate in Rome and while governor of the province of Africa. Once he arrived in Dalmatia, Otho had the legionaries who had killed their officers and thwarted the rebellion brought before him. Instead of rewarding them, he condemned them to death, ignoring the fact that Claudius had promoted them for their deed. [Suet., VIII, 1]

Obviously, Otho was more interested in setting an example that dissuaded legionaries from killing their officers than in encouraging them to put down revolts against their emperor. The unfortunate loyal legionaries of the 7th Claudia Legion and 11th Claudia Legion were beheaded in Otho's presence. At least Otho had no power to take away the legions' new titles. Suetonius was to say that Otho's act may have furthered his reputation as a disciplinarian, but it put him out of favour at the Palatium once it became known that he had executed the very same legionaries who had been rewarded by the emperor. [Ibid.]

AD 43

XVII. INVADING BRITAIN
Four legions versus the Britons

In the spring of AD 43, alarm spread through the Celtic tribes of southern Britain after Gallic merchants trading across the English Channel warned their British cousins that a Roman army and fleet were assembling at the port of Bononia, modern-day Boulogne (originally called Gesoriacum). The talk at Bononia, said the merchants, was of a Roman invasion of Britain. These warnings would have been given credibility by the sighting of Roman warships scouting the coast of Kent (Roman Cantium) that spring.

Stirred into action, the tribal chiefs sent the call around their villages, summoning their warriors. None of the British tribes maintained a standing army as the Romans did. Their chiefs all had permanent troops of bodyguards, some of them Celtic mercenaries or levies. Every British nobleman also maintained a war chariot drawn by a team of two horses. In combat, the standing nobleman rode with a seated driver, hurling javelins then jumping down from the chariot to do battle on foot while the driver waited nearby to provide a quick getaway.

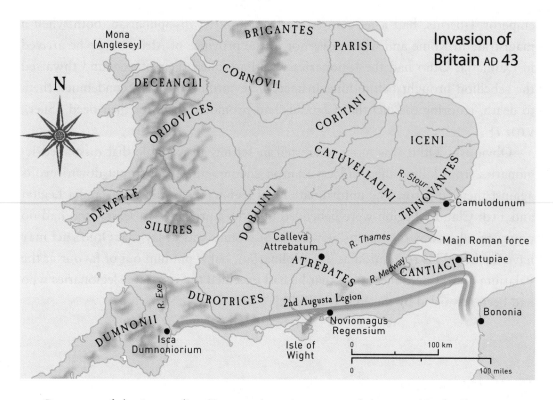

On news of the impending Roman invasion, tens of thousands of tribesmen answered the call to arms, taking up their weapons and congregating on the coast of Kent. Their chiefs waited for weeks, keeping a constant watch on the Channel, as the tribesmen sat impatiently in camp worrying about their crops and their families back home. From their cousins in Gaul, the chiefs knew that the Romans always launched their new military campaigns at the beginning of spring. Finally, when no invasion fleet put in an appearance and it looked as if this was going to be a repeat of the emperor Caligula's British 'invasion' of four years before (which had turned out to be a farcical non-event – Caligula had ordered his artillery to fire into the sea from the French coast, and had his legionaries collect seashells as war trophies), the British tribesmen went home.

The warnings had been based on fact. Four legions and dozens of auxiliary cavalry and light infantry units had marched to the assembly point at Bononia on the orders of the new emperor Claudius, with the intent of crossing the Channel to invade Britain. A Roman invasion of Britain had been on the cards ever since Julius Caesar's two expeditions there in 55 and 54 BC. The emperor Tiberius had contemplated it.

Caligula had toyed with it. Now Claudius, the least martial of the emperors, was carrying it forward, encouraged by a fugitive British tribal ruler named Bericus. [Dio, LX, 19]

By early spring, the legions had assembled at Bononia, among them the 2nd Augusta Legion, which came from Argentoratum (Strasbourg) on the Upper Rhine, their base for the past twenty-five years. Its commander was 33-year-old Titus Flavius Vespasianus, the future emperor Vespasian, who was of praetor rank at this time. As a prefect, Vespasian had commanded a unit of Thracian auxiliaries during his rise up the promotional ladder. According to the Roman biographer Suetonius, Vespasian owed his 2nd Augusta command to his friendship with Narcissus, freedman chief secretary to the emperor. [Suet., x, 4]

Vespasian's son Titus would eventually have a connection with his father's legion, commanding a cohort of auxiliaries attached to the 2nd Augusta in Britain twenty years later. Vespasian's third-in-command of the 2nd Augusta at the time of the invasion was camp-prefect Publius Anicius Maximus, a native of the city of Antioch in Pisidia, a mountainous region in southern Turkey which was then part of the province of Galatia. Anicius would come out of this campaign highly decorated.

The 2nd Augusta was joined at Bononia by another legion from the Upper Rhine, the 14th Gemina, which had been based at Mogontiacum, and the 20th Legion, from the Novaesium (Neuss) base of the army of the Lower Rhine. The fourth legion earmarked for the force, the 9th Hispana, the legion sent to Africa during the Tacfarinas Revolt, marched all the way from its Pannonian base at Siscia, accompanied by the general given overall command of the task force by Claudius, Aulus Plautius. A consul in AD 29, Plautius had been governor of Pannonia at the time of this new appointment.

By this period, praetors were increasingly receiving legion commands, and two of Vespasian's fellow legion commanders in the British task force were also praetors – Vespasian's elder bother Flavius Sabinus, and Gnaeus Hosidius Geta. Geta, who had some six years seniority on Vespasian, had just the previous year led a relatively small force in the province of Mauretania which had twice defeated an army of rebellious Moors. Accordingly, Geta came to this operation with an excellent military reputation.

The auxiliary units involved in the operation included eight cohorts of Batavian light infantry from present-day Holland which supported the 14th Gemina Legion, and among their prefects, almost certainly, was Gaius Julius Civilis, a member of the old royal house of the Batavi tribe, who would have been in his mid twenties. An Equestrian from a wealthy and influential family, Civilis was a soldier with a good tactical mind. Eloquent and confident, he was to become a friend of Vespasian.

The auxiliary cavalry units assigned to the operation included the Batavian Horse, probably the most famous mounted unit in the Roman army. There were also wings of the Thracian Horse, which had become a multinational cavalry unit despite its title, and the Vettonian Horse, a Spanish *equitatae* unit made up of both cavalry and infantry. The Vettonians were commanded by the prefect Didius Gallus, a future governor of Britain.

Claudius' Palatium had made elaborate arrangements for this operation. A troop of elephants stationed at Laurentum outside Rome was even put on standby, for possible use against the British war chariots. Whether the elephants were actually brought up to the staging area at Bononia is unclear. Some modern-day writers have offered colourful descriptions of these elephants in action in Britain, but there is no evidence that they were actually conveyed across the Channel – the marshy conditions and numerous river crossings in the invasion area would have rendered them useless, and this was no doubt realized by task force commander Plautius, who left them behind.

A fleet of transports and a convoy escort of warships had to be built specifically for the job of taking the troops and their horses to Britain, and shipbuilders were brought up to the Channel ports from the Mediterranean for the task. With some 40,000 troops, several thousand cavalry horses, and at least 5,000 baggage animals, hundreds of vessels were required. These ships would form the Roman navy's new Britannic Fleet.

Just as spring began, despite the detailed logistics and efficient arrangements, the operation became bogged down for a very human reason. Rumours spread among the highly superstitious legionaries that unimaginable terrors awaited them in Britain, a place then beyond the outer limits of the known world. Plautius urgently advised Rome that his army had gone on strike as a result. The invasion force sat in camp on the French coast, its rank and file refusing to budge, which was why the waiting Britons saw no invasion fleet off their shore that spring.

Claudius ordered his chief of staff, the freedman Narcissus, to journey to Bononia from Rome to resolve the problem. Plautius called an assembly of all the troops when Narcissus arrived at the embarkation camp. Standing beside Plautius on the general's tribunal, Narcissus began a speech designed to convince the soldiers to proceed with the operation, but he was immediately shouted down. The legionaries knew who Narcissus was, and knew that he was a one-time slave. Someone called out, 'Hooray for the Saturnalia!', a cry taken up by all the soldiers, and soon their chorus drowned out the chief secretary. [Ibid.]

The Saturnalia was the Roman religious festival in late December later adopted and adapted by the Christian world to become Christmas. During the Saturnalia, patrons gave their clients gifts, and slaves could wear the same dress as their masters and enjoy other liberties usually confined to free members of the population. At Bononia, the legions made it clear they would not be lectured by a former slave just because he wore the clothes of a free man.

Embarrassed and frustrated, Narcissus stepped down from the tribunal, with the laughter of the legionaries ringing in his ears. General Plautius then addressed the throng. Narcissus had probably intended to tell the men that the emperor had authorized him to offer the legions a substantial bonus if they undertook this operation. In his stead, Plautius would have informed his troops of the offer. Whatever he said to the troops, it worked. The legions agreed to go ahead with the invasion. By the summer – it was 'late in the [campaigning] season' according to Dio – and with the tribes of southern Britain off their guard, the legions' delayed invasion finally got under way. [Dio, LX, 19]

On the evening tide, the fleet began to pull out from Bononia, passing the giant stone lighthouse that Caligula had built on a point outside the town. Modelled on the Pharos of Alexandria, one of the wonders of the ancient world, the Bononia lighthouse had been the one good thing to come out of Caligula's visit here in AD 39 for his abortive invasion.

Dio wrote that Plautius' legions 'were sent over in three divisions, in order that they should not be hindered in landing, as might happen to a single force'. [Ibid.] In the night, the fleet sailed up through the Strait of Dover, following the long, low stretch of Kent coastline beyond Dover and its white cliffs, passing Deal, where Julius Caesar is believed to have made his landings, and headed for the Isle of Thanet, near Ramsgate. Plautius' invasion troops are believed to have hit the beaches in the vicinity of Pegwell Bay. [W&D, 3, 1–2] (In those times, Thanet really was an island. Over the centuries the Wantsum Channel, the narrow waterway between it and the mainland, silted up and the sheltered harbour there disappeared.)

With dawn's first light the ships of the first wave grounded in the shallows, and the troops jumped over the sides and went splashing to shore. Soon the entire force had landed, with the 2nd Augusta occupying the left flank, and the 20th most probably on the right – it would later take the right flank of the advance up into East Anglia – and the 14th Gemina and 9th Hispana in the centre. With his first priority that of securing the beachhead, Plautius had his troops dig entrenchments to protect the landing zone. A camp, traces of which can still be seen, was built beside the River Stour, in the vicinity of modern Richborough. Troops defending the landing site were housed here, along with the supplies that came ashore from Roman transports plying back and forth between the Gallic and British coasts from then on. This safe harbour would be named Rutupiae and would be used as a Roman supply base for another thirty years. [Ibid.]

One of the four legions, the 9th Hispana, was apparently left behind here to both protect the Roman rear and act as a reserve. Meanwhile, Plautius wasted no time in moving inland with the bulk of his force. Just as Roman commanders such as Germanicus had frequently followed in the recorded footsteps of earlier expeditions when they invaded foreign territory, Plautius would have used Julius Caesar's published and widely read history of his two British campaigns as a guide, for he followed in Caesar's footsteps towards the River Thames – the Tamesa as the Celts called it.

With cavalry scouts and light infantry out in front, the three legions moved west across flat marshlands towards the site of modern-day Canterbury. The invaders had by this time been spotted by the people of the local tribe, the Cantiaci, who fearfully hung back in the forests bordering the marshlands, observing the Roman progress while they sent messengers galloping around the other tribes of southern England with the news that the Romans had landed.

Plautius, leading his invasion force inland from the beachhead, saw no signs of the locals, and 'had a deal of trouble in searching them out'. [Dio, LX, 20] All the while, the tribes were gathering. When the British did finally commit to combat, it was under the command of two brothers, sons of the late Cunobelinus, king of the powerful Catuvellauni tribe. The grandfather of Cunobelinus, King Cassivellaunus, had paid tribute to Julius Caesar after his brief invasions a century earlier. One of these brothers was King Togodumnus, who ruled that part of his father's former kingdom north of the Thames which occupied today's Essex.

The site of the old Catuvellauni capital is occupied by today's city of Colchester, called Camulodunum by the Romans after the Celtic god Camulos, whose shrine the town contained. The Celtic name of the second brother was Caradoc, whom history came to know as King Caratacus, sometimes spelled Caractacus. He ruled the western part of his father's former kingdom from his capital, which the Romans named Calleva Attrebatum, next to the present village of Silchester in Hampshire, in the tribal heartland of the Atrebates people.

After hastily gathering support from subsidiary tribes, the two brothers converged on the Roman advance with their warriors, Togodumnus moving down from the north, Caratacus hurrying from the west. Caratacus was the first to make contact. The numerous sons of the late King Cunobelinus could at times be bitter rivals, and now, without waiting for his brother's forces to join him, to win glory for himself Caratacus attacked the nearest Roman troops, most probably the men of Vespasian's 2nd Augusta Legion.

The Britons were not equipped with armour or helmets. Most of the ordinary tribesman came armed with the simple framea, or spear, and a large, leather-covered rectangular wooden shield. Often barefoot, the Briton habitually went into battle stripped to the waist; some even went naked. The tribesmen who now confronted the Romans, before coming out for battle had sworn an oath to Camulos, their war god, that they would not yield to the weapons of the enemy nor yield to wounds they received in battle.

Despite their oaths, the tribesmen involved in this first attack by Caratacus were quickly routed by the mechanically efficient legion formations, and were soon fleeing back the way they had come. After his attack was swiftly and bloodily repulsed, Caratacus fell back towards the River Medway. As the Romans continued their advance, Togodumnus arrived from north of the Thames with his thousands of tribesmen. He too immediately attacked without giving thought to tactics, and his men were just as quickly cut down. Togodumnus himself appears to have been gravely wounded in this action. Carried away from the battlefield by his bodyguards, he was dead within a few days. In the meantime, his retreating brother Caratacus reached the Medway, where he regrouped his men and was joined by his brother's leaderless, retreating warriors.

In the meantime, part of Caratacus' force, a tribe called the Bodunni by Dio but probably the Dobunni from Gloucestershire, surrendered to Plautius, who had a fort built on the spot to hold them. The Bodunni, who had been subjects of the Catuvellauni for some time, apparently decided it was better to have Roman masters than be ruled by their fellow Celts.

Before long, Plautius came to the broad River Medway. On the far bank, Caratacus had regrouped tens of thousands of tribesmen. By this time, too, chariots had belatedly joined the British force. The Britons 'thought that the Romans would not be able to cross [the river] without a bridge and consequently camped in rather careless fashion on the opposite bank'. [Ibid.] But they had not reckoned on the many skills of the Roman military.

Some distance from the site of his own camp, Plautius sent the Batavian Horse swimming across the river with their horses, fully equipped and ready to go into action as soon as they succeeded in crossing. The Batavians then came downriver on the northern bank. Launching a surprise attack on the British camp, the Batavians were under orders to aim their javelins at the chariots' horses, not their crews. 'In the confusion that followed not even the enemy's mounted warriors could save themselves.' Whilst the Britons were fully occupied fighting the Batavians, Plautius apparently threw bridges of boats across the river. Led by Vespasian and his brother Sabinus, the 2nd Augusta and another legion crossed the Medway upriver, and 'killed many of the foe'. [Ibid.]

Much or all of the Roman army camped on the northern bank of the river that night. But next day the Britons returned in strength, and it took legion commander Gnaeus Geta to lead a counter-attack, 'after narrowly avoiding being captured', that turned the tide and drove off the Britons. For his part in this action at the Medway, even though he was not yet a consul, Geta would be awarded Triumphal Decorations by the emperor.

As the Britons retired to the Thames, the Romans followed. Near to the point where the Thames emptied into the sea and at flood tide formed a lake, the Britons began to cross. The tribesmen, who knew where to find firm ground and where mud would ensnare the unwary, were able to make their way across the mudflats. But when pursuing Roman auxiliary troops tried to follow they were soon in difficulties and had to withdraw. When the main Roman force arrived, Plautius set up camps along the southern bank of the Thames and built a bridge of boats upstream.

Meanwhile, the Batavians again used their swimming skills. Once on the far bank, troops that had crossed the bridge marched to link up with the Batavians. Tribesmen caught in the middle were cut to pieces. But as the Romans gave chase to the remainder, they were led into swamps, and a number were drowned trying to maintain the pursuit. General Plautius pulled his men back and consolidated his position. Envoys were sent out to the chiefs of all the neighbouring tribes, inviting them to surrender on favourable terms. With news of the British defeats at the Medway and the Thames, and with the death of Togodumnus, several chiefs quickly agreed to submit rather than face Roman steel. Once the responses had been received, Plautius sent off a dispatch to Rome, inviting his emperor to come and take charge of the campaign, to accept the surrender of the chiefs, and complete the conquest of the Britons.

Clearly, Claudius had instructed Plautius to do just this once he was in a position to do so, and was expecting the message. Within weeks, Claudius set out for Britain with a massive entourage, leaving the consul Lucius Vitellius in charge at the capital. Several thousand men of the Praetorian Guard and Praetorian Cavalry, under their prefect Rufrius Pollio, provided the imperial escort, along with cohorts of the emperor's imposing German Guard personal bodyguard. Scores of sycophantic senators were in the emperor's party.

As Claudius' guardsmen marched along the Tiber to the port of Ostia, the imperial party was conveyed down the river aboard a fleet of barges. At Ostia, the emperor, his troops and entourage boarded warships from the Misene Fleet, and coasted the short distance to southern Gaul. The storm-tossed and seasick imperial party landed at Masillia (Marseilles), from where it travelled up through Gaul to Germany. From Mogontiacum on the Rhine the imperial progress continued on to Bononia, from where the new Britannic Fleet conveyed the expedition to Britain.

As the emperor made his leisurely way north from Italy to the French coast, taking many weeks to travel the distance that could be covered by the galloping couriers of the Cursus Publicus Velox in a matter of days, Plautius had been busy tying up loose ends. While tribes to the north had sued for peace, and Caratacus had retreated west to Wales, taking his wife, daughter and at least two of his three surviving brothers with him, the tribes of the west stubbornly refused to submit. Plautius therefore ordered Vespasian and the 2nd Augusta Legion to expand the front to the southwest. The 2nd Augusta was still driving along the south coast when the emperor landed in Kent. According to Suetonius, in this sweep along the coast Vespasian's legion fought thirty battles, took more than twenty towns and the entire Isle of Wight, and accepted the surrender of two tribes. [Suet., x, 4]

The remains of some of the fortified hill towns overwhelmed by the 2nd Augusta are still to be found on hilltops through the region today; others were converted into castles by the Normans 1,000 years later. One of the first towns to fall was latter-day Chichester, capital of the Regni tribe of young chief Cogidubnus, who would help convince other tribes to submit to the invaders and continued to be a valued ally of Rome for another fifty years. Downtown Chichester today still retains the layout of the Roman town which grew on the site, Noviomagus Regensium, situated beside a vast, sheltered anchorage.

At a fort of the Durotrige tribe at Spettisbury Rings, near Blandford, over ninety skeletons were found in a mass grave in 1957, many bearing the evidence of sword and javelin wounds. Part of the fort's wall had been pulled down on top of the grave to complete the burial. At the Hod Hill fort, 18 miles (30 kilometres) northeast of Maiden Castle, a number of Roman ballista bolts were found, evidence of the 2nd Augusta's assault. [W&D, 4, 11]

The 2nd Augusta was still pushing along the coast, through today's Dorset and Somerset, when the emperor and the members of his expedition joined Plautius at the Thames. Palatium propaganda would have it that Plautius' legions crossed the Thames under Claudius' command, met and defeated a large army of British tribesmen, then took the surrender of British kings and their disarmed warriors. In reality, with the fighting at the Thames almost certainly over by the time Claudius arrived, Plautius

Claudius overhwelming a female figure representing Britannia. Claudius, who had no military experience, silenced his critics by masterminding the invasion of Britain.

had the kings that were submitting to Roman rule gather at Camulodunum to submit officially to his emperor.

At Camulodunum, the men of three legions, their supporting auxiliaries and the cohorts of the Praetorian Guard would have formed up in full parade dress to awe the locals, standards glittering, decorations shining and helmet plumes blowing in the breeze. Troops of the German Guard would have flanked their emperor as Claudius sat on a raised tribunal. There, in the words of the dedicatory inscription on the Arch of Claudius at Orange in France, 'he received the formal submission of eleven kings of the Britons'. [*CIL*, VI, 920] Sixteen days later, Claudius left Britain for a meandering return to Rome. He walked back into the Palatium the following year after an absence of six months, although he had only spent a little over two weeks in his new province of Britannia.

By the time autumn ended, the 2nd Augusta Legion controlled the south coast of England. Only western Devon and Cornwall remained to be subdued. At the River Exe in Devon, Vespasian and the 2nd Augusta turned the capital of the Dumnoni tribe on the east bank of the river, with its buildings of timber and mud, into what became the substantial Roman town of Isca Dumnoniorium, today's city of Exeter. There, the 2nd Augusta established a base which became the legion's new permanent home, from where it guarded a frontier from Devon up to southeast Wales.

By the end of AD 43, all four invasion legions had spread across southern England and set up permanent forward forts and rear supply bases. The 14th Gemina built its base in the West Country north of the 2nd Augusta's new home, the 20th based itself at Camulodunum, which Plautius made his provincial headquarters, and the 9th Hispana occupied a frontier line north of Camulodunum. The legions had come to stay.

Gold aureus of Claudius, showing his triumphal arch at Orange which celebrated the conquest of southern Britain.

AD 54-58
XVIII. CORBULO'S FIRST ARMENIAN CAMPAIGN
Tough treatment creates victorious legions

Tiridates, a Parthian prince, had now taken the throne of Armenia. With the death of Claudius, the chief advisers to the new teenage Roman emperor, Nero, convinced him that Rome must wrest Armenia from Parthian control. Those advisers, Nero's chief secretary, the famed philosopher Lucius Seneca, and Praetorian prefect Sextus Burrus, recommended that the man for the job in Armenia was Lucius Domitius Corbulo, one of Rome's toughest generals.

In AD 54, Corbulo went east to mastermind an Armenian offensive. Officially, Corbulo was the new governor of the provinces of Cappadocia and Galatia, on the Armenian border, but the Palatium had furnished him with powers superior to those of any provincial governor. When Corbulo arrived, he found the four legions stationed in Syria in a deplorable state. He chose the 6th Ferrata and 10th Fretensis legions to spearhead his planned campaign, but he would not embark on any military operation before he had knocked those units into shape. Many of their soldiers had sold their helmets and shields, most had never stood guard duty, some had become 'sleek money-making traders'. [Tac., *A*, XIII, 35]

Their standards might have identified these units as the 6th and 10th as legions, but they were not legions by Corbulo's standard. Discharging those who were too old or frail, Corbulo put the rest through a rigorous training schedule. At the end of the year, he marched his legions up into the Cappadocian mountains, making them winter there under canvas in the snow. Conditions were so severe that men stand-

Nero was just sixteen years of age when he came to the throne in AD 54, the year he gave Corbulo the task of regaining Armenia for Rome.

ing guard suffered frostbite. Corbulo shared the freezing conditions with his men, and as they toughened up they began to show grudging respect for their uncompromising general.

Corbulo was not a man to rush anything. It was AD 58 before he was satisfied with his men and his preparations. After adding six cohorts of the 3rd Gallica Legion from their station in Judea to the force he assembled in Cappadocia, in the spring of AD 58 Corbulo invaded Armenia. For the operation, legate Cornelius Flaccus led the 6th Ferrata Legion and the hard-bitten Syrians of the 3rd Gallica cohorts. Corbulo himself led the 10th Fretensis supported by auxiliaries. Their opponents were the Armenian army, trained and equipped in the same manner as their allies, the Parthians.

Corbulo, the tough-as-nails general chosen by Nero's Palatium to command the Armenian offensive.

With new Roman allies, the Moschi tribe, running wild in northern Armenia as a diversion, and with his supply lines over the mountains well guarded, Curbulo's legions swept into western Armenia from two directions, taking Tiridates' commanders entirely by surprise. In one day, Roman troops stormed three separate fortresses. At the fortress of Volandum, strongest in Armenia, Corbulo split his units into four groups, each using a different method of assault and in competition with the others to be the first to fight their way into the fortress. Volandum fell to Corbulo within hours, 'without the loss of a [Roman] soldier and with just a very few wounded'. All the adult males found at Volandum were executed. 'The non-military population were sold by auction. The rest of the booty fell to the conquerors.' [Tac., *A*, XIII, 39]

Courage and success were rewarded by Corbulo, but he could not stomach cowardice. Sextus Frontinus, a successful Roman general who knew him, wrote that when two cavalry squadrons and three cohorts gave way before the enemy near the Armenian fortress of Initia, Corbulo made their men sleep outside his camp walls 'until by steady work and successful raids they had atoned for their disgrace'. [Front.,

Strat., IV, I, 21] For the same crime, Corbulo stripped the clothes from the back of cavalry prefect Aemilius Rufus and made him stand naked at the praetorium until he chose to dismiss him. [Ibid., 28]

Linking up, Corbulo's two forces advanced on the Armenian capital, Artaxata, fording the River Avaxes downstream then swinging around to assault the city from the east. Marching in battle order on the plain and flanked by foot archers and squadrons of cavalry extending to the hills, the 6th Ferrata occupied the column's left wing, the 3rd Gallica the right. The 10th Fretensis marched in the middle with the baggage. Cavalry and auxiliaries comprised the rearguard.

King Tiridates brought thousands of horse archers pounding out on to the plain to intimidate the Roman troops, staying out of missile range on the flanks and keeping pace with the column. A young Roman cavalry prefect who had a rush of blood and galloped too close to the shadowing enemy, was filled with Armenian arrows. As night fell, Tiridates' horse archers melted away.

The next day, Tiridates and his army were reported to be withdrawing to the east. When Corbulo arrived outside Artaxata, the inhabitants threw open the gates. Because he had no capacity to hold or defend the exposed city, Corbulo ordered the inhabitants to pack and leave, then burned their city to the ground. He then marched west, with his troops unhappy that they had run out of grain for their daily bread and had only meat to eat. Nonetheless, the legionaries stormed two fortresses before the army reached the second city of Armenia, Tigranocerta, on the River Nicephorius in the southwest.

On hearing from his friend Frontinus that the Tigranocertans were very likely to make an obstinate defence, Corbulo executed Vadandus, a captured Armenian noble, then had Vadandus' head shot into the city by ballista. 'When the leaders of the city saw this,' said Frontinus, it 'so filled them with consternation that they made haste to surrender.' Tigranocerta swiftly opened its gates to Corbulo and his legions. [Front., *Strat.*, II, 5]

Nero had chosen a Cappodocian noble, Tigranes, to be king of Armenia, and the prince now arrived at Tigranocerta. Leaving Tigranes a palace guard of two legionary cohorts, 1,500 auxiliary infantry and some cavalry, Corbulo withdrew to Syria, of which he became governor on the death in office of incumbent Ummidius Quadratus.

After a swift, unstoppable campaign by Corbulo's three legions, Armenia was again in the Roman sphere.

AD 58–60

XIX. RIOTING IN JERUSALEM
Legionaries save the apostle Paul

On a late summer day in AD 58, the guard cohort of the 3rd Gallica Legion stationed at Jerusalem's Antonia Fortress was unexpectedly called to arms. That afternoon, towards the end of the 'hour of prayer' at the Jewish temple up on the Temple Mount, a riot had erupted, and 'all Jerusalem was in uproar'. [Acts, 21; 31]

A Jewish man from Cilicia had been assaulted in the Temple, then thrown out. As temple attendants pushed its massive bronze doors shut, the Cilician was being beaten by a crowd of angry Jews that grew larger by the minute. The 3rd Gallica's camp-prefect at the Antonia, Claudius Lysias, led forth 'soldiers and centurions, and ran down to them'. When the troops arrived on the scene, the crowd drew back. Camp-Prefect Lysias ordered the battered victim, a bald, bearded man in middle age,

The Antonia Fortress, praetorium of the legion cohorts stationed at Jerusalem, the place where Jesus Christ had been scourged decades earlier and where St Paul was briefly imprisoned in AD 58 before being spirited out of Jerusalem by the Roman commander.

to be bound hand and foot with two chains, then demanded to know from the crowd who this fellow was and what he had done. [Ibid., 32]

Lysias was answered by a cacophony of voices, all saying something different, so he ordered his men to carry the prisoner back to the Antonia. With the crowd following them, calling for the man's death, he was carried to the Antonia's gate. At the top of sixty steps that led to the gate, the prisoner, speaking Greek, asked Lysias if he might talk to him. Lysias, who, like many Romans throughout the East, was of Greek extraction, was surprised that the Jew spoke Greek. He then thought that he recognized the fellow as the Egyptian who, four years before, had led 4,000 followers against Jerusalem, only to have his band bloodily dispersed by the Roman garrison. But the man said that he was from the city of Tarsus in Cilicia, then asked for permission to speak to the crowd. Lysias agreed.

From the Antonia's steps, the Jew addressed the mob, which fell silent, as, speaking in their native tongue, he said that he was Saul of Tarsus, a Cilician Jew who had studied at Jerusalem under Gamaliel, a leading rabbi of the day. Later, he said, under the instructions of the Jewish High Priest and the Sanhedrin, he had hunted and imprisoned members of the breakaway Nazarene sect – the Christians. But while on the road to Damascus to collect more Christian prisoners, he had received a vision of Jesus of Nazareth. When he said that Jesus had instructed him to take his teachings to non Jews, however, the mob exploded with rage. 'It is not fit that he should live!' they exclaimed, casting off their clothes and throwing dust in the air in the Jewish custom. [Ibid., 22]

Camp-Prefect Lysias had the prisoner hustled inside the fortress and ordered that he should be interrogated under the lash. As the prisoner was being tied to a column with leather thongs and a flagellator was preparing, the prisoner asked the 3rd Gallica centurion in charge if it was lawful to whip a man who was a Roman citizen without a sentence from a magistrate. It was indeed illegal to punish a citizen without trial, and the worried centurion hurried off to tell the camp-prefect what the man had said. Lysias immediately came to see the prisoner, and demanded to know if he did truly hold citizenship. The man replied that he did. [Ibid., 25]

Apart from having the records checked in Tarsus, there was no way of confirming the prisoner's claim. Lysias was not convinced that the Jew would hold citizenship, saying that he himself had actually paid a large sum to acquire Roman citizenship when he was younger. The fact that Lysias' first name was Claudius suggests that the camp-prefect was a peregrine who had obtained his citizenship during the reign of Claudius, when the empress Valeria Messalina had notoriously taken bribes to arrange for her husband to grant citizenship to large numbers of people. The prisoner responded that he had been born a free man – intimating that he had possessed Roman citizenship since birth.

Lysias believed the man, who used both the Jewish name of Saul and the Roman name of Paulus. This was Paul, the Christian apostle. Lysias kept Paul in the fortress overnight. Next day, he took him before the Sanhedrin, the supreme Jewish religious counsel, to determine what charges they wished to lay against Paul, for the man had not broken any Roman law. When Paul revealed to the Sanhedrin that he had been raised a Pharisee, a Jewish sect which believed in resurrection, dissension broke out between the Sanhedrin's Pharisee and Sadducee members – Sadducees did not believe in resurrection. As the Jewish argument raged, Lysias returned Paul to the Antonia Fortress.

Paul had a sister living in Jerusalem, and later that day her son learned that more than forty Sadducees had vowed not to eat or drink until they had killed Paul. The young man was admitted to the Antonia to visit his uncle, and when he told Paul about this murder plot, Paul informed the camp-prefect. Lysias decided that the best way to avert trouble was to spirit Paul out of Jerusalem and send him to the Procurator of Judea, Antonius Felix, at Caesarea, and let him decide the Jew's fate. Accordingly, that evening Lysias had two of his centurions assemble an escort from the Roman troops stationed at Jerusalem. This comprised two centuries of legionaries, two centuries of auxiliary spearmen and seventy cavalrymen. [Ibid., 23–25]

As soon as darkness fell, in the third Roman hour of the night – roughly between 7.00 and 8.15 p.m. – Paul was led from the Antonia, placed on a mule, and with his escort around him, taken from the city. The centurion in charge took with him a letter from Lysias which urged Procurator Felix to decide what should be done. That night the party travelled as far as Antipatris in the Judean Hills. At dawn, the foot soldiers returned to Jerusalem while the cavalry continued on to Caesarea with Paul. [Ibid.]

Paul was kept at Caesarea for a year. In AD 59, he asserted his right as a Roman citizen to appeal directly to the emperor, and was sent to Rome with other prisoners. They were escorted by a centurion Julius and soldiers who were presumably from the 3rd Gallica Legion. After surviving shipwreck on the Maltese coast, prisoners and escort would arrive in Rome in AD 60. According to Christian tradition, Paul was released by Nero, only to be executed in Rome on other charges, several years later.

AD 60–61

XX. BOUDICCA'S BRITISH REVOLT
14th Gemina versus the warrior queen

'Close up the ranks, and having discharged your javelins, then with
shields and swords continue the work of bloodshed and destruction.'

SUETONIUS PAULINUS, ROMAN GENERAL, PRIOR TO THE BATTLE WITH
BOUDICCA'S BRITONS. TACITUS, *Annals*, XIV, 36.

Intent on subjugating the Welsh island of Anglesey, Gaius Suetonius Paulinus, governor of Britain for the past two years, marched out of Camulodunum in the spring of
AD 60, and, after assembling an army in the Welsh borderlands, pushed through the
mountain valleys towards the northwest coast of Wales. His task force was made up
of the 14th Gemina Legion and auxiliary cohorts including Batavian light infantry
which had fought beside the 14th Gemina for decades, plus the famous Batavian
Horse and other cavalry units.

Ambitious Paulinus had come to Britain with a big military reputation and
something to prove. In AD 42 he had cleared Mauretania of rebellious Moors, and,
according to Tacitus, this 'hard-working and sensible officer' was determined to use
his latest posting to challenge Corbulo, who had recently recovered Armenia for
Rome in the East, for the title of the empire's leading soldier. [Tac., *A*, XIV, 29; *Agr.*, 5]

Paulinus recognized that a unifying strand of the disparate British tribes was the
Druidic religion. The children of British nobles were educated by the Druid priests.
Some of these children themselves later became priests. Others became leaders of their
tribes. And all the tribes appealed to the same Celtic gods to give them the power to
defeat their enemies. Because of its seditious potential, Augustus had made it illegal
for Roman citizens to follow this Druidic religion, and Claudius banned it altogether,
empire-wide. The Druids' religious centre was on Anglesey, which was called Mona
Insula by the Romans. And Paulinus was determined to seize Mona and snuff out this
illegal cult, and so snuff out the Druidic fire at the heart of British resistance.

During the winter, the men of the 14th Gemina Legion had prepared by building
small, collapsible, flat-bottomed boats for river and inshore work. These were car-

ried in the task force's baggage train and unloaded at each river encountered on their progress through north Wales. From their jumping-off point at Deva, today's Chester, there were several major waterways to cross – the Dee, and later the Clwyd and Conway. The Roman force which reached the Menai Strait that summer launched its small boats once more, and began the crossing to Anglesey. They made the crossing in several places, the infantry rowing themselves across, part of the cavalry finding and using a shallow ford, and the Batavian squadrons swimming across with their horses.

Welsh warriors, probably from the Deceangli, Ordovice and Silure tribes, formed up on the southeastern shore of the island in 'dense array' and waited for the Roman troops to land. [Tac., A, XIV, 30] As the legionaries and their auxiliary colleagues clambered from their boats, frenzied women came dashing through the assembled Celtic ranks. Dressed in black, their hair dishevelled, the women waved burning firebrands and shrieked like animals. All around, Druid priests raised their hands to heaven and called down the wrath of their gods on the heads of the invaders.

The sight of these witches' crazy antics dazed the superstitious legionaries, and they froze in their ranks, not even raising their shields to protect themselves as they watched. It took Paulinus himself to take the lead, goading his men into action by asking if they were afraid of women. Without waiting for the cavalry to join them, the legionaries charged forward and cut down warriors and witches alike. Piles of Celtic bodies were soon being consumed in the flames of funeral pyres lit with the women's own firebrands.

Roman troops spread over the island, locating the sacred groves where the Druids reputedly made human sacrifices, and rounding up prisoners. But as the Roman general was congratulating himself on his success, urgent dispatches arrived from the east – there had been an uprising of tribes in eastern Britain. Paulinus ordered his troops to prepare to march.

Prasutagus, king of the Iceni tribe of Norfolk in East Anglia, had died a year or so before. To preserve his kingdom, and his family's control of it, he had willed his Iceni territory jointly to his two daughters and to the Roman emperor Nero. This was designed to keep his family in power, with the protection of Rome. But it had not worked out as Prasutagus had planned. Procurator Decianus Catus, the Roman financial administrator of the province of Britain, had taken the terms of the will literally and sent his staff into the Iceni kingdom to confiscate the homes and property of many nobles in the name of the emperor. The slaves in his employ had not only ransacked the villa of the late king, they had raped his two virgin daughters. And when his widow had tried to intervene, they had stripped and whipped her. Queen Boudicca, young wife of King Prasutagus, had vowed vengeance on the Romans in the name of Andraste, Iceni goddess of war. [Dio, LXII, 6]

Cassius Dio wrote that there was another, financial cause of discontent among the British tribes at this time. The wealthy philosopher Lucius Annaeus Seneca, who was Nero's chief secretary, had loaned the tribes 40 million sesterces, only to call in the money at short notice. Seneca, said Dio, had 'resorted to severe measures in enacting' repayment of the loan. [Ibid., 2]

Insult was added to injury by the legion veterans who had settled in the recently proclaimed military colony at Camulodunum, who 'drove people out of their houses' and 'ejected them from their farms'. Boudicca and her incensed Iceni nobles had met in secret and conspired against their Roman overlords, sending envoys to the Trinovantes tribe in Essex to the south, just above the Thames, bringing them into their revolutionary plot. [Tac., A, XIV, 31]

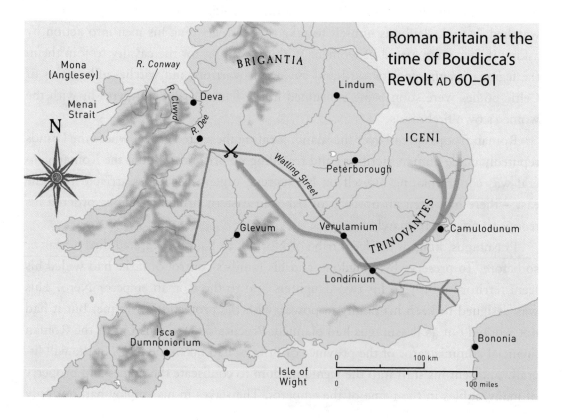

Roman Britain at the time of Boudicca's Revolt AD 60–61

IST ADIUTRIX

IST GERMANICA

IST ITALICA

IST MINERVIA

IST PARTHICA

2ND ADIUTRIX

2ND AUGUSTA

2ND ITALICA

2ND PARTHICA

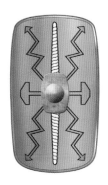

2ND TRAIANA

3RD AUGUSTA

3RD CYRENAICA

3RD GALLICA

3RD ITALICA

3RD PARTHICA

4TH FLAVIA

4TH MACEDONICA

4TH SCYTHICA

5TH ALAUDAE

5TH MACEDONICA

6TH FERRATA

6TH VICTRIX

7TH CLAUDIA

7TH GEMINA

8TH AUGUSTA

9TH HISPANA

10TH FRETENSIS

10TH GEMINA

11TH CLAUDIA

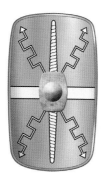

12TH FULMINATA

13TH GEMINA

14TH GEMINA MARTIA
VICTRIX

15TH APOLLINARIS

15TH PRIMIGENEIA

16TH GALLICA

16TH FLAVIA FIRMA

17TH GALLICA

18TH GALLICA

19TH GALLICA

20TH VALERIA VICTRIX

21ST RAPAX

22ND DEIOTARIANA

22ND PRIMIGENEIA
PIA FIDELIS

30TH ULPIA

PRAETORIAN
GUARD

GERMAN GUARD

IMPERIAL
SINGULARIAN HORSE

This golden sword and scabbard would have been the proud possession of an imperial officer. (p.32)

A cameo showing the emperor Augustus early in his reign. Augustus was the father of the imperial legions, improving their organisation and command structure. (p. 18)

Roman officers and marines ready to storm aboard an opposition ship. The ship's oarsmen, out of sight below deck, were paid seamen, not slaves, and were trained to join shipboard fighting also. (p. 56)

This Roman aqueduct along the Mediterranean Sea, in Caesaria, Israel, was built by troops of the 10th Fretensis Legion. (p. 158)

Rome's chariot-racing corporations had first call on horses from stud farms throughout the Empire, even ahead of the Roman army. This charioteer, represented in a pavement mosaic, drove for the Greens corporation. (p. 204)

Scythian fighters such as these shown on a gold ornament were typically armed with bows and arrows. It was for defeating warriors like these that the 4th Scythica Legion gained its title. (p.216)

This sculpture depicts Claudius overwhelming a female figure representing Britannia. Claudius, who had no military experience, silenced his military critics by masterminding the AD 43 invasion of Britain by four legions. (p. 294).

Built by Herod the Great and named after his friend Mark Antony, Jerusalem's massive Antonia Fortress was praetorium of the legion cohorts stationed at Jerusalem. Falling to Jewish rebels in AD 66, it was levelled by Titus' legions in AD 70. (p. 299)

The rocky outcrop of Masada, today, showing the remains of the palace of Herod. Masada was one of the first Roman fortresses to fall to Jewish rebels in AD 66. It was retaken by the 10th Fretensis Legion and auxilary units in AD 73. (p. 355)

Chronicling Trajan's second-century conquest of Dacia after two bloody wars, Trajan's Column was designed to be 'read' by walking around the ramped structure, which no longer exists, that originally wound around it. (p. 409)

Marcus Aurelius spent most of his second-century reign away from Rome, leading the fight against German tribes who invaded Roman territory via the Danube. (p. 464)

Ctesiphon, one of the Parthian capitals, ruins of which are seen here today, was the target of various Roman invasions, and was twice taken by the legions. (p. 452)

The soldier emperor Pertinax, depicted on this gold coin, reigned only for several months. His murder inspired Septimius Severus to take the throne and to punish the Praetorian Guard for the murder. (p. 474)

The soldier emperor Septimius Severus, at right, with his sons, the ambitous Caracalla and the ill-fated Geta. This relief, dating from around AD 203-204, is from the Arch of Severus, in Severus's home town of Leptis Magna, in today's Libya, North Africa.

Elagablus, reigning from AD 218–222, was only 14 when he became emperor through the support of the legions. His eccentric behaviour led to his assassination by his own Praetorian Guard, not an uncommon fate for wayward emperors. (p. 490)

Maximinus was busy fighting barbarians in the Balkans, as depicted here on the Ludovisi Sarcaphagus, when news arrived that the Senate had replaced him with the Gordians, father and son. He led his legions to Italy to defend his throne, only to be murdered by men of his own 2nd Parthica Legion and Praetorians. (p. 494)

The Temple of Bel in the heart of the city-state of Palmyra. The city was destroyed by Rome's legions after the defeat of Queen Zenobia's army. Zenobia would be led through the streets in golden chains during a Triumph. Living at Hadrian's Villa at Tivoli outside Rome, she would eventually marry a Roman senator. (p. 500)

Valentinian I, depicted here on a medallion, was a cavalry commander prior to attaining the throne, and fought in Julian's famous victory at Argentoratum, today's Strasbourg, against a large invading German army. (p. 526)

For years Alaric and his Visigoths were kept beyond these massive Aurelian Walls around Rome by Stilicho and his legions. Once Stilicho was dead, Alaric's AD 410 sack of Rome was inevitable. (p. 574)

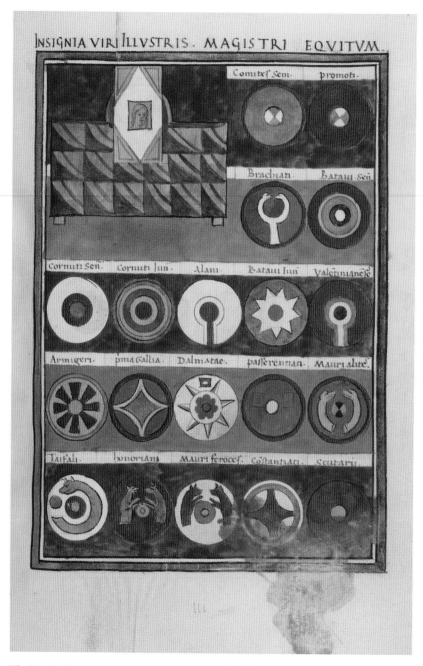

The Notitia Dignitatum, whose pages are variously dated by scholars between AD 360 and 420, depicts shield emblems and shows postings for hundreds of Late Empire units. Many of these units had disappeared by the start of the fifth century, wiped out by the Persians in the East and invaders from beyond the Rhine and Danube. (p. 577)

All tribal thoughts turned to rebellion, and, instead of sowing the new season's wheat crop, tribesmen had devoted their time to making arms, with the intention of helping themselves to the contents of the granaries of the Roman legions' fortresses once the rebellion began. The rebel leadership elected Boudicca their war queen, and deliberately timed their uprising for when the governor and many of his troops were away campaigning, in the summer of AD 60.

The revolt was first felt at Camulodunum, home to tens of thousands of Roman citizen settlers and Romanized Britons. With the Iceni descending from the north and the Trinovantes flooding up from the south, 120,000 wild-eyed rebels swarmed into the city, killing everyone they encountered. The desperate people of Camulodunum sent messengers galloping away seeking help. [Dio, LXII, 2] Some messengers hurried to the southwest to Londinium (London). Others rode northwest to the base of the nearest legion, the 9th Hispana, at today's Longthorpe, near Peterborough.

'There was in the place [Camulodunum] only a small military force,' said Tacitus. [Tac., A, XIV, 32] There were two Roman military camps at Camulodunum at this time. The main camp, originally of more than 40 acres (16 hectares), had been occupied by the 20th Legion for a number of years prior to its transfer west. Archaeological evidence shows that although this camp had been scaled down to half its size, it was still in use in AD 60. There was also a fully operational 26-acre (10.4-hectare) cavalry camp on the southwestern side of the city, which was occupied by the 1st Thracian Ala until AD 71. [Hold., *RAB*, App.]

Auxiliaries of this small force at Camulodunum combined with legion veterans residing there, who hurriedly assembled at the massive nine-year-old temple of Claudius at the centre of the city. The senior centurions decided to attempt to defend the temple, and were joined by thousands of terrified civilians – men, women and children, many of them the families of the retired legionaries. The civilians would have clustered in the temple basement, which still exists today beneath the Norman castle later built over the site of the Roman temple.

From Londinium, Procurator Catus, who had stoked the uprising, sent 200 men 'without regular arms' – probably his slaves, armed merely with cudgels – in response to the call for help. Catus himself boarded a ship at the Londinium wharves, and sailed for Gaul, and safety. The Temple of Claudius at Camulodunum was surrounded by the rebels, and for two days the veterans and their supporters held out. In the end, rebel agents among those inside the temple provided access for the tribesmen.

Thousands of Boudicca's warriors then flooded in and overwhelmed the defenders.

At the Roman base at Longthorpe, the new commander of the 9th Hispana Legion, Quintus Petilius Cerialis Caesius Rufus, received Camulodunum's urgent plea for help, and quickly assembled a relief force. [W&D, 6, n. 15] Cerialis (whose last two names indicate that he had blue eyes and red hair), was married to the cousin of Vespasian, former commander of the 2nd Augusta Legion and future emperor.

Archaeology suggests that the Longthorpe base could only accommodate 2,500 men, or five legion cohorts. Subsequent events indicate that, leaving one cohort to garrison the fort, Cerialis set off for Camulodunum with the 2,000 men of four cohorts of the 9th Hispana and several squadrons of cavalry. With the pace of the relief force dictated by the marching speed of the infantry, at best Cerialis' force would have taken four days to reach Camulodunum, using the paved military highways that led south and east. Unbeknownst to the men of the relief force, when they were only halfway to their destination, Camulodunum fell.

Meanwhile, Boudicca's rebel Britons were plundering and burning the city, and torturing and killing their thousands of Roman captives. According to Tacitus, some Romans at Camulodunum were hanged on gallows while others were crucified. All were subjected to torture by fire. [Tac., A, XIV, 33]

Dio described Roman prisoners being impaled on red-hot skewers and boiled alive. Some were forced to look at their own entrails after they had been cut from their bodies. Dio says that female Romans captives came in for particularly barbaric torture and mutilation at the hands of the Britons. [Dio, LXII, 7]

Approaching Camulodunum, Roman legate Cerialis and his 9th Hispana column were routed by rebels as they were 'coming to the rescue' of their countrymen. According to Tacitus, all 2,000 of Cerialis' infantry were wiped out, after which 'Cerialis escaped with some cavalry into the camp, and was saved by its fortifications'. [Tac., A, XIV, 33]

Many modern writers have assumed this meant that Cerialis returned to his Peterborough camp, but it is more likely that, in darkness, Cerialis and his troopers gained the safety of one of the two camps at Camulodunum, which would have been much closer – probably the smaller cavalry camp. For, as Tacitus also pointed out, 'the barbarians, who delighted in plunder and were indifferent to all else, passed by the fortresses with garrisons and attacked whatever offered most wealth'. [Ibid.] And there is no evidence the rebels went anywhere near Peterborough. Cerialis, behind the walls of the fort at Camulodunum, was saved by the rebels' plundering mindset and lack of siege skills.

From Wales, the province's propraetor Suetonius Paulinus came marching at the double with most of his Anglesey task force, having left several cohorts of auxiliaries on the island. He headed for Deva and then to Watling Street, the military road

This statue of Boudicca and her daughters gracing London's Thames Embankment ironically celebrates the war queen who destroyed London. Boudicca is shown here, incorrectly, in a Roman-style chariot, while the scythes on the wheels are the product of myth.

which sliced across England all the way to Londinium and the Thames. Mounted messengers galloped ahead, summoning reinforcements. Some rode as far as Isca Dumnoniorium, base of the 2nd Augusta Legion. General Paulinus would have carefully weighed his troop options. The 9th Hispana had just lost 2,000 men through Cerialis' rashness. If Paulinus were to take any more men away from the northern frontier forts he would invite tribesmen to the north to come flooding down and join the rebellion. To the west, the 20th Legion was holding the frontier; to withdraw the legion from their western defence line could invite the aggressive Silures to attack the Romans from the rear while they were trying to deal with Boudicca.

Tacitus writes that the army which Paulinus put together comprised 'the 14th Legion with veterans of the 20th and auxiliaries from the neighbourhood'. These 'veterans of the 20th' were almost certainly Evocati militiamen, recalled to their 20th Legion standards by the governor after recently going into retirement, leaving the serving men of the legion to keep guard on the western frontier. Meanwhile, the officer in charge of the 2nd Augusta – both the legate and tribune of the legion were apparently absent – was the camp-prefect Poenius Postumus. Inconceivably, on receiving orders from the propraetor to march the 2nd Augusta Legion to his support, Postumus ignored them. [Ibid., 34]

On the march, Paulinus was met by some 2,500 veterans of the 20th Legion. Combined with the 14th Gemina, which would have been close to full strength with around 5,000 men, plus 2,000 auxiliary infantry and 500 cavalry, Paulinus' force now numbered, said Tacitus, 10,000 fighting men. [Ibid.] With this small force, Paulinus had to confront a rebel army which he knew from initial reports numbered in excess of 100,000 warriors.

Paulinus pressed on to Londinium. By this time a wooden bridge crossed the snaking Tamesa river – the Roman bridge site is occupied today by London Bridge. A settlement had swiftly grown north of the bridge. Gracechurch Street today traces the Roman thoroughfare that led from the bridge up to the hub of the first-century settlement at Cornhill, with today's Bank of England at the centre of Roman London. By AD 60, the settlement had spread west to the hill occupied in modern times by St Paul's Cathedral. Near today's Lloyd's of London, at the site of the present-day Leadenhall Market, stood London's basilica, the settlement's meeting hall and law court.

To one side of the bridge, the riverbank was lined with docks, which at any other time would have been crowded with trading vessels from Europe. Now, those docks were deserted. The merchantmen had fled, and the people of London, who had heard that the rebels were coming, were in a state of panic. They flocked around Paulinus and his troops, urging the governor to prepare defences. Instead, he offered a place in his column to anyone who cared to leave with him, for he could not and would not defend London with so few troops. Thousands of refugees joined him, but other Londoners, convinced they had nothing to fear from the rebels, stayed. Paulinus retreated north, accepting more frightened civilians into his column as he passed through Verulamium, today's St Albans, then continued to withdraw to the northwest.

Boudicca and tens of thousands of warriors from the Iceni, Trinovantes and other tribes who had now joined the revolt descended on Londinium like a horde of locusts. They brought their families with them, in a train of wagons and carts for booty. The tribesmen tortured and killed everyone they found; then, after looting the city, burned it to the ground. Verulamium suffered the same bloody, destructive fate as Londinium and Camulodunum before the rebels moved on to pursue Paulinus' column, leaving Verulamium in flames which soon consumed the corpses of its tortured occupants.

In a few chaotic weeks, Rome's three principal settlements in the province of Britain had been destroyed by the rebels, and 80,000 Roman citizens and their allies had been slain. [Dio, LXII, 1] Tacitus was to marvel that the rebels saved no prisoners to sell as slaves. To him, the Britons had no head for business. As for the rebel killing spree, Tacitus likened it to a man seeking vengeance for his own imminent execution. [Tac., *A*, XIV, 33]

By the time that Paulinus' column reached today's Warwickshire, it would have been clear to the governor that the 2nd Augusta Legion was not going to join him. He realized, too, that if he continued to retreat, within a few days he would be at the frontier, while behind him, the rebels would be in possession of most of Roman Britain. Despite being hugely outnumbered, Paulinus decided that the time had come to fight. He would, in his own reported words, face the rebels and 'conquer them, or die on the spot'. [Dio, LXII, 11]

Precisely where Paulinus and Boudicca did battle is the subject of hot dispute among modern historians. The most likely site is near today's village of Mancetter, on the border between Warwickshire and Leicestershire. Mancetter takes its name from a Roman settlement which later grew here called Manduessedum, or 'place of the chariots' – in the British army that was pursuing Paulinus there were numerous war chariots, which would soon be in action here. Halting his column, Paulinus gave orders for his troops to build a marching camp and for the civilian refugees to continue on, no doubt to seek shelter at the Roman frontier fortresses at Wall and Wroxeter. As his men built their camp, Paulinus went for a ride, looking for a battle site. He settled on a location believed by many historians to be not far from the Anker river. According to Tacitus, it was approached by a narrow defile through the hills, which opened out on to a plain. [Tac., *A*, XIV, 34]

The Romans did not have to wait long before Boudicca and her massive throng came up Watling Street from the south. On a summer's morning, after his scouts had assured him there were no Britons in his rear, Paulinus had his little army form up in battle order at the chosen place. According to Dio, new additions to the rebels' ranks meant that Boudicca's army had almost doubled in size since the attack on Camulodunum, to a massive 230,000 fighting men. [Dio, LXII, 8] It was, said Tacitus, 'a vaster host than ever had assembled'; the largest opposition army ever encountered by the Romans. [Tac., *A*, XIV, 34] It was also by far the largest army to do battle on Britain's shores, ever.

On Paulinus' orders, the Roman troops formed three wedge formations. The men of the 14th Gemina Legion occupied the centre, standing at the head of the defile. The Evocati cohorts of the 20th Legion were joined with them. The auxiliary cohorts were either side of them. The cavalry squadrons occupied the wings. The men of all three wedges were in 'close array'. Across the field, the Britons had 'masses of infantry and cavalry'. [Ibid.]

The rebels were so confident of success that their families had parked their booty-laden wagons in a semicircle at the rear, from where they could watch the battle. On one side of the field, the Roman legionaries wore helmets and body armour. [Dio, LXII, 5] The warriors had neither armour nor helmets, while their first-use weapon was the framea. Each Briton carried a flat oak shield, covered with hide, and longer than the legionary shield. [Warry, *WCW*]

Many British nobles were equipped with captured Roman arms. And they had their chariots – small, light, open-ended, with wheels just 3 feet (30 centimetres) across, and drawn by a pair of nimble ponies. The design of the British chariot had not changed since Caesar encountered 4,000 of them during his 55 BC campaign. The number fielded by Boudicca's rebels is unknown, but they are unlikely to have been numerous, for there had been little time to build them and train chariot horses.

Boudicca herself appeared in a chariot, with her long, red-brown hair flowing.

[Dio, LXII, 2] 'With her daughters before her' in the chariot, Boudicca galloped from one tribe to another to deliver pre-battle speeches. [Tac., XIV, 35] Boudicca urged the warriors to die rather than live under Roman rule. She reminded them how they had punished the 9th Hispana Legion, and assured them that the rest of the Roman troops on the island were cowering in their camps and planning to flee. 'Let us show them that they are hares and foxes, trying to rule over dogs and wolves!' [Dio, LXII, 5]

Against such massive odds of perhaps twenty-three to one, most Roman troops were only thinking of survival. Gnaeus Julius Agricola, a 19-year-old junior tribune on governor Paulinus' staff this day, would later tell son-in-law Tacitus that 'they had to fight for their lives before they could think of victory' in this battle. [Tac., *Agr.*, 5] Yet the Roman commander was confident of success. He too addressed his troops, riding to each of the three divisions. Paulinus' speeches had a common core: 'Close up the ranks, and having discharged your javelins, then with shields and swords continue the work of bloodshed and destruction.' [Tac., *A*, XIV, 36]

And then the British chariots were lumbering forward. Celtic warriors advanced at the walk behind them, roaring out their battle cries. The Roman formations stood their ground, waiting. The chariots gathered speed. As they charged the Roman wedges, their passengers let fly with a volley of spears, which Roman shields parried. The legionaries then let fly with their first flight of javelins, then another. As Roman missiles found targets, wounded chariot horses went down, spewing out passengers. Surviving vehicles swung away and made way for the British infantry.

'At first, the legion kept its position,' Tacitus wrote of the 14th Gemina. [Tac., XIV, 37] Then, Roman trumpets sounded 'Charge'. With a roar, the men of the 14th 'rushed out in a wedge formation', and the two tight-knit wedges either side of them did the same. The two enemy forces crashed together. With shields pumping in and out and swords jabbing over the top, the Roman wedges were like machines. On the flanks, the Roman cavalry also became engaged, using their javelins as lances. [Ibid.]

Romans and Britons 'contended for a long time,' said Dio, 'both parties being animated by the same zeal and daring. But finally, late in the day, the Romans prevailed'. [Dio, LXII, 12] Britons, trying to retreat, created a crush that met the semicircle of their own wagons, which penned them in. Tens of thousands of Britons were trapped, and fell victim to legionary blades as the Roman force pressed all the way to the wagon line. The immense slaughter during this battle was to include British women at the wagon line; it was estimated that 80,000 British warriors and civilians died. Even baggage animals perished in the maelstrom. Total Roman casualties were an estimated 400 dead, and a similar number wounded. [Tac., *A*, XIV, 37]

Ironically, the most deadly battle ever to take place in Britain was never given a name; perhaps it might be called the Battle of Watling Street. Boudicca escaped from the battlefield, but within a few days she too was dead, taking poison, according to Tacitus. [Ibid.] 'The Britons mourned her deeply,' said Dio. [Dio, LXII, 12] When camp-prefect Postumus of the 2nd Augusta Legion at Exeter came to hear of the battle and the signal Roman victory, he fell on his sword rather than face arrest for disobeying orders, which would have resulted in court martial and an inevitable death sentence.

The Palatium rushed reinforcements to Britain to make up for losses suffered during the revolt, among them eight cohorts of auxiliaries and 1,000 cavalry. Uniquely, 2,000 legionaries were also detached from a legion on the Rhine to fill the places of the men of the 9th Hispana lost under Cerialis. [Tac., *A*, XIV, 38] Everything points to these legionaries being recent recruits to the 21st Rapax Legion at Vindonissa. Later events show that the Rapax was well under strength eight years later, missing at least four cohorts, indicating that it never received replacements for the men sent to the 9th Hispana.

Governor Paulinus, stung by the uprising and the destruction that had resulted, kept his troops in the field and 'under canvas' right through the winter of AD 60–61 as he strove to capture those rebels who had escaped, determined to damp out the last fires of rebellion across southern England. [Ibid.] Julius Classicanus, the official sent by the Palatium to replace the cowardly procurator Catus, reported to Rome that the troubles in Britain would continue while the vengeful Paulinus remained in charge. In late AD 61, Paulinus was recalled to Rome, with Petronius Turpilianus replacing him as propraetor of Britain.

Despite the recall, Nero awarded the coveted Triumphal Decorations to Paulinus for his British victory, and six years later Paulinus was given a second consulship by the emperor. The 14th Gemina Legion was also recognized. Tacitus would later report: 'The 14th having particularly distinguished itself by quelling the revolt in Britain, Nero had added to their reputation of by selecting them as his "most effective" troops.' [Tac., *H*, II, 11] There would never again be an uprising by British tribes in southern Britain.

AD 62–63

XXI. CORBULO'S SECOND ARMENIAN CAMPAIGN
Snatching victory from disaster's door

In AD 62, Armenia again erupted in conflict, as Parthia reasserted its claim to the country by invading it. The Parthian invasion force was led by Moneses, King Vologases of Parthia's best general. The Parthians surrounded the new Armenian capital, Tigranocerta, where the king installed by Rome, Tigranes, was fiercely defended by his Roman bodyguard. When word of the invasion reached Corbulo in Syria, he sent two legions under Verulanus Severus marching up into Armenia at full speed to relieve the Roman defenders.

As the two legions approached, the Parthians suspended their siege and withdrew from Armenia. The Roman garrison also withdrew from Tigranocerta and joined the two legions in camp across the border in Cappadocia for the winter. Corbulo now sent to Rome for reinforcements and a senior general to take charge of the defence of Armenia. In response, the Palatium sent out the boastful Gaius Caesennius Paetus,

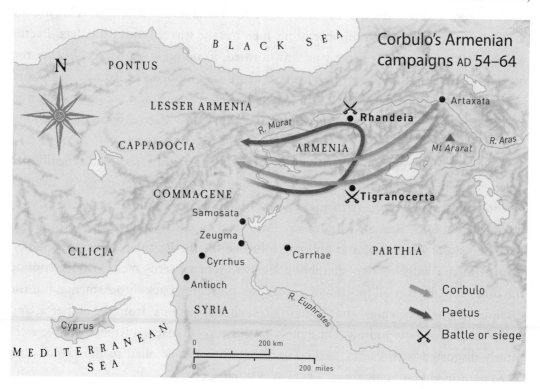

a consul in AD 60, together with the 4th Scythica Legion from Macedonia and the 5th Macedonica Legion from Moesia, the latter having recently replenished its ranks with a new enlistment of recruits in Moesia. Paetus chose to leave the 5th Macedonica in Pontus after it landed from the fleet that had brought it across the Black Sea. Over-confident, Paetus felt sure he would only need two legions in Armenia, and summoned a legion from the Syrian station, the 12th Fulminata, to join the newly arrived 4th Scythica.

In the meantime, the Parthians had sent envoys to Rome, but, unable to reach an agreement with Nero, King Vologases recommenced hostilities, aiming now not only to occupy Armenia but to invade Syria as well. To defend Syria, Corbulo had the 6th Ferrata, 10th Fretensis and cohorts of the 3rd Gallica Legion dig in along the bank of the Euphrates river, Syria's natural border with Parthia. Paetus, meanwhile, declaring that he would achieve total victory, crossed the Euphrates with the 4th Scythica and 12th Fulminata legions and entered Armenia. From the beginning, the omens were not good: the horse carrying Paetus' personal consular emblems across the bridge spanning the Euphrates took fright and bolted to the rear.

The inept Paetus subsequently camped at Rhandeia in northwestern Armenia for the winter, even allowing a number of his men to take leave. From Rhandeia, Paetus wrote a letter to Nero 'as if the war was finished, in pompous language, but barren of facts'. There at Rhandeia, the Parthian army surrounded the Roman camp and subjected it to a gruelling siege. As the weeks passed, Paetus' increasingly hungry and poorly led troops lost the will for offensive action. Now Paetus wrote to Corbulo, begging him to come and rescue him. [Tac., A, xv, 8]

Corbulo, after repulsing the Parthian attack at the Euphrates, methodically put together a relief column, including an ala, or wing, of camels carrying grain. Even as Corbulo was marching to Armenia, Paetus was agreeing to humiliating terms with the Parthians for a Roman withdrawal. After leaving all their baggage and piles of Roman dead at Rhandeia, and building a bridge for the Parthians, Paetus retreated from Armenia with his two shambling legions. When Paetus met Corbulo coming the other way, he was all for joining forces and marching back into Armenia, but the disciplined Corbulo replied that he had 'no such instructions' from the emperor, and both Roman forces withdrew. Once news of this reverse reached Rome, 'people were utterly disgusted with Paetus,' said Tacitus. Paetus was recalled to the capital, but Nero pardoned him 'with a jest'. [Tac., A, xv, 17; 25]

Corbulo, after bolstering his forces with the 5th Macedonica and 15th Apollinaris legions, conducted negotiations with the Parthian king Vologases from a position of strength. In the end, it was agreed that Corbulo would withdrew his troops from Parthian soil east of the Euphrates and the Parthians would withdraw from Armenia. Just as importantly, the peace treaty negotiated by Corbulo and Vologases stipulated that Vologases' brother Tiridates would resume the throne of Armenia, but would become an ally of Rome and swear allegiance to Nero.

Within several years, as part of this treaty, Tiridates would go to Rome to bow down to Nero personally. Meanwhile, Corbulo, one of Rome's best generals, would be forced to commit suicide after his son-in-law Vinianus Annius, who commanded the 5th Macedonica Legion in the last stages of the Armenian operations, foolishly implicated him in a plot against Nero.

AD 66

XXII. FIRST JEWISH REVOLT
Death in Judea

The coals of revolt had been glowing hot in Judea ever since Gessius Florus had been made procurator of the sub-province in AD 64. Florus' rapacity and brutality would soon fan the revolt into all-devouring flame.

On 3 June AD 66, Florus arrived at Jerusalem from the provincial capital, Caesarea on the Mediterranean coast, with two legionary cohorts – almost certainly from the 3rd Gallica Legion – to punish the Jews for recent rioting. After allowing one cohort to loot the city precinct of Betheza, or New City, which resulted in the deaths of hundreds of Jews, a vast mob cut Florus off at the Antonia Fortress. By agreement with the Jews, Florus slipped out of Jerusalem in the dead of night, leaving just a single legionary cohort in the city.

Complaints from Jewish leaders about Florus' heavy-handedness brought no response from his superior Cestius Gallus, propraetor of Syria, so they sent to King Agrippa of Chalcis, asking for help before things got out of hand and local resentment turned into rebellion. Agrippa, a pro-Roman Jew, sent 2,000 troopers from his bodyguard to Jerusalem to dampen the unrest. But by the time they arrived, Eleazar, captain of the Temple Guard, had taken possession of the lower city with thousands of his men and was besieging the lone cohort of the 3rd Gallica stationed at the Antonia Fortress and Herod's Palace. Other rebels were trying to break through the huge Temple doors. From throughout the city, Jews flocked to join the uprising.

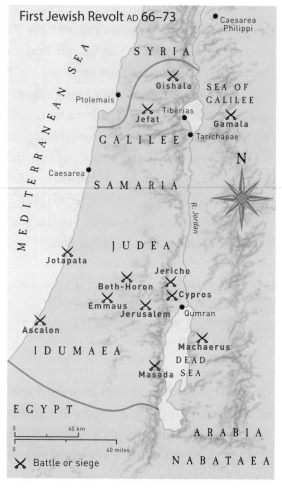

First Jewish Revolt AD 66–73

Some of Agrippa's cavalrymen were let into the temple by pro-Roman priests, while others joined the Roman defenders of Herod's Palace in the west of the city. The Temple, Antonia Fortress and palace were soon isolated. For eight days, battle raged, before attackers managed to trick their way into the Temple and take it over. Most of Agrippa's troops there escaped and fought their way to the legionaries at Herod's Palace. The rebels then concentrated their assault on the massive but lightly defended Antonia Fortress. Two days later, the 250 men of the 3rd Gallica defending the Antonia were overwhelmed by tens of thousands of besiegers and wiped out.

Meanwhile, Jews of the fanatical Zealot faction had hurried to attack other Roman garrisons. Roman troops were stationed at Masada beside the salt lake called the Dead Sea, south of Jerusalem. With these troops unaware of the uprising, the partisans were able to trick their way into the fortress and massacre them. In taking Masada, the rebels gained access to an arsenal for 10,000 men and extensive food stocks stored there since the time of Herod the Great. Most of the conquerors of Masada then hurried back to Jerusalem, where their leader, Menahem, demanded and received the leadership of all partisan forces. Menahem then led a resumed offensive against the 3rd Gallica legionaries holding out at Herod's Palace.

After King Agrippa's troops made an agreement with the partisans and withdrew, the men of the 3rd Gallica were on their own. Soon, with his men out of food, water and ammunition, the senior Roman centurion, Metilius, offered to capitulate if his life and the lives of his legionaries could be saved. The rebels agreed, on condition that the Romans left the palace and disarmed. To seal the agreement, both sides exchanged oaths. Shortly after, the surviving Roman soldiers, probably around 200 of them, emerged from the palace and laid down their weapons. Partisan leader Eleazar then gave a signal, and his men fell on the unarmed Romans and slaughtered them. One Roman was spared, centurion Metilius, who begged for his life and swore to convert to Judaism and submit to circumcision.

Men of the 3rd Gallica garrisoning the fortress at Cypros near Jericho were also caught off guard and exterminated by the partisans. But the 3rd Gallica cohort stationed at the fortress of Machaerus, to the east of the Dead Sea, was prepared for the Jews who surrounded their outpost. The partisans therefore agreed to let these legionaries depart in peace if they surrendered the fortress. Fully armed still, this cohort managed to reach Caesarea intact. By August, most of Judea had been lost, with 1,500 men of the 3rd Gallica Legion killed.

A Roman counter-offensive was inevitable. After three months' preparation, Syria's governor, Cestius Gallus, departed from Antioch to terminate the revolt. According to Josephus, Gallus marched south with the 12th Fulminata Legion and four cohorts from each of 'the others', meaning the other legions stationed in Syria: the 4th Scythica at Zeugma, the 6th Ferrata at Raphanaea and the 10th Fretensis at Cyrrhus. On reaching Caesarea, Gallus would also have added four surviving cohorts of the 3rd Gallica to his force, which also included six auxiliary cohorts and four cavalry wings. King Agrippa of Chalcis joined him with 3,000 foot and 1,000 cavalry. King Antiochus of Commagene sent him 2,000 cavalry, 3,000 foot soldiers and 3,000 archers, and Sohemus, king of Emesa, brought 4,000 men, a mixture of cavalry and foot archers. [Jos., *JW*, 2, 18, 9]

After securing Galilee and destroying the Jewish city of Jotapata, Gallus' army climbed up into the Judean Hills and reached Jerusalem in November AD 66. But after a half-hearted, five-day assault on the city, Gallus unaccountably pulled out his force. On the Beth-Horon road, retreating to the coast, his troops were constantly harassed by the partisans. In this embattled retreat, with fighting going on for days and with 400 Roman volunteers sacrificing their lives at a Beth-Horon village to give the army time to escape, the eagle of the 12th Fulminata Legion was lost to the partisans. Gallus' failed mission cost 5,680 men. He himself died shortly after. And the Jews still controlled much of Judea.

AD 67–69
XXIII. VESPASIAN TAKES COMMAND
Rolling back revolt

In December AD 66, Nero, who was then in Greece, appointed Titus Flavius Vespasianus to lead a new counter-offensive against the Jewish rebels. The 57-year-old Vespasian, renowned as commander of the 2nd Augusta Legion during the invasion of Britain twenty-four years earlier, left the imperial party in Greece and hurried away to put together a task force. At the same time, he sent his eldest son Titus, then a tribune, to Egypt to bring him troops stationed there. At Ptolemais in southern Syria, Vespasian assembled 60,000 men. Ignoring most of the troops involved in Gallus' morale-sapping venture, Vespasian based his force around the 5th Macedonica and 15th Apollinaris legions from Egypt, the Syrian-based 10th Fretensis Legion and the 3rd Gallica's remaining cohorts. The same kings who had supported Gallus' failed expedition also contributed to Vespasian's army, with Malchus, king of Arabia, also supplying 2,000 cavalry and infantry. [Jos., JW, 3, 4, 2]

It took until June AD 67 before Vespasian's army had completed preparations and was marching into Galilee, where the Jewish defenders were led by 30-year-old priest Josephus, the later historian who would write the story of the Jewish Revolt. After the walled town of Gabara swiftly fell, the Roman force swung south and marched on Jotapata. After a gruelling forty-seven-day siege, it too fell, and Josephus, one of 1,200 survivors, surrendered to Vespasian and changed sides. A total of 40,000 Jews had died in the Jotapata siege. [Ibid., 3, 7, 36]

When Jewish forces regrouped in Galilee in August, Vespasian, who had sent his legions into winter camp, led them out again to do battle. The city of Tiberias, on the western shore of the Sea of Galilee, swiftly surrendered, and Vespasian's son Titus led a cavalry force which took Tarichaeae on the southern shore. Vespasian then marched on Gamala, a Jewish city in dry inhospitable territory near Al-Karak in present-day Jordan. With the town built into a hillside, its buildings sat almost on top of each other up the slope. Three massive Roman battering rams went to work on the walls of Gamala, and after weeks of effort all three broke through at the same time.

The legions stormed through the breaches, but in the narrow hill-town streets partisans charged back down the slope and halted the advance in its tracks. As legionaries attempted to clamber over rooftops, houses collapsed under them, and Romans were buried in the rubble. Several nights later, Titus led a party which crept over the town wall and opened the way for a full-scale assault, and Gamala was taken. It now being December AD 67, the legions were again sent into winter camp.

In the spring of AD 68, the Palatium transferred the surviving men of the 3rd Gallica Legion out of Vespasian's army. These Syrian 3rd Gallica legionaries had been at the forefront of Vespasian's offensive as they strove to wreak revenge on the Jews for the deaths of their comrades at the revolt's outset. As the mauled 3rd Gallica went marching away to a

Vespasian, seen here on a coin issued once he was emperor, led the second counter-offensive against the Jewish rebels in Judea after the first failed miserably.

new station in the province of Moesia in Europe, the remainder of Vespasian's army resumed the offensive against the Jews.

The 10th Fretensis Legion advanced down the banks of the Jordan, taking Jericho in May. Not far from the Jewish monastery of Qumran, the curious Vespasian tested the Dead Sea's famed buoyancy by having Jewish prisoners thrown in; they floated. In 1947, the now famous Dead Sea Scrolls were found, located in eleven caves behind the ruins of Qumran, hidden there during Vespasian's offensive. It was only June, but Vespasian ordered a halt to operations. In Rome, Nero's rule was increasingly shaky. In Spain the governor, Sulpicius Galba, was raising the new 7th Galbiana Legion and planning to march to Italy to take Nero's throne, having written to all provincial governors and Vespasian seeking their support.

For the moment, Vespasian suspended his offensive. Until the political air cleared, and with Jerusalem, the last major target in the Roman offensive, still in rebel hands,

Vespasian's legions went into camp: the 10th Fretensis at Jericho, the 5th Macedonica at Emmaus in the Judean Hills and the 15th Apollinaris at Caesarea. A year later, Vespasian's legions still had not moved.

AD 69

XXIV. THE ROXOLANI BATTLE
3rd Gallica's greatest victory

Snow was still on the ground in Moesia in February when 'To Arms' was trumpeted throughout the Danube camp of the 3rd Gallica Legion. The legion, which had been at its new posting for less than a year, was ordered to march at once. Led by their legate Fulvius Aurelius, the 3rd Gallica hurried to intercept a force of many thousands of Sarmatian cavalry from the Roxolani tribe that had crossed the frozen Danube to raid northern Moesia. To counter the Roxolani, both the 3rd Gallica and 8th Augusta legions had been ordered out by Moesia's governor, Marcus Aponius Saturninus.

The 3rd Gallica, several cohorts down after being savaged in the Jewish Revolt in Judea, would have been keen to spill some blood after being transferred away from Vespasian's command. Their Sarmatian opponents were from the Volga river. Natural horsemen who originated in Asia and migrated to the Ural Mountains from today's Iran, the Sarmatian tribes had overwhelmed the Scythians, the original

The Roxolani were armoured Sarmatian cavalry like these shown on Trajan's Column.

inhabitants, to control what is today southern European Russia. Fierce fighters, Sarmatians wore fish-scale body armour and conical helmets, and used long lances and bows but not shields. The sword of the Roxolani Sarmatians was so long that it was worn in a scabbard strapped to the back and was drawn, two-handed, over the shoulder.

Roman cavalry scouts located the Roxolani camp; on ice-covered ground, it extended over a wide plain close to frozen marshes. The Roxolani built no defensive camps. Their hundreds of wagons spread across the landscape, with their thousands of horses tethered in groups. The 3rd Gallica camped some distance away, and lit no fires. Rather than wait to be joined by the 8th Augusta, legion commander Aurelius decided to attack at dawn while he had the element of surprise.

Come morning, with mist overlying the silent countryside, the men of the 3rd Gallica silently moved into position. The mist had risen when Roman trumpets sounded 'Charge'. The Sarmatians, with no sentries, were caught entirely off guard. Desperately they tried to pull on their armour, to saddle their horses, to mount and to fight. Tacitus said of Sarmatian cavalry: 'When they charge in squadrons, scarcely any infantry line can stand against them.' [Tac., *H*, 1, 79] But the Roxolani had no chance to mount a charge. Legionaries employed their javelins as lances, and used their shields to knock heavily armoured opponents off their feet, then quickly dispatched them with the sword. The Roxolani were, says Tacitus, virtually defenceless once knocked to the ground, as the weight of their armour made it difficult to rise again. [Ibid.]

Those Roxolani able to mount found their horses slipping under them on the icy ground. With Roman troops pressing in, the long Sarmatian lances were useless. Many Roxolani were hauled bodily from the backs of their horses and thrown to the ground. And once brought down, the Sarmatians' courage vanished. 'No soldiers could show so little spirit when fighting on foot,' said Tacitus of them. [Ibid.]

A handful of wounded Sarmatians escaped to the marshes, only to freeze to death overnight. Every last member of the Roxolani force was killed – 9,000 men. The 3rd Gallica's losses were not even worth counting. For this victory, commanders Aurelius of the 3rd Gallica, Tettius Julianus of the 7th Claudia and Numisius Lupus of the 8th Augusta were all awarded purple consular ensigns by the Palatium, while provincial governor Aponius was awarded Triumphal Decorations.

AD 69
XXV. YEAR OF THE FOUR EMPERORS
Legion versus legion

> '*A year ... which well nigh brought the commonwealth to an end.*'
>
> TACITUS, *Histories*, I, II

From the moment that 70-year-old Emperor Galba was assassinated in the Forum by a legionary named Camurius from the 15th Apollinaris Legion, on 15 January AD 69, Rome was destined for a year of turmoil.

Galba raised a new 7th Legion to help him seize the throne in AD 68.

Even as Galba's successor Otho was being hailed emperor by the Praetorian Guard at Rome, the legions on the Rhine were preparing to march on the capital to install their choice for emperor, Aulus Vitellius, governor of Upper Germany, on the throne. Three separate task forces marched for Italy in Vitellius' name. From the Rhine came vexillations of between four and six cohorts from each of the 1st Germanica, 4th Macedonica, 5th Alaudae and 15th Primigeneia legions, as well as the entire but under-strength 21st Rapax Legion. From Lugdunum in Gaul came the Italian recruits of the recently created 1st Italica Legion. With these legionaries came as many auxiliaries, so that 75,000 men marched into Italy at the beginning of April, bent on dethroning Otho.

On 14 April, these units clashed with an army taken north from Rome by Otho, at Bedriacum, above the Po river in Italy's central north. Otho's army, commanded by his brother Sextus, comprised cohorts of the Praetorian Guard, the newly formed 1st Adiutrix Legion, the Evocati militia, plus several cohorts from the 13th Gemina and 14th Gemina legions which had just marched all the way from Pannonia.

In the battle, Otho's 1st Adiutrix seized the eagle of the 21st Rapax, only for the Rapax to regroup and overrun the Adiutrix's youngsters and kill their general.

Otho's 13th Gemina gave way to a charge by the 5th Alaudae, exposing the famous 14th Gemina, which had triumphed over Boudicca but which was now surrounded and forced to fight its way back to the Othonian camp. Otho's army negotiated a surrender, and Otho committed suicide. Once Vitellius' generals had secured victory, he himself came down from the Rhine, in July entering Rome and taking the throne. But he soon learned that this very same month the legions in the East had hailed their commander-in-chief, Vespasian, as their emperor.

In the autumn, an army of pro-Vespasian troops marched into Italy to overthrow Vitellius, led by Marcus Antonius Primus – another Mark Antony. A native of Tolosa, today's Toulouse in France, Primus, 'a man of ready audacity' in the opinion of Tacitus, had been convicted of fraud during Nero's reign and sent into exile. [A, XIV, 40] Galba, once on the throne, had cancelled Primus' exile and given him command of his new 7th Legion. Now, seeing an opportunity to become Vespasian's leading general, Primus had entered Italy with just a small force based around auxiliaries and cohorts of the 3rd Gallica Legion – which had led the other legions in Moesia, Pannonia and Dalmatia in swearing allegiance to the Gallica's old commander-in-chief, Vespasian. Those other legions would soon join Primus and the 3rd Gallica in Italy.

Otho, once Nero's closest friend, supported Galba against him and then claimed the throne on Galba's assassination.

As Primus entered Italy, anxious to prevent reinforcements reaching Vitellius from the Rhine, he sent a letter to the prefect of a cohort of Batavian auxiliaries at Mogontiacum on the Rhine, Gaius Julius Civilis. (Tacitus, in his *Histories*, gave Civilis' first name as both Julius and Claudius; other sources say Gaius Julius Civilis.) Civilis, probably now in his early fifties, was a member of the Equestrian Order and a high-ranking descendant of the Batavian royal family, which had ceased to rule after the death of its last king, Chariovalda, during Germanicus Caesar's German campaigns half a century earlier.

Civilis had commanded one of eight cohorts of Batavian auxiliaries until recently attached to the 14th Gemina Legion in Britain, and in the AD 40s he had befriended the then commander of the 2nd Augusta Legion – Vespasian. After the eastern legions had hailed Vespasian emperor in July, Civilis had written to him, pledging his loyalty and offering to help overthrow Vitellius. Now Primus urged Civilis to create the appearance of a revolt in northern Gaul, to keep the Rhine legions busy and prevent them from reinforcing Vitellius in Italy. This letter from Primus to Civilis was to sponsor one of the most devastating and humbling periods in legion history.

Vitellius, commander of the legions on the Rhine, deposed Otho to become emperor.

AD 69
XXVI. THE CIVILIS REVOLT
Blood on the Rhine

During the last months of Nero's reign, Civilis and his brother Julius Paulus had been accused of fomenting revolt in their homeland. Paulus was executed; Civilis had been sent in chains to Nero at Rome. The governor of Lower Germany, Fonteius Capito, the man who imprisoned Civilis, was an opponent of Galba's, and as soon as Galba became emperor he had Capito executed. Civilis was freed and returned to his unit.

Civilis did indeed harbour ambitions to lead a revolt against Roman rule, and when the message arrived from Primus urging him to create a diversion on the Rhine, the Batavian had the excuse and the authority he needed. After being forced from their lands east of the Rhine by the Chatti, the Batavi tribe had occupied that narrow part of the present-day Netherlands between the Waal and Meuse rivers on the North Sea coast which the locals called 'the island'. Since becoming Julius Caesar's allies, the Batavians had provided auxiliary infantry and cavalry to the Roman army as their sole contribution to the alliance; unlike other tribes, they paid no taxes. Their cavalry in particular were valued, for their ability to swim rivers with their horses and in full equipment 'without breaking the order of their squadrons'. [Tac., *H*, IV, 12]

As Vitellius recruited more troops to maintain his disputed rule, he played into the hands of Civilis, for he called up all the Batavian young men for auxiliary service. This was deeply resented by the Batavians, who felt they had contributed enough to Rome. Civilis, the most respected of men among the Batavians for his ability, royal blood and wealth, having inherited numerous estates from his father, hosted a banquet for Batavian elders and young firebrands in a sacred grove. As his countrymen ate and drank, Civilis came to his feet to address them.

Civilis had lost an eye and bore an ugly scar on his face, probably in a battle in Wales, and he likened himself to Carthaginian general Hannibal, and to Sertorius, rebel Roman governor of Spain during Pompey the Great's time, both of whom had also lost an eye. And, like Hannibal and Sertorius, the one-eyed Civilis felt that he could defeat the armed forces of Rome. In an impassioned speech, he fanned the indignation of his fellow Batavians until it burst into revolutionary fire. 'We have a vast force of horse and foot, we have the Germans as our kinsmen, we have Gaul bent on the same object,' he assured his colleagues. [Ibid., 14]

The banqueters enthusiastically swore in the name of their gods to follow Civilis and free their homeland. Messages were sent to the Canninefates, a German tribe which also occupied 'the island', and to the Frisii on the North Sea coast of Germany, to bring them into the revolutionary movement. And Civilis spoke discreetly with Batavian and British nobles who commanded eighteen cohorts of auxiliaries stationed at Mogontiacum, and won over the nobles and their 9,000 men.

In the late summer of AD 69, thousands of Canninefates and Frisians suddenly attacked the Rhine town of Vetera, which was garrisoned by just a Tungrian auxiliary cohort and another cohort of Ubian Germans. Twenty-four ships of the Rhine Fleet were also based there – light, shallow-draught vessels with single banks of oars. The auxiliary cohorts' prefects ordered the warships to escape upriver, then set fire to buildings to prevent the camp falling into German hands, as their men scampered away across the flat Low Country landscape.

After looting the burning camp and slaughtering sutlers and traders who lived outside, the attackers pursued the Roman troops, who made a stand a little way upriver. With the waters of the Rhine at their back, the cohorts were supported by the warships. Meanwhile, a rider galloped to Novaesium, where Civilis and his Batavian cohort were stationed, seeking aid. When the messenger arrived with news of the Vetera attack, Civilis sent a message to Hordeonius Flaccus, the old, lame Roman general left at Mogontiacum in command of both the Upper and Lower Rhine when Vitellius departed for Italy to take the throne. Civilis volunteered to lead a relief force to Vetera, and Flaccus told him to go ahead.

When Civilis and an auxiliary force reached the trapped cohorts, they found them lined up ready for battle at the riverside. The two dozen warships stood close by, their marines and catapults at the ready to support the cohorts. Now Civilis and the so-called relief force changed sides, joining forces with the rebels, with Civilis assuming rebel command. The Tungrian cohort then defected to the rebels. The remaining, vastly outnumbered, Ubian cohort was cut to pieces.

On the ships on the river, Batavian crewmen suddenly turned against their skippers and centurions, killing those who would not join them. Within minutes, the Roman force on land were obliterated, and the ships captured. With these warships, Civilis could control the Lower Rhine. News of this 'brilliant success' for Civilis and his rebels quickly spread throughout Germany and Gaul. Now Civilis remained faithful to a vow he had made when addressing Batavian leaders in the sacred grove, and dyed his hair red, as his ancestors had done when they went to war. [Ibid., 16]

From Mogontiacum, Roman general Flaccus sent orders to Munius Lupercus, commander of the 15th Primigeneia Legion at Novaesium, immediately to take the field against the rebels. Lupercus was senior to Numisius Rufus, legate commanding the other legion at Novaesium, the 5th Alaudae. Both legions were significantly under strength after many of their cohorts had gone to Italy. Between them, they fielded some 5,000 men on the Rhine. Leaving 1,000 men to garrison Novaesium, and adding a number of auxiliaries to their force, including a squadron of Batavian cavalry which had remained loyal to Rome, the young generals set off downriver to put an end to the revolt.

Some 65 miles (104 kilometres) beyond Cologne at Vetera – known as Old Camp – the 5th Alaudae and 15th Primigeneia came on the rebel army in battle array. Behind his troops, Civilis had stationed his mother and sisters, and the wives and children of his men, to encourage his fighters to victory. As rebels sang a war song and women and children cried shrill exhortations, the legionaries of Lupercus and Rufus responded with a roar of defiance.

As if on cue, the Batavian cavalry on Lupercus' wing suddenly rode away, then wheeled and charged the very Roman flank they had been protecting. The remaining Roman auxiliaries fled into the countryside, abandoning the two legions. But when the rebel infantry charged, the discipline of the legionaries held, and they saw off the treacherous cavalry and repelled Civilis' infantry. Maintaining good order, the two legions then retreated to the Old Camp fortification. As legionaries improved defences and destroyed houses around the outside walls to establish clear fields of fire, the rebels encircled the fortress.

Meanwhile, four cohorts of Batavians and Canninefates had recently been sent off to reinforce Vitellius in Italy. When they received a note from Civilis urging them to return and join the revolt, they turned and began retracing their steps towards Mogontiacum. When Flaccus, Roman commander-in-chief, learned this, he timidly kept his legionaries behind the walls at Mogontiacum and sent a message to the 16th Gallica Legion at Bonna. That legion's legate, Herennius Gallus, was ordered to intercept the four cohorts, with Flaccus assuring him that he would come up behind the Batavian and Canninefate column from Mogontiacum with his troops, and between the two forces they would crush the defectors.

But Flaccus made no attempt to leave Mogontiacum. Soon he sent Gallus a new order, countermanding the last, instructing him to let the auxiliaries pass. Gallus was trying to make sense of this when delegates from the column arrived at his Bonna headquarters. They told the general that if he failed to let the column pass, the Batavians and Canninefates would give battle and cut a path through Gallus' legionaries.

Gallus hesitated. But his troops demanded a chance to teach these traitors a lesson. The men of six cohorts of the 1st Germanica Legion left at Bonna when its commander took part of the legion to Italy were especially keen to act, and before Gallus could restrain them they swarmed out of the camp gates accompanied by recently recruited Belgian auxiliary cohorts. On their heels hurried local farmers and merchants, full of bravado and wielding crude weapons, caught up by the confidence of the men of the legion. Gallus' own 16th Gallica men obeyed orders; staying in camp, they manned the ramparts to see what transpired outside.

Although outnumbered, the 2,000 Batavians and Canninefates were experienced soldiers. Forming squares, they held firm against the 1st Germanica's charge. The Roman line broke around the immovable columns, and then the rebels advanced with measured steps. As the attackers fell back on the camp in disarray, they became entangled with panicking civilians. The Belgian auxiliaries fled into the fields, and the 1st Germanica men found themselves hemmed in against the ditch skirting their camp. Scores of legionaries were killed by the Batavians and Canninefates, their bodies filling the trench at the foot of the wall. The remainder surged in through the Bonna camp gates before they closed.

The victorious rebels continued their march, skirting Cologne to link up with Civilis outside Old Camp, where the rebel siege continued. To give credibility to his uprising, Civilis now had all his followers swear allegiance to Vespasian. He then sent envoys to the legions at Old Camp, advising them to throw off their allegiance to Vitellius and also swear for Vespasian. A message soon came back from Old Camp: 'We don't follow the advice of traitors or enemies.' [Ibid., 21]

Civilis now ordered the entire Batavian nation to take up arms. Soon, he was joined in the siege of Old Camp by thousands of Bructeri and Tencteri reinforcements from east of the Rhine. The rebels built crude assault machinery, but this was soon pulverized by stones lobbed from catapults on the fort ramparts, or burned to a cinder by fires started by flaming arrows. When an attempt to storm the walls with siege ladders also failed, Civilis decided to suspend the assault and starve out Lupercus and his legionaries.

Up the Rhine at Mogontiacum, Flaccus was finally on the move. Dispatching orders to Gallus at Bonna to send his 16th Gallica cohorts to meet him at Novaesium, and joined by auxiliary reinforcements from Vindonissa 200 miles (320 kilometres) away in present-day Switzerland, Flaccus sent his army south under his deputy, Dillius Vocula, legate of the recently reconstituted 18th Legion, which had six cohorts at Mogontiacum. Gout-ridden Flaccus himself followed the marching column in a boat on the Rhine.

On the march, rumour flourished among the troops. Those who were strongly pro-Vitellius became convinced that old Flaccus had deliberately muddled the response to Civilis' revolt because he was a secret Vespasian supporter. Becoming aware of the unrest, Flaccus addressed the troops at their next marching camp, reading aloud a letter from Vespasian's generals urging him to go over to Vespasian. To prove to his men where his loyalties lay, Flaccus had the soldiers from Vespasian's army who had brought him the message clapped in irons and sent to Vitellius in Rome. This seemed to satisfy the men, and the march resumed.

When Flaccus and his force reached Bonna they were greeted enthusiastically by the cohorts of the 1st Germanica Legion. As the relief force camped at Bonna, men of the 1st complained bitterly to the new arrivals that Flaccus had failed to give them the promised support for their attack on the Batavians and Canninefates outside Bonna. To quieten his men, Flaccus took the unprecedented step of instructing the standard-bearers of the legions to read aloud his final written order to Gallus not to attack the Batavians and Canninefates, an order the men of the 1st Legion had chosen to flout. Flaccus' most vocal critic in the 1st Legion ranks was then put in chains, but the soldier loudly declared that he had conveyed secret messages from Flaccus to Civilis the rebel and he was only being pulled from the ranks so he could be silenced. General Flaccus hesitated, looking suddenly guilty.

At this knife-edge of a moment, his well-liked deputy Vocula, commander of the 18th Legion, stepped on to the tribunal and ordered the legionary of the 1st executed immediately. Experienced soldiers of the legions voiced their approval; others watched in terrified silence as the legionary was pressed to his knees and deprived of his head with the flash of a centurion's sword. Old Flaccus, knowing that in that moment of hesitation he had lost his men's confidence, handed supreme command of the expedition to Vocula, and retired to his tent. Next day, when the force resumed its march under Vocula's command, Flaccus returned to Mogontiacum by boat.

Overnight, Vocula made his friend Gallus of the 16th Gallica his second-in-command, and attached part of 1st Germanica to the force, leaving its remaining cohorts at Bonna to guard the fort. On reaching Novaesium, the force was joined by the waiting cohorts of Gallus' 16th Legion. The now enlarged army advanced down the Rhine towards the besieged Old Camp, setting up a new camp at Gelduba, today's Gellep, not far from Novaesium.

Vocula seems to have decided to attempt to weld his mutinous troops into a disciplined force before taking on Civilis. Either that or he was a Vespasian sympathizer and was deliberately wasting time – as many of his men suspected. His troops passed the next few weeks building a fortress at Gelduba and going through strenuous exercises on the plain outside it. The rank and file continued to be firmly loyal to Vitellius, and, increasingly convinced that their senior officers leaned towards Vespasian, their confidence in, and trust of, their commanders began to dissolve.

While Vocula was leading a detachment on a raid of pro-Civilis villages of the Gugerni tribe, Gallus, in charge at Gelduba, watched as a supply ship coming down the Rhine from Mogontiacum and laden with grain for his force, ran aground in the shallows just upstream. Northern Europe was experiencing a severe drought at the time, and the depth of the Rhine had fallen so much that in places it was almost unnavigable. German tribesmen soon appeared on the eastern bank, splashed across the river, slaughtered the ship's crew, then tried to drag the vessel off to their side of the river.

Gallus sent a cohort of legionaries to save the ship, but as they reached it, more Germans appeared; the outnumbered Romans were soon fighting for survival. As Gallus sent in additional troops, more Germans kept arriving. This had every appearance of a premeditated plan. Gallus finally gave up the ship and sounded 'Recall', after which the smarting legionaries fought their way back to the fort.

That night, the legionaries involved descended on the general's tent, dragged Gallus out and kicked and beat him, for they were convinced the grain ship episode had been an ambush in which he had been complicit. With a dagger to his throat, Gallus said that their old general Flaccus had been responsible for the ambush. When Vocula arrived back with his raiding party, he found Gallus in irons. Incensed, Vocula freed Gallus, and next morning he summarily executed the ringleaders of the assault on his deputy. But the damage had been done. Soldiers had laid hands on their general. A dangerous precedent had been set.

All this time, Civilis continued the siege of Old Camp. One band of boastful Germans, drunk on Roman wine, tried to scale the walls one night, lighting their way by setting fire to piles of logs. The fire behind them only made the Germans easy targets for legionaries defending the walls. Drunken, half-naked Germans kept on coming, ignoring the men falling in droves all around them impaled by javelins, arrows from catapults and flying stakes. Civilis had to intervene, dowse the fires, and terminate the assault before the entire German contingent was wiped out.

Roman successes like this kept the spirits of the defenders of Old Camp high, but their strength was waning. Having eaten their cavalry and pack animals, they had resorted to eating grass and roots. On the heels of the failed German night assault, Civilis sent a two-storeyed siege tower against the fort's praetorian gate. But as weak as they were, the legionaries used long poles to collapse the tower, crushing many besiegers. A defender also created a crane-like device via which a net would drop down and snare one or more attackers then fly back up; by shifting weights, legionaries then flung ensnared rebels inside the fort, to meet waiting defenders' blades.

It was late October when news reached the Rhine that there had been a seventeen-hour battle at Bedriacum, in northern Italy, between the armies of Vitellius and his challenger Vespasian, followed immediately by a brief siege and four-day sack of the crowded city of Cremona; 50,000 soldiers and civilians had died. Vespasian's army, commanded by Marcus Antonius Primus, had won both encounters, and the men of Vitellius' army were dead or prisoners. Vitellius, now supported by little more than his Praetorian Guard and German Guard, was cut off at Rome. Primus was marching on the capital with one army, with Licinius Mucianus, governor of Syria, not far behind him with another Vespasianist army from the East, led by the 6th Ferrata Legion. Vitellius' end seemed only a matter of time.

For those officers on the Rhine who favoured Vespasian, it appeared to be time that their legions accepted the inevitable and swore for Vespasian. At Mogontiacum, old Flaccus called together his remaining troops and read out a message from Vitellius' general Caecina in which Caecina said that Vitellius' cause was lost. Flaccus' troops refused to believe it, and stood poker-faced as their general read a second letter, from Vespasian's general Primus, requiring the men of the Rhine legions to swear allegiance to Vespasian. Flaccus then brought forward Alpinius Montanus, until recently a prefect of Treveran auxiliaries with Vitellius' army in Italy. Montanus, a Treveran, had served with many of these men at Mogontiacum, and the truth began to dawn on the shocked troops as he told them how he had fought for Vitellius at Bedriacum and Cremona, and how with his own eyes he had seen their emperor's army comprehensively defeated.

Flaccus then administered the new oath of allegiance to the disheartened troops. The Gallic auxiliaries swore for Vespasian without any difficulty. But while the legionaries spoke the words of the oath, most mumbled the name of Vespasian or skipped it altogether. Despite the news from Cremona, and despite the fact that Vitellius was fat and pretentious, to the troops of the Rhine armies Vitellius was *their* general, while Vespasian was the general of the armies in the East, which they considered their inferiors.

Finally, Flaccus read out a letter from Primus to Civilis, instructing him to end his revolt now that Vespasian was on the eve of final victory. But instead of reassuring the troops that peace was at hand, this only confirmed their suspicions that Vespasian's generals had encouraged Civilis to revolt in the first place. The men remained insolently silent as they were dismissed. Montanus was sent to Bonna, Cologne, and Novaesium to repeat his story of Vitellian defeat, and to repeat the administering of the oath to Vespasian to the troops there. Last to be visited was Vocula's relief column at Gelduba; they, too, reluctantly swore for Vespasian.

Montanus next went as Vespasian's envoy to Civilis, passing on Primus' letter requiring the rebel leader to lay down his arms. If Civilis had truly been trying to help Vespasian, said the letter, his purpose had now been fully accomplished. Montanus returned to Flaccus at Mogontiacum to say that Civilis adamantly refused to cease hostilities. What Montanus failed to tell Flaccus was that he and his brother, another officer with a Treveran unit, planned to defect to Civilis.

Civilis now went on the offensive. Putting Batavian countryman Julius Maximus in command of a large force, with Civilis' nephew Claudius Victor as his deputy,

Civilis sent them against Vocula. Maximus cunningly skirted Gelduba then turned and came at the fort from the Roman end of the Rhine. Vocula was literally caught looking the wrong way. The rebels were on the Roman troops so quickly they didn't even have time to form a proper battle line. As his men bunched on the plain, Vocula strove to position the 1st Germanica, 16th Gallica and 18th legions in the centre of his disorganized formation while his auxiliary cavalry charged the rebels.

But the Roman-trained Batavians stood firm. Vocula's cavalry shied away and galloped back to the camp. Now the Nervian auxiliaries on one of Vocula's flanks gave way and fled – through panic, or treachery. The rebels charged the legions' exposed flank. It all had a familiar ring to it. The legions fell back to the camp, leaving countless dead on the field. One after the other, Roman standard-bearers fell and standards were lost to the enemy. Bewildered young legionaries threw down their arms and surrendered. Veteran soldiers were pressed back against the trench outside their fort and cut down in droves. A gate to the fort was forced, and rebels pushed their way inside.

It was now that Fortune smiled on the Romans. For months, Flaccus has been promising to send reinforcements from Mogontiacum; now, several thousand Vascon auxiliaries levied the previous year in Gaul arrived, marching over the hill behind the attackers. Turning to see Roman standards advancing on their exposed rear, rebels thought that Roman troops from Novaesium had arrived, or worse, all of Flaccus' troops from Mogontiacum were approaching.

Seeing the rebels suddenly uncertain, Vocula's legionaries regained the initiative. As the Vascon troops advanced, the rebels outside the camp were caught between them and Vocula's men. Batavians who had fought their way into the camp were trapped and wiped out. Only the Batavian cavalry escaped unscathed, taking with them the Roman standards and prisoners captured earlier. The veteran Batavian infantry and many young Germans were killed. But even so, the legions had suffered heavier casualties. Buoyed by this much needed though expensive victory, Vocula decided at last to raise the siege at Old Camp.

At Old Camp, Civilis paraded the captured standards and prisoners taken by Maximus at Gelduba, for the starving legionaries manning the walls to see. He called to the men of the 5th Alaudae and 15th Primigeneia that Vocula and the relief force had been wiped out, and that here was the proof. But one of the captured legionaries yelled that it was all a lie, that Vocula had actually won the day at Gelduba. His

German captors angrily killed the vocal legionary on the spot, but the damage had been done – now the besieged men knew that Civilis had at last suffered a reverse at the hands of Roman legions. Their defiance redoubled.

Just days later, lookouts at Old Camp spotted fires breaking out in distant farmhouses. Vocula's cavalry was sweeping ahead of his advance, destroying everything in their path. Soon, Old Camp's trapped legionaries saw Vocula's legions and auxiliaries marching to their relief. But then, as Civilis called his men to arms, Vocula ordered his troops to halt and build a fortification before they attacked. His incredulous men refused, declaring they were here to fight, not dig. They demanded that Vocula lead them to the attack. As Vocula hesitated, the legionaries rushed forward anyway, not even bothering to form a line, certain they would repeat the Gelduba victory.

The two armies met in the fields. In loose order the legionaries halted to receive a volley of rebel javelins, then pushed forward and came to grips with the rebel line. Under heavy pressure, the rebels slowly fell back. When Vocula sounded 'Reform', the legionaries formed up in their ranks, behind their standards. Inside Old Camp, Lupercus and Rufus chose their strongest men, opened the fort gates, and sent them hurrying out into the fray. Scrambling over the rebel siege works with renewed strength, these legionaries surged into the rebel rear. In the mêlée, Civilis' horse was felled, sending him crashing to the ground. As Civilis was carried away, word spread through both armies that he was dead. Rebel troops panicked, and fled.

Elated Roman troops started to give chase, but Vocula sounded 'Recall', and they reluctantly obeyed. Vocula's troops marched into Old Camp, where they were greeted as saviours by their besieged comrades. Vocula had food distributed to the starving garrison, then ordered his men to repair and strengthen the walls and towers of the fort. His troops could not believe he would not go after Civilis. But his mind was set. Grumbling among themselves, the troops followed orders.

'Nothing distressed our troops so much as the scarcity of supplies,' said Tacitus of the men at Old Camp. Realizing that the supply situation was critical, Vocula immediately sent his baggage train back to Novaesium to bring grain from the granary there. The baggage train returned laden with supplies, and once it had been unloaded Vocula turned it around and sent it back to Novaesium for more. [Ibid., 35]

On the other side, Civilis had not only survived, but within a few days was well enough to reform his army and revise his plans. As news of his recovery flew down the Rhine, his troops returned to their standards. Meanwhile, rebel cavalry had watched

The emperor Vitellius, who briefly reigned during the civil war that followed Nero's demise. The men of the legions on the Rhine remained steadfastly loyal to him, even after his death, and suspected their officers of supporting Vespasian.

the first supply train go to Novaesium and back. When Vocula attempted to repeat the act, the loaded supply train was ambushed. The fight extended along the full length of the grain train, lasting until darkness gave the escort the opportunity to escape. Civilis' men claimed the train's load.

Despite this loss, Vocula's commissariat officers assured him that there were now enough provisions at Old Camp to keep 4,000 legionaries and a proportionate number of non-combatants fed through the winter. The young general called for 1,000 volunteers from the 5,000 or more men now holding Old Camp – they would march with his army, he said, while the remainder continued to hold Old Camp. Not surprisingly, 2,000 men stepped forward, complaining that they'd had enough of starvation and treacherous legion commanders.

Vocula chose his thousand, left Lupercus in charge of the other 4,000, and marched the remainder of his troops out of the camp gates. As he departed, many men left behind at Old Camp cursed him loudly from the walls for leaving them to their fate. And the men marching with him concurred. As soon as Vocula's column was out of sight, the rebels returned and again surrounded Old Camp. The spirits of the men holding the fort plummeted.

Abandoning Gelduba, Vocula withdrew to Novaesium. There, he was joined by 4th Macedonica Legion cohorts sent from Mogontiacum by Flaccus. Despite these reinforcements, after Civilis' cavalry roundly defeated Vocula's cavalry one chilly day outside Novaesium, Vocula sat inside the walls there and refused to budge. Word now reached Vocula's troops that the emperor Vitellius had some time before sent money to Flaccus as a 'donative' to the troops, to celebrate his coming to the throne. But Flaccus had sat on the money. Vocula's troops now went on strike, demanding their cash.

Begrudgingly, Flaccus paid up, making it clear he was paying in the name of Vespasian, not Vitellius. The money was distributed to all the troops on the Rhine, and they celebrated by promptly getting drunk. One group of legionaries at Mogontiacum, inflamed by too much wine and months of discontent, went to old Flaccus' quarters, dragged him from his bed, declared him a traitor, and plunged their swords into him. Having murdered the governor of the German provinces and commanding general on the Rhine, the troops at Mogontiacum completed their mutiny by overthrowing their officers and restoring the statues of Vitellius that Flaccus had ordered taken down.

Hearing about the revolution at Mogontiacum, Civilis quickly marched a rebel army overland, ignoring the garrisons at Novaesium, Cologne and Bonna, intent on taking Mogontiacum while its troops were in chaos. When the legionaries at Mogontiacum learned that the rebels were coming, they at first formed up in the field to do battle. But, as the rebels drew closer, the legionaries turned and ran. Some deserted their legions. The balance fled back to their fortress and closed the gates. Civilis surrounded the camp, and cut all escape routes.

When a messenger reached Vocula at Novaesium with the news that the troops at Mogontiacum had mutinied and murdered his superior Flaccus, although merely a legion commander he found himself senior Roman commander on the Rhine, with much of the region in rebel hands and Old Camp and Mogontiacum cut off.

On 20 December, Vespasian's army, under his irrepressible general Primus, fought its way into Rome, and Vitellius' own troops murdered the emperor in his Palatium. The following day, the Senate officially proclaimed Vespasian, who was still in Egypt, the new emperor of Rome.

AD 70

XXVII. LOSING THE RHINE
Death, or desertion

On 1 January, Vocula's legionaries at Bonna and Novaesium swore a fresh oath of allegiance to Vespasian. With the civil war at an end, the new administration could focus on Civilis. Yet, far from being promptly extinguished, the flame of revolt was about to grow even larger and threaten to engulf all of Gaul.

Across Gaul, a rumour proliferated that the bases of the legions in Moesia and Pannonia were surrounded by Sarmatian and Dacian invaders. Another rumour had the legions in Britain in trouble against local tribes. And word spread that in Vitellius' final days the sacred sanctuary of Jupiter on the Capitoline Mount had been destroyed by fire. Only the latter was true, but to many provincials this all seemed to signal that the end of the Roman Empire was at hand.

Inspired by the success of Civilis, and encouraged by these rumours, Julius Classicus, descendant of a noble Treveran family and prefect of the Treveran Horse, a unit in Vocula's army, called a covert meeting in Cologne of representatives of four Belgic tribes. Supported by Julius Tutor, Classicus' Treveran Horse deputy, and Tullius Valentinus, a leading noble of the Treveri, Classicus urged the tribes to rise while Rome was on her knees. The meeting broke up with messages being taken away to the other tribes of Gaul urging them to join a rising in the spring to throw off Roman control and join Civilis in creating 'the Empire of Gaul'.

With the arrival of spring, Vocula marched his legions and auxiliaries out of Novaesium and headed down the Rhine to again relieve Old Camp. Leading Vocula's advance was the cavalry under Classicus and Tutor, who, when they reached Old Camp, promptly joined Civilis. Stunned by this treachery, Vocula withdrew.

Classicus and his cavalry shadowed Vocula all the way back to Novaesium, setting up a camp 2 miles (3.2 kilometres) away. Hoping to talk sense into these auxiliaries, Vocula sent centurions and leading legionaries to their camp, where Classicus offered the emissaries massive bribes to change sides. A legionary from the 1st Germanica named Aemilius Longinus deserted then and there. Loyal centurions returning to Novaesium warned Vocula that many legionaries would seriously consider accepting Classicus' offer and would convince others to do the same. Sensing the seditious mood in the Roman camp, Vocula's staff urged him to slip away. Instead, the general called an assembly.

'Never, when I have addressed you,' Vocula began, looking around his assembled troops, 'have I felt more anxious for your welfare, never more indifferent about my own.' He reminded them of the legions' past glories, of the courage of the men besieged at Old Camp who had held out through the winter and could not be shaken by threats or promises. He implored his men not to use their arms against their own country. When he had finished, the men were silent. There was no applause, no cheers, no vote of support. [Ibid., 58]

As Vocula stepped down from the tribunal and walked back to his praetorium, he knew that he had failed. When he unsheathed his sword with the intent of taking his own life, his servants convinced him to put it away. A little later, Aemilius Longinus, the 1st Germanica Legion deserter, was brought to the general's headquarters. He had a message from Julius Classicus, he said, which he must deliver in person and in private. He was ushered into the praetorium. When Vocula asked what the man had to say, Longinus drew his sword: this was Classicus' message. Vocula was prepared for his death. Earlier, he had said, 'Amid so many evils, I look forward to death as the end of my sufferings.' [Ibid.]

On learning that Vocula had been slain in his own tent, Classicus rode up to the fortress at the head of his cavalry. The gates opened, and the Novaesium legionaries of the 1st Germanica, 4th Macedonica, 16th Gallica and 18th legions all went over to the rebels, the waverers swept along with the fanatics. Legion commanders Herennius Gallus and Numisius Rufus were put in irons, and, from the camp tribunal, Classicus led the Roman troops in swearing allegiance to 'the Empire of Gaul'.

Classicus soon joined Civilis at the siege line outside Old Camp, taking the most unprincipled men from the Novaesium legions with him. The rest of the legionaries were left at their camp, as Classicus' deputy Tutor led a force to reinforce the rebels besieging Mogontiacum. When turncoat legionaries spoke with legionaries at Mogontiacum and told them that Vocula was dead and his legions had gone over to the rebels, the legionaries at Mogontiacum arrested their tribunes and joined the revolt. Tutor entered the fortress, and promptly put the arrested tribunes to death. He then made the legionaries, auxiliaries and civilian inhabitants of Mogontiacum swear allegiance to the new empire of Gaul.

From Mogontiacum, Tutor moved on to Cologne. Founded in 12 BC by Marcus Agrippa, the city acquired colony status under Claudius in AD 50. The last legion stationed there had been withdrawn twenty years before. The senators of Cologne signed a peace treaty with Tutor which allied them to the rebel cause and which, they hoped, saved their city. Tutor then made all at Cologne take the oath of allegiance to the Gallic Empire.

At the same time, the cohorts of the 1st Germanica Legion still ensconced at Bonna, finding themselves isolated, voluntarily went over to the rebels and swore allegiance to their cause. The 1st continued to occupy the Bonna camp, awaiting orders from Civilis. Before long, the southernmost Roman military base on the Rhine, at Vindonissa, modern Windisch, also came into rebel hands.

Roman general Lupercus and his 4,000 men at Old Camp were now Rome's last loyal troops on the Rhine. They had exhausted their supplies once more, and after hearing they were alone in their resistance to the rebels, the men of Old Camp lost heart and sent emissaries to Civilis, seeking surrender terms. At first they would not agree to swearing off their allegiance to Rome, but as this was Civilis' prime requirement they finally acquiesced, put Lupercus and other officers in chains, and opened the camp gates that had held Civilis at bay for a year.

As Civilis' troops emptied Old Camp of its valuables, equipment and servants, the men of the 5th Alaudae and 15th Primigeneia legions marched out of the gates. Stripped of their weapons and armour, the weak legionaries shuffled down the road away from the camp accompanied by guards. Five miles (8 kilometres) from the camp, a mass of German tribesmen suddenly rose up from the roadside. The escort stood aside, and the Germans slaughtered the unarmed legionaries. The bravest Romans stood their ground and fought with their bare hands. Their short-lived resistance allowed 1,000 of their number to flee back to Old Camp.

At the camp, these legionaries accused Civilis of treachery, but he denied complicity and upbraided several German chieftains in front of the prisoners. The legionaries were then herded back into the plundered camp and the gates closed. Then, the camp was set alight. Anyone who tried to escape was put to the sword. So died all 4,000 men of the two legions who had resisted Civilis for so long.

Their commander, Lupercus, was kept alive, and taken across the Rhine to be delivered as a gift to Veleda, a virgin German priestess who had predicted the destruction of the legions. But the general did not reach Veleda's tower beside the Lippe river. His bloodthirsty German guards killed him on the road. Roman tribunes and centurions born in southern Gaul were kept alive by Civilis, to be used as bargaining tools when dealing with Gallic tribes which had yet to come over to his cause. According to a later legend, Civilis had junior Roman officers trussed up then watched as his young son used them for target practice with his little bow and arrows.

Civilis had succeeded in capturing every Roman military base on the Rhine from the North Sea to modern Switzerland and either killing the men of the Roman garrisons or bringing them into his rebellion. He had fulfilled the vow he had taken the previous year; he had delivered his people from Roman domination.

AD 70

XXVIII. ROME'S RHINE RESPONSE
Cerialis' offensive

Gallic rebel Julius Sabinus led his Lingone tribe from their home on the River Seine to attack the Sequani, a tribe living between the River Saône and the Jura Mountains. The Sequani, Rome's allies, won decisively, and Lingone survivors fled to Civilis. Sabinus himself went into hiding. He and his entire family would later be executed by Vespasian. [Dio, LXV, 3; 16]

By early AD 70, Mucianus, governor of Syria, had arrived at Rome, where he took charge on behalf of Vespasian, who was still in Egypt awaiting seasonal winds to bring him to Italy. With the war of succession concluded, Mucianus could focus on a counter-offensive on the Rhine. He selected seven legions and a number of auxiliary units then in Italy, Spain, and Britain for a campaign against Civilis, appointing two generals to lead the offensive.

Overall command went to Annius Gallus. A former consul, Gallus been one of Otho's generals in the short war against Vitellius. Injured in a fall from his horse just prior to Otho's death, Gallus had recovered sufficiently to accept this appointment. He would make slow, painful progress from Rome behind the legions, arriving in Germany well into the punitive campaign. The real weight of responsibility fell on the shoulders of younger, fitter Quintus Petilius Cerialis Rufus. Cerialis had married Vespasian's cousin, so his loyalty was unquestionable. A praetor, he had considerable military experience, although his record to date was far from glittering. Ten years before, he had commanded the 9th Hispana Legion in Britain when Boudicca's rebellion broke out, rashly losing 2,000 men to the rebels. More recently, sent with 1,000 cavalry to rescue Vespasian's brother Sabinus from Vitellius' clutches, Cerialis had failed to break into Rome or to prevent Sabinus being murdered by Vitellius' German Guard. Cerialis had much to prove as he rode from Rome to undertake his latest mission.

Tidings of this advance of Vespasian's forces reached the delegates at a Gallic congress convened at Durocortum, today's Reims, capital of the Remi tribe in northern France. Some saw this news as proof that Rome had inexhaustible resources. Conversely, revolutionary delegates welcomed the imminent arrival of fresh legionary fodder for rebel blades, showing off coins minted by Civilis depicting the submission of the Rhine legions.

Many Gauls spoke at the congress, but just two carried the weight of the opposing arguments. Julius Aspex, a respected Remi leader, spoke for peace and reconciliation with Rome. Tullius Valentinus, Treveran noble and avid supporter of the rebellion, came from Augusta Treverorum (Trier) to speak on behalf of Civilis and the war party. When a vote was taken, while the pro-Gaul sentiments of Valentinus were praised, his recommended path to war was not adopted. Only those tribes which had originally risen with Civilis voted for war. Valentinus left the meeting knowing that the rebels were now on their own, that a Gallic empire uniting all the peoples of Gaul could only be achieved by force.

Camped outside the walls of Augusta Treverorum, the men of the turncoat 1st Germanica and 16th Gallica legions found that, with Valentinus away at the conference, they were under lax scrutiny and could discuss their future. All agreed they had committed a shameful act in going over to the rebels. Now, they swore allegiance to Vespasian, and at night, both units slipped away. Heading south, they were prepared to fight anyone who stood in their path.

They marched unchallenged. Civilis was occupied searching Belgium for Claudius Labeo, a Batavian who supported Rome and was stirring up trouble behind his back. Classicus was banqueting. Tutor was east of the Rhine levying more troops among German tribes. Following the Moselle river, the men of the 1st and 16th reached the safety of Divodurum (Metz), capital of the Mediomatrici tribe, which had continued to abide by its alliance with Rome all through the revolt. There, the exhausted men of the 1st and 16th legions were welcomed as friends.

Vespasian, at right. His youngest son, Domitian, shown in the middle here, survived the fighting at Rome to go to Lugdunum with Mucianus to 'oversee' the Roman response to Civilis' revolt.

When Valentinus returned to Augusta Treverorum his foul mood was exacerbated by the discovery that the two legions had gone. He took his anger out on the pair of Roman generals being kept in his city's prison, Herennius Gallus and Numisius Rufus, immediately putting them to death. Now, Valentinus told his people, there was no turning back; there could be no pardon from Rome if the Treveri were to surrender now that two of her generals had died at their hands. The Treveri must fight on.

All the while, the Roman noose was tightening on Gaul. The 21st Rapax, formerly a Vitellianist legion, had reportedly already crossed the Alps. The 6th Victrix and 10th Gemina legions were marching to the Rhine from Spain. The famous 14th Gemina Martia Victrix Legion was being ferried over from Britain by the Britannic Fleet. Three more legions would cross the Alps from Italy, each using different routes: the 6th Ferrata and 8th Augusta from Mucianus' army, and the recently formed 2nd Adiutrix Legion.

Mucianus also left Rome and headed for Gaul. With him went 19-year-old Domitian, Vespasian's youngest son, who was chafing to see action. Mucianus convinced the headstrong teenager that it would be more seemly if the generals were left to do the dirty work, while Domitian stood back and took the credit. Mucianus and Domitian would base themselves at Lugdunum in south-central France, to add the weight of the imperial family to the offensive.

After the forward commander, Cerialis, crossed the Alps, he split his force in two. Sextilius Felix took the auxiliary infantry via Raetia with orders to march up the east bank of the Rhine, while Cerialis led the 21st Rapax Legion along the western bank, with the two forces converging on Mogontiacum. Along the way, Cerialis was joined by the Singularian Horse, an elite cavalry unit formed the previous year by Vitellius from the best German cavalrymen in the Roman army. The unit was ironically commanded by a Batavian, Julius Briganticus, Civilis' nephew. But Briganticus was loyal to Rome, and hated his uncle Civilis with a passion.

As Cerialis neared Vindonissa, the rebels occupying it withdrew. East of the Rhine, the Treveran general Tutor heard that a Roman army was approaching from the southeast, and quickly mustered a rebel force including the legionary defectors from the 4th Macedonica, 5th Alaudae, 15th Primigeneia, 18th and 22nd Primigeneia legions. Tutor prepared an ambush, into which Felix's advance cohort walked; it was wiped out.

Scouts then warned Tutor that a second, much larger Roman force was moving up the opposite bank of the Rhine. When it was learned that it was the 21st Rapax that was approaching, the legionaries under Tutor refused to fight these men who had recently served with them on the Rhine. Tutor was forced to retreat, accompanied by just his loyal Treveran troops, leaving the legionaries to march to Mogontiacum and await Cerialis' arrival.

Skirting Mogontiacum, Tutor withdrew west to Bingium (Bingen), where the Rhine is joined by the River Nahe. Roman commander Felix, crossing the Rhine via a river ford, came up behind Tutor and launched a surprise attack. The rebels were routed, and Tutor fled to join Classicus, further north. At the same time, Cerialis and the 21st Rapax Legion victoriously entered Mogontiacum, to be greeted by the former defectors. He told the once mutinous legionaries that they would soon have their chance to prove themselves, and took them into his force.

With Tutor's comprehensive defeat at Bingium, the Treverans were in a state of panic. Thousands who had taken up arms now disposed of them. Many of their elected officials sought asylum further south with tribes loyal to Rome. Other city senators went north to join Civilis. But Valentinus remained in control of Augusta Treverorum, still with a sizeable force of Treveran fighting men. Civilis and Classicus, stung by Tutor's defeat, assembled their scattered forces, sending messages to Valentinus telling him not to risk a decisive battle with the Romans until they could join him.

AD 70
XXIX. BATTLE OF RIGODULUM
Turning the tide

Cerialis decided to deal with Valentinus at Augusta Treverorum before he ventured further north against Civilis and Classicus. As he approached the Treveran capital, he sent officers to lead the men of the 1st Germanica and 16th Gallica by the shortest possible route back to Augusta Treverorum, from which they had previously escaped, to link up with his army.

With the equally disgraced men of the 4th Macedonica, 5th Alaudae, 15th Primigeneia, 18th and 22nd Primigeneia legions from Mogontiacum in his army, Cerialis marched rapidly west to attack Augusta Treverorum. In three days, his force covered the 75 miles (120 kilometres) to the Moselle, arriving at a place just outside Augusta Treverorum which the Romans called Rigodulum. This is likely to have been where a stream called the Altbach joins the Moselle. Since long before Roman times the Treveri had maintained a sacred sanctuary there.

Ignoring the advice of Civilis and Classicus, Valentinus had brought his Treverans from behind Augusta Treverorum's walls to Rigodulum, having levied every able-bodied man of the city to his standards. Intend-ing to make a stand with the river to one side and surrounded by the foothills of the Eifel and Hunsruck mountains, he built a fortification into a bare hillside, strengthen-ing the position with ditches and stone breastworks.

Cerialis attacked without hesitation. While his infantry made a frontal assault up the hill, the Roman general sent a detachment of Briganticus' Singularian Horse to find an attack route from the rear. The progress of the lines of legionaries and auxiliaries advancing up the hill was slowed briefly as they came within range of the defenders' missiles, but once through, they charged forward and stormed the poorly fortified position. With the benefit of training, experience and superior numbers, and with one-time rebel legionaries keen to prove themselves, it was no contest.

'The barbarians were dislodged and hurled like a falling house from their posi-tion.' [Tac., *H*, 11, 71] As the Romans swept over the defences, Valentinus and his chief lieutenants fell back up the hill, and into the hands of the Roman cavalry, which had found a route through the hills behind the rebel position. Those Treverans not killed were captured. Valentinus was among the captives. The Battle of Rigodulum was a swift and crushing defeat for the 'Empire of Gaul'.

Next day, the gates of Augusta Treverorum were thrown open to the Roman general. Situated on the right bank of the Moselle, the city had been founded as a military post by Augustus in around 15 BC. The Treveri had built a settlement close by which, in the reign of Claudius, had gained Roman colony status and the name of Colonia Augusta Treverorum. In Claudius' reign, too, a large timber bridge had been built across the river, on stone piers, and the city that grew beside the Moselle swiftly became prosperous as a commercial crossroads. As Cerialis entered Augusta Treverorum, his men urged him to destroy the city, the birthplace of Classicus and Tutor. But Cerialis was determined to restore firm discipline to the legionaries who had returned to their standards, and letting them run riot in the city was no way to achieve that.

That same day, the men of the 1st Germanica and 16th Gallica legions arrived from Metz and made a camp outside the city. There were none of the customary cheers and friendly greetings exchanged between the legions of Cerialis and the new arrivals. Swathed in guilt, the men of the 1st and 16th stood around with eyes fixed to the ground. When some of Cerialis' legionaries went to their camp to console and encourage them, they were so ashamed they hid in their tents. Big, strong legionaries from both camps were seen to shed silent tears.

Observing this, Cerialis assembled all the Roman troops and addressed them. The men of the legions caught up in the rebellion must now consider this day the first day of their military service and of their allegiance to Rome and the emperor, he said. He promised them that their past crimes would be remembered neither by the emperor nor by himself. And an order was read to every maniple that henceforth no soldier was to mention past mutinies or defeats. Cerialis then brought the men of the 1st and 16th into the main camp to join the rest of the army; they were outcasts no more. [Ibid., 72]

At an assembly of the Treveri and Lingone people in the city, Cerialis declared, 'It is by my sword that I have asserted the excellence of the Roman people.' [Ibid., 73] He urged the population to swear off rebellion and accept the presence of Roman arms and the payment of Roman taxes as the price of peace. Having heard the legions call for the destruction of the city, the residents welcomed Cerialis' option.

This policy of non-reprisal was applied throughout rebel territory on the orders of Mucianus, who sent the praetor Sextus Julius Frontinus to take the formal surrender of Julius Sabinus' Lingones. Frontinus was to write: 'The very wealthy city of the Lingones, which had revolted to Civilis, feared that it would be plundered by the approaching army of Caesar. But, when, contrary to expectation, the inhabitants remained unharmed and lost none of their property, they returned to their loyalty, and handed over to me 70,000 armed men.' [Front., *Strat.*, IV, III, 14]

Captured Treveran general Valentinus was sent to Lugdunum to appear before Mucianus and Domitian. After hearing the loquacious Valentinus put his case for a free Gaul, the no-nonsense Mucianus ordered his immediate execution. Valentinus went to his death claiming he would be remembered as a martyr to the cause of a free Treveran people. [Tac., *H*, IV, 85]

At the same time, Civilis and Classicus sent a letter to Cerialis claiming that the emperor Vespasian had died. This news had been suppressed by Vespasian's aides, they said. They also assured Cerialis that Italy was once more locked in civil war. The pair suggested that Cerialis leave them as rulers of their own states and go home. Failing that, they said, they would gladly fight him, and beat him, with German reinforcements from across the Rhine. Cerialis merely sent the rebel emissary south to Lugdunum, for the amusement of Mucianus.

Several days later, Cerialis was sleeping peacefully at Augusta Treverorum when he was awoken by panicking staff. Civilis, Classicus and Tutor had swept down from the north in two large columns, one via the Moselle Valley, the other swinging around to the east and coming over the mountains behind Augusta Treverorum. It was a classic pincer movement, perfectly executed. Between them, the two forces had literally caught the legions camped outside the city napping.

AD 70

XXX. BATTLE OF TRIER
Civilis counter-attacks

In the early hours of the morning, Germans had seized the bridge linking Augusta Treverorum with the far bank of the Moselle. Simultaneously, Civilis and his troops had burst into the Roman legionary camp outside the city, where vicious hand-to-hand fighting was taking place. Some parts of the camp had already been lost.

Civilis had been against this attack. Tutor had urged the assault, before Roman reinforcements reached Cerialis from the south. Classicus had voted with Tutor. Outvoted, Civilis had agreed to lead the mission, which now had the appearance of an imminent rebel victory. Cerialis, rising from his bed and picking up his sword without waiting to strap on his armour, hurried to the city gate that opened on to the Moselle bridge. Taking the Roman troops bunched there, the general led a counter-attack that threw the Germans off the bridge.

Leaving a detachment to hold the bridge, the general took the remaining men through the city at the run to the Roman camp beside the river. The first troops Cerialis came upon after he passed through a shattered camp gate were men of the 1st Germanica and 16th Gallica legions. Their standards stood defiantly, but few men defended them; the two eagles looked close to falling into rebel hands.

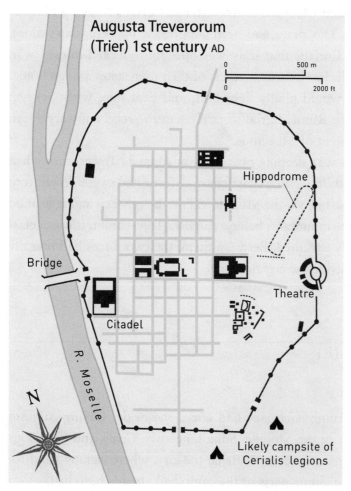

Augusta Treverorum (Trier) 1st century AD

Hippodrome

Bridge

Theatre

Citadel

R. Moselle

N

Likely campsite of Cerialis' legions

'Go tell the emperor,' Cerialis yelled to the men of these two legions, 'or Civilis and Classicus, as they're closer, that you have deserted yet another Roman general on the battlefield.' [Tac., *H*, IV, 77]

This jerked the 1st and 16th into action. Their cohorts rallied, charged the enemy, and saved their standards. While legionaries throughout the camp were compressed among tents and wagons by the enemy onslaught, and were finding it difficult to fight in formation, the men of the 21st Rapax regrouped in open space. Forming a dense line, the Rapax bore in on rebels who had turned their backs on the fighting to loot Roman baggage. Their drive sent tribesmen fleeing from the camp thinking that Roman reinforcements had arrived from Italy and Spain. Maintaining the momentum, Cerialis chased the fleeing rebels down the Moselle Valley towards the Rhine. Late in the day, Cerialis' troops came upon, and overran, the camp where the rebels had camped the previous night.

At Cologne, the city fathers rose against the rebels, burning a cohort of German warriors to death in their quarters in a village near the city. The people of Cologne then butchered Germans found in the city streets, closed the gates, and sent messages to Cerialis, begging him to come to their aid before Civilis reached them. They also offered the Roman general the wife and sister of Civilis and the daughter of Classicus, who had been left at Cologne by the rebel leaders. By forced march, Cerialis hurried his troops to Cologne, receiving the grateful thanks of the city fathers and the three valuable prisoners.

Civilis retreated north, as the 14th GMV Legion, which had been shipped across from Britain, marched into Belgica, crossed the Scheldt river, and accepted the surrender of the Nervi and Tungri tribes, which had gone over to Civilis early in the revolt. Meanwhile, the Canninefates, a seafaring people, had sent their vessels against Rome's Britannic Fleet, which was shadowing the 14th GMV up the coast, sinking half the Roman ships and putting the remainder to flight. The Nervians, to show their loyalty to Rome, spontaneously sent a force of young men against the Canninefates, a force swiftly wiped out by the Canninefates. Meanwhile, near Novaesium, Roman cavalry scouting ahead under Briganticus were surprised by Classicus, who sent the troopers packing. The revolt was still far from over.

At Cologne, Cerialis was joined by the 6th Victrix Legion from Spain and the 2nd Adiutrix Legion from Italy, followed shortly after by 14th GMV. The 6th Victrix's second-in-command was Gaius Minicius, a tribune who, as a prefect, had previously commanded the Treveran Horse and consequently knew how the Treverans fought. Cerialis transferred Minicius to the command of the 1st Wing of the Singularian Horse. This way, Cerialis had a reliable officer keeping watch on Singularian commander Briganticus, Civilis' nephew.

With now over 50,000 men, Cerialis advanced along the Rhine, to find the Novaesium legion camp a blackened ruin. Approaching Old Camp, he discovered that the rebels had dammed the Rhine, which was now flooding his path. Advancing warily across the waterlogged plain, the Roman army was attacked by Germans who seemed perfectly at home in the marshy terrain. Roman officers kept their formations together, reined in panicking horses, and collected their dead and wounded as they went, until the army reached high ground not far from Old Camp and pitched camp. Civilis had returned to the ruins of Old Camp, site of his greatest victory, where, amid the ashes, he had built a new fortress. Here, he would make a stand.

AD 70
XXXI. BATTLE OF OLD CAMP
Cerialis versus Civilis

The two armies lined up beside the Rhine. Cerialis placed his cavalry and auxiliary infantry in his front line. The legions occupied the second line, but the Roman general kept back one group of hand-picked legionary cohorts as a reserve. Across the battle-field, Civilis formed his men up in columns. The Batavians occupied the right wing, with Gugerni Germans on their outside. Ubii and Lingones occupied his centre, and Bructeri and Tencteri Germans took the left flank, beside the river.

Both commanders harangued their troops. Cerialis reminded his newly arrived units of Rome's proud military heritage, and implored the Rhine legions to recover Old Camp, where so many of their comrades had died. On the other side, Civilis reminded his Batavians that this was the site of a great Roman defeat. To the Germans, he said that the gods of Germany were watching them, urging them to give battle remembering their wives, their parents and their fatherland. The Roman legions responded to their general with a determined roar. Batavians and Germans let out a guttural war cry, rapped their weapons on their shields and performed crazy dances.

The sun was high above by the time that Civilis initiated battle by ordering his warriors to let fly with their missiles. The rebels launched stones and lead balls from their side of the marsh, but the Roman front line stood firm as missiles glanced off their raised shields. The rebels kept up the barrage until they exhausted their ammunition, then, yelling and screaming, they advanced to the attack. Their long spears felled auxiliaries in large numbers. A band of Germans now crossed the river via their dam and attacked the right of the auxiliary line, which began to give way.

Now the trumpets of the legions sounded. The legionaries had been standing silent and motionless. Now, they advanced in formation, shields up, swords at the ready. The auxiliaries made way for them. Legions and rebel front line engaged. The opposing sides stood toe-to-toe, slogging it out. As the fighting raged, a Batavian deserter came to Cerialis saying he knew a route through the marches to the west. If given cavalry, he would guide them in a surprise attack on the rebel flank. Cerialis sent two squadrons of cavalry with the deserter. Almost certainly, Minicius, new prefect of the 1st Wing of the Singularian Horse, led the detachment.

The deserter proved to be truthful, and Cerialis' cavalry surprised Gugerni warriors on the rebel right wing and cut them to ribbons. The troopers' victory cheer cued the legions, who then charged the rebel centre. The rebel line broke. Civilis' troops fell back towards the river, pursued by the legions. As heavy rain began to fall, bogging down legionaries and cavalry alike and reducing visibility, many rebels escaped

An inscription in honour of Gaius Minicius. His eminent career would include appointment as Prefect of Egypt. The inscription describes his award of a golden crown by Vespasian, apparently for leading the 1st Wing of the Singularian Horse during the Battle of Old Camp.

upriver. With sunset not far off, Cerialis sounded 'Recall'. As darkness fell, Roman troops began stripping the enemy dead.

Next morning, the 10th Gemina Legion arrived at Cerialis' camp from Spain, bringing news that Cerialis' superior, Annius Gallus, had finally arrived at Mogontiacum from Italy, accompanied by the 6th Ferrata and 8th Augusta legions. Gallus asked that the 14th GMV be sent to him, with the 10th Gemina filling its place. The old general would feel more secure with Rome's most famous legion in his camp.

At the Batavian capital, Noviomagus, Civilis, Classicus and Tutor collected what belongings they could, set fire to the rest, then retreated across the Rhine to 'the island'. With them went the last of their troops, thousands of refugees, 113 senators from Augusta Treverorum, and Roman deserters including the prefect Montanus and his brother Decimus.

The revolt continued to drag on for weeks. The 10th Gemina Legion lost its camp-prefect and five first-rank centurions at Arenacum (Arnhem). The 2nd Adiutrix and auxiliary units faced fierce resistance elsewhere. In another skirmish, Singularian Horse commander Briganticus perished; Cerialis himself appeared on the scene that day with a cavalry escort and drove the rebels back, recognizing the red-headed Civilis trying to regroup his troops before resorting to swimming for it. Civilis, Classicus and Tutor were all plucked from the water by rebel boats and conducted to safety. There was also a German night raid on Cerialis' camp which seriously embarrassed the Roman general, who was with his German mistress at the time.

Yet, despite these rebel successes, the Roman counter-offensive was snuffing the life out of the revolt. Its termination was inevitable, as many rebels came to realize. Once Civilis heard that his men were talking about handing him over to the Romans to save their own necks, he sent word to Cerialis seeking a parley. At the appointed time, the two commanders walked to the opposite ends of a broken bridge. There they agreed terms, and the revolt ended.

It is likely that Civilis spent the rest of his life under house arrest in Italy, as had Bato, Caratacus and other defeated leaders over the decades. Surrendered Batavian and Canninefate fighters were formed into new Roman auxiliary units and sent to Britain. The Batavian Horse was retained; its elite status would only increase. [Hold., *RAB*, App.]

Contrary to Cerialis' promise, a number of the legions that had gone over to the rebels were punished by Vespasian. He abolished the 1st Germanica and 18th legions.

The 4th Macedonica was abolished and reconstituted as the 4th Flavia; the 16th Gallica was similarly abolished and reformed, as the 16th Flavia, with both new units posted well away from the Rhine. Petilius Cerialis was immediately rewarded with a consulship, and appointed governor of Britain the following year. Taking the 2nd Adiutrix Legion to Britain with him, Cerialis would knock the other legions there into shape then lead them on a new mission of conquest, the invasion of northern Britain.

AD 70
XXXII. BESIEGING JERUSALEM
Titus' time to shine

Vespasian, having based himself in Alexandria in Egypt during the winter of AD 69–70, handed the task of resuming and completing the operation against the Jewish rebels in Judea to his 29-year-old son, Titus. To bolster the three legions that had fought under his father, Titus sent for the 12th Fulminata Legion, whose men would have been still smarting after the loss of their eagle under Gallus. Here was their opportunity to make amends. Tacitus says that Titus also reinforced his army with 'some men belonging to the 18th and 3rd [Cyrenaica] whom he had withdrawn from Alexandria'. [Tac., *H*, v, 1]

It was late April when Titus reached Jerusalem with the 5th Macedonica, 12th Fulminata and 15th Apollinaris legions, which immediately began building a vast camp west of the city. The following day, the 10th Fretensis arrived from Jericho and began to make camp on the Mount of Olives. Jewish partisans suddenly swarmed out of the Lower City, dashed across the Kidron Valley and attacked unprepared legionaries of the 10th working on the mountain slope. Titus himself was in the vicinity; he rallied his troops and drove off the attackers.

Jerusalem, surrounded by a series of three high walls, had close to a million Jewish people sheltering inside, many of them pilgrims; it would have to be taken by storm. After Titus' troops had spent weeks clearing the approaches, on 10 May the young general launched an assault on Jerusalem's Third Wall, not far from the present-day Jaffa Gate. All the legions continually fired their catapults at the walls to clear them of defenders, but the artillery of the 10th Fretensis came in for particular mention from

The Arch of Titus shows Roman troops bearing the spoils of Jerusalem, including the Temple's Menorah, in the AD 71 Triumph celebrated at Rome by Vespasian and his sons.

former Jewish general Josephus, who had changed sides. Josephus noted that the 10th was equipped with the most powerful spear-throwing scorpions, with a prodigious rate of fire, and the largest stone-throwing ballistas of all the legions, firing 100-pound (45-kilogram) rounded stones. [Jos., JW, 5, 6, 3]

Three massive wooden siege towers were rolled up to the Third Wall, and on 25 May the wall gave way to their battering rams. As waiting Roman infantry surged over the rubble, defenders withdrew to the Second Wall, which was higher and thicker than the third. The legions pounded away, day in, day out, at this next obstacle. On 30 May, a section of the Second Wall collapsed, forcing the partisans to retreat to the First Wall. Surging triumphantly into the city, legionaries found themselves

trapped in narrow lanes and a Jewish counter-attack forced them to withdraw. On 2 June, new breaches allowed the legions to finally secure the Second Wall, and the Jews again retreated to the First Wall.

Titus now gave each of his legions its own wall section, and pitted them against one another in a competition to see which would be first to breach the wall. The 5th Macedonica Legion was assigned to the Antonia Fortress, with the 12th Fulminata not far away. The 10th Fretensis' sector was near the Amygdalon, the Almond Pool, next to Herod's Palace. The 15th Apollinaris went to work opposite the High Priest's monument.

The legions took fifteen days to build massive, gently sloping embankments of earth against the 60-foot (18.2-metre) wall. As siege towers were being rolled up, partisans were able to undermine the two western embankments and collapse two towers. The 10th and 15th succeeded in rolling their towers into place, only for a Jewish raiding party to dash out of a nearby gate and set fire to the towers, totally destroying both.

Realizing that this siege was going to take some time, Titus suspended offensive operations and surrounded Jerusalem with a wall of his own before resuming the assault. The 5 miles (8 kilometres) of trench and wall, with thirteen forts along its length, was completed in just three days. After a sustained assault and a surprise night raid from men of the 15th Apollinaris, the Antonia Fortress was taken. Amid the ruins of the Antonia, Titus had embankments thrown up against the Temple wall.

Inside the city, partisans were fighting among themselves and killing their own leaders, while civilians starved. Somehow, the weakening partisans continued stiff resistance from the walls, and sent out raiding parties to harass the attackers.

By August, the legions were ready for the final assault on the Temple Sanctuary. It began with a fire. (Josephus would later claim that Titus ordered the Temple spared, and that the fire was accidental.) Legionaries smashed through the giant Sanctuary doors, then went looking for Jews, and plunder. Blood flowed across the Temple flag-stones like water. It was a portrait of hell. The spreading flames, the smoke, the heat, the crashing timbers, wild-eyed Roman troops cutting down everything that moved, officers yelling orders, screaming fugitives, the groans of the dying. The Temple was consumed by fire, but not before the legions had looted it of its treasures.

The last resistance was overcome at Herod's Palace to the west. After four hellish months, Jerusalem had fallen. Close to a million people had died during the siege; another 97,000 Jews had been taken prisoner by the Romans.

When Titus' legions paraded outside the shattered city to receive bravery awards and pay rises, Titus announced the legions' new postings. The 10th Fretensis Legion was ordered to stay at Jerusalem, as resident legion, building themselves a base amid the ruins. In early AD 71, after a triumphant concourse through Judea, Titus would pass by the bleak, razed city of Jerusalem and find the 10th ardently digging up treasure buried by Jews during the bloody siege.

AD 71–73
XXXIII. MACHAERUS AND MASADA
Last Judean sieges

Following the fall of Jerusalem, the 10th Fretensis Legion received a new commander, Lucillius Bassus, and in AD 71 Bassus took the 10th campaigning in southern Judea to terminate the last Jewish resistance. After securing Hebron, Bassus led the legion east of the Dead Sea to the hill fortress of Machaerus. Rebels who had held the fortress since AD 66 left the scene, but the town below it held out briefly. After leaving Machaerus a smoking ruin, the 10th Fretensis wiped out 3,000 partisans hiding in the Forest of Jardes, west of the Dead Sea. But when the legion's commander Bassus died, of natural causes, the 10th Fretensis returned to its new base at Jerusalem.

By the spring of AD 73, only one Jewish centre of resistance remained to be taken. Masada. In March of that year, the 10th Fretensis' new legate, Flavius Silva, led the legion out of Jerusalem and down the western side of the Dead Sea. Masada means, appropriately, 'mountain fastness'. This barren, flat-topped limestone mountain is 1¹/₂ miles (2.4 kilometres) from the lake, and rises 1,700 feet (550 metres) from a desolate landscape devoid of greenery. On the 650-foot (200-metre) by 190-foot (60-

metre) summit, King Herod had built a palace within a fortress. When Silva and his troops arrived below it, the fortress was held by 960 rebels led by Eleazar ben Jair.

The rocky outcrop of Masada, today, showing the remains of the palace of Herod, which was occupied by Jewish rebels from AD 66 until the siege conducted by the 10th Fretensis Legion and auxilary units in AD 73.

Silva had the 10th Fretensis and its supporting auxiliary units set up camps to the west of Masada. Traces of eight of those camps can still be seen today, as can the remains of a 10-foot (3-metre) stone wall that ran for 2 miles (3.2 kilometres) around Masada, dotted with forts and guard posts. To the west there was a promontory called White Cliff, 450 feet (140 metres) below the summit of Masada, and separated from it by a rocky valley. From here, Silva began a massive ramp of earth and rock, targeting the top of Masada's fortifications. While Jewish prisoners were used to ferry water and supplies on their backs to the Masada camps, the men of the 10th Fretensis Legion did all the construction work on the ramp.

Steadily, the ramp closed the gulf at a gradient of 1 in 3. Eventually, the ramp, 695 feet (880 metres) wide at it base, rose 300 feet (90 metres) and was topped by a 75-foot (20-metre) stone pier. A wooden 90-feet (25-metre) tall siege tower was rolled up the ramp. With catapults on the tower keeping up a constant rate of fire to clear

Masada's nearest ramparts of Jewish defenders, a battering ram inside the wooden tower began pounding the base of the wall.

Eventually, the wall gave way, and men of the 10th Legion surged in through the breach, only to find that the defenders had built a second wall, of alternate layers of timber and stone, which was impervious to battering ram blows. So, on 2 May, Silva had the wood in the wall set alight. Expecting the fire to weaken the wall sufficiently for it to be breached at dawn next day, the Roman troops retired.

That night, the Jewish men at Masada, knowing that sunrise would bring the final Roman assault, made a solemn pact. They then went around to their wives and children, and killed them. They then drew lots to decide which of them would die next. By the early hours of the morning, just ten partisans including commander Eleazar ben Jair remained alive. These men burned all their possessions then drew lots for the final act of their suicide pact. In the end, one man remained. He set fire to Herod's Palace, then took his own life.

As the sun rose, men of the 10th Fretensis Legion stormed through the burned second wall and entered Masada, to discover the fortress eerily silent. Throughout the complex they found the bodies of the dead Jews. Then an old woman emerged, and a younger woman, a relative of Eleazar, with five small children. All had succeeded in evading the previous night's murders by hiding in an underground water conduit. Masada had fallen. But it was a hollow victory for the 10th Fretensis.

Detachments of the legion would continue to occupy Masada for another forty years. Today, Israel Defence Force recruits take a vow – never to let Masada fall again.

AD 73
XXXIV. THE 6TH FERRATA TAKES COMMAGENE
The unnecessary invasion

After being part of the army that put down the Civilis Revolt on the Rhine, in AD 71 the 6th Ferrata Legion had marched back to Syria and its old station at Raphanaea beside the Euphrates. The legion found that Gaius Caesennius Paetus had been appointed by the Palatium to replace Licinius Mucianus as governor of Syria. This was the same arrogant and inept Paetus who, in AD 62, had led the 4th Macedonica and 12th Fulminata legions into Armenia, only to be surrounded and cut off by the Parthians at Rhandeia and subjected to humiliating peace terms. At that time, the 6th Ferrata had been in the relief force that had gone to the aid of Paetus' legions. Now, it had Paetus for its commander-in-chief.

In early AD 73, an urgent dispatch reached Rome from Antioch. Governor Paetus advised Vespasian that he had received information that King Antiochus IV of Commagene, a small nation immediately to the north of Syria allied to Rome, was planning to revolt and take his little state over to the Parthians. Paetus recommended immediate preventative action. Vespasian was surprised at this, for Antiochus had long been loyal to Rome, and as a result 'had flourished more than any other kings that were under the power of the Romans'. [Jos., JW, 5, 11, 3]

As proof of his loyalty during the Jewish Revolt, Antiochus had supplied thousands of Commagene troops under his son Epiphanes to support the Roman army. Still, trusting in Paetus' warning, Vespasian authorized the governor to do whatever he felt necessary.

Paetus quickly formed a task force from the 6th Ferrata Legion, auxiliaries and troops from two allied kings, then invaded sleepy Commagene. As the 6th Ferrata led the force up the west bank of the Euphrates into Commagene and advanced on Samosata, the kingdom's capital, Antiochus and his people were taken completely by surprise. The king hurriedly left Samosata and set up camp with his small native army on the plain, 14 miles (22.5 kilometres) from the city. Samosata was occupied by the Roman force without resistance, and, leaving a detachment to garrison it, Paetus advanced on the king's camp with the bulk of his force.

Protesting his innocence, King Antiochus refused to fight the Roman army, but his warlike sons Epiphanes and Callinicus were not prepared to surrender, and they and their few troops stubbornly defended their father's camp for a full day, holding out against the 6th Ferrata. Fighting ceased at dusk, with the Romans encircling the camp. But in the night the old king slipped away with his wife and daughters, and fled to Cilicia. When Antiochus' own troops learned that he had deserted them, they gave up the fight, forcing the king's sons also to flee. With just ten cavalrymen for escort, Epiphanes and Callinicus splashed across the Euphrates and galloped east. On reaching Parthia, they were welcomed by King Vologases, Rome's old enemy.

The king of Commagene took refuge at the city of Tarsus, capital of Cilicia. When Paetus learned this he sent a centurion with a 6th Ferrata detachment to arrest him and take him to Rome to be tried by the emperor. Vespasian knew and liked the king, and could not bring himself to believe the old man had been disloyal to Rome, especially when Paetus was still unable to provide any incriminating evidence. When he heard that Antiochus was being brought to him in chains, the emperor issued orders that the centurion and his party should halt in Sparta, Greece, where the king was to be freed and, for the time being, housed in style and comfort. When the two sons of the king heard that Vespasian was treating their father kindly, they set out for Rome to plead his case. Vespasian then had Antiochus brought to Rome.

So that he did not appear to be overruling one of his most senior provincial governors, Vespasian did not restore the king to his throne. Instead, he took the opportunity to annex Commagene, pulling it into the empire as Rome's latest province. Antiochus and his family spent the rest of their days residing in luxury in Rome and enjoying the patronage of the Flavian family, but deprived of their ancestral kingdom through the actions of a vain general with ambitions to be hailed a conqueror. At Rome in his unhappy old age, and welcoming the prospect of death, Antiochus would complain to Jewish historian Josephus, 'We ought not call any man happy before he is dead'. [Jos., *JW*, 5, 11, 3]

In AD 74, a year after he invaded Commagene, Paetus was recalled to Rome. There is no record of him receiving any reward for his annexation of Commagene. Paetus was replaced as governor of Syria by Marcus Ulpius Trajanus, former commander of the 10th Fretensis Legion and a consul in AD 70. Trajanus' son Marcus would join his father in Syria in AD 75 as a 22-year-old prefect of auxiliaries. In AD 98, that son was to become the emperor Trajan.

AD 83
XXXV. THE CHATTIAN WAR
Domitian's 'sham' victory

Vespasian's youngest son Domitian became emperor of Rome in AD 81, following the death of his brother Titus after just two years in office. Always jealous of the military glory won by his father and brother, Domitian even envied the military success of his generals, men such as Gnaeus Agricola in Britain, even though that success brought spoils and security to Rome. In AD 83, 31-year-old Domitian launched his own military campaign. And to ensure that no one outshone him that year, he deprived his commanders of troops for his campaign; for example, vexillations several cohorts strong were shipped to Gaul from each of the four legions then serving in Britain under Agricola, to join Domitian's task force.

To ensure an easy victory, Domitian chose to make war on an ally, the Chatti Germans. 'The war against the Chatti was uncalled for' and 'unprovoked,' said Suetonius later (he was 14 at this time). [Suet., XII, 6] Because Rome had a peace treaty with the Chatti, Domitian was determined that his attack would be achieved with the benefit of total surprise. So, said Frontinus, three times consul, and governor of Britain during the reign of Domitian's father Vespasian, Domitian 'concealed the reason for his departure from Rome under the guise of taking a census of the Gallic provinces'. [Front., *Strat.*, I, I, 8]

Through this ruse, Domitian was able to meet his assembled legions on the Upper Rhine without raising suspicions in Germany; news of the census-taking allayed any fears of Roman aggression. 'Under cover of this, he plunged into sudden warfare,' said Frontinus. Domitian, 'by advancing the frontier of the Empire along a stretch of 120 miles [193 kilometres], not only changed the nature of the war, but brought his enemies beneath his sway, by uncovering their hiding places'. [Front., I, III, 10]

The Chatti and at least one neighbouring tribe overcame their initial shock and attempted to mount organized resistance. 'All their strength lies in their infantry,'

Domitian conducts a sacrifice prior to departing for his Chattian War.

Tacitus wrote of the Chatti. [Tac., *Germ.*, 30] Said Frontinus of Domitian's campaign, 'When the Germans, in accordance with their usual custom, kept emerging from woodland pastures and unsuspected hiding places to attack our men, and then finding a safe refuge in the depths of the forest', Domitian continued to advance on his broad front, driving the Germans from the Bavarian forests. [Front., I, III, 10]

As Tacitus revealed, the Chatti were the most organized of the German tribes. 'They know how to keep rank, and how to recognize an opportunity or postpone an attack.' A Chattian army, 'in addition to arms, [was] burdened with entrenching tools and provisions' just like the Roman legions. [Tac., *Germ.*, 30] In this war, too, the Chatti succeeded in supporting their fighters with a baggage train carrying supplies, but Roman cavalry tracked it down. Chattian infantry harassed Domitian's cavalry when they were attacking the baggage train, regularly withdrawing into dense forest where mounted troops could not follow, so Domitian ordered his cavalry to dismount and follow the Germans into the trees on foot, and in this way the Chatti were defeated. [Front., *Strat.*, II, III, 23]

All along the broad front, surprise and Roman weight of numbers told. There were no major battles. The Germans were herded like sheep from their territory, and the campaign was over by the time autumn arrived. Frontinus would boast that Domitian 'crushed the ferocity of these savage tribes, and thus acted for the good of the provinces'. [Front., *Strat.*, I, I, 8] As a result of this campaign, Domitian expanded the Roman frontier east of the Rhine in the area of Bavaria and the Black Forest, beyond the frontier originally set by his father Vespasian. Domitian built a new line of forts – the limes – along the new frontier. When forts were constructed in the territory of the Cubii Germans, Domitian actually paid them compensation for the cropland included in the new fortifications. [Front., *Strat.*, II, XI, 7]

Domitian would celebrate a Triumph in Rome for his Chattian War. Tacitus, then a senator, would have seen the celebration with his own eyes. He described it as a 'sham Triumph', and claimed that, to give the impression that large numbers of German prisoners had been taken, Domitian dressed slaves from the marketplace in German attire and had them grow their hair and beards, representing them in his Triumph as Chattian prisoners-of-war. [Tac., *Agr.*, 39]

As for the legionaries who had participated in the campaign, they went back to their original stations. The troops from Agricola's army in Britain returned to their units in time for a real battle on the epic scale.

AD 84

XXXVI. BATTLE OF MONS GRAUPIUS
Rome's most northerly victory

> *'The cavalry do not use swords, nor do the wretched*
> *Britons mount in order to throw javelins.'*
> OFFICER OF 1ST TUNGRIAN COHORT, *Vindolanda Writing Tablets*

Roman general Gnaeus Julius Agricola celebrated his forty-fourth birthday on 13 June. Yet this was a sombre time for him; at beginning of that summer, Agricola and his wife Domitia had lost a son, born the previous year, to illness. It was 'a grievous personal loss,' said Agricola's son-in-law Cornelius Tacitus. But 'the conduct of the war was one means he used to distract his mind from his sorrow'. [Tac., *Agr.*, 29]

That war had been waged by Agricola, governor of Britain, for seven years. Following in the conquering footsteps of his predecessors Cerialis and Frontinus, Agricola had begun by completing the subjection of Wales and had then advanced his troops inexorably into Scotland, defying the piecemeal attempts of the Caledonian tribes to stop him. Now, in the last days of the summer of AD 84, the general watched from the camp tribunal as 20,000 troops assembled in their neat ranks in front of him. [Some authors suggest AD 83 – *see note**.]

In the northern distance, beyond the walls of the Roman marching camp, a bare hill rose up, the nearest of a rolling range that filled the horizon. On that hill, tens of thousands of Caledonian warriors could be seen milling; men of all ages, they had come to make a stand against the Romans. 'Bodies of troops began to move and weapons flashed, as the most adventurous [Caledonians] ran out in front, and all the time their battle-line was taking shape.' [Tac., *A*, 33]

Agricola, according to Tacitus a good-looking man but not striking, wore the armour of a senior officer, with the scarlet waistband of a legate tied around his midriff and the purple cloak of a commander-in-chief draped over his shoulders. He looked intently around his troops, and then began to speak. 'This is the seventh year,

---

*Numerous authorities including Tacitus' translators Professors H. Mattingly and S. Handford [*A&G*, Intro. VI], and Oxford's Professor R. Tomlin, an expert on the north of Roman Britain [*DRA*], have been of the view that Agricola's campaigns extended until late AD 84, with the Battle of Mons Graupius taking place that same year.

comrades,' he said, 'since by loyal service, yours and mine, you began to conquer Britain in the name of imperial Rome's divinely guided greatness.' [Tac., *A*, 33]

Together, Agricola went on, soldiers and general had advanced further north than any previous Roman army. And as they trudged around marshes, crossed mountains and rivers, and warily threaded their way through forests, soldiers had repeatedly asked him, 'When will we meet the enemy? When will they come out and fight?' Well, said Agricola, the Caledonians were coming now, for the Roman army had dug them out of their hiding places. [Ibid.]

Over the last four years, as Agricola's troops had continued their inexorable advance north, the Caledonian tribes had used hit-and-run tactics, sending small groups of warriors to harass the Romans and slow their advance. But the previous year, when the Caledonians had heard that detachments had been taken away from all the Roman legions in Britain to serve in the young emperor Domitian's war against the Chatti on the Rhine, they had found new courage, and had attacked the marching camp of the 9th Hispana Legion at night, in force. It had taken Agricola's arrival with auxiliary units to relieve the embattled 9th to make the tribesmen withdraw.

Pointing to the tribesmen in the distance, Agricola told his troops, 'These are the same men who last year attacked a single legion like robbers in the night, and acknowledged defeat when they heard your battle-cry.' [Tac, *A*, 34] Agricola said that he had long ago made up his mind that generals and armies could not avoid danger by running away. But there would be glory, too, in dying, if die they must. Not that Agricola intended dying this day.

'We have our hands …' he slid his sword from the scabbard on his left hip, and held it high so that every man could see its gleaming blade, 'and swords in them, and these are all that matter!' [Tac., *A*, 33] In response, there was a deep-throated roar from legionaries and auxiliaries alike. With his troops impatient to come to grips with the enemy, Agricola urged them, 'Have done with campaigning. Crown fifty years with one glorious day!' [Tac., *Agr.*, 34] The fifty years referred to the time that Roman troops had been in Britain – it had actually been forty-one years.

The general's speech was met with a 'wild burst of enthusiasm', and the troops hurried off to arm themselves. [Tac., *Agr.*, 35] Before long, a camp gate opened, and the Roman army marched out to meet the Caledonians. Agricola had given explicit orders for the positioning of his troops. The auxiliary light infantry went first – 8,000 auxiliaries in 16 cohorts. They formed the first battle line. The 3,000 cavalrymen of

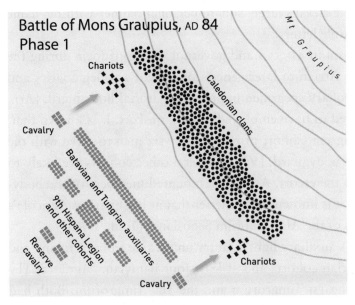

Battle of Mons Graupius, AD 84
Phase 1

Chariots

Mt Graupius

Caledonian clans

Cavalry

Batavian and Tungrian auxiliaries

9th Hispana Legion and other cohorts

Reserve cavalry

Chariots

Cavalry

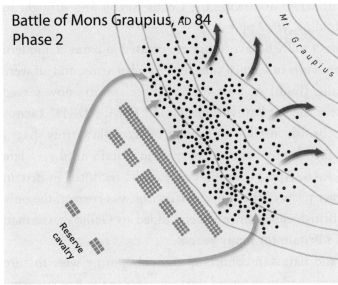

Battle of Mons Graupius, AD 84
Phase 2

Mt Graupius

Reserve cavalry

6 auxiliary alae filed out of the gate next, on foot, leading their horses, then mounted up and divided, with 1,500 troopers swinging out to occupy each wing of the Roman line. Last of all, Agricola's legionaries marched out, to form a second battle line with their backs to the camp ramparts. [Ibid.]

The complete 9th Hispana Legion was here, with all its cohorts now that the detachments from Domitian's Rhine campaign had returned in the spring. Tacitus says that Agricola had 'legions' here, so there would have been cohorts from one and probably two other legions in the battle line. With the 2nd Augusta Legions based in Wales, the two other legions in Britain, the 2nd Adiutrix and the 20th (Valeria Victrix), had their bases closer to the northern frontier and both possibly contributed vexillations of four cohorts of some 2,000 men.

Mounted and in full armour, the general and his staff also came out of the camp together with the men of the gubernatorial bodyguard, and positioned themselves between the two battle lines with all the legion standard-bearers. Close by the general were his mounted trumpeter, and, also on horseback, his own standard-bearer, holding aloft the pole bearing the general's large, square personal banner with his name and title displayed on it in purple letters.

Flavianus Arrianus, a consul in AD 130 and governor of Cappadocia during the reign of Hadrian – known as Arrian to later generations – had 200 legionaries and an unspecified number of auxiliary spearmen in his gubernatorial bodyguard. [Arr., *EAA*] Agricola can be expected to have employed a similar escort. It is known that, around this time, the 1st Tungrian Cohort provided forty-six men to serve with the governor of Britain's infantry bodyguard. [*VWT*] Several other cohorts are likely to have also contributed men to the escort. As for the mounted members of the bodyguard, the *equites singulares*, it is known from a letter that at least part of Agricola's escort was provided by Gauls of the Ala Gallorum Sebosiana. [Tom., *DRA*]

Tacitus says that Agricola's auxiliary light infantry units came from Germany and Gaul and included two Tungrian cohorts and at least four Batavian. [*Agr.*, 35] The two Tungrian cohorts were the 1st Tungrorum and the 2nd Tungrorum. Both had been raised in Gallia Belgica in AD 71 following the Civilis Revolt and brought to Britain by Petilius Cerialis. [Hold., *RAB*, App.]

Nine Batavian units, Cohorts I to IX Batavorum, were created in Batavia, modern Holland, in AD 71, from the remnants of Civilis' surrendered rebel army, and all were also taken to Britain by Cerialis. [Ibid.] At least four of those cohorts now served in Agricola's field army; one was the 1st Batavorum. [Hold., *DRA*, ADRH] Tacitus also indicates that there were British auxiliaries serving in Agricola's army. [*Agr.*, 32] There is no record of any British auxiliary unit serving in Britain until very late in the Roman period. [Hold., *RAB*, App.] Until that time, units recruited in Britain were shipped off to serve in other parts of the empire. If Tacitus was correct, the only conclusion can be that some British replacements were added to Gallic or German units that had been stationed in Britain for many years.

The men of the Tungrian and Batavian cohorts in Agricola's army were mature and experienced soldiers. Not only had they served thirteen years in the Roman army by this point, a number would have previously served with the auxiliary units that had taken part in the Civilis Revolt. This put many of them in their forties, and even older in some cases. 'These old soldiers had been well drilled in sword-fighting,' Tacitus said of them. [*Agr.*, 36] From the way Agricola was to employ the men of these six units in the upcoming battle, he clearly considered them his toughest auxiliaries.

As for the six cavalry wings in Agricola's army, the Ala Gallorum Sebosiana, the unit which supplied part of Agricola's bodyguard, would have been one. Named after an early commander of the ala, the unit had been raised in Gaul before the reign of Tiberius. It had fought for Vitellius during the war of succession, and would also have been brought to Britain by Cerialis. [Hold., *RAB*, App.] The identities of Agricola's five remaining cavalry wings are unknown. There were some fourteen cavalry alae serving in Britain at the time, units from Gaul, Spain, Pannonia and a Thracian ala whose members were recruited from far and wide.

Agricola was prepared to let his foreign auxiliaries take the brunt of the fighting; that was why he put them in his front line. His reason was simple. As his son-in-law Tacitus pointed out: 'Victory would be vastly more glorious if it cost no Roman blood.' [*Agr.*, 35] Many Roman generals showed little faith in their auxiliaries, putting them in the rear or on the wings and assigning the front line and the hard fighting to their legions. Agricola, a student of Roman military history, knew that successful generals had put their auxiliaries in the front line to blunt the enemy attack, reserving their legions for the killer blow. According to Tacitus, Agricola felt that if the auxiliaries were repulsed by the Caledonians after they went forward to the attack, 'the legions could come to their rescue'. [Ibid.]

From his saddle, Agricola watched approvingly as his units were marshalled by their centurions and optios into tight formations facing the enemy. 'To impress and intimidate its enemy', the Caledonian army had occupied the distant hill, with its first line on the plain below it. 'The other ranks seemed to mount up the sloping hillside in close-packed formations.' [Ibid.] Tacitus called this hill Mons (Mount) Graupius and the battle here would take its name from it. In modern times Mons Graupius was taken to refer to the Grampian Mountains, which slant down the middle of Scotland, with the battle thought to have taken place 'at the foot of the Grampian hills', as eighteenth-century British historian Edward Gibbon wrote. [Gibb., 1] More recent opinion has put the battle site in a variety of locations in the northeast of Scotland, with no site yet reliably fixed.

'The flat space between the armies was taken up by the noisy manoeuvring of the chariots,' said Tacitus. [Tac., *Agr.*, 35.] This would

The light British war chariot. The driver is believed to have sat, legs dangling, with a warrior behind.

be the last time that an imperial Roman army faced war chariots in battle. Vegetius was to write that when the Romans first encountered the chariots employed by eastern armies, such as those of Mithradates the Great in the first century BC, they were terrified. But, he said, they later came to laugh at them. [Vege., III] Arrian, who must have seen them first hand whilst serving in Britain in his youth, said that British chariots were light and so could be operated in all kinds of terrain. [Arr., *TH*, 19] Vegetius felt that the main problem with a chariot was that if it did not operate on level ground 'the least obstruction stops it'. [Vege., III]

Arrian wrote that the Britons – the term used by Romans to describe all the native inhabitants of Britain including the Caledonians – normally used pairs of 'small and scruffy' horses to draw their chariots. Despite their looks, these horses were capable of 'harsh labour'. [Arr., *TH*, 19] Yet, as Vegetius was to remark, there was a sure-fire way to render a chariot useless as a weapon of war: 'If one of the horses is either killed or wounded, [the chariot] falls into the opponent's hands.' [Vege., III.] Similarly, it was probable that Agricola's troops had orders to aim their missiles at the horses, not at the chariots.

'The terror inspired by the horses and the noise of the wheels are enough to throw their opponents' ranks into disorder,' Julius Caesar had written of his encounter with chariots in southern Britain 130 years earlier. 'In chariot fighting the Britons begin by driving all over the field, hurling javelins.' [Caes., *GW*, IV, 33]

Here were the Caledonian chariots now, perhaps several hundred of them, racing up and down on the flat between the two armies with pounding hooves and churning wheels, their yelling crews shaking spears in the air as their vehicles careered along. 'The nobleman drives; his dependants fight in his defence,' said Tacitus. [Tac., *Agr.*, 12] In Caesar's day, British chariots had made their way through their own cavalry to deliver one or two fighting men to the battle front, and these men jumped down to engage the opposition on foot, with the chariots waiting to carry them out of the fray if the tide turned against them. [Caes., *GW*, IV, 33]

Tacitus does not identify a role for Caledonian cavalry at Mons Graupius, but it is likely some were present. 'There are very many cavalry,' said an officer of Agricola's 1st Tungrian Cohort, possibly Julius Verecundus, the unit's prefect, in a letter about the natives of northern Britain. 'The cavalry do not use swords, nor do the wretched Britons mount in order to throw javelins.' [*VWT*] In hit-and-run skirmishes, the mounted Caledonians, like the chariot-borne noblemen, would merely use their horses as a means of rapidly delivering them to the fight. There they would dismount and launch their javelins before riding away again.

The Caledonians had 'reddish hair and long limbs', said Tacitus, which he felt indicated they were of German origin. [Tac., *Agr.*, 11] There is no mention of painted faces or limbs among the Caledonians at Mons Graupius or during any of Agricola's seven British campaigns. The first reference in Roman literature to Picts of Scotland – from *pictus*, meaning 'coloured' or 'tattooed' – would not be for another 200 years. The Pict name, and the habit of the warriors of Scotland painting themselves for war, were still a long way off when the tribes of Caledonia assembled to fight Agricola's army.

'The Britons are unprotected by armour,' said the 1st Tungrian Cohort officer. [*VWT*] Neither did they wear helmets. For weapons, apart from spears, Tacitus says that the Caledonians carried small shields and 'unwieldy swords' with rounded ends. [Tac., *Agr.*, 36] While no archaeologist or farmer has to date dug up examples of any especially large Caledonian swords from this period, Tacitus was adamant that the swords used by the Caledonians in this battle were 'huge'. [Ibid.]

When Agricola stepped up on to the tribunal in the Roman camp, he estimated that the Caledonian army numbered in excess of 30,000 men. [Tac., *Agr.*, 29] As he addressed his troops, warriors had continued to flood to Mons Graupius, enlarging the Caledonian army even more. The Caledonian numbers seem to have taken Ag-

Remains of the Roman fort at Vindolanda, base of the 1st Tungrian Cohort, one of the auxiliary units in Agricola's army at Mons Graupius.

ricola by surprise. Only later, from prisoners, would he learn that the previous year the tribes had set aside old differences that had them frequently at war with each other. They had sent envoys around the tribes, a treaty had been signed and ratified by sacrificial rites. Then, the men had sent their women and children away to places of safety, and had vowed to band together to fight Rome. [Tac., *Agr.*, 27]

This uniting of the tribes may well have been the work of a Caledonian chieftain by the name of Calgacus, who was the chosen war chief of the tribes, 'a man of outstanding valour and nobility', according to Tacitus. [Tac., *Agr.*, 29] It was later reported to Agricola that Calgacus delivered a stirring speech to the assembled warriors at Mons Graupius, in which he had reportedly said to his countrymen, 'Which will you choose? To follow your leader into battle? Or to submit to taxation, labour in the mines, and all the other tribulations of slavery?' The future of the Caledonians would be decided here, on this battlefield, said Calgacus. 'On then, into battle! And as you go, think of those who went before you, and those who will come after you.' [Ibid.]

Answering the Caledonian call to arms were 'all the young men and famous warriors', the latter wearing decorations they had earned in previous battles, including, no doubt, trophies from skirmishes with the Romans. By the time that Agricola's army had formed up, the Caledonian numbers had grown to such an extent that the Roman general 'now saw that he was greatly outnumbered', and, fearing that the tribesmen had sufficient numbers simultaneously to make a frontal attack on him and outflank both his wings, he ordered the ranks of his troops to open up so that his lines extended further across the plain. Agricola then dismounted, sent away his horse and took his place in front of the standards. [Ibid.]

With the tribesmen on the hill and the plain singing and yelling, and the Roman troops tense but perfectly silent, battle commenced. 'The fighting began with an exchange of missiles,' said Tacitus. The Caledonian chariots charged forward, and passengers jumped down to launch their javelins. At the same time, the centurions of the auxiliary front line ordered their men to let fly with their spears. 'The Britons showed both steadiness and skill in parrying our spears with their huge swords or catching them on their little shields.' [Tac., *Agr.*, 36]

One hundred and thirty years before, Caesar's cavalry had destroyed the British cavalry sent against him. Now Agricola, keeping four squadrons in reserve, followed Caesar's example, as he ordered most of his cavalry to charge the Caledonian chariots. His trumpet sounded, and the trumpets of the cavalry units repeated the call.

With a roar, the troopers on each Roman wing urged their horses forward, quickly reached the gallop, and charged into the Caledonian chariots, which appear to have begun withdrawing to the Caledonian wings.

As the cavalry engaged the chariots, Agricola gave another order. Trumpets again sounded. The standards of six auxiliary cohorts in the front line inclined forward. Yelling their battle cry, the 3,000 men of the two Tungrian cohorts and of four Batavian cohorts leapt forward and charged the Caledonian infantry, quickly surging into the opposition line on the plain. The auxiliaries' commanders rode into battle; Aulus Atticus, young Roman prefect of one of these six cohorts, either driven by youthful impetuosity or carried on by an uncontrollable horse, pushed too far into the tribal ranks and found himself isolated. The Roman officer was quickly hauled from the saddle by Caledonians and slaughtered.

Roman auxiliaries behind the prefect maintained formation as they drove into the tribesmen. 'The Batavians, raining blow after blow, striking them with the bosses of their shields and stabbing them in the face, felled the Britons posted on the plain and pushed on up the hillsides.' [Ibid.] Now the 5,000 remaining Roman auxiliaries were sent charging forward to join the fight. Meanwhile, the Roman cavalry had swiftly overwhelmed the Caledonian chariots, massacring their drivers and passengers. With the noblemen of all the tribes piloting these chariots, the Caledonians were deprived of many of their leaders. The Roman troopers now turned their attention to the infantry mêlée.

The Caledonian ranks on the slopes held firm against the impact of the Roman cavalry, and the rough ground made it hard going for horses. As a result, the Roman cavalry came to a standstill, and the troopers had to fight for their lives as the lanky tribesmen pressed forward around them. Roman auxiliaries, meanwhile, found themselves crushed up against the horses' flanks. Occasionally, said Tacitus, a driverless chariot or a panic-stricken riderless horse would come crashing blindly into the mass of fighting men.

Higher up the hill, many Caledonians had yet to become engaged in the battle. An astute chieftain, perhaps Calgacus, seeing an opportunity to surround the outnumbered Roman auxiliaries, now sent these as yet unbloodied men rushing down the sides of the hill to outflank the Romans and attack them from the rear. Hundreds of yards away, Agricola, still standing outside the Roman camp with 9,000 stock-still legionaries aching to enter the fight behind him, saw the tribesmen come down off the hill and sweep around to the rear of his auxiliaries. The general gave another order. In response, his four reserve cavalry squadrons galloped off and thundered across the plain, smashing into the Caledonians attacking the rear of the Roman auxiliary cohorts.

This cavalry charge turned the battle. The Caledonians, intent on attacking the auxiliaries, did not see the cavalry coming, and many were cut down from behind. Survivors from this group of Caledonians broke off the fight and ran for their lives, with Roman cavalry chasing them across the moorland. Overtaking tribesmen, Roman troopers would force them to disarm, taking them prisoner – they would bring a good price from the slave merchants who had followed the army north. But then, said Tacitus, troopers saw more Caledonians fleeing their way, and to prevent their first prisoners from escaping, they killed them, and then galloped off to make fresh captives of the latest terrified tribesmen on the run. [Tac., *Agr.*, 37]

The sight of the slaughter of their countrymen on the plain robbed the Caledonians still fighting on the hill of their spirit. The battle disintegrated into a rout. Large groups of warriors, while retaining their arms, deserted the hill fight and ran for the protection of distant forests. Auxiliaries gave chase. Agricola now ordered the legions forward, to mop up on the hill as he himself joined the pursuit by the auxiliaries.

As Caledonian dead littering the battlefield were being stripped by legionaries, Caledonian clans regrouped in the forests, and cut down the first rash Roman pursuers who ventured into the trees after them. Agricola ordered the auxiliary infantry to surround the forests, then sent the cavalry into the trees to finish the day's work. 'The pursuit went on until nightfall and our soldiers were tired of killing,' said Tacitus, who numbered the Caledonian dead at 'some 10,000'. Agricola, he said, lost just 360 auxiliaries in the fighting. Not a single legionary had died, while the young prefect Atticus was the most senior of the Roman casualties. At nightfall, the Romans returned to their marching camp, exhausted but victorious.

'For the victors, it was a night of celebrating over their triumph and their booty,' said Tacitus. For Caledonian civilians, it was a night of searching the battlefield and the mounds of stripped bodies for their dead and wounded, and carrying them away. The Romans heard both men and women wailing in their grief that night. In the far distance, farmhouses glowed orange after being put to the torch by their owners, who fled with the survivors of the battle. [Tac., *Agr.*, 38]

Next day, with the naked Caledonian dead lying where they had fallen, 'an awful silence reigned everywhere'. [Ibid.] The hills were deserted. Smoke rose lazily from the ruins of distant farmsteads. Agricola sent cavalry scouts ranging for miles around. They found not a living soul. [Ibid.]

The most northerly battle ever fought by an imperial Roman army, and the last against war chariots, was a bloody victory for Agricola and for Rome, yet, apart from 10,000 bodies, glory and booty, it achieved little. With the summer almost at an end, Agricola and his troops withdrew to the south. No Roman army would ever progress this far north again.

The emperor Domitian recalled Agricola to Rome at once, and the Senate granted Agricola Triumphal Decorations. Agricola, fully aware that Domitian was jealous of his British success, immediately went into retirement and declined to be considered for any future official appointment.

AD 85–89
XXXVII. DECEBALUS THE INVADER
Prelude to Dacian conquest

Dacia, which encompassed much of modern-day Romania, was a mountainous country north of the River Danube populated by a Germanic people. Although theirs was primarily a rural economy, the Dacians had a high degree of commercialization and industrialization. Members of the Dacian ruling class were well educated, reading both Latin and Greek, and they also had substantial wealth, from Dacia's rich gold, silver, iron and salt mines.

Up to this point in their history the Dacians had only seriously challenged Rome twice, and then only briefly, with raids into Moesia during the reign of Augustus and again in AD 69, when the Roman Empire was in turmoil during the war of succession following the demise of Nero. On both occasions the Dacians had come off badly from their encounters with Rome's legions. That situation was about to change.

In AD 85, the elderly ruler of Dacia, King Dura, voluntarily abdicated in favour of a younger, more energetic man. Decebalus, the new king, was renowned for his military skills, both tactical and physical. The aggressive king Decebalus and his senior general Susagus, whose name meant 'grandfather', quickly assembled an army of foot soldiers from the tribes of mountainous Dacia, and led it across the Danube to invade the Roman province of Moesia, taking the Roman garrison there completely by surprise.

'One after the other,' Tacitus was to complain, 'experienced officers were defeated in fortified positions.' [Tac., *Agr.*, 41] The Roman governor of Moesia, Oppius Sabinus, hurriedly marched against the invaders with the 5th Macedonica Legion, then stationed at Oescus. [Suet., XII, 6] In the ensuing battle the governor was killed by the Dacians, and the mauled 5th Macedonica fell back in disarray. The Palatium rushed the 4th Flavia Legion and auxiliary units to Moesia from Dalmatia, but the damage had been done. By the time the reinforcements arrived, Decebalus and his troops had sacked cities, towns and farms and taken thousands of prisoners, and, by the end of the year, had withdrawn across the Danube with their loot and their prisoners.

Domitian mounted an AD 86 counter-offensive against the Dacians. He personally led an army into Moesia, but waited in the comfort of a Danube city as the prefect of the Praetorian Guard, Cornelius Fuscus, crossed the river with several legions, cohorts of the Praetorian Guard and numerous auxiliary units. In a mountain pass, Fuscus' army was ambushed by Decebalus and his waiting Dacians. Fuscus was killed. One of his legions was wiped out, with its eagle and artillery carried away by the enemy. This legion was almost certainly the 5th Alaudae, which disappeared from the records at this time.

The 5th Alaudae was apparently commanded by Marcus Laberius Maximus, who perished with his unit. Laberius' personal slave Callidromus, made a prisoner by Dacian general Susagus, was sent by King Decebalus as a gift to King Pacorus of Parthia. Thirty years later, Callidromus would escape back to his home town, Nicomedia, in Bithynia-Pontus.

The bloodied remnants of Fuscus' army flooded back across the Danube to bring Domitian the news of the brutal defeat in Dacia. Survivors would tell horrific stories of curved Dacian swords that sliced through Roman helmets and heads, and hacked off Roman limbs. As the Dacians occupied positions along the south bank of the Danube, Domitian issued orders for more troops to garrison Moesia and keep watch on the Dacians, then scurried back to Rome to plan a new counter-offensive in safety.

Domitian's counter-offensive of AD 88 was led by Tettius Julianus, a former consul who had commanded the 7th Claudia Legion. Julianus' army crossed the Danube and pushed over the mountains into central Dacia behind the back of Decebalus and his troops on the Danube. Late in the year, at Tapae, west of Decebalus' capital of

The only known depictions of King Decebalus are on Trajan's Column. Here, he is shown killing himself when surrounded by Trajan's Thracian cavalry, which had been tracking him for months.

Sarmizegethusa (today's Varhely), Julianus' legions met a Dacian army led by a leading Dacian general, Vezinas, 'who ranked next after Decebalus'. [Dio, LXVII, 10] The next most high-ranking individual in Dacian society after the king was the high priest of Zamolxis; Vezinas may well have been the high priest.

The Roman troops were fully aware that these Dacians had wiped out an entire legion only two years before, so, to inspire his men to great deeds, Julianus ordered each of his legionaries to paint their name and that of their centurion on their shield.

This way, the most valiant fighters could be readily identified for later reward. Julianus' incentive to excel had the desired effect. His troops routed the Dacians at Tapae, and 'slew great numbers of them'. [Ibid.] Vezinas, the Dacian commander, finding himself trapped, threw himself down on the ground among the sea of Dacian corpses, and pretended to be dead. Once night fell, Vezinas rose from the dead and made good his escape.

When news of this defeat reached Decebalus, he ordered trees to be cut down to form barricades across the valley leading to his capital, and had armour nailed to tree trunks to give the impression that the barricades were manned. With the winter of AD 88–89 approaching, Julianus camped at Tapae, in position to advance on Sarmizegethusa the following spring. But Julianus' plans were about to be influenced by events on the Rhine.

AD 89

XXXVIII. SATURNINUS' REVOLT
Clash of the legions

'Only an amazing stroke of luck checked the rebellion.'
SUETONIUS, *The Twelve Caesars*, XII, 6

Several times during the first century, provincial governors had led rebellions against sitting Roman emperors. The AD 21 revolt of Julius Sacrovir in Gaul and Julius Florus of the Treveri had been put down so quickly by Tiberius, according to his subordinate Velleius Paterculus, 'that the Roman people learned that he had conquered before they knew he was engaged in war'. [Velle., II, CXXIX, 3] Scribonianus' AD 42 revolt against Claudius in Dalmatia was snuffed out five days after it had begun. Vindex's AD 67 Gallic revolt was bloodily terminated in a battle between rebel Gauls and legions from the Rhine, but sparked the rebellion of Galba in Spain and demise of Nero the following year. By AD 89, Domitian had ruled for eight forgettable years when Lucius Antonius Saturninus, governor of Upper Germany, set a new revolution in motion.

Saturninus' plan revolved around his own legions of the army of the Upper Rhine – the 14th Gemina and 21st Rapax, both based at his provincial capital, Mogontiacum, plus the 8th Augusta at Argentoratum and 11th Claudia at Vindonissa. In addition, Saturninus planned to bring German tribes from east of the Rhine into the uprising, paying them to take part. To raise the money to pay the Germans, Saturninus dipped into the savings banks of his own legions. Into these banks, administered by legion standard-bearers, legionaries deposited their savings – from their salaries, imperial donatives and the sale of war booty.

The revolt was scheduled to take place late in the winter, with the German tribesmen crossing the ice of the frozen Rhine to join Saturninus' legions. It appears that once Lucius Maximus, governor of Lower Germany, heard of this plan, he marched his legions up the Rhine to take on Saturninus. With a pitched battle looming between the two Roman armies, 'only an amazing stroke of luck checked the rebellion', according to Roman biographer Suetonius, who was aged around 20 that year. 'The Rhine thawed at the very hour of battle,' preventing Saturninus' German allies from crossing the ice to join him. In the light of this turn of events, 'the troops who remained loyal disarmed the rebels'. [Suet., XII, 6]

As for Saturninus, 'Lucius Maximus overcame him and destroyed him,' said Cassius Dio. [Dio, LXVII, 11] The heads of Saturninus and those men who had been in league with him were sent to Rome and exhibited in the Forum on Domitian's orders. 'It would be impossible to say how many he killed,' Dio was to say of Domitian's subsequent retribution. Domitian did not bother to inform the Senate of the identities of those of its members who fell to the swords of his Praetorian execution parties, and he prohibited the entering of the victims' names in the official records.

Julius Calvaster, a senior tribune with one of Saturninus' Upper Rhine legions, pleaded not guilty to involvement in the conspiracy, declaring that the reason he had spent so much time in private with Saturninus prior to the revolt was because he was involved in a homosexual liaison with the governor, and knew nothing of the planned rebellion. He was believed, and acquitted. Lucius Maximus burned all the late governor's correspondence, so that Domitian could not implicate and then execute any other leading Romans. 'For his action,' said Dio approvingly, 'I do not see how I can praise him enough.' [Ibid.]

As a result of Saturninus' revolt, Domitian increased the annual salary of all Roman legionaries from 900 to 1,200 sesterces a year, to elevate his popularity with the rank and file. He also decreed that legionaries could in future only keep a maximum of 1,000 sesterces in their legions' banks, to limit the temptation that these legion savings might offer rebellious spirits. In addition, Domitian ordered that no longer could two or more legions share a base – to limit the opportunities for legions to conspire against him. From that time forward, said Domitian, only one legion could occupy each base. Both the salary increase and regulation regarding the number of legions per base were to involve significant expense by Rome's Military Treasury, with the latter requiring several legions to leave their long-time bases and build new homes for themselves elsewhere.

AD 89
XXXIX. RETREAT FROM DACIA
Domitian's humbling treaty

News of the Saturninus Revolt on the Upper Rhine spread fast. North of the Danube, Sarmatian tribesmen learned of it late in the winter. Believing that the Romans would be preoccupied by the Rhine affair, and with the Danube still frozen and passable, the Sarmatians mounted a raid into Moesia, surprised and savaged auxiliary garrisons, and ravaged towns and farms.

At Tapae in Dacia, as spring sunshine melted the winter snows, Tettius Julianus, preparing to march his Roman army against the Dacian capital, received word that the legions of the Upper Rhine were in revolt, and, worse, that the Sarmatians were swarming all over Moesia to his rear. He also learned that Decebalus, Susagus and their Dacian troops were withdrawing from the Danube to defend Sarmizegethusa. Fearing that he would be cut off in Dacia between the Dacians and the Sarmatians, Julianus fell back from Tapae and crossed the Danube to re-enter Moesia.

By this time Domitian had come up from Rome and was again personally leading an army north, aiming to deal with the Sarmatians. As he and Julianus linked up in Moesia, the Sarmatians withdrew across the Danube. Decebalus the Dacian king now offered Domitian a peace treaty, but only if the Romans paid him a vast amount. Domitian turned him down, executing the Dacian envoys who brought the peace offer.

Determined to exact revenge on someone, anyone, for the losses to the Sarmatians and the Dacians, and flushed with the success that Julianus had achieved at Tapae, Domitian sent his army marching into the province of Pannonia. The Quadi and the

Marcomanni Germans beyond the Danube had earlier refused to assist him against the Dacians when he had asked them to, and he was intent on punishing them for that refusal. Hearing that the Romans were coming after them, the Marcomanni marched from their home territory in Bohemia, crossed the Danube into Pannonia and attacked and repulsed Domitian's army, then returned to Bohemia laden with booty.

With his troops in Pannonia retreating, Domitian lost his nerve. When another Dacian envoy, the princely Diegis, came to him, Domitian agreed to a peace treaty with Dacia, even sending Diegis home wearing a crown. In this treaty, Domitian agreed to pay the Dacians large amounts of gold every year in return for peace, and to also provide Decebalus with engineering and military advisers. Apart from a Dacian withdrawal from the Moesian bank of the Danube, and a promise of future peace, all Rome received in exchange was the return of a few Roman prisoners from among large numbers of Roman captives held by the Dacians.

Back in Rome, Domitian celebrated a double Triumph, as if he was a victor. One Triumph was for his small-scale success against the Chatti in AD 83, when 'he plundered some of the tribes beyond the Rhine that enjoyed treaty rights', according to Dio, 'a performance which filled him with conceit, as if he had achieved some great success'. [Dio, LXVIII, 3] Domitian's other Triumph was for Julianus' victory at Tapae. 'He did not insist on recognition for his [failed] Sarmatian campaign,' Suetonius wrote, 'contenting himself with the offer of a [victor's] laurel crown to Capitoline Jupiter.' [Suet., XII, 6]

Following the signing of the treaty with the Dacians, Domitian divided Moesia into two provinces, Upper Moesia to the west, Lower Moesia to the east. This was intended to ensure that in future the defence of Moesia did not become the lot of just one rash or cowardly consular commander who proved unequal to the task, as had been the case with the late Oppius Sabinus.

But much damage had been done to Rome's pride at home and to her prestige abroad by Domitian's capitulation. Cornelius Tacitus, who himself commanded a legion around this time, would rage at the incompetence that had cost Rome dearly: 'It was no longer the frontier and the Danube line that was threatened, but the permanent quarters of the legions and security of the empire.' [Tac., *Agr.*, 41]

Four legions were now stationed in the provinces of Moesia, with another four in neighbouring Pannonia. They stood watch on the Danube, tensed for another attack from across the river by the Dacians or their allies. For, said Tacitus several years later, the Dacians were 'a people which can never be trusted'. [Tac., *H*, III, 46] Over the next decade, there was an uneasy peace along Rome's Danube frontier. But it was not to last.

AD 101

XL. FIRST DACIAN WAR
Following Trajan's Column

> '*The Dacian war! There is ... no subject so poetic and almost legendary, although its facts are true.*'
>
> PLINY THE YOUNGER, *Letters*, VIII, 4

Rome's new emperor Trajan was going to war. It was March AD 101, and Trajan rode out of Rome followed by thousands of foot soldiers of the elite Praetorian Guard and hundreds of troopers of the Singularian Horse household cavalry, and headed for the Danube. Where Domitian had failed to cower the Dacians, Trajan was determined to succeed.

Trajan, a powerfully built man of 47 with a thick neck, long nose and hair combed in a severe fringe, had come to the throne in AD 98 on the death of Nerva, the elderly senator who had succeeded Domitian as emperor in September AD 96 – after the unpopular Domitian was assassinated by a wrestler. Nerva, who reigned for less than two years, had in AD 97 adopted Trajan and made him his heir. An experienced general and son of a general, Trajan, one-time commander of the 7th Gemina Legion in Spain, had been made a consul by Domitian in AD 91 and appointed commander of the army of the Lower Rhine by Nerva. It was on the Rhine in February AD 98 that Trajan learned that Nerva had died in the last week of January and that the Senate had endorsed him as Nerva's successor.

Trajan was in no hurry to go to the capital. Remaining on the Rhine, he ordered the creation of additional auxiliary units, such as a 1,000-strong light infantry cohort raised in Britain that spring, the Cohors I Brittonum Ulpia. Through AD 98 Trajan inspected all the troops on the Rhine, and the following spring he toured the Danube, ordering the legions there to construct new forts, military roadways and a canal in the Iron Gates region of the Danube. At the same time, the new emperor intensified the training of the legions stationed in the Danubian provinces.

After he finally reached Rome in AD 99, Trajan had his Palatium begin preparations for a major military campaign. Trajan had never forgiven Domitian for the humiliation of the peace terms with the Dacians. He 'was grieved by the amount of money they were receiving annually,' said Dio, 'and he also observed that their power and pride were increasing.' [Dio, LXVIII, 15] Decebalus was welcoming Roman deserters into his army, which continued to grow stronger with each passing year.

Roman military preparations intensified throughout AD 100, with weapons and ammunition being produced and stockpiled in Moesia, where the resident 1st Italica, 4th Flavia, 5th Macedonica and 7th Claudia legions would have been training for river crossings. More ships would have been added to the Moesian and Pannonian fleets on the Danube. Food supplies were brought in. Baggage animals were procured, and legion carpenters built carts and collapsible boats. By the spring of AD 101, a further six legions had been quietly moved closer to the Danube or were on the march to Moesia from stations throughout Europe, accompanied by scores of auxiliary units from as far afield as Britain.

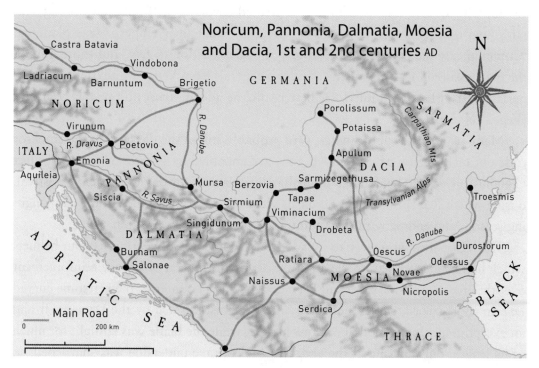

At Brigetio on the Rhine in Pannonia, the regulation imposed by Domitian stipulating that only one legion could occupy any military base was flouted as the 11th Claudia arrived from Vindonissa in today's Switzerland and joined the 1st Adiutrix. The 14th Gemina arrived at Vindobona, modern-day Vienna, after marching from Mursa to free up the 13th Gemina, which was ready to march for Moesia. Not far away, at its Pannonian base at Carnuntum, the 15th Apollinaris was also preparing to march. The 1st Minervia Legion was tramping down the Rhine from Bonna in company with the 10th Gemina Legion from Noviomagus. And the 2nd Adiutrix was on the march from its base at Aquincum, today's Budapest.

The logistical arrangements for the Dacian operation were enormous, involving 100,000 troops, almost as many non-combatants, thousands of sailors, plus up to 30,000 horses, mules and oxen, so it was no wonder that it took Trajan's staff at the Palatium two years to bring the operation to fruition. The other factor that had to be borne in mind was the need for secrecy – the Dacians could not be permitted to know that Trajan was coming after them, for Decebalus had shown himself to be a wily military tactician who could be expected to launch a pre-emptive strike against the Romans if he learned that they were preparing to invade his country.

So, with Dacian ambassadors being treated cordially at Rome, few among Trajan's own officers would have known precisely what their emperor was planning. 'Communicate the plans you intend to put into execution to few, and those only of the most assured loyalty,' was the advice to generals from Vegetius, adviser to the imperial court of Late Antiquity. 'Or better still,' he added, 'trust no one but yourself.' [Vege., DRM, III]

Many of Trajan's subordinates were probably still in the dark when the emperor rode out of Rome on 25 March AD 101, accompanied by Praetorian Guard prefect Claudius Livianus. The date fell immediately after the four-day Quatranalia Festival, during which Roman military standards were blessed prior to the annual campaigning season, and ending with the anointing of trumpets on 23 March.

The legionaries who were to invade Dacia would do so wearing Roman helmets which had been modified by the addition of cruciform iron or bronze reinforcement over the crown. This measure had been designed as a counter to the fearsome curved Dacian short-sword, called the *falx* by the Romans, the *sica* by the Dacians. It had an exceptionally long wooden or bone handle, while the blade was straight for much of its length, only curving at the end. Just the concave underside was sharpened, so that when the weapon was wielded the curved end projected towards the target. For maximum destructive effect, the user crashed his falx down on to the target double-handed, then drew the blade back towards himself in a sawing motion.

As the sword-makers of Japan were to discover centuries later, a curved blade is a much more efficient cutting edge than one that is straight. In modern tests, a two-handed downward strike by a falx has cut through a wooden Roman shield with comparative ease. While the falx could be used one-handed, allowing the user still to carry a shield on his left arm, it was this double-handed strike that could be lethal. Conversely, double-handed use meant that the user had to discard his shield, making him more vulnerable to attack.

To prevent the overhead blow from a falx, it was essential that Roman legionaries came close to their Dacian opponents, and quickly so, to jab horizontally with the pointed end of their straight gladius. A scene on the Roman monument at Adamclisi, later erected by Trajan beside the Danube, shows a Dacian warrior stripped to the waist and poised to crash his falx down two-handed on a Roman legionary's head. But at the same time, the legionary, too quick for the Dacian, thrusts his gladius into the man's exposed midriff, killing him first. In the months leading up to the invasion of Dacia, the men of the legions involved would have undergone intensive training to close swiftly with the enemy in this manner.

Another tactic used by Dacian swordsmen was to aim blows at a Roman adversary's lower right arm – the exposed sword arm. Dacians didn't have to kill their opponents to neutralize them; by chopping off or shattering the sword arm, a Dacian could take a Roman out of the fight. As shown by a metope on the Trajan monument at Adamclisi, to counter that tactic many of the Roman legionaries going into Dacia wore segmented metal arm protectors on their lower right arms.

Now, the operation was about to begin. The very first scene on Trajan's Column shows serene farmland beside the River Danube, with farmhouses dotted here and there, surrounded by protective circular wooden palisades. Next, we see auxiliaries setting off from Moesian forts, waving goodbye to the comrades who were remaining behind. Meanwhile, from watchtowers, long thin beacons project with their ends burning, a signal for the auxiliary units to march. The spring of AD 101 had begun, and so too had the First Dacian War.

In northwestern Moesia, auxiliary units and legions converged on the Danube town of Viminacium, today's Kostolac in Serbia. Here too, says Trajan's Column, fleets of transport ships were busy unloading supplies for the operation. Trajan and senior officers joined the assembling troops. Apart from Praetorian prefect Livianus, Trajan's deputies for this campaign included the wealthy ex-consul Lucius Licinius Sura, Trajan's trusted confidant. The elderly Sura, close to the previous emperor Nerva, had been influential in Nerva's decision to adopt Trajan and make him his heir. Trajan also took along another consular general, Lucius Appius Maximus, as well as a general named Longinus, another of the emperor's good friends. This Longinus may have been the Pompeius Longinus who, as a tribune in AD 68–69, had been a solid supporter of the emperor Galba at Rome. If so, he was now in his fifties. Dio indicates that Longinus had previously fought the Dacians, serving under Julianus during the Roman victory at Tapae in AD 88. [Dio, LXVIII, 12]

One of Trajan's staff officers was the 25-year-old quaestor Publius Aelius Hadrianus, the future emperor Hadrian, and Trajan's nephew and ward. Like Trajan, Hadrian had been born in Spain. By the age of 19 he had served his six-month junior tribuneship with the 2nd Adiutrix Legion in Upper Moesia. In AD 96, apparently after just one season commanding an auxiliary unit, Nerva had promoted him, at the age of just 20, to senior tribune with the 5th Macedonica Legion in Lower Moesia. Hadrian's meteoric rise was clearly designed by old Nerva to please Trajan. In AD 100, the year that Trajan had made him a quaestor, Hadrian had married Trajan's grand-niece Vibia Sabina. Now on Trajan's staff, Hadrian had the opportunity to put his eye for detail and talent for organization to good use.

Trajan's legionaries had constructed the components for two boat bridges, and in the late spring, as soon as the spring floods on the Danube subsided, these temporary bridges were thrown across the river. Trajan's Column shows two lines of troops crossing the bridges into Dacia, with the standards of legions and cohorts bunched together in front. One line is clearly made up of the men of a legion. The troops wear full segmented armour and are led by an officer wearing the insignia of a commander, followed by a bareheaded eagle-bearer and a manipular standard-bearer wearing a bearskin headdress and cape. The legionaries crossing the bridge carry their shields on their left arms and have their helmets around their necks. From the poles over their left shoulders are suspended their bedrolls, entrenching tools, and mess kit. The second line of troops is similarly equipped to those in the foreground, but they are led by bunched eagle-bearers, standard-bearers of legion maniples and the lion-caped standard-bearers of at least four cohorts of the Praetorian Guard.

Trajan's army of 100,000 men arrived in Dacia without meeting any initial resistance. As Trajan had planned, surprise was complete. Dacians farmers fled ahead of them as the Roman troops marched quickly north through rugged, heavily forested Transylvania. Auxiliary light infantry and cavalry pushed on ahead, followed by road-making detachments from the legions which cleared the way for the main body and the baggage trains. Trajan himself rode in the vanguard.

At his mountain capital of Sarmizegethusa in the centre of today's Romania, King Decebalus received word of the Roman invasion. Decebalus was shaken by the news, because, as Dio observed, 'he knew that on the previous occasion it was not the Romans that he had defeated, but Domitian'. [Dio, LXVIII, 15] Nothing in the demeanour of the Romans prior to this had indicated Trajan's military intentions north of the Danube, but Decebalus knew that 'now he would be fighting both Romans and Trajan'. [Ibid.]

Calling his fighting men to arms and summoning help from his Sarmatian allies to the east and north, Decebalus dispatched ambassadors to meet the Roman army on the march and seek a conference with Trajan. Decebalus only deigned to send junior officers, long-haired warriors, to meet with the Roman emperor, not *pileati*, or 'cap-wearers', as Dacian nobles were called after the close-fitting leather skull caps they wore as a sign of their rank. Decebalus was playing for time.

Trajan's legions were soon building strong marching camps. Trajan's Column shows legionaries hard at work building exterior walls from turf bricks. Three hundred years later, the Roman army was still using the same technique. In their kit, legionaries carried turf cutters. 'The sods are cut with [these] iron instruments,' said Vegetius. 'If the earth is held strongly together by the roots of the grass, they are cut in the form of a brick a foot and a half high, a foot [30 centimetres] across, and a foot and a half [45 centimetres]

Trajan was planning his invasion of Dacia from the moment he became emperor in AD 98.

long.' [Vege., III] On top of the turf wall went a palisade of wooden stakes carried on the march by the infantry. Meanwhile, legion carpenters were building gateways, gates and watchtowers.

Even as a camp was being built, Trajan and his senior officers were conducting a *souvetaurilia* ceremony, a sacred sacrifice of bulls to earn the blessings of the gods for the new campaign. With all the pomp of official robes, chants, the burning of incense and the blaring of trumpets and horns of the legions, animals were sacrificed, and the augurs found auspicious omens in their entrails. The Dacian envoys now reached the Roman emperor's camp, but Trajan was not interested in parleying, especially not with junior ambassadors. The Dacians were sent away. Shortly after, the Roman advance parties met the first resistance from the locals; a party of auxiliaries crossing a river came under heavy attack from Dacian warriors before the attackers withdrew into the forest.

By now, with summer warming the mountain valleys, the numbers of Dacian fighters had begun to swell. As many as 140,000 Dacians would confront the Romans in this war, supported by some 20,000 allies from north of the Danube. Few Dacians went to war fearing death; they worshipped the god Zamolxis, whose high priest told them that in dying they went to a better life. Said to have been a follower of Greek mystic, mathematician and philosopher Pythagorus 800 years before, Zamolxis had gone to Egypt before settling in Dacia, where he died in a mountain cave. Three years later, Zamolxis had reputedly risen from the dead to guide his people. The Dacian capital Sarmizegethusa and a number of other Dacian cities and citadels were located in the hills around Cogaionon, Zamolxis' holy mountain – from which the enemy had to be kept at all costs.

With their faith in Zamolxis, the Dacian warriors who went off to fight the Romans now did so almost welcoming death, yet made confident of victory by the remembrance of the way they had slaughtered the Romans in Domitian's reign. Behind their dragon standards they marched – metal wolves' heads and snake-like bodies in the form of windsocks which, when filled with air on the run, trailed majestically behind their standard-bearers while a mournful moan was emitted from the head.

Tens of thousands of bearded, long-haired Dacians came streaming down from the Transylvanian Alps and launched stinging attacks on Roman marching camps. In one scene on Trajan's Column, Dacian bowmen attack a Roman camp. In another, Dacians employ a battering ram against the gate of a camp. But the attacks on the

Roman camps were repulsed, and the Roman advance continued. Using small boats brought up in a baggage train, the advance guard crossed the river, then began the climb into the mountains.

Decebalus' plea to allies paid dividends, for Roman auxiliary cavalry was met by Sarmatian cavalry in pointed helmets and fish-scale armour covering their entire bodies, arms and legs. Even the Sarmatians' horses were covered by scale armour. But the heavy armour made Sarmatian horses and riders slow and unwieldy, while the nature of the ground favoured lighter, more nimble riders. The Roman cavalry prevailed – the Sarmatians were thrown back with heavy losses.

The Roman advance continued, with two columns working their way north via different routes. Ahead of them, Dacians carrying their children on their shoulders fled from their villages. It was well into summer as the legions pressed further north, building marching camps as they went. At a forward Roman camp, fresh envoys arrived from Decebalus; this time, three of 'the noblest among the cap-wearers'. [Dio, LXVIII, 9] And this time Trajan gave the ambassadors a hearing.

Discarding their arms and prostrating themselves before the emperor, the bearded Dacian nobles begged Trajan to meet personally with Decebalus, who would, they swore, do whatever Trajan commanded. But, Dio was to write, Trajan was not interested in a meeting with Decebalus. The envoys then asked him at least to send representatives to agree peace terms with the Dacian king, so Trajan sent two of his most senior advisers to Decebalus, Lucius Sura and Praetorian prefect Livianus. [Ibid.]

Decebalus was moving his army west to intercept the Roman invaders as Trajan and the legions crossed the Transylvanian Alps then swung east. Scouts informed the emperor that Decebalus and his army had arrived at Tapae, scene of the bloody AD 88 battle when Tettius Julianus had been victorious for Rome. When Trajan's two envoys reached the Dacian camp, Decebalus refused to see them personally, sending subordinates to speak with them. When it was obvious to Sura and Livianus that the Dacian king was only playing for time, they returned to Trajan.

Trajan's army and the second column now linked up, and pushed east through the mountains. Finding Dacian watchtowers and forts on hilltops overlooking the passes and river valleys, the Romans attacked them and quickly overwhelmed their defenders. At several fortresses Trajan's troops found artillery and personal weapons taken from the 5th Alaudae Legion in Moesia in AD 85. Most importantly, to Trajan and his men, they also recovered the eagle of the destroyed legion. [Dio, LXVIII, 9]

The Roman advance reached Tapae and the sprawling camp of the Dacian army. As Roman catapults of the *cheiroballistra* type were brought up in carts for the assault on the Dacian defences, Trajan received a message from Germanic tribes of the region which were allied to Rome, beseeching Trajan to 'turn back and keep the peace'. [Dio, LXVIII, 8] But, despite the fact that autumn had arrived and the days were becoming shorter and colder, Trajan was not going to turn back.

There outside Tapae, in the middle of a thunderstorm, the two armies came together to do battle. Over 200,000 men fought there in the mountain valley at Tapae, in the pouring rain and amid flashes of lightning and crashing thunder. The Dacians did not have the Romans' organization, but they did have superior numbers and physical superiority, with their scraggy warriors being taller than the average Roman legionary. And at this latest Battle of Tapae, the curved Dacian falx again did great damage to the Romans, as the auxiliaries in the front line took the brunt of the wild enemy charge. The legions also felt the effect of the curved Dacian blades.

So many Romans were wounded in this battle and carried off to the medical attendants working in field dressing stations that the Romans ran out of bandages, and Trajan even had his own linen clothing cut into strips to make bandages for his troops. [Dio, LXVIII, 8] But the legions held firm, and won the day. Decebalus' bloodied army fell back to Sarmizegethusa, leaving large numbers of their countrymen lifeless on the muddy battlefield. Ignoring the atrocious weather, the victorious Roman army stripped the enemy dead of their weapons, valuables and clothing.

Trajan, after honouring his own dead, ordered an altar to be raised on the site of the battle, where funeral rites were to be performed annually in memory of the Romans who had perished there. Despite his victory, Trajan realized that it was pointless to proceed any further. He could see from the deteriorating weather that winter would set in early here in the mountains, and that further military operations would soon become bogged down in mud, snow and ice. The campaign would have to be suspended until the following spring.

In an assembly during which Trajan praised his troops, he doled out rewards to many of them. Trajan's Column shows auxiliaries bowing to the seated emperor, kissing his hand, and going away bent double with weighty sacks on their backs – filled with captured Dacian gold perhaps, or even salt, which the Dacians mined in this area and which was a valuable trade item. One of the auxiliary units which is known to have performed well for Trajan in Dacia was the 1st Brittonum Ulpian Cohort, raised by Trajan in Britain in AD 98. All its surviving members would be given honourable discharges by Trajan thirteen years ahead of their prescribed discharge time – for valiant service in the Dacian Wars, their discharge diplomas record. Perhaps this was the very unit seen on the Column being rewarded in AD 101.

The Roman army now upped stakes and withdrew via a direct route almost due south to the Danube. According to Trajan's Column, as the Romans were pulling out of the Dacian interior, Roman prisoners in Dacian hands in the mountains, stripped naked, were being tortured by Dacian women.

Trajan, leaving auxiliary units to spend the winter in forts along the northern side of the river, crossed the Danube at the gorge called the Iron Gate. The emperor and his staff were transported in ships of the Moesian Fleet, which also ferried many troops and their equipment to the southern bank. The boat bridges were also used once again. Opposite Drobeta, the legions built winter camps along the Moesian bank of the Danube, storing away their weapons, not expecting to use them again until the new year. But King Decebalus was not waiting for the Romans to return.

As the winter set in, Decebalus brought together a revitalized coalition of Dacian and Sarmatian fighters. Early in the new year, as the winter weather improved, Decebalus seized the initiative. Without warning, Dacians launched attacks on Roman auxiliary forts on Dacian soil along the lower Danube. At the same time, thousands of Sarmatian cavalry crossed the frozen Danube to the east and entered Moesia behind the backs of the legions.

At the forts in Dacia, fighting desperately, using anything that came to hand as ammunition, auxiliary units were close to being overrun when reinforcements arrived – infantry coming down the river by boat, and cavalry led by Trajan himself which crossed the river by the two boat bridges. A series of carved metopes on the Trajanic monument at Adamclisi tells what happened next. While the infantry fought off the attacks on the Danube forts, Trajan led his cavalry inland, cutting off and surrounding a Dacian baggage train in the hills. In what came to be called the Battle of the Carts, most of the Dacians accompanying the train as escorts or animal handlers were killed, but among the prisoners taken by Trajan were a number of cap-wearing Dacian nobles.

All this time, Trajan was unaware that the Sarmatians had entered Moesia behind him. The legions in Moesia, called to arms by their officers in the last weeks of winter, marched from their camps and hurried to intercept the Sarmatian invaders in eastern Moesia. The first encounter between the two sides was a brief night skirmish near the village of Nicopole. Then, on a plateau at Adamclisi in the Urluia Valley of today's Romania, as many as ten legions met some 15,000 Sarmatian cavalry. The battlefield was level ground ideally suited to infantry tactics, and while there are no details of the battle itself, nor of who commanded the Roman army, it is known that the legions slaughtered their mounted opponents that day.

Roman generals had always known that cavalry unsupported by foot soldiers could be beaten by infantry. Here in Moesia, a little over thirty years before, the well under-strength 3rd Gallica Legion had proved that by wiping out 9,000 Roxolani Sarmatian cavalry. The 15,000 Sarmatians who had crossed the Danube on this offensive had not learned any lessons from the earlier brutal defeat, and paid the price now. Very few of the Sarmatian invaders survived the battle. Those that did managed to retreat to the Danube. Even then, with the river ice beginning to break up, a number of heavily armoured Sarmatians drowned when the ice gave way under their horses. Not that this had been a cheap victory for the Romans; it has been suggested that as many as 4,000 legionaries died in the hectic Battle of Adamclisi.

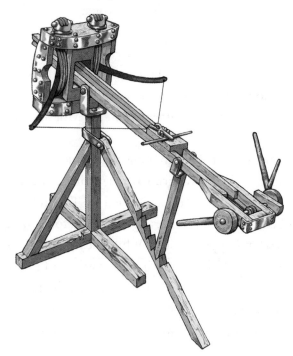

Defeated on both sides of the Danube, Dacians and Sarmatians withdrew to the Carpathian mountains. As Trajan returned to the Moesian side of the Danube with his prisoners and congratulated his victorious legions, King Decebalus, at Sarmizegethusa, ordered every possible preparation for the next Roman offensive that he knew must come in the wake of the spring

The fifty-five Scorpio catapults, like this one, of the obliterated 5th Alaudae Legion, along with its eagle standard, were recaptured by Trajan in AD 101.

thaw, and Dacian forces regrouped and completed hurried repairs to mountain fortresses that had been burned during the last Roman campaign. The next stage of the war would be crucial, to both sides.

XLI. OVERRUNNING DACIA
The first, false victory

With the spring of AD 102, Trajan conducted the new year's lustration ceremony. Trajan's Column shows him then addressing an assembly of legions and auxiliary units, no doubt hoping to inspire them to victory and make this year's campaign the last in Dacia.

At Drobeta, the Roman army re-crossed the Danube and marched into the fertile sheep lands of Wallacia. As auxiliary infantry and cavalry scouted ahead, legion work parties cut roads through forests. For this campaign, Trajan again divided his army in two. A flying column of cavalry and light infantry under the command of Lucius Maximus would advance on the Dacian capital from the southwest. At the same time, Trajan would cross the plain of Wallacia then follow the Aluta river to the Red Tower Pass with the legions and the baggage. If all went according to plan, the two columns would link up at Sarmizegethusa in the Orastie Mountains.

One mountain stronghold after another was stormed by Trajan's legions as they pushed on across the Transylvanian Alps. Pliny the Younger, the noted Roman author, and a consul in AD 100, describes Roman marching camps 'clinging to sheer precipices' during this campaign. [Pliny, VIII, 4] Trajan's Column shows the Roman army assaulting a stone-walled citadel. On poles outside the walls sit severed heads of bearded men – either those of captured Roman auxiliaries or of Dacians who had wanted to surrender. The Column next shows auxiliaries setting fire to wooden buildings inside the captured Dacian citadel, then moving on.

Trajan himself followed close behind the advance, and in the Column's narrative he was at this point crossing a wooden bridge placed across a ravine. As the Roman advance guard erected another marching camp near a Dacian town which had several round shrines in the background, Dacians assembled behind their standards in the hills. The main Roman column arrived on the scene with legion musicians playing their trumpets and horns. The baggage train lumbered in, its oxcarts laden with equipment. From this camp, Trajan directed the next stage of the operation.

Now Dacian forces descended from the heights and attacked advancing Roman cavalry and light infantry. Following a fierce struggle, the bloodied Dacians withdrew into the forests. Another day's advance, another marching camp thrown up. Artillery was brought forward for an assault on the next Dacian hilltop fortress on the road to Sarmizegethusa.

To save time, wooden hurdles, usually employed to cover enemy trenches, were used to create protection for the Roman catapults' firing positions, for the Dacians possessed excellent archers. Trajan's Column shows crates of catapult ammunition opened and ready for use, revealing catapult balls packed neatly inside. [Vitr., x.3] Small balls were for anti-personnel use; larger ones were fired at emplacements.

On the Column, eastern archers with conical helmets and barefoot slingers without armour are shown launching a rain of missiles against the walls of the Dacian fortress. Behind them, the catapults let fly their balls. Between them, archers, slingers and catapults would have cleared one section of the wall of defenders. Dacians raising their heads above the parapet at that point would have invited death. Waiting Roman infantry rushed forward, clambered over outer palisades, hurdled ditches, then dashed for the wall with assault ladders.

Trajan's Column shows that, to try to drive the Romans back from the wall, Dacian defenders poured out of a fortress gate to the attack. But Trajan had been expecting this and thousands of auxiliaries surged towards the Dacians, who were slaughtered in the open; only a few escaped, fleeing into the forest. After that the fortress was swiftly taken. Relentlessly, the Roman army moved on. Dacians cut down trees to slow the Roman advance up the valley, and laid ambushes in expectation of catching legionaries as they tried to clear the roadblocks. But Trajan merely diverted via another route through the forest, with his advance guard cutting a road through the trees.

As the advance guard emerged into open country from the forest, a large Dacian force fell on them. Roman auxiliaries fought off the Dacians, who fell back to another hilltop fortress. Trajan assaulted the fortress, where a wounded Dacian noble – perhaps the fortress commander or one of Decebalus' generals – is shown, on the Column, in the arms of subordinates at the wooden palisade line.

With the palisade overcome, a legion went against the fortress's walls under the cover of raised shields in a *testudo*, or tortoise formation. Many ranks deep, the testudo was impervious to missiles rained down from defenders on the parapet above, and under its cover the legionaries undermined the wall. Creating a breach, the legionaries flooded inside, killing every Dacian they found. As the citadel fell, auxiliaries brought Trajan the heads of two Dacian leaders killed in the fighting; one probably belonged to the wounded noble previously depicted. These two Dacian leaders were unidentified, but Susagus is never again mentioned in classical texts, and he may have been one of them.

Only a few Dacian villages now stood between Trajan and Sarmizegethusa. As the Romans pushed on, Dacian warriors withdrew ahead of them and climbed to the ridge-tops. There was fighting in forests and outside villages, as, with increasing desperation and decreasing effectiveness, the Dacians tried to halt the Roman advance. As Trajan drove towards Sarmizegethusa from one direction, Maximus' flying column was surprising the Dacians from another. Inflicting heavy casualties on a disorganized defence, destroying settlements, causing mayhem, Maximus progressively decreased the distance between Trajan's force and his own. At one stronghold, Maximus even captured King Decebalus' sister. The arms of the pincer came together outside Sarmizegethusa, where the two forces linked up and surrounded the city.

Sarmizegethusa, sited on a bend in the Sargetia river and covering 4 square miles (6.4 square kilometres), occupied several hills below Cogaionon, the holy Dacian mountain. The city was divided into two residential districts and a holy precinct which climbed up the hillsides via a series of stone terraces, on which were built mostly wooden buildings with stone foundations. The local stone was so brittle that limestone and andestite had been carried in from miles away. Sarmizegethusa had paved streets, running water and a sewer system. There were residences, workshops and shops, while in the sacred precinct there were circular temples and one large rectangular temple, of wood and stone.

The city was protected by a meandering limestone block wall 45 feet (13.7 metres) high, with rectangular stone towers at its corners. That wall consisted of two layers of stone blocks with rubble fill and wooden beams in between – which would have helped absorb the shock of catapult balls. Decebalus had made Sarmizegethusa his capital because of its nearness to the holy mountain and the cave of Zamolxis. In addition, it was at the heart of the gold, silver, iron and salt mining areas that had made Decebalus such a wealthy monarch.

Dacian envoys seek a parley with Trajan. From Trajan's Column.

As the Roman army made visible preparations to begin a siege of the city, which was packed with both residents and tens of thousands of refugees from elsewhere, Decebalus sent out cap-wearing envoys to discuss an end to hostilities. Trajan again delegated Lucius Sura and Claudius Livianus, who offered terms for a Dacian surrender to the envoys. Those terms were speedily agreed and the siege was suspended. Truth be known, Trajan probably knew that his troops were as exhausted as were those of Decebalus after the two grinding campaigns that had brought him to the gates of Sarmizegethusa. Unable to sustain a prolonged siege of the Dacian capital, if he was to come away from this war the victor he had little choice but to grant Decebalus equitable terms.

The Dacian defenders came out of the city, laid down their arms and fell to their knees, begging Trajan's mercy. Trajan's Column depicts the emperor seated on a tribunal, surrounded by the standards of the legions, Praetorian Guard and auxiliary units, as the cap-wearing Dacian nobles prostrated themselves before him. Then it was the turn of Decebalus himself. The bearded king cast away his curved sword and dagger, prostrated himself before Trajan and swore to abide by the terms of the peace treaty.

Those terms required Decebalus to surrender an area in western Dacia called the Banat, and the flatlands of Wallacia extending from the Danube to the mountains. He was totally to evacuate these regions of Dacian citizens, who would be replaced by Roman settlers. Decebalus agreed to demolish those of his forts that still stood. He would hand over deserters from the Roman army who had fought for him, and surrender all artillery and advisers previously loaned to him under the treaty with Domitian. Decebalus was also forbidden to give shelter to, or to employ, soldiers from the Roman Empire in future. He was also to follow forthwith the foreign policy of Rome, recognize Rome's allies and enemies as his own and not send ambassadors to foreign nations. And, of course, Rome immediately ceased paying the hefty tribute that it had been sending to Sarmizegethusa since AD 89.

Following the surrender, Trajan conducted an *ad locutio* thanksgiving ceremony, with sacrifices to the gods of war, and with the army assembled in ranks and the officers in ceremonial white robes. Addressing the troops, Trajan thanked them for their grit and courage, and called forward individual soldiers by name to receive bravery awards. Raising their right arms in salute, the men of the legions hailed Trajan *imperator* – the fourth time in his career that he received this honour.

As Trajan set off back to Rome, where he would be welcomed as a hero, the legions withdrew from Dacia. Some returned to their bases, others set to work on major building projects in Moesia – a bridge and a monument. Trajan's Column shows Dacian farmers abandoning their homes in Wallacia and the Dacian Banat, driving their stock before them, carrying their portable possessions and babies in arms, and with infants walking beside them. Auxiliary units were left to garrison occupied Dacian territory and protect Roman settlers who would soon cross the Danube. Trajan gave his old friend General Longinus the job of administering occupied Dacian territory and overseeing the treaty with Decebalus. Meanwhile, Dacian envoys appeared before the Senate at Rome with their hands behind their backs, to secure ratification of the peace treaty.

Trajan had reversed the Dacian situation and avenged the legions that had perished under Domitian. All was peace along the Danube. For now.

TRAJAN'S ADAMCLISI MONUMENT
The Tropaeum Trajani

Literally meaning 'Trajan's trophy', the Tropaeum Trajani was built following the First Dacian War of AD 101–102. The commencement of its construction can be dated to AD 102 or shortly afterwards, because the monument itself is depicted between the two wars on the chronological panels on the later Trajan's Column.

The monument is located south of the River Danube at Adamclisi, on a plateau in the Ueluia Valley in today's Romania, site of the battle that took place during the winter of AD 101–102, in which Trajan's legions defeated a force of Sarmatian heavy cavalry from north of the Danube. Dedicated to Mars the Avenger, the monument was intended to commemorate the sacrifice of the 4,000 Roman troops who fell at Adamclisi.

The identity of this monument's designer is unknown, but it is likely to have been Apollodorus of Damascus, who, on Trajan's commission, designed the bridge, the massive arches of which spanned the Danube at Drobeta. Apollodorus was also responsible for Trajan's elegantly curved Forum at Rome, and probably also Trajan's Column, the unique circular monument that stood in the middle of Trajan's Forum. The base of the Tropaeum Trajani is also circular, and this repeated use of the circular form was Apollodorus' trademark. The monument was built at the same time as, and not far from, Apollodorus' bridge at Drobeta, making it all the more probable that he was responsible for both.

Around the monument's frieze were fifty-four marble panels, called metopes, on which three sets of carved reliefs represented scenes from the Battle of Adamclisi, the Battle of the Carts, which took place in Dacia at the same time, and the Dacian countryside. The metopes, each about 4 feet (1.56 metres) high and 3 feet 6 inches (1.16 metres) wide, are not as realistic or skilful as those on the later Trajan's Column at Rome, but they serve the same purpose, telling the story of Rome's victory over the barbarians.

At the top of the cone-shaped monument a 15-foot (4.5-metre) human figure in armour and helmet was erected. Although thought by many observers to represent a Roman legionary, the figure wears Sarmatian fish-scale armour and a conical Sarmatian helmet. In each hand are Sarmatian shields. These represent Sarmatian arms taken as trophies by the Romans. At the figure's feet are three life-size statues, two of seated

women with their hands bound behind their backs, the third of a standing male. The females represent two nations subjected by Rome – the Dacians and the Sarmatians. Frequently on Roman monuments and coins a subjected nation was represented by a female figure. The male probably represents Decebalus, the Dacian king who surrendered to Trajan.

The monument that stands at Adamclisi today is not the original. Trajan's Tropaeum was repeatedly damaged and ultimately destroyed by barbarian invaders from north of the Danube during the Marcomanni Wars of AD 167–180, just sixty-five years after the monument was raised. The present-day monument is a 1977 reconstruction based on remnants of the original.

AD 103–104

XLII. BETWEEN THE DACIAN WARS
Both sides rebuild

During the summer of AD 103, Trajan celebrated a Triumph in Rome for his Dacian success, and received the title Dacicus from the Senate. He had already commissioned architect Apollodorus of Damascus to build him a permanent bridge across the Danube at the Drobeta ravine, where the river was at its narrowest. Twenty monstrous piers of squared stone, each 60 feet (18 metres) thick, 150 feet (45 metres) high and 170 feet (52 metres) apart, would be erected across the river, connected by a lacework of graceful wooden arches over which a wide wooden roadway would pass. A marvel of engineering which took the breath away of all who saw it once it was built, Trajan's Danube bridge was by far the largest bridge ever built anywhere in the world to that time. Simultaneously, at Adamclisi, work proceeded on the Tropaeum Trajani, Trajan's circular monument to his victory over the Dacians and Sarmatians.

Yet, Trajan did not rest on his laurels. Though he had won a famous victory, he had lost thousands of troops in the battles of AD 101–102. Besides, he did not trust Decebalus. As Dio was to write, Decebalus had no intention of abiding by the peace agreement, but had only entered into it to 'secure a respite from his temporary reverses'. [Dio, LXVIII, 9] By the summer of AD 103, it was reported to Trajan that Decebalus was 'acting contrary to the treaty in many ways'. [Ibid.]

The irrepressible Dacian king was collecting arms, welcoming Roman deserters, rebuilding forts destroyed during the war, and sending envoys to neighbouring nations seeking new alliances. He even sent envoys and gifts to the king of the Parthians in the East. As for those nations that had not supported him in the last war with Rome, Decebalus threatened them with dire consequences if they let him down again, and as an example of what they could expect, he sent his troops to annex a portion of the territory of his Germanic neighbours the Iazyges, Roman allies who lived between the Danube and the River Tisa west of Dacia.

Trajan knew that he could only terminate the threat posed by Decebalus by terminating Decebalus and his troops. A new war was inevitable. But first Trajan had to rebuild his bloodied army. It might be expected that he would have replaced losses suffered by his existing legions by levying masses of new recruits for those units. Yet this was not the Roman way; legions frequently operated well under strength, without replacements. Instead, Trajan raised two brand-new legions – the 2nd Traiana, named after Trajan himself, and the 30th Ulpia, which, like auxiliary units raised by Trajan, took his family name. By the last legion pay period of AD 103, the 30th Ulpia Legion was at Brigetio in Pannonia. The 2nd Traiana Legion, meanwhile, was sent to the East, making its temporary base at Laodicea, chief port of Syria.

In the summer of AD 104, when Decebalus learned that Trajan was building up his forces on the Danube, he sent Roman deserters into Moesia to gain an audience with Trajan and then either kill or kidnap him. But one of the conspirators was arrested on suspicion, and under torture he revealed the plot. Undaunted, the wily Decebalus next sent for Trajan's legate in Dacia, Longinus, 'who had made himself a terror to the king in the wars'. [Dio, LXVIII, 12] Decebalus' message said that he would do whatever was demanded of him, so Longinus rode to Sarmizegethusa with an escort – only to be made a prisoner by the crafty king.

Decebalus questioned Longinus in public about Trajan's plans, but Longinus would say nothing. The Roman general was then bustled about behind Decebalus, under guard, wherever the king went. Decebalus sent a message to Trajan, informing him that Longinus was his prisoner, and offering to ransom him in exchange for the return of all Dacian territory as far as the Danube now occupied by Roman forces, as well as financial reimbursement of all Dacian expenses for the last war.

An ambiguous reply duly came back from Trajan – he would certainly like to have Longinus returned to him, but he did not think Longinus worth the price that Decebalus was asking. Cassius Dio would later comment that the emperor did not want to appear desperate for Longinus' return, but he did not want him to seem unimportant to him either, in case Decebalus felt he was no longer of value and killed him. [Ibid.] Trajan was stalling for time. As the messen-

The massive bridge built for Trajan by Syrian architect Apollodorus of Damascus across the Danube to Dacia is only depicted in two places – on Trajan's Column, and on this sestertius coin.

gers headed for the Danube with his reply, he gave his Palatium the order to prepare to launch a new war.

Decebalus was still considering his next step when Longinus unexpectedly offered to write to Trajan urging him to agree to Decebalus' terms for his return, on condition that his freedman secretary be permitted to take his letter to Rome. Decebalus agreed, but required that the freedman personally return with the emperor's reply. Longinus wrote the letter, which Decebalus approved, and the freedman then set off for the Danube with a Dacian escort.

Trusting the amenable Longinus more now, Decebalus relaxed the guard on him, which was exactly what the general had been hoping for. Once he had learned that his secretary had left Dacian territory, Longinus drank poison which his freedman had procured for him in the Dacian capital. Longinus died that same night. Now, the emperor would not have to worry about his loyal friend's safety when he decided his course of action regarding Dacia.

Decebalus was furious. He sent messages demanding the return of the freedman, promising to exchange him for the body of Longinus and ten of the Roman troopers of his escort now languishing in a Dacian prison. There was no response from Rome. Decebalus was becoming more and more determined to have his own way, to the point of irrationality. He paroled the centurion in charge of Longinus' escort, and sent him to Rome with instructions to bring back the freedman, whom, no doubt, he planned to execute for his part in the general's suicide. Not surprisingly, Trajan retained both freedman and centurion.

AD 105–106
XLIII. SECOND DACIAN WAR
Trajan's total war

> '*A great and glorious victory in the finest tradition of Rome.*'
> PLINY THE YOUNGER, *Letters*, X, 14

For three years the Dacians had been preparing to renew hostilities with Rome, and, although King Decebalus had not been able to convince any allies to join him in a new challenge to Trajan, in the spring of AD 105 he went on to the offensive. Dacian fighters poured down from the mountains and attacked Roman auxiliary forts throughout occupied territory. They even attacked the fortress at Drobeta, which guarded Apollodorus' handsome new Danube bridge, a structure which the Dacians detested – as much for the Roman subjugation of their land that it represented as its strategic importance.

Trajan's Column shows the Dacians surprising legion work parties in Dacian territory. Separated from their stacked shields, the legionaries fight back with axes and entrenching tools, but their chances of survival appear slim. At forts, surrounded auxiliaries fight desperately. A legion, or more than one, is shown arriving by forced march to relieve the defenders of one particular fort.

Come the first days of summer, Trajan was still in Rome, but news of the Dacian offensive spurred him to action, and he left on 4 June. The date was significant in the Roman religious calendar, being the day on which the god Hercules Magnus Custos (Hercules the Great Protector) was honoured. Within two years, Trajan would be expressing his thanks to Hercules Invictus (Hercules the Unconquerable) on his coins. [Dus., *DRA*]

To speed his progress to Moesia, Trajan hurried along the Valerian Way to Picenum and Italy's east coast. Trajan's Column picks up the story of the Second Dacian War with Trajan at a major Italian port, thought to be Ancona. From there he, his staff, and troops of the Praetorian Guard and Singularian Horse boarded warships of the Ravenna Fleet and were quickly conveyed across the Adriatic to Dalmatia. Word of the emperor's impending arrival went before him, and a vast crowd of officials and townspeople waited for him at the dock of a Dalmatian port, probably Salonae near present-day Split in Croatia. There, with a grand drama theatre behind him, and surrounded by standards of the Praetorian Guard, Trajan is seen on the Column performing ritual sacrifices.

As cargo ships brought supplies across the stormy Adriatic behind him, Trajan marched inland towards the Danube, preceded by Singularian Horse squadrons. Just south of Siscia, the emperor would have swung east to march to Sirmium. Trajan's Column shows that all along the route men, women and children crowded the roadsides to see their emperor and cheer his passing. From Sirmium, Trajan followed the Danube east to Viminacium and then to Drobeta, collecting legions along the way – including the 1st Minervia, which had marched from its base at Bonna, a legion that now had a new commander, Trajan's nephew Hadrian.

While Trajan was on the march, auxiliaries at Drobeta had been reinforced by legionaries from Moesia who beat off the Dacians attacking the approaches to Apollodorus' new bridge. On the Moesian side of the Danube, Roman legions and tens of thousands of auxiliaries assembled. At the height of the summer Trajan arrived, accompanied by the Praetorian Guard. He inspected Apollodorus' impressive new Danube bridge, built entirely by the labour of soldiers of Rome's legions.

Historian Cassius Dio, whose father governed Dalmatia and who also later governed the provinces of Dalmatia and Pannonia, saw this bridge some seventy years after it was built. By that time, the superstructure had been removed by Trajan's successor Hadrian – to prevent it being used by barbarian invaders. [Dio, LVIII 13] Despite the fact that 'the bridge is no use to us', Dio would say, it appeared to him as if the piers 'had been erected for the sole purpose of demonstrating that there is nothing which human ingenuity cannot accomplish'. [Ibid.] Today, at low water, the remains of those piers can still be seen. As for its designer, Apollodorus, like his bridge, would be destroyed by Hadrian; following a quarrel, Hadrian was to execute Trajan's great architect in AD 130.

As Trajan dedicated the bridge and conducted the lustration of the legions' standards, with Hadrian in his entourage, at least six different foreign delegations waited on the emperor. Dacian envoys promised peace on Decebalus' behalf provided Trajan elected not to go to war. There were Suebi German ambassadors, with their long hair tied up in the Suebian knot that distinguished free Suebian from slave. 'They occupy more than half of Germany,' said Tacitus of the Suebi. [Tac., *Germ.*, 38] There were also ambassadors present from Grecian states such as the Bosporan kingdom; even from as far away as India. Some ambassadors had come to offer friendship, others to beg the emperor not to go to war with the Dacians. He accepted the former, and rejected the latter – Trajan's Column next shows him leading the Roman army across the Apollodorus bridge into Dacia.

Trajan's army advanced across the Dacian lowlands to join legions camped near a circular Dacian religious sanctuary. With the end of summer near, Trajan ordered his forces to camp for the winter where they were, and the legions passed the winter of AD 105–106 at marching camps deep inside Dacia.

With the spring thaw of AD 106, Trajan once again conducted the Lustration Exercise. Once the ceremony had been completed, the Column shows the emperor being approached by a cavalry officer. This was Lusius Quietus. A dark-skinned Moor from Morocco, Quietus had once commanded a cavalry unit in the Roman army but had been 'condemned for base conduct' and 'dismissed from the service'. But when the First Dacian War commenced he had approached Trajan and offered his services. Trajan, who 'needed the assistance of the Moors', re-employed him. [Dio, LXVIII, 32] Quietus had 'displayed great deeds of prowess' in the First Dacian War, and 'being honoured for this, he performed far greater and more numerous exploits in the Second War'. [Ibid., 17] At his own suggestion, Quietus led a cavalry column which set off to take the most difficult mountain route to Sarmizegethusa.

Trajan's army, now consisting of twelve legions and scores of auxiliary units, advanced over the Transylvanian Alps from four different directions – Trajan led one force, Sura another, Maximus the third and Quietus the fourth. In their rear, supplies were brought up from the Danube by baggage train, but the further they advanced the more difficult the supply situation became. Even the residents of Sarmizegethusa habitually brought in foodstuffs from the fertile Mures river valley, many miles from the Dacian capital, to the inhospitable high country.

At Trajan's marching camp in the mountains, supplies were stockpiled as a major Dacian fortress was reconnoitred. Dacian scouting parties led by cap-wearers watched the Roman build-up from the trees, but were driven back into the forests by auxiliary attack. The siege of the Dacian fortress now began.

Chief among the fortresses assaulted by Trajan were those at Costesti, Blidaru and Piatra Rosie. With outer defences of two wooden palisades and high main walls of limestone blocks many feet thick, the fortresses' citadels typically featured five defensive stone towers and a single gate. Yet there was nothing sophisticated about these fortresses, and they were only capable of holding a few thousand defenders each. To Roman legionaries, with a vast array of equipment and tactics for assaulting fixed emplacements, taking the hill fortresses would have been child's play. The legions soon marched on, leaving the fortresses looted, strewn with Dacian dead and in flames.

By the beginning of summer, Sarmizegethusa was reached by one Roman column. Too impatient for victory and booty, these troops could not wait until artillery and archers arrived to clear a section of the wall of defenders. Trajan's Column shows a mixed group of legionaries, auxiliaries and cavalrymen going against the wall with scaling ladders. Above the Roman attackers, Dacian defenders on the wall lobbed anything they could lay their hands on, including boulders, at the climbing Romans.

The Dacians were renowned bee-keepers, and according to Romanian lore Dacian defenders even resorted to throwing beehives at the Romans. The attack was beaten off.

Trajan's Column reveals that soon, another Roman force of both legionaries and auxiliaries reached the city from a different direction. Catapults were set up, and Roman archers took up firing positions. Now Dacians sallied out of a city gate to attack the Romans before they could renew the assault. From the city walls, other Dacians anxiously watched the battle below.

Cassius Dio tells of a Roman cavalry trooper who was severely wounded during this fighting and taken to his tent. Believing that he would not live, the trooper picked himself up, found his equipment, and went back to the battle. 'Taking his place in the line once again,' said Dio, the trooper 'perished after displaying great feats of courage.' [Dio, LXVIII, 14] This battle outside the city was a bloody affair, in which the Dacians were ultimately overwhelmed. Trajan's Column shows piles of mangled Dacian bodies.

Once all four Roman columns arrived, the assault on the city walls resumed. After a barrage from the missile-launchers, legionaries equipped with dolabrae attacked the stone foundations to undermine the wall. But the hail of missiles from above forced them back. Now Trajan gave orders for entrenchments to be built and siege equipment constructed. This operation was going to take time.

Trajan's Column shows Roman troops preparing major siege works. Sarmizegethusa was surrounded by trenches and marching camps. On the Column, legionaries are seen cutting timber and building wooden siege towers. While auxiliaries stood guard, the men of the legions removed their helmets, laid aside their shields and javelins, and in their armour built massive earth ramps at strategic locations that increased in height as they crept closer to the walls. The siege of Sarmizegethusa dragged on for months through the summer.

With the distance between ramps and walls expected to be closed within days, Decebalus sent out a cap-wearing envoy to plead for surrender terms. But this time Trajan was not interested in Decebalus' surrender. He only wanted his head. As for Trajan's troops, they did not want the Dacians to surrender; under the rules of plunder, they could only loot the city if they took it by storm. The envoy was sent back to Decebalus without terms for surrender.

Trajan's refusal to treat caused consternation among senior Dacians. They knew that when the Romans did storm the city, all Dacian men of military age were likely to be killed, and the women raped, while survivors would be enslaved. Decebalus, if he were taken alive, could expect to be the star attraction of Trajan's next Triumph at Rome, after which he would be garrotted, as Roman tradition required. The prospects, for all those inside Sarmizegethusa, were grim.

In the twilight, as the last tons of earth were carried up the ramps by legionaries protected from missile attack by high wooden screens, the siege towers were pushed and pulled into position at the base of the ramps, and the men who would man them prepared for the final assault the next day. Now fires began breaking out in Sarmizegethusa. The Dacians were setting light to their own capital. The Dacian buildings, built mostly of wood, with wooden shingle roofs, burned well. As night fell and fires raged in those parts of the city nearest the Roman ramps, Decebalus met with his nobles in his citadel.

On a stove in the king's apartments, a cauldron was bubbling. Decebalus dipped a precious metal cup into the liquid bubbling in the cauldron. Eight hundred years before, Zamolxis had promised his Dacian followers eternal life, and now Decebalus was offering his nobles a swift route to the afterlife. He proffered the cup to a woman – a wife of the king, or a daughter perhaps? His sister was already in Roman hands. The woman drank, and fell dead to the floor. Decebalus refilled the cup. A bearded young man stepped up and took the cup from the king – the king's son, or perhaps the high priest of Zamolxis? Or was this the princely Diegis whom Domitian had sent back to Decebalus wearing a crown seventeen years earlier? The young man drank the poison, and he too died there in front of the watching nobles.

The bodies of the woman and the young man are shown on Trajan's Column at the feet of Decebalus as the king and one of his nobles offer poison to other cap-wearers. Most of the nobles eagerly reach for the fatal cups. One of them has rent open his clothes and is reaching heavenwards, beseeching a Dacian deity to help his people. But not all the Dacian nobles took their own lives, and Decebalus himself had no intention of committing suicide while there was a chance of escaping and continuing the fight against Rome.

In the dead of night, Decebalus, his closest followers and his bodyguards escaped from the city. Trajan's Column shows them using what appears to be a secret tunnel under a city wall, quite possibly emerging at the riverbank. Horses were waiting for them, and Decebalus and his party made good their escape, perhaps following the river shallows northwards to evade the encamped Roman army.

At dawn the next morning, the Roman siege towers were moved into position and the legions came over the city walls. The defenders were overwhelmed, the fires extinguished and the Roman army sacked Sarmizegethusa and took tens of thousands of prisoners. From captives, Trajan learned of the escape of Decebalus. He gave the job of finding the king to his cavalry. Thousands of cavalry troopers now spread out from Sarmizegethusa in search of Decebalus.

Several captured retainers of Decebalus begged for their lives, and one, Bicilis, offered to tell Trajan where the king had hidden much of his vast treasure. Some was in mountain caves, while more lay buried beneath the bed of the Sargetia river right outside the Sarmizegethusa city walls. To achieve the latter, said Bicilis, the king had used prisoners to temporarily divert the course of the river before excavating a hole for gold, silver, and other valuables. Once the treasure had been deposited in the ground, stones were heaped over the hiding place and the river was directed back to its old course over it. The prisoners had then been killed so that none could identify the hiding place.

Trajan now set several of his legions to work redirecting the river. A levy bank was created, and once the dried riverbed had been exposed beside the city walls thousands of legionaries made short work of digging it up. Sure enough, the king's treasure hoard was unearthed. It was so immense that, combined with gold and silver produced by the mines of Dacia, it was to finance all the major new building works in Rome over the next few years. The Basilica Ulpia, in Trajan's Forum, would bear plaques declaring that it was built *E Manubiis* – 'from the spoils'. [Carc., 1, 1]

News that Dacians were regrouping in the mountains to the north, under the direction of Decebalus, prompted Trajan to send several legions north. At this point on Trajan's Column, some legionaries are seen tramping over a Roman bridge that spans a river; others build boats to cross it. Decebalus soon led an attack on a Roman marching camp. But his troops were too few, and, soon dispirited, were beaten off and retreated into the forest.

By the second week of August, outside the ruined city of Sarmizegethusa, Trajan conducted an *ad locutio*, a religious ceremony designed to give thanks to the gods for Rome's great military victory. To crown Trajan's success, another hoard of Decebalus' valuables was now found in caves on the Dacians' holy mountain. Meanwhile, in the mountains to the north, Decebalus addressed the last of his loyal followers; Trajan's Column shows some of them pleading with him. It seems the king told them he intended seeking asylum with former Sarmatian allies, hoping to convince them to return him one day to Dacia at the head of an army that would throw out the Romans. Decebalus, accompanied by his closest advisers, bodyguards and several children, then mounted up and rode away. Some of the Dacians that Decebalus left behind took their own lives, others went to Trajan and surrendered.

A little later, in the Carpathian Mountains, snow was thick on the ground as Roman cavalry of the 2nd Pannonian Ala closed in on a party of riders that had paused in a forest clearing. As revealed by his later gravestone, decurion Tiberius Claudius Maximus from Philippi in Macedonia, formerly with the 7th Claudia Legion, led a Pannonian Horse detachment that caught up with King Decebalus. Outside Porolissum, not far from where the borders of Romania, Moldova and the Ukraine meet today, the elated troopers encircled the exhausted king and his party.

Decebalus had dismounted. Decurion Maximus urged his horse forward, aiming to make the king a prisoner. Decebalus reached to the sheath at his waist and drew a curved dagger. In one quick movement, the king drew the blade across his neck, and slit his own throat. Maximus quickly dismounted, but the king, lying in the snow, drowning in his own blood, could not be kept alive. Trajan's Column shows one of the troopers on horseback surrounding the Dacian party making an obscene two-fingered gesture towards the dying monarch. With Decebalus dead, Maximus drew his long cavalry sword, and with carefully aimed blows, severed the king's head and right arm.

The decurion and his men took Decebalus' remains south to Trajan, who rewarded the cavalry officer with a golden torque, the second such decoration that Maximus received during his career, which would also include service for the emperor in Parthia. The head of King Decebalus was subsequently taken to Rome and displayed on the Gemonian Stairs – proof positive to the Roman people that their great enemy of the past twenty-one years had finally been eliminated, that the Dacian wars were at last at an end, and that the legionaries who had perished at the hands of Decebalus and the Sarmatians had been avenged.

Dacia was now a Roman province. Trajan left the 13th Gemina Legion building a base for itself at Apulum in northern Dacia, and numerous auxiliary units were stationed throughout conquered Dacian territory. The remainder of the invasion force withdrew to bases south of the Danube. Four legions would now make their homes along the Danube in Moesia in support of the 13th Gemina – the 1st Italica at Novae, the 5th Macedonica at Troesmis, the 7th Claudia at Viminacium and the 11th Claudia at Durosturum.

The emperor himself set off back to Rome. According to Trajan's personal physician Crito, Trajan brought 50,000 Dacian prisoners back to Rome, all of whom were put up for auction, creating a significant boost to the Roman slave market. [Carc., III, 3] Trajan sent orders ahead of him for preparations to be made for 123 days of spectacles at the Colosseum; 11,000 animals were to die in the arena during these spectacles, and 10,000 gladiators did battle. [Dio, LXVIII, 15]

When news of the complete victory of Roman force of arms in Dacia reached Rome ahead of Trajan's return, Trajan's friend and client Pliny the Younger dashed off a brief note to him: 'May I congratulate you, noble emperor, in my own name and that of the State, on a great and glorious victory in the finest tradition of Rome.' [Pliny, X, 14]

AD 106
XLIV. TRAJAN ANNEXES ARABIA
Eyeing eastern expansion

Even as he was delivering the knockout blows to King Decebalus in Dacia in AD 105–106, Trajan had his eye on further conquest in the East. The new 2nd Traiana Legion arrived in Syria by the end of AD 105, and with it came orders for the governor of Syria, the propraetor Aulus Cornelius Palma. Orders also went to the prefect commanding the 3rd Cyrenaica Legion based at Alexandria, telling him to prepare to march his legion north.

In the spring of AD 106, the 3rd Cyrenaica left Alexandria, crossed the Nile, and marched across Egypt, through Judea, and into Syria, where it linked up with propraetor Palma, his gubernatorial bodyguard, and almost certainly the newly arrived 2nd Traiana Legion and detachments from legions based in Syria. Led by Palma, this army marched into the kingdom of Nabataea, in present-day Lebanon. Nabataea, which had its capital at the famed city of Petra, had long been a Roman ally, supplying valued cavalry to the Roman army. Palma annexed it for Trajan, creating the new Roman province of Arabia Petraea.

As Palma and the other troops returned to Syria, the 3rd Cyrenaica Legion established a new base at Bostra in the new province, as the 2nd Traiana took the 3rd Cyrenaica's place in Egypt. After Palma returned to Rome from his Syrian posting, Trajan was so pleased with the job he had done in Arabia he appointed him a consul for the second time, in AD 109.

For the moment, this was the extent of Trajan's moves in the East. But, the time was not far off when he would set out to achieve what Julius Caesar had planned to do but had never accomplished – the conquest of Parthia.

CREATING TRAJAN'S COLUMN

'He set up an enormous column, to serve at once as a monument to himself and as a memorial of his work in the Forum.'

DIO, *Roman Histories*, LXVIII, 16

Between the close of the Second Dacian War in AD 106 and AD 113, a team of artists and sculptors worked on the creation of the most unique war memorial in the world. Standing 125 feet (38 metres) tall, Trajan's Column is one of the few monuments of ancient Rome to remain almost completely intact in Rome today, with the sculpted marble scenes circling it from bottom to top in a continuous spiral band 800 feet (244 metres) long, telling the story of the emperor Trajan's Dacian Wars.

The Column's creator was probably Apollodorus of Damascus, responsible for the massive bridge across the Danube at Drobeta, as well as Trajan's new odeum and gymnasium buildings at Rome, and, more famously, Trajan's Forum, where Trajan's round Column was to stand. [Dio, lxix, 4] Apollodurus was fond of the curve – his bridge was a series of graceful arches, while Trajan's Forum is based on two hemicycles of brick.

Trajan's Column is hollow. Inside, it measures 12 feet 2 inches (4 metres) across, and in this narrow space a staircase winds to the top. Forty-three small window slits admit a little light to the interior. The curving exterior Parian marble panels, each roughly 4 feet (1.2 metres) high, would have been sculpted in an artist's studio over several years. The varying quality of the sculpting, from astonishing detail on the fingers and faces of some of the 2,500 figures, to no more than adequate chisel and rasp work on others, shows that a few master craftsmen worked on the project aided by a number of less skilled assistants.

The craftsmen's studio was probably in Rome, not far from the chosen site for the Column in the new Forum of Trajan. The staged nature of each scene, and the way that many groups of figures are stepped, with one figure slightly above the other, indicates that models stood in place on a series of tiers in the studio. First, the designer would have consulted with the emperor to determine what

Trajan's Column has survived down through the ages reasonably intact. It was designed to be 'read' by walking around the ramped structure, which no longer exists, that originally wound around it.

Trajan wanted depicted on the Column, and once the hundreds of scenes had been mapped out, the human and animal models would have been brought in. Each panel was designed as a separate unit, with one scene sometimes flowing into the next; while at other times a device such as trees was used as a scene break. The less lifelike backgrounds would have been added later from descriptions or rough sketches drawn from memory or on location by officers who had taken part in the two campaigns.

Throughout the drafting stage, troops stationed in Rome would have been used as models – primarily men of the Praetorian Guard, which had actually taken part in the campaigns. This is indicated by the fact that most of the emblems on Praetorian and legion shields depicted on the Column are of similar thunderbolt designs. For many years this was taken by historians to mean that by the beginning of the second century all legion shield emblems had standardized on the thunderbolt theme. Designs shown in the later Notitia Dignitatum indicate that this was unlikely. It is more likely that the shield designs we see on the Column represent different cohorts of the Praetorian Guard. Each Praetorian cohort was like a mini legion, and another second-century engraving said to represent men of the Praetorian Guard shows each with different though similar thunderbolt emblems on their shields. [See page 192]

Artists and sculptors of Roman times were invariably of Greek origin. Those responsible for Trajan's Column would have had no sensibility of the corporate nature of legion shield emblems, and would have drawn the emblems in front of them – those of the Praetorian Guard. For cavalry scenes, troopers of the Augustan Singularian Horse, the imperial horse guard at Rome, may have played the part of all the Roman auxiliary cavalry shown on the Column. Singularians would probably have donned captured enemy armour to act the role of Sarmatian cavalry. A detachment of auxiliary light infantry was probably sent to Rome to model for the Column; we see these auxiliaries in various scenes, with the same auxiliary unit shield design often recurring.

Many, though not all, of the auxiliaries depicted on the Column are clean-shaven, which was untypical of auxiliaries by the second century. Some have moustaches, a Gallic trait. Intriguingly, most of the 'legionaries' seen crossing the Danube in an early panel wear full beards, which historians have believed did not become the fashion until the reign of Hadrian, himself a beard-wearer, a decade after the Dacian Wars. Either the Column disproves that theory, or these 'legionaries' shown crossing the Danube behind legion standards and in full legionary equipment were auxiliaries modelling the part.

There are several authentic-looking auxiliary slingers and archers on the Column, and it is likely that a handful of each were sent to Rome to act as models; a troop of Lusius Quietus' Numidian cavalrymen is depicted, with dreadlocked hair, flowing robes and riding bareback as was the Numidian custom. Imperial slaves were probably used to play the roles of Dacians, using captured Dacian weapons displayed in Rome during Trajan's AD 103 Triumph.

The Column was dedicated by Trajan on 13 May AD 113. [Carc., I, 1] By that time, the Column's panels were all in place, providing their continuous visual narrative. Like the statues of classical times, all the figures and all the scenery on the Column were originally highly painted in lifelike colours –which would wear away over time – and along the length of the spiral, here and there figures on the relief were seen to be holding weapons and implements made from iron, bronze, even silver and gold. When Rome was sacked by the Vandals early in the fifth century, or during later sackings, these were looted, leaving many men on the Column we see today in an empty-handed state.

As a crowning glory, a bronze Roman eagle was set on top of the Column, which stood in the middle of the Forum courtyard flanked by Trajan's new Latin and Greek libraries. A series of platforms surrounded it, and it was possible to walk around the Column, climbing from platform to platform, and follow the story of the two wars from bottom to top. There is no record of whether these viewing platforms were open to the public or were reserved for Palatium guests.

When Trajan died in AD 117 his ashes were placed in the base of the Column. His successor Hadrian had the eagle on the top removed and replaced by a bronze statue of Trajan. During the Middle Ages, the Column was again looted, with locals this time attacking it, and damaging it, to remove the iron pins holding the marble panels in place. In 1588, the Christian Church removed Trajan's statue, replacing it with the statue of St Paul seen today.

AD 113–116
XLV. TRAJAN'S PARTHIAN WAR
Empty victories

'Trajan was wont to make good his threats by his deeds.'

CASSIUS DIO, *Roman Histories*, LXVIII, 16

At his death in 44 BC, Julius Caesar had been days away from leaving Rome to embark on a major military operation – the invasion of Parthia. Over the next 150 years, several emperors seized on the idea of realizing Caesar's dream of conquering Parthia. In AD 66, Nero was marshalling his forces for an invasion of Parthia when the Jewish Revolt forced him to abort the plan and divert his legions to counter the revolt. With Nero's death, the Parthian plan died too. It seems that Trajan had also long harboured the desire to become the conqueror of Parthia. Once he had brought Dacia into the Roman Empire and had consolidated the Dacian conquest, he was able to turn his full focus to the East.

Trajan was presented with an excuse to go to war with the Parthians. The current king of Armenia, Exedares, had been crowned by the Parthian king, Osroes, and had sworn loyalty to Parthia. Traditionally, the emperors of Rome had reserved the right to choose the kings of Armenia. But Trajan had another motive. According to Dio: 'His real reason was a desire to win renown.' [LXVIII, 17]

In AD 113, Trajan gave orders for the legions of the East to prepare for a major campaign the following spring. He also ordered several of his European-based legions to transfer to Syria in preparation for the new campaign. He himself set off to sail to Syria via Greece accompanied by his wife, the empress Plotina, and elements of the Praetorian Guard and Singularian Horse. They travelled aboard ships of the Roman navy's Misene Fleet from Misenum commanded by fleet prefect Quintus Marcius Turbo, who would later become prefect of the Praetorian Guard under Hadrian. [Starr, App., & Add.] A large part of the fleet remained in the East throughout Trajan's eastern campaign. [Starr, viii]

One of the legions sent east for Trajan's new campaign was the 1st Adiutrix. Founded in AD 68, it would have undergone a new enlistment over the winter of AD 108–109, so by AD 113 its numbers were up and its new recruits were settled and trained. The 1st Adiutrix marched west from Brigetio in Pannonia to the next legion base on the Danube, Carnuntum, and there its column was joined by the 15th Apollinaris Legion. Both legions then marched down to Ravenna in northeastern Italy to board warships of the Ravenna Fleet, which ferried them to Syria.

The 2nd Traiana Legion, raised by Trajan in AD 105 and sent to the East to support the annexation of Arabia Petraea, came up to Syria for the offensive from its base in Egypt. At the same time, the 3rd Cyrenaica at Bostra in Arabia Petraea prepared its weapons, ammunition and stores for a campaign the following year. In Cappadocia, just to the south of Armenia, the province's governor Marcus Junius sent word to his two legions, the 12th Fulminata at Melitene and the 16th Flavia at Satala, to be ready to march in the spring.

Word soon reached the Parthian king that Trajan was heading to the East with an army, and immediately he saw himself as the Roman emperor's target. By the time that Trajan reached Athens in Greece on his way east, Parthian envoys were awaiting him there. The envoys offered Trajan gifts and, telling him that Osroes had removed Exedares from the Arme-

One of the captive cap-wearing Dacian nobles who was led through the streets of Rome in chains in Trajan's Triumph following the Dacian Wars.

nian throne, sought a peace agreement. As part of the Parthian peace initiative, King Osroes asked that Trajan authorize him to make his nephew Parthamasiris the new king of Armenia. 'The emperor neither accepted the gifts nor returned any answer, either oral or written,' said Dio, 'except the statement that friendship is determined by deeds and not words, and that accordingly when he reached Syria he would do all that was proper.' [Dio, lxviii, 31]

Trajan's nephew Hadrian had been a consul and governor of Lower Pannonia following the Dacian Wars, but his career had slowed dramatically after that. Hadrian had a great liking for Greek customs, and by AD 112 he was archon, or governor, of Athens, and was no doubt in the city when Trajan arrived there in AD 113 on his way to Syria. It seems that Trajan added Hadrian to his party at the urging of his wife

Plotina, who was close to Hadrian, giving him the post of governor of Syria, for Dio wrote that Hadrian 'had been assigned to Syria for the Parthian War'. [Dio, lxix, 1]

After Trajan's fleets arrived at Laodicea, he and the imperial party spent the winter at Antioch. The facilities at Laodicea were apparently so overburdened by the influx of naval and military personnel that sailors and marines of the Misene Fleet were quartered at the long-deserted quarters of the 10th Fretensis Legion at nearby Cyrrhus. [Starr, Add.; and *AE* 1955, 225]

Trajan was joined at Antioch by his lieutenants for the campaign. Chief among these was the Moor Lusius Quietus. Quietus had served Trajan so loyally and effectively throughout the Dacian Wars that the emperor had, over the past seven years, made him a praetor, consul and provincial governor. Quietus was serving as governor of Judea when the emperor arrived in the East. Trajan's other senior general, the trusted Lucius Appius Maximus, came out from Rome with him. Like Quietus, Maximus had served Trajan well in Dacia. Trajan no longer had the services of tough old Sura, the third of his successful Dacian War generals, who had died a natural death in around AD 108.

In the spring of AD 114, leaving his wife with Hadrian at Antioch, Trajan launched his eastern offensive; as governor of Syria, Hadrian had the task of ensuring that Trajan's lines of supply were efficiently maintained. For the first stage of the campaign, Trajan marched his army north to Melitene in Cappadocia. As the army tramped along the Roman highways at a steady 18 miles a day, Trajan neither rode nor was carried in a litter; he marched on foot at the head of his troops, bareheaded. Each day, he personally decided the marching order. [Dio, lxviii, 23]

By the end of March, Trajan had reached Melitene and added the two Cappadocia-based legions to his column; from there, he swung east, crossing the Euphrates and entering Armenia. [Guey] The summer was still young when Trajan's troops completed the seizure of southern Armenia, driving a wedge between the Armenians to the south and the forces in the north loyal to Parthamasiris, the nephew of Osroes, whom the Parthian king had proceeded to install on the Armenian throne.

When Marcus and his army reached the Armenian city of Elegeia, Parthamasiris left the rebuilt Armenian capital, Artaxata, and came to Trajan's camp seeking an audience. Trajan was seated on a tribunal when the young Parthian prince approached, saluted him, and removed his crown and placed it at Trajan's feet. Parthamasiris fully expected the Roman emperor to return his crown to him, just as Nero had returned that of Tiridates fifty years before. But Trajan did no such thing. Instead, he sent the prince and the Parthian members of his entourage away under Roman cavalry escort, and told the Armenians in the party to stay right where they were, as they were now his subjects. Soon, Trajan's legions had brought all of Armenia under Roman control.

Trajan, after crossing the Tigris river and securing key frontier cities including Nisibis and Batnae, and leaving garrisons at strategic points, marched west to Edessa, modern Urfa in southeast Turkey. Situated on the plain of Haran, the city controlled a strategic hill pass to Mesopotamia and the Parthian heartland. At Edessa, Trajan received various eastern potentates before pushing south through the pass and occupying part of northern Mesopotamia. With the end of the year approaching, Trajan left the army camped in Parthian territory and returned to Syria to winter at Antioch. As he departed the army, he left orders for the legions to fell trees in the forests around Nisibis then use the wood to build collapsible boats for the new year's campaign in Mesopotamia.

Over the winter, Antioch and many cities of the region were hit by a severe earthquake. The Syrian capital was badly damaged, and 'multitudes' killed. [Dio, lxviii, 25] Among the casualties were foreign ambassadors waiting on the Roman emperor, and Marcus Vergilianus Pedo, who had just arrived in Syria after briefly serving as a consul in Rome and giving his name to the year. Trajan himself managed to escape with minor injuries, via a window of his quarters, being led from the ruins by men 'of greater than human stature'; Dio was possibly referring to large Germans of the emperor's Singularian Horse bodyguard. [Ibid.] For some days, Trajan lived in a tent in the Antioch chariot-racing stadium, the hippodrome, as aftershocks continued to shake the region.

The spring of AD 115 saw Trajan back with the army in Mesopotamia, and again on the advance. The six legions of the task force moved east through a landscape 'destitute of trees'. A convoy of wagons had brought the newly constructed fleet of collapsible boats down from Nisibis, but as Trajan tried to send his troops across a river in his path – probably the Nighr – an opposition force that had assembled on the far bank made life difficult for the invaders by peppering them with missiles. [Ibid.]

This was the first mention in Cassius Dio's narrative of the campaign of organized resistance in the field. It turned out that Trajan's invasion had taken place at an opportune time, for 'the Parthian power had been destroyed by civil conflicts and was still at this time the subject of strife'. [Dio, LXVIII, 22] The Parthians were locked in a civil war. It is likely that the troops who opposed Trajan at this river crossing comprised the small army of the kingdom of Adiabene, a Parthian ally in northern Mesopotamia.

After assembling their vessels, Trajan's legions began to build a bridge of moored boats across the river. In the usual Roman textbook fashion, there were several craft at the forefront of this growing bridge, equipped with towers and screens, and manned by archers and heavy infantry with javelins who rained missiles down on the enemy. At the same time, various Roman units dashed this way and that, up and down the western bank of the river, giving the impression that they were going to cross in boats at various points. This forced the outnumbered enemy to divert detachments from their army to hurry up and down the bank in order to be in position to counter these crossings. With the main enemy defence weakened, Trajan was able to send his troops across the bridge of boats in force.

There was a brief battle on the eastern side of the river, but Trajan had overwhelming numbers – his army would have comprised 60,000–70,000 fighting men at the commencement of the offensive the previous year. 'The barbarians gave way,' said Dio. [Dio, LXVIII, 21] Once across the river, the Roman army quickly gained possession of the kingdom of Adiabene.

To Trajan, this was a special moment. Like so many Roman generals including Julius Caesar, Trajan had a desire to emulate the deeds of Alexander the Great. Alexander had brought his army here to Adiabene. [Ibid.] And it was here, on the plain in the vicinity of the ancient cities of Nineveh, Arbela and Gaugamela, that the Macedonian army had defeated King Darius' Persian army in 331 BC.

Further to the south, at Adenystrae, modern-day Irbil, 70 miles (112 kilometres) north of Kirkuk in today's northern Iraq, there was a strong Parthian fort. When Trajan sent a legion centurion named Sentius ahead to give the Adenystrae garrison a chance to surrender, the Parthian commander, Mebarsapes, rejected the offer and imprisoned the centurion. In the Adenystrae dungeon, Sentius convinced other prisoners to help him. The centurion duly escaped, found Mebarsapes, then killed him, and opened the fort gate as the Roman army approached. Centurion Sentius' rewards from a grateful Trajan can only be imagined.

As the Roman army continued its advance down the Euphrates, 'quite free from molestation' from the enemy and apparently using the collapsible boats to transport its supplies, Trajan conceived the idea of building a canal between the Euphrates and the Tigris. [Dio, LXVIII, 26, 28] This was to allow him to follow the Tigris all the way to the

Persian Gulf, or the Erythreaean Sea as the Romans called it. The courses of the two rivers come tantalizingly close near to where the later city of Baghdad would rise, but Trajan's engineers warned him that his canal was not practical because the Euphrates flowed at a higher elevation than the Tigris, and a canal would only run the Euphrates dry. The determined emperor therefore had his troops drag the boats overland to the Tigris.

On the eastern bank of the Tigris, the legions came to Parthia's winter capital, Ctesiphon. Its Parthian defenders put up some resistance, but the legions soon captured it, and, apparently, also captured neighbouring Seleucia. At an assembly in Ctesiphon, Trajan was hailed imperator by the legions. It seems that Trajan and the bulk of his army spent the winter of AD 115–116 there at Ctesiphon, with Trajan occupying the palace of the kings of Parthia. From there, Trajan sent his latest dispatches to the Senate at Rome. Following the AD 114 campaign, the Senate had granted Trajan the title Optimus, meaning 'Most Excellent'. When news of the emperor's latest successes in the East arrived, especially the taking of the Parthian capital, the Senate granted him the additional title of 'Parthicus'.

In the spring of AD 116, Trajan and part of his army sailed down the Tigris in his fleet of boats, almost coming to grief when, on reaching a point in the river's lower reaches where the current met the incoming tide, a storm broke over the vessels. The Romans took refuge on an island in the river, Mesene, whose ruler treated Trajan kindly. Trajan continued on to the Persian Gulf. There, on seeing a ship departing for India, reminding him that Alexander the Great had marched that far, Trajan is reported to have said: 'I would certainly have crossed over to the Indi, too, if I were still young.' [Ibid., 29]

The Romans then retraced their course up the Tigris. Whether on water against the current, or on land, this return progress would have been slower than the exhilarating trip down the river to the Gulf. Trajan deliberately paused at the ancient ruins of Babylon, 55 miles (88 kilometres) south of today's Baghdad. Babylon's original culture had been more than 1,500 years old when Alexander the Great died here during his great eastern campaign of conquest. At Babylon, Trajan was shown the room where Alexander had reputedly breathed his last, and there he conducted a religious sacrifice in memory of the great Macedonian king.

As he lingered at Babylon, Trajan received unsettling news. While he had been playing tourist and sailing down to the Gulf and returning again, 'all the conquered districts were thrown into turmoil and revolted, and the garrisons placed among the various peoples were either expelled or slain'. [Ibid.] Nisibis and Edessa were among the cities that had revolted, as had Seleucia, only a comparatively short distance from Babylon. In response, Trajan quickly sent his best generals, Quietus the Moor and Maximus, hurrying north with flying columns, and dispatched a force under legion commanders Ericius Clarens and Julius Alexander to retake Seleucia, a city with a population of as many as 600,000 people.

Maximus' troops were engaged in battle in the field by the Parthians. The Romans were defeated, the loyal Maximus slaughtered in the fighting. Lusius Quietus made up for Maximus' failure by recovering several key cities including Nisibis and storming a stubbornly defended Edessa, which his troops sacked and left in flames. Seleucia was also recaptured, by Clarens and Alexander, and it too was put to the torch after being sacked, although it appears not to have been totally destroyed.

Trajan himself returned to Ctesiphon, the Parthian capital, and on the plain outside the city he called an assembly of his troops and of all Parthians in the vicinity. Trajan, after mounting a lofty platform in front of the assembly, told his audience of all he had achieved in this war, and announced that he had chosen a new king of Parthia – it would be, he said, Parthamaspates, a Parthian prince, whom he now produced and crowned king.

Parthamaspates was left at Ctesiphon to rule over the Parthians while vowing fealty to Trajan and Rome. Trajan, in the meantime, led his troops north to Hatra, a little west of the Tigris, where the Atreni Arab residents had also revolted and closed their gates to Romans. The city of Hatra was not large, and it sat on the edge of the desert with little water and no trees in the vicinity. But these very qualities made it difficult to besiege. Trajan had a camp built, and surrounded the city, then sent his legionaries against its walls with mining equipment.

Before long, the troops had created a breach by causing a section of Hatra's wall to topple. Trajan, commanding the assault from the saddle and keeping close to the action, immediately sent cavalry to force their way through the breach. But the Atreni counter-attacked so fiercely that they drove the Roman cavalry back into their own camp. So that he would not be recognized by enemy archers, Trajan had removed his purple commander-in-chief's cloak and other imperial trappings, but now, as his troopers came flooding back in disarray, the pursuing Hatran archers, 'seeing his majestic grey head and his august countenance, suspected his identity' and let off a volley of arrows in his direction. Trajan himself escaped unhurt, but one of the cavalrymen of his bodyguard was killed in the deluge of arrows. [Ibid., 31]

As the siege of Hatra dragged on, the Roman besiegers were sometimes drenched with rain and pelted by hail, while at other times they endured fierce heat and were plagued by flies that settled in masses on their food and drink. With the siege making no progress, the morale of his troops drooping and the campaigning season nearing its end, Trajan gave up his attempt to take Hatra, and ordered his troops to pack up and pull out. As the army marched north, Trajan began to feel increasingly unwell.

The year had seen the legions and auxiliary units involved in the campaign suffer heavy casualties. With supplies low, Trajan, now sick and exhausted, withdrew his forces from Mesopotamia. Leaving his army in Armenia and Cappadocia for the winter, he returned to Antioch, where he rejoined his wife and nephew, who had been supervising the metropolitan rebuilding efforts in the wake of the earlier earthquake.

Early the following year, AD 117, at Antioch, Trajan was making plans for a new spring offensive in Mesopotamia when he was struck down by a serious stroke which left him paralysed down one side. As he struggled to recover, the emperor put his Parthian plans on hold. And then, in the spring, news reached Antioch that there had been Jewish uprisings around the eastern Mediterranean. In Cyrenaica in North Africa, a reported 220,000 Romans and Greeks living in the province had been killed. In Egypt, more civilians died, and on Cyprus 240,000 people were said to have perished at the hands of the Jewish rebels. [Ibid., 32]

Now, all thoughts of resumed operations in Mesopotamia were forgotten as Trajan set out to eliminate the Jewish problem. The Jews of Judea, however, had not risen with their compatriots elsewhere in the East, so to ensure that Judea remained secure Trajan detached the 6th Ferrata Legion from his army and stationed it at Caparcotna in Galilee, just 15 miles (24 kilometres) from Nazareth, in the heart of Jewish territory.

Simultaneously, Trajan gave Lusius Quietus, fleet prefect Turbo and his other senior commanders orders to take more troops from his army and put down the Jewish rebellions elsewhere. Units quickly set off for Egypt and Cyrenaica to the south, and, by sea, for Cyprus to the west. Meanwhile, to consolidate the Roman hold on Armenia, Trajan sent the 16th Flavia Legion to the city of Samosata, in southwestern Armenia, to establish a new base there, with the 15th Apollinaris Legion making the 16th Flavia's former base at Satala its new home.

In the summer of AD 117, Roman troops swept into Egypt and Cyrenaica to terminate the revolts, and triremes of Turbo's Misene Fleet glided into harbours at Cyprus and disgorged thousands of troops. Under the leadership of Quietus and his colleagues, Roman soldiers who had so recently been fighting a gruelling war in Armenia and Parthia swiftly and brutally put down all the Jewish uprisings. Those Jews on Cyprus not killed in the Roman reprisals would have been taken away as prisoners, for the island was cleared of Jews, who were from that time forward banned from even setting foot on Cyprus. [Ibid.]

By the middle of the summer, with his poor health sorely affecting him, Trajan decided, or was convinced by those around him, to go home to Rome. In late July, he set sail for Italy with Plotina, leaving Hadrian at Antioch still in charge of Syria. Tracing the Turkish coast, the emperor's flotilla put in at Selinus in the province of Cilicia, today's Anatolia region in southern Turkey. There in early August AD 117, shortly after his arrival, Trajan apparently suffered another stroke, and died.

So it was that after almost twenty years on the throne, and with his Parthian expedition up in the air, Trajan left the scene. In a letter signed by his wife but supposedly from Trajan, 41-year-old Hadrian was named as his heir. As a result, Hadrian was proclaimed the new emperor of Rome by the legions in the East, and this was subsequently endorsed by the Senate.

In the end, apart from glory for Trajan and booty aplenty for those of his troops who survived the campaign, Trajan's Parthian War achieved nothing, at considerable cost. Many thousands of legionaries and auxiliaries perished in the campaign, and, while numerous cities and towns had been briefly occupied or destroyed, no new territory or sources of income had been acquired by Rome.

The Parthians, meanwhile, rejected and ejected Trajan's choice for king, Parthamaspates, and appointed a new ruler of their own choice. As for the balance of power in the region, it was left unchanged. The Euphrates continued to serve as the boundary between the Roman world and the Parthian world. And the Parthians rebuilt their power in the region, to the extent that they would be in a position to invade Syria before half a century had passed.

Hadrian set off for Italy, making a leisurely perambulation through the eastern provinces. By the summer of AD 118 he had arrived in Rome. With no intention of following in Trajan's expansionist footsteps, Hadrian officially terminated the campaign in the East and sent the 1st Adiutrix Legion back to its longtime Danube base in Moesia. Hadrian's self-appointed task from this point on would be consolidation of the frontier throughout the empire.

Before the year was out, several of Trajan's leading advisers and generals were arrested on what were probably trumped-up charges of conspiracy against Hadrian, and executed. Among the generals who perished in this pogrom were Palma, who had annexed Arabia Petraea for Trajan, and Quietus, the Moor who had proved to be Trajan's most reliable and effective field commander in Dacia and the East.

As Hadrian removed Trajan men from power and put his own stamp on the Palatium, even Trajan's brilliant but arrogant architect Apollodorus of Damascus was sidelined, and eventually executed, by the new emperor. Hadrian went as far as removing the superstructure of Apollodorus' famed bridge over the Danube, leaving just the massive piers standing. Hadrian's excuse for this act was a fear of barbarian invaders using the bridge to cross the river into Roman territory. Some writers have suggested he may merely have been so jealous of Apollodorus he wanted to destroy one of the greatest monuments to his genius.

Under Hadrian, Rome now moved from the financially unsustainable offensive stance taken by Trajan in both the West and the East, to one of defence. From this time on, the Roman Empire would be forever on the defensive.

AD 122

XLVI. DISAPPEARANCE OF THE 9TH
Solving the mystery

Some time after AD 120, the 9th Hispana Legion disappeared from the face of the earth, with no explanation in any classical text or on any inscription. Later historians came to believe that the legion, whose last known posting was northern Britain, had been wiped out by Caledonian tribes in Scotland in AD 122, with the disaster being hushed up by Roman authorities. This was, at least, the theory.

A popular British children's novel of 1954, Rosemary Sutcliffe's *The Eagle of the Ninth*, was based on the scenario that the 9th Hispana was wiped out in 'Pictland' in AD 117. No Roman writer identified tribes in Scotland as 'Picts' (painted ones) until the end of the third century, and the term Pictland was not used until several centuries later, but the basic premise of a legion being wiped out in Scotland, with a legionary's son embarking on a quest to determine what fate befell his father, a soldier of the 9th Hispana Legion, made for a bestseller and a widely viewed television series.

This popularity may have been unsettling for academics, and before long a counter-theory took hold in academic circles – that the 9th Hispana had actually been wiped out a decade later in Judea, during the Second Jewish Revolt of AD 132–135. Yet, there was absolutely no proof to support this latter theory other than the fact that Roman historian Cassius Dio had written that 'many Romans, moreover, perished in this war'. [Dio, LXIX, 14]

Several other writers have suggested that the 9th Hispana was the legion which Dio describes being wiped out by the Parthians at Elegeia in Armenia in AD 161, at the beginning of the reign of Marcus Aurelius. But the legion involved on that occa-sion is much more likely to have been the 22nd Deiotariana, which was based in the East throughout its career. AD 161 was, after all, four decades after the last known reference to the 9th Hispana.

The theory of the 9th Hispana's annihilation in Judea some time between AD 132 and 135 came to hold sway in academic circles even though there was no record of the legion leaving Britain, of it being stationed in the East, or of it even being in existence during that decade between AD 122 and 132. The evidence does point to the two legions stationed in Judea in AD 132, the 10th Fretensis and the 6th Ferrata being severely mauled during the revolt, but no classical source states that a legion was totally destroyed in Judea.

Nonetheless, to support the theory that the 9th Hispana had been wiped out in Judea some time during the revolt, and to scotch the idea that the 9th Hispana had been destroyed in Britain in AD 122 or earlier, some authors pointed to the evidence of two inscriptions in Holland which, they said, put the 9th Hispana out of Britain and on the Lower Rhine after AD 122. It was assumed that, as the legion had been based in Britain since AD 43 and had never previously been stationed on the Lower Rhine, these inscriptions must have dated from some time after AD 122, meaning the legion had been transferred out of Britain not long after AD 120, the dating of the last numismatic evidence of the legion's presence in Britain.

There was also the fact that another legion took the 9th Hispana's place in Britain in AD 122, and some authors have suggested that this indicated an orderly transition from one resident legion to another that year. It has also been pointed out that two officers known to have served as *laticlavius* tribunes with the 9th Hispana, Lucius

Aemilius Karus, around AD 119, and Lucius Norvius Crispinus Martialis Saturninus, in AD 121, both lived to enjoy long and distinguished careers, and therefore the legion could not have been wiped out in or before AD 122 and must have existed after that time.

The latter point is worth examining in detail. With only one *laticlavius* tribune serving with a legion at any one time, Karus, who went on to become a consul and the governor of Arabia, would have left the legion by AD 121, to be replaced by Saturninus as senior tribune and second-in-command of the 9th Hispana. Yes, Saturninus also lived to become a praetor, legion commander, consul and provincial governor. But here is the intriguing thing – following his posting as a tribune with the 9th Hispana Legion, Saturninus did not receive another official appointment for twenty-five years. Only then, after all that time, was he given command of a legion.

Normally, after leaving a legion, a man who had served as tribune could be expected to soon take a seat in the Senate and over the succeeding years work his way up the promotional ladder, with a legion command quickly following. After AD 122, Saturninus' career stopped dead. Hadrian would have nothing more to do with him. It was only in AD 147, under the emperor Antoninus Pius, that Saturninus at last received his legion command, that of the 3rd Augusta in Africa. He was by that time aged around 50. A legion commander of that maturity, at any time in Roman history, was rare. Two years later, Antoninus gave Saturninus a new imperial appointment, and his stalled career was on the move again, with a consulship not far off. [*CIL*, VIII 2747, 18273.]

In contrast, Saturninus' predecessor at the 9th Hispana, Lucius Karus, had joined the Senate, been a praetor, commanded a legion, been made a consul and become governor of Arabia by AD 142. [*AE* 1909, 236, Gerasa] All this had been achieved while Saturninus was ignored, with Karus' peak career appointment as a provincial governor taking place five years prior to Saturninus' career restarting with his appointment to the command of the 3rd Augusta Legion.

What was it that suddenly put the brakes on Saturninus' career and would leave him in the official doldrums for a quarter of a century? Could it be that he was present at the annihilation of the 9th Hispana Legion in northern Britain in AD 122? Was he, a mounted officer, among the few men of the legion to escape the slaughter, perhaps galloping away accompanied by a few cavalry, in the same way that Petilius Cerialis had escaped Boudicca's British rebels in AD 60 when he commanded the 9th

Hispana? Or was Saturninus taken prisoner, and later returned by the Caledonians? The disgrace of defeat, and of surrender or capture, hung like a dead bird around the necks of Romans. Many officers and enlisted men throughout Roman history committed suicide rather than live to face either. Was this why Lucius Saturninus was made to pay the price of ignominy for twenty-five years?

This was not the first time a senior officer had been banned from the promotion lists after his legion had suffered at the hands of the enemy in Britain. In AD 51, during the reign of Claudius, 'the legion under Manlius Valens had meanwhile been defeated' by the Silures in Wales. [Tac., *A*, XII.40] Neither this battle nor its location was described by Tacitus. The legion in question was not identified, but it is likely to have been the 20th, which had recently arrived in the west of England after being transferred from Colchester in the late AD 40s. The legion's commander, Manlius Valens, survived the battle, but the defeat of his unit saw him removed from the lists for the next seventeen years.

Through the remainder of the reign of Claudius and the entire reign of Nero, Valens received no further official appointments. Only in AD 68, when Galba came to power, was Valens restored to the promotional ladder, starting, uniquely, with a second legion command, that of the new 1st Italica Legion. Valens went on to become a consul much later, in his ninetieth year. His case demonstrates a precedent for a senior legion officer being sidelined by the Palatium for many years as punishment for the defeat of his legion when serving in a command position.

Now consider the evidence of the two 9th Hispana inscriptions in Holland. At Nijmegen, tile stamps of the 9th Hispana put men of the legion there, on the Lower Rhine, some time between AD 104 and 120, according to one authority. [Web., *IRA*, 2] Nearby, at Aachen, there is an altar dedicated by Lucius Latinius Macer, camp-prefect of the 9th Hispana Legion. [Ibid.] There is no numismatic evidence to show that the legion as a whole ever left Britain. That the altar at Aachen was dedicated by the legion's camp-prefect indicates that he was leading a vexillation of the unit on detached duty on the Lower Rhine. If the entire legion had been present, its legate or tribune could have been expected to make the dedication.

Another authority has proposed that a detachment of one or more cohorts from the 9th Hispana Legion was transferred from Britain to Nijmegen in AD 113 when Trajan was preparing for his AD 114–116 Parthian campaign in the east. [Hold., *RAB*, 1] The theory is that the 9th Hispana detachment replaced troops taken from the Rhine and sent to the East for Trajan's Parthian operation. [Ibid.]

It has been pointed out that several auxiliary units including the Ala Vocontiorum were transferred from Britain to the Lower Rhine in around AD 113, and so probably accompanied the 9th Hispana detachment. [Hold., *RAB*, 1] All these auxiliary units that had transferred with the 9th Hispana vexillation were back at their old stations in Britain by AD 120. [Ibid.] This suggests that by AD 120, the 9th Hispana detachment had also rejoined the mother legion in Britain, where numismatic evidence put the 9th Hispana that year.

There is another intriguing fact. Five auxiliary units known to be based in Britain up to this time, a cavalry wing and four light infantry cohorts, also disappeared from the face of the earth in Britain in the same year, AD 122 – the Ala Agrippiana Miniata, and the 1st Nervorium Cohort, 2nd Vasconum CR Cohort, 4th Delmatarum Cohort and the 5th Raetorum Cohort. [Hold., *DRA, ADRH*] There is no record of the existence of these units after AD 122, just as there no evidence of them being transferred or disbanded. They simply disappeared. And this ala and these cohorts constitute the type and minimum number of support units that a legion on campaign might be expected to take with it.

Were the 9th Hispana Legion and its auxiliary support units ambushed by Caledonian tribes in Scotland in the late summer of AD 122 as they marched unsuspectingly through the lowlands of Scotland? Was the legion exterminated by the Caledonians, with the bodies of the fallen Romans stripped and the 9th Hispana's sacred eagle and all its other standards carried away by the victorious tribes? And did the legion's second-in-command Lucius Saturninus survive the bloody battle and escape back to Roman lines, only to live in shame for the next twenty-five years?

In the spring of AD 122, the new emperor Hadrian arrived in Britain as part of a long inspection tour of the empire. That same year, work began on the construction of an east-west wall across southern Scotland, from one coast to the other, to keep the barbarian tribes out of Roman Britain. It might be suggested that the annihilation of the 9th Hispana Legion that year sponsored the order to build Hadrian's Wall. But, during his tour of the empire, Hadrian ordered the construction of strengthened defences including walls on frontiers in numerous places, not just in Britain.

Here is another interesting fact. In the summer of AD 122, men from thirteen cavalry alae and thirty-seven auxiliary cohorts stationed in Britain were given honorary discharge after serving the required twenty-five years in the Roman military. [Birl.,

Once Hadrian became emperor, he took a defensive posture, pulling Roman units out of unsustainable locations and building frontier defences such as Hadrian's Wall. But did the 9th Hispana disappear before or after construction of the wall began?

DRA, CEO] It is hardly likely, with a legion just recently destroyed on the province's frontier, that the emperor would permit any such discharges. Could it be that these discharges took place prior to the annihilation of the 9th Hispana, and also played a part in it?

Via traders, word would have reached the tribes of Scotland that the Roman emperor was touring Britain and had ordered the construction of a wall to keep them out. They may well have also known that many Roman auxiliary units would be discharging men that summer, with the auxiliaries concerned looking forward to their retirement. Here was a window of opportunity for the tribes – before the wall was erected and while the auxiliary units were weakened by the discharge of experienced men.

The 9th Hispana Legion had moved up to Carlisle from Eburacum (York) some time after AD 108. In all probability the move took place in the summer of AD 122, to permit the legion to commence the earthworks on the wall that Hadrian had ordered to be erected; this brief occupation would explain why the legion left no epigraphic evidence at Carlisle. The move made the 9th Hispana the most northerly based of the legions stationed in Britain and the Empire. The Roman fortress at Carlisle, which occupied a site alongside the town that served as the capital of the local Carvetti tribe, became a military base second only in the province to the capital Eburacum. [Tom., *DRA*, DRAC]

Perhaps in the late summer, once Hadrian had left Britain, the Caledonians sent a message to the commander of the 9th Hispana Legion, to entice him north of his base at Carlisle. Perhaps that commander was told that his emperor's wall would not be necessary, that the tribes were prepared to sign a lasting peace with Rome – but the commander must come quickly, while the chieftains were all of one mind, and he should bring as many troops as he could to awe the locals and ensure that wavering tribes did not back out of the treaty.

The officer commanding the 9th Hispana would have been well aware that Hadrian was all for consolidating the empire's borders; in some cases Hadrian had given up territory acquired by his predecessor Trajan and withdrawn troops from what he saw as untenable positions. Unlike Trajan, Hadrian had no desire to expand the Roman Empire; he preferred making peace to making war. So, taken in by the Caledonians, and imagining how pleased his emperor would be with him if he could give him a peace treaty with the Caledonians, the commanding officer of the 9th Hispana marched his legion, four auxiliary cohorts and a cavalry wing north from Carlisle. And in doing so, he led 7,500 men into a trap.

The tribes of Caledonia had assembled more than 30,000 fighting men in AD 84, to take on the Romans at the Battle of Mons Graupius in Scotland. [Tac., A, 29] It is conceivable that a similar number would have taken part in the ambush of the 9th Hispana thirty-eight years later, among them survivors of Mons Graupius and the

The remains of Hadrian's Wall track across the Cumberland hills, with the original ditch still visible on the northern side. Over the centuries, the wall has been much reduced with stones removed from it used to build farm fences and farmhouses.

sons and grandsons of men who had fallen in that battle, all thirsting for revenge. And in a short, sharp bloodbath, these men surprised and destroyed the 9th Hispana – a legion that had taken part in the Mons Graupius defeat of the Caledonians – and its accompanying auxiliary units. With their ambush, the Caledonians had avenged their people for the defeat at Mons Graupius.

In late AD 122, before the last salary payment period of the year, the 6th Victrix Legion marched out of its base at Vetera on the Lower Rhine. Soon the legion arrived in southern Britain aboard the ships of the Britannic Fleet, then hurried north to make its new headquarters at Eburacum. It had come to fill the gap left by the 9th Hispana. Soon, too, three new auxiliary units freshly raised by Hadrian arrived in the province. [Hold., *DRA*, *ADRH*] Replacements for the men discharged at the beginning of the summer would also have been rushed to Britain. And work on Hadrian's Wall took on a new urgency.

Yet no one said a word about what had happened to the 9th Hispana Legion, the legion that had served Julius Caesar and eight emperors through the Roman Empire's rise to its zenith. Officially, it was as if the annihilated 9th Hispana had never existed.

The remains of a guard tower on Hadrian's Wall. Four auxiliaries manned each such tower.

AD 132–135

XLVII. SECOND JEWISH REVOLT
Shimeon bar-Kokhba's uprising

If Trajan had been a soldier emperor, Hadrian was a tourist emperor, spending more time visiting the provinces and seeing the sights than he did in Rome. In AD 131, his latest travels brought him to Judea. Hadrian was now 55. He had been emperor for almost fourteen years. He had consolidated Rome's frontiers, inspecting garrisons and forts, abolishing some installations and relocating others. And he had lectured his legionaries and auxiliaries, and drilled them, reforming practices that he felt were too luxurious for soldiers. He tightened the discipline governing his men, and 'taught them all that should be done'. [Dio, LXIX, 9]

By the time he had climbed up into the Judean Hills in the summer of AD 131 to the site of the once mighty Jewish city of Jerusalem, Hadrian was thinking about his legacy to history. In AD 70, following the defeat of the Jewish rebels holding Jerusalem, Roman general and future emperor Titus had ordered the 10th Fretensis Legion to raze the city to the ground and then build themselves a permanent camp amid the ruins. When Hadrian and his entourage, including men of the Praetorian Guard and Singularian Horse, reached Jerusalem, they found a devastated landscape where once stood a city that had hosted more than a million people at the Jewish Passover every year.

There were few structures of note here. Only the towering Temple Mount, from which the Jews' Second Temple, built by Herod, had been removed. And the fortress of the 10th Fretensis Legion, apparently built in the vicinity of the former palace of Herod. A small ramshackle *vicus*, or civilian settlement, had also grown outside the legion base to house camp followers.

Hadrian now instructed his subordinates to build a new city on the site of Jerusalem. He would give it *colonia* status and settle retiring legionaries there. He named the new city Aelia Capitolina, incorporating his family name of Aelius. Meanwhile, the soaring Temple Mount begged a new adornment, and Hadrian ordered a Roman temple dedicated to Jupiter erected there. He also issued an edict that circumcision, a rite among the Jews which Hadrian considered a barbaric form of mutilation, was forthwith illegal throughout the empire. In addition to founding the new city of

Aelia, said Eusebius, who was the Christian bishop of Caesarea in the fourth century, 'before its gate, that by which we go to Bethlehem, he [Hadrian] set up an idol of a pig in marble, signifying the subjugation of the Jews to Roman authority'. [Eus., *Chron.*, 2, HY 20]

Because Jerusalem was then the site of the base of the 10th Fretensis Legion, later historians would assume that this pig, or boar as they perceived it, was forthwith adopted as the new emblem of the legion. But with the 10th Fretensis' old emblems of bull, dolphin and war galley reoccurring on its coins after it left Jerusalem and transferred to Arabia, it is clear that Hadrian's pig identified the city, not the legion that occupied it. As Eusebius made clear, this idol of a pig at the city gate was intended by Hadrian to be a deliberate double-edged slight to the Jews, whose religion required them to avoid both the pig and graven images.

Hadrian, the emperor who prided himself on maintaining a state of peace, departed for Egypt. But he had lit a fuse under Judea. 'The Jews deemed it intolerable that foreign races should be settled in their city and foreign religious rites planted there,' said Dio. [Dio, LXIX, 12] There was a leader among the Jews of Judea by the name of Shimeon bar-Kosiba who now directed Jewish anger at Hadrian's acts into a well-planned resistance movement, with him at its head. His leadership was given credibility by his claim that he descended from King David, and by the most influential rabbi of the day, Akiva ben Yosef, who called him Bar-Kokhba, or 'Son of the Star', which implied that he was the long-awaited Jewish Messiah.

Calling himself *nasi*, or prince, Bar-Kokhba, as he was to become known far and wide, launched his revolt quietly, and cunningly. Through the remainder of that year of AD 131, according to Dio, while Hadrian remained close by, first in Egypt and then in Syria, Bar-Kokhba and his followers continued to make the weapons that their overlords required them to produce as part of their tribute to Rome; but they made them with faults, so that they would be returned to them to be corrected. In this way, they actually made arms for themselves. At the same time, the rebel leadership began to build underground strongholds in out-of-the-way places, 'and they pierced these subterranean passages from above at intervals to let in air and light'. [Ibid.]

Had Roman officials in Judea been more observant, they would have realized that something was afoot among the locals, but they took no heed of the signs of looming insurrection. They would pay the price for their laxity. By the spring of AD 132, 'all Judea had been stirred up'. [Dio, LXIX, 13] Jews were gathering everywhere, sometimes in public, sometimes in secret. Dio talks of overt and secret acts of Jewish defiance – among other things, Roman statues would have been torn down. And help for the rebel movement was coming from foreign countries – there were large Jewish communities east of the Euphrates in Parthia, and elsewhere. [Ibid.]

And then, one day in the first half of AD 132, the revolt exploded across the province, no doubt in a number of simultaneous and coordinated attacks, taking the Romans completely by surprise. The two legions stationed in the province, the 10th Fretensis at Jerusalem, or Aelia Capitolina as the Romans now called it, and the 6th Ferrata at Caparcotna in Galilee, took the brunt of the uprising.

The province's governor, Tineus Rufus, survived the initial revolutionary outbreak by virtue of the fact that he was headquartered at Caesarea, on the coast, but it was a different matter for Romans inland. Meanwhile, anyone in the Jewish territories who did not support the revolt suffered at the hands of the rebels, who, according to the later Christian bishop, Eusebius, 'killed the Christians with all kinds of persecutions' for refusing to help them against the Romans. [Eus., *Chron.*, 2, HY 17]

When news of the revolt reached Hadrian, he was in Greece. He immediately ordered one of his best generals to Judea to command the Roman response to the revolt. The task fell to Sextus Julius Severus, then governor of Britain. With one of the consuls for the year in Rome stepping down to hurry to Britain to take Severus' place there, the general, who is likely to have made his military reputation in Trajan's Parthian campaign – a general identified only as Severus was named by Dio among the successful Roman commanders against the Parthians – set off for the East.

Clearly, the militarily conservative Hadrian would not release any legions from the west to help Severus, for there is no record of legions being transferred to the East at this stage of the revolt. Severus would have to put down the uprising using whatever resources he found in the East, together with the few auxiliary troops that accompanied him from Britain.

But Hadrian did give Severus sweeping powers that placed him above provincial governors, whose authority did not extend beyond the borders of their individual provinces. Those powers would enable Severus to bring in units from outside Judea. They also allowed him almost *carte blanche* authority in the region whilst acting in the name of the emperor – as demonstrated by the term *ex indulgentia divi Hadriani*, meaning, at the indulgence of Hadrian, which was used on special military discharge diplomas issued by Severus in Judea. [Starr, V, 2]

Severus probably took several British-based auxiliary units to Judea with him, plus detachments from various other units as his personal bodyguard. One of the units likely to have contributed to, or been part of, Severus' British contingent was the 1st Hispanorum Cohort, based at Maryport on the Solway Firth – the unit's prefect Marcus Censorius Cornelianus is known to have gone to Judea with Severus. [Hold., *RAB*, 4]

Coins issued by rebel leader Shimeon bar-Kokhba proclaimed him prince of Jerusalem and a free Judea.

It is probable that Severus did not reach Judea until the spring or summer of AD 133. The situation that confronted Severus and his accompanying troops when they arrived at Caesarea on the Mediterranean coast, having been brought from a port in southern Gaul or western Italy aboard warships of the Misene Fleet, can only be imagined. [Starr, VIII] Modern-day writers have speculated that a legion was wiped out by the Jewish rebels during Bar-Kokhba's revolt. But while Dio wrote that the Romans suffered grievously during this revolt, neither he nor any other classical author stated that a legion was totally destroyed, nor even lost its eagle.

Of two legions known with some certainty to have been wiped out in the second century, one, the 9th Hispana, disappeared after AD 120, and can be demonstrated to have perished in northern Britain. [*See pages 421–8*] The other legion that disappeared from the records, the 22nd Deiotariana, is likely to have been the unit which, according to Dio, was most definitely wiped out in Armenia in AD 161.

What Dio did say about Roman losses in the Second Jewish Revolt was that 'many Romans' perished in this war, and that, as a consequence, when Hadrian sent one of his annual new year's letters to the Senate during this conflict, to be read to the House on 1 January – probably in AD 133, after the first bloody year of the revolt – he omitted the traditional opening of, 'If you and your children are in health, it is well; I and the legions are in health.' [Dio, LXIX, 14] But this does not constitute evidence that a legion had been wiped out.

Certainly, the two legions stationed in Judea, the 10th Fretensis and 6th Ferrata, would have taken heavy casualties in the opening stages of the revolt. The 10th Fretensis in particular must have suffered severely. As evidence of this, newly arrived Roman commander Sextus Severus was forced to take an almost unprecedented step in order to bring the 10th Fretensis up to some sort of fighting strength. As discharge diplomas show, Severus granted Roman citizenship to a number of sailors and marines crewing ships of the Misene Fleet that had brought him to Judea, and whom he transferred into the ranks of 10th Fretensis Legion. [Starr, VIII] Such a heavy toll was taken on the ranks of the centurions of the 10th Fretensis that Severus took the equally rare step of transferring the prefect of the 1st Hispanorum Cohort to this legion as a senior centurion. [Hold., *RAB*, 4] No doubt other transfers of a similar nature also took place.

Shimeon bar-Kokhba established his headquarters at the hilltop fortress of Bethar, 8 miles (12 kilometres) southwest of Jerusalem. Today, the village of Bittir sits at the bottom of the hill, and the rail line to Tel Aviv runs by it. There had been a small fortress on the hill here since the time of the First Temple at Jerusalem, and Bar-Kokhba's fighters rebuilt the tumbled-down stone walls that ran for 1,000 yards (915 metres) around the hill, repaired the semicircular bastions set along the walls, and dug out the 15-feet (4.5-metre) deep and 50-feet (15-metre) wide moat which ran across the saddle of earth connecting the hill to a mountain ridge to the south. The roughly oval-shaped fortress covered 25 stony acres (10 hectares). [Yadin, 13]

It is certain that the rebels succeeded in taking and destroying the fortress of the 10th Fretensis Legion in Jerusalem at the outbreak of the revolt, and tearing down the offensive marble pig that stood above the city gate. All the men of the legion caught there would have been put to the sword by the rebels, in the same way that the Roman garrison of Jerusalem had been slaughtered in AD 66. Only those cohorts of the 10th Fretensis occupying outstations, and its 1st Cohort stationed with the legion's eagle at the provincial capital of Caesarea, escaped the fate of their comrades at Jerusalem.

Bar-Kokhba remained at Bethar for the next three years, ruling Judea as its self-proclaimed 'prince' and 'president' with the help of his Sanhedrin, the supreme Jewish religious council. He also appointed Jewish administrators to various parts of Palestine. Surviving documents reveal that several of those administrators were still approving land leases in their areas three years later. [Yadin, 12] Bar-Kokhba also minted his own coins – possibly melting down captured Roman coinage, for Roman coin images representing the emperor and his legions were alien to the Jews. On those new coins were inscribed legends such as, 'Year 1 of the Liberty of Israel', and 'Shimeon, President of Israel'. [Ibid., 1]

Roman general Severus was faced with the very same task that had awaited Vespasian in AD 67 – the recovery of Jerusalem and much of Judea from rebel Jewish hands. To achieve that, he needed many more men. Numismatic evidence reveals that, to consolidate the Roman position in Judea, for the duration of the revolt Severus brought in two legions from neighbouring provinces – from Arabia, the 3rd Cyrenaica, and from Raphanaea in southern Syria, the 3rd Gallica.

In all likelihood Severus also used vexillations from other legions in the East. A vexillation from the 4th Scythica Legion, for example, which was based at Zeugma in Syria, was very likely to have taken part in Severus' Judean counter-offensive, because a centurion of the 20th Valeria Victrix Legion, Ligustinius Disertus, accompanied Severus from Britain to Judea and subsequently served with the 4th Scythica during the revolt. Disertus' name suggests that he was a Syrian native, like a number of men of the 20th vv. Centurion Disertus' local knowledge may have been the reason that Severus took him to Judea. After the revolt, Disertus returned to his own unit, the 20th vv, in Britain. [Hold., *RAB*, 4]

The fourth-century author Eusebius gave the province's governor Tineus Rufus credit for supervising the Roman offensive against the rebels, writing that 'Rufus, the governor of Judea, once military aid had been sent to him by the emperor, moved out against them treating their madness without mercy'. Severus outranked Rufus, and Roman command in this war was his. According to Eusebius, too: 'He destroyed in heaps thousands of men, women and children, and under the law of war, enslaved their land.' [Eus., *EH*, IV, VI] There can be no doubting that the Roman response was indeed harsh and merciless, just as the rebel slaughter of Romans had been when the uprising began. But the counter-offensive was not as swift or as sure as Eusebius implied. It would prove to be a long, grinding war.

With just the two full-strength 3rd legions, the battered remnants of the 6th Ferrata and 10th Fretensis, vexillations from several more legions and his auxiliary units, Severus devised a brutal but effective strategy for the best deployment of his vastly outnumbered troops against hundreds of thousands of armed rebels and their supporters. 'Severus did not venture to attack his opponents in the open at any one point, in view of their numbers and their desperation,' said Dio. [Dio, LXIX, 13] Severus broke up his units into a number of wide-ranging smaller groups. These parties intercepted Jews in small groups, captured them, locked them up, deprived them of food and allowed them to die. Elsewhere, Roman flying columns made lightning raids in which they located the hidden Jewish outposts, destroying fifty of them. [Ibid.]

As the outposts were eliminated, surviving Jewish fighters and their families withdrew to remote hiding places. Numerous such rebel hiding places were located by twentieth-century Jewish archaeologists in the rocky heights west of the Dead Sea. Between Engedi and Masada, the archaeologists found several caves along the cliffs of the Nahal Hever wadi, one containing ancient skeletal remains of eighteen men, women and children plus clothing and implements, which were dated to around the second century.

Tellingly, in one of the caves, the archaeologists also came upon an archive of Jewish documents written on papyrus. Among them were letters from Shimeon bar-Kokhba himself to his subordinates, giving them orders. In one of those letters, Bar-Kokhba wrote, 'Get hold of the young men and come with them. If not, a punishment. And I shall deal with the Romans.' Other letters, from Bar-Kokhba and his deputies, urged the capture of traitors. [Yadin, 10]

These Nahal Hever caves, some precariously placed in cliff faces, were difficult to reach and even more difficult to locate, making them ideal hideouts for the rebels, from were they could emerge to make hit-and-ruin raids on Roman forces. Eventually, the Roman military became aware that there were Jewish hiding places somewhere in this vicinity, for the remains of two small Roman camps are located in the area, high on opposite clifftops overlooking the Nahal Hever wadi. Both camps were capable of housing eighty men – a unit of century strength. [Ibid.] This fits the story told by Dio, of a number of small units being separated from their legions, cohorts and wings and sent out into the countryside relentlessly to track down the rebels.

A papyrus of AD 124 put the 1st Thracian milliaria Cohort at Engedi, not far from the Nahal Hever caves. [Hold., *DRA*] This 800-man cohort continued to be based in the area following Bar-Kokhba's revolt. [Yadin, 10] It would seem likely that the two Roman camps of the Nahal Hever belonged to centuries of the 1st Thracians, and that these troops eventually caught and dealt with most of the Jews hiding out in the region – with the exception of the group of eighteen, never found by the Romans, who must have starved to death in what became known as the Cave of the Letters.

While some rebels were being hunted down in the barren Dead Sea region, to deny them shelter and support other Roman troops progressively destroyed one Jewish village after another across the length and breadth of Palestine, as Roman control edged closer and closer to Jerusalem and Bar-Kokhba's headquarters at Bethar. According to Cassius Dio, in the application of this scorched earth policy, 985 villages were destroyed. [Ibid., 14] It was a slow process, said Dio, but the Roman troops were gradually able to 'crush, exhaust and exterminate' the Jews. It was an ethnic cleansing operation which, over three years, took the lives of 580,000 Jewish men; Dio could not calculate how many Jews also died from famine, disease, or in those villages put to the torch, but between these remedies and the sword 'nearly the whole of Judea was made desolate'. [Ibid.]

Roman operations against the rebels continued in Judea for three years, but it appears that by the winter of AD 134–135, two years after the revolt first erupted, only Bar-Kokhba's headquarters at Bethar remained to be taken, and had already been isolated. The Judean situation had stabilized sufficiently for Hadrian's Palatium to remove auxiliary units from the province and transfer them north to the command of Arrian, governor of Cappadocia, for a campaign against the invading Alans in Lesser Armenia.

That transfer was also made possible by the fact that legionary reinforcements had arrived from Europe. Probably assured by Severus that one final, reinforced push would bring about the downfall of the rebels holed up at Bethar, and that the legions in the East were exhausted, Hadrian sent vexillations from the 5th Macedonica Legion, then based at Troesmis in Moesia, and from another legion based in Moesia, the 11th Claudia, whose base was at Durosturum. [Yadin, 13]

Cohorts from these two Moesian legions would have been shipped from Europe together, arriving in time for the spring offensive of AD 135. Severus marched his army to Bethar, surrounding it with a siege wall 4,000 yards (3,656 metres) long, and setting up two major camps on the dry, rocky soil, camps which can still be traced today. One of those camps measured 400 yards (365 metres) by 200 yards (182 metres), and was large enough to accommodate 5,000 men, the equivalent of a full legion, while the other was roughly half the size of the first camp. [Ibid.]

Using the loose stones littering the area, the Roman troops built low walls around their tents in the camps, and these walls remain to this day. There is a spring close to one of the camps, and idle legionaries of a water-carrying party cut an inscription into the rock there – 'LEG V MAC ET XI CL', identifying two of the legions taking part in the siege of Bethar, the 5th Macedonica and 11th Claudia. [Ibid.]

According to the Jewish *Midrash*, 200,000 Jews congregated in the Bethar fortress with Bar-Kokhba. Other Jewish sources give a far greater number. Either way, the hilltop compound would have been crowded beyond belief. Standing more than 2,000 feet (609 metres) above sea level, the fortress was surrounded by a deep natural canyon on three sides, with the rocky saddle connecting the hilltop to the surrounding mountains to the south – where the defenders had dug their moat. [Yadin, 13]

In undertaking the siege of Bethar, Severus followed the model used in the siege of nearby Masada sixty-two years before. Once he had surrounded the Jews and cut them off from outside supply, he commenced to build a ramp of earth across the southern saddle towards the fortress wall. Once completed, the ramp would fill in the defensive moat and lead to the summit of the hill, allowing the legions to drive up it as if it were a highway and gain entry to the fortress over the wall. In the meantime, Roman catapults maintained steady fire against the Jewish defenders.

'The siege lasted a long time,' said Eusebius, 'before the rebels were driven to final destruction by famine and thirst, and the instigator of their madness paid the penalty he deserved.' [Eus., *EH*, IV, VI] The siege was terminated before the summer had ended – traditional Jewish sources say that Bar-Kokhba was dead by September AD 135. [Yadin, 10] From Eusebius' narrative it would seem that Bethar fell, and Shimeon bar-Kokhba died – probably at his own hands – before the Roman legions' assault ramp was completed.

With the fall of Bethar and massacre of all those within its walls, the Second Jewish Revolt had come to its bloody conclusion. On the orders of Hadrian, Jews were banned from ever setting foot in Jerusalem again, or of even approaching it, 'so that even from a distance' they 'could not see [their] ancestral home'. [Eus., *EH*, IV, VI] Roman colonies would progressively be built at Jerusalem and throughout the province in previously Jewish areas. On Hadrian's orders, to expunge any reference to the Jews, the name of the province was changed from Judea to Syria Palestina – the Palestina referring to the Philistines, age-old foes of the Jewish people.

Shimeon bar-Kokhba's bloody revolt and his brief reign as the prince of Israel had brought about a predictably fierce response from Rome. This had been the second time that Romans had paid a painful price at the hands of the Jews in Judea. Hadrian was determined that there would not be a third time. The Jewish people had been expelled from their homeland, and Judea would never again be a flashpoint for Rome.

AD 135
XLVIII. ARRIAN AGAINST THE ALANS
Throwing the barbarians back

By the winter of AD 134–135, Roman forces had all but quashed the Second Jewish Revolt in Judea. With the last of the rebels confined at Bethar, and legionaries arriving from Europe to undertake a siege of Bethar through the summer, the situation in Judea had been sufficiently turned around for Hadrian's Palatium to turn its attention to another threat in the East.

In the summer of AD 134, after learning from Pharasmanes, king of Iberia, today's Georgia, that Rome's forces were tied up fighting the Jews in Judea, many thousands of mounted warriors of the Alani tribe, Sarmatians from the Caucasus region between the Caspian and Black Seas, had pushed southeast. [Dio, LXIX, 15] According to Dio, the Alans invaded the territory of the Albani and also the kingdom of Media, where they 'caused dire injury'. [Ibid.] From there, the Alans threatened Armenia, Lesser Armenia, Cappadocia, Pontus and the neighbouring Roman provinces.

Originating from north of the Black Sea, the nomadic Alani, or Alans, were renowned both as horse-breeders and as fierce mounted warriors. Hadrian's military policy, unlike that of his predecessor, the soldier emperor Trajan, was one of defence rather than offence. But an offensive operation against the Alans, designed to drive them back across the mountains and seal the western passes from the Caucasus, had a defensive objective, that of securing existing Roman territory and that of Rome's allies.

Now that much of the pressure had been taken off the Roman military in Judea, sufficient Roman resources could be redirected for an offensive against the Alans. The man chosen to lead the operation was Flavianus Arrianus, or Arrian, as later writers would dub him. Then Roman governor of the province of Cappadocia, Arrian had been born at Nicomedia in Bithynia around AD 90. Working his way up the Roman promotional ladder, Arrian had entered the Senate in Rome in approximately AD 120, becoming a consul ten years later.

To reach the Senate and later achieve a consulship, Arrian had to serve as a junior officer with Rome's auxiliary forces and legions, the culmination of his military career being the command of a legion. During this early stage of his career he had almost certainly served in Britain, for in one of his written works, he describes the Britons' chariot horses as if from first-hand knowledge. Of Greek stock, Arrian was a fan of Alexander the Great, writing a biography of the Greek king in seven volumes which was to become one of our key sources on Alexander and his military conquests.

Arrian also wrote a handbook on military matters, which, while hankering back to the Greek-style military of Alexander, who had used armies made up of phalanxes of spearmen, still reveals much about the Roman army of Arrian's day, and earlier. Arrian was a man who both led from the front and who organized his military campaigns in fine detail, well in advance. A copy of his orders for the AD 135 expedition against the Alans, *Aries contra Alanos*, has come down to us, and from this we have an excellent idea of how the mission developed.

At his immediate disposal for the campaign, Arrian had the 15th Apollinaris Legion at Satala in Cappadocia. This, Arrian knew, was a vastly experienced legion with a lengthy history; it had a long roll of battle honours in the east and in Europe, including the First Jewish Revolt and the Dacian Wars. The 15th would form the core of Arrian's army, and the legion's commander, the legate Marcus Vettius Valens, would be Arrian's second-in-command.

To the 15th, Arrian added his other locally based legion, the 12th Fulminata, which had been based at Melitene in Cappadocia since taking part in the First Jewish War in AD 66–70. For this campaign, the 12th Fulminata was led by its senior tribune, just as it had been during the Jewish War. The 12th had lost both its eagle and its commander to the Jewish rebels in AD 66, and it is tempting to think that, after that disgrace, the legion was not given a commander of senatorial rank.

One of the auxiliary units in Arrian's army was the 1st Apamenorum Cohort, an equitata unit of both horse and foot archers raised at Apamea in Syria. For some time prior to this, the unit had been based in Egypt, but more recently, before being sent up to Cappadocia, it had probably taken part in Sextus Severus' operations in Judea. Two factors indicate that this Alani operation was not a knee-jerk offensive initiated locally, but was an operation planned and directed by the Palatium in Rome. Firstly, for Arrian to lead the legions based in Cappadocia out of his province he required specific permission from the emperor; otherwise, he was breaking the law and could be declared an enemy of the state by the Senate. Arrian, therefore, had been granted special powers by Hadrian for this operation, as Severus had been in Judea.

Secondly, of the auxiliary units tasked with the Alani operation, six were specialist units of foot and horse archers, indicating that they had been very carefully chosen for this mission. This was the single largest concentration of archers in any Roman province at that time. In Britain, for example, there was then not a single unit of archers, while there was just one in Syria. [Hold., *DRA*, *ADRH*] Arrian's planned tactics for the operation against the Alans would depend heavily on archers, indicating that he had specifically asked for the bowmen. Alternatively, knowing that the Alans, like so many Eastern tribes, were themselves strong in archers and were all mounted, the Palatium may have chosen to equip Arrian with a large contingent of bowmen to enable him to fight fire with fire.

Auxiliary units and allied units supplied by Roman allies marched to Armenia Minor either late in the autumn of AD 134, to spend the winter in Cappadocia or Armenia Minor, or made the journey at the beginning of the spring of AD 135. Either way, before the spring of 135 was over, all the elements of Arrian's army including local troops had come together at the assembly point. From Caesarea Mazaka, capital of Lesser Armenia, Arrian's army marched east towards the Caucasus, intent on throwing the Alans back across the mountains.

Arrian's army, in addition to the two legions, comprised four cavalry alae including one of dark-skinned Moors, a force of allied cavalry from the Getae tribe, originally from Thrace, and a large number of horse archers supplied by the king of Armenia. For auxiliary infantry, Arrian had ten cohorts of auxiliary light infantry, as well as mounted infantry and foot and horse archers – not all of them at full strength according the Arrian's figures – and two groups of fighters of unspecified size, provided by Roman allies. In all, there were over 20,000 men in the Roman force.

It seems that Arrian had personally scouted the territory into which his troops were now marching. Either that, or someone whose judgment he trusted implicitly had scouted for him. For, based on prior knowledge of the locale, Arrian had chosen a particular valley in the foothills of the Caucasus where he intended to fight the Alans after they crossed the mountains – in his orders to his officers he wrote of 'the appointed place' for the battle. [Arr., *EAA*, 11] This was a valley where the infantry could readily form up in its battle lines on the flat, with rising ground on either flank where Arrian planned to post archers and stone-throwers.

Arrian also very carefully dictated the order of march. A stickler for orderly formations, he knew that Roman armies on the march – such as that of Varus in the Teutoburg Forest in Germany in AD 9 – had been destroyed while proceeding in disorder, by enemies sometimes inferior in numbers and/or equipment. Arrian's orderly formation as he led the army east in AD 135 began with cavalry scouts well out in advance, in pairs. The army's vanguard consisted of auxiliary cavalry, infantry and archers, followed by the two legions, then carts carrying Arrian's catapults, with horse archers protecting the flanks. More auxiliaries followed, then the main baggage train, with a cavalry rearguard provided by Getae allies.

On Arrian's orders, his troops marched in silence; the only sounds were those of tramping feet and hoofs, rolling wheels, the tinkling of the bells on the thousands of mules in the baggage train, and the rattle of harness and equipment. Each unit looked much the same as the next, with similar uniforms and equipment. Frequently the only way to tell one from the other was to look at the unit designs on their shields. Only the allied Armenian horse archers stood out, in their loose trousers and fish-scale armour, riding horses that also sported armour.

On reaching the chosen valley – the exact location is unknown – mounted scouts were sent by Arrian to clamber up into the surrounding heights to keep watch for the enemy. Meanwhile, the Roman cavalry formed up in a vast square on the flat ground, ready to defend the infantry should the enemy appear unexpectedly. Inside the cavalry screen, and still without uttering a word, the Roman infantry armed themselves with additional ammunition from the baggage train, and then moved to their prearranged battle positions.

Arrian's army, following the battle plan he had carefully mapped out back in Mazaka, spread across the plain and up on to the rising ground on either side of it. Arrian did not use the standard Roman formation for countering cavalry attack – the wedge. Instead, the majority of his front line was flat and straight. The 15th Apollinaris Legion took the right side of the battlefront, four lines deep. The legion's commander, Valens, was to command all troops on the right – which included auxiliary light infantry, stone throwers and horse archers from Armenia under their chiefs Vasakes and Artbelos. Here, Arrian introduced a tactic of his own creation – these units on the wing curved around the foothills to project ahead of the straight battlefront, like the horn of a bull.

The 12th Fulminata Legion occupied the left of the battlefront, again four lines deep. Its tribune commanded the left of the line. As on the right, there were light infantry, horse archers and cavalry stationed on the left flank, likewise following the rising ground to form a projecting horn. The cavalry were stationed in front of the infantry on the wings, with orders not to hurl their lances at the enemy but to extend them in front, with each trooper running the rear part of his lance along the flank of his horse for added strength. These projecting lances formed a sharp wall to discourage the enemy from approaching the Roman wings, and prevented the Alans from reaching the archers stationed behind the cavalry.

Immediately behind these front lines, to the left and right, the artillery was quickly set up, the gunners under orders to fire their missiles over the heads of the legionaries and auxiliaries lined up in front of them. A long line of auxiliaries including the foot archers extended between the catapults, behind the legion lines. Arrian positioned himself to the rear of the lines of archers, with more catapults. Here, from his saddle, the general could see over the archers to the legion lines, and could quickly spot any problems that might develop with the legions – the core of his army – and relay orders to correct those problems. [Arr., *EAA*, 23]

The commander-in-chief was accompanied by his staff, all mounted, including his personal standard-bearer and trumpeter, and the governor's bodyguard – his mounted *equites singulares*, who were detached from various cavalry units for the prestigious task of providing protection for Arrian, plus 200 hand-picked legionaries from the 15th Apollinaris and 100 carriers of light spears.

Arrian's dispositions meant that the Romans blocked the valley. The Alans' passage would only be over the dead bodies of Arrian's men. Whether the planned battle actually took place or not is not recorded, but the outcome of Arrian's campaign against the Alans suggests that it did. If the battle ran according to Arrian's plan, it went with Arrian sending cavalry to encourage the Alans to pursue them, and so draw them into the the valley where the Romans waited. On the other hand, perhaps the nomadic Alans were simply moving west now that the winter had passed and the snows in the mountain passes had melted, and Arrian stood in their way.

The Alans approached from the northeast. Their exact number is unknown, but they were a large tribe and this force was probably not less than 10,000 strong; it may well have numbered many more men. They were all mounted, with, Arrian noted, both riders and their mounts lightly armoured. [Arr., *EAA*, 31] Confident of their ability to ride down any foot soldiers foolish enough to oppose them, the Alans would have enthusiastically charged the stationary Roman army in their path.

Because the horns of the Roman battle line occupied high ground, the charge of the Alans funnelled through the valley to crash into the Roman legions on the flat ground in the centre, ignoring the auxiliaries on the wings. On Arrian's orders, the

Roman army was silent as the thousands of barbarian horsemen pounded towards them armed with long lances, swords and battleaxes.

The commander-in-chief's trumpeter sounded a call. The curved, rectangular shields of the four lines of legionaries of the 12th and 15th came up from the rest position, and the men of the first three lines locked their shields together to create three solid walls. The second and third lines shuffled forward, until they had created a dense mass of men and shields. There they stood, like sardines in a can, with shields raised and left foot forward, ready to take the impact of the charging horsemen. Behind them, the men of the fourth legionary line stood back a little in the throwing stance, with a javelin in their right hand.

On the wings, stone-throwers and javelin-throwers stood ready to release their missiles; they were under orders to concentrate their fire on a particular point in the front ranks of the charging enemy cavalry. Behind them, the catapults had been drawn into the firing position and loaded with long, metal-tipped bolts. On the wings and in a close-packed line stretching along behind the legions, the archers raised their bows to the heavens and drew back their first arrows.

On his horse, Arrian waited, watching the Alani charge bring the mass of enemy horsemen closer and closer. Timing was critical; the general could not afford to give his order too soon, or too late. Around him, men and horses would have been becoming edgy. Arrian was waiting for the precisely the right moment. He had to allow time for his order to be transmitted, first by his trumpeter, then by the trumpeters of the legions, then for the troops to react and for their missiles to fly to the point where Arrian wanted them to land, right at the forefront of the enemy charge.

Now, the general gave the much anticipated order. As Arrian noted in his *Tactical Handbook*, the noise of battle could sometimes make it difficult for the troops to hear commands. For this reason, the general's banner would visually show what the latest command was. As the keyed-up troops heard the trumpet call they had been waiting for, the general's banner also motioned – with the standard-bearer possibly quickly pumping it up and down. Arrian's pre-battle orders required his men at this moment to 'all cry out most grandly and frightfully to [the god] Ares' and let fly with their missiles. [Arr., *EAA*, 25]

The men of the first three lines of the legions, waiting to receive the enemy charge with their raised shields hard up against their left shoulders, now would have seen and heard thousands of arrows and catapult bolts fly over their heads from behind them. They saw the missiles fall from the sky like rain, right on to the front ranks of the mass of charging horsemen. Dead and dying horses would be going down; others shying in terror. Riders would be toppling from the saddle with multiple wounds. The massive charge had its own momentum, and continued forward, over the top of fallen men and steeds.

Another Roman trumpet call. The bowmen had swiftly reloaded; they fired again. From the flanks, the shorter range missiles now began to fly. Stones, arrows and javelins filled the air, coming in from the 'horns' towards the centre of the charging mass. At the same time, the legionaries of the fourth line let fly with their javelins, then reached for their next missile. The catapults had reloaded; with a thwack and a whoosh they too let fly, and their missiles again soared over the heads of the infantry. 'Altogether,' Arrian wrote in his battle plan, 'the shooting should be from all sides, to one dense point, for the confusion of horses and the destruction of the enemy.' [Arr., *EAA*, 25]

The Alans' horse charge would have devolved into chaos. Some of the Alans would have made it through the carnage and confusion caused by the missiles, which continued to fall from the sky in their thousands, to press home the attack. The legionary shield line held firm; horses literally bounced off it. As the Alans closed in with lances, swords and axes, the men of the legionary front line pushed javelins out through slender gaps in their shield line, and jabbed into the nearest horses. With shrieks of pain horses reared up, badly injured, or fell dead to the ground, dislodging their riders.

Once confronted by a solid legionary wall, the Alani cavalry was brought to a halt. From the rear, missiles flew over the heads of the tightly packed front lines of Arrian's two legions, to impale the Alans.

The charge had come to a rude halt. Alan riders further back continued to push forward, crushing comrades against the shield line. With the momentum of the charge gone, using their small shields to try to protect themselves from the hail of missiles, and with their horses going down under them or going mad with fear, panic broke out in the Alani ranks. More and more horsemen withdrew from the fight in wide-eyed terror.

If the enemy were repulsed by his tactics, Arrian had written, his foot soldiers were to advance, in good order, to give pursuit and drive home the advantage. As for the Roman cavalry on the wings, half – those in the frontal formations on the 'horns' – were permitted to charge in pursuit, while the remainder were under strict orders to follow in formation and at the trot. If the enemy continued to flee, once the horses of the first division of pursuing Roman cavalry tired, then the second division was permitted to continue the chase and complete the destruction of the enemy. They were under orders not to throw javelins at the Alans but to get in close on their heels and butcher them in the saddle, or on the ground if their horses went down, with sword and axe.

On the other hand, should the enemy regroup and suddenly wheel to stage a counter-attack, a common tactic among the cavalry of eastern peoples, the cavalry that were slowly following up the pursuit could then charge to the attack. To prevent the enemy from wheeling about, Arrian placed the Armenian horse archers with the first cavalry division, and they had orders to keep up a discouraging rate of fire as they took part in the pursuit.

Apparently, Arrian's battle went precisely to his carefully conceived plan: the Alans were slaughtered in their thousands and the survivors fled back across the mountains. According to Dio, the Alans then not only accepted gifts from the king of Armenia and agreed not to invade his country, but they 'also stood in dread of Flavius Arrianus'. [Dio, LXIX, 15] For the Alans to be in dread of Arrian, who had not possessed a significant military reputation prior to his Cappadocian appointment, strongly suggests that they had suffered a terrible defeat at the hands of his army.

Arrian's apparently stunning victory had another result, for Dio reported that the Iazyges Germans, who had gone to war with Rome during the reign of Domitian and who would launch a savage new war during the reign of Marcus Aurelius, less than thirty years later, quickly sent envoys to Hadrian in Rome following the withdrawal of the Alans, for they 'wished to confirm the peace'. [Ibid.] The Armenians also sent envoys to Hadrian in Rome blaming Pharasmanes, the Iberian king, for encouraging the Alan invasion. Pharasmanes himself would later travel to Rome to vow his allegiance to the Roman emperor.

It would be another 200 years before the Alans pitted themselves against the might of Rome in strength, and then it would be in the West. After their sound defeat by Arrian, the Alans would not again take the road south to the Roman East. As for the men of the two legions who had taken part in the battle, there was the glory of a great victory, and a cheap one at that. And there was booty galore from the dead Alans and their horses – which were famously decorated with gold horse ornaments.

ARRIAN'S ORDER OF BATTLE

This is the most detailed extant order of battle for any Imperial Roman army.

ARMY COMMANDER:
Flavius Arrianus, Propraetor of Cappadocia.

DEPUTY COMMANDER:
Marcus Vettius Valens, legate of the 15th Apollinaris Legion.

LEGIONS:
15th Apollinaris Legion, normally stationed at Satala, Cappadocia. Commanded by the legate Valens (above).

12th Fulminata Legion, normally stationed at Melitene, Cappadocia. Commanded by its senior tribune.

ARTILLERY:
Approximately 110 spear-throwing catapults (55, the standard legion complement, from each of the two legions), operated by men from the legions.

CAVALRY:
1st Ala Augusta Gemina Colonorum. From Lesser Armenia, formed by combination with another existing unit, this wing had fought in the Second Jewish War. It is probable that casualties in that conflict had been so high that it had been necessary to combine this wing with another.

1st Ala Ulpian Dacorum. Raised in Syria during the reign of Trajan; these troopers had also fought in the Second Jewish War.

2nd Ala Gallorum. Raised in Galatia.

2nd Ala Ulpian Auriana. Raised in Spain by Trajan.

Getae allied cavalry, strength unknown. Commanded by a tribal leader.

INFANTRY:
1st Cohort Apula CR. Italian light infantry; former slaves. Commanded by the Roman prefect Secundius.

1st Cohort Bosporanorum Sagittaria. Foot archers, raised in the kingdom of the Bosporus.

Commanded by Lamprocles, a Bosporan who, like many of his countrymen, descended from Greek settlers.

1st Cohort Germanorum. A milliaria equitata unit from northern Gaul, of approximately 1,000 light infantry and mounted infantry. Although labelled Germans, the men of this unit were described as Celts by Arrian. Their mounted element was led by a senior centurion from one of Arrian's legions.

1st Cohort Italica Volunt CR. Former slaves, recruited in Italy. Commanded by the Roman prefect Pulcher.

1st Cohort Ituraeorum Sagittaria. Arabian foot archers. Their ancestors had been nomads.

1st Cohort Numidarum Sagittaria. Equitata unit of foot archers and horse archers from Numidia in North Africa. Commanded by the Numidian prefect Beros.

1st Cohort Raetorum. Spearmen from Raetia, raised in the mountains of the Tyrol. Commanded by the Greek-born prefect Daphnes of Corinth.

3rd Cohort Augusta Cyrenaica Sagittaria. Foot archers from Cyrenaica in North Africa.

3rd Cohort Ulpian Petraeorum Sagittaria. Horse archers from Arabia Petraea.

Unspecified light infantry cohort of from Trapezous (modern Trabzon) on the Black Sea coast of Pontus. Could be any one of three units known to then be stationed in Cappadocia.

ALLIED INFANTRY AND ARCHERS: Armenian horse archers. Unspecified number. Under their chieftains Vasakes and Arbelos.

Lesser Armenian slingers. Unspecified number.

Unspecified number of allied spearmen from River Rhixia, east of the Black Sea.

In Britain, the 10-foot-high (3-metre) earthen Antonine Wall, erected AD 142–143 by the emperor Antoninus Pius, ran for 36.5 miles (58.5 kilometres) from the River Clyde to the Firth of Forth, 100 miles (160 kilometres) north of Hadrian's Wall. By AD 196 it was abandoned, with Roman troops withdrawing to Hadrian's Wall.

AD 161

XLIX. A LEGION DESTROYED
Overrun by the Parthians

On 7 March in the year AD 161, 74-year-old Antoninus Pius, Roman emperor for the past twenty-two years, died peacefully in his sleep. His death uniquely left Rome with two emperors – his adopted sons Marcus Aurelius and Lucius Verus. Seeing this as a time when Rome could be expected to be weak and indecisive, Vologases III, king of Rome's age-old enemy in the East, Parthia, gathered his forces and invaded Armenia, which had been within Rome's sway since the time of Trajan.

An unidentified legion, at that time stationed at Elegeia in Armenia and commanded by Publius Aelius Severianus, stood in the way of the Parthian invasion. Given no warning, the legion was surprised at or near its base by the Parthian invaders. Scholars are divided as to which legion this was, as several legions disappeared from the records during this century. It is most likely to have been the 22nd Deiotariana, which had been stationed in the East since its inception 191 years before.

On an inscription in Rome from later in the reign of Marcus Aurelius, the 22nd Deiotariana Legion was missing from a listing of the twenty-eight legions then in existence. [*ILS*, 2288] The other possible candidate for destruction at Elegeia, the 9th Hispana Legion, had been last heard of forty years before on the far side of the Roman world, in Britain. The weight of evidence supports an old scenario that the 9th Hispana was wiped out in Scotland in AD 122. [*See pages 421–8*] It is likely that the 22nd Deiotariana had been based in Armenia ever since Arrian's defeat of the Alans in Lesser Armenia in AD 135, removed from the backwater of Egypt to front-line Armenia by the defensively minded Emperor Hadrian as a deterrent against further barbarian incursions.

Vologases commenced the invasion of Armenia by 'hemming in on all sides the Roman legion under Severianus,' wrote Dio, 'then shooting down and destroying the whole force, leaders and all'. [Dio, LXXI. 1] Cataphracts, heavily armoured cavalrymen whose powerful horses also carried armour, formed the core of Parthian armies. But the Parthian mainstay was the mounted horse archer, who, with small nimble mounts, galloped in to launch a quiver of arrows before darting away again. Infantry opponents caught in the open could be mown down by their hail of arrows, and this appears to have been the fate of the 22nd Deiotariana Legion.

Once the news reached Rome that a legion had been annihilated by the Parthians, and that the 'powerful and formidable' Vologases was advancing against the cities of the province of Syria, 40-year-old Marcus Aurelius acted quickly, dispatching his 31-year-old adoptive brother and co-emperor Lucius Verus to the East to take charge. [Dio, LXXI, 2] Lucius sailed to Syria from Brundisium, taking several legions and a large part of the Misene Fleet with him; the warships would remain in the East throughout the coming war. [Starr, VIII]

The European legions accompanying Lucius for this operation were the 1st Minervia from Bonna on the Rhine, the 2nd Adiutrix from Aquincum on the Danube, and the 5th Macedonica from Troesmis in Moesia. All three seasick legions had landed at Laodicea in Syria by the end of AD 161. They would be away from their home bases for five years.

The destruction of a legion in Armenia occurred in the first year of the joint rule of Marcus Aurelius, depicted in this bust, and his co-emperor Lucius Verus.

Lucius appointed the governor of Syria, Gaius Avidius Cassius, to command the counter-offensive, and over the winter Lucius 'made all the dispositions and assembled all the supplies for the war', knowing that with the new year Vologases would launch a major attack on Syria aided by allies from east of the Euphrates. [Dio, LXXI, 2]

AD 162–166
L. CASSIUS' PARTHIAN WAR
Conquering for Marcus Aurelius

A Syrian, born at Cyrrus, Gaius Avidius Cassius was the son of a Greek freedman, Helidorus, who had been Hadrian's secretary of correspondence and later served as Prefect of Egypt. Exhibiting great ability and loyalty, Cassius had risen above his father's freedman status to enter the Senate, becoming a praetor and serving as a consul before receiving the governorship of Syria, the most prestigious and highly paid of the provincial postings.

Cassius could potentially draw on eleven legions for this operation against Vologases. There were the three legions that Lucius had brought with him from Europe, as well as the two legions based in Syria, the 3rd Gallica and 4th Scythica, plus those stationed in nearby provinces – the 3rd Cyrenaica in Arabia, 10th Fretensis in Judea, and the 12th Fulminata and 15th Apollinaris in Cappadocia. Some of the eastern-based legions would take part in the offensive complete, others would send vexillations while leaving some cohorts garrisoning their frontier bases. Perhaps the 2nd Traiana at Nicopolis in Egypt was the only legion left undisturbed.

The eleventh legion in the region, the 16th Flavia, had been based at Samosata in southwest Armenia ever since Trajan's Parthian War. Dio writes that Marcus Statius Priscus, imperial legate in Armenia and commander of the 16th Flavia, placed a 'garrison of Romans' at the 'new city' in Armenia immediately after Vologases' invasion. [Dio, LXXI, 3] In the northeast, the city of Artaxata, Armenia's ancient royal capital and today's city of Yerevan, had been destroyed in AD 64 by Roman general Corbulo when he had overrun Armenia during Nero's reign. King Tiridates of Armenia, given his throne by Nero on condition that he swear loyalty to Rome, had built a new city on the ruins of Artaxata, calling it Neronia in honour of Nero. This was Dio's 'new city'.

It is clear that, on hearing of the Parthian invasion of Armenia, and of the fate of the 22nd Deiotariana, Priscus had marched 16th Flavia Legion north from the Samosata legion base to the new city at Artaxata. Leaving the majority of the legion's cohorts to garrison the city, Priscus and the remaining elements of the 16th Flavia escorted the king of Armenia, Sohaemus, out of the country to safety in Syria. Those 16th Flavia cohorts had been cut off at Artaxata ever since, with the Parthian army between them and Roman forces to the south. Part of Cassius' task now was to push a relief force through to the legionaries trapped at Artaxata. But first, he had to stop the rampaging Parthian army in its tracks, before it ravaged the wealthy cities and mini-states of Syria.

For two years, beginning in the spring of AD 162, Cassius and his legions fought the Parthians on Rome's Syrian doorstep. This 'noble stand' by Cassius' legions tested the patience of Vologases' allies, many of whom, by early AD 164, had deserted the Parthians, and Vologases begrudgingly 'began to retire' from Syria. [Dio, LXXI, 2] Now Cassius could go on the offensive.

The Roman general divided his army in two. One part he gave to legion commanders Publius Martius Verus, whose task was to drive northeast to Artaxata. With him went exiled King Sohaemus and his entourage. 'This general,' said Dio, referring to

Ctesiphon, one of the Parthian capitals, ruins of which are seen here today, was the target of various Roman invasions.

Martius Verus, 'thanks to the terror inspired by his arms and to the natural good judgment that he showed in every situation, kept pressing vigorously forward' against the Parthians to the north. [Dio, LXXI, 3]

Not only did Martius Verus have the ability to overpower the enemy with his force of arms, said Dio, he was also a brilliant strategist who anticipated and out-thought his opponents at every turn. This was 'the true strength of a general', in Dio's opinion. But, if necessary, the general also parlayed with the enemy, giving them promises and gifts. [Ibid.] In this way, sometimes fighting, sometimes parlaying, Martius Verus and his legions ground north through mountain valleys on a slow but determined advance towards Artaxata.

At the same time, with the Parthians distracted by Martius Verus' advance and throwing the majority of their forces against him, Cassius led the balance of the Roman army east into Parthia. Throwing a bridge of boats across the Euphrates, he protected it with wooden towers and screens. Legion catapults on the towers, and archers behind the screens, drove off a force of enemy spearmen on the far bank, allowing tens of thousands of Roman troops to pour across the Euphrates. Cassius then turned southeast, and followed the river towards the city of Seleucia, and the Parthian capital, Ctesiphon.

Now Vologases was forced to divide his forces in an attempt to counter both Roman offensives. Martius Verus, facing weakened opposition, drove on to Artaxata and relieved the 16th Flavia garrison. He arrived just in time; the 16th Flavia legionaries, cut off for two years and starved and deprived of their commander, had mutinied against their officers by the time Martius Verus reached the city. 'He took pains, by word and by deed, to bring them to a better temper,' said Dio, and, reunited with their commander and the rest of the legion, they returned to the command of their officers. Verus now reinstalled King Sohaemus on his throne and 'made this place [Artaxata] the foremost city of Armenia'. [Ibid.]

To the south, Cassius' army drove to the Tigris river in today's central Iraq, where he camped for the winter. The following year, AD 165, after marching 800 miles (1,290 kilometres) since leaving Antioch, Cassius took Seleucia. The city held a population variously estimated at between 300,000 and 600,000, including a large Jewish community and many people of Greek extraction. The legions sacked and razed the 500-year-old city, which would never be rebuilt. Among the spoils removed from burning Seleucia was a massive statue of Apollo Comaeus torn from its pedestal in a Parthian temple. Taken to Rome, it would be installed in the temple to Apollo on the Palatine Hill. [Amm., 11, xxiii, 6, 24]

Crossing the Tigris river, Cassius' army fought its way into nearby Ctesiphon, looted Vologases' palace, then put it to the torch. But this was the extent of the Roman conquest. Trajan had reached Ctesiphon in his AD 114–116 campaign, only to withdraw. And so it was with Cassius. In inhospitable country, a long way from support and with vulnerable communications, after coming all this way Cassius turned his army around, and set off back to Syria.

But it would not be an easy passage for Cassius. 'In returning,' said Dio, 'he lost a great many of his soldiers through famine and disease.' With Roman corpses lining the route of his withdrawal, Cassius eventually 'got back to Syria with the survivors'. Co-emperor Lucius, waiting anxiously at Antioch, was overjoyed at Cassius' success. Overlooking Cassius' high casualty rate, 'Lucius gloried in these exploits, and took great pride in them'. [Dio, LXXI, 2]

Armenia had been reclaimed, the eastern frontier stabilized, and the Parthians punished, but at the price of a legion lost and many thousands of other casualties. As Lucius was celebrating at Antioch an urgent dispatch arrived from his co-emperor Marcus Aurelius – bring back the European legions at once, for the Germans had flooded across the Danube frontier.

The three legions that returned to their bases on the Danube and Rhine in AD 166 took back more than just spoils from Parthia; they brought back 'the germ of that pestilence,' said Ammianus Marcellinus, 'which, after generating the virulence of incurable diseases in the time of the same [Lucius] and Marcus [Aurelius] polluted everything with contagion and death, from the frontiers of Persia all the way to the Rhine and Gaul'. [Amm., II, xxiii, 6, 24] The plague brought back by the victorious legionaries would sweep through Europe.

AD 166–175
LI. MARCUS AURELIUS' DANUBE WARS
Decade of death

Marcus Aurelius could not wait for the return of Lucius and his legions from the East. To counter German tribes now threatening Italy, he urgently raised two new legions, in Italy, the 1st Italica and 2nd Italica. By the end of AD 165, both new legions were stationed at the city of Aquileia in northeastern Italy. This was the first time in 200 years, apart from the civil war of AD 68–69, that legions had been stationed in Italy, and the move signalled the seriousness of Rome's situation.

As soon as the seasonal winds had brought Lucius and his three depleted legions back to Italy by sea, Marcus and Lucius sat down to plan how they would counter the German tribes pressuring the northern frontier. Dacia, the only Roman province north of the Danube, and with just the 13th Gemina Legion at Apulum, stood particularly exposed. The 5th Macedonica Legion had been based at Novae in Moesia prior to going to the East; now, Marcus and Lucius sent it to Dacia, to establish a base at Potaissa.

That summer of AD 166, 6,000 Suebi of the Langobardi and Obii tribes from along the Elbe in northwestern Germany crossed the Danube into Pannonia. But their incursion was cut short by Praetorian Prefect Marcus Macrinus Vindex. Sent north by Marcus and Lucius with a cavalry column, Vindex intercepted the Germans and delayed the enemy until joined by infantry. 'The barbarians were completely routed,' said Dio. As a result, King Ballomarius of the Marcomanni, and ten other German leaders met with the governor of Pannonia, Jallius Bassus, to discuss a peace treaty. [Dio, LXXII, 3]

The Marcomanni and their cousins the Quadi and Iazyges had been allies of Rome since the reign of Augustus, with just one blemish on their record when the Marcomanni had made a pre-emptive strike into Pannonia during the reign of Domi-

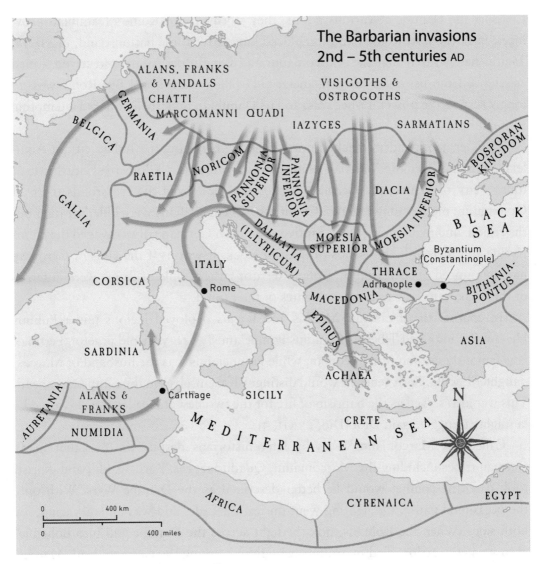

The Barbarian invasions
2nd – 5th centuries AD

tian. Time and again over two centuries, the Marcomanni had sided with Rome for the sake of peace. As for the Iazyges, they had not even complained when Trajan kept a parcel of their territory won from the Dacians and incorporated it into the province of Dacia. The German leaders now ratified a peace treaty with the Roman governor, the raiders withdrew across the Danube, and all seemed well again on the frontier.

But in AD 167, more German tribes came flooding down through Raetia, Noricum and Pannonia and into northern Italy. This time, intent on plunder and unimpressed by Rome's imperial duopoly, the Marcomanni, Quadi and Iazyges joined the surge.

Crossing the Danube at various points, they stormed into Rome's Danubian provinces. In times past, Rome had even placed kings over these nations, and, in AD 98, Tacitus had written that the Marcomanni and Quadi 'occasionally received armed assistance from us; more often financial aid'. [Tac., *Germ.*, 42] But Rome was no longer seen as the power it once was, and its Danubian underbelly offered a tempting route to riches.

The German invaders reached northern Italy, besieging the Italian city of Aquileia, sweeping over the Venetian plain, and, 50 miles (80 kilometres) northeast of today's city of Venice, the Germans sacked and destroyed the crossroads town of Opitergium, modern-day Oderzo. Countless Roman civilians were killed throughout the region, and many more taken captive as a dozen German tribes ravaged the countryside and drove off thousands of head of stock. It was as if the gods of Germany had announced open season on Roman territory; the people of Rome were in terror of the barbarians reaching the very gates of the capital.

To counter the invasions, Marcus and Lucius deployed legions under Publius Helvius Pertinax and Tiberius Claudius Pompeianus. A 40-year-old praetor, Pertinax was famously the son of a freedman, while Pompeianus was the husband of Marcus' daughter Lucilla. Both generals would distinguish themselves in the campaigns ahead. This war also served as the baptism of fire for the two new Italica legions. It would be 'a mighty struggle,' said Dio. [Dio, LXXII, 3]

Called the Marcomanni Wars by later historians despite the fact that many German tribes including the Marcomanni, Quadi, Iazyges, Buri, Vandili and Naristi took part, the conflict would be better described as the Danube Wars. With only the occasional pause, the fighting went on for a decade, and was all embracing, for both sides. When the Romans took the fight across the Danube and into Bohemia, even women warriors clad in armour were found among the German dead. Marcus' co-emperor Lucius did not live to see the end of it; he died in AD 169; as the result of poisoning, according to Dio. The following year, several lesser German tribes sued for peace, but it was when the Quadi came to the treaty table that year that it seemed as if 'a brilliant victory' had been gained by Rome. [Ibid.]

To be closer to the battlefront, Marcus had relocated from Rome to Carnuntum, modern-day Petronell in Austria, 20 miles (32 kilometres) east of Vienna. Carnuntum was a pleasant if undistinguished Pannonian village in rolling hills south of the wandering Danube. The permanent stone-walled base of the 14th Gemina Martia Victrix

Legion stood here. Marcus' wife, the empress Faustina, who was the daughter of the previous emperor Antoninus Pius, joined Marcus at Carnuntum.

There at Carnuntum in AD 170, the emperor received peace envoys from Furtius, king of the Quadi. To seal the peace, the Quadi delivered thousands of captured horses and cattle into Roman hands, and promised to hand over 13,000 Roman captives and military deserters at once. Marcus granted the Quadi peace, in the hope, said Dio, that this would separate them from the Marcomanni. Furtius also promised not to accept Marcomanni or Iazyge fugitives, nor to let them pass through Quadi territory. Although he agreed to the peace with them, Marcus banned the Quadi from markets in Roman territory while the war lasted, in case other Germans posed as Quadi to reconnoitre Roman positions and purchase provisions. [Dio, LXXII, 11]

Before the year was out, several other German tribes surrendered. Marcus formed their fittest fighting men and returned deserters into auxiliary units and sent them to serve in the farthest reaches of the empire. Other surrendered Germans were settled on land in Dacia, Pannonia, Moesia, the Rhine provinces, and even in Italy. Some were settled in the Italian naval city of Ravenna, but that proved a mistake – dazzled by the wealth around them, the Germans rose up before long and seized control of the city. They were soon dealt with, probably by marines and sailors from the Ravenna Fleet, and removed from the country. Marcus would not make the same error again.

In AD 171, while Marcus was launching into the writing of his famous Meditations at Carnuntum, one of his armies, led by Praetorian Prefect Vindex, was defeated in Bohemia by the Marcomanni, with Vindex himself falling. Marcus, never a well man, was forced to assume a more prominent military role, and personally led one of his armies on the next campaign against the Iazyges. Marcus was so frail and sickly, said Dio, that when he stepped up on to the tribunal to address an assembly of his troops one wintry day he was chilled by the cold and could not open his mouth, and had to retire to the warmth of his praetorium. [Dio, LXXII, 6]

In Bohemia, the legions under Pertinax and Pompeianus fought the Marcomanni to a standstill, and by AD 172 the king of the Marcomanni, Ballomarus, had sealed a peace treaty with Marcus and withdrawn from the conflict. 'In view of the fact they had fulfilled all the conditions imposed on them, albeit grudgingly and reluctantly', Marcus restored to the tribe half of what had previously been considered a neutral zone along the northern bank of the Danube, permitting them to settle to within 5 miles (8 kilometres) of the river. Both sides exchanged prisoners, and days for regular trading between Roman and Marcomanni merchants were established. [Dio, LXXII, 15]

In theory, both the Quadi and the Marcomanni were now out of the war, leaving just the Iazyges further east to confront. But Marcus did not trust the Quadi. Since King Furtius had signed the peace treaty he had been overthrown by his own people, who had given themselves a new king, Ariogaesus. And under the new king's reign, contrary to the peace conditions signed by his predecessor, Marcomanni fugitives fleeing Roman troops were helped by the Quadi.

When envoys came to Marcus from Ariogaesus to confirm the treaty signed by Furtius and offering to return another 50,000 Roman prisoners, the emperor steadfastly refused to recognize the new king. Furtius had been placed over the Quadi by Antoninus Pius, Marcus said, and he reserved the right to appoint a king of the Quadi of his choice. The envoys of Ariogaesus were sent away empty-handed. To encourage the Quadi to hand over their new ruler, Marcus offered a reward for Ariogaesus, alive, of 100,000 sesterces (the equivalent of eighty-three years' salary for a legionary), half that for his head. [Ibid.]

When the Quadi failed to hand over their new king, Marcus lost patience with them. They did send back some Roman captives, but only the old and infirm; or, if they were in good physical condition, the Quadi retained the captives' families so the men would come back to their territory to be with their loved ones. Marcus determined that the only way that Rome could remove the threat posed by the Quadi was with the sword.

AD 174
LII. THE THUNDERING 12TH
Triumphing for Marcus

With the Danube Wars dragging on and casualties mounting, Marcus Aurelius sent for reinforcements from the East. By the summer of AD 174, the 12th Fulminata Legion had arrived in Pannonia from its long-time base at Melitene in Cappadocia. The 12th Fulminata Legion had not long been on the Danube when it was called out to follow the emperor to intercept a Quadi offensive. Led by King Ariogaesus, the tribe had re-entered the war, launching a surprise campaign across the Danube.

Marcus, with just the newly arrived 12th Fulminata plus auxiliaries and no doubt elements of the Praetorian Guard and Singularian Horse, marched to deal with them.

At the height of summer, on a battlefield in Pannonia, the two armies met. It was on ground favourable to the Quadi, and a blisteringly hot day, according to Dio, when the German tribesmen, 'far superior in numbers', apparently caught the legionaries on the march early one morning. [Dio, LXXII, 8]

'Only a few of them have swords or large lances,' Tacitus wrote of German warriors. 'They carry spears called *framea* in their language, with short and narrow blades.' These were so sharp and easy to handle that they could be used at close quarters or in long-range fighting, for the Germans could hurl them great distances. The tribesmen frequently went into battle naked, or merely wearing a short cloak. Occasionally a breastplate could be seen, and here and there a helmet of metal or leather. Their most distinctive piece of equipment was the small wooden shield, painted with bright colours. Singing battle songs in honour of Donar, the German Hercules, and shaking their weapons at the Romans, the barefoot, long-haired and bearded Quadi were confident of victory. [Tac., *Germ.*, 6]

The situation looked grim for Marcus Aurelius and the surrounded 12th. With their shields locked together, said Dio, and apparently in orbis formation, the legionaries created a solid wall around themselves, with the cavalry and the emperor's party in the middle of their formation. Despite expending several hours, many of their spears and much energy, the Quadi could not break through the legionary line. [Dio, LXXII, 8] King Ariogaesus therefore halted the attack and pulled his warriors back, continuing to encircle the 12th Fulminata and their emperor, waiting for a Roman capitulation. For Marcus and the 12th Fulminata Legion, said Dio, 'were in a terrible plight, from fatigue, wounds, the heat of the sun, and their thirst'. [Ibid.]

With Marcus Aurelius was Arnuphis, an Egyptian who was, said Dio, a magician. Arnuphis now began to chant incantations to various deities, in particular the Egyptian equivalent of Mercury, god of the air, seeking intervention on behalf of the emperor and his troops. Clouds soon gathered; heavy rain began to fall. 'At first, all turned their faces upward and received the water in their mouths. Then some held out their shields, and some, their helmets, to catch it.' The Roman troops not only drank deeply of the rainwater but also gave it to their horses. The blood of some wounded Roman soldiers flowed into their helmets, but that did not deter them; they gratefully drank the bloody water. [Ibid.]

Marcus Aurelius' Column, erected between AD 176 and 193, depicts Marcus' victories against the Germans on the Danube, including the famous victory of the 12th Fulminata Legion in a thunderstorm.

The Quadi, seeing that the Romans were preoccupied slaking their thirst, suddenly charged the legion line. Some legionaries who had lowered their curved shields to drink, or held them up to catch the rain, were felled by German spears. As the Quadi closed in for hand-to-hand combat the Roman defence was shaky. But the storm increased in intensity; hail now lashed the two armies, the hailstones pounding down like slingers' bullets. The legionaries, in helmets and armour, could withstand the hail, but the unprotected Germans took the full force of it. The Quadi broke off the attack and ran for the cover of trees.

The storm intensified. Thunder boomed in the heavens, lightning bolts lanced down into the trees, with terrifying results. Not only did trees burst into flame, Quadi warriors and their weapons, too, were struck by lightning. Said the poet Claudian of the scene: 'Spears glowed, molten by lightning, and swords vanished suddenly into smoke.' Here a Quadi warrior 'sank down beneath his fire-wasted helmet', there a cavalryman was left trembling on the smoking back of his charger. [Claud., *SCH*, 341–6] The terrified Germans, some of them on fire, ran from the trees and to the Romans, begging for their aid and protection. The battle disintegrated into a disaster for the Quadi. By the time that the storm had passed, the battle was over, and many Quadi, including King Ariogaesus, had been taken prisoner.

Claudian, writing two and a half centuries later, said that while some attributed Marcus Aurelius' famous victory in a thunderstorm to 'Chaldean seers' and 'their magic spells' he was of the opinion that 'Marcus' blameless life had the power to win the Thunderer's [Mars'] homage'. [Ibid., 347–50] Marcus himself seems to have attributed the victory to the legionaries of the 12th Fulminata Legion. It would have been pointed out to the emperor that the legion was known as the 'Thundering 12th'. Now, the 12th had truly become the thundering legion, defeating the Quadi in a thunderstorm summoned by the Egyptian priest. According to Dio, Marcus now officially conferred the title Fulminata on the legion. [Dio, LXII, 9]

In a later interpolation to Dio's work, a Christian writer replaced the reference to Arnuphis and his prayers to the Roman gods with a passage that made all the men of the 12th Fulminata Christians, and it was they who did the praying, he wrote. This was historically impossible. During Marcus Aurelius' reign, Christians were crucified if they did not repent and sacrifice to the Roman gods. An entire legion of 5,000 men could not have been Christians at that time. It would be hundreds of years before Christianity had such a hold in the Roman military. Intriguingly, Claudian, a man of consular rank, writing in around AD 400, eighty years after Constantine the Great had made Christianity the official State religion, still spoke of the Christians as a mere sect, and gave full credit for the 12th Fulminata's AD 174 victory to Mars, god of war.

At an assembly convened by the emperor following the victory, the men of the 12th Fulminata hailed Marcus Aurelius imperator. Normally, said Dio, Marcus would not have accepted such an honour before the Senate voted it to him, but this time he felt that Heaven had made his victory possible, so he sent a dispatch to the Senate telling them that the Quadi had been vanquished and that he had accepted the title of imperator from the troops. [Ibid.] The Senate, in its gratitude, not only confirmed the emperor's latest grant of the imperator title – he had previously received it six times for his generals' victories – it granted the influential empress Faustina the title of *Mater Castrorum*, or Mother of the Camp.

As for the captured Quadi king, Ariogaesus, Marcus sent him to Britain, to live out the remainder of his days in exile there. Twenty thousand Roman soldiers were now stationed in the Marcomanni and the Quadi homelands, to ensure that the Germans could not assemble in number. [Dio, LXXII, 20]

Marcus could now concentrate on the Iazyges, the last German combatants left in the ring with Rome. As soon as the Iazyges heard of the defeat of the Quadi by a single legion, one of their two kings, Banadaspus, sent envoys to Marcus seeking peace. But Marcus was not interested in signing a treaty. After the Quadi had broken their promises and again gone to war with him, he would not trust their cousins the Iazyges; Marcus saw just one solution – he 'wished to annihilate them utterly'. [Dio, LXXII, 13] Once the Iazyges heard that Banadaspus' peace feelers had been rejected, they locked him up, threw their support behind second king, Zanticus, and prepared to receive the full weight of Marcus' legions.

AD 174–175
LIII. BLOOD ON THE ICE
Victory on the frozen Danube

Over the winter of AD 174–175, Marcus' best general, Publius Pertinax, led a Roman army from Pannonia towards Iazyge territory above the Danube. The Iazyges had been expecting this offensive, and King Zanticus sent a large mounted column to confront the Romans, crossing the ice on the frozen Danube to engage Pertinax in Roman territory. The initial battle, in bitter winter conditions, went against the Iazyges, with Pertinax using cavalry and infantry to combined effect, forcing the Iazyge cavalry to withdraw in disorder to the northern side of the Danube.

With the enemy on the run, Pertinax and his legions hurried in hot pursuit, but on the far side of the river German leaders were able to reform their riders. The Roman legionaries began to slip and slide as they gingerly made their way across the frozen Danube; it was then that regrouped Germans attacked. 'Some of the barbarians dashed straight at them, while others rode round to attack their flanks, as their horses had been trained to run safely even over a surface of this kind.' Yet the Roman troops 'were not alarmed, but formed in a compact body, facing all their foes at once'. [Dio, LXII, 7]

Pertinax's legions formed the square, also called the brick and the box by Romans, a standard formation for defence against cavalry attack, and still used by infantry to counter cavalry as late as the 1815 Battle of Waterloo. The legionaries stood many ranks deep to create a large hollow square, with each man facing outward, and with the cavalry, auxiliaries, standards, non-combatants and senior officers inside the square.

On command, 'most of them laid down their shields [on the ice] and rested one foot on them, so that they might not slip so much'. As Iazyge cavalrymen closed with their lances, some firm-footed legionaries grabbed the bridles of horses. Others grasped the shields and lance shafts of German riders. Often, horses were dragged off their feet on the ice, or riders were dragged from their mounts. If a legionary lost his footing, he kept his grip on his opponent and dragged him to the ground with him. Countless wrestling matches took place on the ice. More than once, Roman soldiers used their teeth as weapons in these desperate tussles. The barbarians were overwhelmed by these unorthodox tactics, said Dio, and 'few escaped out of a large force'. [Ibid.] With the ice stained crimson with blood, the battle on the Danube was a decisive victory for Pertinax's legions.

As Pertinax invaded their homeland, and deserted by all their German allies, the Iazyges saw the futility of continued resistance. King Zanticus and his fellow Iazyge leaders came to Marcus at Carnuntum, suing for peace and seeking to restore the old alliance with Rome. Zanticus even prostrated himself before the emperor. But Marcus did not trust the Iazyges, and still wished to 'exterminate them utterly'. [Dio, LXXII, 16] The Iazyges were saved from extermination by disturbing news that now reached Marcus from Martius Verus, governor of Cappadocia. Marcus' friend Avidius Cassius, governor of Syria, had declared himself emperor of Rome. Worse still, the provinces of Syria, Cilicia, Judea and Egypt and the troops they contained had all hailed Cassius emperor.

Cassius had seemed the most loyal of Marcus' adherents. Three years earlier he had marched an army down to Egypt to relieve the resident 2nd Traiana Legion which was under siege at Alexandria by Egyptian partisans led by a priest named Isidorus who opposed Marcus' rule. Why, now, had Cassius suddenly decided to usurp Marcus?

AD 175
LIV. CHALLENGING FOR MARCUS' THRONE
The accidental pretender

Avidius Cassius had declared himself emperor of Rome because he believed that Marcus Aurelius was dead. This had arisen out of a misunderstanding involving Marcus' wife Faustina, a powerful behind-the-scenes player. Marcus had not been well for some time, and in AD 175 his health worsened. He himself was to say this same year that he was 'already an old man and weak, unable to either take food without pain or sleep without anxiety'. [Dio, LXII, 24]

The empress Faustina had thought that Marcus was close to death, and, deciding that Cassius would make a better successor as emperor than Marcus' unpleasant son Commodus, she had sent Cassius a secret message urging him to take the throne for himself as soon as Marcus died, promising to support him. Cassius had subsequently received a report that Marcus was dead, and had immediately claimed the throne. But Marcus was still very much alive. Even when Cassius learned the truth, he would not recant; he had already shown his hand.

At Carnuntum, treating with Iazyge peace envoys when he would have preferred to exterminate the tribe, Marcus knew that he had to march to the East to put an end to the usurper's claim. And to do that, he could not afford to have a Danube war continuing behind his back. As the 12th Fulminata Legion received orders to prepare to return to the East with the emperor, Marcus reluctantly sealed a peace agreement with the Iazyges.

This equestrian statue of Marcus Aurelius, which still stands in Rome, portrays him as a dashing military figure. He was in fact frail and frequently unwell.

Marcus granted the Iazyges similar peace terms to those enjoyed by the Marcomanni and Quadi, with several exceptions. He stipulated that the Iazyges must live twice as far away from the Danube as their former German allies, and must contribute 8,000 of their most superior surviving cavalry to the new alliance. These men would be posted to the fringes of the empire – 5,500 would go to Britain as members of numeri units, for example. In this way Marcus deprived the Iazyges of their best fighting men, and of their capacity to go to war against Rome again. The Iazyges also gave up all Roman captives taken during the ten-year war.

Even after some prisoners had died in captivity and others had escaped, the Iazyges still held 100,000 captive Roman civilians, who were now returned. [Dio, LXXII, 16]

Rewarding Pertinax, his most successful and loyal general, for his 'brave exploits' with a consulship for the year, the emperor set off east to confront Cassius, taking along the empress Faustina and a large body of troops. [Dio, LXII, 22] En route to the East, Marcus received word that Cassius was dead. Just three months after declaring himself emperor, Cassius had been assassinated. One of his own centurions had stabbed him, then galloped off, leaving him seriously wounded. A decurion, apparently from Cassius' escort, had finished the job. Cassius' severed head was sent to Marcus.

Marcus continued on to the East to cement the loyalty of the legions there before he returned to Rome. When he did finally return home in AD 177, he conducted a Triumph through the streets of the capital for his victory over the Germans, and erected a triumphal arch in Rome. Marcus Aurelius' Danube wars had come to an end. But the peace he had won was not to last long.

AD 177–180
LV. MARCUS AURELIUS' LAST CAMPAIGNS
Victory and death

The empress Faustina had passed away in AD 176 while she and Marcus Aurelius were returning to Rome from the East. Her death shattered Marcus, and back in Rome the following year he threw himself into public business. At the same time, he declared his 16-year-old son Commodus his co-emperor.

By this time, Rome was again at war with northeastern neighbours. Not the Germans, but a Scythian tribe from east of Dacia that had crossed the Danube into Lower Moesia. The brothers Quintilius, Maximus and Condianus, were apparently the governors of Rome's two Moesian provinces at the time. The talented pair, who uniquely shared everything, including official appointments, and, eventually, death by the sword, had consolidated Rome's position on the Danube during Marcus' absence but 'had been unable to end the war' for the emperor. By AD 178, 'the Scythian situation again demanded his attention'. [Dio, LXXII, 33]

At Rome, the sickly Marcus hurled the bloody spear kept in the Temple of Bellona, in a traditional ceremony that signalled he personally was going to war in foreign territory. As Marcus set out for the Danube, to base himself in Pannonia, as before, he sent Palatium secretary Tarrutenius Paternus ahead with the main force to reinforce the Quintilius brothers and aggressively prosecute the war against the Scythians.

Paternus and the army arrived just as the legions of the Quintilius brothers were locked in a battle with the Scythians. The battle site is likely to have been north of the Black Sea mouths of the Danube, above Troesmis, base of the 5th Macedonica Legion prior to its transfer east for the Parthian campaign. Here Hadrian had built a line of fixed defences, the *limes*, manned by auxiliary units. But no legion had replaced the 5th Macedonica at Troesmis, leaving this sector exposed to barbarian inroads. Alternatively, the fighting could have taken place on the Dacian border north of Novea; Hadrian had also built a line of walls and forts there. Both locations would have come under attack during this period. Once Paternus' army reached the disputed territory and joined the fighting, the Scythians held out for a full day before being wiped out. For Paternus' victory, Marcus was hailed imperator for the tenth time.

But this was not the end of hostilities. Other barbarians had avaricious eyes on Rome's Danubian territory, among them the Buri Germans from the River Oder, who began raiding into Dacia and dragging many Roman settlers back to their homeland. Other German tribes possessing peace treaties with Rome also became restive. Three thousand men of the Naristi tribe, disturbed by talk of war, deserted their bellicose leaders and came over to Marcus, who settled them in Roman territory.

The Quadi, meanwhile, became so fed up with Roman troops garrisoned on their territory telling them where they could graze their flocks and till the land, that they decided to migrate en masse north across the River Elbe to join their cousins the Semnones. When Marcus heard of this, he mobilized his forces in Bohemia. The Quadi, finding their route to the Elbe blocked by Roman troops, were forced to return to their homes. The Iazyges could not take any more from Roman garrisons either, and sent envoys to Marcus asking for

Commodus, errant son and successor of Marcus Aurelius, seen here in the guise of Hercules, his favourite deity.

more lenient treatment. So that the tribe did not become completely alienated, and in recognition of their recent good behaviour, Marcus granted some of their requests.

Cassius Dio, whose father was alive during the reign of Marcus Aurelius, had no doubts that Marcus would have subdued the entire region in time. But, in March AD 180, while Marcus was at Vindobona (Vienna), a day's march to the west of Carnuntum, he fell seriously ill, and on 17 March he died. Dio wrote that he had been told that Marcus' physicians killed him, as a favour to his son and heir. [Dio, LXII, 21] At just 19 years old, Commodus, who was at his father's deathbed, was hailed emperor of Rome.

Commodus 'hated all exertion and was eager for the comforts of the city'. [Dio, LXXIII, 2] So, he quickly made a truce with the barbarians threatening Moesia and sealed new peace treaties with the German tribes beyond the Danube above Pannonia and Noricum. As his part of the agreement, Commodus withdrew all Roman occupying forces from the German tribes' territories to the 5-mile (8-kilometre) neutral strip north of the Danube. In return, the Quadi provided 13,000 cavalry to serve in the Roman army, and the Marcomanni sent a lesser number of foot soldiers. Fifteen thousand Roman captives still in the hands of these tribes were returned to Rome. Commodus also agreed a peace treaty with the Buri, who provided hostages and returned Roman prisoners. Commodus then went home to Rome, and an idle life.

Under Marcus, Rome may have been almost constantly at war, but the ship of state had been in good hands. Insecure, unstable young Commodus soon executed many of his father's wisest advisers and best generals. As a consequence, the Roman Empire, said Cassius Dio, now descended 'from a kingdom of gold to one of iron and rust'. [Dio, LXII, 36]

AD 193–195
LVI. SEVERUS VERSUS NIGER
Defeating the eastern usurper

Septimius Severus, the 47-year-old governor of the province of Upper Pannonia, was a slight yet vain man with curly hair and a curly beard that was deliberately grown into two points to set him apart from others. He had been an admirer of the soldier emperor Pertinax, who had succeeded the murdered Commodus at the start of AD

193. Severus was so incensed by the murder of Pertinax by 200 men of the Praetorian Guard after a reign of less than three months that he called on his troops to avenge Pertinax's death. On 13 April, the legions of Pannonia – the 10th Gemina and 14th Gemina Martia Victrix in his own province, and the 1st and 2nd Adiutrix legions from neighbouring Lower Pannonia – had hailed Severus the new emperor, and joined him in a march on Rome to take the throne.

Severus had three rivals. One was the senator Marcus Didius Julianus, who, on Pertinax's death, had won the support of the Praetorian Guard in a bizarre auction for their loyalty in which he had outbid the city prefect, Titus Flavius Sulpicianus, after which the Praetorians proclaimed Julianus emperor. There was also the ambitious Decimus Clodius Albinus, governor of Britain – Severus placated him for the time being by appointing him his Caesar, or deputy emperor. And then there was Gaius Persennius Niger, governor of Syria, who also claimed the throne and won the backing of much of the Roman East. To make the throne his, Severus would have to deal with all three rival claimants.

Persennius Niger, one of Severus' two rivals for the throne.

Sixty-year-old Julianus soon departed the scene, murdered in his bath on 1 June by the very Praetorian Guard that had proclaimed him emperor just two months earlier, after the approaching Severus had sent the Guard letters promising to punish only those Praetorians who had participated in the murder of Pertinax. With the murderers of Pertinax put in chains by their own comrades, the Senate met and named Severus emperor.

But Severus was unimpressed by the Praetorians. He did indeed execute the men responsible for the murder of Pertinax, but he went much further. On arriving outside Rome shortly after Julianus' murder, he summoned the full Praetorian Guard to an assembly. There, the unsuspecting Praetorians were surrounded by Severus' legions, stripped of their arms, and their officers deprived of their horses. All former Praetorians were then banished from Rome. Severus would recruit a new Praetorian Guard by transferring the most meritorious legionaries into it from legions throughout the empire.

Severus wasted no time in proceeding against his most threatening rival, Niger. A native of Italy whom Commodus had made governor of Syria even though he was only a member of the Equestrian Order, Niger had by this time come west to Byzantium, on the European side of the Hellespont. The city, like all the Roman East, had come out for Niger. In July, just weeks after arriving in Rome, and after conducting an elaborate funeral service for the dead emperor Pertinax, Severus set off for the East to deal with Niger. While Severus marched overland, the Misene and Ravenna Fleets transported his legions across the Adriatic to Dyrrachium, from where they marched into Macedonia. The fleets then sailed around Greece to participate in the campaign against Niger. [Starr, VIII]

From Byzantium, Niger attacked nearby Perinthus, but, unsettled by unfavourable omens, returned to Byzantium. [Dio, LXXV, 6] As Severus' forces drew near, Niger and most of his forces withdrew into Asia, but Byzantium remained loyal to him and closed its gates against Severus. While Severus launched a siege of Byzantium, he sent his generals in pursuit of Niger's army. Niger's chief lieutenant, a senator named Aemilianus who was a relative of Albinus, governor of Britain, did battle with Severus' generals near Cyzicus, on the northern coast of Asia. Severus' troops were victorious – Aemilianus was killed in the battle, and his army defeated.

Niger himself was tracked to Nicaea, today's Iznik, and was drawn into battle beside Lake Ascania (Iznik), by Severus' general Tiberius Claudius Candidus. Niger marshalled his army on the plain, while Candidus occupied the higher ground on the nearby hillsides. Some enterprising troops, apparently from Severus' army, commandeered local fishing boats and, using these, discharged arrows at Niger's troops from the lake. Candidus' troops had the better of the early part of the battle, until Niger himself took personal command. Niger forced Candidus' men to fall back, and Severus' general had to seize hold of his standard-bearers and turn them to face the enemy again before he could take the offensive once more. Candidus' troops had gained the upper hand by the time that darkness descended. It was a moonless night, and this enabled Niger and his surviving troops to escape to the safety of nearby Nicaea.

This so-called Battle of Nicaea had been a moral victory for Severus' troops, but Niger was able to continue his withdrawal to the East towards Syria. Severus' troops gave chase, and come the spring of AD 194 they had overtaken Niger's regrouped army camped at Issus in Cilicia, near the Cilician Gates. A narrow pass between the mountains and the sea which offered entry to Syria, the Cilician Gates had been the scene of many a battle down through the centuries. Even Alexander the Great had fought and won here. At the pass, the two Roman armies again met in mortal combat.

Niger had in excess of 20,000 infantry, but no cavalry to speak of. Having built a well-fortified camp on a hill, he formed up his army on the sloping ground outside, with his legions in the front ranks, then javelin and stone-throwers behind them, and archers in the last line. His baggage train was arrayed in the rear, to prevent his men from retreating. Severus' general Publius Cornelius Anullinus, who had less infantry than Niger but a sizeable force of cavalry, mimicked Niger's battle formation with his infantry but ordered his mounted troops under his deputy Valerianus to attempt to skirt the forest that was protecting Niger's rear and find a way to attack him from behind.

The battle began under a clear sky. As Niger's troops held their ground, Anullinus' infantry ran to the attack. Fighting raged for some time, as Niger's troops, with superior numbers and the high ground, held their positions against Anullinus' men. Out of the blue, a storm sprang up, and, just as it looked as though Niger's army would prevail, amid thunder and lightning, heavy rain swept in from behind Anullinus' army and into the faces of Niger's troops. Anullinus' troops were given courage, believing that the gods were with them, while Niger's troops lost heart for the same reason. Men began to peel away from Niger's rear ranks. Now the Severan cavalry under Valerianus appeared, having found their way through the forest, and attacked from the rear.

Niger's men who had fled were forced back to the battle by the onset of the cavalry. Meanwhile, Niger's remaining troops had begun to give ground to Anullinus' infantry. Niger's ranks disintegrated. Men ran in all directions trying to save themselves. In the carnage that ensued, '20,000 of Niger's followers perished'. [Ibid., 7, 8] Niger himself managed to escape the battle, and fled south to Antioch. Severus' army then advanced down into Syria and easily took Antioch, forcing Niger again to flee. Niger had plans to cross the Euphrates, but he only got as far as the suburbs of Antioch, where he was killed by 'a common soldier'. [Amm., II, xxvi, 8, 15] Severus, who was himself hastening to Syria at the time, ordered Niger's head sent to his forces besieging Byzantium, to be displayed on a pole to the defenders of the city in the hope that the sight would induce the Byzantines to surrender.

Despite Niger's death and the sight of his severed head, Byzantium held out. Under cover of a storm, the city's defenders had sent ships from its fleet of 500 mostly single-banked vessels to pillage nearby coastal towns and bring back supplies. But the next time the Byzantine fleet attempted a similar breakout to find desperately needed provisions, it was met by the triremes of the combined Roman fleets from Misenum and Ravenna and utterly destroyed, by which time the starving people of Byzantium had resorted to eating leather, and even, it was said, to cannibalism. [Ibid., 13] Following the loss of its fleet, the city surrendered to Severus' army, which put to death all the fighting men and magistrates of Byzantium. As a further reprisal for opposing him, Severus ordered the massive walls surrounding the city to be demolished.

Severus himself was in Mesopotamia when news reached him of the fall of Byzantium, and he gloated about it to his troops. He had been brought to Mesopotamia by a revolt of the people of the Osroene kingdom. Situated east of the upper Euphrates, with the famous city of Edessa as its capital, Osroene had been garrisoned by Roman troops at several forts for a number of years. Seeing the civil war between Niger and Severus as an opportunity to throw off Roman overlordship, both Osroene and its neighbour the kingdom of Adiabene had revolted, seizing several Roman forts in their territory and making prisoners of survivors from the Roman garrisons. They then laid siege to the Roman-occupied city of Nisibis.

Severus had linked up with his victorious legions in Syria, and now, as he approached the Euphrates, the rebels withdrew from Nisibis and the Osroenes sent envoys to the Roman emperor, offering to return the Roman captives if he withdrew the remaining Roman garrisons from their territory. Ignoring this offer, Severus crossed the Euphrates with his army. Tramping through the desert, he went close to losing a number of men to lack of water and a dust storm. When they did find a spring, the water looked so strange that the men refused to drink until Severus himself drank it in clear view of his troops.

Severus now based himself at Nisibis and, sending his army in three divisions ranging throughout Osroene under his generals, he captured all its cities. They then crossed the Tigris river and did the same to the mountainous kingdom of Adiabene. With its capital at Arbel, the present-day city of Irbil in Iraq, Adiabene straddled today's Kurdish Iraq and parts of southern Armenia and Iran. Towards the end of AD 196, Severus' war in the East was brought to a conclusion by the conquest of Adiabene.

But now Severus had to turn his attention to his rival Albinus in the West, who had entered Gaul from Britain and been hailed emperor by his troops. As he himself set off west, Severus ordered the navy to ferry his Danube legions and Praetorian Guard back to Europe.

AD 197
LVII. BATTLE OF LUGDUNUM
Severus versus Albinus

'Roman power suffered a severe blow.'
CASSIUS DIO, *Roman History*, LXXVI, 7

The February air was still wintery when two armies came together on the plain north of the River Rhône near Lugdunum, today's Lyon in central France. Both armies were Roman; each was determined to destroy the other; and between them they fielded 150,000 men.

After Septimius Severus, governor of Upper Pannonia, had been declared emperor by the Pannonian legions on 13 April AD 193, he had given the governor of Britain, Decimus Clodius Albinus, the title of Caesar, or deputy emperor, to conciliate him. While Severus was in the East dealing with his rival Niger, in AD 195 Albinus had moved to take the throne for himself, after Severus had declared his sons Caracalla and Geta his new Caesars and heirs.

Crossing the English Channel from Britain, Albinus had brought men of the three legions stationed in Britain – the 2nd Augusta, 6th Victrix, and 20th Valeria Victrix – to Gaul, where he had installed himself at Lugdunum. The principal city of Gaul and capital of the province of Gallia Lugdunensis, Lugdunum housed an imperial mint and a cohort of Rome's City Guard, which appears to have gone over to Albinus. He was hailed emperor by his troops and the people of Lugdunum, and there at Lugdunum he was soon joined by Lucius Novius Rufus, governor of one of the Spanish provinces, who brought him reinforcements from the 7th Gemina Legion and auxiliary units based in Spain.

After Severus had defeated Niger, he brought his Danube legions and the Praetorian Guard to Gaul to take on Albinus, also sending word to the legions on the Rhine to send troops south to join him. As legions from the Rhine, commanded by Virius Lupus, neared Lugdunum ahead of Severus' army, Albinus led the majority of his forces from Lugdunum to intercept them. At Tinurtium, today's Tournus, 40 miles (64 kilometres) up the Saône river from Lugdunum, Lupus' force were repulsed by Albinus with heavy loss. When Severus himself approached with his main army, the victorious Albinus withdrew, leading his army back to their camp outside Lugdunum to consolidate his forces.

Now, on 19 February, the battle that would decide who would rule the Roman Empire took place outside the city. For this battle, both Severus and Albinus would be actively involved. Both men knew that this battle would make or break them. Albinus' legions formed up in battle order outside their camp. Severus' army then marched out of its camp on the plain and formed up in battle lines opposite them.

Both Severus and Albinus were experienced generals. Severus was a self-made man. A native of Leptis Magna in the province of Africa and son of an Equestrian, he had overcome his provincial background with a steady rise through the military ranks to become a consul in AD 190 at the age of 43, before taking up the post of governor of Upper Pannonia.

Albinus, on the other hand, came from a good senatorial family and was well educated. He had made a name for himself commanding a victorious Roman army in campaigns against invading barbarian tribes east of Dacia during the reign of Commodus. In the opinion of Cassius Dio, who knew him, Severus was 'superior in warfare and was a skilful commander'. Just the same, Albinus had more experience at the head of his troops in battle, while Severus had previously let subordinates lead his armies. [Dio, LXXVI, 6]

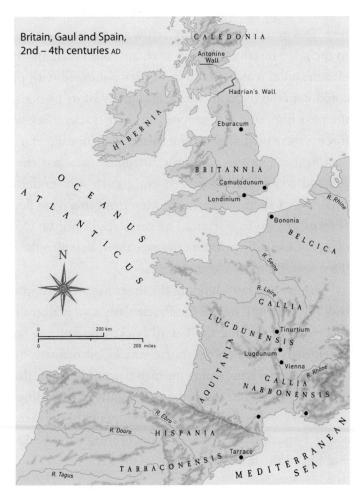

Britain, Gaul and Spain, 2nd – 4th centuries AD

The Battle of Lugdunum was long and drawn out, with numerous shifts of fortune. It opened in time-honoured fashion. With both sides lined up facing each other in numerous ranks, both charged forward. Prior to the battle, probably in the night, the men on Albinus' right wing had been able to dig a long pit, unseen by the other side. This pit had been given a covering, apparently of hides, with an overall layer of earth to conceal it. At the battle's commencement, Albinus' men here on his right dashed forward to the edge of the hidden pit, launched their javelins, then withdrew, as if through fear. This had drawn Severus' left wing forward, on

It was the murder of the emperor Pertinax, who is depicted on this coin, that inspired Septimius Severus to take the throne. But he had to fight Niger and Albinus to keep it.

to the pit. The covering gave way, and both men and horses of the first line tumbled into the hole, which would have been equipped with pointed stakes. The second line could not stop its momentum, and many of its men also went into the pit. Troops in the next lines not only stopped in their tracks, they withdrew in horrified disorder, forcing their own men behind them over the edge of a cliff.

On the opposite wing, the fortunes were just the opposite. After hectic hand-to-hand combat, Albinus' left wing gave way under pressure from Severus' more experienced right-wing troops. Men from this wing fled back to Albinus' camp, with Severus' troops in pursuit. The gates could not be closed in the crush of panicking men, allowing the pursuers to force their way into the camp, where they slaughtered those inside and looted their tents.

Severus had been holding the Praetorian Guard in reserve. Seeing his left wing in trouble at the pit, he led the Praetorians into action on the left. But Albinus' troops succeeded in pushing the Guard back. The fighting 'came very near destroying the Praetorians', and Severus' horse was killed beneath him. [Ibid.] Finding himself on the ground, Severus, seeing his men fleeing the fight, threw off his heavy riding cloak, drew his sword, and ran among the fugitives, intending to either turn them around or die fighting. After halting the flight of many of his men and reforming them, he led a counter-attack that cut down many of those who had been pursuing Severus' troops, and forced the others to retreat.

At this point Severus' general Maecius Laetus intervened with the cavalry. According to Dio, Laetus had ambitions to himself become emperor and had been holding Severus' cavalry back in the hope that both Severus and Albinus would be killed, after which he would claim the vacant throne for himself. But seeing Severus' troops having the better of Albinus' men, Laetus brought the cavalry into play to support Severus. [Ibid.] This turned the tide, and allowed Albinus' army to be overrun. Albinus fled the battlefield, and took refuge in a farmhouse beside the Rhône. But he was followed, and the house was surrounded by Severan troops. Rather than fall into Severus' hands, Albinus took his own life.

Albinus' body was brought to Severus. After taking in the corpse, and angrily denouncing the dead man for opposing him, Severus ordered his head severed and sent to Rome to be displayed on a pole; the rest of the body was discarded with neither burial nor cremation. When Severus returned to Rome he would execute a number of senators who had supported Albinus. Meanwhile, Severus' loyal general Lupus received Albinus' former post of governor of Britain, while the ambitious Laetus was sent to the East to become governor of Mesopotamia.

Because Lugdunum had supported Albinus, Severus allowed his victorious troops to loot the wealthy city. He would have been all the more incensed at the city's disloyalty because his son Caracalla had been born there, yet still its people had turned against him. Severus' 1st Minervia Legion, which had been located at Bonna on the Lower Rhine since the reign of Trajan, was now detached from Severus' army and based at Lugdunum. Treating it as an occupied enemy city, the legion would remain at Lugdunum until AD 211, after which it would return to Bonna. Lugdunum would never regain its previous prestige or importance among the cities of the empire. [Pelle.]

With this battle outside Lugdunum, the brief civil war was brought to an end, but the Roman army had been devastated by the internecine conflict. 'Countless numbers had fallen on both sides,' at Lugdunum. 'Even the victors deplored the disaster, for the entire plain was seen to be covered with the bodies of men and horses,' Dio lamented. 'Roman power suffered a severe blow.' [Dio, LXXVI, 7]

But Severus was not finished with making war. Once he was back in Rome, news reached him that the Parthians, knowing that the Romans were fighting among themselves in the West, had launched 'an expedition in full force'. After invading and capturing most of Mesopotamia from the Romans, the Parthians were laying siege to the governor, Laetus, at Nisibis. [Ibid., 9] Severus issued orders for a major campaign in the East. Not only did he plan to throw the Parthians out of Mesopotamia, he set his sights on achieving what Julius Caesar had dreamed of doing, what Hadrian had abandoned after Trajan's brief excursion east of the Euphrates, and what Commodus had failed to achieve – the conquest of Parthia and the elimination of the Parthians as a future threat to Rome.

AD 197–203
LVIII. SEVERUS' PARTHIAN WAR
An eastern disaster

In the light of the massive losses sustained by all the legions taking part in the battle outside Lugdunum in February AD 197, Severus ordered the raising of three new legions. So that there was no doubt about their purpose, he named them the 1st Parthica, 2nd Parthica, and 3rd Parthica legions – Parthica meaning 'of Parthia'. All three legions took the centaur as their emblem. As the mythological centaur was said to have originated in Macedonia, it is thought likely that all three legions were in the main raised there and in neighbouring Thrace. [Cow., *RL AD 161–284*]

Using the Misene and Ravenna Fleets, and taking with him some of his existing European-based legions and part of the Praetorian Guard, all of which had suffered heavy casualties in the February Battle of Lugdunum in Gaul, Severus set off for the East late in the year, departing from the port of Brundisium in southern Italy. [Starr, VIII] The three new Parthica legions would have marched from their recruiting grounds to nearby Byzantium, where they were probably collected by ships of the Pontic Fleet to be ferried around the eastern Mediterranean to link up with Severus in Syria.

By the spring of AD 198, Severus was leading his army north into Mesopotamia to relieve Nisibis, modern Nusaybin in southeast Turkey. This ancient city, surrounded by massive walls, had been under extended siege by the Parthians. The approach of Severus and his army forced the Parthian king, Vologases, to withdraw back into central Parthia. Severus' general Laetus, a 'most excellent man', according to Dio, who was acquainted with the general, had defiantly held out through the siege for many months. 'In consequence, Laetus acquired still greater renown.' [Dio, LXXVI, 9]

The scenes on the carved panels on the Arch of Septimius Severus, erected in AD 203 not far from the Senate House in the Forum in Rome, show Severus then going to war once again with the kingdom of Osroene, which had been an age-old ally of the Parthians and several years before this had rebelled against Severus. According to the panels on Severus' arch, he employed elaborate 'war engines' against Edessa, the capital of Osroene.

Some of these engines – massive mobile towers, catapults and cranes – were designed by the engineer Priscus of Bithynia. Priscus had been involved in the defence of Byzantium during the siege of that city by Severus' forces, building exotic war machines that had made life difficult for the besiegers. Severus had ordered that Priscus be spared when Byzantium fell, and subsequently took him east with him. [Dio, LXVV, 11] Severus' arch in Rome shows the city of Edessa surrendering to Severus, and then Abgar, the king of Osroene, also surrendering.

Dio says that, using timber from a forest beside the Euphrates, Severus' legions then constructed boats which they launched on the river, and down the Euphrates the Roman army sped, with part – the baggage, no doubt – on water, and part marching along the riverbank. [Dio, LXXVI, 9] Severus' arch shows Vologases, king of the Parthians, fleeing on horseback ahead of Severus. Dio reports that when Severus reached Seleucia, the city on the Tigris previously destroyed by Trajan, he found it totally abandoned. [Ibid.] Marching south, Severus found ancient Babylon also abandoned.

The Parthians put up a fight for their capital Ctesiphon, and again Severus brought in war engines. Despite the surrender of the city's defenders, Severus allowed his legions to enter Ctesiphon and loot it. Severus then pulled out of Parthia – partly, said Dio, due to a lack of provisions. It seems that he withdrew all

The Parthian enemy. A scene from the Arch of Septimius Severus, which he raised in the Forum at Rome following his Parthian campaign.

the way to Nisibis, where he would spend the winter. His army, again partly in boats and partly on land, also followed the Tigris river to winter in the north.

In the spring of AD 199, having prepared large stores of food and built numerous war engines, Severus launched a new campaign. This time he marched across the desert to the city of Hatra, capital of the Atreni Arabs, to which he laid siege. Hatra may have been remote, but it was a rich city, for it was the famous centre of the worship of a sun god and contained numerous valuable offerings and vast amounts of money. Eighty-three years before, Trajan had also besieged Hatra; he had given up in disgust after both the defence and the locale had proved too much to overcome. Ammianus, a Roman officer who was to pass this way with a Roman army 164

years later, wrote that Hatra lay in the midst of desert, and that on the desert plain here it was possible to march for 70 miles (112 kilometres) and find that the only water available was 'salty and ill-smelling'. [Amm., II, XXV, 4]

Despite the conditions, Severus was determined to take the city, which was surrounded by a series of high walls, employing a range of war engines against it. Again Priscus of Bithynia created massive engines for the attack, as did the legions' own engineers. Many of these war engines were destroyed by fire arrows shot from the city walls, to Severus' frustration. 'His siege engines were burned, many soldiers perished, and vast numbers were wounded.' [Dio, LXXVI, 11] Severus withdrew, and set up camp in a more hospitable area for the winter.

Over the winter, Severus had supplies stockpiled for a protracted campaign in the new year, and had numerous new

On the weathered Arch of Septimius Severus at Leptis Magna in Libya, Severus is shown addressing his troops, top left, after their capture of Ctesiphon, the Parthian capital.

war engines constructed. There was obviously a mood of dissatisfaction in Severus' camp at the human cost of the campaign to date, for Severus lashed out at those around him. Maecius Laetus had become his most successful general; more than that, Laetus had gained great popularity with the troops and the public; now Severus had him arrested, and executed. Then, when it was reported that one of the tribunes of the Praetorian Guard, Julius Crispus, had quoted a line from the poet Virgil that 'we are meanwhile perishing all unheeded', Severus took it as seditious criticism of his leadership, and had the tribune executed. The soldier who had informed on Crispus was promoted into the tribune's post. [Ibid., 10]

The spring of AD 200 found Severus and his army back outside Hatra for a renewal of the siege, for Severus was galled by the fact that this one city should be allowed to resist him when all others in the region had fallen. Severus' latest siege engines were brought up as the struggle was renewed, but the Atreni tribe defending Hatra were also equipped with destructive weapons, some of which were massive catapults that launched two large arrows at a time. These had such a long range that they hit Severus' bodyguards as the emperor sat on a lofty tribunal from which he was watching the siege progress, no doubt scattering both emperor and attendants.

Severus' legionaries were subsequently sent against one of the walls of Hatra using covered mantlets on wheels. They managed to break down a small part of the wall, and assault troops massed at the breach. In response, the defenders fired containers of burning bituminous naphtha against the wooden siege sheds; these burst over them and 'consumed the engines and all the soldiers on whom it fell'. [Dio, LXXVI, 11] The horrible fate of these men soured the enthusiasm of the other Roman troops who witnessed it, and the attack faltered.

Except those built by Priscus, all the siege machines were destroyed by fire as a result of Hatran barrages. Fireproofing precautions, which often involved a layer of earth on the top of wooden siege machines, may have prevented Priscus' engines from being engulfed in flame. Eventually, another large breach was made in a wall by Priscus' surviving siege machinery. Severus' troops were eager to force their way through the breach, but Severus unaccountably decided to give the enemy twenty-four hours to surrender. A day later, the Hatrans had not only failed to give up but had secretly rebuilt the breached wall during the night.

Of Severus' legions, Dio said that those that had come from Europe 'alone had the ability to do anything'. [Dio, LXXVI, 12] Yet even they shied away from tackling the wall now that the Arabs had been given time to strengthen their defences. 'They were so angry' about Severus' twenty-four-hour delay that 'not one of them would any longer obey him'. [Ibid.] 'The others, Syrians,' said Dio – apparently the Syria-based legions such as the 3rd Gallica, the 4th Scythica, the 6th Ferrata and the 10th Fretensis – were ordered to make the assault in the place of the European legions but they were 'miserably destroyed' and the attack repulsed. [Ibid.]

One of Severus' generals said that if the emperor gave him 550 men from the European legions he would take the city, but Severus sourly pointed out that he could not even find that many European soldiers because of the disobedience of their legions. [Ibid.] After twenty days of bloody failure, like Trajan before him, Severus gave up the siege of Hatra. He withdrew from Mesopotamia, leaving garrisons at various cities and forts, and travelled to Palestine. At the temple to Jupiter built on the site of the Jewish Temple at Jerusalem, Severus sacrificed to the memory of Pompey the Great, the first Roman general to take Jerusalem.

The campaign had cost the lives of thousands of Roman troops and secured no great lasting benefits for Rome, other than buying a little time before her assets beyond the Euphrates were again besieged and overrun. Now, Severus turned his back on military affairs and played tourist. He went to Egypt, and at Alexandria locked up the tomb of Alexander the Great so that no one in future could view his mummified body. He then sailed down the Nile, halting only when he learned that disease was ravaging Ethiopia ahead.

By AD 202, Severus was back in Rome. He had left the new 1st Parthica and 3rd Parthica legions in the East, and they built bases for themselves in Mesopotamia – the former at Singara, the latter at Rhesana. Severus brought the 2nd Parthica Legion back to Italy with him following the Parthian expedition. Even though Severus had reformed the Praetorian Guard after he came to power, he never totally trusted it; Praetorians had, after all, murdered his predecessor Pertinax. The 2nd Parthica Legion was now installed at Alba Longa, in the Alban Hills, just 12 miles (19 kilometres) south of Rome, becoming the first legion based in Italy south of the River Po since the late days of the Republic, some 230 years before.

Here at Alba, the 2nd Parthica, which had proved its loyalty to Severus in the East, became the emperor's pseudo lifeguards. Now the Praetorians knew that the emperor's pet legion was just several hours' march away at Alba should they ever have thoughts of murdering the occupant of the throne. The 2nd Parthica Legion, or the Alban Legion as it would colloquially become known, was now serving as Severus' life insurance.

The following year, the triumphal Arch of Septimius Severus was inaugurated in Rome. In one of the panels, a Roman soldier is seen escorting an eastern prisoner who may well have been King Abgar of Osroene, who had surrendered to Severus following the fall of Edessa. Abgar did subsequently go to Rome, with a massive escort. [Dio, LXXX, 16] He may have taken part in Severus' triumphal procession. On an inscription on the arch, Severus claimed to have restored the state and enlarged the empire. For the moment, the Roman Empire's extended borders were secure, the frontier lands quiet. But peace, in the third century, would be a rare phenomenon for Romans.

AD 208–210
LIX. SEVERUS' SCOTTISH INVASION
Invigorating idle legions

The emperor Septimius Severus, feeling that the legions 'were becoming enervated by idleness', and having concluded that Rome controlled less than half of Britain, decided to correct both situations by invading the island's northern unconquered portion. [Dio, LXXVII, 11] In AD 197, while Severus was planning his Parthian campaign, the Maeatae tribe of Scotland, which lived beside Hadrian's Wall, was being troublesome – their neighbours, the Caledonians, having failed to abide by their promises to Rome that they would keep the Maeatae under control. With his focus on the East, as a temporary solution Severus had authorized the governor of northern Britain, Virius Lupus, 'to purchase peace from the Maeatae for a large sum'. [Dio, LXXVI, 5]

But by 208, Severus was now ready to turn his attention to Scotland personally. In the spring, he arrived in Britain with his wife, sons and a large army. Then, from his headquarters at Eburacum, he advanced past Hadrian's Wall and launched an offensive against the Maeatae, near the wall, then against the Caledonians in the Highlands. 'But as he advanced through the country he experienced countless hardships in cutting down the forests, levelling the heights, filling up swamps, and bridging the swamps.' [Dio, LXXVII, 13] Cassius Dio, a senator at the time, says that the warriors of Scotland, who lived in tents, were 'very swift in running and very firm in standing their ground'. They were armed with a shield, short spear and a dagger. The tribes also still used war chariots drawn by small, fast horses, as they had at the time of Agricola's campaigns 120 years before. [Ibid.]

The tribes avoided pitched battles but instead used their livestock as bait, luring the Roman troops intent on plunder into swamps and bogs. The tribesmen would 'plunge into the swamps and exist there with only their heads above water,' said Dio. While 'the water caused great suffering to the Romans', the tribesmen only attacked the Romans 'when they became scattered'. Wounded Roman soldiers who could not walk 'would be slain by their own men, in order to avoid capture'. [Ibid.]

Over the three years of the campaign, Roman losses were enormous: 'Fully 50,000 died,' said Dio. But Severus 'did not desist until he had approached the extremity of the island'. [Ibid.] By this time suffering from severe gout, he himself was carried the length of Scotland in a litter. By the end of the summer of AD 210, Severus' expensive campaign had not subjugated the tribes of northern Britain, but it forced them to parley.

A family portrait of Septimius Severus, his wife Julia Domna, and one of his children.

At 64 years old, Severus rode at the head of the Roman army to meet the tribal leaders to finalize a peace treaty. With him rode his ambitious eldest son, 22-year-old Caracalla – a nickname, derived from his habit of always wearing a particular type of cloak. Caracalla's actual name, which changed several times, was Marcus Aurelius Severus Antoninus. Ahead on the moorland, the Caledonians had formed up in battle array for the parley. Caracalla rode just behind his father, but in front of the emperor's escort. As they came up to the Caledonians, the young prince drew his sword and appeared to prepare to plunge it into his father's back. Other Romans of the party cried out a warning to Severus, who turned, saw Caracalla's sword, and gave his son a cold stare, which checked the youth.

Severus, short but well built, said nothing, just dismounted and walked to the tribunal prepared for the negotiations, which then proceeded. The treaty was agreed – Roman troops would not enter tribal territory, but in return the Maeatae had to give up their lands and withdraw north. Issuing an invitation for Caledonian chiefs and their dependants to visit him at his headquarters at Eburacum, Severus withdrew.

Back at Eburacum, Severus sent Praetorian Prefect Papinian to bring Caracalla to his quarters. When the pair arrived, they found the emperor unwell on a couch. Severus' influential freedman, chief secretary Castor, was also present. A sword lay on a table in front of the emperor, with the handle pointing towards Caracalla. Severus castigated his son for daring to draw a sword against him, and in public. He then dared Caracalla to take up the sword in front of him and slay him; or, to order Papinian to kill him. Caracalla slunk away.

Shortly after, a delegation of Caledonian chieftains arrived at Eburacum, and were treated as the special guests of the emperor and the empress, Julia Domna. The empress even entertained the wife of Caledonian leader Argentocoxus and was impressed with her wit. [Dio, LXXVII, 16] With winter closing in, the treaty was sealed, and the tribal leaders returned to Scotland. But the peace would be temporary.

AD 210

LX. EXECUTIONS AT YORK
Legionaries or Praetorians?

Caracalla simmered with humiliation until one day, late in AD 210, he burst from his quarters at Eburacum, 'shouting and bawling that he was being wronged by Castor', his father's right-hand man. 'Thereupon certain soldiers who had been got ready beforehand assembled and joined in the outcry.' But 'they were quickly checked when Severus himself appeared among them and punished the more unruly ones'. [Dio, LXXVII, 14] What form that punishment took was not revealed. Not many weeks later, on 4 February 210, Severus died at Eburacum.

Discoveries of the skeletons of beheaded men in a Roman cemetery at modern-day York in 2004 led the press and BBC Television to suggest that these were victims of a massacre carried out at Eburacum by Caracalla following his father's death. A number of graves, including those of fifty adult males, were found outside the old city walls, in a graveyard bordering the old Roman road from the southwest. Many of these men had been beheaded; one had manacles around his ankles. Pottery shards at the burial site suggested that the graves dated from early in the third century. In

2005, another grave containing the remains of a further twenty-four men was found nearby; at least eighteen of these men had also been decapitated. [Girling]

The decapitations had taken place from behind, and had been rough affairs; in one case, thirteen sword or axe blows had been required to sever a victim's head. Scientific analysis of the bones showed that none of the men in the graves was older than 45. All were quite tall for the time, at around 5 feet 9 inches (174 centimetres). All were powerfully built, and their arms showed evidence of extreme exertion over a number of years. Isotope analysis of their teeth indicated that these men originated from the Mediterranean, the Alps, even from Africa. [Ibid.]

Even though the evidence suggested that these men were connected to the Roman military – Eburacum was the base of the 6th Victrix Legion in the third century and headquarters of Severus' army of numerous legions during his Scottish campaigns – a story that these skeletons were evidence of a bloody wave of executions of Severus' courtiers carried out by Caracalla quickly gained media currency.

However, the York Archaeological Trust in its Annual Report for 2005–6 played down the Caracalla massacre theory, pointing out that these skeletons came from four different periods. Additionally, while Cassius Dio reported that Caracalla did execute many of his father's courtiers, including Castor, once he became emperor, those executions apparently took place later, in Rome.

But perhaps one group of York's beheaded skeletons was connected to Caracalla's AD 210 outburst against Castor; perhaps they were Praetorian guardsmen;

Remains of one of the tall, decapitated Romans unearthed at York, likely to have been one of the Praetorians who made the mistake of showing mutinous support for Caracalla.

Caracalla, depicted in this bust, murdered his younger brother Geta while he was in their mother's arms. Ambitious Caracalla was subsequently the cause of the punishment of soldiers who supported him at York.

members of Caracalla's severely punished 'cheer squad'. These men were Roman citizens – it was the right of every citizen to be beheaded if convicted of a 'capital crime' – and their uniformly large physical size marks them as possible Praetorians. Ever since Severus' AD 193 reforms, serving legionaries had been made Praetorians – on the strength of their physicality and bravery. And Severus' Praetorian recruits came from all areas of the empire, just like the decapitated men at York. Cassius Dio, who had contact with Severus' Praetorians, described them as 'soldiers most savage in appearance, most terrifying in speech, and most boorish in conversation'. [Dio, LXXV, 2]

It is quite possible that here, then, unearthed at York, was the gruesome evidence of Caracalla's tantrum, and of the price that Praetorian guardsmen had paid for their obedience to his wishes.

AD 217

LXI. KILLING CARACALLA
Eastern retreat

Spring had come, the standards of the legions had been sanctified in the lustration during March's Quatranalis ceremonials, and in Mesopotamia, the emperor Caracalla, now 29 years old, was planning to resume the war against the Parthians. It was 8 April when Caracalla set off from Edessa with a mounted column, planning to ride to Carrhae (modern-day Harran in Turkey), to set the campaign in motion. Some distance along the road, the column came to a halt for a rest break. Caracalla dismounted and stretched his legs. Around him, others followed suit. Among them were men of his personal bodyguard unit, the Lions. These bodyguards were Scythians and

Germans, for Caracalla did not trust the Praetorians or any other Roman soldiers to protect him. These bodyguards were former prisoners who had been slaves before Caracalla had taken them from their Roman masters, armed them, given them the same privileges and pay as centurions, and made them his closest companions.

A mature soldier named Julius Martialis now approached the emperor on foot, looking as if he wanted to discuss something with him. Martialis was a retired legionary now serving in the Evocati militia. Apparently living in the East after leaving his legion, he had been recalled to service for Caracalla's campaign. Martialis had recently asked the emperor for promotion to centurion, but his request had been denied. This, said Dio, was enough motivation for what Martialis was about to do. [Dio, LXXIX, 5]

Coming up to Caracalla, Martialis leaned close, as if about to confide something to him, then jabbed him with a small dagger. No one saw the strike, and Martialis hurried away. Only when the emperor collapsed to the ground was the alarm raised among the bodyguards. Martialis, instead of throwing the murder weapon away, kept hold of it, and a Scythian of the Lions bodyguard, seeing the bloodied blade in his hand, launched a javelin at him as he tried to make his escape. The javelin transfixed the assassin, who fell down dead.

But Caracalla was not dead. As soldiers and staff members crowded around the seriously wounded emperor on the roadway, two tribunes of the Praetorian Guard, the brothers Aurelius Nemesianus and Aurelius Apollinaris, pushed through the crowd and huddled over Caracalla. But instead of helping him, the brothers finished the job, killing the emperor. Like other mad emperors before him, notably Caligula and Commodus, Caracalla died at the hands of his own people.

According to Cassius Dio, who was with the imperial party in Mesopotamia at the time, all three of Caracalla's assailants had been put up to the deed by Caracalla's prefect of the Praetorian Guard, Marcus Oppellius Macrinus. [Ibid.] Macrinus had already been in secret communication with the troops stationed throughout Mesopotamia, promising to end the unpopular war with the Parthians, which the legions considered 'especially burdensome'. For three days following the assassination of Caracalla, Macrinus kept a

A coin of Caracalla issued to the troops who would soon assassinate him on the road to Carrhae.

low profile. Then, on 11 April, which happened to be the birthday of the late and well-remembered emperor Septimius Severus, Macrinus was hailed by the troops as their new emperor. [Ibid.]

At 53 years old, Macrinus was a native of Mauretania in North Africa, and even wore an earring as the Moors did. Of Equestrian rank at the time of Caracalla's death, Macrinus became the first man to obtain the Roman throne without having been a senator. To keep his word to the army that he would end this Parthian war, Macrinus immediately sent a friendly message to the Parthian king, Artabanus V, together with freed Parthian prisoners, hoping to bring about a peace treaty between them. In response, Artabanus demanded that the Romans rebuild all the cities and fortresses that they had destroyed throughout Parthia, make large financial reparations, and then withdraw entirely from Mesopotamia.

Macrinus had barely received this haughty proposal when he learned that Artabanus and a large Parthian army of mounted archers and heavy cataphracts, even camel units, was advancing on the Roman headquarters at Nisibis. There, the two armies warily camped opposite each other beside a water source, and before long blows were exchanged between Romans and Parthians over control of the water. This soon exploded into a full-scale battle outside the Roman camp.

Macrinus himself, who was described as 'exceedingly timorous' by Dio, apparently panicked when the tide of battle turned against his troops. [Dio, LXXIX, 27] When it looked as if the Roman camp would fall, Macrinus departed with his entourage, leaving his soldiers to their own devices. The non-combatants in the Roman camp, the armour-bearers and baggage attendants, then rushed out of the camp and charged the Parthians who, thinking these men were armed Roman reinforcements, reeled away.

The onset of night saved the Roman army from total defeat, but the flight of Macrinus dejected the troops he had deserted, and they were subsequently 'conquered' by the Parthians. Macrinus then purchased an end to the war, paying 200 million sesterces in gifts and cash to the Parthian king and the nobles around him. Macrinus also ceased Roman military operations in Armenia against Tiridates, the Armenian king, who had won the support of the Parthians. Macrinus even sent Tiridates a crown, recognizing his sovereignty over Armenia. Both sides then withdrew from Mesopotamia, with the Parthians returning to their own territory and the Romans pulling back to Syria. [Ibid.]

Macrinus sent word to the Senate that the war was over, but he failed to tell the senators at home that he had paid for peace and given up territory that since the time of Severus had been considered Roman. The Senate sacrificed to the goddess Victory in the deceitful Macrinus' honour, and offered him the title of Parthicus, an honour he guiltily declined. Still, Macrinus had kept his word to the legions; he had terminated the war. But the way he had done it was 'exasperating because of their defeat', as far as some Roman soldiers were concerned. [Dio, LXXIX, 29] Others perceived Macrinus as weak and easy to manipulate. While the legions were encamped en masse in Syria prior to marching back to their individual bases, a mood of mutiny swept through their ranks.

This mood was exacerbated when Macrinus ordered reductions to pay and conditions for future legion recruits. Caracalla had introduced higher pay and certain exemptions from duty for legionaries, and this had achieved its aim of making him highly popular with the legions. But it had also increased the annual salary bill for the legions by 280 million sesterces a year. [Dio, LXXIX, 36] Macrinus was at Antioch in the late spring when word reached him that his own troops were in revolt against him. A new civil war was about to begin.

AD 217–218
LXII. MACRINUS AGAINST ELAGABALUS
Praetorians versus legions

Seventeen-year-old Varius Avitus Bassianus had been born at Emesa in Syria, where his mother's family provided the hereditary high priests of the eastern sun god Baal – known as Elagabalus among the Romans. The youth's grandmother Julia Maesa, sister-in-law of the late emperor Septimius Severus, was determined that a grandson of hers would occupy the throne and restore the Severan dynasty that had ended with the death of Caracalla earlier that year, AD 217. The wealthy grandmother promoted her grandson's claim to the throne, which had been seized on 8 April by Praetorian prefect Macrinus on the death of the young emperor

Macrinus was not popular with either soldiers or civilians. As a result of his capitulation to the peace demands of the Parthians, 'the soldiers despised him and paid no heed to what he did to win their favour,' said Dio. [Dio, LXXIX, 20] In September,

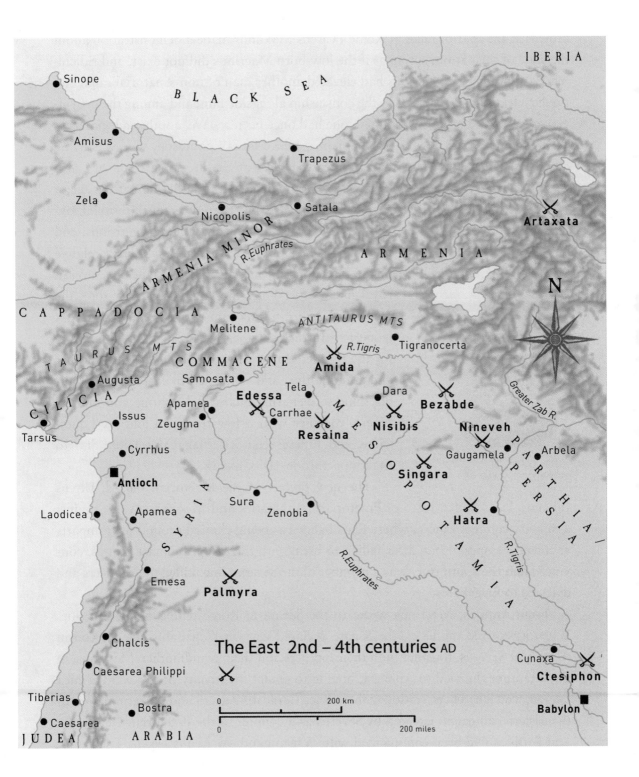

The East 2nd – 4th centuries AD

crowds at the chariot races at Rome's Circus Maximus made a demonstration about the state of the nation, acting as if the low-born Macrinus did not exist, and ridiculing his appointees – Macrinus had elevated another man of non-senatorial rank, city prefect Oclatinius Adventus, to the consulship alongside him, and among the provincial governors Macrinus appointed, one had once been a slave, another a legionary.

By the new year of AD 218, Bassianus, Julia Maesa's grandson, who was living at Emesa with his grandmother, claimed that he was the illegitimate son of Caracalla – who would have had to father him at the age of 11 if the claim was true. There was much residual loyalty to the murdered Caracalla among the troops, and they chose to believe the story and support a relative of the late emperor Severus and continue the Severan royal line. Before long, the young pretender took the name Elagabalus, to link him with the sun god of that name and further enhance his prestige and suitability for the throne. On 16 May, encouraged by his mother and grandmother, and supported by just the small unit of ethnic soldiers that guarded the shrine and mint at Emesa, together with a few freedmen and six Equestrians and Emesa senators, Elagabalus laid claim to Macrinus' throne. [Dio, LXXIX, 31]

Elagabalus was only fourteen when he became emperor.

The new prefect of the Praetorian Guard, Ulpius Julianus, led a mixed force of Praetorians, auxiliaries and Moorish cavalry against a military camp at Emesa, where Elagabalus was being chaired around the ramparts as the new emperor. But, after failing to break into the camp, Julianus' troops, convinced that the youth truly was a member of the Severan line, killed their officers and defected to Elagabalus.

From Antioch, Macrinus wrote to the Senate in Rome telling of the uprising. When it received the letter, the Senate declared war on Elagabalus and his cousin Alexander Severus, together with their mothers and their grandmother. Macrinus, in the meantime, hurried to Apamea, hoping to secure the loyalty of the 2nd Parthica Legion, which had been stationed there since Caracalla's death and the termination of the eastern campaign. Created by Severus as a counter to the Praetorian Guard, the 2nd Parthica had been commanded with 'a firm hand' by Aelius Decius Triccianus, the present governor of Pannonia, who had enhanced its loyalty to Macrinus. [Dio, LXXX, 4]

In late May AD 218, in front of the men of the 2nd Parthica, Macrinus announced that he was making his 10-year-old son Diadumenianus his co-emperor, as if to counter Elagabalus' dynastic claims by creating a dynasty of his own. He also promised every legionary of the 2nd Parthica 20,000 sesterces, and handed out 4,000 sesterces to every man on the spot. [Dio, LXXIX, 34] While he was throwing a banquet for the locals, a soldier brought him a severed head – of his Praetorian prefect Julianus. Unnerved by this, Macrinus returned to Antioch. Once he had gone, the 2nd Parthica and other units wintering in the region of Apamea lost faith in him and swore loyalty to Elagabalus.

In the first week of June, joined by the 2nd Parthica Legion and other troops who had defected to him, Elagabalus set off for Antioch. Macrinus, with only cohorts of the Praetorian Guard staying faithful to him, marched to intercept the young usurper. By this period the Praetorians were wearing scale armour in preference to the heavy segmented metal armour they are seen wearing on Trajan's Column a century earlier. But even this lighter armour was considered too heavy by some soldiers, and at their request Macrinus gave his Praetorians permission to dispense with the armour and their heavy 'grooved' shields, which 'thus rendered them lighter for battle'. [Ibid., 37]

At a village 24 miles (38 kilometres) northeast of Antioch, the two comparatively small armies met on 8 June. Elagabalus' mother and grandmother had even come along, riding in chariots. Young Elagabalus himself was riding a horse in the column, but he was not in command. For her grandson's military commander, Julia Maesa had chosen not a general but Elagabalus' longtime Greek tutor, Gannys, who, according to the contemporaneous Dio, 'was utterly without military experience and had spent his life in luxury'. [Ibid., 38] Seeing Macrinus' column approaching from the direction of Antioch, Gannys was anxious to occupy a pass in the column's path. There, he marshalled his troops in good order.

Elagabalus' troops, no doubt unimpressed at being commanded by a slave, put up a half-hearted defence when Macrinus' stripped-down Praetorians came running to the attack. When men began pulling out of Elagabalus' rear ranks, the boy's mother and grandmother jumped down from their chariots and ran among them, urging the soldiers to return to the struggle. Then the youngster himself was seen riding towards the fight with sword in hand. The defence stiffened, but Elagabalus would not have been victorious had not Macrinus again lost his nerve. The emperor rode off back to Antioch accompanied by a few men, leaving his troops to continue the fighting. Seeing this, his Praetorians lost heart, and capitulated.

On entering Antioch, Macrinus told the Antiochans that he had won the battle. He then put his son in the care of a trusted freedman and sent them riding east, making for Parthia, where, the freedman was instructed, they should seek the protection of King Artabanes. Macrinus then shaved off his bushy beard and shaved his head. That night, wearing a dark, hooded civilian cloak, he slipped out of the city with a few loyal companions. He succeeded in reaching Cilicia, where, pretending to be a soldier, he secured a carriage of the Cursus Publicus Velox, the government courier service. Using this he drove all the way through Cappadocia, Galatia, and Bithynia, to reach the port of Eribolon.

From Eribolon, planning to return to Rome, where he was sure he would still have the support of the Senate, Macrinus took a merchant ship around the Bithynian coast to Chalcedon, modern Kadekoy in Turkey. This was just across the water from Byzantium. From Chalcedon, Macrinus sent a message to a local procurator seeking money to enable him to continue his journey. But this was a mistake. The procurator, choosing Elagabalus over Macrinus, had the fugitive emperor arrested. A centurion who had orders to return Macrinus to Syria took him as far as Cappadocia. There, Macrinus learned that his 10-year-old son had been arrested at Zeugma by a centurion of the 4th Scythica Legion while trying to cross the Euphrates.

Macrinus now threw himself from the carriage carrying him, only to frac-

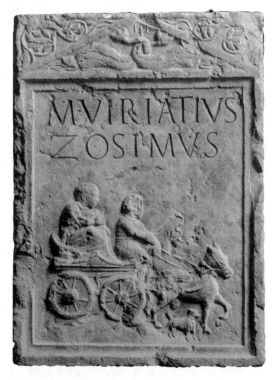

Defeated by the legions of Elagabalus, Macrinus succeeded in escaping using a *raedae* carriage, like this one, of the Cursus Publicus Velox courier service.

ture his shoulder. Another centurion, Marcianus Taurus, under orders to ensure that the emperor did not reach Antioch alive, met Macrinus' party in Cappadocia shortly afterwards, and put Macrinus to the sword. Young Elagabalus saw Macrinus' body when he passed by some time later on his way from Syria to Bithynia, and gloated over it. [Dio, LXXIX, 40] An emperor made by the Praetorian Guard had been destroyed by the legions. His successor, made by the legions, would be destroyed by the Praetorians.

Ironically, opposition to young Elagabalus' rule swiftly bubbled over in his own back yard. Within months of his taking the throne, in the province of Syria Phoenicia, Verus the governor attempted to lead the one legion resident in his province, the 3rd Gallica, in a rebellion against Elagabalus. The son of a centurion of the 3rd Gallica serving in the ranks of his father's legion had already stirred up the unit against the new emperor; Governor Verus himself had been a centurion before being elevated to the Senate.

Meanwhile, at the base of the 4th Scythica Legion at Zeugma in Syria proper, that legion's commander, Gellius Maximus, the son of a physician, also came out against the new emperor. But, said Cassius Dio, these men 'took leave of their senses' in opposing Elagabalus without ensuring their legionaries were solidly behind them. With their legions remaining loyal to the emperor, these rebellious officers were soon arrested, and that same year, AD 218, they met the executioner's blade. [Dio, LXXX, 7]

But Elagabalus did not have long to live. After he imposed the worship of Baal on the Roman world and indulged in homosexual orgies, the young emperor lost popular favour and in AD 222 was murdered by the Praetorian Guard, who also killed his manipulative mother. His grandmother survived, as, in his place, the Guard hailed Elagabalus' cousin, Severus Alexander, as Rome's new emperor.

AD 238
LXIII. FOR AND AGAINST MAXIMINUS
The price of loyalty

Gaius Julius Verus Maximinus was the first soldier from the ranks of the legions to become emperor of Rome. Born in Thrace, before enlisting in the legions he was a shepherd. A large man, his great physical strength and determination equipped him to rise rapidly through the ranks to become a legion commander under Septimius

Severus. Under Severus' nephew and Elagabalus' successor as emperor Severus Alexander, Maximinus was a consul and commander of the army on the Rhine. When Alexander was murdered in AD 235, Maximinus was declared emperor by the Rhine legions, an appointment reluctantly endorsed by a Senate unimpressed with his lowly background.

In AD 236, Maximinus departed from Rome leading cohorts of the Praetorian Guard and the 2nd Parthica Legion from the Alban Mount – a unit in which he may well have served as an enlisted man, for it was recruited in his home territory of Thrace. Basing himself in Pannonia, where he brought an army together from the Rhine and Danube legions, over the next two years Maximinus aggressively countered the inroads of Germans and Sarmatians.

By March of AD 238 Maximinus and his troops were preparing to launch a spring offensive against Goths occupying Moesia. Meanwhile, in the province of Africa, wealthy young landowners rebelled against high new taxes imposed by Maximinus, killing the imperial tax-collectors and declaring the provincial governor and his son co-emperors. The Senate in Rome immediately endorsed their action, and the cities of

Maximinus was busy fighting barbarians in the Balkans, as depicted here on the Ludovisi Sarcophagus, when news arrived that the Senate had replaced him with the Gordians, father and son.

Italy also came out for father and son and against Maximinus, whom the Senate declared deposed. Both new emperors were named Marcus Antonius Gordianus Sempronianus Romanus Africanus. The father, Gordian I, who was aged around 70 and was more interested in literature than politics, gave his son and now co-emperor Gordian II the task of raising

The town of Tebessa, today's Timgad in Algeria, was built by the 3rd Augusta, resident legion of the province of Africa for hundreds of years.

an army of levies in and around the provincial capital, Carthage.

There was just a single legion stationed in Africa, the 3rd Augusta, inland at Tebessa, to the southwest of Carthage. Once news of events at Carthage reached Tebessa, the legion prepared to march on the provincial capital in support of Maximinus. For the legionaries, the Gordians were not rulers in the stamp of the soldier emperor Maximinus, and, remaining loyal to Maximinus, they were determined to deal with the usurpers.

In the first week of April, leading an army of raw recruits, Gordian II and rebel leaders came face to face with the 3rd Augusta Legion on the plain outside Carthage. Silently, the legionaries of the 3rd Augusta spread into battle formation in front of Gordian's army, then stood stock still in their battle lines and awaited the order to charge. The very sight of the highly disciplined and unflinching legionaries in formation was enough to unnerve the rebels' recruits. Gordian's men broke; 'throwing away their equipment [they] ran without waiting for the charge. Pushing and trampling each other, more were killed by their own side than by the enemy.' [Herod., VII, IX, 7]

When the 3rd Augusta did charge, they met little opposition, quickly routing the rebel force and killing the younger Gordian. When the news of the defeat of his army and death of his son reached Gordian I at Carthage, this, along with the fact that the 3rd Augusta was advancing on the city, prompted the old man to take his own life. The Gordians, father and son, had shared the title of emperor of Rome for just three weeks.

At Rome, the news of the deaths of the Gordians caused the Senate to elect from their ranks a 'board of twenty' consuls and ex-consuls to govern, and from these, two senators who would be co-emperors – Decimus Balbinus and Pupienus Maximus. Balbinus had been a consul, and governor of Asia, while Pupienus was an unpopular former City Prefect of Rome. The pair was so disliked by the public that, at the insistence of the men of the Praetorian Guard cohorts at the capital, the Senate proclaimed as Caesar, or deputy emperor and heir to the throne, Gordianus, the 13-year-old grandson of the late Gordian I.

Meanwhile, Maximinus, the deposed emperor, had not been idle. On the news of the elevation of the Gordians he had marched his army from Pannonia into northeastern Italy, intent on dealing with his opponents. The first major city he came to – Aquileia – closed its gates and, led by the co-emperor Pupienus, offered sharp resistance. Maximinus ordered his troops to besiege the city. As the siege of Aquileia dragged on for months, the loyalty of the men of one of Maximinus' legions began to fray. His 2nd Parthica Legion was normally based at Alba, just outside Rome, and the legion's troops became increasingly concerned that the senatorial forces might harm their wives and children, who lived outside the legion camp at Alba, or at the very least make them hostages.

During a break in the fighting outside Aquileia, Maximinus, his son Maximus, and most of their troops retired to their tents. Now men of the 2nd Parthica acted. They 'went to Maximinus' tent about noon and with the help of the Praetorians tore his image from the standards. When Maximinus and his son came out of their tent and attempted to reason with the troops, they were killed without being heard'. The 2nd Parthica completed the deed by also killing the Praetorian Prefect and Maximinus' other senior advisers. [Herod., VIII, V, 8–9]

Pupienus returned triumphantly to Rome, bringing many of Maximinus' troops with him, but he soon became suspicious of his co-emperor Balbinus, who had been in sole command in Rome during his absence. The pair began to quarrel bitterly. To settle matters, the Praetorian Guard kidnapped both of them, but as the men of the German bodyguard that Pupienus and Balbinus had created for themselves rushed to save the co-emperors, the Praetorians killed them.

Gordian I's teenage grandson now became the emperor Gordian III. His mother and later his father-in-law would rule in his name. One of the first acts of the administration of Gordian III was the abolition of the 3rd Augusta Legion, the unit that had remained loyal to Maximinus and had been responsible for the deaths of Gordian III's grandfather, Gordian I, and uncle, Gordian II. The 2nd Parthica Legion, meanwhile, was honoured by Gordian and returned to its base and its families at the Alban Mount.

Ahead lay half a century of almost interminable civil wars, with the Roman throne changing hands with alarming regularity and with the legions fighting off invaders on the one hand, and forced to fight each other on behalf of various imperial incumbents and pretenders on the other, as the empire lurched towards collapse.

AD 242–268
LXIV. VALERIAN CAPTURED
Rome's great humiliation

King Shapur I was the son of Ardashir I, first ruler of the Sasanian Persian dynasty, which gained power in the former Parthian Empire in the third century. Shapur proved to be as able a ruler, as capable a soldier, and as violent an opponent of Rome as his father had been. By AD 242, Shapur had successfully taken up where his father had left off in the war against the Romans. Invading Roman Mesopotamia, Shapur took the cities of Nisibis and Carrhae from the legions of Gordian III. In AD 243, Shapur suffered a reverse at Resaina, home base of the 3rd Parthica Legion. The following year, after young Gordian III was murdered by his troops and his Praetorian Prefect Marcus Philippus replaced him as emperor – he would become known to later historians as Philip the Arabian – Shapur sealed a favourable peace with the Romans, which left him controlling significant portions of former Roman territory, knowing that Philip was anxious to hurry to the West to deal with Gothic invaders who were threatening Italy.

Over the next dozen years, Philip was murdered and four other Roman emperors came and went in swift and bloody succession, so that by AD 256 Shapur felt the Roman Empire to be so vulnerable that he launched a new campaign, leading his army into Armenia and Syria, penetrating even as far as Cilicia. Swatting away the legions that attempted to stop him, he sacked all the wealthy cities of Syria, including the capital, Antioch.

It fell to the latest Roman emperor, the elderly Valerian, to attempt to repulse the Persian invaders. Valerian had been a consul under Severus Alexander, and was one of the consuls and ex-consuls who in AD 238 supported the rebellion of Gordian I and Gordian II against Maximinus, then appointed Pupienus and Balbinus co-emperors, and finally hailed Gordian III as their successor. In AD 253, Valerian was commanding the legions on the Upper Rhine when the then emperor Gallus summoned him to help fight off rival Aemilius. Valerian marched an army from Mogontiacum to Rome, but arrived too late to save Gallus, who had been killed by Aemilius. He avenged him by executing Aemilius, then took the throne for himself.

When news of Shapur's invasion of the Roman East reached Rome, Valerian appointed his son Gallienus to rule the West, then headed east with fresh troops. Fortunes subsequently waxed and waned as the Roman and Persian armies slugged it out, with Valerian pushing Shapur back into Mesopotamia. With the Roman garrison at Edessa on the Euphrates (considered to have the most formidable walls of any city in the East), under siege from the Persians, Valerian led an army to its relief. But outside Edessa in June AD 260, Shapur's Persians caught the Romans in the open and routed them. Valerian himself was captured, and forced to surrender on bended knee to the Persian king.

As many as 40,000 of Valerian's troops were killed or captured. The Roman prisoners, the men of several proud legions, were herded east and put to work on major construction projects by the Persians. Valerian's captured legionaries used their building skills to erect the new Persian city of Gondeshapur, and the massive dam at Shaushtar which Shapur named, with some irony, Band-e-Qeysar – Dam of Caesar.

A Persian relief shows Roman emperor Valerian on bended knee as he surrenders to Persian emperor Shapur I. Valerian died two years later in Persian custody.

Valerian died in Persian captivity two years later. While his son Gallienus ruled in Rome for the next eight years, the influx of invaders across the Rhine and Danube meant that Spain was in the hands of the Franks; Gaul and Britain had declared independence; and the Danube provinces were occupied by German and Gothic tribes, so that Gallienus was effectively only in control of Italy and the Balkans, even fighting invaders on Italian soil. In AD 268, Gallienus too would be murdered – in Milan, while fending off a claimant to his throne. His assassination generated yet another succession of short-lived emperors. In both the East and the West, the Roman Empire and its legions were in a shambles.

AD 267–274
LXV. THE PALMYRAN WARS
A queen in golden chains

Zenobia was the young and beautiful wife of Odenatus, king of Palmyra, a rich city state and Roman ally in the desert, at the junction of caravan routes to India. After the capture of Roman emperor Valerian by Shapur, King Odenatus had led his small Palmyran army against the Persians, capturing one of their columns – loaded down with Roman booty following the defeat of Valerian's legions. Over the next several years, with the Roman command structure in the East non-existent, Odenatus brought surviving Roman troops in the region under his command. Using the skills of his own army, which was based on cavalry and archers in the eastern fashion, plus the infantry and siege machinery abilities of the Roman troops, Odenatus was able to whittle away the Persian hold on Roman assets in the East, earning the gratitude of the Roman emperor, Valerian's son Gallienus. In AD 267, a year before Gallienus was himself murdered, Odenatus and his eldest son were assassinated – by whom, was never established. As a result, Zenobia's young son Vaballathus became sovereign of Palmyra, with his ambitious mother ruling through him.

In 269, Zenobia, who already occupied Syria in Rome's name, led the Palmyran army south to seize Egypt, then took most of Asia Minor. But instead of doing this in Rome's name, she declared all the annexed territory part of her son's Palmyran kingdom. The Romans, in the West, were too occupied with civil war and invaders from the north to immediately address the loss of the Roman East to the Palmyran queen, but by AD 270 the then emperor Aurelian was able to turn his eyes east.

By AD 272, Aurelian had arrived in Syria with an army which included new units only recently raised for this expedition – such as the 1st Illyricorum Legion,

The Temple of Bel in the heart of the city-state of Palmyra. The city was destroyed by Rome's legions after Queen Zenobia's defeat.

recruited in the Balkans. Aurelian conducted a steady campaign of attrition against the Palmyran army. At Antioch and then at Emesa, he defeated Zenobia's army, then pushed east through the desert to surround Palmyra. Zenobia and her young son attempted to escape the Roman siege, but were caught. The city surrendered, and Roman control of the East was re-established, and Palmyra lost its client status. Aurelian took Zenobia and several of her sons back to Rome with him. When Palmyra revolted against Roman rule the following year, Roman legions marched on the city, stormed it, then razed it to the ground. The famous crossroads city ceased to exist.

In AD 274, the same year that Aurelian surrendered the Roman province of Dacia to the barbarians and withdrew all Roman troops south of the Danube, he celebrated a Triumph through the streets of Rome for his victory over the Palmyrans and for restoring Roman control to the eastern provinces. It had been a long time since Rome had anything to celebrate. The hundreds of thousands of Romans lining the streets saw Zenobia and two of her sons on display in the triumphal procession. According to legend, Zenobia was led in golden chains. Just to prove she was no ordinary prisoner, she was kept at the famous villa of the emperor Hadrian at Tivoli, just outside Rome. Zenobia later married a Roman senator, and lived out the remainder of her life in Italy.

AD 305–312

LXVI. CONSTANTINE FIGHTS FOR THE THRONE
Victory under a new standard

The Roman Empire of the fourth century was rent from within by civil wars and eroded from without by the inroads of numerous foreign invaders. Peace, security, stability, these were all things of which fourth-century Romans could only dream. Yet the century started on a promising note. The emperor Diocletian and his co-emperor Maximian had vowed that they would rule for twenty years and then retire, handing over power to others. Uniquely, in AD 305 the two emperors abdicated, with Diocletian famously secluding himself in his vast palace at Salonae in Dalmatia, today's Split in Croatia.

The two emperors had prepared for an orderly transition of power by appointing a pair of co-emperors for both the East and the West, also appointing a Caesar under each co-emperor. While sharing power around eight men may have seemed to Diocletian and Maximian a sure way to prevent a single despot gaining power, it was in fact a formula for bitter internal rivalry. For, in leaving power in the hands of eight men, the pair created a recipe for in-fighting that would dominate Roman affairs for nineteen years and cost the lives of thousands of Roman soldiers in a series of costly civil wars.

It was Flavius Valerius Constantinus, or Constantine the Great as we know him, who would eventually emerge from the chaos as the sole victor. As Constantine I, he would go into the history books

After the abdication of co-emperors Diocletian and Maximian, seen here embracing, the scene was set for civil conflict that would result in Constantine the Great fighting his way to the throne to become sole ruler.

On the Arch of Galerius at Thessalonica in Greece, the army of the emperor Galerius, in which Constantine distinguished himself as a young cavalry officer, fights the Persians.

as the first Christian emperor, an excellent general and a man of intelligence, and the emperor who gave the city of Constantinople its name. He was all those things. But he was also cunning, ruthless, brutal, vindictive, paranoid and obsessed with glory. Diocletian had separated military and civil commands in the provinces. But it was the subsequent changes that Constantine wrought on the Roman army, from the organization and distribution of units to the structure of the officer corps, combined with the losses suffered in wars internal and external, that weakened the army to such an extent that within 100 years the Roman military would prove incapable of preventing the barbarians from sacking Rome. The army would also prove incapable of preventing the Roman Empire in the west from disappearing altogether within little more than 150 years.

Classical authors put Constantine's age when he died, in AD 337, at between 62 and 66. [Eus., *EH*, LIII] Born in Upper Moesia, Constantine was the son of Constantius Chlorus, great-nephew of the emperor Claudius II, one of Rome's crowd of emperors during the last half of the third century. Constantine's father pursued a military career, starting out with the imperial bodyguard and rising to become governor of Dalmatia and then Caesar for the west. Constantine himself was educated as part of the court of the emperor Diocletian at his capital of Nicomedia in Asia, and served as a tribune in the army which Diocletian took on an expedition to Egypt in AD 296.

Constantine fought the Sarmatians under the deputy emperor Galerius, the son of Diocletian, and is likely to have also served under him in his wars with the Persians. According to an anonymous contemporary biographer, 'When Constantine, then a young man, was serving in the cavalry against the Sarmatians, he seized by the hair and carried off a ferocious barbarian, and threw him at the feet of the emperor Galerius.' Later in the same campaign against the Sarmatians, Constantine 'slew many and won the victory for Galerius'. [Vale., 2, 3]

On the abdication of Diocletian and Maximian, young Constantine was not named as a Caesar to his father, the new co-emperor of the west, as he would have expected. When Constantius sought permission from the new Eastern emperor Galerius for his son to join him on an expedition to Britain to counter troublesome Picts in the north, at first Galerius was reluctant to release young Constantine, but he eventually agreed. Constantine left the palace at Nicomedia that same evening in a carriage of the Cursus Publicus Velox and hurried west, laming the horses at each Cursus Publicus station he passed through so that no message could overtake him rescinding the emperor's permission. [Ibid., 2, 4]

At Bononia on the coast of Gaul, Constantine joined his father, and from there the pair crossed the English Channel by ship, then hurried north. In the spring of AD 306, father and son led Roman forces in a campaign north of Hadrian's Wall, and won 'a victory over the Picts'. [Ibid.] But in the middle of the summer Constantius fell ill, and had to return to the provincial capital, Eburacum. There, in July, with all his children around him and having anointed Constantine as his successor, Constantius died. On 24 July, the Roman troops in Britain hailed Constantine as the new emperor in the west. As soon as news of the death of Constantius reached Rome, the Praetorian Guard hailed Maxentius, son of the abdicated emperor Maximian, as their choice of Emperor of the West. This creation of a rival emperor to Constantine sparked a series of civil wars that would last for years.

From the East, the emperor Galerius reluctantly granted Constantine the title of Caesar, but would not recognize him as his equal as Emperor of the West. For the moment, Constantine accepted the role of deputy emperor, and to cement his claim to ultimate power, married the daughter of abdicated emperor Maximian and sister of Maxentius.

Galerius, meanwhile, would not accept Maxentius' claim to be Emperor of the West, and sent his deputy emperor Severus marching to Rome with an army to unseat him. Severus was 'low both in character and in

A bust of a youthful Galerius, son of Diocletian, under whom Constantine served, and from whom he fled to join his father.

origin' and 'given to drink'. [Ibid., 4, 9] His troops did not respect him, and when Severus reached Italy in AD 307 he was deserted by his army and was forced to flee to Ravenna. Maxentius' father Maximian now came out of retirement at his son's behest and went to Severus at Ravenna. Through deception, Maximian made Severus a prisoner and took him to Rome, after which Severus was kept at an imperial villa at Tres Tabernae, 30 miles (48 kilometres) south of Rome. [Ibid., 3, 11]

Determined to punish Maxentius, Galerius himself then marched an army from the East to Rome. Camping at Interamna, today's Terni in southern Umbria, just to the north of the eternal city, Galerius sent envoys to Maxentius in Rome to convince him to submit to his authority. Not only did Maxentius send the envoys packing, he offered bribes to Galerius' troops, and some of them even defected as a result. Unsettled by this, Galerius withdrew from Italy, but, 'in order to supply his men with whatever booty he could' and so placate their greedy demands, he gave them permission to sack the Italian towns they passed through on the Flaminian Way north. [Ibid., 3, 7] As Galerius and his looting army marched away, Maxentius ordered the execution of his prisoner, the deputy emperor Severus, humiliatingly 'in the midst of his own troops, as it were'. [Eus., *EH*, XXVII]

Galerius' health was in decline; he would be dead within four years. He now retreated to Illyricum, and let Maxentius and Constantine fight it out to see who would become sole emperor of the Western Empire. According to Eusebius, who spoke to Constantine on the subject, Constantine resolved to overthrow Maxentius after 'those who had attempted it', Severus and Galerius, 'had experienced a disastrous termination of their enterprise'. [Ibid., XXVI]

On the other hand, historian Zosimus wrote that it was Maxentius who made the first move towards war with Constantine. To begin with, Maxentius supposedly fell out with his father Maximian, who sought refuge with Constantine in Gaul. [Zos., 2, 14] From there, Constantine efficiently dealt with a series of raids by the Bructeri and the Franks, 'barbarians who dwelt on the banks of the Rhine', and made allies of the Alemanni. [Eus., *EH*, XXV] Once he had Constantine's confidence, the elderly Maximian then twice tried to betray him, the second time paying for his treachery with his life. Now, said Zosimus, Maxentius used the pretext of avenging his dead father to prepare for war with Constantine. [Zos., 2, 14]

Throughout his career, Constantine had a habit of moving much more rapidly than his opponents expected. In the spring of AD 312, before Maxentius could mobilize his forces for an expedition to Gaul, Constantine crossed the Alps into Italy with an army made up of men from the garrisons of Britain, Gaul and the Rhine. The identity of individual units in his force is not known, but it was particularly strong in mounted troops – Constantine had much personal experience with the cavalry arm.

The 'obscure and imperfect narrative' of Zosimus, in the words of Gibbon, put the number of men in Constantine's force at this time at an excessive 90,000 foot and 8,000 horse, and gave Maxentius an amazing 170,000 foot and 18,000 horse. [Gibb., XVIII, n. 22] This total, of close to 300,000 men, would have been by far the largest number of Roman troops in Italy at any time during the imperial era, a number that, at that time, is simply not credible. A more reliable ancient source put Constantine's force at less than 40,000 men. [Eus., *HE, Prole.*, n. 3014] From later events, 8,000 cavalry would seem a realistic figure, while his infantry probably numbered 30,000. The same source gave Maxentius 100,000 men. [Ibid.] These lesser numbers are supported by the fact that within a few years Constantine would be leading an army of just 20,000 men into battle, with his opponent the then Eastern Emperor, Valerius Licinius, commanding 35,000. [Vale., 5, 27]

Meanwhile, from where did Maxentius amass so many troops at Rome? Even 100,000 soldiers was a huge army by the standards of the Late Empire. A number of cohorts of the Praetorian Guard were permanently stationed in Rome, but how many there were at this time is not known. Septimius Severus increased the Praetorian Guard to 15,000 men, but some Praetorians may have been serving with the Eastern Emperor Galerius and his successor Licinius. Likewise the household cavalry, the Imperial Singularian Horse, numbered 2,000 men at this time, but how many, if any, of those troopers were with Galerius is unknown.

The 2nd Parthica Legion, stationed at Alba Longa just south of Rome, was without doubt in Maxentius' army. In addition, Maxentius had incorporated Severus' eastern troops into his forces after they had changed sides on reaching Italy. According to Zosimus, Maxentius' army also included troops from Carthage, Sicily and Italy. [Zos., 2, 15] These men may have been freshly levied by Maxentius, in which case they could barely have been trained by the time that Constantine marched into Italy. The troops from Carthage, in addition to Moor and Numidian cavalry, may have also included the 3rd Augusta Legion; the only legion then based in North Africa, this unit would not be located in North Africa when the Notitia Dignitatum was written later that century. [Not. Dig.]

Once Constantine's army crossed the Crottian Alps from southern Gaul it stormed its way into the pro-Maxentius town of Sigusium (modern Susa in Piedmont), in northern Italy. Constantine's troops set fire to the town after they crashed through its gates, but Constantine had them extinguish the flames and save the town, and treated his prisoners well – so that word of his clemency would go on ahead of him and incline other Italians towards his cause and against that of Maxentius.

As Constantine proceeded southeast, 40 miles (64 kilometres) from Susa a large opposing cavalry force arrived from its base at Mediolanum, today's Milan, and formed up in his path on the plain near Augusta Taurinorum, modern-day Turin. The mainstay of Maxentius' cavalry force were units of heavily armed cataphracts in chain mail, with their horses also clad in mail, and the even more heavily armoured cavalry, called the Clibarnii, who wore suits of segmented armour that presaged the armoured knights of the Middle Ages. This style of heavy cavalry had been 'borrowed from the nations of the East' by the Romans. [Gibb., xiv] Maxentius himself was still at Rome, 450 miles (725 kilometres) away, so that the force that now opposed Constantine was commanded by Maxentius' subordinates.

The Maxentian cavalrymen, who had formed up in a massive wedge, point forward, 'flattered themselves that they should easily break and trample down the army of Constantine'. [Ibid.] Constantine sent his mixed force of cavalry and infantry against the opposition cavalry using complex manoeuvres which 'divided and baffled' the Maxentians. Soon the Maxentian troopers were fleeing in disarray to Turin, with Constantine's army in hot pursuit. The city of Turin closed its gates and refused to admit the retreating Maxentian cavalry, and outside the city walls Constantine's men isolated and butchered their mounted opponents. 'Very few escaped.' [Ibid.]

Following this comprehensive victory, Constantine led his army on to Milan, which, like Turin before it, welcomed him. Briefly, he occupied the city's imperial palace, as envoys arrived from cities throughout northern Italy with vows of allegiance. One city that did not submit to him was Verona. Under the command of Ruricius Pompeianus, an experienced general, the city closed its gates and prepared to defy Constantine. A cavalry force ordered west by Pompeianus to intercept Constantine's army was sent reeling in retreat after an engagement near Brescia, and Constantine arrived outside Verona and surrounded the city. A sally outside the walls by Pompeianus' troops was easily repelled, and Constantine prepared for a protracted siege of the city.

The resourceful Pompeianus was able to slip out of Verona by night, and he assembled a force of pro-Maxentius troops which he then led against the army besieging the city. Constantine, on hearing that Pompeianus' force was approaching, divided his army, leaving part to continue the siege and leading the remainder to meet Pompeianus in the field. On forming two battle lines on the plain, and finding that Pompeianus' troops outnumbered his, with the opposition front line extending much further than his and threatening to wrap around his flanks when both sides engaged, Constantine depleted his second line to fill out the front line to match the opposition.

This battle began towards the end of the day, and raged right through the night.

Constantine the Great.

Constantine, a tall man with great bodily strength and with considerable combat experience, was in the thick of the fighting. Dawn revealed a battlefield littered with mounds of bodies, and a victory for Constantine. Among the dead was Pompeianus, Maxentius' loyal and diligent general. On 28 August, when word of Pompeianus' defeat reached Verona, the city capitulated to Constantine, who imprisoned every member of the Maxentian garrison. [Gibb., XIV]

In the early autumn, as Constantine prepared to march on Rome, his subordinates begged him not to expose himself to danger by personally taking part in the next round of fighting, and in so doing putting the future of the Roman state at risk. He was, after all, one of the few Roman commanders-in-chief since Julius Caesar who physically took up sword and shield and fought alongside his men in battle.

At Rome meanwhile, Maxentius did not allow news of the defeats in the north to become public. Instead, he levied more troops locally and made plans for a deciding battle outside the capital. There, he was confident, he would destroy the threat posed by his brother-in-law Constantine in the same way that he had dealt with the feeble efforts of Severus and Galerius to dethrone him.

AD 312

LXVII. BATTLE OF THE MILVIAN BRIDGE
Deciding who rules

The site for the deciding battle between the rivals for the western throne was chosen by Maxentius, Constantine's Rome-based co-emperor and brother-in-law. That site was the flat river plain north of the Tiber river, just under 2 miles (2.4 kilometres) from the city. The plain was reached from the Field of Mars by the Milvian Bridge, the stone piers of which dated back to the first century BC. As part of his battle strategy, Maxentius had the wooden decking of the bridge removed, and gave orders for a bridge of boats to be built across the river nearby.

In October, Constantine and his army came marching down the Flaminian Way towards Rome. Constantine would later tell Eusebius that one day just after noon – usually the time that a Roman army ended its marching for the day and made camp – 'he saw with his own eyes the trophy of a cross of light in the heavens, above the sun, and bearing the inscription, "Conquer by this"'. [Eus., *EH*, XXVIII]

Eusebius claimed that all of Constantine's army also saw this sign in the heavens, but no other classical author confirms this. In fact, there would be much scepticism voiced down through the ages about the entire episode, even by Christian theologians. Dr Ernest Richardson, Eusebius' nineteenth-century translator, was to say, 'There are all sorts of explanation, from that of an actual miracle to that of pure later invention.' Richardson, himself a theologian, suggested that perhaps what Constantine, under intense mental strain at the time, actually experienced was 'some natural phenomenon of the sun', or 'a simple dream, or an hallucination'. [Ibid., n. 3019]

Or perhaps Constantine was a very clever tactician who saw an opportunity to let his highly superstitious soldiers think that he was divinely guided and so, therefore, were they. Nor was he averse to lying to Bishop Eusebius – at the same time that he described his vision of the cross in the sky to Eusebius, he assured him that he had marched on Italy because 'life was without enjoyment to him as long as he saw the imperial city thus afflicted' by Maxentius' rule. And that accordingly 'he resolved to deliver Rome from Maxentius'. [Eus., *EH*, XXVI] He told Eusebius this many years later, after he had emasculated Rome and made his capital elsewhere; in fact, Rome was a city Constantine disdained so thoroughly he would only visit it twice after AD

312, and only then to preside over the tenth and twentieth anniversaries of his rule and rub the noses of the Romans in his authority.

That night after his 'vision', Constantine told Eusebius, as he slept, 'the Christ of God' came to him in a dream 'and commanded him to make a likeness of that sign he had seen in the heavens'. [Ibid., *EH*, XXIX] Next day, when Constantine rose from his bed he told his closest associates of his dream, then called together artisans of gold and precious stones and, sitting in the midst of them,

The Porta Palatina, one of the city gates at Augusta Turinorum, today's northern Italian city of Turin. Constantine's forces routed the cavalry of Maxentius, his brother-in-law, outside this gate, on his push to Rome.

instructed them to create him a new imperial standard based on the sign of the cross in his vision, in gold and jewels.

Eusebius, who subsequently saw for himself the new battle standard created to Constantine's design, was to describe it: 'A long spear, overlaid with gold, formed the figure of a cross by means of a transverse bar laid over it.' What Eusebius described was the usual vexillum design used by the standards of emperors for hundreds of years prior to this; the vexillum, a standard also common to units of the Roman army, had always naturally, but incidentally, formed the sign of a cross. 'On the top of the whole was fixed a wreath of gold and precious stones,' Eusebius went on. The wreath, representing Victory, was also a common feature of legion and auxiliary unit standards. 'And within this, the symbol of the saviour's name, two letters indicating the name of Christ by means of its initial characters [in Greek], the letter P being intersected by X at its centre.' Eusebius added that 'these letters the emperor was in the habit of wearing on his helmet at a later period'. [Eus., *EH*, XXXI]

From the new imperial standard's crossbar was suspended a piece of square cloth, as was the usual style with a vexillum, 'covered with a profuse embroidery of the most brilliant precious stones' and 'richly interlaced with gold'. Below the golden wreath with its ☧ monogram the pole bore a golden portrait of Constantine and his children – such an imperial *imago* had long been a common feature of legion stand-ards. In fact, the only really novel and distinctly Christian aspect of the new standard was the relatively discreet ⚔ monogram. [Ibid.]

As Richardson was to remark, in the same way that Eusebius made Constan-tine's new cruciform standard sound as if it was something entirely new and solely inspired by Christian faith, the same ancient Christian chronicler attributed a number of things to Constantine alone that were in fact 'entirely customary with other emper-ors'. [Eus., *EH*, XIX, n. 3178]

A later legend, repeated by modern authors, had it that Constantine also had his troops paint the ⚔ monogram on their shields. This comes from a lone classical author, Lactantius. Yet it was not mentioned by Eusebius, who was otherwise effusive about Constantine's adoption of Christian symbols. Later Christian writers such as Gibbon and Richardson gave no credence to the legend concerning the use of the ⚔ on the shields of Constantine. The balance of evidence suggests that Constantine did not instruct his soldiers to paint ⚔ on their shields until some years later, when, says Eusebius, Constantine also commanded that his troops should no longer be preceded by their golden eagle standards but only by his new imperial standard. [Eus., *EH*, XXI] It seems that Constantine's Christian symbolism prior to doing battle with Max-entius extended no further than the ⚔ on his glittering new personal standard.

Fifty hand-picked men from Constantine's bodyguard formed the escort for that new standard, men 'who were most distinguished for personal strength, valour and piety'. Their sole duty 'was to surround and vigilantly defend the standard, which they carried each in turn on their shoulders'. [Eus., *EH*, 2, VIII] Constantine's stand-ard came to be called the Labaram. Richardson suggested this title may have had a Spanish origin, coming from the Basque word *labarva*, which means a standard. [Ibid., 1, XXXI, n. 3010] Constantine's spiritual adviser, from perhaps as early as his years in Gaul, was a Spaniard, Bishop Hosius, and he may have given the standard its name.

On the morning of 26 October, Constantine and his army arrived at the village of Saxa Rubra, 9 miles (14.5 kilometres) north of Rome. Constantine would have planned to set up camp there at Saxa Rubra, within easy striking distance of the capital, but he was surprised to learn from his cavalry scouts that Maxentius and his army were marching out of Rome and forming up for battle north of the Tiber, near the Milvian Bridge. Constantine immediately called a conference of his officers and assigned the units their positions. 'We are informed, and we may believe, that Constantine disposed his troops with consummate skill,' said Gibbon. [Gibb., XIV] And then Constantine ordered his new standard raised – the signal that today his army would be doing battle.

It took a little over an hour for Constantine's army to march down to where Maxentius' army was deployed and waiting. Ahead of Constantine, several deep lines of infantry spread across the river plain, extending all the way to the river, which created a bulwark against retreat by Maxentius' troops. Behind them, a bridge of boats stretched across the swift-flowing Tiber. The Praetorian Guard, whom Maxentius considered 'the firmest defence of his throne', probably occupied his prestigious right wing. [Gibb., XIV] Positioned on both outer wings, the thousands of heavy cavalry of the Imperial Singularian Horse, clad in fish-scale armour, and unarmoured Moorish and Numidian light cavalry from North Africa, tried to settle their restless horses. [Ibid.]

Maxentius himself was there between the lines, mounted on a charger and wearing heavy armour, surrounded by his bodyguards. Before he had ordered his troops to march from the city that morning, he had consulted the Roman priests who kept the Sibylline Books, which were supposed to foretell the future. When Maxentius asked whether he would be victorious if he were to fight Constantine, he was informed that the enemy of Rome would fall that day. [Ibid.] This prophecy, together with his secret scheme involving the bridge of boats, had given Maxentius the courage to proceed.

Preceded by a cacophony of trumpet calls, both sides charged. Constantine had ignored the counsel of his officers to keep himself out of danger; placing himself on one wing, he led the charge of his cavalry, which slammed into the other side. After only brief fighting, the cavalry facing Constantine gave way and withdrew towards the bridge of boats. At the same time, Maxentius and his bodyguards also withdrew. Constantine and his cavalry gave chase.

Constantine would only later learn that this withdrawal by Maxentius and his cavalry was part of a preconceived plan. The cunning Maxentius realized that, if he could do away with Constantine, his leaderless army would be much easier to destroy; it might even come over to him in the same way that Severus' troops had done. So Maxentius had conceived a way of isolating and killing Constantine. The centre of the bridge of boats had been rigged to give way at Maxentius' signal, and dump whoever was on the bridge at the time into the Tiber. The scheme required Constantine to be lured on to the bridge. And the early withdrawal of Maxentius and his cavalry after Constantine's initial charge had this as its objective – Maxentius' troopers were under orders to deliberately retreat and lure Constantine on to the bridge. [Eus., *EH*, 1, XXXVIII; Zos., 2, 15]

But Maxentius' ploy, while it began as planned, quickly went awry, and spectacularly so. It was when Maxentius and the troopers of his Singularian Horse were on the middle of the bridge of boats that it gave way. Perhaps it had been poorly constructed. Perhaps the signal to pull the pins holding the bridge together was given too early. Or perhaps a Constantine sympathizer among Maxentius' troops was responsible. Whatever the cause, the bridge broke under Maxentius, sending the emperor and men of his bodyguard tumbling into the river, horses and all.

A marble panel on the Arch of Constantine, later erected beside the Colosseum to commemorate Constantine's victory, shows Maxentius and his men in fish-scale armour struggling to swim in the swift-flowing river, while Constantine's cavalrymen line the bank and throw javelins at them. There is even a distinctive eastern archer

A scene from Rome's Arch of Constantine showing the Battle of the Milvian Bridge, where Maxentius' booby-trap backfired on him.

among the men on the riverbank, in long robe and angular helmet, firing arrows into the men in the water. Maxentius attempted to clamber up the southern bank of the river, but it was too steep and too crowded by other fugitives also intent on saving themselves. Carried away by the swirling waters and weighed down by his armour, Maxentius, Roman emperor of the west for six years, disappeared beneath the surface.

With their commander-in-chief gone, the cavalry on both wings of Maxentius' army gave way, and fled. The infantry was left to fend for itself, and the less experienced troops were also soon fleeing. Only the Praetorian Guard stood its ground. Conscious of the fact that they had made Maxentius their emperor, the Praetorians shared his fate. The Praetorians were surrounded, and javelins and arrows poured into their ranks. Gibbon was to say, 'it was observed that their bodies covered the same ground which had been occupied by their ranks'; none had attempted to run. [Gibb., xiv] In an eerie repeat of history, 1,503 years later, Napoleon's Imperial Guard would make a similarly brave but fatal last stand after their emperor had been defeated, at Waterloo.

After just a few hours, the battle was over. Thousands of Maxentius' troops had died; thousands more surrendered. Constantine rode into Rome as the victor, and was greeted as a hero by the members of the Senate and crowds of Roman people. Maxentius' fate soon became known. 'The following day his body was recovered from the Tiber, and the head was cut off and taken to Rome.' [Vale., 4, 12] Even as Maxentius' head was being paraded around Rome on the point of a spear, the former emperor's closest advisers were being arrested and executed by Constantine's troops. [Zos., 2, 17]

Constantine remained in Rome for nearly three months. In that time he made sweeping changes to Rome and to the Roman military. On his orders, the Praetorian Guard, the force that had put Maxentius on his throne, was abolished, along with its supporting troops. [Zos., 2, 17] The Praetorians' massive fortress, the Castra Praetoria, built in the northeast of the city by the notorious Praetorian prefect Sejanus early in the reign of Tiberius, was razed to the ground.

Under the same directive, the household cavalry, the Imperial Singularian Horse, was abolished. Its bases below Rome's Caelian Hill, the Old Fort and the New Fort, were demolished. Constantine even donated the Singularians' graveyard to the Christian Church, which built the Basilica Constantiniana, the later San Giovanni in Laterano, over it; 609 Singularian gravestones would be discovered beneath the building by modern archaeologists. Other Singularian gravestones were used as building material. In that part of the graveyard not built over, troopers' gravestones were deliberately smashed to pieces. [Speid., 10]

Constantine did not abolish Maxentius' 2nd Parthica Legion. Instead, its survivors were transferred from their comfortable base at Alba Longa south of Rome to the dry wastes of Mesopotamia in the East, to face the Persians. The 2nd Parthica's base at Alba Longa, and the civilian *vicus*, or township, outside its walls, where the families of the soldiers had lived, were given by Constantine to the Christian Church.

At the same time, Constantine reduced the power of the Senate of Rome to that of a town council, and taxed the senators for the privilege of sitting in the Senate. No longer would the promotional path of senior Roman military officers be via the Senate of Rome. Now, the emperor appointed men of Equestrian rank to the command of his legions and auxiliary units. They would come from throughout the empire, and from beyond, with an increasing number of foreigners rising to command Roman armies in the coming decades.

Legion commanders would now be prefects, not praetors of Rome, and tribunes would command auxiliaries. A pair of tribunes would now be second-in-command and third-in-command of the legions. The old officer cadet system involving junior tribunes was replaced by the Candidatii Militares, two cohorts of officer cadets attached to the emperor's bodyguard from which suitable candidates were promoted by the emperor to the rank of tribune and given commands of their own. And, like the 2nd Parthica, legions that supported Constantine's rivals would be relegated to frontier postings, while new so-called Palatine legions formed the mobile field army with which Constantine dealt with enemies foreign and domestic.

Yet, Constantine was not yet ruler of the entire Roman world. Galerius had appointed a new Caesar, Licinius, to replace the executed Severus. In May AD 311, on the death of Galerius in Illyricum, his deputy Licinius had become emperor of the Eastern Empire. Licinius swiftly removed his fellow Caesar for the East, Maximinus Daia, from the scene. For now, Constantine was prepared to work with Licinius. In early AD 313, Constantine and Licinius met at Mediolanum and discussed joint policy for the administration of the Roman Empire, issuing joint decrees as a result. To cement their alliance, Licinius married Constantine's sister Constantia, there at Mediolanum.

Within seven years, the eight-man leadership group established by Diocletian and Maximian on their abdication in AD 305 had been whittled down to two by sword and sickness. But neither of these two surviving emperors was content to share power for long. Soon, Constantine and Licinius would pit their legions against each other to decide the ultimate ruler of the Roman Empire.

AD 316–321
LXVIII. CONSTANTINE AGAINST LICINIUS
The final struggle

With Valerius Licinius ruling the Roman East from Illyricum, Constantine appointed Bassianus as his Caesar, or deputy, giving him as his bride Constantine's sister Anastasia. Leaving Bassianus in charge in Italy, Constantine returned to Gaul in AD 313, where, over subsequent years, he would make several cities including Augusta Treverorum in the Moselle his capital. But when Constantine learned that Bassianus was secretly dealing with Licinius, he executed Bassianus and in AD 316 marched an army into Illyricum to do battle with its ruler.

Licinius had been born in New Dacia, or Dacia Ripensis, the province carved from the old Moesia south of the River Danube following Rome's forced surrender of the province of Dacia north of the Danube to barbarian invaders in AD 274. Licinius was, according to one source, 'of somewhat common origin'. [Vale., 5, 13] He was a heavy drinker, but a fearless soldier. Licinius, at his capital of Sirmium in Illyricum (today's Sremska Mitrovica in Bosnia), seems to have been taken by surprise by Constantine's march into his domain, for he and his army only met Constantine 50 miles (80 kilometres) from Sirmium, at Cibalae (modern Vinkovci in Croatia), on the Sava river. [Gibb., XIV]

Licinius' army consisted of 35,000 infantry and cavalry. Constantine had 20,000 foot plus cavalry. [Vale., 5, 16] Constantine, forewarned of Licinius' approach, spread his compact battle lines across a defile half a mile (0.8 kilometre) wide, with a steep hill on one flank and a deep morass on the other. This meant that Constantine could not be outflanked, and his opponent was committed to a narrow frontal attack. Licinius and his army came up shortly after dawn. Once they had formed their battle lines, both sides exchanged missiles before Licinius' troops charged, with Constantine's outnumbered men holding their ground. Toe to toe, the men of the two Roman armies fought it out there in the defile through much of the day, with neither side giving way. Late in the day, Constantine himself led a cavalry charge from his right wing which finally broke the deadlock. 'After an indecisive contest in which 20,000 of Licinius' foot and part of his mail-clad cavalry were slain, he himself made his escape with most of his other cavalry under cover of night to Sirmium.' [Ibid.]

Collecting his wife, Constantine's sister Constantia, and his children, from Sirmium, Licinius hurried north to New Dacia, and gave his deputy Valens the task of collecting more troops to continue the war against Constantine. Constantine had proceeded after Licinius, and when he reached Philippi in Macedonia he received envoys from his opponent seeking peace terms. Constantine ignored the peace overture, and, hearing that Valens had assembled a large force at Adrianople in Thrace, marched towards it. At Mardia, in Thrace, Constantine confronted Licinius' deputy. Once again, the missiles flew from both sides, and two Roman armies became locked in battle.

Constantine's glittering new standard was now prominent between the lines. Eusebius was to relate a story, which he said had come to him direct from Constantine's own lips, about Constantine's new standard. In one battle, the standard-bearer carrying the Labaram lost his courage as the battle heated up, and, handing the emperor's standard to a colleague of the escort, the standard-bearer ran for his life. The fleeing soldier did not get far, according the Eusebius, as 'he was struck in the belly with a dart, which took his life'. The man to whom he had passed the standard, meanwhile, survived the battle unscathed. [Eus., *EH*, IX]

Both sides fought shield-to-shield for indecisive hours. At one point Constantine detached 5,000 men and led them via high ground to attack the other side's rear, but the two battle lines of Licinius' army continued to stand firm until nightfall, and then withdrew. [Gibb., XIV] Licinius and Valens linked up, and, suspecting that Constantine would pursue them, pretended to withdraw towards Byzantium but turned aside towards the Thracian town of Beroea. Sure enough, Constantine marched right by them. [Vale., 5, 18] Surprised to learn that his opponents were behind him, Constantine swung about. [Ibid.]

But Licinius had lost his best troops, and sent one of his generals to Constantine again suing for peace. This time, Constantine, whose own troops were 'worn out from fighting and marching', agreed. [Ibid.] Under the peace terms, Licinius'

Rome's fourth-century triumphal Arch of Constantine was decorated almost entirely by material plundered from earlier works.

able deputy Valens was removed from office, and Licinius' power was defined as the eastern provinces plus Asia, Thrace, Moesia and Lesser Scythia. Constantine would control the remainder of the empire, with the aid of his sons Crispus and Constantius, whom he appointed his Caesars and heirs.

There was now a brief, uneasy peace, with Constantine provocatively basing himself at Thessalonica in Macedonia. This was one of his provinces, but it was right on the border of the two emperors' realms. Licinius, having twice been unable to defeat Constantine in battle, did not trust him and concentrated his troops around himself in Illyricum, seeking allies from among barbarian tribes. Encouraged by Licinius, 'the Goths broke through the neglected frontiers, devastated Thrace and Moesia, and began to drive off booty'. [Ibid., 21] From Thessalonica, Constantine reacted quickly. Marching his army against the invaders, he marched into Licinius' territory, surprised the Goths and forced them to return their Roman civilian captives and booty. [Ibid.] Licinius was enraged, complaining that Constantine had breached their peace agreement by using force of arms in Licinius' provinces.

To mollify Licinius, Constantine, in rebuilding the Moesian city of Tropaeum Trajani, which rose beside Trajan's famous monument to the Dacian Wars and was destroyed by the Goths in AD 170, placed an ironic inscription over the restored city's eastern gate. That inscription, which survives today in the museum at Adamclisi, describes Constantine and Licinius as 'our leaders' and 'defenders of Roman security and liberty', saying that 'through whose virtue and wisdom foreign peoples have been subjected in order to assure a lasting border'. Just as that border would not last – the Goths and then the Huns would before long mock the inscription and the legions of Rome by overrunning the city – neither would the shaky partnership between Constantine and Licinius.

In AD 324, Constantine launched a new campaign against his fellow emperor. Sending his son Crispus with a fleet to occupy Asia and seal off Licinius' back door, Constantine himself led his army into Thrace. Licinius and his army occupied a mountain near Adrianople, and Constantine's troops slowly made their way up the mountain slopes. A series of small battles took place all over the mountain, as Licinius' 'confused and disorganized' army was defeated piecemeal. Constantine himself was wounded in the thigh in this fighting, although not seriously. [Ibid., 24] Licinius escaped to Byzantium.

Off Callipolis (today's Gallipoli), Constantine's fleet, commanded by his son Crispus, did battle with Licinius' fleet, commanded by his admiral Amandus, with the result that 'part of Licinius' fleet was destroyed, part captured'. [Ibid., 26] On hearing this, Licinius fled to Chalcedon in Asia, and Constantine entered Byzantium. In Asia, Licinius put together another sizeable army including Goths led by the Gothic prince Alica. The persistent Constantine crossed to Asia with his army, and opposite Byzantium at Chrysopolis (modern Scutari in northwestern Turkey), the two rivals came together for yet another battle.

By this time, the Labaram, Constantine's new standard, had come to be perceived as a lucky charm by Constantine's superstitious soldiers, and when troops in a particular part of the battle were hard pressed, Constantine would send his standard there, lifting the spirits of his men and turning the tide. [Eus., *EH*, VII] Eusebius wrote that Licinius instructed his soldiers not to direct their attack where Constantine's standard was known to be, and not even to look at it, while his own troops 'advanced to the attack preceded by certain images of the dead and lifeless statues' – the traditional form of Roman military standard. [Ibid., *EH*, XVI]

After he was reinforced by his son, the Battle of Chrysopolis was a total victory for Constantine. 'When they saw Constantine's legions coming in Libernium galleys [with Crispus] the survivors threw down their arms and surrendered.' [Ibid., 28] Licinius himself and his leading supporters were taken prisoner. The following day,

Licinius' wife, Constantine's sister Constantia, went to Constantine and begged for her husband's life. Constantine granted Licinius his life on condition that he give up all claim to the throne. Licinius agreed.

Constantine entertained Licinius at a banquet that night, after which Licinius was sent to Constantine's headquarters at Thessalonica. There, Constantine 'had him murdered'. [Ibid., 29] While praising Constantine's 'excessive humanity', Christian bishop Eusebius neither condemned the murder of Licinius, nor that of Licinius' generals and chief advisers that followed on its heels, because those men had all worshipped Rome's old gods. Bishop Eusebius felt that Constantine acted 'according to the laws of war' and consigned Licinius and his subordinates to 'fitting punishment'. [Eus., *EH*, XI; XVIII]

With his brother-in-law out of the way, Constantine was now the Roman emperor of both the West and the East. 'In commemoration of his splendid victory', he renamed Byzantium, calling it Constantinople, after himself. He 'adorned it with great magnificence and wished to make it equal to Rome'. But he 'lavished such wealth on the city that in doing so he all but exhausted the imperial fortunes'. [Vale., 6, 30]

To refill his empty treasury, Constantine forbade the worship of idols and ordered all the temples of the Roman gods throughout the empire to be looted of their statues, sending around parties of his 'friends' to perform the task. Marble statues of the classical gods were removed to Constantinople to add to its adornment. Gold, silver and brass statues were melted down on the spot. One or two temples were completely razed – Constantine had a special dislike of the 'foul demon' goddess Venus, and her temples were particularly singled out for destruction. With others, he merely removed their doors or their roofs, leaving them derelict. [Eus., *EH*, LIV–LVI]

Constantine also ordered that Romans were to observe a day of rest, in the Jewish fashion. But instead of adopting the Jewish Sabbath, which runs from Friday evening to Saturday evening, Constantine inaugurated Sunday as the Christian Sabbath. This was not coincidental; Constantine had long venerated Sol Invictus, the Roman sun god, and Sunday was the day in the Roman calendar dedicated to him. For a number of years to come, Constantine's coins depicted Sol Invictus, and some authorities believe that the divinity that he venerated while emperor was a blend of Sol Invictus and Christ.

Constantine also required that his soldiers observe the day of rest, even giving them a short prayer to be recited on Sundays. Christians in the ranks were given time off on Sundays to offer prayers. But Constantine did not require his troops to convert to Christianity. He probably realized that it could lead to unrest among his legions, even revolt – Gibbon estimated that at that time no more than 5 per cent of the population of the Roman Empire was Christian. [Gibb., XVI] There were probably even fewer Christians in the army than in the general population. In fact the army would prove slower than civilian society to adapt to Christianity over the coming decades.

In the second half of this same century, noted Roman historian Ammianus Marcellinus, himself an officer in the Roman army, would venerate the classical Roman gods in his writings and almost totally ignore the followers of the Christian faith, which he would describe as a sect rather than as the state religion. Likewise, seven decades after Constantine, at the beginning of the fifth century, leading Roman poet Claudian, who chronicled in verse the brilliant career of the last great Roman general Stilicho, wrote in celebration of the old Roman gods, and noted that he gave public recitals at Rome's temple of Apollo, where he received the award of a statue in recognition of his talent.

As further evidence of the lack of penetration of Christianity into the Roman army of the Late Empire, the Notitia Dignitatum, which was last updated around a century after Constantine's death, reveals that Christian symbols had almost entirely failed to find their way into the army. Apart from two angels incorporated into the shield emblems of the two household bodyguard units of the emperor of the East of the Late Empire, there were no identifiably Christian symbols on any of the hundreds of unit emblems depicted in the Notitia. On the other hand, some of the old pagan legion symbols such as the eagle survived, and pagan symbols including the wheel of the goddess Fortune and symbols associated with Bellona, Roman goddess of war, were common among unit emblems depicted in the Notitia.

Whatever Constantine's personal view of Christianity, he knew that his popularity with the troops could only be maintained by retaining a corporate continuity that did not threaten the security of his men. Meanwhile, he kept his soldiers busy – there were no more civil wars during the thirteen years of his sole reign, but there were foreign wars aplenty. A soldier at heart, Constantine personally led campaigns against the invading Goths and the Sarmatians, and when he died in AD 337 at an imperial villa outside Constantinople, he was preparing to launch a war against the Persians.

That Constantine was a brilliant soldier there is no doubt. In his later years, he gave himself the primary title of Victor, and headed his letters with an astonishing string of titles in which he claimed victory over, among others, the Alemanni, the Goths, the Sarmatians, the Germans, the Britons and the Huns. He was never defeated in battle. But during his reign, tens of thousands of Roman soldiers died in civil wars, with no doubt just as many perishing in the wars with the barbarians. The Roman legions that Constantine left to his sons and successors when he died had been weakened by decades of internal strife and eternal wars with barbarians. They had also been diluted by foreigners, and, with Constantine's organizational restructuring, changed beyond recognition from the legions of the first, second and third centuries.

Constantine's leadership qualities, his personal physical and mental strength and his ruthlessness, had won him sole power. On his death, his legions decided among themselves that they would recognize as equal co-emperors his three surviving sons, Constantius, Constantine and Constans – their jealous father had executed as a threat to his throne his popular eldest son and heir Crispus. 'And these resolutions they [the legions] communicated to each other by letter, so that the unanimous desire of the legions became known.' [Eus., *EH*, LXVIII] Once again, through the agency of the army, the empire was opened up to rule by division.

LXIX. JULIAN AGAINST THE GERMANS
Countering the Alemanni

On a wintery day in the second half of December AD 355, a small mounted column trotted into the city of Vienna (today's Vienne) in southern Gaul. At the head of the column rode 23-year-old Flavius Claudius Julianus, the new Caesar, or deputy emperor; he would be referred to by later historians as Julian.

The bearded young man, of medium height but broad-shouldered and with a strong face, had been studying philosophy in Greece when he was summoned to Milan by his cousin, the emperor Constantius II. [Amm., XXV, 4, 22] The third son of Constantine the Great, Constantius had become sole emperor after the death of his brothers Constantine in AD 340 and Constans in AD 350. On 6 November, Constantius had presented Julian to the household troops at Milan, his imperial capital – Rome had ceased to be capital of the Roman Empire the previous century – and announced the youth's appointment as Caesar. As a sign of approval, the assembled

Constantius II, shown here, sent
Julian to Gaul to counter
the German invasion.

troops had rapped their shields against their knees.
[Ibid., XV, 8, 15]

Young Julian had set off for Gaul on 1 December
with a small retinue. His mission was to rally the forces
in Gaul and counter the invasion of the Gallic provinces
by a coalition of Franks and Alemanni German tribes.
That invasion had resulted in the sacking of forty-five
famous Rhine and Gallic cities, including modern-day
Tongres, Trier, Strasbourg and Worms, and the burning of many of them. [Gibb., XIX] Just prior to Julian's
departure from Milan, word had reached the emperor
that a lengthy siege of Cologne by the Franks had resulted in that city's fall and destruction. The German
invaders had penetrated as far as central Gaul, and the
mood that Julian found in Vienna was one of fear and
dread. Despite the dire situation, his arrival served to
buoy local spirits, even though the new deputy emperor
had absolutely no military experience and very little
military training.

Julian remained at Vienna until the spring of AD 356. Sending orders to the
Roman units stationed in the region to assemble at today's Reims with provisions
for a month, he then advanced north, aiming to relieve the city of Augustodunum,
today's Autun on the Arroux river in central France, which was under siege from the
Alemanni. He marched with cataphract heavy cavalry and an artillery unit whose
ballistas were mounted on two-wheeled carts. After linking up with the main army
at Reims, Julian marched for Autun with a force of little more than 13,000 men. On
a misty day, Alemanni forces attacked the two Roman legions forming the column's
rearguard as the column approached Autun. Those two unnamed legions were cut off
from the column and 'would nearly have been annihilated', said Ammianus, had not
allied troops rushed back to relieve them. [Ibid., XVI, 2, 10]

Autun's besiegers withdrew as Julian approached, and Autun was relieved on
24 June. Julian then swung east, and near the town of Brumath, in eastern Gaul, a
force of Germans met Julian's advance and offered battle. Forming his army into a
crescent formation, Julian closed on the over-confident Germans, who were swiftly

overwhelmed. Julian continued on to the Rhine, and entered the ruined city of Cologne – the invaders had no interest in occupying cities; they preferred to live in huts in the countryside. From Cologne, Julian made a peace pact with the kings of the Franks, then moved to Senonas (modern Sens), to spend the winter.

Julian distributed his troops among Sens and neighbouring towns, and when the Alemanni learned this from Roman deserters they surrounded Sens and laid siege to it. All through this siege, the Roman Master of Horse, Marcellus, who was at a nearby town, made no attempt to collect his cavalry and come to the young deputy emperor's aid. If Julian had not realized it before, he would now have been under no illusion that Rome's established military commanders were his friends. When the emperor Constantius learned of Marcellus' behaviour, he dismissed him from office. After a month, the Alemanni tired of the siege of Sens, and withdrew.

For the AD 357 campaign against the Germans in Gaul and on the Rhine, Constantius made Julian his co-consul for the year, and sent to him 25,000 troops under Count Barbatio, Master of Infantry, whose father was a Frank. As soon as spring arrived, Julian, knowing that Count Barbatio was drawing near, advanced his army down the Rhine towards the Batavian 'island', at the North Sea mouth of the Rhine in today's Holland. His plan was for Barbatio to take a different course with his army, with both Roman forces meeting at Batavia in a pincer movement to catch the Alemanni in a trap.

As the two arms of the pincer closed on Batavia, the Laeti, an Alemanni tribe, slipped between them both and drove down to Lugdunum. That city just managed to close its city gates in time to keep out the Germans, who ravaged the surrounding farms and villages before withdrawing. When Julian heard about this he sent three squadrons of light cavalry to watch the three roads the Laeti were likely to use on their way back to the Rhine. One of these squadrons was commanded by the able 36-year-old tribune Valentinianus, who was destined to become the emperor Valentinian I in seven years' time. Sure enough, one of these squadrons ambushed the returning Germans and slaughtered them, recovering all the booty from the Lugdunum raid.

Master of Infantry Count Barbatio was another officer determined not to help the young Caesar. First, he allowed the few survivors from the ambushed Laeti column to slip by him, and then when Julian sent orders for Barbatio to provide him with seven of the ships he had acquired on the Rhine as part of a planned bridge of boats to the eastern bank, Barbatio disdainfully burned them.

Called Julian the Apostate by Christian writers because he reinstated official worship of the old Roman pantheon, the emperor Julian was a charismatic and successful young general despite his lack of military training or experience.

Young Julian had wanted to use the ships to ferry his troops to the islands held in the Rhine by the Alemanni. Undaunted, he gave the Germans of several Cornuti auxiliary units the task of crossing the river; according to the Notitia Dignitatum these were the Palatine auxiliary units the Cornuti Seniors and the Cornuti Juniors. The Cornuti had a custom of swimming rivers on their wooden shields, and in this manner Julian's auxiliaries successfully crossed the Rhine. Landing on the island, they wiped out every man, woman and child of the Alemanni living there. News of this was enough to terrify the other Alemanni settled on Rhine islands, and they quickly withdrew to safer territory east of the river.

This allowed Julian to occupy and rebuild a fortress at Savernes previously destroyed by the German invaders. But after Julian's troops had collected winter supplies in the district, Count Barbatio's men confiscated their foodstuffs, burning what they could not use themselves. Even though it was still only midsummer, Barbatio proceeded to distribute his troops to various winter quarters and then retired to Milan. The rumour soon spread that Barbatio was doing all this on the paranoid orders of Constantius, to ensure that Julian was defeated and would cease to be a threat to his throne. [Ibid., XVI, 11, 13]

The Alemanni tribes soon learned from a Roman informant that Barbatio had departed for Italy, and that Julian only had 13,000 men with him. Seven kings of the Alemanni – Chonodomar, Vestralp, Ur, Ursicin, Serapio, Suomar and Hortar – decided to combine for an attack on Julian while he had such an inferior force at his command. [Ibid., 12, 1] From former Roman territory east of the river, the Black Forest and the so-called 'Rhine re-entrant' area previously annexed by Vespasian and Domitian, the kings wrote to Julian, ordering him to depart from the western Rhineland, which they considered theirs by conquest. Julian ignored the demand, and prepared to counter the invasion of a combined Alemanni army that he knew must follow on the heels of the kings' demand.

AD 357

LXX. BATTLE OF ARGENTORATUM
Decision at Strasbourg

It was early August when Roman scouts reported that an army of Alemanni tribesmen had made camp not far west of the Rhine between Argentoratum, today's Strasbourg, and Drusenheim. Camped 21 miles (33.8 kilometres) away, Julian, Rome's young deputy emperor, gave the order for his army to move. The sun was just rising as Roman trumpets sounded the order to march and the troops tramped from their camp. As the infantry led the way, cavalry units fell in beside them to guard the column's flanks.

This was a very different Roman army from those that had marched this very road in centuries past: the armies of Julius Caesar, and of Drusus, Tiberius and Germanicus Caesar, and of Cerialis, the general who had put down the Civilis Revolt here on the Rhine. Four centuries earlier, those Roman armies had comprised as many as fifteen legions plus auxiliaries, with well over 100,000 men. Julian's army totalled just 13,000.

Of Julian's units only two legions are known. One was the Legio Primani, or 1st Legion. This may well have been the former 1st Minervia Legion, with the pagan goddess stripped from its title in these (officially) Christian times. The 1st Minervia, unlike the 1st Legion, was not to be listed in the Notitia Dignitatum, compiled shortly after this; but the 1st (or Primani) Legion was. The 1st, a Palatine legion, came under the control of the 2nd Master of Military Readiness. It was one of six legions and thirty cavalry and auxiliary units making up a 'ready' force which was supposed to be thrown into any trouble spot in a hurry.

Julian's other known legion was the Legio Regii, a reasonably recent creation of unknown provenance. The Regii was one of thirty-two *legiones comitatenses*, or 'escort' legions, and was subject to the Master of Infantry. No other legions in Julian's force are identified, if indeed there were any others. The majority of Julian's troops were auxiliary units. There were one or more cohorts of Batavian infantry – both the Batavian Seniors and Batavian Juniors came under the control of the Master of Infantry. And Julian's force also included several cohorts of Germans of the Bracchiati and the Cornuti tribes.

For cavalry, Julian had at least three squadrons of light cavalry including one commanded by the future emperor Valentinian. Julian also had the Equites Cataphractii, a heavy cavalry 'ready' squadron whose men and horses both carried extensive mailed armour. Also coming under the Master of the Military, this unit appears to have accompanied Julian to Gaul from Milan, where the ready cavalry units were based. In Julian's force the unit was led by a tribune by the name of Innocentius. Julian's deputy was Severus, the emperor's Master of Horse.

When the later emperor Valentinian I, depicted here on a medallion, was a cavalry commander, he fought under Julian in Gaul and in Julian's famous victory at Argentoratum, today's Strasbourg.

Despite the summer heat, Julian's little army made good progress on the march during the morning. Just before noon, not far from Argentoratum, Julian called a halt, for his scouts had just warned him that the enemy were over a rise ahead. From the back of his horse, Julian addressed his troops. They had marched all morning, he told his men, so he now proposed that they build a marching camp with ditch, walls and palisade, and attack the Germans first thing next morning after a good night's sleep. But his troops disagreed, and rapped their javelins on their shields to let him know it. They did not want rest, they wanted to come to grips with the enemy, now.

Julian's troops, many of whom had come off the worst against the Alemanni in previous encounters, had come to respect their young commander after his successful campaigning of the past two seasons, and considered him a lucky general. [Amm., XVI, 12, 13] Even the civilian administrator of Gaul, the Praetorian prefect Florentinus – Praetorian prefects having become financial officers since the abolition of the Praetorian Guard – urged the young Caesar to give the men their head and lead them to battle without delay. Seeing that his troops could not be dissuaded, Julian gave the order to recommence the march.

The standards went ahead with the troops of the vanguard, bunched together in time-honoured fashion, with the first rank centurions of the legions marching with the standard-bearers. [Ibid., 12, 20] The gentle hill climbed by the marching Roman army was covered with ripened wheat wafting in the late morning breeze. On the summit ahead, three mounted German scouts and several comrades on foot were watching the Romans approach. But the scouts lingered too long. As Roman light cavalry suddenly burst from the marching column and galloped towards them, the mounted Germans realized their danger, turned and rode off, leaving their unmounted companions to fend for themselves. All but one of the running Germans was sufficiently fleet of foot to get away; the odd man out was snared by Julian's cavalry, and brought to Julian. Under questioning, the prisoner revealed that German forces had been crossing the Rhine for the last three days.

As the Romans broached the hill, they saw the German army spread not far below them on the river plain, formed up in close-packed wedge formations and waiting for them. The Roman vanguard halted, and spread in a solid line. Auxiliary units formed a front line. The legions came up and took the centre of a second line, flanked by more auxiliaries. As had been the case for hundreds of years, the standard-bearers took their station between the lines, accompanied by the trumpeters. At Julian's command, all his cavalry wheeled to one side and formed up on his right, for his scouts had warned him that the Germans had dug trenches on his left.

As was their custom, the Alemanni had elected two of their kings to act as generals for this campaign. The commander-in-chief was Chonodomar, and the Romans could see him riding along his left wing mounted on a massive charger – it had to be a large horse, for Chonodomar was a huge man, tall and of 'mighty muscular strength' despite his immense weight. He wore shining armour, and a gleaming helmet distinguished by a red plume. In the opinion of Ammianus, who was then a junior officer in the imperial bodyguard, Chonodomar was both a tough fighter and the most skilful general in the Alemanni ranks. [Ibid., XVI, 12, 24]

Chonodomar's deputy was his brother's son, Serapio, a young man who had yet to successfully grow a beard yet who possessed ability and maturity well beyond his years. Serapio's father, previously a hostage of the Romans in Gaul for many years, had changed the boy's name from Agenarich to Serapio after studying the Greek-Egyptian mysteries involving the all-powerful god Serapis, who was variously likened to a bull and to the sun. Young Serapio had command of the German right wing. The clans and tribes of the army were led by the other five Alemanni kings and ten princes. Around them spread the German wedges, made up of 35,000 warriors drafted from the various tribes. [Ibid., 12, 26]

Chonodomar and his fellow German leaders knew that their fighters outnumbered young Julian's army by close to three to one. And as they spied the Roman units forming up on the rise, they recognized many of the unit emblems on their shields as belonging to the same units that had run before them in battles in Gaul over the past few years. [Ibid., 12, 6] The confidence of the Germans, already high, soared.

Julian had taken up his position. Trumpets blared orders on both sides. Julian's left wing began to advance down the slope. Severus, the Roman commander on the left, was aware that trenches dug by the Germans lay in the path of his advance. The Germans had planned to spring out of the trenches and assault the Romans when they came close, but Severus, anticipating this, ordered his troops to halt well short of the Alemanni trenches.

Julian, accompanied by a bodyguard of 200 cavalry, moved along the front of the stationary Roman lines at the centre, stopping every now then to give a brief speech to the troops in front of him. Each speech was a little different to the last. 'The real time for fighting' had come, he told one group. When another part of the line called on him to give the signal to attack now, he urged them not to ruin their coming victory by disobeying orders and chasing the enemy too far on the one hand or in giving ground on another. To men in the rear ranks, he said, 'Fellow soldiers, the long hoped for day has arrived.' It was time 'to wash away the old stains and restore majestic Rome's due honour'. [Ibid., 12, 31–2]

As Julian was still talking, a roar went up from the German ranks. As one, the Alemanni called on their kings and princes to fight on foot with their men. Without hesitation Chonodomar sprang from his horse, and his fellow royals followed suit and sent their horses away. Trumpets sounded. Missiles were exchanged by both sides for a time, with the air filling with arrows, javelins, spears and stones. And then, with a deep-throated roar, the long-haired, bearded warriors on the German left dashed forward to engage the stationary Roman cavalry, wielding their massive swords in their right hands as they ran. 'Their flowing hair made a terrible sight, and a sort of madness shone from their eyes,' said Ammianus. [Ibid., 12, 36]

The Roman cavalry closed up. Auxiliary infantry moved close to protect their flanks. The Germans surged into their line. All the Roman infantry used their shields to protect their heads from the raining sword blows, jabbing back with their swords and hurling darts when they could. Soon, clouds of thick dust were raised by the struggling combatants. As the Romans stood their ground, forming a solid barrier with their oval shields, whose bottom edges sat on the ground, Germans used their knees in an attempt to push the shields back while they swung their swords at the same time. Behind the combined weight of the Germans, some front-line Roman infantry on the right began to give a little ground.

On the Roman left, impatient Germans in the trenches had sprung out and launched themselves at Severus' stationary front line. But Severus' infantry beat them back, and, on Severus' command, began to slowly advance in tight formation, wheeling a little to the right to avoid the trenches. With triumphant shouts, Severus' men pushed into the German centre.

On the right, the hard-pressed Roman cavalry, unaccustomed to standing and fighting in the one spot, lost its nerve, and broke. Many riders fell back, only to be confronted by the men of closed-up second-line infantry, who refused to let them through. The Roman cavalry officers were regrouping their formations when the cataphracts saw their commander Innocentio sustain a wound, and then a cataphract's horse went down, catapulting the rider over its head to the ground. The heavy cavalry panicked, infecting all the Roman cavalry, which attempted to scatter. Again the second-line Roman infantry held their positions, and refused to let their own cavalry break their close-knit ranks.

Seeing the cavalry disperse this second time, young Julian kicked his horse into motion, and rode into their path, urging them back to the fight. Behind him rode his standard-bearer, with his purple draco standard streaming in the breeze. The tribune of one squadron, coming face to face with the deputy emperor, paled with guilt, turned his horse around, and dived back into the fight.

The Alemanni on the Roman right, having dispersed the cavalry, threw themselves on Julian's front-line infantry, the Cornuti and the Bracchiati. These German auxiliary units gave their national battle cry, which, said Ammianus, 'rises from a low murmur and gradually grows louder, like waves dashing against the cliffs'. [Ibid, 12, 43] But the Alemanni, taller, stronger and fiercer than their opponents, succeeded in encircling the Cornuti and Bracchiati, who seemed to be in dire trouble as the Germans repeatedly crashed their swords against the raised Roman shields, attempting to hack through them as they would hack through a forest. Among the Cornuti who now fell was a tribune commanding a cohort.

The Roman second line had been waiting and watching. On Julian's command, the Batavian auxiliaries, and the 'formidable' troops of the Regii Legion, who bore the emblem of a thirteen-pointed star on their oval shields, advanced in formation at double quick time, and smashed into the Alemanni, to 'rescue' their comrades. [Ibid., 12, 45; & Not. Dig.] But the Alemanni would not give way. Some were seen to drop to their left knee in their exhaustion, yet from that position they would continue to flail at the nearest Romans with their long swords.

In the centre, a 'fiery band of nobles' burst through the Roman first line, and dashed to the second line. These Alemanni nobles ran on to the immovable orange shields of the 1st Legion. The legion had taken up a close-packed formation called Praetorian Camp – a square – and with their shields locked together and employing iron discipline that kept them rooted to the spot, these men created an impregnable barrier. Through gaps in the shield line the Romans jabbed at the Germans' unprotected torsos, and soon Alemanni were piled in front of them; the ground flowed with blood that made it difficult under foot for the next wave of Alemanni that came up to replace the first.

As the blood flowed, despair began to flow through the Alemanni ranks. The Romans held firm and dealt out death with each passing minute. Here, a German warrior broke and fled the battle, there another. Soon, it was an epidemic. The Germans were turning and running in their thousands. The Romans gave chase, overtaking many and slashing them down from behind. Now, the Germans' size counted for nothing; it merely meant that they made larger targets for Roman weapons as they ran. Piles of corpses soon blocked retreat. Many Germans ran to the bank of the Rhine. A number jumped into the river to escape their Roman pursuers, and in the water some were transfixed by Roman spears, while others were swept away and drowned. Thousands of Alemanni swam the river, others floated away clinging to their shields. On the bank, Julian and his officers yelled to their men not to go into the river after the enemy, for that would be a death trap.

And then it was all over. The Battle of Argentoratum, or Battle of Strasbourg as some modern historians dub it, was at an end. For the Roman soldiers, who had not tasted success against the Germans for a long, long time, Argentoratum was a total victory. Roman losses were 243 rank and file and four tribunes including the commander of the cataphracts. Six thousand Alemanni dead were counted on the battlefield; many more had been killed in the Rhine. [Ibid. 12, 62] King Chonodomar was tracked by a Roman cohort to a wooded hill beside the Rhine. There, the Alemanni leader surrendered, together with three close friends and 200 men.

On the orders of the emperor Constantius, King Chonodomar was subsequently sent to Rome, where he was kept a prisoner at the Castra Peregrina, the Caelian Hill barracks used by allied troops based in Rome. Chonodomar would end his days there. Young Julian's reputation as the general who had dealt the previously unstoppable Alemanni a bloody defeat, and restored the Rhine frontier, swept throughout the Roman world. Within four years, Julian would be emperor of Rome.

AD 359
LXXI. SURVIVING THE SIEGE OF AMIDA
100,000 Persians, 73 bloody days

From a clifftop, two Roman officers and their Armenian guide watched in awe as the Persian army of 100,000 men passed below them, filling the plain for 50 miles (80 kilometres). Out in front rode Shapur the Great, Persian 'king of kings', tenth ruler of the Sasanian dynasty that had overthrown the Parthian kings to rule the former Parthia. Shapur was leading his army on a campaign to invade the Roman Empire's eastern provinces.

The senior of the two Roman officers observing the slowly passing Persian multitude was 29-year-old Ammianus Marcellinus, a young gentleman of Greek ancestry and a native of Antioch in Syria. As a teenager, at Mediolanum in Italy, Ammianus had become a junior officer with the Protectores Domestici, or Household Protectors, the personal bodyguard of the emperor Constantius II. Five years later, in the year 353, Ammianus had returned to his home town of Antioch to join the staff of Ursicinus, who had been the comes, or count, in overall command of the military in the Roman East since AD 348. Ammianus had been the count's faithful aide ever since.

Just a week or so before this, as spring edged towards summer and there was no news of Persian intentions, Ammianus had been sent into enemy territory by Count Ursicinus, accompanied by a centurion, to gather intelligence on Persian movements. A local satrap friendly to Rome had told the pair to occupy a certain escarpment, and wait. Sure enough, after Ammianus and his companions had camped on the ridge for two days, the Persian army had appeared on the horizon and moved across the plain before their eyes. To Shapur's left, Ammianus could see King Grumbates of the Chionitae, an old and shrivelled man 'but of a certain greatness of mind and distinguished by the glory of many victories'. [Amm., XVIII, 6, 22] To the right of the Persian monarch rode the king of the Albani, the tribe that then peopled modern-day Georgia.

The rulers and their entourages of generals and bodyguards were followed by a multitude of troops of every kind – infantry spearmen, foot archers, wave after wave of horse archers, men of the cataphract heavy cavalry in armour from head to toe, a camel corps of light cavalry and even lumbering war elephants whose fighting towers filled with spearmen swayed from side to side on the elephants' massive backs with each step the animals took. These eastern troops had been 'chosen from the flower of the neighbouring nations and taught to endure hardships by lengthy continued training'. [Ibid.]

Ever since the year AD 337, Shapur had regularly sent his army across the Tigris river against Roman strongholds in Armenia and northern Mesopotamia, trying to force the Romans out of the region. Over thirteen years of sieges and skirmishes in which the countering Roman army had been led by the emperor Constantius himself, the Persian king had achieved some successes, notably the razing of the Roman fortress at Hileia in AD 348. In that same year there had also been a battle at the fortress of Singara in Mesopotamia (modern-day Sinjar in northern Iraq), where, Ammianus was to write, a 'furious contest took place at night and our troops were cut to pieces with great carnage'. The Romans had lost a great many men at Singara, but had either retained, or soon after reclaimed, the fortress, with both sides touting victory in the contest. [Ibid., 5, 7]

Yet Shapur had not reached the prize city of Edessa or seized the bridges across the Euphrates that acted as the gates to the rich Roman provinces further west. A few small fish, tasty though they may be, do not a banquet make. Besides, following Rome's disasters of AD 348, a new Roman commander had arrived in the East – Ursicinus. And ever since Ursicinus had taken command, the legions of the East had fought without loss. [Ibid., XVIII, 6, 2]

Tired of the contest with Rome, and stymied by Ursicinus, in AD 350 Shapur had suspended his war against Rome to concentrate on subduing troublesome neighbours. This had allowed Constantius to return to Europe and deal with Vetranio and Magnentius, a pair of usurpers who had led uprisings against his rule in his absence. Magnentius, a barbarian-born officer in the Roman army, had killed Constantius' brother and co-emperor Constans in his bid to seize power.

Eight years later, as Ursicinus was on his way home to Italy to accept promotion to the post of Rome's Master of Infantry, having handed over command in the East to his successor Sabinianus, King Shapur launched his latest initiative against Rome. For by that time, the Persian ruler had made his regional enemies his allies, and had prepared and trained a vast army for the new enterprise. Shapur also knew that Ursicinus had departed, and that Constantius and much of the Roman army were tied up in a bitter campaign in Illyricum against Sarmatian, Quadi and Suebi invaders from beyond the Danube.

Shapur had begun by writing to Constantius to demand all territory held by Rome in the East as far as Macedonia, which he claimed was historically the property of Persia. Constantius had declined to oblige. Suspecting that Shapur was intending to launch a new campaign, Constantius had sent a message to Ursicinus ordering the general to turn around and go back to the East to counter whatever Shapur attempted.

Ursicinus, on his way to Italy, had just arrived in Thrace when the emperor's dispatch reached him. Ammianus had been with his general when he opened his orders, and he saw that Ursicinus had been deeply troubled by them. The emperor was leaving Sabinianus in overall command in the East, so, technically, Ursicinus would be answerable to him. Neither was the emperor permitting Ursicinus to take any troops apart from his bodyguard to the East with him. Ursicinus knew that these orders had been framed by his enemies at court; he was, it seemed, being set up to fail.

Nothing is known about Ursicinus' background. Many senior Roman commanders of this era had barbarian blood: Vandal, Frank and German. And there was a king of the Alemanni Germans named Ursicinus at this same time, so it is quite likely that Ursicinus was also of German extraction. He had clearly shown great military skill over the past decade, but at the same time had made many enemies at the court of Constantius. Yet he had never wavered in his loyalty to the emperor. 'The most valiant of men', in the opinion of his aide Ammianus, Ursicinus could not disobey his emperor, and neither could he allow Shapur to go unchecked. Taking Ammianus and the remainder of his staff and his escort from the Household Protectors with him, the general reversed his course and hurried back to Syria. [Ibid., XVIII, 5, 4]

Over the winter of AD 358–359, as Ursicinus and Ammianus were returning east, a Roman official by the name of Antoninus had crossed the Tigris river in the dead of night in a Persian fishing boat. With the help of the Persian governor on the eastern bank, Antoninus took his entire family with him, and was conducted to the winter quarters of King Shapur.

Antoninus was a former wealthy merchant who served on the staff of Rome's Duke of Mesopotamia. A financial scandal had erupted in the province, implicating Antoninus. When Ursicinus had been in charge in the East he had been sympathetic to Antoninus' plea of innocence, but Ursicinus' successor Sabinianus had ignored Antoninus' appeals that other, much more powerful men were responsible for the fraud, and had laid down a date by which he must personally repay the missing money. As that date approached, Antoninus had determined to have his revenge. After making careful note of all the Roman military dispositions throughout the region, he had defected to the Persians.

Serving as an adviser to King Shapur, the defector Antoninus was riding with the Persian army as the two Roman officers watched from their hilltop observation post. Antoninus had been welcomed by the Persian king and given a turban that denoted him as a satrap entitled to vote with the king's other advisers. The Roman defector had urged Shapur to forget his old policy of reducing Roman strongholds one at a time. Instead, Antoninus had said, producing the details of the location of Roman units and arsenals, the Persians should drive to the Euphrates river, cross it to the west, and then push up through Roman provinces all the way to the west coast of Asia before the Romans had time to organize. It was a plan that Shapur had enthusiastically endorsed.

Once the Persian army had passed, Ammianus and his centurion companion came down off their hill and trailed the enemy at a safe distance as the Persian horde followed the Tigris river. The two Romans were able to observe the Persian king and his adherents sacrificing in the middle of a bridge of boats across the Anzaba river (today's Greater Zab in northern Iraq), with their army formed up beyond the river. There were shouts of joy from those on the bridge, indicating that the priests had found the omens auspicious for a campaign against the Romans, and the Persians had commenced to traverse the bridge. Estimating that it would take at least three days for the entire Persian army to cross the river, Ammianus and the centurion slipped away. [Ibid., 7, 1]

Crossing the mountains, 'deserted and solitary places', Ammianus returned to his general. Ursicinus had made his headquarters in southern Armenia, at the city of Amida (modern-day Diyarbakir in Turkey), on the western bank of the Tigris, where

The basalt walls of ancient Diyarbakir in today's Turkey. In the fourth century, this was Amida, the city subjected to siege by Shapur's 100,000-strong Persian army.

seven legions had gathered. [Ibid., 7, 2] The count listened to Ammianus' report, and considered the situation. Sabinianus, the official Roman commander in the East, was at Edessa in Osroene, to the west, near the Euphrates, with another large body of Roman troops.

Sabinianus, 'a cultivated man' and 'well to do' despite an obscure family background, was nonetheless 'unfit for war' and 'inefficient', in Ammianus' opinion. With Sabinianus showing no interest in leading his troops to intercept the Persians before they reached the Euphrates, Ursicinus sent couriers galloping across the Roman province of Mesopotamia with orders for the governor and for the province's military commander. [Ibid., XVIII, 5, 5]

In response to the general's orders, Roman troops were soon compelling Mesopotamian farmers and their families to move with their flocks to safer quarters to the west. At the same time, the city of Carrhae was totally evacuated, for it was only surrounded by weak fortifications and could not be successfully defended. Then, also on Ursicinus' orders, Roman troops set fire to all the farmland of the province, to deny grain and fodder to the advancing Persians. The flames swept across the plain, and mile after mile of yellowing corn that was almost ready for harvesting was consumed, as were many wild animals including lions, as Mesopotamia was blackened from the Tigris to the Euphrates. As the plains burned, Roman troops erected fortifications at potential crossing places along the eastern bank of the Euphrates. [Ibid., 7, 3–4]

Bypassing the Roman-held city of Nineveh, the Persian army continued west towards Edessa. But then, at the village of Bebase, a scout arrived with the news that the past winter's melting snows had flooded the Euphrates, making it impassible for the time being. On the advice of the defector Antoninus, the Persian army now turned sharply right and marched north, to attack Amida. At Amida, Ursicinus was preparing to pull out. Believing that Shapur was still pushing on towards the Euphrates, the Roman general had decided to hurry west, cross the Euphrates at Samosata in Commagene, and then move down the river and destroy the bridges at Capersana and Zeugma in Syria to deny the Persians an easy Euphrates crossing.

On the road to Amida, guided by Antoninus, an advance force of 20,000 cavalrymen under the Persian generals Tamsapor and Nohodares galloped ahead of the main Persian army. Two Roman cavalry wings recently arrived from Illyricum had been stationed on the approaches to Amida to guard against just such a surprise attack. Come nightfall, the 700 Roman troopers of the two wings withdrew from the public roads they were supposed to be watching and were soon 'overcome with wine and sleep'. In the darkness, the Persian advance force slipped by. Come daylight, the Persian commanders had hidden their men and horses behind sand dunes outside Amida. [Ibid., 8, 3]

This was the summer's day on which Ursicinus set off for Samosata, leaving his departure until late in the afternoon so that he rode through the cool of the night. As twilight was falling, the Roman general and his staff and escort of both infantry and cavalry had not gone far from Amida before, as they topped a rise, they saw the 'gleam of shining arms' in the distance, as the Persian cavalry force made its appearance. 'An excited cry was raised that the enemy were upon us,' said Ammianus, who was riding with his general. Ursicinus' standard was raised, and the small Roman force concentrated in close order. [Ibid., 8, 4–5]

As Persian light cavalry came up at the gallop, 'some of our men rashly ran forward, and were killed' by the arrows of the Persians. When both sides pressed forward, Ursicinus recognized Antoninus leading the enemy force, and yelled that he was a traitor and a criminal. Antoninus, removing the turban that the Persian king had presented him, sprang from his horse.

Antoninus, bowing before Ursicinus, called to him, 'Pardon me, most illustrious Count. It is through necessity and not voluntarily that I have had to descend to this conduct, which I know is iniquitous. As you know, it was the unjust demands of scoundrels that drove me to it. Not even you, with your high position, could protect me from their avarice.' With that, Antoninus withdrew, respectfully walking backwards, until he had disappeared into the descending night. [Ibid., 8, 6]

From the rear of the Roman column, which was on higher ground, came another warning cry. A mass of Persian cataphracts, heavy cavalry, was galloping up to join the fight. Without waiting for orders, men of the general's party scattered in all directions, hoping to escape into the darkness. Ammianus saw his chief surrounded by Persian horsemen, 'but he was saved by the speed of his horse and got away, in company with the tribune Aiadalthes and a single groom'. With just these two companions, Ursicinus was able to make good his escape to the west. [Ibid., 8, 10]

In the darkness, Ammianus, on horseback, found himself in a throng of Romans who were driven, fighting all the way, to the high, steep bank of the Tigris. Some Roman soldiers jumped from the bank, only to be weighed down by their equipment and stuck fast in the mud at the river's edge. Others, caught by the swirling water, were drawn out into the swift-flowing stream and drowned. Some men stood their ground on the bank and tried to fight off the Persians, with varying degrees of success. Some tried to break through the ranks of enemy horsemen.

Ammianus became separated from the others. '[I] was looking around to see what to do when Verennianus of the Household Protectors came up with an arrow in his thigh.' Ammianus tried to remove the arrow. But suddenly finding himself surrounded by 'the foremost Persians', Ammianus kicked his horse into motion and galloped away 'at breathless speed, and aimed for the city' of Amida. [Ibid., 8, 11]

Amida was situated on a rocky plateau beside the River Tigris. From the direction that Ammianus approached it, there was a single narrow ascent up the cliffs. When Ammianus arrived, he found that thousands of Persians were attempting to assault the city using that same precarious route. It was clear that they had been met on the slope by Roman infantry from Amida who had inflicted heavy casualties on them before withdrawing inside the city walls. In the darkness, after discarding his horse, and, with a companion – probably the wounded Household Protector Verennianus – the young officer began to climb the rise, picking his way past Persians living and dead, the living being too focused on their attack to notice the two Romans in their midst.

Unable to proceed any further, the pair lay down among the dead to await sunrise, using night and the mounds of corpses to cover their presence. So crowded together were the Persian bodies, said Ammianus, that many dead men stood upright among the throng, prevented by the crush from falling. 'In front of me,' said Ammianus, there was 'a soldier with his head cut in two and split into equal halves by a powerful sword stroke'. The dead Persian 'was so pressed in on all sides that he stood erect like a stump'. [Ibid., 8, 12]

With the dawn, 'showers of missiles from all kinds of artillery flew from the battlements' of Amida, aimed at the Persian attackers on the slope below. But Ammianus and his companion had pushed up so close to the wall in the night that these missiles passed harmlessly over their heads. The two Romans rose up, and dashed for the wall, making for the rear gate. Recognized by those inside, Ammianus and his colleague were admitted to the city by the rear gate which was opened for just enough time for them to dash inside.

Amida had once been a small frontier town until Constantius, in the reign of his father Constantine, had expanded it, building extensive defensive walls and towers around it and permanently equipping those walls with a range of artillery. The Tigris wound past its eastern wall, with a defensive tower on the southeast of the city rising up directly beside the meandering waterway. To the north, the peaks of the Taurus Mountains were visible, while the barren plains of Mesopotamia extended to the southern horizon and the distant Persian heartland. Inside the city walls, Ammianus could hardly move for the crush of people. All around him, wounded lay dying and distraught civilians wailed the names of loved ones they had lost. Others called out the names of missing relatives, hoping to find them in the unhappy throng.

There were 120,000 people crowded into Amida. Ammianus' original Latin text read 20,000, but later scholars increased this to 120,000, considering the original figure a transcription error. In the eighteenth century, Gibbon took the figure at face value, accordingly putting 1,000–1,500 men in each of the seven legions present; but the true figure was likely to have been double that. [Gibb., XVII, n. 133]

A fair had been taking place in the city at the time the Persian advance guard had flooded to its doorstep, so that the metropolis was crammed with its own residents, visiting farmers, foreign merchants and Roman soldiers. Ammianus reported to the most senior officer in Amida, a count by the name of Aelianus. The young officer also acquainted himself with the identity of the units in Amida. He wanted to assure himself that the city could withstand a siege from an army of the magnitude of the one he had witnessed just days before from his hilltop observation post.

As Ammianus knew, the city's garrison was normally provided by a single legion, the 5th Parthica, a unit originally raised some 130 years before. To it had been added six other legions. Several of these had supported the German-born usurper Flavius Magnentius when he had risen against Constantius at Cologne in AD 350. One of these legions was the 30th Ulpia, which dated back to Trajan and which had been based at Vetera on the Lower Rhine at the time of the Magnentius rebellion.

Two of the other legions had been raised by Magnentius and his brother Decentius in Gaul in AD 350 to support the bid for the throne. Constantius rated their legionaries 'untrustworthy and turbulent', but Ammianus considered these Gallic soldiers 'brave, energetic men'. Constantius had sent all these disgraced units east to face foreign foes after first defeating Magnentius at Mursa in Dalmatia in AD 351 and then his brother Decentius in the Cottian Alps two years later. [Ibid, 9, 3; XIX, 5, 2]

Of the other legions at Amida there was the 10th Fortenses, which had been formed from a vexillation from one of the two existing 10th legions. There were also the Superventores and Praeventores, legions raised in AD 348 by Constantius for service in the East. These latter three legions had been stationed at Singara in AD 348, and with their commander Aelianus these 'raw recruits' had broken out of that doomed city at night, killing 'great numbers of Persians while they were buried in sleep'. [Ibid., XVIII, 9, 3] But, at the same time, those Roman legions had suffered heavy casualties at Singara.

Among the auxiliary units also stationed in the besieged city was a squadron of horse archers whose members were freeborn foreigners. The Roman force holding Amida and several smaller fortresses nearby numbered fewer than 30,000 men. Soon, they would face assault from 100,000 determined Persians. [Ibid., 9, 9]

While Antoninus and the Persian advance guard had pushed on to Amida to seal off the city, King Shapur and the Persian army's vanguard had paused to assault two smaller Mesopotamian fortresses, at Reman and Busa. The Roman garrisons at both had swiftly surrendered. The men of these Roman garrisons were made prisoners; the women, including a company of young Christian nuns, were set free.

On the third day of the Persian siege of Amida, a hot July day, Shapur arrived with the main Persian army. Behind the army came a massive baggage train, carrying everything from captured Roman artillery to tents and couches for the officers and materials for conducting sieges. Said Vegetius, writing thirty years later, 'The Persians, following the example of the Romans of old, surround their camps with ditches and, as the ground in their country is generally sandy, they always carry with them empty bags to fill with the sand taken out of the trenches, and raise a parapet by piling them one atop the other.' Shapur's baggage train also carried a number of wives; at least those of the senior Persian officers and their allies. [Vege., III]

Ammianus was one of the Roman soldiers crowding the walls of the city that day to watch the vast enemy column arrive. 'When the first gleam of dawn appeared, everything as far as the eye could see shone with glittering arms, and mail-clad cavalry filled hill and hollow.' King Shapur, mounted on a massive charger, accompanied by the riders of his bodyguard and followed by kings, princes and satraps from many eastern nations, boldly rode up to the main gate of the city, his royal crown replaced with a golden helmet in the shape of a bejewelled ram's head set with jewels, complete with projecting horns. [Amm., XIX, 1, 2–3]

Roman defector Antoninus had advised Shapur that it would be a mistake to become bogged down here in a lengthy siege, for that would give the Romans time to prepare for them west of the Euphrates. The Persian king had therefore decided to awe the occupants of Amida into submission. He came so near to the front gate in his bid to call for a parley that Ammianus could clearly make out his features – his large nose, close-shaved beard and moustache, and long, dark, curly hair that fell to his shoulders. But the over-confident Shapur was in for a rude surprise. The garrisons at Reman and Busa may have been overawed by the sight of him, but the Romans at Amida were not that easily dazzled by his presence. With a thwack of ropes and a clang of iron firing arms against restraining bars, ballistas on the front wall let fly with their deadly cargoes.

Lethal iron-tipped darts and slender lances went scything by the king on the still morning air. The king and his escort quickly turned about, raising a cloud of dust which helped to cover their retreat, as more missiles were launched from the city walls. Had Shapur been killed that day, the history of the region may have been very different, but he survived the episode unscathed but for a torn robe caused by a Roman lance. But the king's pride was hurt, and he raged against the occupants of Amida and ordered a full-scale assault to begin. Only once he had calmed down were his generals able to talk him into giving the city one more chance to surrender before he invested too much time and effort besieging it.

At dawn the following day, King Grumbates of the Chionitae rode up to the city's eastern wall accompanied by a mass of followers including his teenage son. Grumbates had volunteered to call the occupants of Amida to sit down with the Persians at a peace conference. But before the king could utter a word he was spotted by the crew of a Roman ballista on the wall, and they let fly. The steel-headed bolt flew by Grumbates and struck his son. That son, a tall, handsome young man who, having just turned 16, had come of age, took the bolt in the chest; it passed right through his expensive armour and penetrated his breast. To the horror of his father and comrades, the prince toppled from his horse, dead. As more missiles flew their way, Grumbates and the others quickly galloped out of range, leaving the prince's body lying in the dust.

The affronted Chionitae roused other tribes to action, and thousands of men came charging up the slope to help recover the body of the fallen prince, as the Romans on the walls rained down missiles on them. Slingers and archers from the ranks of the Persians and their allies answered their fire with volleys of slingshot and thousands of arrows. These exchanges went on all day, as many men sacrificed their lives trying to retrieve the body of Grumbates' son. By day's end, the bodies of dead and dying were piled all around the dead prince, their blood running like rivers across the dry earth. After dark, the young man's body was successfully dragged back to the Persian lines.

For seven days the Persians suspended operations to mourn the death of the much-loved prince. His body was placed on a high platform, along with the bodies of ten others who had also perished, all laid out on couches. Throughout the week, the tribes all conducted mourning feasts by community and by military company, with funeral dances and songs of lamentation. The women, meanwhile, in customary fashion beat their breasts and wept loudly for the prince.

At the end of the week the funeral platform was burned, and the prince's ashes placed in a silver urn. As the ashes were carried away to be buried in the earth of his homeland, a meeting of Shapur and his war council decided that the young man's spirit would be best propitiated by destroying the city that had been the cause of his death. Antoninus' plan to cross the Euphrates was put in abeyance; Shapur and his army would not now leave this place until Amida had been razed, no matter how long it took.

Over the next two days, Persian light cavalry ranged the countryside destroying the crops of the region. Then Shapur raised his flame red banner, signalling to his troops that battle was to begin. Amida was encircled by a line of shields five men deep. It had been decided by the Persian council of war that the assault on Amida would be launched from all sides at once. Lots were drawn by the principal nations, and three days after the prince's funeral pyre had been consumed by fire, the Persians and their allies left their camp at dawn and silently moved into position for the assault on the city. [Ibid., xx, 6, 3]

Grumbates and his Chionatae had drawn the eastern sector, where the king's son had perished. The Gelani lined up to attack the southern gate, the Albani the northern gate, the Segestani the western gate. Beyond the battle lines, captured Roman catapults, their Persian crews trained by legionary prisoners, were set up, trained on the city, and loaded. From a city tower, Ammianus watched the enemy take up their positions, and, with them, lines of war elephants 'with their wrinkled bodies and loaded with armed men'. It was, he said, 'a hideous spectacle, dreadful beyond every form of horror'. Ammianus and those around him could not hope to survive against such a massive and determined force, and they vowed 'to end our lives gloriously'. They would, they agreed, die fighting. [Ibid., xix, 2, 3–4]

Yet that day, the Persians did not make a move. To unnerve the defenders, the Persian battle lines stood in perfect silence, without even a neigh from a horse, all day long. Then, in equal silence, they withdrew to their camp for the night. At dawn the next day the besiegers returned, and resumed their previous positions. But this time they would not be standing around. After King Grumbates ceremoniously launched a bloodied spear towards the city, the assault began, with infantry and cavalry dashing towards the walls to the sound of blaring trumpets.

In response, the Roman catapults lining the walls let fly. 'Heads were shattered, as masses of stone hurled by the scorpions crushed many of the enemy. Others were pierced by arrows. Some were struck down by spears.' The ground outside the city was soon strewn with bodies. But the defenders also took heavy casualties. 'A thick cloud of arrows darkened the air, while the artillery that the Persians had acquired from the plunder of Singara inflicted still more wounds.' [Ibid., 2, 7–8] Persian wounded frequently returned to the fight after having their wounds patched up, or called on their comrades from where they lay on the battlefield to pluck out the arrows that had pierced their bodies.

The assault did not stop with nightfall. The Persian forces worked in relays at the walls, and only late in the night did they retire. Every dawn they began all over again.

The assault lasted throughout the next day until the Persians withdrew to their camp after dark. Inside the city, Roman defenders who did not die at once from arrow wounds died slowly from loss of blood. There was nowhere to bury Roman dead, so they were simply piled in the streets. Predictably, disease broke out in the city. The pestilence would pass after ten days; the defenders put the end of the plague down to a fall of light rain.

Count Ursicinus, meanwhile, had reached Edessa, the Roman headquarters for the region. There, he tried to convince Count Sabinianus to send troops with him to relieve Amida, or at least to harass the besiegers, but Sabinianus produced letters from the emperor Constantius ordering him not to put the troops under at him at risk, and refused to release any men to Ursicinus for the relief of Amida. The powerless count, compared by Ammianus to a lion robbed of its claws and teeth, was restricted to sending scouts to Amida to find out the latest state of affairs there. [Ibid., 3, 1–3]

The siege dragged on through the 'steaming heat' of summer. The Persians had learned the art of siege from the Romans, and as the daily attacks by bowmen and slingers continued they also built mantlets to protect men trying to undermine the city walls, and began building earth ramps designed to reach the top of the walls. Ammianus saw tall wooden towers with iron protection on the front being built at the foot of the growing ramps, each with a ballista mounted on top. [Ibid., 5, 1–2]

The two legions raised by Magnentius in Gaul had received no training in the use of artillery, and neither did these Gallic farmers have any skills in the building of fortifications. They were experienced in battle in the open field, said Ammianus, but in the type of fighting in which they were now engaged they proved more of a hindrance than a help. Several times the Gauls slipped out of the city to harass the mound builders, dashing back inside after having inflicted some casualties and causing panic. The Gallic legionaries were brave and fierce, said Ammianus, but their reckless efforts achieved little, and were like pouring a single handful of water on a fire; they only resulted in diminishing their own numbers. In the end, the Gauls' officers forbade them to again venture out, and additional bars were put on the gates to keep them inside. [Ibid., 5, 2–3]

Although a fresh water spring bubbled up at the foot of the citadel in Amida, a tunnel had been hollowed out of the rock leading from the tower on the southeast corner of the city down to the Tigris river, to allow water to be brought up to the inhabitants in emergencies. A Roman deserter knew about this tunnel, and he now led seventy archers from Shapur's bodyguard to its entrance. In the night, these men crept up the tunnel, entered the tower, and positioned themselves on its topmost third floor. As the sun rose, they waved a red cloak, signalling to the Persian lines that they were in position. As the Persian army launched a fresh assault, with waves of attackers sweeping towards the walls equipped with scaling ladders, the archers that had infiltrated the tower fired down into the city with deadly accuracy, causing mayhem inside Amida.

At first, the Romans could not work out where the devastating shower of arrows was coming from. Once the Persians were spotted on the southeast tower, Ammianus was among those given the task of relocating five light ballistas to adjacent towers. Using these, the Romans were able to cut down the Persian archers with their ballista spears. Devoid of cover, and seeing comrades fall all around them, some of the Persian bowmen jumped from the tower, to be killed on the river rocks below. The tower was soon cleared, but the infiltrators had caused numerous casualties in Amida.

Meanwhile, outside, many Persians had succeeded in reaching the walls and scaling the ladders to fight hand-to-hand with the defenders on the battlements. The five redirected ballistas were now turned on the Persians, clearing the walls of attackers by midday. The Persians suspended the assault for the remainder of the day and returned to their lines.

The following day, from Amida's elevated central citadel, a long line of prisoners could be seen, being herded to the Persian camp below. Detachments from Shapur's army had taken several forts in the area, including a large emplacement called Zatia, whose walls ran for more than 3 miles (4.8 kilometres). Leaving the fortifications of Zatia in flames, the Persians had brought their thousands of Roman prisoners to the siege of Amida. Many of the captives were elderly men and women; those who could not keep up with the column and fell by the wayside had their calf muscles slashed or their hamstrings cut by their Persian guards, so that they could not escape and would starve to death where they fell. From the walls of Amida, this could all be seen happening.

The hot-headed Gauls of the two Magnentian legions, infuriated at the way the prisoners were being treated and by the loss of the neighbouring fortresses, attempted to smash through the wooden bars on the gates with their swords. This convinced the commanders at Amida to give the Gauls their head, so they were instructed to launch a night attack on the Persian guardposts that stood just a little out of arrow range around the city, and then push on to wreak as much havoc as they could inside the walls of the vast Persian camp. The Gauls hurried off to their quarters to prepare for their mission.

The night chosen for the Gallic raid was overcast and moonless. In the early hours of the morning, a rear gate was quietly opened, and the men of the two legions slipped out, armed with swords and battleaxes, their national weapons of choice. Without making a sound they crept up to Persian guardposts. Guards were quietly dispatched where they stood. Off-duty Persians of the guard units in their beds nearby were killed in their sleep. The Gauls were planning to sneak all the way to King Shapur's quarters, but as they pushed on through the gates in the sandbagged Persian rampart the alarm was raised. Persians rushed to arms, and fell on the attackers as they penetrated the Persian encampment.

Faced by raging Persians on every side, the Gauls formed up, and stood their ground. Clouds of arrows came out of the night, bringing down many a Gallic legionary. Slowly, they backtracked from the camp and towards the city walls, walking backwards, fighting as they went, in step 'as if retreating to music' said Ammianus. Persian trumpets were sounding the alarm throughout the massive camp as the Gauls withdrew towards the city, losing men to arrows with each pace. [Ibid., 6, 9]

On the city walls, Ammianus and other Romans had been waiting breathlessly for the outcome of the attack. Realizing that the Gauls were returning, the defenders opened a gate for them, as, up on the walls, the artillery 'roared constantly' – going through the motions of firing but without letting go with any ammunition, so that the Gauls weren't hit by friendly fire. The Persians in pursuit, on hearing the familiar sounds of catapults firing, ducked and hugged the ground. This gave the Gauls enough time to flee in through the open gate, just as the sun was rising. Before the pursuing Persians could reach it, the gate was swiftly closed again.

The raid had cost the Gauls 400 dead, and many of those who returned were wounded. Among the dead were the senior officers of both legions, their prefects and tribunes. Prior to this mission the officers had strived to hold their men in check, but once their units had been given the task of penetrating the enemy camp, the officers had been at the forefront of the fighting, and had paid with their lives. When the emperor Constantius heard about the bravery of the fallen officers he ordered statues of them to be made, wearing full armour, and to be erected in the provincial capital, Edessa.

Once the sun rose, the Persians, surveying the thousands of dead at the outposts and in their camp, found officers of grandee and satrap rank among the casualties, and wails of grief rose up from all quarters. Shapur sent a message to the Roman commanders asking for, and being granted, a three-day truce to enable proper funerals to be carried out for their men.

The Romans had time to take breath, and take stock. At two places outside the city, toiling Persian infantrymen had been slowly raising their earth ramps. To counter these, inside the city, whenever there was a break in hostilities, defenders had been working on raising mounds of their own opposite the location of the Persian mounds, so that a substantial number of Romans could meet the enemy should they come over the walls at those places, on equal ground. Work on the Roman mounds continued uninterrupted through the three-day truce. But the Romans knew that once the Persian mounds were completed, they would be like sloping highways into Amida, permitting the attackers to flood into the city in their tens of thousands. The end of Amida might be delayed, but not prevented.

With the truce at an end, the Persian attack resumed with renewed intensity; the Persians were determined to avenge their dead comrades. The ironclad Persian towers were now rolled up into artillery range, and Persian infantry rolled forward the wooden sheds on wheels. Others took positions behind mobile wicker screens. The entire Persian army seemed to be massed around the city, in precise, ordered lines of infantry and cavalry. Persian trumpets began to play 'slow notes', to which the attackers walked forward with onerous precision, not in a mad rush as before. As soon as the slowly advancing enemy lines were within range, the Romans' wall-mounted catapults opened fire.

'Almost no form of dart failed to find its mark. Even the mail-clad horsemen were checked and gave ground.' The Persians broke formation, and, in open order, returned fire with their bows. At the same time, the ballistas mounted on top of the two massive assault towers, which were even taller than the towers of Amida, 'caused terrible carnage on our side,' said Ammianus, as they shot down from their great height. The bloody battle lasted all day. The attackers were beaten off yet again, and withdrew at sunset. [Ibid., 7, 4–5]

That night, Count Aelianus and the surviving Roman officers held a conference to try to devise a tactic against the ballistas on the enemy towers. Many ideas were discussed, but finally it was agreed that four stone-throwing catapults would be quietly moved into positions on the walls directly opposite the enemy towers, from where they would open fire at sunrise.

Taking pains not to make any noise, the Romans relocated the weapons. It was 'an act calling for the greatest skill,' said Ammianus, for, if the tactic was to work, the Persians must not know that with the coming of the dawn the Roman artillery was positioned at such point-blank range. As soon as the first streaks of daylight lit the sky, the defenders could see lines of Persian attackers forming up below, supported by trumpeting war elephants. Before the sleepy Persian gunners in the assault towers opposite realized what was happening, the four Roman catapults let fly at the pair of towers. Massive stones flew through the air, with immediate effect. The wooden towers' framework was shattered, and the towers collapsed, throwing the two ballistas and their crews to the ground, destroying both. [Ibid., 7, 6]

The Roman catapults then directed their aim at the Persian elephants, firing a stream of burning arrows at them. If a flame touched an elephant, the beast turned and fled in terror, with its driver unable to control it. Burning arrows were then shot into the wreckage of the two tumbled towers, and they were soon in flames. King Shapur considered this turn of events sufficiently bad to enter the battle himself, which was unheard of, said Ammianus; Persian rulers never usually took part in combat. Shapur's large bodyguard served to draw Roman attention to the king, and artillery fire was aimed at the royal party. When many of those around him were cut down by Roman missiles, Shapur was forced to retire out of range. But the siege continued, with fresh units being thrown into the fight by the Persians in the afternoon.

For day after day the battle continued in this way, until the focus shifted to the two Persian mounds and the countering Roman mounds inside the walls, with archers on both mounds fighting each other across the void. But then luck deserted the defenders. One of their earth mounds, standing well above the wall to match the enemy mound outside, gave way, collapsing towards the wall. Earth from the collapsed Roman mound filled the gap between Persian mound and wall, creating a causeway between the two. The attackers flooded up the Persian mound and over this causeway in their tens of thousands. Defenders rushed to the spot, becoming so densely packed together that they got in each other's way.

Hectic hand-to-hand fighting decided by the sword followed, as the Persians flooded over the wall and into Amida. Persians ran amok in the streets of the city. Armed and unarmed, male and female 'were slaughtered like so many cattle' by the

Persians. As darkness approached, most of the surviving Roman defenders massed in the one place to make a final stand, at the citadel. Ammianus, meanwhile, was cut off from the bulk of his comrades. With two Roman rank and file soldiers he hid in 'a secluded part of the city'. In the night, the three of them slipped out of a rear gate, and fled. Behind them, the last defenders at the citadel were overwhelmed, and Amida fell to the Persians.

After travelling 10 miles (16 kilometres) from Amida, Ammianus and his two companions reached a horse-changing station of the Cursus Publicus Velox. But all the horses had been taken. 'I was already unequal to the excessive walking, to which, as a gentleman, I was unaccustomed,' said Ammianus, and he was not looking forward to continuing the escape bid on foot. Then – a stroke of luck for Ammianus – the trio came on a horse. A groom had used it in an attempt to escape. Because the horse had no saddle, the groom had wrapped the reins around his wrist to help him keep his seat on its back. At some point the groom had fallen off, and the terrified horse had dragged him through forest and over desert. The groom was a bloody pulp, and very dead. Separating corpse and horse, Ammianus mounted up, and the two soldiers led the young officer and his steed west. [Ibid., 8, 6]

At a spring on their route, the trio found a deep well. All three of them stripped off their military tunics and tore them into strips to make a length of rope. One of the soldiers then removed the cap he wore under his helmet for comfort's sake, and this was tied to the end of the rope, which was lowered into the well. With this device they were able to quench their burning thirst. They reached the Euphrates river north of Edessa, and, after spotting a detachment of Roman cavalry being hotly pursued by a large force of Persian riders, realized that some Persian units had advanced as far as the Euphrates.

Keeping to the cover of trees and undergrowth, the trio made their way north, following the river, to the city of Melitene, then capital of the province of Armenia Minor and longtime base of the 12th Fulminata Legion. From there, Ammianus and his companions accompanied an officer heading to Antioch, where Ammianus would report the fall of Amida. Ammianus would go on to become a noted Roman historian.

At Amida, King Shapur crucified Count Aelianus and the surviving Roman tribunes. Persian troops scoured the city for any soldiers from east of the River Tigris who had served with the Romans, and these men were executed no matter what their rank. Several officers who had served on the staff of the Master of the Cavalry in the Roman east and with the Protectors were marched away with their hands bound behind their backs, as were the surrendered men of the numerous units that had defended Amida. All would become slaves of the Persians.

Seven legions had taken part in the defence of Amida, and with the city's fall all seven ceased to exist. Legions such as the 30th Ulpia, created by Trajan in AD 103, and the more recently raised 5th Parthica, were removed at a stroke from Rome's list of serving legions. With them went short-lived legions raised for the unsuccessful defence of Singara, and the Gallic rebellion of Magnentius. Their men were now either dead or slaves of the Parthians. This was a defeat that in its scope exceeded the shame of Crassus' 53 BC defeat at Carrhae and the shock of the annihilation of Varus' three legions at the Teutoburg in AD 9.

Once, Roman historians had boasted of how Roman legions had successfully conducted sieges, from Alesia to Jotapata. In AD 70, four legions had achieved the capture of Jerusalem after a bloody summer's siege. Now, 289 years later, the tables had been turned. Now it was the barbarians, having learned siege skills taught to them by the Romans, who applied those skills to become the victors.

The Persians marched many thousands of Roman prisoners from Amida and looted the city before burning it to the ground. But the seventy-three days taken to complete the siege had robbed Shapur of the summer, and of many thousands of men – Ammianus noted that a Roman official estimated that 30,000 Persians lost their lives during the siege of Amida. [Ibid., 9, 9] By the time it was all over it was October, and too late for Shapur to continue the advance to the Euphrates. Taking their prisoners and their plunder with them, the Persians and their allies crossed back to the eastern side of the Tigris, and went home. But they would be back.

AD 360–363
LXXII. LOSING MESOPOTAMIA
Singara and Bezabde fall

With the emperor Contantius rushing troops to the East to try to fill the void left by the seven lost legions, Antoninus' plan for the Persians to invade all the Roman East was held in abeyance. But in the spring of AD 360, the Persians and their allies returned to Roman Mesopotamia, their numbers bolstered by new recruits and bringing new siege equipment with them. Shapur and his men had acquired a taste for victory and for plunder, and before they looked beyond the Euphrates there were many Roman fortresses with which to deal.

The first objective was Singara, which Shapur had besieged several times in the past fourteen years. This time, he was determined to deprive the Romans of the city permanently. The 1st Parthica Legion had been based at Singara ever since the end of Septimius Severus' Parthian campaign in AD 199. After the Persian wars had begun in AD 337, the 1st Parthica was joined by the 1st Flavia Legion, a probable creation of Constantius or his father Constantine – the first name of both was Flavius – and more recently also joined by a few cavalry.

After several days of fighting at the walls of Singara, Shapur brought up 'a ram of uncommon strength' at twilight. This went to work against a round tower that had been breached in the last Persian assault on Singara, twelve years before. The breach had been repaired by the Romans since then, but Shapur reasoned that the tower would have been weakened by the previous destruction, and this proved to be the case. The massive battering ram brought the tower tumbling down, and Persian hordes poured through the wreckage. The city was quickly taken. Most of the men of the 1st Parthica and 1st Flavia legions were taken alive. They were 'led off with their hands bound' to become slaves in the farthest reaches of Persia. [Ibid., xx, 6, 6; 8]

The Persians then moved on to the town of Bezabde near the Tigris (today's Cizre in southeastern Turkey), which was then a hilltop town with strong walls. Bezabde was defended by the 1st Parthica's brother legion, the 2nd Parthica. This unit had been tipped out of its comfortable base at Alba Longa, outside Rome, by Constantine the Great in AD 312, following his victory at the Milvian Bridge. They were then sent to the farthest reaches of the empire in punishment because of their support for Constantine's opponent Maxentius. At Bezabde, the 2nd Parthica was joined by the 2nd Flavia, and another relatively new legion, the 2nd Armenia. The garrison also included a large number of archers of the Zabdiceni tribe, whose territory around Bezabde this was.

After a surrender offer was rebuffed by the Roman defenders, the Persians launched a siege of Bezabde, and attempted to bring a number of battering rams into action. On the difficult sloping ground, and against determined opposition from defenders raining down stones, arrows and firebrands, it was only the largest of the rams, which had a covering of wet bull hides that could not be set alight, that succeeded in doing damage to the wall. Inevitably, the ram, 'with its huge beak', weakened a tower in the wall, which crumbled and fell. [Ibid., xx, 7, 14]

As usual, Persians attackers surged through the opening created by the fallen tower. 'Bands of our soldiers fought hand-to-hand with the enemy,' said Ammianus. [Ibid.] Vastly outnumbered, the defenders were overwhelmed, as the Persians ran amok in the city, killing everyone who fell into their path, male and female, as Bezabde was mercilessly plundered. But unlike Amida and Singara, the city was not levelled; Shapur decided to retain and strengthen Bezabde as a Persian fortress. Meanwhile, from the surrendered legions and civilian survivors of Bezabde, 'a great throng of captives' was led off to the Persian camp. The 2nd Parthica Legion and the other units with it ceased to exist.

The Notitia Dignitatum, which is believed by some scholars to have been updated, in part, in around AD 420, still showed the 1st Parthica and 2nd Parthica legions as part of the garrison under the Duke of Mesopotamia at that time, together with twelve cavalry units and two cohorts of auxiliary foot soldiers including the Zabdenorii. Ammianus shows that these legions perished at Amida and Singara. The listing in the Notitia Dignitatum for Mesopotamia actually appears to reflect the situation there prior to Constantius' Persian wars – that is, prior to AD 337. Because, at the time the Notitia Dignitatum was said to have been last amended, the Roman province of Mesopotamia had not existed for many years.

In AD 361, Constantius arrived in the East with a large army. Having blamed Count Ursicinus for the losses in Mesopotamia and dismissed him from office, Constantius personally led his army into Mesopotamia. He wept over the ruins of Amida, and attempted to lay siege to Persian-held Bezabde. But unlike the Romans before them, the Persian defenders held out. With the rainy season approaching, the Roman army, unable to achieve what the Persians had achieved at the very same place a year earlier, gave up the siege of Bezabde and withdrew to Syria.

Constantius died in AD 361. He was on his way back to the west at the time, for his cousin and deputy Julian had been hailed as emperor by the troops in Gaul in opposition to Constantius. Julian, victor against the Germans at Argentoratum in AD 357, became the undisputed new emperor. Called Julian the Apostate by later historians because he personally renounced Christianity, he removed Christians from the Roman army, with whom he was enormously popular. Julian would take up where Constantius left off in the East, leading an army to recover Mesopotamia.

But on 26 June AD 363, after just twenty months as emperor, 31-year-old Julian died while leading a Roman army of 65,000 men in a bloody but ultimately indecisive battle against Shapur the Great's army deep inside Persia. Rushing into the fight without his armour, Julian was mortally wounded by a flying spear from a Persian cataphract that pierced his liver.

Finding itself in the heart of Persia with neither leader nor direction, the Roman army hastily hailed as Julian's successor 30-year-old Jovianus, or Jovian, who had little claim to the throne, being a middle-ranking commander of the bodyguard and son of a retired count. Jovian immediately agreed to the demands of those around him that the Roman army pull out of Persia and Mesopotamia.

So it was that, in the summer of AD 363, four years after the end of Amida and three years after the fall of Singara and Bezabde, the new Roman emperor Jovian surrendered five Roman provinces in Mesopotamia and southern Armenia to King Shapur the Great, and gave up all claim to fifteen key fortress locations including those at Nisibis and Singara. Harried by the Persians all the way, the Roman army withdrew beyond the Euphrates.

Eight months after ascending the throne, Jovian himself was dead, to be succeeded in turn by Valentinian, who had served as a cavalry tribune under Julian at the Battle of Argentoratum. But the damage in the East had been done; Roman Mesopotamia ceased to exist, just as the legions that had unsuccessfully attempted to defend it ceased to exist.

In just three sieges in AD 359 and 360, the Persians had deprived Rome of twelve legions. Many authorities believe that by this time the number of men in each legion was substantially less than had been the case in early imperial times. Gibbon spoke of legions of this time being 'of the diminutive size to which they had been reduced in the age of Constantine'. Legions of 2,000 to 3,000 men by this time seem the norm. [Gibb., XIX]

Such losses of manpower and equipment to the Persians, combined with the number of Roman fighting men lost in the interminable revolts within the empire in the fourth century, could not be sustained. Within half a century, the drain on Roman resources would mean that there would not be the men to spare from distant provinces when crises arose in the west. The Roman East had its own battles to fight. Only brilliant generalship would keep the empire's countless enemies off the road to Rome.

LXXIII. BATTLE OF ADRIANOPLE
Valens' legions destroyed

> 'The diminished legions, destitute of pay and provisions, of
> arms and discipline, trembled at the approach, and even the name,
> of the barbarians.'
>
> EDWARD GIBBON, *Decline and Fall of the Roman Empire*, XIX

Ever since AD 364, Flavius Valens had been Rome's co-emperor for the East, based at Antioch in Syria, while his elder brother Valentinian I had been emperor in the West. Valentinian had spent most of his reign based in Gaul fighting off Germanic invaders.

Valens had led Roman armies with mixed success in the past. Twice, in AD 367 and 369, he had defeated the Visigoths north of the Danube, in what had once been the Roman province of Dacia. And in the East he had won a victory against the Persians in Mesopotamia before having to concede territory and withdraw. Now, 49-year-old Valens was intent on defeating the Visigoths once again, as they ravaged Thrace and threatened nearby Constantinople.

Driven across the Danube river by the territorial expansion of the Hun people from beyond the Volga river, the Visigoths had in AD 376 come to an arrangement with Valens' generals, who had permitted them to settle in Roman Moesia and Thrace south of the Danube. But in Thrace the locals had resented their presence, and Valens had decided to move the refugees to Asia. The Visigoths, whose religion was anchored to the Danube, which they considered sacred, had refused to move. So the people of Adrianople in Thrace decided to take matters into their own hands. Adrianople, also called Hadrianopolis – it was named after the emperor Hadrian – is the modern-day town of Edirne in European Turkey. The Adrianopolese attempted to forcibly remove the Visigoths who were settled nearby. This backfired, badly, with the Visigoths rising up, laying siege to Adrianople for a time, and ravaging rural Thrace.

Twice, Valens' generals fought the itinerant Visigoths, with bloody but indecisive results. As the Visigoths received reinforcements from their cousins the Ostrogoths and other allies from north of the Danube, and turned their attention to Constantinople, Valens marched from Antioch to Constantinople with much of the eastern army, sending to the west for Roman reinforcements.

The Roman emperor in the west by this time was Valens' nephew Gratian, who had succeeded Valentinian on his death in AD 375. Now 29 years old, Gratian had been making a name for himself in Gaul by leading his army in repelling the Alemanni, who had recently made a fresh incursion across the Rhine. Just prior to receiving his uncle's plea for support, Gratian had decisively defeated the Lentiensi, a branch of the Alemanni, at Horburg beside the Rhine. From the Rhine, young Gratian set off for Thrace, planning to lead part of his army to link up with Valens in Thrace for a decisive combined offensive against the Goths.

In July, with the main body of the Visigoths known to be encamped near Adrianople, Valens' senior general Sebastianus was marching to Adrianople with the advance element of Valens' army. He had detached 300 men from each of his legions and sent them ahead to destroy a large band of Visigoth looters spotted by his scouts. The legionaries achieved the objective, and recovered so much plunder from the butchered Visigoths that there was not enough room for it all inside Adrianople. The emperor Gratian, meanwhile, while hastening east with his troops to link up with Valens, was delayed in Pannonia when his column was attacked by Scythians of the Halani tribe.

According to the Roman writer Ammianus, who had been an officer of the Roman army under the three previous emperors, Valens was jealous of his nephew's military success against the Alemanni, and even jealous of the initial success of his own general Sebastianus on the road to Adrianople. [Amm., XXXI, 12, 1] He therefore set off with the bulk of his army, intending to demonstrate his prowess in controlling the Goths. As he approached Adrianople with his troops marching in square formation, his scouts reported that a slow-moving column of Gothic wagons had made its way through the hill passes to the north and was 15 miles (24 kilometres) from Adrianople. According to the scouts, there were 10,000 Gothic fighting men with the wagon train along with their family members.

On reaching Adrianople in the first week of August, Valens had his troops build a camp outside the town, with ditch and rampart topped by wooden stakes, in the old Roman manner. There at the Adrianople camp, while impatiently awaiting the arrival of Gratian and his army, Valens was joined by Richomeres, a count commanding Gratian's household troops. Count Richomeres brought a letter from

Gratian in which the emperor of the west assured his uncle he would soon join him, and urged him not to venture anything before his arrival.

On a hot August day, a council of war took place in Valens' pavilion at Adrianople, as Valens sought the opinions of his subordinates on what to do. Should he wait for Gratian, or should he attack the Goths at once? Sebastianus urged him not to wait, but launch an attack on the Goths immediately, a view supported by a number of others. But Victor, Valens' Sarmatian-born Master of Cavalry, counselled his emperor to wait for the arrival of Gratian's army from Gaul, and he was supported in that view by numerous other officers.

In reality Valens did not want to share a victory with his nephew. He wanted to attack at once. He chose to accept the advice of Sebastianus, perhaps reminding his courtiers that Constantine the Great had won a great victory near Adrianople in AD 324, against his rival Licinius, to make himself emperor of the entire Roman Empire. That famous victory probably encouraged the hawks among Valens' counsellors to think that this would be the place where Valens should similarly gain great glory. Orders were therefore issued for the army to prepare for battle next day.

As preparations were under way, a Christian elder came as envoy from the Theruingi tribe's Fritigern, king of the Visigoths, and presented Valens with a letter from Fritigern saying that if Valens would grant his people all of Thrace, together with its crops and flocks, he would guarantee a lasting peace between the Visigoths and Rome. Valens sent the envoy away.

At dawn on 9 August, Valens' army passed out of the gates of its camp outside Adrianople in battle order. According to some modern authorities, that army numbered 60,000 men. [Warry, *WCW*] With the cavalry taking the roads and the infantry marching over open country, 'a suitable guard of legions' was left behind at the camp, which contained Valens' imperial treasury, the emperor's personal insignia, the individual packs of the soldiers and all the army's baggage. [Amm., XXXI, 12, 10] These legions would also be guarding the arms in the Adrianople arsenal, for Adrianople was one of thirty-four cities across the empire which then housed a state arms factory. [Gibb., *DFRE*, XVII]

Valens had received a report from his scouts that the enemy had formed a vast circle of wagons on a hill some miles away. It was towards this hill encampment that the army marched all morning, over rough ground and in intense heat. At around two o'clock in the afternoon, the men of the Roman army could see the massive Gothic

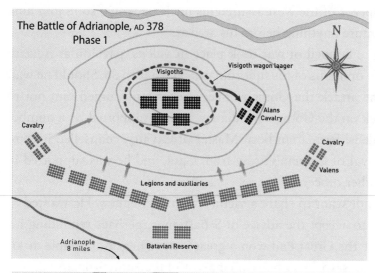

The Battle of Adrianople, AD 378
Phase 1

Visigoths

Visigoth wagon laager

Alans Cavalry

Cavalry

Cavalry

Valens

Legions and auxiliaries

Adrianople 8 miles

Batavian Reserve

N

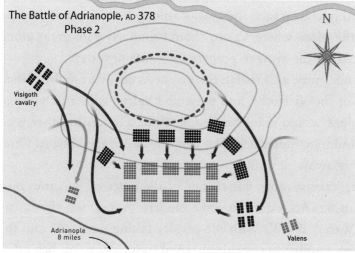

The Battle of Adrianople, AD 378
Phase 2

Visigoth cavalry

Valens

Adrianople 8 miles

N

wagon circle on the hill ahead, perfectly formed and looking like a wall of wood around the slope.

Although his men had been marching for something like eight hours, and were tired, thirsty and hungry, Valens ordered battle lines to be formed. Roman trumpets sounded the order, and the infantry spread into lines, taking positions allotted to them at that morning's assembly. The leading elements of the Roman cavalry moved to occupy the right wing. Other troopers assigned to the left wing were still coming up country roads, so that the left was not yet properly filled out. In the centre, the Roman infantry stood glaring across the parched expanse of earth separating them from the Visigoths who, summoned by their horn-blowers, were taking position at their wagons in their thousands. The Romans began to clash their javelins and lances rhythmically against their shields.

From the Visigoth encampment, King Fritigern again dispatched envoys seeking peace, but Valens sent them away, saying that a peace agreement could only be negotiated by men of rank. So Fritigern sent a message to say that the Romans should send several high-ranking Romans to his encampment to discuss peace terms. Valens did not know that Fritigern was playing for time. The Visigoth cavalry, led by the kings Saphrax and Alathe of the Greuthingi tribe, was absent from the camp, apparently only gathering fodder in the vicinity, and as soon as the Roman army had been spotted approaching, Fritigern sent messengers galloping to find them and bring them to the aid of their people. The Roman leaders discussed who should go as envoy to Fritigern, and Richomeres, the count from Gratian's household command, volunteered to go to the Goths' camp.

As Richomeres was about to ride up to the massive circle of wagons on the hill, some of Valens' mounted troops, apparently stationed on the Roman left, lost patience and commenced an attack of their own accord, urged on by their over-confident officers. These men, Armenian horse archers of the Comites Sagiittarii Armeni led by the tribune Bacurius of Hiberia, from northern Armenia, and cavalrymen of a Scutarii squadron led by a tribune named Cassio, charged up to the wagon line and engaged the Visigoths. But they were met by such a hail of arrows and other missiles that they turned tail and galloped back the way they had come before many minutes had passed, which did nothing for the confidence of the remainder of the Roman army.

Now, the Goth cavalry under Saphrax and Alathe arrived, accompanied by Halani allies, and thundered into the rear of the Roman army. Valens had not put out cavalry patrols to warn him of the approach of enemy reinforcements – which meant that he and his army were taken completely by surprise as the Goth cavalry charged into his stationary army and mowed down Roman soldiers in their path. The charge broke up the Roman lines and a number of battles followed.

Roman infantry and some cavalry were locked in combat with the Goth cavalry. On the left, the Roman infantry advanced of its own accord all the way to the wagon line. But the Roman cavalry on the left had been so disorganized by the rash charge by the horsemen of Bacurius and Cassio that the infantry lacked cavalry support. They were met by a wave of Goths that came out of the wagon line like water from a breaking dam and washed over the Roman left. The Roman infantry here was so crushed together that 'hardly anyone could draw his sword or pull back his arm'. [Ibid., 13, 1] The fighting raised a dust cloud which cut visibility dramatically. This prevented Roman infantry from spotting Gothic arrows that came in clouds from the wagon line, killing or wounding them in their thousands.

Describing the battle, Ammianus spoke of Romans and Goths wielding the battle-axes that had become common weapons for infantrymen: 'On both sides, the strokes of axes split helmet and breastplate.' He described Goths who'd had their hamstrings severed or right hands lopped off in the fighting yet who still fought with defiant courage. One Goth, he said, though pierced through the side and near death, was still 'threateningly casting about his fierce glance'. Romans, their lances broken, and seeing no way of escape, weighed into the enemy with their swords, determined not to sell their lives cheaply. [Ibid., 13, 4]

The Roman lines had been completely broken by the rush of Goths from the hill. The number of 10,000 that Valens' scouts put on the Gothic warriors proved woefully short of the truth. Modern-day authorities suggest that there were 200,000 Goths present that day – men, women and children – and that as many as 50,000 of them were warriors who took part in the battle. [Warry, WCW] Not only did they almost match the Romans in numbers, the Goths had in their favour the element of surprise with the unexpected arrival of their cavalry, plus the impetus of their infantry charge from the wagon line on higher ground.

All over the body-strewn field, Roman units broke and their men ran. Valens, never one to inspire devoted loyalty from his troops, was even deserted by most of his imperial bodyguard. In the middle of the Roman line, two Roman legions had un-flinchingly held their ground. One was a Mattiarii legion, either the Mattiarii Seniors or the Mattiarii Juniors, which were Palatine legions. The other was a Palatine legion made up of foot lancers – either the Lanciarii Seniors or Lanciarii Juniors. All the Palatine legions were considered elite units, and were paid more and received more imperial favours than other units. Valens took refuge with these two steadfast but encircled legions, as they fought off each barbarian attack.

Seeing the emperor with these two legions, old Count Trajanus, the former commander-in-chief of Valens' troops who had been recalled from retirement by Valens for this campaign, yelled out from the back of his horse that, as Valens had been abandoned by his bodyguard troops, all hope was gone unless he called up the foreign auxiliaries that he had placed in reserve.

Valens agreed, and above the din of battle Trajanus instructed the Sarmatian Victor, his Master of Cavalry, to ride with all speed to summon up the famously tough Batavian auxiliaries who had been held in reserve – the Batavi Seniors and/or the Batavi Juniors – and the Palatine auxiliary units. Bent on his mission, Victor turned his horse around and slashed his way through the surrounding Visigoths, but when he reached the place where the Batavian troops should have been, there was no sign of them. They too had fled. So Victor kept riding. [Ibid.]

The fighting, which had raged all afternoon, continued into the twilight. And then night fell; an inky, moonless night. With its arrival, the battle ended. The Roman army had been destroyed. Ammianus estimated that no more than one third of the troops in Valens' army escaped with their lives. Modern authorities put the Roman losses at 40,000. [Warry, *WCW*] Certainly Roman casualties were massive. Ammianus said that the roads were blocked with the dead and the dying. 'With them also mounds of fallen horses filled the plains with corpses.' [Amm., XXXI, 13, 11]

Valens' most senior generals, the counts Sebastianus and Trajanus – one who encouraged the early battle, the other who had stayed with his emperor to the last – both fell on the battlefield. Thirty-five Roman tribunes also perished in this bloody defeat that became known as the Battle of Adrianople. One of the Roman officers to fall that day was Potentius, a tribune 'in the first flower of his youth' who had commanded a Palatine mounted unit, the Equites Promoti Seniors, which was apparently made up of men promoted from other units. Potentius would have been a personal friend of the historian Ammianus, for he was the son of Ammianus' former chief, Count Ursicinus, who had been Roman commander-in-chief under the emperor Constantius II. [Ibid., XXXI, 13, 18]

As for the emperor Valens, he was never seen again, dead or alive. Ammianus related a story told by a young officer cadet of the Candidati Militares relating his fate. The soldier said that Valens, though wounded by an arrow, had escaped from the battlefield late in the day with a few officer cadets, including the teller of the tale, and some eunuchs from the Palatium staff, and found refuge in a two-storey farmer's cottage nearby. While Valens' companions were attempting to treat his wound, the cottage was surrounded by Gothic warriors. As the Goths were attempting the break down the bolted doors, one or more of the officer cadets from Valens' party loosed off arrows at the attackers from an upper window and drove them back. The Goths then piled firewood against the house, and set it alight.

As the cottage burned, the storyteller decided to take his chances with the Goths, and dived through a window. None of the other occupants of the cottage emerged from the flames, and all perished. The young officer cadet was made a prisoner by the Goths, who were appalled when they learned from him that they had just fried the Roman emperor, for they would have won great glory among their people had they captured Valens alive. The young officer cadet later escaped from his captors, found his way to Roman forces and told his story. [Ibid., XXXI, 13, 14–16]

The Roman defeat at Adrianople was a staggering blow to Roman prestige. 'The annals record no such massacre of a battle except the one at Cannae,' said Ammianus, referring to the defeat of the Romans in Italy by Hannibal many centuries before. [Ibid., 13, 19] But worse than the stink of defeat, these were 'ever irreparable losses,' Ammianus lamented, 'so costly to the Roman state'. [Ibid., 13, 11] Poor generalship had been to blame. The barbarian nations in both the West and the East took heart from this telling defeat and renewed their savage inroads into the Roman provinces. The conquest of Italy now seemed achievable. Rome itself now beckoned.

Who would or could save the Roman Empire from collapse now?

AD 401–403
LXXIV. STILICHO SAVES ITALY
Rome's last hope

> 'You and you alone, Stilicho, have dispersed the darkness that enshrouded our empire and have restored its glory.'
>
> CLAUDIAN, *The Gothic War*, AD 36–39

It was the middle of the winter of AD 401–402, and a Roman cavalry column was warily picking its way across the snowbound Swiss Alps, urged on by their impatient young commander; Rome's most senior general was attempting to come to the rescue of his emperor after Italy had been invaded by the Visigoths.

Flavius Stilicho was just 36 years of age. Yet, according to the poet Claudian, who knew him, Stilicho had 'shining grey hair'. [Claud., *TGW*, 458] The weight of command had apparently sent him prematurely grey, for on his young shoulders Stilicho carried the command of all of Rome's military in the west of the Roman Empire as Master of Both Military Services, a post previously occupied by two men that combined the roles of Master of Foot and Master of Cavalry. Stilicho's mother was a Roman, his father a Vandal from Scandinavia who had been a tribune of Roman cavalry.

As a teenager Stilicho had embarked on a career within the Roman military, swiftly becoming an outstanding soldier and an extremely confident and inspiring leader. Both qualities meant that he was swiftly propelled to the rank of tribune of cavalry. In

AD 385, at the age of just 20, Stilicho had been appointed by the emperor Theodosius to the post of *Comes Domesticorum* – Count of the Household troops, the imperial bodyguard that succeeded the Praetorian Guard abolished by Constantine the Great. Theodosius had also given Stilicho the hand in marriage of his favourite niece, Serena. Two years before Theodosius died in AD 395, he had made Stilicho Master of all his forces in the west, and guardian of his 10-year-old son and successor Honorius. This, in effect, made Stilicho regent of the Western Empire. Young Honorius had subsequently married Stilicho's daughter Maria.

Now, Stilicho faced his greatest test – saving Italy from the invading hordes. The Visigoths, originally from the Ukraine, had crossed the Danube thirty years before. After the massive Gothic defeat of the army of the emperor Valens at Adrianople in AD 378, the Visigoths had occupied Moesia, making their capital Novae, previously the base of the 1st Italica Legion. Two years after the death of Theodosius, in AD 395, the Visigoths had elected a new king and war leader, 25-year-old Alaric, who had previously served as commander of Goth auxiliary troops in the Roman army. Since then, the Visigoths had invaded Thrace, occupied all of Greece, and seized Pannonia and Illyricum from Rome, forcing Roman settlers to flee. Alaric had been placated by the emperor of the Eastern Roman Empire, Arcadius, Theodosius' eldest son, apparently with a bribe, and for six years the Visigoths had controlled their Balkan empire on Italy's eastern flank while maintaining an uneasy peace with the Romans.

As the autumn of AD 401 was coming to an end, Alaric led his people – men, women and children – along a recently built path that traversed the Julian Alps, and entered northeastern Italy unheralded. As Alaric had hoped, the Romans were caught completely off guard. The Visigoths supposedly had a treaty of peace with them, while the looming winter gave the residents in Italy a false sense of security – no one, they thought, would launch an invasion at this time of year. In late October, once the invaders' presence in northeastern Italy became known, a hastily assembled Roman army met the Visigoths at the Timavus, the Timavo river, northwest of Trieste. In the battle that followed, the Roman army was destroyed, after which Alaric's forces flooded unimpeded across northern Italy as far as Liguria to the west, overwhelming farms and villages, and laying siege to cities and towns.

Community after Roman community fell to the invaders. Walls reinforced with steel, mighty defensive towers and iron gates, none of these could keep the invaders out. No rampart or palisade could withstand the onrush of the Visigoth cavalry, said Claudian; it was almost as if the city gates opened of their own accord. [Claud., *TGW*, 213–16] The people of northern Italy resorted to praying for foul weather which would bring rain that flooded the rivers and kept the invaders from reaching their towns and villages. But through the winter and into the spring the rain stayed away, and the people complained that even the sunshine seemed to conspire against them. [Ibid., 48] Nothing stopped the invaders; they glutted themselves with booty, and took tens of thousands of Roman civilian captives – some to ransom, others to retain as slaves.

Rome was no longer the seat of emperors. In northwestern Italy, the young emperor Honorius had made his capital at Mediolanum, today's city of Milan, just as his father and several previous emperors had done since early in the fourth century. And now the invaders surrounded the imperial city, cutting off Honorius and his court from the outside world. In southern Italy, as news arrived that the north was being overrun, Rome and every other city and town closed their gates and levied every able-bodied man to their defence. A massive earthen wall was thrown up around Rome's outer suburbs and equipped with numerous wooden watchtowers – Claudian, who was in Rome to see it being built, said that the wall's architect was fear. [Claud., *SCH.*, 533] Yet, while many were industrious in their preparations to defend Rome, the wealthy prepared to evacuate their families and their valuables to the islands of Sardinia and Corsica. [Claud., *TGW*, 218]

Stilicho rose to command all Roman forces in the West under the emperor Theodosius I (shown here on the Missorium of Theodosius with troops of his bodguard), who also gave Stilicho his niece's hand in marriage.

At Honorius' court in Milan there was talk of giving up Rome to the invaders and transferring the city's population to southern Gaul at the junction of the Saône and Rhine rivers, making Lugdunum the new capital, the new Rome. [Ibid., 296–300] In Gaul itself, and in Spain and Britain, the news of the Visigoth invasion generated a rumour, which quickly spread, that Rome had fallen. [Ibid., 201–204] Meanwhile, messengers from the emperor had been sent on a desperate mission to find Stilicho and beg him to return to Italy at once to direct the defence.

When tidings of the invasion reached Stilicho, he had been in Vindelicia, a region taking in parts of modern-day Switzerland, Germany and Austria. He had been busy putting down an uprising by Ostrogoth tribesmen who had settled in Vindelicia and Noricum under a peace settlement with Rome. [Warry, *WCW*]

The seal of Alaric. Elected king of the Visigoths at the age of 25, he vowed never to remove his breastplate until he had walked the Forum at Rome as the city's conqueror.

Apparently encouraged by Alaric, the barbarian settlers had broken their treaties. [Claud., *TGW*, 364–6] Once Stilicho arrived in Vindelicia, despite being accompanied by only a small number of Roman troops, he had soon quelled the rebellion. His soldiers from Raetia had then sacked the Ostrogoth farms across Vindelicia and generated a 'mass of spoil'. [Ibid., 415]

Another barbarian tribe which had also settled in Roman territory in Switzerland under an agreement with a previous administration. They were Alans, and were reported to have been ready to participate in the uprising, or at the very least had supported it. The (unnamed) king of the Alans had protested his innocence, and volunteered to lead his mounted fighting men in Stilicho's service. So Stilicho enrolled the Alans, 'setting such number to their forces as should best suit' to ensure that he did not take over many of them to Italy with him, where, if there were too large a number, they might have been a burden to the country or a threat to him. [Ibid., 400–403] Stilicho would soon have plenty of bloody work for the Alani cavalry.

To speed his journey south, Stilicho had used a small boat to cross 'the lake' – Lake Como, according to Gibbon. He then joined a waiting mounted column quite probably made up of the Alani volunteers, for the passage of the Alps, which were considered 'inaccessible in winter'. [Ibid., 320–23] As Stilicho hurried towards Italy, messengers were carrying the youthful Master of the Armies' orders to legion commanders throughout western Europe, telling them to march their units to join him with all speed in northern Italy.

From their station at Castra Regina (Regensburg) in Raetia, the 3rd Italica Legion set off to join their general. From faraway Britain, the only legion that remained intact in the British Isles, the 6th Victrix, hastened from Eburacum to the Kent coast, from where it was ferried to Gaul for the march to Italy. This was the legion, said Claudian, 'that had kept the fierce Scots in check, [and] whose men had scanned the strange devices tattooed on the faces of the dying Picts'. [Ibid., 416–18]

From the Rhineland came the last two legions left guarding the Rhine frontier. The 1st Minervia left its base at Bonna, where it had 'held the Chatti and wild Cherusci in subjection' since the reign of Trajan. The 22nd Primigeneia marched from Mogontiacum, where it had been based without interruption from the days of Claudius, and where it had lately 'faced the flaxen-haired Sugumbri'. With these legions' departures, said Claudian, the Rhine was defended by just one thing – the fear of Rome. [Ibid., 421–4] While Stilicho lived, his reputation alone guarded the west bank of the Rhine from German attack, despite the removal of Rome's best frontier troops.

The path that Stilicho took across the Alps to reach Italy was deep with snow, and men commonly froze to death trying to use this route in winter, or were carried away by avalanches of ice and snow, while ox-carts plunged from icy paths into crevasses. There was no wine and little food for Stilicho's mountain crossing, and what food they had Stilicho and each man ate with sword in hand, 'burdened with rain-soaked cloak', before urging on 'his half-frozen steed'. At night, Stilicho slept in caves or shared the huts of alpine shepherds, using his shield for a pillow. [Ibid., 348–56]

Despite the bitter conditions, Stilicho and his escort pressed on and succeeded in crossing the Alps. As soon as they reached the foothills of northern Italy, Stilicho sent riders galloping south with a message for the people of Rome, urging them not to abandon hope, but patiently to await the defeat of the foe. [Ibid., 268–9] He himself set his course for Milan, which was crowded with Roman refugees. At Milan, refugees and residents, 'herded together like sheep', had to watch glumly from the city walls as Alaric's Visigoths put farmland to the torch, and flames swept through the fields around the city. [Ibid., 45–7]

Twilight was descending as, from one of the city's Palatine towers, the 17-year-old emperor Honorius surveyed the depressing scene around Milan. The city had been surrounded by the Visigoths since February, but they were not making any effort to storm it; Alaric was convinced that, without any hope of relief from outside, the boy emperor would soon be forced to come to terms with him 'on any conditions he chose'. [Claud., *SCH*., 448–9] Claudian was to quote Honorius directly about this night. A leading poet in Rome at the time, he was close to Serena, Stilicho's wife, so it is likely that the emperor spoke to him about these events. 'Wherever I looked I saw the watch fires of the enemy shining like stars,' the young emperor recalled. [Ibid., 453–4]

Somewhere out there, Honorius hoped, his wife's father was trying to reach him, for he was counting on Stilicho getting through to lift the siege of the city. [Claud., *SCH*, 450–51] 'But the enemy held the road between my father-in-law and myself,' Honorius said. 'What was Stilicho to do? Halt? My danger forbade the slightest delay. Break through the enemy's line? His force was too small – in hurrying to my aid he had left behind him many troops, both of our country and foreign.' [Ibid., 462–3]

Stilicho was in fact very close by. After coming down out of the mountains east of the River Adda, his mounted column had followed the Adda south towards Milan without encountering Visigoth patrols. Opposite Milan, where a bridge crossed the churning river's icy mountain waters, Stilicho had came on a Visigoth encampment barring the way over the bridge. From Milan, just across the river, Roman trumpets could be heard summoning the men of the first watch to their guard posts. [Ibid., 444–5] Stilicho decided not to wait for his other forces to join him. Time was of the essence. In the fading light, Stilicho and his cavalry escort charged into the Visigoth camp at the Adda bridge. Surprising the sentries, he rode right through the camp, 'sword in hand, cutting down all who stood in his path'. [Ibid., 488–9]

The sentries in the tower at Milan's main gate recognized their general at once as he and his small force of heavy cavalry galloped up from the bridge with their dragon pennants flying. Tall and slim, with large eyes, small mouth, a neat beard and his grey hair shorn in the page-boy style that had become the fashion, Stilicho wore a richly embroidered cavalry cloak that reached all the way to his knees, while his helmet gleamed. As the gate rose up and Stilicho was admitted to the embattled city, the troops in Milan came running to him. 'The cohorts, such love they bore their commander, hurriedly assembled from everywhere, and at the sight of Stilicho their courage revived and they burst into tears of joy.' [Claud., *TGW*, 404–407]

Alaric would have been furious that Stilicho had managed to push through to link up with his emperor. But that was only the beginning of Alaric's problems. The news that Roman reinforcements were crossing the Cottinian Alps from Gaul now reached both Alaric and Stilicho, probably at much the same time. Using the main military highways of Gaul, the legions had marched from Britain and the Rhine. The 6th Victrix, 1st Minervia and 22nd Primigeneia legions would have linked up in Gaul and marched south in one large column, passing through Lugdunum and Vienna on their way to the Cottinian Alps. Then, in March, as the spring thaw made the Alps passable to legions with their heavy baggage, the units crossed the mountains to Turin in northeastern Italy. From there it was only several days' march to Milan to join Stilicho and lift the siege.

The Visigoth leaders were made uneasy, despite the successes of the past few months. According to Claudian, a council of war was convened at Alaric's camp by Visigoth chieftains. Many were elderly, with some using spears as walking sticks. Most bore the scars of battle, and all were long-haired and clad in garments of animal fur. All were aware that Alaric was intent on pressing south and taking Rome. When he was made king of his people six years earlier, Alaric had made a vow to the River Danube, which he and his forefathers considered sacred. That oath was 'that he would never unbuckle his breastplate until he had marched in triumph through the Forum' in Rome. [Ibid., 81–3] Now, Alaric proposed to fulfil that vow.

At the meeting of the Visigoth senate, the most elderly tribal leader came to his feet. Like him, the older men here had participated in the rout of the emperor Valens' Roman army at Adrianople twenty-three years before, when Alaric was just 8 years old. This same warrior chief had given Alaric his first bow and arrows when he was a boy. In times past, the old warrior had counselled Alaric to observe the treaty with Rome and keep the peace. Now, in grave tones, he warned the young king that he had pushed his luck, and that of his people, further than was prudent.

It was time to collect their spoils and go home, the Visigoth elder said, while the approaching legions were still far off. Wait any longer, he cautioned, and their people could be trapped in Italy. No one had succeeded in taking Rome; it was said that in the city's defence the gods hurled thunderbolts from her walls. It was folly even to consider it. Further, he reminded Alaric that in the not so distant past, a Roman army under Stilicho had inflicted a severe defeat on the Visigoths in Greece. 'If you are not afraid of the gods,' said the old man, 'beware the might of Stilicho.' [Claud., *TGW*, 469–515]

Alaric was furious. Declaring the old man a coward, he reminded the other leaders that he had never been defeated, and never took a backward step. He intended to either conquer Italy or to die there. Even now, he said, Italian blacksmiths in occupied towns were being forced to forge weapons that the Visigoths would use against Stilicho and his Roman troops. The gods had told him to conquer Italy, he said, and he would not defy Heaven's rule – there would be no retreat from Italy. Equally unwilling to defy their gods, the Visigoth leaders on the council of war backed their king. Then, 'exhorting them to combat', Alaric 'made ready his army to take the road [west]', to meet and defeat the approaching legions. [Ibid. 518–52]

By the beginning of April, Alaric had concentrated his forces at the town of Pollentia, today's village of Pollenza. On the Tanaro river, Pollentia straddled the main paved Roman military highway that led from Turin to Asti and on to Milan. Clearly, it was Alaric's intention to intercept and destroy the Roman reinforcements marching from Gaul before they could reach Stilicho.

Once the Visigoths had pulled out of the encirclement of Milan, Stilicho could venture out of the city and march west with the hope of linking up with the legions coming from Gaul. But he had to do it before the Visigoths attacked the column. Addressing his legions at Milan before he set out, he told them it was time to exact vengeance. 'Wipe out the disgrace which the encirclement of your emperor by his foes has brought on you, and let your swords end the shame which the defeat on the Timavus and the enemy's passage of the Alps has caused to Rome.' Rome's enemies were watching, he said – the fierce tribes in Britain, the Germans beyond the Rhine, the barbarians north of the Danube. 'The empire's frame is tottering. Let your shoulders support it. A single battle, and all will be well. Just one victory, and the world's peace will be assured.' [Ibid., 562–73]

Sending a similar message to be read to the auxiliaries, Stilicho gave his invigorated troops the order to prepare to march. He now dispatched Honorius under escort to Ravenna, on the east coast of Italy, from where the young emperor could escape by ship if the campaign went against the Romans. Stilicho himself combined some of the legionary and auxiliary troops that had garrisoned Milan, the 3rd Italica Legion, which had by now arrived from Raetia, and the king of the Alans and his cavalry; on the eve of Easter, 'at full speed he advanced his army, clamorous for battle', to the southwest, on the heels of the enemy. [Ibid., 560–61]

It was 6 April, Easter Sunday, when Stilicho chose to engage in battle with the enemy. The Visigoths may have felt Christian Romans would not fight during an important religious festival, but Stilicho had no scruples about fighting at Easter. The two armies formed up on the plain outside the vast Visigoth camp. It is unclear whether Stilicho had by this time managed to link up with the three legions that had been marching from the west to reinforce him, but it is likely, for he took the initiative and lined up outside the Visigoth camp in battle order. His formation was a standard one, with infantry in the centre and cavalry on the wings. It seems, from his later battle tactics, that he placed the majority of his legionaries in the front rank, with auxiliaries behind them. [Claud., *SCH*, 220–21]

Flavius Vegetius Renatus, a senior adviser to the emperor Valentinius II just a decade or so earlier, described the nature of the disposition of the cavalry and infantry in the battle line during this time. The heavy cavalry, those troopers wearing armour from head to toe and whose horses were also armoured, stood next to the infantry with their massive spears projecting well out in front of them, together with the lancers, who were equipped with four or five lances. Light cavalry – the horse archers and troopers without any armour – occupied the extremities of the wings. The task of the infantry line, said Vegetius, was to stand its ground and repulse or break up the enemy attack. [Vege., III] The heavy cavalry's role was to stay with the infantry and protect its flanks. At the same time, the light cavalry was to gallop forward and surround the enemy's wings and disorder them. [Ibid.]

Stilicho posted the Alani cavalry in his rear as a reserve. But the men of the cavalry were to play a key role in his battle tactics, for Stilicho planned to use them in a manoeuvre designed to capture Alaric alive. At the Romans' final council of war this secret plan was shared with the king of the Alans, who, according to Claudian, was short in stature, 'but great was his soul, and anger blazed fiercely from his eyes'. He was covered in battle scars, and a spear wound had left a particularly savage scar on his face. [Claud., *TGW*, 581–5] When he left the conference with Stilicho, the king of the Alans knew precisely what he had to do, and he was determined not to fail the Roman general, just as he was determined to throw off the accusation of treachery levelled at him after the Alans had been implicated in the uprising in Vindelicia the previous year. [Ibid., 590–93] Alani heavy cavalry took their position in the rear, probably joining a legion assigned by Stilicho to his reserve. That legion, like all by this time, would have numbered little more than 1,000 men.

The Notitia Dignitatum illustrates how the legions were equipped at this time. They wore trousers and boots, and were attired in tunics that were in some cases white, in others red. Some wore light chain-mail armour. Their helmets were like those of firemen today. While archaeological finds from earlier centuries indicate that Roman helmets were then lined with felt, by the fourth century it had become the habit for Roman soldiers to wear a conical felt cap under their helmets for comfort.

The weapons carried by Stilicho's legionaries were a handful of javelins, a sword that was longer than the old gladius short-sword, a dagger, and as many as three battleaxes of differing design, some double-headed, jammed into the belt. Their shields were wooden, oval, almost flat, and bore a painted unit emblem as in the past.

On the other side, Alaric deployed long-haired, bearded Visigoth infantry with spear, sword, and wooden shields that were sometimes oval and sometimes oblong. Few of the Visigoths wore armour or helmets. Alaric's cavalrymen were likewise unarmoured, and were equipped with spear, shield and sword. Some leaders, including Alaric himself, wore Roman armour and helmet. As the Visigoth men poured from their camp to form battle lines, their women and children waited in the camp to enjoy the spoils of another anticipated victory, while thousands of chained Roman prisoners in the camp prayed for Roman success.

Rome's armies no longer charged the enemy as in the day of Julius Caesar – who had been fiercely critical of Pompey the Great's decision to have his army stand firm to receive Caesar's charge at Pharsalus in 48 BC. As Vegetius indicates, by the time of the Battle of Pollentia it was the norm for the legions to stand and receive an enemy charge. So it would appear that this is how the battle outside Pollentia opened, with the Visigoths charging the stationary Roman army and the two front lines becoming locked together.

It was soon heavy going for Roman troops fighting in the centre. As legionaries in 'wearied ranks' began to flag, Stilicho ordered whole cohorts out of the battle line, throwing in waiting auxiliaries of the second line to replace them. Among those now brought into the fight against the Visigoths were units of Goth auxiliaries. The poet Claudian would gloat over this move by Stilicho: 'Thus he cunningly weakens the savage tribes of the Danube by opposing one tribe against another.' This, in Claudian's opinion, meant that either way barbarians would perish in battle for Rome's sake. [Claud., *SCH*, 220–23]

Once battle had been under way for a time and the Roman and Visigoth warriors were shield to shield, Stilicho, positioned behind the lines, spotted Alaric, mounted, and with a strong horse-guard, on the opposite side of the battlefield. It was then that Stilicho ordered a particular trumpet call to be sounded. This was the signal that the Alans had been waiting for. Led by their diminutive, battle-scarred king, the armoured Alani cavalrymen kicked their horses into motion and, with their standards flying in the wind, came charging around from behind the Roman army and swept into one flank of the Visigoth army.

Carried by momentum and received with surprise, the Alans cut their way through opposing troops towards Alaric and his escort. The Alans were desperately close to achieving their goal when, in his enthusiasm, their king pressed too far ahead of his men, and was surrounded by Goths with hacking blades. Before the eyes of his men, the king was toppled from his steed and killed. His death threw his followers into confusion. Many turned away from the fight. 'The entire host would have reeled had not Stilicho swiftly gathered a legion, and hurrying to the spot, rallied the cavalry to the fight with infantry support,' said Claudian. [Claud., *TGW*, 594–7]

'The rash Alan chief [had] upset his carefully laid scheme,' said Claudian of Stilicho's plan to capture his opposite number. 'All but a prisoner', Alaric managed to escape, and galloped from the battlefield. [Claud., *SCH*, 224–5] The Visigoth king rode back to his camp. There, gathering what pack animals he could, he had them loaded with valuables, then fled east with his entourage. Thousands of Visigoth fighting men did the same, leaving their wives and children behind. Stilicho's troops swept into the camp, where they took the Visigoth non-combatants prisoner and released from their chains throngs of Roman captives, who planted 'thankful kisses on their deliverers' bloodied hands and hurried back to their long-lost homes and their dear children'. [Claud., *TGW*, 616–19]

The Visigoths hoped their retreat would be aided by the Roman troops pausing to loot the enemy camp of its spoils, for the invaders had brought all their valuables to Italy with them. But, says Claudian, the majority of the Roman troops gave chase, ignoring Visigoth carts laden with gold and silver. To further slow the pursuit and speed their escape, the Visigoths discarded their war trophies along the highway in their wake – everything from Greek mixing bowls to life-size statues looted from Corinth in Achaea before that famous Greek city was burned by Alaric's hordes. In desperation, Visigoth leaders threw away scarlet robes that had belonged to the Roman emperor Valens and which they had looted from his baggage at Adrianople more than two decades earlier. None of these things tempted Stilicho's men, said Claudian, for these things were connected with past Roman defeats and were considered 'ill-omened'. [Ibid., 613]

After weeks of retreat, Alaric was able to regroup a number of his men and make camp in the foothills of the Apennine Mountains in central Italy. Stilicho hung back, keeping watch on the Visigoth encampment but not surrounding it, and posting troops at every point to warn him of enemy movements. According to Claudian, Alaric, bitter at his defeat at Pollentia, had initially considered marching over the Apennines to Rome. [Claud., *SCH*, 291–2] But once his youthful temper had cooled he decided to find a route across the Alps into Raetia, or even Gaul. Yet each time his scouts ventured in one direction or another they ran into Roman patrols, as if Stilicho could read Alaric's mind, and were forced to turn back. [Ibid., 231–41]

There, as the heat of summer beat down on Italy, without fodder, Alaric's horses were forced to eat leaves and tree-bark. Disease raged in the Visigoth camp. Alaric's followers berated him, complaining that they had lost all their worldly goods, and that their wives and children were prisoners of the Romans. Yet, he felt the same loss – Alaric's own wife and children had been captured, and his wealth had also been taken. [Ibid., 296–7] The warriors urged him to do battle with the Romans once more, but he would not venture to fight Stilicho again.

Disillusioned with their king's leadership, whole sections of Visigoth infantry and squadrons of cavalry began to desert Alaric, going over to Stilicho or heading for Pannonia. Some of his most senior commanders went with them. Alaric rode after deserters, at one moment cursing them, at another imploring them to stay faithful to him, and reminding them of their past glories together, even offering to let them kill him as an alternative to turning their backs on him. But they ignored him, and rode on. [Ibid., 250–55]

Claudian wrote that, finally, 'with Stilicho pressing hard upon him', Alaric 'fled in terror before our eagles'. [Claud., *SCH*, 320–21] The indications are that Stilicho actually negotiated the departure of Alaric and his depleted force from Italy, perhaps paying him a sum in gold and probably returning wives and children. One way or another, by the end of the summer the Visigoth threat had been terminated and Alaric's invaders had left Italy's soil.

Stilicho was able to send Honorius from Ravenna down across the Apennines to Rome, where the young emperor's arrival was applauded by adoring crowds, their cheers ringing through the Palatium that had stood empty and neglected on the Palatine Hill for so many years. The last time that Honorius had been in Rome he had been a mere child. Many senators of Rome had never as much as heard him speak before this day; they would 'learn to know him' now, said Claudian. [Ibid., 593–4]

But the true hero's welcome was reserved for Stilicho. Having satisfied himself that Alaric had truly left the country, and after posting his infantry to guard the alpine passes, Stilicho rode south for Rome with his cavalry. Word sped through Rome on a million tongues that Stilicho was coming with the army. This, to the people of Rome, was certain proof that the war with Alaric was over and that they were saved. As Honorius and the courtiers rushed out to greet the conquering general and escort him into the city, the people lined the city walls to catch a glimpse of him, recognizing his distinctive helmet, 'glittering like a star' and his 'shining grey hair'. [Claud., *TGW*, 458–9]

The residents of Rome surged out of the city gates as far as the Milvian Bridge to swarm around their hero. They yelled their greeting to Stilicho, and shouted their congratulations to the 'mail-clad' equites of the heavy cavalry who rode 'brazen-armoured horses' in their squadrons behind the general. [Claud., *SCH*, 569] The poet Claudian was in that throng, and in the crowd again on New Year's Day AD 403 when Honorius drove into Rome in a four-horse chariot with Stilicho at his side, celebrating a Triumph for the defeat of the Visigoths. The triumphal procession was then followed by a lion hunt and a military display by 1,000 men in the packed Circus Maximus. Although a pale emulation of the great Triumphs of Pompey, Caesar, Vespasian and Trajan in previous centuries, where Rome truly was glorious and victorious, at least in Stilicho the Romans had a general to equal great commanders of the past.

There was as much relief as joy in the air in Rome that day. 'Gone for ever are our miserable impressed levies,' Claudian exulted. No longer, said he, would the security of Rome depend on conscript farmers who laid aside the sickle to attempt to hurl the javelin. Stilicho was the saviour of city and empire. 'Here is Rome's true strength, her true leader, Mars in human form.' [Claud., *TGW*, 463]

Claudian's rejoicing would prove to be premature. Seven years later, Rome would fall. To the Visigoths. Led by Alaric.

AD 410
LXXV. THE FALL OF ROME
Alaric keeps his vow

Alaric was just 25 when he was chosen king of the Visigoths in AD 395, and made his vow to the river god who the Visigoths believed resided in the Danube that he would not remove his armour until he trod the Forum of Rome as the city's conqueror. [Claud., *TGW*, 81–3]

Three times this one-time commander of Gothic auxiliaries in the Roman army came close to keeping that vow. In AD 401–402 he had led a Visigoth army that rampaged through northern Italy, only to suffer defeat at the hands of the young Roman general Stilicho. Humiliated at the Battle of Pollentia in the spring of AD 402, Alaric had been forced to retreat from Italy, following which Stilicho and his young emperor and son-in-law Honorius had celebrated a Triumph.

In AD 403, Alaric and his Visigoths had again invaded Italy, and this time Stilicho had stung Alaric with defeat before he could cross the River Po, at the Battle of Verona. Alaric, like his luck, had survived the encounter, and he had negotiated his way back to Pannonia. Two years later, Honorius, Roman emperor of the Western Empire, had more to worry about than Alaric. A massive German coalition led by Ostrogoths under Radagaisus had flooded down through Raetia and invaded northern Italy. Again Stilicho was called on to save Italy; he came on the barbarians when they were attacking the city of Florentia, latter-day Florence. He drove the invaders north, cut off their supplies, then massacred them at Fiesole. Radagaisus was captured by Stilicho, and featured in a Triumph celebrated by Honorius in August, after which the German leader was executed.

But the following year, a coalition of Suebi Germans, Vandals and disenchanted Alans had crossed the undefended Rhine and plundered their way through Gaul and into Spain. In AD 407, Alaric led his Visigoths into the Roman province of Noricum, demanding 4,000 pounds (1,812 kilograms) of gold to leave. Stilicho convinced a reluctant Senate in Rome to pay up, and Alaric had withdrawn with his gold. But he had not yet finished with the Romans.

By early AD 408, 23-year-old Honorius' wife Maria, the daughter of Stilicho, had died. Honorius then married Stilicho's younger daughter Thermantia. But relations

The massive Aurelian Walls of Rome could not prevent Alaric and his Visigoths from sacking Rome.

between Honorius and his father-in-law and one-time guardian began to sour when it was rumoured that Stilicho was plotting to put his son Eucherius on the throne. Then came the news that Honorius' brother Arcadius, Roman emperor of the Eastern Empire, had died at Constantinople. When Stilicho proposed to go to Constantinople to play a role in the settlement of the succession there, suspicions grew about his intentions, and renewed rumours circulated about his plans for his son. In August, on the orders of Honorius, Stilicho was arrested in Ravenna. On 23 August, Stilicho was beheaded. His son was executed shortly after.

Rome had just lost her last great general, and her last hope. And Alaric knew it. He immediately marched his Visigoths into Italy. With numerous auxiliary units from barbarian tribes defecting to him from the Roman army, and apparently disposing of Stilicho's leaderless legions with ease, Alaric reached Rome and laid siege to it. The Senate of Rome granted Alaric another payment in gold, and agreed to assist him in negotiations with Honorius, who had taken up residence at Ravenna.

But when Honorius refused to consider paying Alaric anything more, the Visigoth king returned to Rome in AD 409, laying siege to the city anew. This siege was lifted after a negotiated peace deal permitted Alaric to install a puppet emperor of his own choice, Attalus, in Rome. At this same time, Roman officials in Britain wrote desperately to the emperor Honorius at Ravenna, begging him to send back the legion that Stilicho had taken from them several years before, the 6th Victrix, together with any other Roman troops he could spare, for the Picts and the Scots had burst across Hadrian's Wall and were ravaging Britain.

There would be no record in the Notitia Dignitatum of the four legions that Stilicho had withdrawn from Britain, the Rhine, and Raetia to fight Alaric. It is probable that since Pollentia, all these units had been ground down to nothing by the continual fighting in Italy, and Honorius wrote back to the officials in Britain to say that he could offer Britannia no hope of military assistance. No more Roman troops would ever be sent to Britain; the locals would have to provide for their own future defence.

In AD 410, Alaric was again outside Rome with his army – to depose Attalus, who had turned against him – laying siege to the city once more. On 24 August AD 410, almost exactly two years to the day since Stilicho's death, Visigoth agents inside Rome opened a city gate, and Alaric's army flooded into the capital. With pitiful ease, Rome had fallen, and for three days the Visigoths sacked the eternal city.

Rome's buildings were pillaged, some set alight. The fate of the city's defenders is unknown, although the civilian population was generally not harmed. All the gold and silver that adorned the city, from the statue of golden-winged Victoria that once stood in the Senate House to the gold and silver glittering around Trajan's Column, and even the *milliarium aureum*, the gilded column in the Forum from which all distances in the Roman world were said to be measured, all these would have fallen to the invaders, who, there in the city, would have industriously melted down their loot for ease of transport.

Following the AD 402 rebuff to Alaric at Pollentia, the Roman poet Claudian had boasted that Stilicho had saved Rome, and that she would never again have to fear the barbarian. But Stilicho's brilliant generalship, like all things, was doomed to be lost with time. Under his steadying hand, Rome had been like the dying man who seems to experience a remarkable and unexpected improvement in health, only to collapse and perish soon after. Claudian himself seems not to have lived to have seen the day, in August 410, when Alaric the Visigoth kept his vow to his pagan god and walked the well-trod paving stones of the Forum, as conqueror of Rome.

Just a matter of weeks later, as Alaric was leading his victorious army on a pillaging progress through southern Italy after the sack of Rome, the Visigoth king fell ill at Cosentia, today's Cosenza in Calabria. At just the age of 40, he died there. Legend has it that Alaric was buried in the bed of the Busento river, along with loot from Rome.

Alaric was dead. But he had demonstrated that mighty Rome could fall. Forty-five years later, Gaiseric, king of the Vandals, would invade Italy from the south after conquering North Africa, and he too would sack Rome. The imperial legions of Rome were no longer invincible. After dominating the western world in the first century, they had been fighting a long losing battle ever since, to hold Rome's frontiers. The legions of Rome and the empire they had created were no more.

LXXVI. WHY DID THE LEGIONS DECLINE AND FALL?
Explaining Rome's end

Vegetius, attempting to advise the child emperor Valentinian II (reigned AD 371–392), shortly before Rome fell to the barbarians, complained that the Roman soldier of his day had become soft. During the AD 367–383 reign of Gratian, he said, the legions had sought permission to lay aside their armour, because it was too heavy, and later their helmets, too. [Vege., *MIR*, I] 'After the example of the Goths, the Alans and the Huns, we have made improvements in the arms of the cavalry,' Vegetius said, 'yet it is plain the infantry are entirely defenceless.' [Ibid.]

'The name of the legion indeed remains to this day in our armies,' Vegetius told his emperor, 'but its strength and substance are gone.' He complained that vacancies in the legions of his day were no longer filled – not surprising considering the huge drain in manpower caused by the numerous civil wars and defeats served out on Rome's armies by invaders in Vegetius' day. Vegetius complained that the men of the legions had come to find 'duty hard, the arms heavy, the rewards uncertain, and the discipline severe'. [Vege., II]

Since the year AD 212, once Roman citizenship was conferred on all free men, the distinction between legion and auxiliary unit had virtually disappeared, and to avoid service in the legions, said Vegetius, young men of his day enlisted in auxiliary units, 'where the service is less laborious and they have reason to expect more speedy recompense'. [Ibid.]

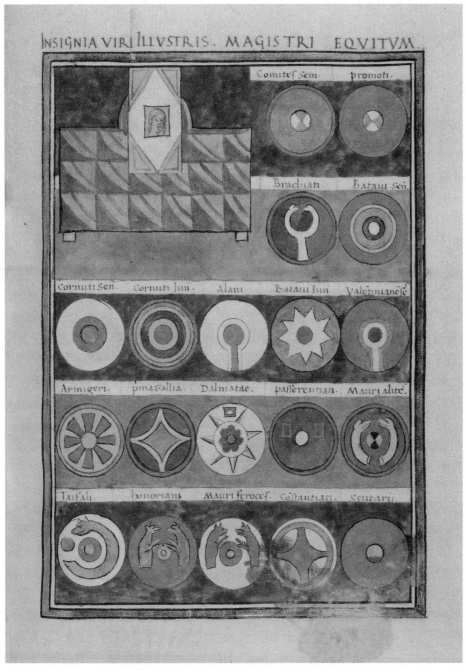

A page from the Notitia Dignitatum, showing shield emblems for various Late Empire units. By the time the Notitia was created, Roman troops were complaining about the weight of their armour, helmets and shields, and sometimes fought without them, to their cost.

By the end of the fourth century, Rome's legions, once considered glamorous to Roman youth and perceived as formidable fighting units by Rome's enemies, were routinely chewed up in the endless wars in both the East and West. But even men whose legions were outnumbered and who had previously suffered defeat at the hands of their enemies could be turned into victors by good generals; in the Western Empire's last years both Julian and Stilicho proved that. But in the end, Rome ran out of good generals, just as she ran out of time.

From the time of Trajan, Rome was in decline. Considering the number of poor emperors, assassinations and civil wars, the most remarkable thing about the Roman Empire is that it lasted as long as it did. That longevity can only be attributed to her legions. Despite all that inept commanders and ambitious throne-seekers did to it, the institution that was the imperial legion nonetheless served Rome well for more than 400 years.

KEY TO SOURCES

AE – *L'Annee Epigraphique*, Paris

Alex. W. – *The Alexandrian War* (Caesar, CW)

Amm. – Ammianus Marcellinus

Arr. *TH* – Arrian, *Tactical Handbook*

Arr. *EAA* – Arrian, *Expedition Against the Alans*

A.V. – Aurelius Victor, *De Caesaribus*

Birl. *DRA* – Birley, *Documenting the Roman Army*, 'The Commissioning of Equestrian Officers'

Bon. *B&B* – Bonet, *Bulls & Bullfighting*

Caes. *GW* – Caesar, *The Gallic War*

Caes. *CW* – Caesar, *The Civil War*

Carc. – Carcopino, *Daily Life in Ancient Rome*

CAS – Chester Archaeological Society, Table 1

Cic. *Phil.* – Cicero, *Philippics*

CIL – *Corpus Inscriptionum Latinarum*, Berlin

Claud. *OSC* – Claudian, *On Stilicho's Consulship*

Claud. *SCH* – Claudian, *Sixth Consulship of Honorius*

Claud. *TGW* – Claudian, *The Gothic War*

Cow. *RL 58–69* – Cowan, *Roman Legionary, 58 BC–AD 69*

Dio – Cassius Dio, *Roman Histories*

Dus. – Dusanic, *Documenting the Roman Army*, 'The Imperial Propaganda of Significant Day-Dates'

Eus. *Chron.* – Eusebius Pamphilius, *Chronicle*

Eus. *EH* – Eusebius Pamphilius, *Ecclesiastic History*

Eus. *LC* – Eusebius, *Life of Constantine*

Front. – Frontinus, *Stratagems*

Guey – *Essai de la Guerre Parthique de Trajan*

Herod. – Herodian, *History of the Empire*

Hold. *DRA* – Holder, *Documenting the Roman Army*, 'Auxiliary Deployment in the Reign of Hadrian'

Hold. *RAB* – Holder, *The Roman Army in Britain*

Horr. – Horrocks, *Secrets & Stories of the War*, Foreword

ILS – *Inscriptiones Latinae Selectae*, H. Dessau, Berlin

Jos. *JA* – Josephus, *The Jewish Antiquities*

Jos. *JW* – Josephus, *The Jewish War*

Kepp. *CVSI* – Keppie, *Colonisation & Veteran Settlement in Italy 47–14 BC*

Kepp. *MRA* – Keppie, *The Making of the Roman Army*

Livy – *History*

Not. Dig. – *Notitia Dignitatum*

Pelle. – Pelletier, *Histoire de Lyon*

Petr. – Petronius, *The Satyricon*

Plut. – Plutarch, *Lives of the Noble Grecians & Romans*

Poly. – Polybius, *History*

Res Gest. – Augustus, *Res Gestae*

Speid. – Speidel, *Riding for Caesar*

Starr – *Imperial Roman Navy*

Suet. – Suetonius, *Lives of the Caesars*

Tac. *A* – Tacitus, *The Annals*

Tac. *Agr.* – Tacitus, *The Agricola*

Tac. *Germ.* – Tacitus, *The Germania*

Tac., *H* – Tacitus, *The Histories*

Tom. *DRA* – Tomlin, *Documenting the Roman Army*, 'Documenting the Roman Army at Carlisle'

Vale. – *Excerpta Valesiana*

Vege. – Vegetius, *De Rei Militaris*

Velle. – Vellius Paterculus, *Roman History*

Vitr. – Vitruvius, *On Architecture*

VWT – *Vindolanda Writing Tablets*

W&D – Webster & Dudley, *The Roman Invasion of Britain*

Warry – *Warfare in the Classical World*

Web. – Webster, *Roman Imperial Army*

Wells – *The Day that Stopped Rome*

Yadin – *Bar-Kokhba*

Zos. – Zosimus, *Historica Nova*

BIBLIOGRAPHY

BOOKS

Abbott, F. F., and Johnson, A. C., *Municipal Administration in the Roman Empire*. Princeton, NJ; PUP, 1926.

Ammianus Marcellinus, *History*, and *The Excerpts of Valesius* by Anonymous (J. C. Rolfe transl.). Cambridge, MA; 1935.

Appian, *Roman History* (H. White transl.). London; Loeb, 1913.

Arrian, *Expedition Against the Alans*, J. G. DeVoto (ed.). Chicago; Ares, 1993.

Arrian, *History of Alexander, and Indica* (P. Brunt transl.). London; Loeb, 1976.

Arrian, *Tactical Handbook*, J. G. DeVoto (ed.). Chicago; Ares, 1993.

Augustus, *Res Gestae Divi Augusti* (F. W. Shipley transl.). Cambridge, MA; HUP, 1924.

Aurelius, M., *Meditations* (G. Long transl.). Chicago; Encyclopaedia Britannica, 1952.

Aurelius Victor, S., *De Caesaribus*. Liverpool; LUP, 1994.

Azzaroli, A., *A History of Early Horsemanship*. London; Brill, 1985.

Berger, P. C., *The Insignia of the Notitia Dignitatum*. New York; Garland, 1981.

Birley, A., *Marcus Aurelius*. London; Eyre & Spottiswoode, 1966.

Birley, E., *Roman Britain and the Roman Army*. Kendal, UK; Wilson, 1953.

Boardman, J., Griffin, J., Murray, O., *The Oxford History of the Classical World*. Oxford; OUP, 1986.

Bonet, E., *Bulls & Bullfighting: History, techniques, spectacle*. New York; Crown, 1970.

Bouchier, E. S., *Spain under the Roman Empire*. Oxford; Blackwell, 1914.

Bowman, J. D., and Thomas, A. K., *The Vindolanda Writing Tablets*. Newcastle; Graham, 1973.

Boyne, W., and Jones, S., *A Manual of Roman Coins*. Chicago; Ammon, 1968.

Brogen, J., *Roman Gaul*. London; Bell, 1953.

Broughton, T. R. S., *The Romanization of Africa Proconsularis*. New York; Greenwood, 1968.

Bryant, A., *The Age of Elegance*. London; Collins, 1954.

Buchan, J., *Augustus*. London; Hodder & Stoughton, 1937.

Caesar, J., *Commentaries on the Gallic & Civil Wars* (W. A. M'Devitte and W. S. Bohn transl.). London; Bell, 1890.

Carcopino, J., *Daily Life in Ancient Rome*. London; Pelican, 1956.

Cave, W., *Lives, Acts, and Martyrdoms of the Holy Apostles*. London; Hatchard, 1836.

Chevalier, R., *Roman Roads*, (N. H. Field transl.). London; Batsford, 1976.

Church, A. J., *Roman Life in the Days of Cicero*. London; Seeley, 1923.

Cicero, M.T., *Letters to Atticus* (O. E. Winstedt transl.). Cambridge, MA; HUP, 1912.

Claudian, *On Stilicho's Consulship; Panegyric on the Sixth Consulship of Honorius; The Gothic War*. Cambridge, MA; HUP, 1922.

Colledge, M. A. R., *The Parthians*. Leiden; Brill, 1986.

Collingwood, R. C., *Roman Britain*. Oxford; OUP, 1932.

Cottrell, L., *Enemy of Rome*. London; Pan, 1962.

Cottrell, L., *The Great Invasion*. London; Evans, 1958.

Cowan, R., *Roman Legionary 58 BC–AD 69*. Botley, UK; Osprey, 2003.

Cowan, R., *Roman Legionary AD 161–284*. Botley, UK; Osprey, 2003.

Cowell, F. R., *Cicero and the Roman Republic*. London; Penguin, 1956.

Croft, P., *Roman Mythology*. London; Octopus, 1974.

Cunliffe, B., *Rome and Her Empire*. Maidenhead, UK; McGraw-Hill, 1978.

Cunliffe, B., *The Celtic World*. London; Bodley Head, 1979.

Cunliffe, B., *The Roman Baths at Bath*. Bath; BAT, 1993.

Dando-Collins, S., *Blood of the Caesars: How the Murder of Germanicus Led to the Fall of Rome*. Hoboken, NJ; Wiley, 2008.

Dando-Collins, S., *Caesar's Legion: The Epic Saga of Julius Caesar's Elite Tenth Legion & the Armies of Rome*. New York; Wiley, 2002.

Dando-Collins, S., *Cleopatra's Kidnappers: How Caesar's Sixth Legion Gave Egypt to Rome and Rome to Caesar*. Hoboken, NJ; Wiley, 2006.

Dando-Collins, S., *Mark Antony's Heroes: How the Third Gallica Legion Saved an Apostle & Created an Emperor*. Hoboken, NJ; Wiley, 2007.

Dando-Collins, S., *Nero's Killing Machine: The True Story of Rome's Remarkable Fourteenth Legion*. Hoboken, NJ; Wiley, 2005.

Delbruck, H., *History of the Art of War* (J. Walter Renfroe Jr transl.). Lincoln, NE; University of Nebraska Press, 1990.

Depuy, R. E. and T. N., *The Encyclopaedia of Military History, From 3500 BC to the Present*. London; MBS, 1970.

Dio, C., *Roman History* (E. Cary transl.) Cambridge, MA; HUP, 1914.

Duff, J. D., *Lucan*. Cambridge, MA; HUP, 1977.

Emile, T., *Roman Life under the Caesars*. New York; Putnam, 1908.

Eusebius Pamphilius, *Church History; Life of Constantine; Oration in Praise of Constantine*. Cambridge, UK; Hayes, 1683.

Forestier, A., *The Roman Soldier*. London; Black, 1928.

Frank, T. (ed.), *An Economic Survey of Ancient Rome*. New Jersey; Pageant, 1959.

Frere, S. S., *Britannia, a History of Roman Britain*. London; Routledge & Kegan Paul, 1987.

Frontinus, S. J., *Stratagems* and *The Aqueducts of Rome* (C. E. Bennet transl.) Cambridge, MA; HUP, 1969.

Fuller, J., *Julius Caesar: Man, Soldier and Tyrant*. London; Eyre & Spottiswoode, 1965.

Furneaux, R., *The Roman Siege of Jerusalem*. London; Hart-Davis, 1973.

Gardner, J. F., *Family & Familia in Roman Law & Life*. Oxford; OUP, 1998.

Gibbon, E., *The Decline and Fall of the Roman Empire*. Chicago; Encyclopaedia Britannica, 1932.

Goldsworthy, A., *Roman Warfare*. London; Cassell, 2000.

Goldsworthy, A., *The Complete Roman Army*. London; Thames & Hudson, 2003.

Grant, M., *History of Rome*. Harmondsworth; Penguin, 1978.

Grant, M., *Julius Caesar*. Harmondsworth; Penguin, 1969.

Grant, M., *Roman History from Coins*. New York; Barnes & Noble, 1995.

Grant, M., *The Army of the Caesars*. Harmondsworth; Penguin, 1974.

Grant, M., *The Jews of the Roman World*. Harmondsworth; Penguin, 1973.

Grant, M., *The Roman Emperors*. Harmondsworth; Penguin, 1985.

Haywood, R. M., *Ancient Greece and the Near East*. London; Vision, 1964.

Haywood, R. M., *Ancient Rome*. London; Vision, 1967.

Herodian, *History of the Empire*. Harvard; HUP, 1995.

Highet, G., *Juvenal the Satirist*. Oxford; Clarendon, 1954.

Hill, W. T., *Buried London*. London; Phoenix, 1955.

Holy Bible: Acts of the Apostles, King James version.

Home, G. C., *Roman London*. London; Eyre & Spottiswoode, 1948.

Jimenez, R., *Caesar Against the Celts*. Conshohocken, PA; Sarpedon, 1996.

Jones, A. H. M., *Augustus*. New York; W. W. Norton, 1972.

Josephus, F., *The New Complete Works* (W. Whiston transl., 1737). Republished Grand Rapids, MI; Kregel, 1999.

Keppie, L., *Colonisation & Veteran Settlement in Italy, 47–14 BC*. London; BSR, 1983.

Keppie, L., *Roman Inscribed & Sculpted Stones in the Huntorian Museum University of Glasgow*. London; SPRS, 1999.

Keppie, L., *The Making of the Roman Army: From Republic to Empire*. New York; Barnes & Noble, 1984.

Ker, W. C. A., *Martial*. London; Loeb, 1919–20.

Laking, G. F., *A Record of European Armour & Arms Through Seven Centuries*. New York; AMS, 1934.

Leach, J., *Pompey the Great*. New York; Croom Helm, 1978.

Livy, *The War With Hannibal* (E. de Selincourt transl.). Harmondsworth; Penguin, 1965.

MacMullen, R., *Soldier and Civilian in the Later Roman Empire*. Cambridge, MA; HUP, 1967.

Margary, I. D., *Roman Roads in Britain*. London; Phoenix, 1957.

Marsden, E. W., *Greek and Roman Artillery*. Oxford; OUP, 1969.

Mattingly, H., *Roman Coins from the Earliest Times to the Fall of the Western Empire*. London; Methuen, 1927.

Merrifield, R., *London: City of the Romans*. London; Batsford, 1983.

Mommsen, T., *The History of Rome*, D. A. Saunders and J. H. Collins (ed.). Clinton, MA; Meridian, 1958.

Mommsen, T., *The Provinces of the Roman Empire*, T. R. S. Broughton (ed.). Chicago; UoC, 1968.

Mothersole, J., *In Roman Scotland*. London; Lane, 1927.

Napthali, L., *Life in Egypt under Roman Rule*. Oxford; Clarendon, 1983.

Parker, H. D. M., *The Roman Legions*. New York; Barnes & Noble, 1958.

Payne-Gallwey, R., *The Crossbow. Mediaeval and Modern. With a Treatise on the Ballista and Catapults of the Ancients* (1903). Reprinted London; Holland, 1995.

Pelletier, A., *Histoire de Lyon: de la capital des Gaules à la métropole Européenne*. Lyon; Editions Lyonaises, 2004.

Petronius Arbiter, G., *The Satyricon* (M. Heseltine transl.). London; Loeb, 1913.

Philo Judaeus, *The Works of Philo* (C. D. Yonge transl.). Peabody, MA; Hendrickson, 1993.

Plato, *The Dialogues* (B. Jowlett transl.). Chicago; Encyclopaedia Britannica, 1952.

Pliny the Elder, *Natural History* (H. Rackman transl.). London; Loeb, 1938–63.

Pliny the Younger, *Letters* (W. Melmoth transl.). London; Loeb, 1915.

Plutarch, *The Lives of the Noble Grecians & Romans* (J. Dryden transl., 1683–1686). Republished, Chicago; Encyclopaedia Britannica, 1952.

Polybius, *The Histories of Polybius* (P. Holland transl., 1606). Republished New York; LEC, 1963.

Raven, S., *Rome in Africa*. London; Longman, 1969.

Robertson, D. S., *Greek and Roman Architecture*. Cambridge; CUP, 1943.

Robinson, H. R., *The Armour of Imperial Rome*. Oxford; OUP, 1975.

Rossi, L., *Trajan's Column and the Dacian Wars*. London; Thames & Hudson, 1974.

Rostovtzeff, M. I., *The Social and Economic History of the Roman Empire*. New York; Biblio & Tannen, 1957.

Salway, P., *Roman Britain*. Oxford; OUP, 1981.

Seager, R., *Tiberius*. London; Eyre Methuen, 1972.

Seneca, *Letters from a Stoic* (R. Campbell transl.). Harmondsworth; Penguin, 1969.

Sherwin-White, A. N., *The Roman Citizenship*. Oxford; OUP, 1939.

Simkins, M., *Warriors of Rome*. London; Blandford, 1988.

Smith, F. E., *Waterloo*. London; Pan, 1970.

Speidel, M. P., *Riding for Caesar: The Roman Emperors' Horse Guards*. Cambridge, MA; HUP, 1994.

Starr, C. G., *Roman Imperial Navy, 31 BC–AD 324*. NJ; Westport, 1975.

Statius, *Collected Works* (J. H. Mozley transl.). Cambridge, MA; Loeb, 1928.

Strabo, *The Geography of Strabo* (H. L. Jones transl.). Cambridge, MA; Loeb, 1924.

Sulimirski, T., *The Sarmatians*. New York; Praeger, 1970.

Syme, R., *Ammianus and the Historia Augusta*. Oxford; OUP, 1968.

Syme, R., *History in Ovid*. Oxford; OUP, 1979.

Tacitus, P. C., *The Agricola* and *The Germania* (H. Mattingly transl.). London; Penguin, 1948.

Tacitus, P. C., *The Annals* and *The Histories*. Chicago; Encyclopaedia Britannica, 1952.

Todd, M., *The Early Germans*. Oxford; Blackwell, 1992.

Todd, M., *The Northern Barbarians, 1000 BC–AD 300*. New York; Blackwell, 1987.

Trench, C. C., *A History of Horsemanship*. New York; Doubleday, 1970.

Valerius Maximus, *Memorable Deeds and Sayings: One Thousand Tales from Ancient Rome* (H. J. Walker transl.). Indianapolis, IN; 2004.

Vegetius, *The Military Institutions of the Romans* (J. Clark, transl.). Harrisburg, Penn.; 1944.

Velleius Paterculus, *Compendium of Roman History* (F. W. Shipley transl.). Cambridge, MA; HUP, 1924.

Vernam, G. R., *Man on Horseback*. New York; Doubleday, 1964.

Vitruvius, *On Architecture* (F. Granger transl.). Cambridge, MA; HUP, 1934.

Waldeck, C., *Secrets and Stories of the War*. London; Reader's Digest Assoc., 1963.

Wallace, L., *Ben Hur*. London; Ward, Lock, 1890.

Warmington, E. H., *Nero*. Harmondsworth; Penguin, 1969.

Warry, J., *Warfare in the Classical World*. London; Salamander, 1989.

Watson, G. R., *The Roman Soldier*. Ithaca, NY; Cornell UP, 1969.

Webster, G., *The Imperial Roman Army of the First & Second Centuries*. London; Black, 1979.

Webster, G., and Dudley, D. R., *The Rebellion of Boudicca*. New York; Barnes & Noble, 1962.

Webster, G., and Dudley, D. R., *The Roman Conquest of Britain*. London; Pan, 1973.

Weigall, A., *Nero, Emperor of Rome*. London; Butterworth, 1930.

Wells, P. S., *The Battle That Stopped Rome: Emperor Augustus, Arminius, & the Slaughter of the Legions in the Teutoburg Forest*. New York; Norton, 2003.

Wheeler, R. M., *Rome Beyond the Imperial Frontiers*. London; Bell, 1954.

White, K. D., *Greek & Roman Technology*. Ithaca, NY; Cornell UP, 1983.

Wightman, E. M., *Roman Trier and the Treveri*. New York; Praeger, 1970.

Wilkes, J. J. (ed.), *Documenting the Roman Army*. London; ICS, 2003.

Wiseman, F. J., *Roman Spain*. New York; Bell, 1956.

Yadin, Y., *Bar-Kokhba: The Rediscovery of the Legendary Hero of the Last Jewish Revolt Against Imperial Rome*. London; Weidenfeld & Nicolson, 1971.

Yadin, Y., *Masada: Herod's Fortress & the Zealots' Last Stand*. New York; Grosset & Dunlap, 1966.

Zosimus, *Historica Nova*. Oxford; Hindmarsh, 1684.

NEWSPAPER & JOURNAL ARTICLES

Guey, J., 'Essai sur la Guerre Parthique de Trajan (114–117)', Bibliotheque d' 'Istos', II (1987), p. 157.

Gurling, R., 'A Cemetery of Secrets', *Sunday Times*, 26 March 2006.

Salmon, E. T., 'Trajan's Conquest of Dacia', *Transactions & Proceedings of the American Philological Assoc.*, Vol. 67 (1936), pp. 83–105.

Southern, P., 'The Numeri of the Roman Imperial Army', *Britannia*, Vol. 20 (1989), pp. 81–140.

Speidel, M. P., 'Raising New Units for the Late Roman Army: Auxilia Palatina', *Dumbarton Oaks Papers* (Harvard University), Vol. 50 (1996), pp. 163–70.

REPORTS

York Archaeological Trust Annual Report 2005–6.

OTHER

Chester Archaeological Society, 'Table 1, Recruitment to Legions II Adiutrix and XX Valeria Victrix in Britain', http://chesterarchaeolsoc.or.uk

INDEX

Page numbers in *italics* denotes an illustration

INDEX
Page numbers in *italics* denotes an illustration